**BILINGUAL EDUCATION AND BILINGUALISM 2**
Series Editor: Colin Baker

# Policy and Practice in Bilingual Education

## A Reader Extending the Foundations

### Edited by

### Ofelia García and Colin Baker

**MULTILINGUAL MATTERS LTD**
Clevedon • Philadelphia • Adelaide

**Library of Congress Cataloging in Publication Data**

Policy and Practice in Bilingual Education: A Reader Extending the Foundations
Edited by Ofelia García and Colin Baker.
(Bilingual Education and Bilingualism: 2)
Includes bibliographical references.
1. Bilingual Education. 2. Bilingualism. I. García, Ofelia. II. Baker, Colin, 1949- . III. Series.
LC3715.P65       1995
371.97–dc20        94-25145

**British Library Cataloguing in Publication Data**

A CIP catalogue record for this book is available from the British Library.

ISBN 1-85359-267-6 (hbk)
ISBN 1-85359-266-8 (pbk)

**Multilingual Matters Ltd**

*UK*: Frankfurt Lodge, Clevedon Hall, Victoria Road, Clevedon, Avon BS21 7SJ.
*USA*: 1900 Frost Road, Suite 101, Bristol, PA 19007, USA.
*Australia*: P.O. Box 6025, 83 Gilles Street, Adelaide, SA 5000, Australia.

Printed and bound in Great Britain by WBC Ltd, Bridgend.

# Contents

## Section 4: Using the Bilingualism of the School Community: Teachers and Parents

# Introduction

## The Contents of the Reader

This Reader contains a selection of the most important and influential recent contributions on bilingualism and bilingual education. Each has become a 'classic' or a pivotal paper. The Reader provides an instant introduction to recent fundamental and formative ideas on bilingualism and bilingual education in four Sections:

1.  Policy and Legislation on Bilingualism in Schools and Bilingual Education
2.  Implementation of Bilingual Policy in Schools: Structuring Schools
3.  Using Bilingualism in Instruction: Structuring Classrooms
4.  Using the Bilingualism of the School Community: Teachers and Parents.

## Use of the Reader by Instructors and Students

The Reader can be used as a comprehensive introduction for instructors, researchers and students in a variety of courses. It is also designed for 'interactive' use by students. After each article, there is a set of **student questions**. Such questions invite students to review some of the essential themes of each article. Following the questions, there is a set of **student activities**. Each activity aims to extend reading by generalization to the student's locality or experience. Some activities require research, others group discussion or a project. Such activities are designed to make the reading more relevant to a student, to widen an understanding of the topic, and to stimulate a process of introspection, generalization and personalization. A short list of 'Further Reading' is given at the end of some activities to extend relevant ideas.

We have designed the Reader so that the instructor can structure the course in ways that reflect practices recommended in the readings. For example, questions and activities can be performed in **cooperative learning groups** and are meant to engage students in a process of inquiry modelled after what Ada calls 'creative education'. Many of the activities extend beyond the classroom, involving students in a process of collaboration with the community, creating familiarization with, and incorporation of, their cultural and linguistic resources.

Students working through the questions and activities will be exposed to a form of 'mediated' instruction that will help them become **critical thinkers** and allow them to take on an advocacy-oriented role. This is accomplished by giving students practice in 'critical pedagogy', involving them not only in reading and reflection, but also in actual practice. This then becomes the source for further reflection and action. Thus, students can themselves experience some of these practices and their relationship to their own learning, while reflecting on how to use such practices in their teaching.

Following recent advances in teacher education, the activities involve students in **critical reflection** and **direct observation** of classrooms and students. When the student is already a teacher, her classroom may become the laboratory for her study. Those who are still training to become teachers can visit classrooms and engage administrators, educators, parents and students for their answers.

The student questions and activities are designed to give instructors and students plenty of **choice**. Some questions and activities will be more relevant to some classes and contexts than others. All questions and activities can easily be **adapted** by instructors to fit a particular class in a particular educational and geographic context. Where United States contexts are cited, instructors in other countries will be able to adapt questions and activities to ensure local relevance.

Although the totality of the questions form an integrated review of the reading, the activities are independent of each other. The **instructor** will need to decide whether to give the students the option to choose how many activities to complete, and will need to select those activities that are most relevant to their students and community. Questions may be completed in small groups, but the activities are the real source for cooperative learning. The instructor may need to give students further direction and advice to structure these cooperative tasks.

Because teachers need to be researchers and inquirers, the activities give teachers practice in some of the most common methods of research: ethnographic observation, surveys, interviews and content analysis. Many of the activities involve teachers in humanistic forms of research, enabling them to express themselves in writing, acting and drawing, and extend themselves by reading further. Such a multiple 'process' approach to student learning reflects the best of contemporary educational practice.

The Reader relates to the experience of both **language minority** and **language majority** students, to those directly involved in any form of bilingual education, and those that have or will have students of different language backgrounds in their classrooms. For language minority students, the Reader is structured in ways that reflect what the literature considers effective educational practices for language minorities. **Bilingual teachers** will have a better understanding of present policy and practices, and how these could be structured to develop the bilingualism and biliteracy of all students. Language majority students will become more familiar with issues surrounding language minorities and their education, as well as the importance of bilingualism and biliteracy for all individuals, and of cultural and linguistic pluralism in society. All teachers can benefit from a perspective of how to incorporate languages and cultures in their classroom, and how to turn their teaching into effective anti-racist practices. 'Creative education' is offered here for all.

While the Reader is designed to be a 'stand alone', it links with *'Foundations of Bilingual Education and Bilingualism'* (also published by Multilingual Matters). By concentrating on policies and practices in bilingual education, students who have first read that introduction will find this Reader deliberately extends and enlarges that book. Many instructors using the *'Foundations'* book also require students to read individual articles. This book is designed to fulfill that need.

## Rationale of the Reader

In the process of compiling the Reader, we started with a 'long list' of potential articles to include. We then consulted a sample of Instructors and Experts in the field of bilingual education and bilingualism. The final selection represents a balanced, comprehensive and challenging set of articles. Each article has been chosen because it does one, and usually many, of the following:

- summarizes well an important topic;
- provides fresh and original thinking;
- challenges through its ideas and beliefs;
- authoritatively analyzes a topic;
- is historically important in the development of a major issue;
- provides a seminal and creative case study.

Together, the articles, followed by questions, activities and further readings, construct a comprehensive and thorough review of recent bilingual education policies and practices within the context of the United States, Canada and Europe.

# Glossary

**Accommodation:** Adjusting speech to make oneself understood.

**Acculturation:** The process by which an individual adapts cognitively and emotionally to a new culture, as well as adapting to its communication system.

**Additive Bilingualism:** The second language adds to, and does not replace, the first language.

**AIR:** American Institutes for Research.

**Balanced Bilingualism:** Approximately equal competence in two languages.

**Barrios:** Spanish for 'neighborhood'. Used in the United States for areas where many Latinos live.

**Basal Readers:** Reading texts that use simplified vocabulary and syntax and are used in class sets.

**BEA:** Bilingual Education Act (United States legislation: part of ESEA — see below).

**BICS:** Basic Interpersonal Communicative Skills.

**Big Books:** Used frequently in 'whole language classrooms,' they are teachers' books that are physically big so that students can read along with the teacher.

**BSM:** Bilingual Syntax Measure (attempts to establish the dominant language of a bilingual).

**CALP:** Cognitive/Academic Language Proficiency.

**Chicanos:** Mexican-Americans.

**Cloze:** A procedure whereby every $n$th word is deleted in a text. Used to determine readability of text and the reading ability of a student.

**Code-switching:** Moving from one language to another, inside a sentence or across sentences.

**Communal Lessons:** Lessons in which linguistically heterogeneous students are mixed for very contextualized activities, such as working in projects, doing art or physical education. The European Hours in the European Schools are considered Communal Lessons.

**Communicative Competence:** Proficiency to use a language in everyday conversations. This term accentuates being understood rather than being 'correct' in using a language.

**Compensatory Education:** see Deficit Model.

**Comprehensible Input:** Language delivered at a level understood by a learner.

**Core Language Class:** Teaching the language as a subject. Used mostly to describe foreign language instruction.

**Core Subject:** A subject that is of prime importance in the curriculum. In Britain the three Core Subjects are Mathematics, English and Science.

**CUP:** Common Underlying Proficiency (in two languages).

**DBE:** Developmental Bilingual Education: Also known as Two-way Dual Language Programs and Two-way Bilingual/Immersion Programs. Two languages are used for approximately equal time in the curriculum.

**Decoding:** In learning to read, the deciphering of the sounds and meanings of letters, combinations of letters, whole words and sentences of text.

**Deficit Model:** The child has a perceived language 'deficit' that has to be compensated by remedial schooling. The problem is located in the child rather than in the school system or society or in the ideology of the perceiver. The opposite is an enrichment model (see Enrichment Bilingual Education).

**DES:** Department of Education and Science (Britain).

**Dialect:** A regionally or socially distinctive variety of a language. Often with a distinctive pronunciation or accent.

**Diglossia:** Two languages existing together in a society in a stable arrangement through functional distribution.

**DL:** Dual Language (School).

**Double Immersion:** Schooling where subject content is taught through a second and third language (e.g. Hebrew and French for first-language English speakers).

**Early Exit/Late Exit Bilingual Education Programs:** Early Exit Programs move children from bilingual classes in the first or second year of schooling. Late Exit Programs provide bilingual classes for three or more years of elementary schooling. Both programs exist in Transitional Bilingual Education.

**EC:** European Community (EU = European Union; EEC = European Economic Community).

**EFL:** English as a Foreign Language (ESL = English as a Second Language).

**Ego-permeability:** A willingness to change, adapt or develop oneself.

**Equilingual:** Someone who is approximately equally competent in two languages.

**ERA:** Education Reform Act (British).

**ERASMUS:** A European program for students to take part of their higher education at one or more European universities as well as their 'home' university.

**ESEA:** Elementary and Secondary Education Act (United States).

**ESOL:** English for Speakers of Other Languages.

**Enrichment Bilingual Education:** Develops additive bilingualism, thus enriching a person's life.

**Ethnic Mosaic:** Immigrants of different geographical origins co-existing in a country (e.g. United States) and retaining colorful constituents of their ethnicity.

**Ethnocentrism:** Discriminatory beliefs and behaviours based on ethnic differences.

**Ethnographic Pedagogy:** Teaching practices and learning strategies that are derived from Ethnography (see below) and conducted in the classroom. An ethnographic researcher becomes involved in a classroom, observing, participating and helps transform teaching practices. In Delgado-Gaitán's article, the Ethnographic Pedagogy includes learning to read by harnessing students' prior cultural knowledge and experience, and encouraging peer interaction.

**Ethnolinguistic:** A set of cultural, ethnic and linguistic features shared by a social group.

**Ethnography:** Research that is qualitative rather than quantitative in approach (e.g. engages in fieldwork, interviews and observation). Such research is often intensive and detailed, hence small-scale.

**Franco-Ontarian:** French speakers from Ontario, Canada.

**GAO:** General Accounting Office (United States).

**Gastarbeiter:** An immigrant or guestworker.

**Gemeinschaft:** A society based on close community bonds, kinship, close family ties, and an emphasis on tradition and heritage. Sometimes portrayed stereotypically as village life.

**Gesellschaft:** A society with less emphasis on tradition and more on rational goals and a duty to organizations with many secondary relationships. Sometimes portrayed stereotypically as one type of urban existence.

**Graphology:** The way a language is written.

**Guest Workers:** People who are recruited to work in another society. Also known as Gastarbeiter.

**Hegemony:** domination; the ascendancy of one group over another, expecting compliance and subservience by the subordinate group.

**Heterogeneous Grouping:** The use of mixed ability and/or mixed language groups or classes. The opposite is 'homogeneous grouping' or Tracking (see below).

**Hispanics:** Spanish speakers in the United States. Officially used in the US census.

**Immersion Bilingual Education:** Schooling where some or most subject content is taught through a second, majority language.

**In-migrants:** Encompasses immigrants, migrants, refugees.

**Instrumental Motivation:** Wanting to learn a language for utilitarian reasons (e.g. to get a better job).

**Integrative Motivation:** Wanting to learn a language to belong to a social group (e.g. make friends).

**Interlanguage:** A language integrating aspects of the first and second language used by a second-language learner while learning the second language.

**Involuntary Minorities:** Also known as 'caste-like minorities', according to Ogbu. They differ from immigrants and 'voluntary minorities' in that they have not willingly migrated to the country.

**L1/L2:** First Language/Second Language.

**Language Demographics:** The distribution of the use of a language in a defined geographical area.

**Language Minority:** A person or a group speaking a language of low prestige or having low numbers in a society.

**Latinos:** Spanish speakers of Latin American extraction. It is the Spanish term which is now used in English, especially by US Spanish speakers themselves.

**LEP:** Limited English Proficiency.

**Lexical Competency:** Competence in vocabulary.

**Lexis:** The vocabulary or word stock of a language.

**LMS:** Language Minority Students.

**LINGUA:** A European program to increase majority language learning across Europe. The program funds scholarships, student exchanges and teaching materials to improve language learning and teaching in the twelve European (EC) countries.

**Lingua Franca:** A language used between groups of people with different native languages.

**Linguicism:** The use of languages to legitimate and reproduce unequal divisions of power and resources in society.

**LM:** Language Minority.

**LMP:** Linguistic Minorities Project (Britain).

**Mainstreaming:** Putting a student who has previously been in a special educational program into classrooms for everybody.

**Marked Language:** A minority language distinct from a majority one, and usually not highly valued in society.

**ME:** Medium of Education. Using a language to teach content. Also medium of instruction.

**Melting-pot:** The amalgamation of a variety of immigrant ethnic groups to make a 'US American citizen'.

**OCR:** Office of Civil Rights (United States).

**Ordinary Level:** A British examination for 16-year-olds. Each subject of the curriculum has its own examination (now called GCSE — the General Certificate of Secondary Education).

**Personality Principle:** The right to use a language based on the history and character of the language.

**Parallel Teaching:** Where bilingual children experience two teachers working together as a team — each using a different language. In Corson's article the term specifically means a second-language teacher and the class teacher planning together but teaching independently.

**Phonics:** A method of teaching reading based on recognizing the sounds of letters and combinations of letters.

**Phonology:** The sound system.

**Polyglot:** Someone competent in two or more languages.

**Process Instruction:** An emphasis on the 'doing' in the classroom rather than creating a product. A focus on procedures and techniques rather than on learning outcomes, learning 'how to' through inquiry rather than learning through the transmission and memorization of knowledge.

**Pygmalion Effect:** The self-fulfilling prophecy. A student is labeled (e.g. by a teacher) as having 'limited English'. The label is internalized by the student who behaves in a way that confirms the label.

**Racism:** A system of privilege and penalty based on race. It is based on a belief in the inherent superiority of one race over others, and acceptance of economic, social, political and educational differences based on such supposed superiority.

**Reception Classes/Centers:** For newly arrived students.

**Register:** A variety of a language closely associated with different contexts or scenes in which the language is used (e.g. courtroom, classroom, cinema, church) and hence with different people (e.g. police, professor, parent, priest).

**Remedial Bilingual Education:** Also known as Compensatory Bilingual Education. Uses the mother tongue only to 'correct' the students' presumed 'deficiency' in the majority language.

**SAIP:** Special Alternative Instructional Programs (United States).

**Scaffolding Approach:** Building on a child's existing repertoire of knowledge and understanding.

**Sheltered English:** Content classes with integral English language development.

**Skills-based Literacy:** Where the emphasis is on the acquisition of Phonics and other forms, rather than in ways of using those forms.

**SL Extension:** Corson uses this term to denote an option in a secondary school where the second language is given extra time on the curriculum. Other students choose different subject options or further time on their first language.

**SLT:** Second Language Teaching.

**Standard Language:** A prestige variety of a language (e.g. Standard English).

**Submersion:** Schooling that does not allow the child to use his or her home language for learning. The child works solely through a second, majority language.

**Subtractive Bilingualism:** The second language replaces the first language.

**Syntax:** Word order. Rules about the ways words are combined.

**Target Language:** The language being learned or taught.

**TBE:** Transitional Bilingual Education.

**TEFL:** Teaching English as a Foreign Language.

**Territorial Principle:** A claim to the right to a language within a territory.

**TESOL:** (a) Teachers of English to Speakers of Other Languages; (b) Teaching English as a Second or Other Language.

**Threshold Level:** A level of language competence a person has to reach to gain benefits from owning two languages.

**TPR:** Total Physical Response — a method of second language learning.

**Tracking:** The use of homogeneous groups (also called setting, streaming, banding, ability grouping).

**Two-way Programs:** (see DBE above).

**UK:** United Kingdom (England, Scotland, Northern Ireland and Wales).

**UN:** United Nations.

**UNESCO:** United Nations Educational, Scientific and Cultural Organization.

**US English:** An organization committed to making English the only officially functioning language in US society.

**Vernacular:** A indigenous or heritage language of an individual or community.

**Wanderarbeiter:** A nomadic, seasonal worker, usually from a 'foreign' country. An itinerant worker in a 'foreign' country.

**Whole Language Approach:** An amorphous cluster of ideas about language development in the classroom. The approach is against Basal Readers (see above) and Phonics (see above) in learning to read. Generally the approach supports an holistic and integrated learning of reading, writing, spelling and oracy. The language used must have relevance and meaning to the child. Language development engages cooperative sharing and cultivates empowerment. The use of language for communication is stressed; the function rather than the form of language.

**Withdrawal Classes:** Also known as 'pull-out' classes. Children are taken out for special instruction.

**Zone of Proximal Development:** New areas of learning within a student's reach. Vygotsky saw the zone of proximal development as the distance between a student's level of development as revealed when problem-solving without adult help, and the level of potential development as determined by a student problem-solving in collaboration with peers or teachers. The Zone of Proximal Development is where new understandings are possible through collaborative interaction and inquiry.

## Acknowledgement

The Editors wish to thank Ricardo Lopez, a graduate student at the City College of New York, for making many valuable suggestions about the nature of the Glossary. We are indebted to him for his important contribution.

# The Past and Future Directions of Federal Bilingual-Education Policy

## James J. Lyons

On 17 January 1967, Texas Senator Ralph Yarborough and six cosponsors introduced S. 428, the American Bilingual Education Act (BEA), an amendment to the Elementary and Secondary Education Act of 1965. The legislation was designed to address 'the special educational needs of the large numbers of students in the United States whose mother tongue is Spanish and to whom English is a foreign language.'[1] Senator Yarborough explained the motivation behind the bill:

> The failure of our schools to educate Spanish speaking students is reflected in comparative dropout rates. In the five Southwestern States…, Anglos 14 years of age and over have completed an average of 12 years of school compared with 8.1 years for Spanish-surnamed students. I regret to say that my own State of Texas ranks at the bottom, with a median of only 4.7 years of school completed by persons of Spanish surname.[2]

Full-scale change, according to the senator, would require 'money, coordination, and inspiration.' Confident that the 'inspiration will come from the many eager teachers, researchers, administrators, parents, and students, who are impatient with the failure of the old methods and anxious to work for a better tomorrow,'[3] S. 428 was meant to supply the money and coordination. It provided a three-year authorization of appropriations, with a first-year limit of $5 million and annual increases of $5 million, for grants to local education agencies — to plan, establish, maintain, and operate programs for students 'whose mother tongue is Spanish.' Authorized activities included

(1) bilingual-education programs;
(2) the teaching of Spanish as the native language;
(3) the teaching of English as a second language;
(4) programs designed to impart to Spanish speaking students a knowledge of and pride in their ancestral culture and language;
(5) efforts to attract and retain as teachers promising individuals of Mexican or Puerto Rican descent;
(6) efforts to establish closer cooperation between the school and the home.[4]

S. 428 was referred to the Special Subcommittee on Bilingual Education of the Senate Labor and Public Welfare Committee. During seven days of hearings virtually all of the more than 100 witnesses testified in support of the bill and its underlying objectives. The witnesses advanced five major arguments in favor of bilingual education. For Spanish-speaking students, bilingual education was necessary

- to prevent the academic retardation resulting from the provision of monolingual English instruction to children who, though proficient in Spanish, were limited in their English proficiency;
- to stem the psychological damage sustained by Spanish-speaking students who enter the linguistically and culturally alien environment of English-only schools; and
  to prevent the loss of potential bilingualism among Spanish-speaking students.

For Spanish-speaking parents, many poorly educated, witnesses argued that bilingual education helped to foster strong and effective home–school cooperation. Finally, some witnesses stressed the potential importance of bilingual education in conserving the nation's dwindling language and cultural resources.

While much of the testimony relied on basic research in education and psychology, some witnesses presented data derived from experimental bilingual school programs. Officers and

staff of the National Education Association testified to the success of pilot projects recently
inaugurated in Phoenix and Tucson, Arizona;
Pueblo, Colorado; Albuquerque and Pecos, New
Mexico; and El Paso and Laredo, Texas. The
projects were summarized in a 1966 publication,
*The Invisible Minority: The NEA-Tucson Survey on
the Teaching of Spanish to the Spanish-Speaking,*
which became an important part of the Senate
hearing record.

Several witnesses cited a program at the Coral
Way Elementary School in Miami, established in
1963 with assistance from the Ford Foundation.
The Coral Way program was developed to assist
the children of Cuban refugees who had moved
to Miami in the late 1950s and early 1960s.
Although most of the Cuban refugee parents
were educationally and economically advantaged, many of their children performed poorly
in Miami's monolingual English school programs. Unlike the southwestern bilingual
programs summarized in the National Education
Association's report, the Coral Way program was
structured to provide bilingual instruction to
both Spanish- and English-language-background
children in an integrated setting. High test scores
for both the Cuban and Anglo students attested
to the program's academic success; teacher observations confirmed the social benefits of this
innovative two-way bilingual-education program.

## The First Bilingual Education Act: Origins of the Misnomer

The concept of a federal bilingual education
program proved politically popular, and soon
more than three dozen bilingual-education bills
were introduced in the House of Representatives.
The bill that emerged from conference committee
and was signed into law, however, differed from
the vision of Senator Yarborough and the cosponsors of S. 428 in two major respects.

First, the focus of the law changed from 'Spanish-speaking children' to 'children of limited
English-speaking ability.' This broadening fundamentally transformed the focus into a remedial
or compensatory program to serve children who
were 'deficient' in English-language skills. The
new perception of eligible children as deficient in
English rather than as proficient in another language was reinforced by another provision
added to the law in conference committee, that
grantee schools have a high concentration of
students from low income families.

Second, three activities specifically authorized
in the Senate bill were dropped from the final law,
with profound implications for the purpose of the
Bilingual Education Act and federally supported
bilingual programs. The Senate bill's authorization of 'the teaching of Spanish as the native
language' could have been redrafted to refer to
'home languages.' Instead, it was dropped, ren-
dering unlikely the establishment of bilingual-
education programs that would fully develop the
native-language skills of students. Elimination of
'the teaching of English as a second language'
withdrew recognition of the importance of spe-
cially designed English-development programs
for non English-language-background students.
As a result, many early federally funded bilingual
programs provided English language instruction
geared inappropriately to native-English-speak-
ing students. Finally, the law deleted reference to
'efforts to attract and retain as teachers promising
individuals of Mexican or Puerto Rican descent'
rather than redrafting it to reflect the broader
focus on all non-English speakers.[5] With it was
dropped the notion that our schools could benefit
from the linguistic skills and cultural experiences
of ethnic language-minority Americans.

## Education Amendments of 1974

Six years after its enactment, Congress
reauthorized and substantially revised the BEA.
The 1974 amendments expanded the program by
authorizing new grants for state education-
agency technical assistance; training programs
separate from instructional programs; and a
national clearing house to collect, analyze, and
disseminate information about bilingual education programs.

The 1974 amendments also defined a 'program
of bilingual education.' In a pertinent part, the
definition provided that 'there is instruction
given in, and study of, English and, to the extent
necessary to allow a child to progress effectively
through the educational system, the native language of the children of limited English speaking
ability.' The native-language instruction thus
provided for was not designed to develop the
child's native language but only to allow children
to progress in academic subjects while acquiring
English.

This limitation on the objectives of federal
bilingual-education programs was reinforced by
another provision of the 1974 amendments,
which authorized 'the voluntary enrollment to a
limited degree' of English-speaking children in

bilingual education programs, accompanied by the prohibition that 'in no event shall the program be designed for the purpose of teaching a foreign language to English-speaking children.'

Thus, while the 1974 amendments expanded the structure and operation of the BEA, they also reinforced the acts's focus on English-language development and neglect of native-language development. The amendments also barred federal support for two-way bilingual-education programs such as the successful Coral Way model.

## Education Amendments of 1978

In 1978, Congress again reauthorized and revised the BEA, again expanding the scope and size of the program. The amendments increased the authorization of appropriations to $200 million for fiscal year 1978, with annual $50 million increases through fiscal year 1983, authorized new grant programs and directed the commissioner of education to collect and publish information on a wide range of issues relating to language-minority students and bilingual education.

The 1978 amendments clarified the definition of eligible children. The term 'limited-English-proficient' (LEP) supplanted 'limited-English-speaking' in recognition of the importance of reading, writing, understanding, and cognitive skills in addition to speaking. The new definition, while arguably clearer and more comprehensive, reinforced the deficit approach to educating language-minority students.

The amendments also clarified the 1974 provision authorizing the voluntary enrollment 'to a limited degree'[6] of English language-background students by specifying that up to 40 percent of the students could be native-English speakers 'to prevent the segregation of children on the basis of national origin.'[7] The amendments eliminated the 1974 ban on programs that were designed to teach a foreign language, substituting a gentler though equally narrow requirement that 'the objective of the program shall be to assist children of limited English proficiency to improve their English language skills, and the participation of other children in the program must be for the principal purpose of contributing to the achievement of that objective.'

## Bilingual Education and Civil Rights Policy, 1968–80

Modern federal bilingual-education policy has proceeded along two parallel tracks. The first,

propelled by both parties in Congress, involved federal financial and programmatic assistance through the BEA to schools serving language-minority students. The executive branch, under two Democratic and two Republican presidents, and the federal courts propelled movement along the second track of federal bilingual-education policy — civil rights enforcement.

### Title VI of the Civil Rights Act of 1964

Title VI of the 1964 Civil Rights Act prohibited discrimination on the basis of race, color, or national origin in federally assisted programs and activities and imposed on grant-making agencies responsibility for ensuring compliance. To enforce Title VI compliance in federal education programs, the Office of Civil Rights (OCR) was established in the Department of Health, Education and Welfare (DHEW).

In 1968, the last year of the Johnson administration, DHEW issued general Title VI guidelines, which held 'school systems...responsible for assuring that students of a particular race, color, or national origin are not denied the opportunity to obtain the education generally obtained by other students in the system.'

In 1970, just a year after President Nixon took office, the director of OCR followed up on the general 1968 guidelines with a memorandum providing specific information on responsibilities to school districts whose national-origin minority group enrollments exceeded 5 percent.[8] The memorandum noted a 'a number of common educational practices which have the effect of denying equality of educational opportunity to Spanish-surnamed pupils.' 'Similar practices,' it continued, 'which have the effect of discrimination on the basis of national origin exist in other locations with respect to disadvantaged pupils from other national origin minority groups, for example, Chinese or Portuguese.'

The compensatory character of the directive, exemplified by its reference to 'disadvantaged pupils,' found expression in the memorandum's primary injunction:

> Where inability to speak and understand the English language excludes national origin-minority children from effective participation in the educational program offered by a school district, the district must take affirmative steps to rectify the language deficiency in order to open its instructional program to these students.

The memorandum prohibited 'the assignment of national origin-minority students to classes for the mentally retarded on the basis of criteria which essentially measure or evaluate English language skills' and denial of access to 'college preparatory courses on a basis directly related to the failure of the school system to inculcate English language skills.' It specified that ability grouping and tracking systems must meet 'language skill needs as soon as possible and must not operate as an educational dead-end or permanent track.' Finally, the memorandum noted that to adequately notify national-origin minority-group parents of school activities, notices may 'have to be provided in a language other than English.'

### Lau v. Nichols

The full significance of OCR's 1970 Title VI memorandum would not be realized until 1974, when the United States Supreme Court handed down its first and only substantive decision concerning the legal responsibilities of schools serving LEP students. The case was *Lau v. Nichols*, a class-action suit by the parents of nearly 3000 Chinese pupils in the 16,500-student San Francisco public school system. Approximately one-third of the Chinese students received supplemental instruction in the English language; the remainder received no special instruction. The plaintiffs alleged that the school district's conduct violated both the Fourteenth Amendment to the Constitution and Title VI of the Civil Rights Act of 1964, but they did not seek a specific remedy — 'only that the Board of Education be directed to apply its expertise to the problems and to rectify the situation.' Because the Court unanimously found the San Francisco system in violation of Title VI, it declined to rule on the plaintiffs' constitutional claims. The logic of the Court's decision, authored by Justice William Douglas, was straightforward. Justice Douglas reviewed provisions of the California Education Code pertaining to English-language and bilingual instruction in the state, to English-proficiency requirements for high school graduation, and to the compulsory full-time education of children between the ages of 6 and 16 years.

> Under these state-imposed standards there is no equality of treatment merely by providing students with the same facilities, textbooks, teachers, and curriculum; for students who do not understand English are

> effectively foreclosed from any meaningful education.

> Basic English skills are the very core of what these public schools teach. Imposition of a requirement that, before a child can effectively participate in the educational program, he must already have acquired those basic skills is to make a mockery of public education. We know that those who do not understand English are certain to find their classroom experiences wholly incomprehensible and in no way meaningful.[9]

Justice Douglas then cited the general Title VI regulations promulgated by DHEW in 1968 and the 1970 memorandum guidelines. 'It seems obvious,' he wrote, 'that the Chinese-speaking minority receive fewer benefits than the English speaking majority from respondents' school system which denies them a meaningful opportunity to participate in the educational program — all earmarks of the discrimination banned by the regulations.'[10] Regarding the validity of the DHEW regulations the Court noted, 'The Federal Government has power to fix the terms on which its money allotments to the States shall be disbursed. Whatever may be the limits of that power, they had not been reached here.'[11]

### Lau Remedies of 1975

After the Supreme Court's *Lau* decision, DHEW officials in the Ford administration launched a major Title VI enforcement program. Recognizing that few school districts were providing any type of special instruction to LEP students, DHEW began the effort by developing 'remedial' rather than 'compliance' guidelines for districts not in compliance with Title VI under *Lau*.

The guidelines, announced by Education Commissioner T. H. Bell in 1975 and informally called the '*Lau* Remedies,'[12] specified proper approaches, methods, and procedures for (1) identifying and evaluating national-origin-minority students' English-language skills; (2) determining appropriate instructional treatments; (3) deciding when LEP students were ready for mainstream classes; and (4) determining the professional standards to be met by teachers of language-minority children.

Under the *Lau* Remedies, elementary schools were generally required to provide LEP students special English-as-a-second-language instruction as well as academic subject-matter instruction through the student's strongest language until the student achieved proficiency in English sufficient to learn effectively in a monolingual English classroom.

Three alternative instructional models were specified for elementary schools, all requiring schools 'to utilize the student's native language and cultural factors in instruction.' Under the transitional model, native-language instruction was provided only until the student became 'fully functional in English.' Bilingual-bicultural programs were to provide ongoing instruction in and development of both English and the student's native language, 'the end result... [being] a student who can function, totally, in both languages and cultures.' Multilingual-multicultural programs were even more ambitious, providing instruction in and development of English and at least two other languages.

The *Lau* Remedies quickly evolved into *de facto* compliance standards as DHEW moved aggressively to enforce Title VI during the Ford and Carter administrations. Between 1975 and 1980, OCR carried out nearly 600 national-origin compliance reviews, leading to the negotiation of 359 school-district *Lau* plans by July 1980.

In 1978, Alaskan school districts sued DHEW to block use of the *Lau* Remedies as a Title VI compliance standard, claiming that the *Lau* Remedies lacked the force of formal regulations since they had not been officially published for public comment. DHEW Secretary Joe Califano settled the case through a consent decree, agreeing to publish, at the earliest practicable date, formal regulations to determine a school district's compliance with the requirements of Title VI under *Lau*.

### Political controversy over 1980 rule making

The task of issuing formal Title VI *Lau* regulations fell to the new Department of Education, established in 1979 after a hard-fought highly partisan contest between the Carter administration and conservatives in Congress. To head the new department, President Carter chose Shirley Hufstedler, a federal judge on the Ninth Circuit Court of Appeals.

Secretary Hufstedler may have been new to Washington and to the field of education, but she was no stranger to the Supreme Court's *Lau* ruling. Indeed, as part of the appeals-court panel that heard the case, she authored a dissenting opinion foreshadowing the Supreme Court's

unanimous decision. On 5 August 1980, Secretary Hufstedler announced the issuance of proposed Title VI regulations applicable to language-minority students.[13] These regulations required school districts receiving federal assistance to provide special instruction to all LEP national-origin-minority students and, under most conditions, to provide some native-language instruction in academic subjects to LEP students who were more proficient in their native language than in English.

In response to prior criticism about ambiguities in the *Lau* Remedies, the department's 1980 proposed rules included objective specifications for the identification of language-minority students; the assessment of their English proficiency; the provision of proper instructional services; and exiting LEP students from special instructional programs. Although prescriptively written, the proposed regulations authorized 'waivers' from most requirements if a school district was making good-faith efforts to achieve compliance.

The proposed rules, the first major regulations to be issued by the fledgling Department of Education, drew criticism from many quarters; over 4000 letters, most of them critical, were received. Members of Congress who had opposed establishment of the Education Department seized on the regulations as proof of their worst predictions about federal control of local education. Editorial writers generally concluded that the proposed rules went too far.

Coming just three months before the presidential election, the proposed regulations became a campaign issue. Reagan campaign officials cited them as another example of the need to get the federal government 'off the back' of the American public. Ronald Reagan vowed that, if elected, he would eliminate the new Department of Education. After meeting with senior congressional officials, Education Secretary Hufstedler agreed not to take further action finalizing the new Title VI regulations. While the secretary's action extinguished an immediate legislative brush fire, it did not retard the political conflagration over bilingual education.

## Bilingual-Education Policy During the Reagan Administration

In off-the-cuff remarks shortly after taking office, President Reagan stated his personal views on bilingual education.

'Now, bilingual education, there is a need, but there is also a purpose that has been distorted again at the federal level. Where there are predominantly students speaking a foreign language at home, coming to school and being taught English, and they fall behind or are unable to keep up in some subjects because of the lack of knowledge of the language, I think it is proper that we have teachers equipped who can get at them in their own language and understand why it is they don't get the answer to the problem and help them in that way. But it is absolutely wrong and against American concepts to have a bilingual education program that is now openly, admittedly dedicated to preserving their native language and never getting them adequate in English so they can go out into the job market and participate.'[14]

The president's statement on bilingual education was remarkably consonant with the position taken by the Heritage Foundation in *Mandate for Leadership*, a transition document prepared to help Reagan design a 'conservative agenda.' The Heritage Foundation report charged:

> This well-intended program, in effect, keeps children out of American society by delaying the learning of English. By delaying the emphasis on learning English, this federal program requires duplication of teachers in the classroom, and the spending of a great deal of taxpayers' money on recruitment, training, and certification of bilingual teachers and instructional aides. Not only that, the program requires that textbooks and teaching materials have to be developed in scores of languages other than English. Our schools should concentrate on teaching English to these children. They are going to have to learn English sooner or later — so why not sooner?'[15]

Reagan's first education secretary, T.H. Bell, moved quickly to change federal bilingual-education policy.

### Civil rights policy: Flexibility and neglect

As one of his first acts of office, Education Secretary Bell officially withdrew the 1980 proposed Title VI regulations, calling them 'harsh, inflexible, burdensome, unworkable, and incredibly costly.' The secretary promised that the department would 'protect the rights of children who do not speak English well' by 'permitting school districts to use any way [type of education program] that has proven to be successful.' Secretary Bell's promise overshot the performance of his OCR. Guidelines were rescinded but not replaced, and the number of Title VI complaint investigations and compliance reviews conducted pursuant to *Lau* plummeted. In the years 1981–86 school districts were nine times less likely to be scheduled for a Title VI *Lau* review than in the period 1976–81. Yet, even under the flexible, permissive, and unpublished compliance standards of the Reagan administration, OCR found legal violations in 58 percent of the *Lau*-related investigations carried out after 1981.[16]

### Bilingual Education Act appropriations: Cut to serve a growing population

The Reagan administration moved quickly to cut funding for the Bilingual Education Act. In 1982, BEA appropriations were cut by $23 million. The following year, the administration tried to cut nearly $40 million more from the program. Real spending under the BEA was reduced 47 percent between fiscal year 1980 and fiscal year 1988. Real support for all education programs declined by 8 percent during this period.

These drastic funding cuts in bilingual education coincided with dramatic increases in the number of LEP children needing BEA-funded programs and services. Secretary Bell's 1982 report *The Condition of Bilingual Education in the Nation* estimated that at least 3.6 million LEP students were attending school in the United States. The LEP school-age population was projected to grow, through the year 2000, two and one half times as fast as the general school-age population. The nation's schools, according to Secretary Bell's 1982 report, were not meeting the needs of their LEP students. 'Many schools are not assessing the special needs of language minority children. They are not assessing the English language proficiency of these children, much less the home language proficiency, as a basis for planning programs and providing services.'[17]

What programs and services were LEP students receiving? Few. According to Bell's report, only a third of the LEP children identified in a 1978 federal study were receiving any kind of special instructional services, and less than 6 percent were enrolled in a bilingual program that provided at least five hours of home-language medium instruction a week.[18]

Contrary to the Heritage Foundation's claims that bilingual education delayed and subordinated English-language development, Secretary Bell's report noted that 'LEP students receiving bilingual instruction receive somewhat more instruction in the English language arts than do students in English-medium programs. In Title VII [BEA] programs, most subjects are taught in English, irrespective of teaching in the home language.'[19]

### 1982 Bilingual Education Act amendments

In 1982 Secretary Bell transmitted to Congress draft legislation to amend the BEA. The primary change sought was elimination of the requirement that BEA funded programs make some instructional use of a LEP student's native language. (California Republican Senator S.I. Hayakawa introduced the bill. Most of the public testimony and expert evidence presented during two days of subcommittee hearings contradicted the administration's position on English-only instruction, and no further action was taken on the legislation in the 97th Congress.

### 1984 Bilingual Education Act amendments

With virtually no input from the administration except for the recommendation to strike native-language instruction from the BEA, Congress turned to education and language-minority groups for help in developing legislation to reauthorize and revise the act. The resulting legislation strengthened and expanded the BEA, clarifying that the goal of all BEA programs was enabling LEP children 'to achieve competence in the English language... [and] to meet grade-promotion and graduation standards.' It also required that all BEA programs provide LEP students with intensive 'structured English language instruction.'[20]

The legislation replaced the existing single basic BEA grant for instructional programs with assorted special efforts: Family English Literacy programs for adults and out-of-school youths; preschool, special-education, and gifted and talented programs for LEP students; development of instructional materials for LEP students; and identifying bilingual-education programs of demonstrated academic excellence. The two general-purpose instructional programs authorized were transitional bilingual education (TBE) and developmental bilingual education (DBE). In

keeping with the fact that TBE had been the model underlying successful, previously funded BEA programs, the legislation reserved 75 percent of instructional grant funds for TBE programs.

The legislation's authorization for DBE programs represented a major breakthrough in federal bilingual-education policy. Not since key provisions of the original 1967 American Bilingual-Education bill were dropped in conference committee had federal policy countenanced native language development as an objective of BEA programs. The legislation specified that DBE programs must enable LEP students not only to become proficient in English and to meet grade-promotion and graduation requirements but also to become proficient in a second language. In keeping with the finding 'that both limited English proficient children and children whose primary language is English can benefit from bilingual education programs, and that such programs help develop our national linguistic resources,'[21] the legislation specified that 'where possible,' DBE programs should enroll approximately equal numbers of native English-speaking children and children 'whose native language is the second language of instruction and study in the program.'[22]

The Reagan administration opposed the 1984 BEA amendments on the grounds that they did not authorize monolingual English instructional programs for LEP students. A bipartisan group of House members sought to resolve the impasse through legislative compromise. The product of the compromise was authorization of a third category of general instructional grants, for special alternative instructional programs (SAIP), that is, monolingual English programs. The authorization for SAIP was premised on the finding 'that in some school districts establishment of a bilingual education program may be administratively impractical due to the presence of small numbers of students of a particular native language or because personnel who are qualified to provide bilingual instructional services are unavailable.'[23] Preference in awarding SAIP grants was to be based on the existence of such factors.

To prevent diversion of BEA resources from bilingual programs, the compromise legislation contained a formula to control SAIP funding — 4 percent of the first $140 million in BEA appropriations would go to SAIP. To stimulate administration support for higher BEA funding, the formula stipulated that SAIP would received 50 percent of all appropriations in excess of $140 million until SAIP grants equaled 10 percent of total BEA funding. In the fall of 1984, the compromise bilingual-education legislation was signed into law.

### Secretary Bennett's bilingual-education policies

Before the Education Department had developed regulations to implement the 1984 amendments to the BEA, Education Secretary Bell resigned and President Reagan appointed William J. Bennett to be his successor. In a September 1985 speech, the secretary lashed out against federal bilingual-education policy. Citing the high drop-out rates of Hispanic students, Bennett termed the 17-year-old BEA a 'failure.' 'This, then is where we stand: After seventeen years of federal involvement, and after $1.7 billion of federal funding, we have no evidence that the children whom we sought to help...have benefitted.' Federal bilingual-education policy, he charged, had 'lost sight of the goal of learning English as the key to equal educational opportunity.'[24]

During 1986 and 1987, Secretary Bennett and other department officials pushed to remove the funding limit on SAIP grants, asserting that English-only instructional programs were as effective for LEP students as bilingual instructional programs. These assertions motivated a request by House Education and Labor Committee Chairman Augustus F. Hawkins for a 1987 General Accounting Office report, *Bilingual Education: A New Look at the Research Evidence*, which contradicted the department's assertions about the relative effectiveness of monolingual English instruction and bilingual education.

### The education amendments of 1988

As in 1984, the Reagan administration did not become actively involved in the 1988 legislative reauthorization of the BEA except to insist on removing all restrictions on the amount of BEA funds that could be devoted to English-only SAIP programs. Both the House and Senate passed legislation that compromised with the administration on this issue.

The House bill achieved the compromise through an extremely complex funding formula. The Senate compromise, eventually adopted by the House in conference committee, set aside 75 percent of all BEA grant monies for TBE; it also

permitted the secretary of education to reserve up to 25 percent of BEA appropriations for SAIP. The remaining four BEA grant programs, including DBE, could be funded from either set-aside. The intent of the Senate funding compromise was explained by its architect, Edward M. Kennedy, chairman of the Labor and Human Resources Committee:

> Inclusion of the Senate bill's new funding reservations in H.R. 5 accommodates the Education Department's quest for greater funding flexibility without mandating increased spending for monolingual instructional programs. This enhanced funding flexibility should be exercised in a responsible fashion, and I urge both the Department of Education and my colleagues on the Senate and House Appropriations Committees to allocate non-reserved funds to those Part A programs which, on the basis of objective program evaluation and research data, are shown to be most effective in helping limited English-proficient students achieve academic success. In this regard, I am troubled by the fact that the Department of Education currently provides only two grants, amounting to less than one-quarter of 1 percent of all Part A grant funds, for two-way developmental bilingual education programs. Locally funded two-way bilingual education programs have proven effective in meeting the second-language learning needs of both limited-English-proficient students and monolingual-English students in a positive, integrated educational environment... Programs like these deserve additional Federal support, support made possible under the bill's new funding reservations.[25]

Contrary to Chairman Kennedy's advice, the Education Department's invitation for fiscal year 1989 grant applications projected that between $12 and $24 million would be available for new SAIP grants. The department did not even invite applications for fiscal year 1989 DBE grants. Senator Paul Simon, a member of the Labor and Human Resources Committee, observed that 'the Department has used its expanded discretionary funding authority as a noose to choke off support for Developmental Bilingual Education Programs — the most promising and thc most underfunded of the three major alternative programs supported under Title VII [BEA].[26]

## English Monolingualism: A Negative Educational Outcome

Weeks before he left office, Education Secretary Bennett issued his 'final report to the American people.' *James Madison Elementary School* detailed a model curriculum, including prescribed learning objectives and reading lists and some sound advice regarding foreign-language instruction:

> Early study of foreign languages makes sense. The imitative capacities of young children give them natural advantages as language students. And language study is good for them. It allows children a taste of the size and diversity of human experience and helps them to distinguish similarities and differences between their own and other cultures and peoples. It may even have a positive effect on their command of English.[27]

Bennett's voice joins a chorus of support for expanded foreign-language education. Declining American influence in a shrinking world has forged a national consensus on the importance of language and culture studies. Second-language study is now viewed as an essential, albeit often missing, part of the American core curriculum.

The discussion of foreign-language study highlights the failure of federal bilingual-education programs to develop our students' native-language skills. If bilingualism is a positive educational outcome, the transformation of language-minority students from monolingual speakers of a language other than English into monolingual English speakers must be viewed as a negative educational outcome, one that may violate Title VI's guarantee that all students have an equal opportunity to 'participate in and benefit from' federally assisted education programs.

Some states and local school districts are already moving to exploit the native language skills of their students. The New York State Board of Regents recently revised state bilingual-education policy to emphasize native-language development and two-way bilingual education. The Los Angeles Unified School District has replicated in more than two dozen schools a demonstrably successful bilingual educational program developed at the Eastman Elementary School. The Eastman program provides intensive native-language — Spanish — development in kindergarten and early grades. Once the children have achieved literacy in Spanish, generally in the middle-elementary grades, English language development is emphasized. By the end of elementary school, Eastman students academically outperform other district students in English; they are also functionally bilingual.[28]

## The Goal of American Bilingual Education

Today, nearly one of every five American students entering school knows a language other than English. Nearly half of these students are limited in English language proficiency. In the future, language-minority and LEP students will compose a greater proportion of our school-age population. This demographic reality coupled with our long-term need to promote bilingualism and multilingualism compel a shift in federal bilingual education policy from a language wrecking-ball to a language building-block approach.

Time certainly seems to be on the side of monolingualism in America. Even if we were to pursue foreign-language study with the noted fervor of the Japanese, and if local, state, and federal legislatures were quick to appropriate the billions necessary for teacher training, retraining, and materials development, it would be well into the twenty-first century before a significant portion of our children left school bilingual, simply because it takes time to become proficient in a second language. At the Defense Language Institute — a highly regarded, well-funded, intensive foreign-language program serving well-educated and highly motivated professional adults — a 47-week program providing 35 hours of instruction per week supplemented by hundreds of hours of structured homework generally enables program graduates to achieve a score of 2 or 2+ on the US Government Interagency Language Round Table Oral Proficiency Interview scale. This level of proficiency is described as follows:

> Able to satisfy routine social demands and limited work requirements...can get the gist of most conversations on nontechnical subjects and has a speaking vocabulary sufficient to respond simply with some circumlocutions; accent, though often quite faulty, is intelligible; can usually handle elementary constructions quite accurately but does not have a thorough or confident control of grammar.[29]

To put the institute's training into focus, consider that an undergraduate student preparing to be a teacher would receive in four years only 600 hours, at five hours per week, of foreign-language instruction. The average graduate of such a teacher-training program lacks the skills to use properly, much less teach, a foreign language to children. Only rarely would he or she possess foreign-language skills suitable for the 'imitative capacities of young children.'

Time could be turned to our advantage, however, if we were to conserve, develop, and capitalize on the language skills of the language-minority students in our schools. These skills, developed through tens of thousands of hours of mother-tongue instruction, offer both a quick fix and a long-term solution to the problem of American monolingualism.

The average language-minority child entering kindergarten has a higher level of language mastery than the average graduate of the intensive and expensive 47-week Defense Language Institute program.[30] But language skills seldom remain static; either they are developed or they atrophy. The cost of further developing the already substantial native-language skills of our language-minority students is marginal. The payoff, however, is big and relatively immediate — the production, within a generation, of millions of bilingual, biliterate Americans.

Expansion of two-way developmental-bilingual-education programs could also dramatically accelerate the mastery of second languages by students who are monolingual in English. For more than 25 years, the Miami Coral Way Elementary School has developed students' Spanish skills. Since the early 1970s the Oyster Elementary School in Washington, DC, has followed the same basic approach for a racially and ethnically mixed student population with tremendous success. Currently, several dozen locally funded two-way bilingual-education programs — including one serving more than 3000 students in San Diego, California — are helping elementary school students achieve something most of their parents have still not developed, the ability to communicate effectively in English and at least one other language and to understand and respect other cultures.[31]

Whether federal support for such programs grows is up to Congress and the president. Influential members of Congress have already announced their desire to expand developmental and two-way bilingual-education programs. President Bush has not yet shared his views.

## Notes

1. S. 428, 90th Cong., 1st sess. (1967).
2. US Congress, Senate, Committee on Labor and Public Welfare, Special Subcommittee on Bilingual Education, *Hearings on S.428*, 90th Cong., 1st sess.. 1967. pp. 1–2.
3. Ibid., p. 2.
4. S.428.
5. Ibid.
6. Pub. L.93-380, §703(a)(4)(B)(21 Aug. 1974).
7. Pub. L.95-561, §703(a)(4)(B)(1 Oct. 1978).
8. J. Stanley Pottinger, 'Identification of Discrimination and Denial of Services on the Basis of National Origin' (Memorandum, Department of Health Education and Welfare 25 May 1970).
9. 94 S.Ct.786.788 (1974).
10. Ibid. p. 789.
11. Ibid.
12. US Department of Health, Education and Welfare, *Task Force Findings Specifying Remedies Available for Eliminating Past Educational Practices Ruled Unlawful under Lau v. Nichols*, 11 Aug. 1975.
13. Notice of Proposed Rulemaking under Title VI or the Civil Rights Act of 1964, *Federal Register*, 5 Aug. 1980, 45:52052.
14. James Crawford, *Bilingual Education: History, Politics, Theory and Practice* (Trenton, NJ: Crane, 1989).
15. Ronald F. Docksai, 'The Department of Education'. In *Mandate for Leadership: Policy Management in a Conservative Administration* ed. C.L. Heatherly (Washington, DC: Heritage Foundation, 1981), pp. 186–87.
16. James Crawford 'US Enforcement of Bilingual Plans Declines Sharply'. *Education Week*, 4 June 1986, p. 1.
17. T.H. Bell, *The Condition of Bilingual Education in The Nation, 1982* (Washington, DC: Department of Education. 1982), p. 3.
18. Ibid.
19. Ibid.
20. Pub. L. 98-511, §§ 703(a)(4)(A), (5)(A), (6) (19 Oct. 1984).
21. Ibid., § 702(a)(11).
22. Ibid., § 703(a)(5)(B).
23. Ibid., § 702(a)(7).
24. William J. Bennett, Address to the Association for a Better New York, New York City, 26 Sept. 1985.
25. US Congress, Senate, *Congressional Record*, 100th Cong., 2d sess., 20 Apr. 1988, p. S4367.

26. Senator Paul Simon to Secretary of Education Designate Lauro F. Cavazos, 8 Sept. 1988 pp.3–4.
27. William J. Bennett, *James Madison Elementary School: A Curriculum for American Students* (Washington, DC: Department of Education, Aug. 1988), pp 47–48.
28. See, for example, Kenji Hakuta, *Mirror of Language: The Debate on Bilingualism* (New York: Basic Books, 1987); US General Accounting Office *Bilingual Education: A New Look at the Research Evidence*, GAO/PEMD-87-12BR. Mar. 1987; Crawford, *Bilingual Education*.
29. Russell N. Campbell and Kathryn Lindholm, 'Conservation of Language Resources' (Los Angeles: University of California, 1987). p. 5.
30. Ibid.
31. Deborah L. Gold, 'Two Languages, One Aim: "Two-Way" Learning,' *Education Week*, 20 Jan. 1988, p. 7.

## Questions

(1) Why does Lyons call the Bilingual Education Act (Title VII of the Elementary and Secondary Education Act) a misnomer? Ensure you refer to the Act's origins, as well as its goal when it was passed in 1968.

(2) Make a table to explain the changes to the Bilingual Education Act since its adoption in 1968. Refer to the amendments of 1974, 1978, 1984, 1988. (You may want to read Casanova's article, this volume, before expanding on this question.)

(3) The Bilingual Education Act of 1968 referred to 'limited English-speaking' (LES) students. By 1978, the term 'limited English-proficient' (LEP) was adopted. Explain what the difference is between the two. Discuss why Lyons says that the term LEP 'reinforces the deficit approach to educating language minority students.' What other terms have you heard referring to students who are learning a second language? How would you evaluate them? What comment does Casanova make about this? (See Casanova, this volume.)

(4) Explain the case of *Lau* v. *Nichols* and the Supreme Court's decision of 1974. Refer to the legal basis for this judicial decision. Does *Lau* v. *Nichols* mandate bilingual education? Then discuss the Lau Remedies and their history, including the relationship of Title VI of the Civil Rights Act and the Office of Civil Rights (OCR) to bilingual education.

(5) What is the contradiction between (a) opposing bilingual education for language minorities and (b) supporting foreign language instruction. Refer to some manifestations of this contradiction in policy. (You may also include other examples given in the last section of Casanova's article, this volume.)

(6) What was the Coral Way Elementary School? Following the typology of bilingual education given below, which type of bilingual education would you say this was? Given its success, why do you think it was not an option from 1968 to 1984? How did the 1984 bilingual education amendments change this situation?

## Activities

(1) Select a school with which you are familiar. Interview parents, teachers and administrators. Write a historical account of the changes that have taken place in the student population of the school, the education of language minority students, and the presence of a minority language(s) in education.

(2) In the library, read testimonies given during the Senate Hearings for the authorization of the 1968 Bilingual Education Act. Write an essay with the following information:
(a) Who gave testimony?
(b) What were the opinions expressed?

# A TYPOLOGY OF BILINGUAL EDUCATION

## WEAK FORMS OF EDUCATION FOR BILINGUALISM

| Type of Program | Typical Type of Child | Language of the Classroom | Societal and Educational Aim | Aim in Language Outcome |
|---|---|---|---|---|
| SUBMERSION (Structured Immersion) | Language Minority | Majority Language | Assimilation | Monolingualism |
| SUBMERSION with Withdrawal Classes / Sheltered English) | Language Minority | Majority Language with 'Pull-out' L2 Lessons | Assimilation | Monolingualism |
| SEGREGATIONIST | Language Minority | Minority Language (forced, no choice) | Apartheid | Monolingualism |
| TRANSITIONAL | Language Minority | Moves from Minority to Majority Language | Assimilation | Relative Monolingualism |
| MAINSTREAM with Foreign Language Teaching | Language Majority | Majority Language with L2/FL Lessons | Limited Enrichment | Limited Bilingualism |
| SEPARATIST | Language Minority | Minority Language (out of choice) | Detachment/ Autonomy | Limited Bilingualism |

## STRONG FORMS OF EDUCATION FOR BILINGUALISM AND BILITERACY

| Type of Program | Typical Type of Child | Language of the Classroom | Societal and Educational Aim | Aim in Language Outcome |
|---|---|---|---|---|
| IMMERSION | Language Majority | Bilingual with Initial Emphasis on L2 | Pluralism and Enrichment | Bilingualism & Biliteracy |
| MAINTENANCE/ HERITAGE LANGUAGE | Language Minority | Bilingual with Emphasis on L1 | Maintenance, Pluralism and Enrichment | Bilingualism & Biliteracy |
| TWO-WAY/DUAL LANGUAGE | Mixed Language Minority & Majority | Minority and Majority | Maintenance, Pluralism and Enrichment | Bilingualism & Biliteracy |
| MAINSTREAM BILINGUAL | Language Majority | Two Majority Languages | Maintenance, Pluralism and Enrichment | Bilingualism & Biliteracy |

Notes: (1) L2 = Second Language; L1 = First Language; FL = Foreign Language.
　　　(2) For an explanation of this table, see *Foundations of Bilingual Education and Bilingualism* (Baker, 1993) where the table was first presented.

(c) Was there a difference between testimony offered by members of the majority and of the language minority?

What can you conclude about the motivation for the Bilingual Education Act?

(3) Search through the index of a major US daily, such as *The Washington Post* or *The New York Times*. Look for articles on the following:

(a) Passage of the First Bilingual Education Act, 1968.

(b) *Lau* v. *Nichols* decision, 1974.

(c) Withdrawal of Title VII regulations, 1980.

Different groups might search different newspapers and compare the reporting both with regard to coverage and attitudes expressed. For example, New York might be compared to Los Angeles; an English-language daily might be compared to a non-English-language daily. On a particular day, compare the number of articles, the length of the articles, and whether the attitudes are positive or negative. Make a chart with your results.

(4) Select a school with which you are familiar. Interview parents, teachers and administrators. Find out the school's policy with regard to:

(a) The education of language minority students.

(b) The use of minority languages in education.

(c) Bilingualism and biliteracy.

(d) Language and cultural awareness for all.

Also find out whether the school's policy responds to any societal policy or demands. Summarize answers on a chart.

Different groups might select schools with different characteristics. For example, an urban school might be compared to a suburban or rural one; a private one to a public one; a large one to a small one. Share your answers.

(5) Find out whether the city or state or community you live in has a specific policy on the education of second language learners, the use of minority languages in instruction, bilingual education, or multicultural education. Find relevant documents. Share them with the class. Write a short report in which you summarize the policy, quoting from the documents.

(6) Research the recent history of the US Bilingual Education Act. What is its present status? What is some of the discourse surrounding reauthorization? Write a summary report.

## Further Reading

More in-depth coverage of bilingual education policy in the United States is offered in the following:

Brez Stein, Colman, Jr (1986) *Sink or Swim: The Politics of Bilingual Education*. New York: Praeger.

Castellanos, Diego (1983) *The Best of Two Worlds*. Trenton: New Jersey State Department of Education.

Crawford, James (1991) *Bilingual Education: History, Politics, Theory and Practice* (2nd edn). Los Angeles: Bilingual Educational Services.

Leibowitz, Arnold H. (1980) *The Bilingual Education Act: A Legislative Analysis*. Rosslyn, VI: National Clearinghouse for Bilingual Education.

Malakoff, Marguerite and Hakuta, Kenji (1990) History of language minority education in the United States. In Amado M. Padilla, Halford H. Fairchild and Concepción M.

Valadez (eds) *Bilingual Education: Issues and Strategies* (pp. 15–26). Newbury Park, CA: Sage.

Matute-Bianchi, María Eugenia (1979) The Federal mandate for bilingual education. In Raymond Padilla (ed.) *Bilingual Education and Public Policy in the United States* (pp. 21–31). Ypsilanti: Eastern Michigan University.

Teitelbaum, Herbert and Hiller, Richard J. (1977) Bilingual education: The legal mandate. *Harvard Educational Review* 47, 138–70.

# Bilingual Education: Politics or Pedagogy?

## Ursula Casanova

### Introduction

My first contact with bilingual education in the United States came in 1971, only three years after the passage of the first Bilingual Education Act, when I assumed a position as assistant principal for instruction in an urban elementary school. One of my major responsibilities was the supervision of the school's bilingual program.

My professional experience previous to bilingual education was similar to that of many Hispanics at the time. I had been a teacher of Spanish as a foreign language for five years. A veteran of one of the many blips in the US educational landscape: the foreign language in elementary schools (FLES) program implemented during the sixties. When bilingual education came upon the scene, everyone assumed that if you could teach a foreign language, or even if you were only a competent speaker of one, then you knew how to teach students in bilingual education. It was soon evident that we had much to learn.

In 1971 bilingual education was little more than an idea, a step-child of the Civil Rights Act. Bilingual programs were being implemented much quicker than materials were made available or teachers trained. And a knowledge base to support the instructional activities being initiated was practically non-existent. We operated more out of instinct than anything else, and everyone worked exceedingly hard trying to keep ahead of the demands presented by their classes. With characteristic bluntness Fishman & Lovas (1970) called attention to those very lacks in bilingual education: lack of funds, lack of trained personnel, and lack of evaluated programs.

The next few years were accompanied by growth in all areas of bilingual education. Early experimental efforts culminated in the passage of the 1974 Bilingual Education Act, the first one accompanied by a respectable budget, and consciously targeted to the needs of non-English speaking students. By that time moneys for training had been made available and publishers were producing materials more or less suited to the needs of our students. The mood was optimistic, the energy level high. Barely four years later, and not too surprisingly, those early tentative efforts would be negatively evaluated in the AIR report which will be discussed below.

It is useful to remember that the late sixties and early seventies were a time of ferment for bilingual education when politicians spoke passionately about their hopes for children. Bilingual education was a friendly concept then. But it was also a time of struggle for those of us in the schools. Although bilingual education had existed in various guises throughout the country's history, and was alive and well in many parts of the world, we had no maps. (For a review of that history, see, for example, Heath, 1981; Keller & Van Hooft, 1982.) Our energy and commitment made up for our ignorance as we invented programs and curricula to respond to the new legislation. Under the current attacks from US English we tend to forget the hope and promise of those years. But the past remembered serves as context for the present. And understanding the historical context is particularly important in an area as young and conflicted as bilingual education.

In this chapter I will attempt to shed light on the persistent conflict over bilingual education through a comparison of the evolution of bilingual education policy at the federal level against the knowledge base on bilingualism and bilingual education. My focus will be on the relationship between these two strands of influence on bilingual education.

### Bilingual Education: Policy

#### The early years

Perhaps the most important characteristic to remember about the 1968 Bilingual Education Act is what it was not. It was not a pedagogical response to a previously documented problem but rather the result of political strategies designed to funnel federal poverty funds to the Southwest. This is not to say that children lacking English skills were not failing in the schools, but while the need existed, there was no great demand for the type of federal political intervention represented by the Bilingual Education Act. The problem remained at the local school and district levels.

In 1965 the Johnson administration, besieged by urban riots, sought to direct Federal funds to the poor in US cities. With the passage of the Elementary and Secondary Act (ESEA) of 1965 Johnson succeeded not only in targeting money to the poor, but also in overcoming historical opposition to federal aid to education. Title I of the ESEA was the first attempt by Congress to pledge money for children of low-income families (Schneider, 1976).

The sweetener tossed for Hispanics into the 1968 Title VII Amendments to ESEA was not based on knowledge about language learning or bilingualism. The move has been attributed to Sen. Yarborough's (Democrat from Texas) interest in funneling a portion of the federal anti-poverty funds to the Southwest. He, and those who joined him in the effort, appealed to the needs of Mexican-Americans who were described as the second largest minority, very poor, and with a language deficiency (descriptors that unfortunately continue to haunt the program). Hispanic leaders were recruited to testify and they also described the great injustices suffered by this newly discovered 'culturally disadvantaged' group. A few experts were also called to testify, among them Joshua Fishman. Their combined effort resulted in the Title VII Amendments, the first categorical Federal law authorizing bilingual–bicultural educational programs (Betances *et al.*, 1981).

Other pressures also contributed to the acceptance of the Title VII Amendments. One was the presence of hundreds of immigrants from Cuba who saw themselves as only temporary residents of the United States. They were ready to leave as soon as Castro was chased away and were therefore eager to maintain their culture and their children's Spanish language skills. In 1963 the Ford Foundation had already helped Cuban refugees to set up an experimental program in bilingual education. The program was considered a success and provided a viable model for later efforts. Unlike later government funded

programs, the Dade County program was oriented toward enrichment instead of remediation (Hakuta, 1986).

The Civil Rights movement was also beginning to inspire demands for equal educational opportunity from other linguistic minorities, including Native Americans. Those pressures contributed to the extension of bilingual education beyond the original Hispanic target group. And from Alaska to the Mexico border, poor children from homes where English was not the dominant language became the beneficiaries. The nation's newspapers proclaimed that Public Law 90-247 would establish 'bilingual education programs for children of Indian, Puerto Rican and Mexican descent' (Schneider, 1976).

From its conception then, bilingual education was a political artifact; born not of knowledge, or even of expressed need, but of political maneuvering perhaps heavily laced with a sense of social responsibility. Such serendipitous beginnings had unintended consequences. Bilingual education rapidly became a rallying point for Hispanics. It was a cause that could, and did, unite Hispanic people across the country, across cultural, educational, and even class barriers. As a result, the political climate surrounding the Education Amendments of 1974 was drastically different.

### Legal support

In 1974 the Supreme Court of the United States handed down its decision in the landmark Lau vs. Nichols case. In this decision the Court ruled that students were being denied equal educational opportunity when school officials took no steps whatever to help speakers of other languages (SOLs)[1] participate meaningfully in the school program. The decision came at a fortuitous time, in the midst of congressional hearings about bilingual education. Through this ruling the Court legitimized the need for bilingual instruction: '...there is no equality of treatment merely by providing students with the same facilities, textbooks, teachers, and curriculum; for students who do not understand English are certain to find their classroom experiences wholly incomprehensible and in no way meaningful' (Lau vs. Nichols, 1974). Thus, through the Court's commonsensical decision Congress' previous political actions were translated into a pedagogical need.

The importance of this ruling was not lost on members of Congress who could now see themselves as being on the side of the law, and perhaps even ahead of it. It is likely that the court's resolute statement encouraged legislators to accept a requirement for native language instruction in the legislation. In addition, eligibility was broadened through elimination of the poverty requirement. For Hispanics the court's decision provided needed encouragement. Schneider (1976) found that non-English dominant populations exerted a significant influence in the passage of the 1974 Bilingual Education Act. They did this directly as lobbysts and active participants in the drafting of the legislation, and indirectly as constituents to senators such as Edward Kennedy of Massachusetts and Alan Cranston of California, both from states with large SOLs populations and, therefore, strong advocates of the legislation. In contrast, Schneider found that public opinion had little influence on the passage of the law. But once again, four years later the climate was vastly different.

By 1978, the next reauthorization cycle, research on bilingual education had begun to accumulate and the findings were generally supportive of the programs (see, for example, Dulay & Burt, 1978 and Troike, 1978). Bolstered by this research, reauthorization should have been easily accomplished. However, critics had also found their voice and the 1978 hearings gave them a national forum. Noel Epstein's *Language, Ethnicity and the Schools* became a much cited source in the attacks on bilingual education. As a reporter for The Washington Post, Mr. Epstein's opinion was assured wide dissemination, even though his position was sharply criticized by some of the very people he had cited in his support. Fishman, for example, called it 'an ignorant critique...heaps bias upon bias, suspicion upon suspicion, misinterpretation upon misinterpretation...' (Fishman, 1978: 16). Albert Shanker, then president of the American Federation of Teachers, also had a ready soap-box from which to promulgate his opposition through his editorials and position papers, and he used them often to attack bilingual education.

The Congressional committee heard more substantial criticism from Malcolm Danoff, of the American Institute of Research (AIR). Under his direction, this organization had conducted a study which less than four years after its uncertain beginnings had concluded that Title VII did not appear to have a significant impact in meeting the goals of the legislation. Although the study was severely criticized on methodological

grounds by O'Malley (1978) and others, the findings received wide publicity from the press and became a rallying point for the opposition during the 1978 hearings. In spite of this formidable opposition, bilingual education was retained in language close to the original legislation.

This temporary reprieve masked the gradual erosion of support for bilingual education. The program, and its sister programs in the Great Society collective were not well received by politicians. Their political power depended on the disbursement of federal funds to their constituents. By circumventing traditional relationships through direct assignment of funds to the barrios and ghettos, the Great Society offended these politicians and generated hostility toward the programs (Piven & Cloward, 1971).

The Lau decision was followed by the creation of Lau Centers to provide technical assistance and support to school districts. These centers applied the Lau Guidelines which did not have the force of law but were implemented through the Department of Health, Education and Welfare's (now the Department of Education) monitoring responsibilities. The Lau Guidelines encouraged the use of the native language in the bilingual/bicultural education for SOLs. In 1980 the Guidelines were reviewed by the newly created Department of Education and its first Secretary, Shirley Hufstedler. Formal regulations, mandating bilingual instruction in any public school enrolling 20 or more speakers of a given language emerged from that review but were never implemented. They were withdrawn soon after President Reagan took office in 1980. His election also led to the softening of the government's advocacy role in civil rights and, therefore, the weakening of Title VI, the Equal Educational Opportunity Act of 1974, which had provided legislative support for the Bilingual Education Act.

The drastic change in climate was heralded in an early address by President Reagan to the National League of Cities where he characterized bilingual programs as 'absolutely wrong and un-American' (Reagan, March 2, 1981). Instead of demands for compliance, the Reagan White House engaged in activities directed at discrediting bilingual education. In September 1981 the Baker/de Kanter report was issued to the press in draft form and before formal review. Although the authors claimed to have conducted an independent study, they acknowledged that it had been initiated 'at the request of the White House

Regulatory Analysis and Review Group for an assessment on the effectiveness of bilingual education' (Seidner & Seidner, 1982).

The report was roundly criticized on methodological grounds by many researchers, nonetheless it succeeded in gaining the attention of the media.

### Increased opposition

The Bilingual Education Act was reauthorized most recently in 1988. Conflict over the relative emphasis on native-language instruction has been continuous since, in spite of its name, the Act did not originally require 'bilingual' instruction. In addition, although transitional goals have been emphasized, the possibility for other instructional programs has never been excluded. The requirement for native language instruction has nonetheless been maintained throughout, although lately portions of bilingual education funds have been set-aside for the implementation of competing instructional strategies advocated by its opponents.

Previous to the 1988 reauthorization, William Bennett, then Secretary of Education attempted to remove the specific reservation of funds for programs using the students' native language from the law altogether. His department cited the supposed ambiguity in research and evaluation reports as the reason to oppose continuation of that requirement. In an effort to clarify the issues, the House Committee on Education and Labor requested the Government Accounting Office (GAO) to conduct an independent review of the research evidence in bilingual education. Their review culminated in the GAO's *Bilingual Education: A New Look at the Research Evidence* (1987). In their summary analysis the GAO reports that:

> The experts' view on the official statements…indicate that the department interpreted the research differently in several major ways. First, only 2 of the 10 experts agree with the department that there is insufficient evidence to support the law's requirement of the use of native language to the extent necessary to reach the objective of learning English. Second, 7 of the 10 believe that the department is incorrect in characterizing the evidence as showing the promise of teaching methods [such as immersion] that do not use native languages. Few agree with the department's suggestions that long-term school problems experienced by Hispanic youths are associated with native-

language instruction. Few agree with the department's general interpretation that evidence in this field is too ambiguous to permit conclusions. (GAO, 1987: 3)

Thus, the GAO comparison of statements by Department of Education officials with the research evidence suggests either that department officials were unfamiliar with or misinterpreted the evidence, or that, for their own reasons, they chose to misquote and misuse it. Mr Bennett, and other Reagan administration officials, succeeded, nevertheless, in shifting the policy debate. Discussions about the preferred goal for bilingual education pre-1980 addressed the relative value of maintaining the native language alongside English instruction vs. using the native language purely as a transitional stage (see, for example, Gonzalez, 1978, and Trueba, 1979). The debate has now shifted.

Immersion programs conducted solely in English for SOLs were endorsed particularly by William Bennett during his tenure as Secretary of Education (1985–1988). And although Canadian researchers had warned against the transfer of successful immersion Canadian programs to the different US context (Tucker, 1980), the 1988 BEA increased the funding set-aside for 'Special Alternative Instructional Programs' under which immersion programs are categorized. In addition, and perhaps most damaging, the 1988 Act required students to exit from BEA funded instructional programs at the end of three years, and under no circumstances may a student continue to be enrolled in such programs for more than five years.

Under the threat of total loss of support for bilingual education, the possibility of maintenance is no longer discussed, we now speak of immersion vs. transitional. Ironically, this shift has occurred while the proposed evidence supporting positive effects for both bilingualism and bilingual instruction continues to mount.

It is this contrast between public policies on bilingual education, and the research evidence that is of interest to this writer. In the following pages I will cite selected findings to document the evolving evidence favoring bilingual education and bilingualism against the policy backdrop of the last twenty-one years discussed above.

### Bilingual Education: The Research

The research I will cite falls across three categories: research about bilingualism, research about bilingual education, and research about the effects of bilingual education. The questions that guide me are: Is bilingualism an asset or a handicap? If an asset, is there reason to believe that bilingual education is an appropriate vehicle for instruction? If so, how do we know? This is not intended to be a full review of the literature regarding these broad topics, that task has been accomplished elsewhere (see, for example, Larter & Cheng, 1984). The purpose is, instead, to contrast the robustness of positive research findings against eroding government support.

### Bilingualism: An asset or a handicap?

Most of the research conducted until the early sixties concluded that bilingualism was a language handicap. This research was sharply questioned in 1962 by Peal & Lambert. They reported that bilingual children performed better than monolinguals in a series of cognitive tests, when sex, age, and socioeconomic status were appropriately controlled. These researchers attributed the negative findings of earlier studies to the failure to differentiate degrees of bilingualism and to control for socioeconomic status.

Diaz (1985: 72) in a well-substantiated review intended as a plea of support for bilingual education in the Southwest United States lists a number of studies which show the advantages of bilingualism: '...in measures of conceptual development (Bain, 1974; Liedtke & Nelson, 1968), creativity (Torrance *et al.*, 1970), metalinguistic awareness (Cummins, 1978), semantic development (Ianco-Worrall, 1972) and analytical skills... (Ben-Zeev, 1977)'. Diaz (1985: 72) also reports that children with higher levels of bilingual proficiency perform at a higher level than their peers on measures of analogical reasoning and tests of spatial relations.

Kessler & Quinn (1987) have compared the performance of 6th grade bilingual children in a southwestern barrio school to private school Anglo children in the same grade in the northeast in the solution of science problems. In spite of the Anglo children's superior reading level (7.38 compared to 3.0) children from the barrios of San Antonio achieved higher scores in their ability to generate more (1,945 to 579) and higher quality (176 to 53) scientific hypotheses, to use more complex metaphors (26 to 19), and to produce more syntactically complex statements (182 to 130) while attempting to solve science problems.

### Is bilingual education effective?

Assessing the effectiveness of bilingual education will always be a problem. The term 'bilingual education' has no specific definition. It tends to be applied to any program directed at SOLs. Some of these programs may use the native language very little, if at all. In addition, the transitional nature of bilingual schooling ensures frequent turn-over in student population and the accumulation, especially as students move up the grades, of students who may require a longer period of native language support. Those are also the students who are least likely to perform well in standardized tests.

Both the AIR study of 1974 and the Baker/de Kanter report of 1981 were criticized for the researchers' lack of discrimination among various programs purporting to be 'bilingual education'. Rigorous assessment of instruction would require careful attention to program content and structure, as well as to student population. But this has not been the case in most assessments of bilingual education.

Willig (1985) has conducted a 'partial replication' of the Baker/de Kanter review by using all but five of the original set of studies. The excluded studies were conducted on programs outside of the US or, in one case, outside of a regular public school setting. Willig also controlled for methodological inadequacies such as initial group differences in language dominance, in environmental language exposure, in need for the bilingual program, inappropriate comparisons with 'graduates' of bilingual programs, and differences, due to exiting of successful students and addition of newcomers, between pre- and post-test population. Willig found that participation in bilingual programs consistently produced small to moderate differences favoring bilingual education. Willig concluded that the predominance of inadequate research designs, and inappropriate comparisons of children in bilingual programs to children who were dissimilar in many crucial aspects, has done a disservice to bilingual education: 'In every instance where there did not appear to be crucial inequalities between experimental and comparison groups, children in bilingual programs averaged higher than the comparison children on criterion instruments' (Willig, 1985: 312).

Researchers have also been criticized for limiting their criteria to those easily measured through standardized achievement tests. Paulston (1980a), for example, noted that the 1976 dropout rate for Native Americans in Chicago public schools was 95% while it was only 11% in the bilingual–bicultural Little Big Horn School in Chicago. She argued for the use of broader criteria and longitudinal studies to determine a program's success. Also excluded from the criteria used to evaluate bilingual education is the value of bilingual competence which is added to an individual's linguistic repertoire. In studies of 4th and 5th grade bilingual children, Hakuta (forthcoming) found that the translation skills of these young students were comparable to those of foreign language adult students. Hakuta suggests that the students' translation skills are related to a variety of metalinguistic skills.

In spite of the scarcity of rigorous, comprehensive studies, the experts judging the available data for the GAO report did conclude that the data favored programs using native language instruction. They were also clear in stating that there were no data to support the assertion that bilingual education was impeding the educational progress of Hispanic students.

### Is there evidence for positive outcomes?

The notion that bilingualism impedes the educational achievement of Hispanic students is also belied by data from the National Center of Education Statistics' 'High School and Beyond' study. Fernandez & Nielsen (1986) found that exposure to Spanish during upbringing was not a handicap but an asset, greater Spanish proficiency was associated with greater achievement in both verbal and nonverbal tests.

Data is also available regarding differences in aspirations. One might infer that students with higher aspirations are likely to also achieve at a higher level. This was the position taken by Nielsen & Lerner (1982) in an analysis of language skills as they affected the school achievement of high school seniors. These researchers considered three measures of school achievement: educational aspirations, grade point average, and age. They found ability and socioeconomic status to be the strongest determinants for achievement, effects that are well substantiated in the literature. However, they also found that Hispanicity was the third strongest determinant of aspirations. That is, among the group of bilinguals, those who used Spanish more often also had higher aspirations. Conversely, English proficiency had no significant effect on these students' aspirations.

Along a similar vein, García (1981) also found positive associations with bilingualism among Latinos. He found that when Spanish dominant homes enhanced the Spanish fluency of children, the offspring developed higher levels of self-esteem, more ambitious economic plans, greater assuredness of achieving such plans, greater locus of control, and higher grades in college. The research evidence thus tends to favor Spanish language maintenance. The benefits of bilingualism are now widely recognized and they appear to accrue not just to advantaged populations, but also to the children of the barrio. Over and over we find that native language competence appears to contribute, rather than detract, from academic achievement. There does not appear to be any evidence to the contrary.

So, how has this recent, and consistently positive research knowledge influenced policymakers? Not much.

## Social Science Research and Government Policy

Hakuta notes that 'bilingual education has received a disproportionate amount of public horn-locking by politicians, educators, and ordinary citizens alike' (1986: 206). This has been true even though in its richest year (1984) the bilingual education budget was less than one percent of the total United States federal education budget. He ascribes this mismatch between funding level and the amount of controversy generated to the emotional loading of the issues represented by bilingual education.

And this is the real battle for bilingual education advocates. After 21 years we now have the research to support our instinctive beliefs. We can now argue with a measure of confidence about the benefits of bilingual education. Through the years we have become more knowledgeable about effective instructional strategies and even about language assessment, although we still have much to learn about both. In spite of all this progress, the battle has become more, rather than less, difficult.

The conflictive situation of bilingual education contrasts sharply with the easy acceptance of educational funding for other federal programs, for example, for the gifted and talented. The allocation of special funding for this population was probably as much a creature of the political climate as was the original allocation of moneys for bilingual education. However, unlike bilingual education, programs for the gifted and talented have never received judicial support or the support of research in the social sciences resulting in the positive findings reviewed above, nor do programs for the gifted and talented have the obvious potential for satisfying a national need such as that for increased language fluency. Programs targeted for the gifted and talented have not been proven effective against any criteria. And yet, funding for these programs continues to be accepted by the public and our legislators without question.

It is ironic that the conflict over bilingual education occurs side by side a gathering tide of concern over US students' lack of competence in foreign languages. In November of 1980 the Presidential Commission on Foreign Languages and International Studies, appointed by President Carter, described the national state of incompetence in foreign languages as 'scandalous'. The need for foreign language education appears to be a cause everyone can comfortably espouse. Even the former Secretary of Education, William Bennett, in spite of his aversion to bilingual education, included two years of foreign language in his proposed model high school.

What are we to make of these conflicting positions? Steve Muller, commenting on the Presidential Commission's report, notes that bilingualism in the US has seldom been a learned achievement, more often it has been a stigma of recent immigration. He argues that inspiring greater national receptivity to the languages of other people will require a persistent assault on the American consciousness (Muller, 1980). But resistance to foreign languages is selective.

Lambert & Taylor (1986) found that citizens of the majority culture tend to be favorably disposed towards the maintenance of heritage cultures and languages for all ethnic groups. But their generosity stops at the schoolhouse door since they also consider instruction in languages other than English inappropriate in the public school setting. However, this same group of parents considers bilingualism developed through schooling as a social, intellectual, and career advantage for their own children. They want their children to achieve skills in another language and become bilingual, but they do not endorse native language instruction for language minority students. These students, they believe, should be taught in English, though they might want to maintain their language in informal settings. The less successful white, working class parents, tend to reject the preservation of heritage cultures and languages in or out of school. However, they also see advantages for their children if their children become bilingual.

The negative associations that tend to accompany bilingual education may also reflect early identification of the program with poverty and educational deficiency. Those labels served a convenient purpose, they made the program possible, but they have also contributed to the confusion of language difference with language deficiency. Students who may, in fact, be competent in two languages, continue to be described as language deficient.

These conflicting values are reflected in public policy. In Arizona, for example, bilingual education programs are at best, transitional. SOLs are expected to receive only minimal instruction in their native language before being mainstreamed into English only classrooms. While these children are being encouraged to forget their mother tongue, recent legislation demands that other Arizona children begin to learn a second language in the elementary school. Thus we may shortly find classrooms where students are being alienated from their native language adjacent to those where their age-mates are struggling to learn a second language.

Hakuta (1986) argues for dissolution of this paradox of admiration for school-attained bilingualism on the one hand, and scorn and shame for home-brewed immigrant bilingualism on the other. He proposes the development of all students, including monolingual English-speakers, as functional bilinguals by substituting linguistic, cognitive, and enrichment purposes for current compensatory goals. This writer shares his opinion that there are only two possible solutions to the conflict over bilingual education. Advocates will either have to convince the general public of the pedagogical value of bilingualism, or they must manage to dilute the identification of bilingual education with ethnicity, poverty and compensatory education. This could be achieved through programs that integrate monolingual English speakers with SOLs in mutually productive instructional relationships.

The intimate connection between bilingual education and foreign language competence has also been noted by prestigious organizations: the Carnegie Corporation, through its Presidential Report (Pifer, 1979), and in a joint report, the Academy for Educational Development and the Hazen Foundation (AED & E.W. Hazen Foundation, 1982). All have endorsed the value of bilingual education, and its potential for complementing a national effort at advancing foreign language competence in the nation.

In spite of such strong and prestigious endorsement, and of the commonsensical notion of connecting two national issues of pedagogical significance, bilingual education continues to be treated as a threat. The lack of influence of relevant scientific data to the debate is particularly surprising in a country that prides itself on its positivism.

The contrast between the scientific/pedagogical argument and public policies puts in question the relevance of the social sciences to the conduct of public policy. In so doing the question of how to preserve the benefits of bilingual education for the increasing number of SOLs remains. The pedagogical avenue appears to be weak in relation to the emotional loading of the concept. If so, only the political avenue remains. This will require a united flexing of the emerging minority voting muscle and appeals to the interests of liberal monolingual populations. Bilingual education as a remedial program will not survive. Its only hope is in the embracing of those who understand that language competence of whatever variety is not a deficiency but an advantage.

## Note

1. I consider the acronym LEP offensive because 'limited' puts a negative cast on the linguistic skills of these students and it calls to mind a historically oppressed population. I have therefore adopted 'speakers of other languages' as a more descriptive and accurate way to identify these children. The phrase results in a much more positive acronym as well: SOLs.

## References

Academy for Educational Development and the Edward W. Hazen Foundation (1982) A new direction for bilingual education in the 1980's. *Focus* 10, 1-4.

Bain, B. (1974) Toward a general theory. In S.T. Carey (eds) *Bilingualism, Biculturalism and Education: Proceedings from the Conference at College Universitaire Saint Jean, Edmonton*. Alberta: The University of Alberta.

Ben-Zeev, S. (1977) The influence of bilingualism on cognitive strategy and cognitive development. *Child Development* 48, 1009–18.

Betances, S., Fernández, R.R. and Baez, L.A. (1981) Hispanics, educational policies and the politics of bilingual education. Typescript.

Cummins, J. (1978) Metalingusitc development of children in bilingual educational programs: Data from Irish and Canadian Ukranian-English Programs. In M. Paradis (ed.) *The Fourth Locus Forum 1977* (pp. 127–138). Columbia, SC: Hornbeam Press.

Diaz, R.M. (1985) The intellectual power of bilingualism. *The Quarterly Newsletter of the Laboratory of Comparative Human Cognition* 7, 16-22.

Dulay, H. and Burt, M. (1978) *Why Bilingual Education? A Summary of Research Findings*. San Francisco: Bloomsbury West.

Fernández, R.M. and Nielson, F. (1986) Bilingualism and Hispanic scholastic achievement: Some baseline results. *Social Science Research* 15, 43–70.

Fishman, J.A. (1978a) A gathering of vultures, the 'Legion of Decency' and bilingual education in the USA. *NABE* 2, 13–16.

Fishman, J.A. and Lovas, J. (1970) Bilingual education in a sociolinguistic perspective. *TESOL Quarterly* 4, 215–22.

García, H.D.C. (1981) *Bilingualism, Confidence and College Achievement*. Center for the Social Organization of Schools: John Hopkins University.

González, J. (1978) The status of bilingual education today: Un vistazo y un repaso. *NABE* 2, 13–20.

General Accounting Office (GAO) (1987) Bilingual Education: A new look at the research evidence. US General Accounting Office Briefing Report to the Chairman, Committee of Education and Labor, House of Representatives.

Hakuta, K. (1986) *Mirror of Language: The Debate on Bilingualism*. New York: Basic Books.

Heath, S.B. (1981) English in our language heritage. In Ferguson and Heath (eds) (pp. 6–20).

Ianco-Worral, A.D. (1972) Bilingualism and cognitive development. *Child Development* 43, 1390–1400.

Keller, G.D. and van Hooft, K.S. (1982) A chronology of bilingualism and bilingual education in the United States. In J.A. Fishman and G.D. Keller *Bilingual Education for Hispanic Students in the United States*. New York: Teachers College Press.

Kessler, C. and Quinn, M.E. (1987) Language minority children's linguistic and cognitive creativity. *Journal of Multilingual and Multicultural Development* 8, 173–86.

Lambert, W.E. and Taylor, D.M. (1986) *Cultural and Racial Diversity in the Lives of Urban Americans: The Hamtramck/Pontiac Study*. Preliminary Report. Toronto, Canada: McGill University.

Larter, S. and Cheng, M. (1984) *Bilingual Education and Bilingualism: A Review of Research Literature*. Toronto, Canada: Toronto Board of Education.

Lau vs. Nicholas (1974) 414 US 563.

Liedtke, W.W. and Nelson, L.D. (1968) Concept formation and bilingualism. *Alberta Journal of Educational Research* 14, 225–32.

Muller, S. (1980) *America's International Illiteracy*. New York Times Higher Education Supplement, November 11.

Nielsen, F. and Lerner, S.J. (1982) Language, skills and school achievement of bilingual Hispanics. Unpublished manuscript. Chapel Hill: University of North Carolina.

O'Malley, J.M. (1978) Review of the evaluation of the impact of ESEA Title VII Spanish/English bilingual education program. *Bilingual Resources* 1, 6–10.

Paulston, C.B. (1980a) *Bilingual Education: Theories and Issues*. Rowley, MA: Newbury House.

Peal, E. and Lambert, W.E. (1962) The relationship of bilingualism to intelligence. *Psychological Monographs* 76, whole no. 546.

Pifer, A. (1979) *Bilingual Education and the Hispanic Challenge*. New York: Carnegie Corporation.

Piven, F.F and Cloward, R. (1971) *Regulating the Poor: The Function of Public Welfare*. New York: Vintage.

Schneider, S.G. (1976) *Revolution, Reaction or Reform: The 1974 Bilingual Education Act*. New York: Las Americas Publishing Co.

Seidner, S.S. and Seidner, M.M. (1982) In the wake of Conservative reaction: An analysis. *Bilingual Education Paper Series* (November). Los Angeles: California State University.

Torrance, E.P., Wu, J.J., Gowan, J.C. and Aliotti, N.C. (1970) Creative functioning of monolingual and bilingual children in Singapore. *Journal of Educational Psychology* 61, 72–5.

Troike, R. (1978) Research evidence for the effectiveness of bilingual education. *NABE Journal* 3, 13–24.

Trueba, H.T. (1979) Bilingual education models: Types and designs. In Trueba and Barnett-Mizrahi (eds) (pp. 54–73).

Tucker, G.R. (1980) Implications for US bilingual education: Evidence from Canadian research. *Focus* 2, 1–4. National Clearinghouse of Bilingual Education.

Willig, A.C. (1985) A meta-analysis of selected studies on the effectiveness of bilingual education. *Review of Educational Research* 55, 269–317.

## Questions

(1) Explain what Casanova means when she says that the most important characteristic to remember about the 1968 Bilingual Education Act is what it was not. What was it?

(2) Identify the following studies on the effectiveness of bilingual education, and indicate how they have impacted on the discussions surrounding reauthorization of the Bilingual Education Act:

    (a) The AIR Study (1978).

    (b) The Baker/de Kanter Report (1981).

    (c) The Willig study (1985).

    (d) The GAO Review (1987).

    (You may want to refer to '*Foundations of Bilingual Education and Bilingualism*,' Chapter 12, for more on these reports, or read Cummins (1986, this volume), to expand on this question. See also Meyers, Michael and Fienberg, Stephen (eds) (1992) *Assessing Evaluation Studies: The Case of Bilingual Education Strategies*. Washington, DC: National Academy Press.)

(3) Summarize the findings of Díaz (1985) and Fernández and Nielsen (1986) on the cognitive advantages of bilingualism. (You may want to consult '*Foundations of Bilingual Education and Bilingualism*,' Chapter 9, for more on the cognitive advantages of bilingualism.)

(4) After reading Lyons and Casanova, consider whether the United States has been involved in language planning for bilingualism? How has it or has it not?

## Activities

(1) Make a poster that portrays SOLs. Be as creative as you can. Select the best entries and display them in the class.
(2) Interview five students who are bilingual on:
   (a) Whether native language competence contributes or detracts from academic achievement.
   (b) The benefits of bilingualism.
   Different groups might select students with different characteristics. For example, some may interview language majority students, others may question language minority students; some might include students who are fully bilingual, and others those who are still acquiring the second language. Record their answers and share them with the class. Write an essay with conclusions derived from the class's research.
(3) Interview five language majority parents. Find out their view on bilingualism and whether they want their children to become bilingual. Then ask about their views on bilingual education for minority students. Find out whether they think public schools in the United States should be teaching non-English languages to language minority students. Record their answers on an answer sheet. Then write an essay with your conclusions.
(4) If you are bilingual, reflect on your own experience. Write an essay about a specific instance in which you have benefited from your ability to speak two languages. If you are not bilingual, write an essay about a specific experience when speaking a second language might have come in handy.

## Further Reading

A similar view to that of Casanova is offered in:

Cummins, Jim (1991) The politics of paranoia: Reflections on the bilingual education debate. In O. García (ed.) *Bilingual Education: Focusschrift in Honor of Joshua A. Fishman*. Amsterdam: John Benjamins.

Secada, Walter G. (1990) Research, politics, and bilingual education. *Annals of the American Academy of Political and Social Science* 508, 81–106.

An early warning of these events was offered in:

Fishman, Joshua (1978) A gathering of vultures, the 'Legion of Decency' and bilingual education in the USA. *NABE Journal* 2, 13–16.

Readers may also want to consult the following classical works on the socio-educational context of bilingual education:

Fishman, Joshua. A. (1976) *Bilingual Education: An International Sociological Perspective*. Rowley, MA: Newbury House.

Gaarder, Bruce A. (1977) *Bilingual Schooling and the Survival of Spanish in the United States*. Rowley, MA: Newbury House.

# Educational Language Planning in England and Wales: Multicultural Rhetoric and Assimilationist Assumptions

## Michael Stubbs

*Language – Bilingualism* (handwritten)

Britain is often recognised as a country with profoundly monolingual assumptions and a widespread apathy towards learning other languages. This paper is a case study of some major changes which are currently taking place in the British education system. These changes involve a great deal of discussion of language issues, both in official documents and in the press, and they do have some bright spots, notably:

- for the first time, learning a modern foreign language will be compulsory for all secondary school pupils;
- an element of language studies (language awareness) will be a compulsory component within the English curriculum.

However, despite much government rhetoric about increased opportunities for linguistic diversity, I will conclude pessimistically, that basic attitudes are unchanged, and that there are major attempts to further strengthen the dominant position of Standard English in Britain, rather than to attempt a more balanced relationship between English and other languages. The essential theme of the article is expressed by Williams (1965: 145) in his discussion of the selective tradition in British education:

> ...the way in which education is organized can be seen to express, consciously and unconsciously, the wider organization of a society, so that what has been thought of as simple distribution is in fact an active shaping to particular social ends.

His comment about distribution is intended to apply to selections of content in the curriculum and therefore applies equally to the way in which languages are chosen for the educational system.

The essential structure of the argument is provided by a very pointed and aggressive attack in current government language policy, formulated by Rosen (quoted in the *Times Education Supplement*, 24 June 1988): 'liberal words (which are used) to disguise sinister messages of state coercion.'

In this paper, I discuss to what extent such judgements are true, and conclude that they are, to a large extent, justified. There is much talk in government statements about ethnic diversity, and about opportunities for children to study a wider range of languages. But much of this looks like empty rhetoric when seen against the background of

- other statements;
- the lack of resources to implement such policies;
- the complete absence of any overall language planning.

(For other articles with the same basic argument that there is a gap between the rhetoric and the reality, between appealing formulations which give only an illusion of change and social facts, see Skutnabb-Kangas (1989), and several papers in Skutnabb-Kangas & Cummins (1988), especially Tosi (1988), who discusses the 'depressingly vague and ambiguous notion' of multicultural education in the UK.)

## The Education Reform Act (ERA) and the 'National' Curriculum

This paper discusses only England and Wales: Scotland and Northern Ireland have different education systems, and the Secretary of State for Education and Science (i.e. the Minister of Education) has responsibility only for England and

Wales. He cedes this responsibility to the Secretary of State for Wales in Welsh matters, including the Welsh language in schools. I will comment further below on this geographical definition of language matters in Britain.

The organization of education in England and Wales has changed very sharply since 1988, when the ERA came into force: this is the largest piece of educational legislation (hundreds of pages in length) since the Education Act of 1944, and makes very large scale changes to the organization of primary, secondary and tertiary education. One of the main planks of current British conservative government policy is the National Curriculum. This is a misnomer, since it applies only to state schools in England and Wales. (Private schools may follow it if they wish.) However, it is within the so-called National Curriculum that a great deal of language planning is taking place, not explicitly and overtly, but in a fragmented and uncoordinated way, so that its effects are more difficult to monitor and predict.

What mainly concerns us here is that previously there was no National Curriculum in schools. Pre-1988, in the years BNC (before the National Curriculum):
- many educational responsibilities were delegated to around 110 Local Education Authorities (LEAs);
- the curriculum in schools was the responsibility of individual schools, departments and teachers (with examination boards effectively controlling the content of the curriculum for upper secondary age pupils).

Whereas now:
- there is enormous centralization of control over the content and assessment of the curriculum: the Act gives the Secretary of State about 400 new powers with which to manage the whole system.

These changes have taken place very fast indeed, with only minimum consultation with teachers and others. Amongst very many other provisions, the ERA established a National Curriculum comprising English, mathematics, science, technology, history, geography, one modern foreign language, music, art and physical education, and, in Wales, Welsh.

I will discuss here the work of various government committees (only some of which were overtly concerned with language), whose work amounts to *de facto* language planning. My main

references will be to the following Reports and Orders:

1975 Bullock (DES, 1975)
1985 Swann (DES, 1975)
1988 Kingman (HMSO, 1988)
1989 Cox (DES, 1989a)
1989 Orders for Modern Foreign Languages (DES, 1989b)
1990 Harris (DES, 1990).

There is no national language planning commission (as there has been, for example, in Australia: Clyne, 1988). CDE (1982) is a very clear Australian statement on the inadequacy of uncoordinated, *ad hoc* responses to language diversity, and on the need for an explicit national language policy, with clear discussion of the different roles of languages in the country, local, nation and international.

It has not been customary for the British government to do any language planning at all. For example, it has collected no statistics of languages spoken in the UK in the 10-yearly censuses (except for Welsh, Scottish Gaelic and Irish). Figures, where they have been collected at all, have been collected at Local Education Authority level (e.g. LMP, 1985; Bourne, 1989a,b; and see Printon, 1986, who gives some basic statistics from various sources.)

However, language planning has suddenly simply started to be done, on a very large scale. But it is not generally presented as such: it is seen merely as a natural concomitant of the National Curriculum, an inevitable effect of the work of various government committees concerned with English and foreign language teaching. Language planning is introduced by the back door. The approach is uncoordinated, perhaps deliberately so: it could be denied that this is language planning at all.[1] It is either a muddle or a conspiracy, depending on your wider view of British history. But certainly, when there is no explicit policy, it is more difficult to monitor the language rights of different groups.

Skutnabb-Kangas & Phillipson (1989: 8) point out that countries differ significantly in the degrees of explicitness with which language rights are formulated. Britain is far at the implicit end (see Figure 1). The British government has always avoided any basic policy commitments on languages (except for Welsh). It is, I think, a widespread and justifiable view of the Thatcher government, but also more widely of British

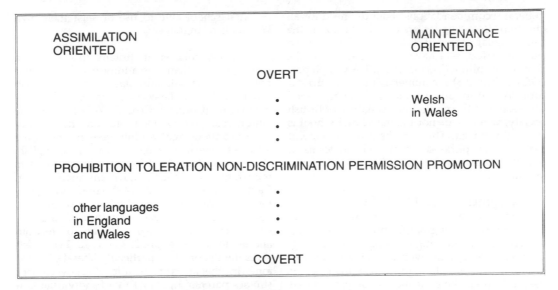

ASSIMILATION
ORIENTED

MAINTENANCE
ORIENTED

OVERT

· Welsh
· in Wales
·
·

PROHIBITION TOLERATION NON-DISCRIMINATION PERMISSION PROMOTION

·
other languages · 
in England ·
and Wales ·

COVERT

**Figure 1** After Skutnabb-Kangas & Phillipson (1989)

politics, that there is a lack of underlying theory: things are done in an *ad hoc*, pragmatic, piecemeal fashion. But an absence of a policy is a policy, whether intended or not. And an indifference to languages is likely to lead to an endorsement of the status quo.

It is doubtful, in fact, if the term *language planning* would mean anything at all to most people (including most politicians and educationalists) in Britain. It might mean 'teaching English to immigrants' or 'choosing which foreign languages to teach in schools'. The majority could probably not conceive what else it might mean, because of the profoundly monolingual assumption which are regarded as natural in Britain.

Language planning of a far-reaching kind has, then, suddenly started to be done, via different committees which are isolated from each other. One effect of the lack of explicit planning is that advice and decision making are all split. The Swann Report (1985) was about the education of minority group children. The Kingman Report (1988) was about English language in the mother tongue curriculum.[2] The Cox Report (1989) was about teaching English as a mother tongue in the National Curriculum.[3] The Harris Report is about modern foreign languages in the National Curriculum. But no committee has had a national language policy *per se* as part of its terms of reference. And there are large areas, obviously

relevant to general policy, which are not covered at all in the present reforms: e.g. adult literacy; the education of the deaf; language disabilities; translation and interpretation services, in the courts or social services.

Consultation is also muddled and split. Therefore groups of subject teachers or bilingual speakers have to make the same points over and over again to different committees. They have no participation rights, and the process of divide and rule leads to exhaustion and demoralization.

## The Swann Report (DES, 1985)

The Swann Committee was set up to advise not on language planning, but on the role of education in race relations and equal opportunities. The concern was with social cohesion, in a situation where the government was deeply worried about possible race riots in an ethnically divided country. The Committee recommended a policy of mainstreaming: i.e. of giving bilingual children better access to the curriculum, by having them taught, with support, alongside their peers, rather than being withdrawn to separate remedial language classes or special language centres (as had been the strategy to deal with large waves of immigrant children into Britain from the 1960s). The policy of mainstreaming is now widely accepted.

But this change is, by definition, limited to schools with multilingual populations. Swann's general recommendations about the need for all children, in whatever area, to learn about the multilingual nature of Britain, have hardly been put into effect, and have had little effect on the dominant culture (Verma, 1989). The Cox Report (DES, 1989a: 2.8) recommends that the curriculum for all pupils should include informed discussion of the multi-cultural nature of British society, whether or not the individual school is culturally mixed. This may be a pious hope. It may also be phrased too vaguely in terms of multilingualism with no specific demands about languages.

### The Kingman Report (DES, 1988)

In the immediate run up to the National Curriculum, the Kingman Committee was set up to recommend on English language teaching. This was widely perceived as having to do with grammar teaching, though the Kingman Report itself interprets the issue more widely, as indeed its terms of reference required it to do.

The Report proposes a model of language comprising: the forms of the English language (essentially phonology, graphology, syntax and discourse), communication and comprehension, acquisition and development, and variation. This is a standard type of model, very familiar to linguists. Much of it is, however, almost incomprehensible to many English teachers, who have received little or no training in English language or linguistics.

In addition, the model has come under heavy attack. It provides an extraordinary description of language variation, which is seen as historical and geographical, but not social. No social class or ethnic divisions are mentioned, although social class is obviously a major concomitant of language diversity in Britain. (The Cox Report also avoids the term 'social class', and talks coyly of 'social groups'.) The implicit denial of social class differences in the Kingman Report is clearly politically loaded; it is also simply false. The language of a particular class is passed off as the language of the nation.

But there is considerable confusion in the Kingman Report over whether the Committee are talking of the English language or of language in general. For example, consider these paragraphs (p. 33, paras 1 and 2):

> It is the purpose of this chapter to illustrate the relevance of the language model to English teaching... Children arrive at their

first school able to use at least their own spoken language.

For many children in Britain, this will be a language other than or in addition to English, but there is no unambiguous statement that English can be better understood in relation to other languages. (Contrast Cox, 2. 7–17.) Since the educational recommendations are not clearly focused on language learning needs in general, the effect is to give more weight, yet again, to English.

On the surface, the Kingman Report appears moderate and liberal, though many analyses (e.g. Cameron & Bourne, 1989: 12–13) see it as authoritarian It recommends social cohesion around one variety of English. It uses a rhetoric of language entitlement and language rights, and of freedom and democracy (e.g. pp. 2, 3, 4, 7, 10, 11), which gives the Report its superficially liberal pluralist tone. (In other areas of education, the government stresses parents' rights.) Talk of individual language rights makes the correct moral noises, but it has no legislative basis, and is therefore empty. There is talk of entitlement, but not of the discrimination which many children face; and talk of equality of opportunity, but not equality of outcome. (Cf. Rampton, 1989 on the 'entitlement' rhetoric; Skutnabb-Kangas & Phillipson, 1989 on the myth that language rights are a reality in many countries.)

### Language and Nationality

In the debate over language and nation, the Kingman Report is a key ideological text (Cameron & Bourne, 1989). The focus was on a claimed crisis of falling standards. 'Grammar' carried an enormous symbolic weight of authority, hierarchy, order, tradition, and elitism. The Report has been widely interpreted as taking an authoritarian, national unity position, ethnocentric and nostalgic, with the covert function of strengthening and protecting English.

A characteristic of the current debate in Britain about language, especially English in the National Curriculum, is the enormous press coverage which the Kingman and Cox Reports have had, and essential to an understanding of the debate is the nature of the rhetoric which is used. For example, *The Times* leading article (30 April 1988), when Kingman was published, wrote:

> English ought to be the queen of the curriculum for any British child. It is one of the things that define his or her nationality.

This claimed relationship between language and nationality, which has very little basis in British law, occurs very frequently. Marenbon (1987) is published by the Centre for Policy Studies, a right-wing think tank set up by Margaret Thatcher and Keith Joseph in 1974. Marenbon ends his attack on current trends in English teaching in this way:

> ...in the future of its language there lies the future of a nation.

The Kingman Report itself uses a general formulation (p 43, para 32):

> ...language above all else is the defining characteristic of an individual, a community, a nation.

There are certainly many cases in the world where language has been the focus of separatist, nationalist demands. But the Kingman Report is presenting as the only, obvious, 'natural' view, what is, in fact, a particular 19th century European Romantic view (Leith, 1989), that a language expresses individual, creative, poetic genius (there is a lot of literary criticism in the Report on biblical translations, Shakespeare and Dickens), and the Volksgeist, the genius of a people.

## The Cox Report (DES, 1989a)

The main job of the Cox Committee was to recommend programmes of study and attainment targets for English mother tongue teaching from 5 to 16. Its recommendations have been amended, after limited consultation, by the National Curriculum Council, and turned into law. The Report also contains other chapters on Standard English, linguistic terminology, knowledge about language, equal opportunities, bilingual children, and Wales: these chapters have no statutory force.

There is no space here for a detailed account of the very substantial debates around teaching English as a mother tongue. (For more detailed analysis of the Cox Report see Stubbs, 1989.) The Report is discussed elsewhere in this article for its relevance to the other languages of England.

The essential general point is that the ERA defines separate subjects on the school curriculum: 'English' is different from 'Modern Foreign Languages'. Different Committees are responsible for the curriculum, with only poorly defined requirements of 'cross curricular themes'

between subjects. It has been pointed out that the list of subjects in the National Curriculum is almost identical to the list of subjects for grammar schools proposed in the early 1900s.

## Modern Foreign Languages in the National Curriculum: Statutory Orders

In connection with the ERA, the government has published Statutory Orders (DES, 1989b), which came into effect in August 1989, specifying which languages may be taught in the National Curriculum. Nineteen languages are listed as possible foundation subjects, to be taught between 11 and 16 years (probably for 4 periods per week).

The positive aspect is that, for the first time, a modern foreign language will be compulsory for all secondary age pupils, whereas previously a foreign language has been seen as a subject for the academic elite. This new 'languages for all' policy is a major step forward, in the context of facilitating communication between citizens of EC countries. However, there are several aspects of the policy which are disappointing.

The permitted languages are in two schedules. Schedule 1 contains the working languages of the EC (minus English). These are unconditionally specified as foundation subjects, and schools must offer at least one:

> Danish, Dutch, French, German, Modern Greek, Italian, Portuguese, Spanish.

Schedule 2 contains 11 languages, which are a mixture of international languages and languages of major linguistic minorities in Britain. As long as they offer an EC language, schools may in addition offer one or more of:

> Arabic, Bengali, Chinese (Cantonese or Mandarin), Gujerati, Modern Hebrew, Hindi, Japanese, Panjabi, Russian, Turkish, Urdu.

The schedules do explicitly give legal status to a relatively wide range of languages, and one must welcome the formal recognition of non-European languages. This enhancement of their status may look very progressive in a European context, where non-European languages are often totally unrecognised except in low status 'migrant worker programmes'. But it has been quickly pointed out that the schedules also establish a caste system of grade 1 and grade 2 languages. (See also below on some of the implications of territorial descriptions such as 'non-European'.) Again, we have a proposal which appears superficially to encourage language diversity. However, there are problems:

- Children are obliged to study only one language in the National Curriculum: they may study second and subsequent languages, but outside the National Curriculum, and very little time is available outside the compulsory subjects. In practice, the opportunity to study a second language will seldom be available.

- The publication of such lists creates the expectation of adequate resourcing, but, in fact, no resourcing is available for the wider range of languages proposed. There are no teachers of Danish or Dutch, for example. Nor are there any incentives to offer schedule 2 languages. French will therefore continue to be taught because there are teachers of French. The government has published schedules of languages, to which it can rhetorically refer in talking of opportunities for pupils, but is has shown no commitment to turning the schedules into reality.

- In practice, there are few resources to teach much apart from French. But there is actually a current shortage even of French teachers, and this is when over 60 per cent of pupils now drop French at age 14. Under the National Curriculum, they will be obliged to continue with a language until 16, and the teacher shortage will therefore be more acute.

- Although 19 languages are listed, others are thereby excluded: schools need special permission to teach them. The central specification of particular languages is inevitably a partial and arbitrary estimation of future needs, but no mechanisms are proposed whereby the schedules might be changed. In general, the Orders fossilize provision. The schedules embody a superficial and mechanical definition of Europe: simply 1992 as visualized in 1989. If Turkey or Sweden join the EC, for example, does the government have to change the law? After the events of summer and autumn 1989, this view of Europe looks very dated indeed.

The Orders are accompanied by a non-statutory Circular (DES 9/89) which contains a brief discussion of which languages are of relevance to Britain. There is a weak classification into: working languages of the EC, major trading languages, and languages used by ethnic communities in Britain. But there is no real theory of such language types or functions. (Again, contrast CDE, 1982.)

Watertight categories are clearly useless, and any theory would have to allow multiple categorization (Clyne, 1988). Starting categories might be:

- traditional foreign languages, i.e. languages for which teachers are available;
- community/heritage languages;
- languages of neighboring countries and/or trading partners;
- EC languages;
- world/international languages, e.g. languages used for scientific communication;
- classical languages (which are completely omitted from the National Curriculum;
- 'easy' versus 'difficult' languages, e.g. languages with a non-Roman writing system (though such a description may be very ethno- or Eurocentric).

It would not be possible to define such categories in more than a common sense way. In fact, it is evident that the categories above are not neutral, since they signal the status of languages: *international language* sounds important, *community language* less so. But planners and decision makers need such categories because they imply policies and actions.

The Circular attempts no basic justifications for language education (Clyne, 1988: 278), in terms, for example, of social justice, enrichment for all British citizens, or the maintenance of languages already spoken in Britain. Even on cost–benefit grounds, the economic arguments look very shortsighted: there is likely to be an enormous waste, allowing languages already spoken in the home and community to be eroded, whilst starting from scratch to teach other languages in schools and colleges. Only a narrow version of economic strategies in relation to Britain's external relations is clearly spelled out.

This will need careful analysis of the implications of some very simple facts. For example, in Europe, German is the first language in terms of numbers of speakers, and of the number of different countries in which it is the main language (Germany, Austria and Switzerland, with sizeable numbers of speakers in other countries. In the world, in terms of numbers of speakers, German ranks below English, Spanish and Portuguese (and many other languages) (Ammon, 1991).

The Circular gives only a very sketchy rationale, based on personal motivations (practical skills, understanding of other cultures), and national motivations (economic and cultural, trade, tourism and international relations). This needs to be substantially developed by an analysis of increased personal mobility, of increased opportunities to meet migrants and tourists, of the increasing importance of languages in international life, including increased access to radio, television and films in other languages, etc. Nor is there anything but the vaguest discussion of the internationalization of business and commercial life in which an adult is very likely to have to use a foreign language, but probably not the one s/he learned at school (Trim, 1989). The implications of the global village are hardly recognised.

In a word, there is still great confusion over what modern foreign languages are *for* in British schools. The range of political, social and historical factors which lead to lists of languages such as those in the schedules must be publicly debated and justified. Language planning depends on a problem being defined, alternative solutions being formulated so that they can be evaluated, and so that one can then be chosen and implemented, and its implementation in turn evaluated (O Riagáin, 1991).

In addition, the rationale for teaching heritage/community languages is very different from teaching traditional modern foreign languages (in practice, French and German), and very different programmes of study are needed. Expectations of linguistic competence could be much higher than with *ab initio* teaching of a foreign language. The main motivations may be cultural and or religious, and the maintenance of a language spoken in the local community.

In summary, the overt ideology has changed in favour of widening the available languages. But when this rhetoric is translated into concrete actions in institutions, little will change. If anything, the present status quo could be even more rigid than at present, because some aspects of it are now enshrined in law. English exists in a web of institutions, woven even tighter in England and Wales by the National Curriculum.

In a review of language planning in the USA from the 1960s to the 1980s, Fishman (1981: 516, 522) reaches pessimistic conclusions, very similar to this article:

> *plus ça change, plus c'est la même chose.* On the surface a great deal has changed...but basically ours is not a society whose peculiar genius is along the lines of linguistic sophis-

tication, sensitivity or concern. ...the exasperated know-nothingism of 'this is, after all, an English-speaking country' ...Language maintenance...is not part of public policy because it is rarely recognised as being in the public interest.

## Modern Foreign Languages in the National Curriculum: The Harris Committee

The National Curriculum Modern Foreign Languages Working Group was set up in September 1989, to design the programmes of study and attainment targets which will come into force from autumn 1992.

The press statement, from the Education Minister at the DES who introduced the Committee, emphasised, in a narrow way, the 'challenge of 1992' and the need for languages in 'today's increasingly competitive world'. The Committee's terms of reference were, however, wider than many people had predicted: the group was asked both to reconsider the two schedules of languages and also whether only one language in secondary education is appropriate. At the time of writing (March 1990), the Committee has produced an interim report, which does not significantly change the terms of the debate.

## Welsh

The Welsh Act of 1967 asserted the 'equal validity' of English and Welsh, and gave both languages equal status in legal proceedings. However, when the effects of the Act were reviewed 10 years later, it was concluded that such legislation had not strengthened Welsh. This required active promotion in all domains. The National Curriculum Welsh Working Group envisages a variety of different kinds of provision: Welsh medium education, Welsh mother tongue teaching, and Welsh as a second language within English medium education. In 1988, only 13 per cent of young primary age Welsh children were fluent in Welsh. The proportion of bilinguals does not therefore look very different in Wales and in England.

But the legal situation of Welsh in Wales is very different from the situation of other languages in England or Wales. A particular form of territoriality principle, with unfortunate consequences, is used for Welsh in Wales (Cameron & Bourne, 1989; Bourne, 1989a,b). Geography is used to define provision and rights. Welsh has legal status only in Wales, so that as soon as a Welsh speaker crosses the border into England those rights vanish for that individual. This territorial conception of language rights is not only enshrined in law: it is the conception which has been acceptable to Welsh language activists themselves. (The territorial view is, of course, found widely elsewhere under very different political circumstances: many separatist political demands are based on a language-territory claim; even in Switzerland, despite the notion of a multilingual federation, languages are linked to territory (Nelde, 1991; Watts, 1991)).

The Welsh Act is the only explicit legislation in the UK concerning language rights, and is therefore significant for its covert implications for other languages. And this discourse of national boundaries has dangerous implications. The territorial conception may well have benefited Welsh itself, but have created unfortunate precedents for other languages. If Welsh is the natural language of Wales, then it seems to follow that English is the natural language of England, and that languages in general belong to territories not to speakers. Since the languages of England (e.g. Asian languages, Chinese, etc.) have geographical homes elsewhere, then they have no natural home in Britain Their speakers belong elsewhere, and should presumably forget their languages or return to where they came from. They certainly cannot expect any language rights in Britain. This seems to be the unacceptable logic of this way of thinking.

It is such assumptions which have to be extracted from covert statement. The Kingman Report (e.g. p. 30) also sees languages as things which spread over territories:

> As populations are dispersed and separated, they typically develop regular regional changes in their language forms. These changes may mark different dialects (or eventually different languages).

This expresses a strange model of populations 'dispersing', independently of other populations who might be making them disperse: agency is strangely missing. Further, there is no notion that, having dispersed, the populations might come into contact with other populations who speak different languages. Language contact often leads to language *con*vergence.

## The Other Languages of England and Wales

Bhatt & Martin-Jones (1989) summarize the changing policies concerning minority languages

in Britain. The major waves of immigration into Britain in the 1960s were accompanied by firmly assimilationist assumptions: Britain should respect, but could not be expected to perpetuate, different cultural values. Groups were seen as a problem needing compensatory English teaching: bilingualism was seen as bewildering for the individuals involved (DES, 1971: 9). The Bullock Report (1975) took a liberal pluralist view that minority languages are a resource and a right: in a famous statement (quoted by Cox, DES, 1989a: 2.7.), they asserted that children should not be expected to cast off the language and culture of the home as they cross the school threshold. The EC Directive (EC, 1977) on the education of the children of migrant workers was interpreted by the DES (1981) as requiring an exploration of how minority languages might be taught inside or outside school, but not as the right of children to have such tuition. In the 1980s, there was discussion of the possibility of minority languages in three places in the curriculum: as examination subjects in secondary schooling; as bilingual support in the classroom, especially for young children in reception classes and as a resource in language awareness courses. (Tosi (1988) provides a comparable analysis, of a rhetoric which shifts from 'assimilation' to 'integration', with little changing but the words.)

Surveys of minority languages spoken in Britain tend to stress their diversity. For example, the Cox Report (10.3) emphasises that:

> The 1987 Language Survey conducted by ILEA (Inner London Education Authority) found 23 per cent of the Authority's school population using a language other than or in addition to English at home, with 170 different languages spoken by its pupils.

This argument is probably a strategic blunder, because it makes planned provision seem impossible (Bourne, 1989a,b). In fact, of the 170 languages spoken by London school children, 37 languages were spoken only by one child, and the overall distribution of the languages was very uneven. For example, Bengali accounted for over 20 per cent of bilingual children (some 12,600 pupils), who were concentrated in certain areas. There were large numbers of speakers of Bengali, Gujerati, Panjabi and Urdu, and substantial numbers of Turkish, Greek and Chinese speaking children. In England some 5 per cent of children are bilingual, but in many schools over 60 per cent of the children speak the same language other than English, and in some schools it is over 90 per cent. Such a presentation of the figures makes planned provision seem much more realistic.

It is important, in a wider European context, to stress that such children are not from migrant worker or immigrant families. They are not *Gastarbeiter* or *Wanderarbeiter*. They are second or third generation British citizens.

Pupils who have recently arrived in the UK may be exempted for only 6 months from the National Curriculum, but the DES (Circular 15/89) expects such exemptions to be very rare. Even if exempted, they are still entitled to a 'broad and balanced' curriculum: i.e. there are no explicit language recommendations even here (that they should receive special English language teaching help, for example.) Otherwise, bilingual children are subject to the same programmes of study and attainment targets as any other pupils. This might seem, on the face of it, like equality of treatment. But again, the point is that there are no general principles for language education, only specific programmes of study which pupils have to follow. The *ad hoc* language planning is hidden. Furthermore bilingual children do not anywhere get credit for their knowledge of two (or more) languages.

The Kingman Report (p. 58, para 17) dismisses bilingual children in a single paragraph, saying simply that the Report is concerned with English as L1, and that English as L2 is outside their terms of reference. This is all extremely weak and arguably quite false. The Committee's terms of reference asked them to advise on a model of the English languages which could inform 'all aspects of English teaching', but the committee narrowed its own terms of reference quite sharply.

The Cox Committee, in contrast, was given much more sharply defined guidance by the Secretary of State, and contested it by trying to find a better formulation. However, the formulations which it did find stand only as an assertion of principle, with no financial backing or legislative force. They amount only to recommendations that other languages should be valued and respected.

In a statement (in the Notes of further guidance to the Chair of the Committee) the Secretary of State said this, in an extraordinary paragraph on equal opportunities:

> The group should take account of the ethnic diversity of the school population and soci-

ety at large, bearing in mind the cardinal point that English should be the first language and medium of instruction for all pupils in England.

In this unprecedentedly explicit statement, English is given priority, and the assumption appears to be that bilingual education is ruled out in Britain: only English-medium education is assumed (except for bilingual schools in Wales). Furthermore, the assumption appears to be that English should become (?) the 'first language' of children themselves: the monolingual assumptions underlying this statement are quite extraordinary. Language loss appears to be recommended. Given that the paragraph is about 'equal opportunities', it is just double speak.

The statement is contested in the Cox Report itself, but only weakly. The Report points out that English is not the first language of all children. But it admits that English is the 'first language' of the education system. Overall, the rhetoric is one of rights and entitlements. It appears tolerance- and promotion-oriented: and some of the minority languages are explicitly listed in the schedules. But there is no actual promotion or financial support. Such languages may be a subject on the curriculum, but not a language of instruction. There is no explicit right even to use such languages in education (or any other institution). There is only weakly supported co-existence in very narrow domains

## Assimilationist Assumptions

Researchers (e.g. LMP, 1985) have struggled to have linguistic diversity accepted as the norm, on a continuum from dialects of English to languages other than English. And some of these ways of talking have been picked up in government reports. The overt rhetoric is often of ethnic diversity and multiculturalism but always held in check by ethnocentric and assimilationist assumptions.

Schools have always been the most powerful mechanism in assimilating minority children into mainstream cultures. Skutnabb-Kangas & Phillipson (1989) discuss the symbolic violence involved in a shift from physical to psychological control over groups of people. This is a new and more sophisticated control, which recognises ethnic diversity, but confines it to the home, which pays lip service to multilingualism, but is empty liberal rhetoric. They argue that declarations of language rights must be explicit. Even overt permission does not protect languages: compare the lack of effect of the Welsh Language Act cited above. Languages are oppressed, not by active opposition, but by lack of resources (also Phillipson, 1989).

There are no social justice arguments used in favour of minority languages. There is no thought of whose interests are served, or of what policy for language provision would be formulated by a speaker of one of the minority languages, from the point of view of the bilingual him or herself. (See Rawls, 1972).

There is an unstated premise: that the situation of the monolingual majority should be altered as little as possible. Language planning (such as it is) avoids any challenge to the practice of the currently privileged. The policies operate systematically and consistently to the advantage of speakers of Standard English. But this is nowhere stated: this is the advantage of *not* having a language policy. Implicit ideologies are used to legitimate unequal resources. The discourse of multiculturalism excludes questions of social, economic and political power.

In a swingeing attack on such situations in different countries, Skutnabb-Kangas & Phillipson (1989) talk of the implicit paranoia ideology of a country which is monolingual in an international language. Multilingualism is thought to be inevitably negative, and one widely held, but seldom explicitly expressed, myth or assumption, is that many languages divide a nation (Skutnabb-Kangas & Phillipson, 1989: 55). There is an implicit assumption that societal monolingualism is the norm and that language diversity means conflict. Behind the rhetoric, *bilingual* is often a euphemism for 'Black' and 'poor'.

Educational statements often refer to societal multilingualism as a fact. For example, the Secretary of State's notes of guidance to the Cox Committee refer to:

> the ethnic diversity of the school population and society at large.

But they tend not to refer to individual bilingualism as a goal In the present context, this goal is formulated only with reference to Welsh in Wales.

## Knowledge About Language

One bright spot on the horizon is the explicit requirement that language study itself, or language awareness, become an explicit part of English teaching. A prerequisite of successful foreign language learning is a positive attitude towards multilingualism. The monolingual ideology must be contested if the aim is to be a more linguistically aware nation.

Widdowson (1989) discusses Britain as a profoundly monolingual nation which has no concept of multilingualism as an asset. The pervasive attitude is of cultural and linguistic self-sufficiency, and of a contempt of anything foreign which does not contribute to material well-being. As an example of ethnocentric complacency and prejudice, he quotes an article in *The Sun* with the headline *Di foxed by Frog Lingo*. The article reported Princess Diana sympathising with children at the British school in Paris because of their difficulties in learning French: i.e. the language of the country they were living in… This was reported with indulgent tolerance and approval. Widdowson makes the point that simply putting an obligatory language in the National Curriculum will not magically improve the image of modern languages: it might just provoke mass disaffection. (Esarte-Sarries (1989) reports research on primary age children's stereotypes of France and the French: onion sellers in stripy shirts. At the end of a depressing article, she makes the point that 'the continuation of negative attitudes amongst secondary boys was disquieting').

Along with supporting chapters on Standard English and Linguistic Terminology, the Cox Report has a complete chapter on knowledge about language. This will become an obligatory part of programmes of study in Speaking and Listening, Writing and Reading from ages 11 to 16, covering forms of language, language variation and language in social institutions.

A major problem, however, will be teachers' own lack of knowledge and confidence in this area. The Bullock, Kingman and Cox Reports all point out that almost 30 per cent of teachers of English as a mother tongue have no qualifications in English past their own schooling, and that such teachers are responsible for about 15 per cent of all English teaching. Bourne (1989b) points out that many teachers of English as a second language have come from other subjects, and are not much better qualified. And Kingman and Cox both point to the huge teacher training programme which is necessary if teachers themselves are to know enough about language to teach about it coherently. A £15 million training programme is now underway: possibly a drop in the ocean of prejudice and stereotypes, but at least a start. Even this programme is being developed by and for English teachers themselves. Modern language and community language teachers are certainly not systematically involved. Again, there is monolingual vision.

## Conclusions

Language planning is, by definition, interventionist, goal-oriented, and institutional. It ought to be explicit and, ideally, systematic (Christian, 1988: 197). The British government now has a highly interventionist policy in the state education system: but the nature of their intervention in language planning is not explicit, even if it is conscious and deliberate. It is goal-oriented, but its goals are often unclear. It is pervasive, but it is neither systematic nor rational. It is not based on any careful analysis of the range of relevant factors and of the desired outcomes. The alternatives are not clearly laid out: there are, for example, no genuine consultations between central government, local authorities and smaller groups with different language interests. And I see little possibility of the present British government, in the current political climate, setting up the national language commission which would be necessary to move beyond the *ad hoc* uncoordinated and disguised language planning which is taking place.

Nevertheless, ideologies are never static. Hegemonies are constantly adjusted and renegotiated. Although little is likely to change in the profoundly monolingual assumptions in Britain, the ways in which the linguistic domination is maintained have changed rapidly and significantly. These mechanisms therefore require analysis, to discover where they might be challenged.

Rational argument is clearly not enough on its own. Linguists have been exposing linguistic myths for years, with some genuine effects, but only in restricted domains, such as initial teacher training. What is required may include a range of small-scale strategies and publicity campaigns aimed at changing people's attitudes. Over time, modest changes in the image of other languages might affect people's assumptions about languages and their speakers. For example, British television is gradually using more sub-titles in place of voiceovers when speakers of languages other than English are broadcast. In this small way, other languages gain a higher profile in a natural way, people get used to hearing them,

and sometimes understanding them, if only a little. Such initiatives should be encouraged. In addition, languages need institutional support: for example, university chairs in minority languages are a concrete sign that they are valued in British society. British academics, as a whole, have done little to encourage such developments, or even to prevent cuts in the few such chairs which have existed.

Concessions have been made, in British law, to Welsh in Wales, and this could support movements for change elsewhere, if alliances could be forged. The ideology of multilingualism is strong at local levels, where approaches to language diversity are unavoidable, but it is hampered by lack of central resourcing. Relations with the European Community have had some effect: witness the schedules of languages in the National Curriculum. The British government has previously used the decentralized education system as an excuse for not acting (e.g. on the EC Directive on the education of the children of migrant workers), but with a highly centralized system, it no longer has this excuse.

When the possibilities for rational and systematic planning are so restricted, then perhaps small, ad hoc strategies are the best hope. In general, more linguists should be encouraged to get involved with the policy making and to influence decisions where they are made.

## Summary

This article has discussed the failure of current British government policies to address the dilemma of pluralism: how can a country both sustain cultural differences and also promote national unity? (Widdowson, 1989). The symbolic functions of language as both a separatist and a unifying force are evident from the media hype and hysteria which accompanied the publication of the Kingman and Cox Reports (Stubbs, 1989). But there is no planning for the possible co-existence of the lower order bonds of community and of the higher order bonds of national unity: no discussion of pluralist *Gemeinschaft* and national *Gesellschaft* (Fishman, 1981).

A great deal of language policy is currently being formulated in England and Wales, but, due to a lack of an explicit general statement, and the (deliberate?) fragmentation of the consultation process, it is difficult to see its implications. The present article is a very partial study of some of the mechanisms which legitimate the dominance of one language over others. The partial nature of the analysis is partly due to the very speed at which the legislative changes are taking place in the British education system.

Skutnabb-Kangas & Phillipson (1989) have provided a way of charting the positions on language rights adopted in different countries. For example, Phillipson (1988) points out that discrimination against languages may be *overt* (e.g. a language may be prohibited in schools), or *covert* (e.g. certain languages are simply not used in schools or teacher training), or *conscious* (e.g. teachers tell their pupils not to use their home languages in case this interferes with their learning of another language), or *unconscious* (e.g. English is just assumed to be the 'natural' language for education or whatever). They also provide a way of mapping the positions adopted by different countries in their language planning provisions: Figure 1 provides a brief summary of my argument.

## Acknowledgements

I have learned a great deal about the topics discussed here from Jill Bourne, both from her published work and from her detailed critical comments on an earlier draft of this paper. I have also drawn on papers by Ben Rampton and Ros Mitchell submitted as evidence to the DES on language issues. I am grateful to Gabi Keck, Robert Phillipson and Tove Skutnabb-Kangas for critical comments on an earlier draft. Many points made in discussions at the conference in Bad Homburg have also been integrated into the argument.

## Notes

1. The term *language planning* is used explicitly by Peter Gannon HMI, Secretary of the Kingman Committee (Gannon, 1988).
2. I will use the term *English mother tongue* in places in this article. But the term is misleading, since many English teachers teach children who have mother tongues other than English.
3. I was a member of the Cox Committee.

## References

Ammon, U. (1991) The status of German and other languages in the European Community. In F. Coulmas (ed.) *A Language Policy for the European Community.* Berlin: Mouton de Gruyter.

Bhatt, A. and Martin-Jones, M. (1989) Bilingualism, inequality and the language curriculum. Paper read at British Association for Applied Linguistics Meeting. University of Lancaster, September 1989.

Bourne, J. (1989a) The teaching of language in the English school system. Paper read to European Colloquium on Language Planning Policies in a Context of Cultural Pluralism. Brussels, May 1989.

— (1989b) *Moving into the Mainstream: LEA Provision for Bilingual Pupils.* London: NFER-Nelson.

Bourne, J. and Bloor, T. (eds) (1989) Kingman and the linguists. Committee for Linguistics in Education (mimeo).

Cameron, D. and Bourne, J. (1989) Grammar, nation and citizenship: Kingman in linguistic and historical perspective. *Language and Education* 2 (3), 147–60.

CDE (Commonwealth Department of Education) (1982) *Towards a Language Policy.* Canberra.

Christian, D. (1988) Language planning: The view from linguists. In F. J. Newmeyer (ed.) *Language: The Socio-Cultural Context.* Cambridge: Cambridge University Press.

Clyne, M. (1988) Australia's national policy on language and its implications. *Journal of Educational Policy* 3 (3), 237–80.

DES (Department of Education and Science) (1971) The Education of Immigrants. Education survey 13. London: HMSO.

— (1975) *A Language for Life.* (Bullock Report). London: HMSO.

— (1981) *Directive of the Council of the European Community on the Education of the Children of Migrant Workers.* Circular 5/18. London: DES.

— (1985) *Education for All.* (Swann Report). London: HMSO.

— (1988) *Report of the Committee of Inquiry into the Teaching of English Language.* (Kingman Report). London: HMSO.

— (1989) *English for Ages 5 to 16.* (Cox Report). London: DES and Welsh Office.

— (1989b) *The Education (National Curriculum) (Modern Foreign Languages) Order 1989.* Statutory Instruments, 825. London: HMSO.

— (1990) *National Curriculum Modern Foreign Languages Working Group. Initial Advice.* London: DES and Welsh Office.

European Community (1977) *Council Directive on the Education of the Children of Migrant Workers.* 77/486/EEC. Brussels: EC.

Esarte-Sarries, V. (1989) 'Onions and stripey tee-shirts' or how do primary pupils learns about

France? *British Journal of Language Teaching* 27 (2), 65–71.

Fishman, J. (1981) Language policy: Past, present and future. In C.A. Ferguson and S. Brice Heath (eds) *Language in the USA*. Cambridge: Cambridge University Press.

Gannon, P. (1988) Kingman: Setting the scene. In E. Ashworth and L. Masterman (eds) *Responding to Kingman*. University of Nottingham (mimeo).

Lawlor, S. (1988) *Correct Core*. London: Centre for Policy Studies.

Leith, D. (1989) Three criticisms. In Bourne and Bloor (eds).

Letwin, O. (1988) *Aims of Schooling*. London: Centre for Policy Studies.

LMP (Linguistic Minorities Project) (1985) *The Other Languages of England*. London: Routledge & Kegan Paul.

Marenbon, J. (1987) *English our English*. London: Centre for Policy Studies.

Nelde, P. H. (1991) Language conflicts in multilingual Europe: Prospects for 1993. In F. Coulmas (ed.) *A Language Policy for the European Community*. Berlin: Mouton de Gruyter.

O Riagáin, P. (1991) National and international dimensions of language policy when the minority language is a national language: The case of Irish in Ireland. In F. Coulmas (ed.) *A Language Policy for the European Community*. Berlin: Mouton de Gruyter.

Philipson, R. (1988) Linguicism: Structures and ideologies in linguistic imperialism. In Skutnabb-Kangas and Cummins (eds).

— (1989) Human rights and the delegitimation of dominant languages. Paper presented at Fourth International Conference on Minority Languages. Ljouwert/Leeuwarden, June 1989.

Printon, V. (ed.) (1986) *Facts and Figures: Languages in Education*. London: Centre for

Information on Language Teaching and Research.

Rampton, B. (1989) Almost passionate in its advocacy: Kingman on entitlement. In Bourne and Bloor (eds).

Rawls, J. (1972) *A Theory of Justice*. Oxford: Oxford University Press.

Skutnabb-Kangas, T. (1989) Legitimating or delegitimating new forms of racism: The role of researchers. Paper presented at Fourth International Conference on Minority Languages, Ljouwert/Leeuwarden, June 1989.

Skutnabb-Kangas, T. and Cummins, J. (eds) (1988) *Minority Education: From Shame to Struggle*. Clevedon: Multilingual Matters.

Skutnabb-Kangas, T. and Phillipson, R. (1989) Wanted! Linguistic human rights. Rolig-Papir, 44, University of Roskilde (mimeo).

Stubbs, M. (1989) The state of English in the English state: Reflection on the Cox Report. *Language and Education* 3 (4), 235–50.

Tosi, A. (1988) The jewel in the crown of the modern prince. In Skutnabb-Kangas and Cummins (eds).

Trim, J.L.M. (1989) Language Teaching in the perspective of the predictable requirements of the twenty-first century. Prepared for AILA for submission to UNESCO.

Verma, G. (ed.) (1989) *Education for All: A Landmark in Pluralism*. London: Falmer.

Watts, R.J. (1991) Linguistic minorities and language conflict in Europe: Learning from the Swiss experience. In F. Coulmas (ed.) *A Language Policy for the European Community*. Berlin: Mouton de Gruyter.

Widdowson, H.G. (1989) Language in the National Curriculum (Unpublished lecture). Institute of Education: University of London.

Williams, R. (1965) *The Long Revolution*. Harmondsworth: Penguin.

## Questions

(1) What are the similarities and differences between the United States and Great Britain with regard to languages other than English, their speakers (both indigenous minorities and in-migrants), and their place in the school curriculum? Are there differences in their 'language planning' (for English and for LOTES, Languages Other than English)?

(2) From a list of the documents below, in one column define the policy contained in the document. In the second column, discuss its limitation, according to Stubbs:

   (a) Bullock (1975).

   (b) Swann (1985).

   (c) Kingman (1988).

   (d) Cox (1989).

(e)  Draft Order for Modern Foreign Languages (1989).

(f)  Harris (1990).

(3)  The Swann Report recommends mainstreaming language minority students. Define what is mainstreaming. What are the advantages of mainstreaming language minority students? Could there be disadvantages? Why or why not? What is the practice in your local school?

(4)  Define the territoriality principle in the granting of language rights. Say how it relates to Wales. (You may want to refer to Baker, this volume, to expand on the Welsh situation.) Why does Stubbs criticize the territoriality principle? Does granting language rights according to the territoriality principle have any advantages? For whom? What other situations in the world can you think of where linguistic rights are granted according to the territoriality principle, and why is the principle used?

What do you think of the territoriality principle?

(5)  Stubbs reports that surveys of minority languages spoken in Britain stress how varied they are. He then goes on to say, 'This argument is probably a strategic blunder, because it makes planned provision seem impossible.' Do you agree with Stubbs? Why or why not? Discuss the linguistic heterogeneity of the student community in your local school. Could planned bilingual instruction be possible for all groups, some groups, none? What would you do if planned bilingual instruction were not possible? Discuss the possibilities for both language minorities and language majorities.

## Activities

(1)  Survey a school community. Find out which languages are represented and how many children speak those languages. Make a graph showing your results. Then, interview a school administrator or teacher. Find out how minority languages are used in:

(a)  Education of language minority students when they are learners of the majority language.

(b)  Education of language minority students when they are bilingual.

(c)  Education of all students, including language majority students.

(d)  Examinations, including teacher-made assessment and more official assessment.

(e)  Evaluations, including psychological and learning evaluations.

(f)  School life, including assemblies, announcements, correspondence, offices.

Make a chart with your results.

(2)  Write your own document outlining an explicit language policy that supports linguistic and cultural pluralism in education in your community. Make sure that you take your local community's sociolinguistic profile into account. Read your document to your class. The class may then select the document with the most appropriate language policy for education in that community. Read that language policy to a teacher or school administrator in your area. Write up their reactions and share them with the class.

(3)  Write a story on the school life of Jagdish, a Gujarati speaker who goes to a secondary school in Britain. Then write a story on the school life of Hilary, a British student who is learning French. Compare their stories.

(4)  For a specific grade level, make a list of objectives for a language awareness curriculum. Then design one unit of lessons to include activities and materials used. Share the results with the class.

(5)  Interview at least three people you know using the following quote taken from *The Times* (London) article, 30 April 1988. (Substitute 'American' for 'British' in the US):

'English ought to be the queen of the curriculum for any British child. It is one of the things that define his or her nationality.'

Tape and transcribe your interviews. Share the transcriptions with the class.

Different groups might select to interview people with different characteristics. For example, the following characteristics might be considered: language majority vs. language minority, racial majority vs. racial minority, professional vs. working class, urban dweller vs. suburban dweller, speakers of international languages vs. speakers of community/heritage languages, bilingual speakers vs. monolingual speakers. Compare differences between groups. Make a summary chart of the class's results.

(6) Ask two language minority persons, one a monolingual speaker of the minority language who is a non-professional, and the other a bilingual person who is a professional, to tell you about a specific instance in which they have experienced:
   (a) overt language discrimination;
   (b) covert language discrimination.

Tape and transcribe their answers. Then compare them. Write an essay summarizing your findings.

## Further Reading

For more on the situation of language in education in Britain, readers may consult the following works:

Alladina, Safder and Edwards, Viv (eds) (1991) *Multilingualism in the British Isles*. London: Longman.

Edwards, Viv (1983) *Language in Multicultural Classrooms*. London: Batsford.

Edwards, Viv and Redfern, Angela (1992) *The World in a Classroom: Language in Education in Britain and Canada*. Clevedon: Multilingual Matters.

Ghuman, P.A. Singh (1994) *Coping with Two Cultures: British Asian and Indo-Canadian Adolescents*. Clevedon: Multilingual Matters.

Mills, R.W. and Mills, J. (1993) *Bilingualism in the Primary School: A Handbook for Teachers*. London: Routledge.

Tomlinson, Sally (1983) *Ethnic Minorities in British Schools: A Review of the Literature, 1960–1982*. London: Heinemann.

Tosi, Arturo (1984) *Immigration and Bilingual Education: A Case Study of Movement of Population, Language Change and Education Within the EEC*. Oxford: Pergamon Press.

Language planning is treated extensively in the following:

Cooper, Robert L. (1989) *Language Planning and Social Change*. New York: Cambridge University Press.

Eastman, Carol M. (1983) *Language Planning: An Introduction*. San Francisco: Chandler and Sharp Publishers.

Tollefson, James W. (1991) *Planning Language, Planning Inequality: Language Policy in the Community*. London: Longman

For work specifically on language planning and bilingual education, see especially:

Hornberger, Nancy (1990) Bilingual education and English-Only: A language-planning framework. *Annals of the American Academy of Political and Social Science* 508, 12–26.

Rubin, Joan (1983) Bilingual education and language planning. In Chris Kennedy, (ed.) *Language Planning and Language Education* (pp.4–16). London: George Allen and Unwin.

# Multilingualism and the Education of Minority Children[1]

## Tove Skutnabb-Kangas

'A linguistic science which is aware of these political involvements can only be militant. And it is the duty of linguists in their respective countries and regions to assume responsibility for this task, this struggle for the defence and development of their own language and culture. ' (Postface to L.-J. Calvet, *Linguistique et Colonialisme*)

### Introduction

The topic of multilingualism and the education of minority children is fascinating to work with in several different ways:

- it is a socially important — and controversial — topic, with immediate implications for most societies in the world. It forces the researcher to penetrate questions of ethics and the philosophy of science more deeply than do many other areas of inquiry, when pondering over the relationship between research and policy.
- it is multidisciplinary and problem-oriented, and forces the researcher to familiarize herself with many disciplines, in addition to her original one(s), and to ponder over the relationship between the definitions of social reality inherent in different disciplines.

In this chapter it is possible only to introduce some of the issues. I hope, though, that both their fascination and their complexity become clear and that the reader is intrigued and wants to find out more. The chapter starts by presenting the tension between the fact that a majority of the fewer than 200 states of the world are officially monolingual (have one official language only), and the fact that these states contain speakers of some 4–5,000 languages. Is state monolingualism, then, a stupid and irrational state of affairs, or a rational necessity? Is monolingualism in fact a reflection of an ideology, akin to racism, namely

*linguicism*, the domination of one language at the expense of others (see a more detailed definition later), or is it a sign of a mature state which has reached far in an inevitable but at the same time desirable development?

Those individuals whose mother tongues do not happen to be official languages in the countries where they live, *have* to become bilingual (or multilingual). If they want to be able to speak to their parents, know about their history and culture, know who they are, they have to know their mother tongue. If they want to get a good education (which is usually not available in their own language, at least not to the same extent as in the official language) and if they want to participate in the social, economic and political life of their country, they have to know the official language. It should be the duty of the educational systems to help them become bilingual, since bilingualism is a necessity for them, and not something that they themselves have chosen. The next question is: Does education in fact try to do so or not? In order to examine this question, definitions of both a mother tongue and of bilingualism/multilingualism are needed. The definitions used by the educational authorities are then examined, so as to see whether or not they reflect linguicism. In order to counteract the threat of linguicism, a declaration of children's linguistic human rights is proposed.

The next section of the chapter introduces a way of comparing the success of educational programmes in different countries in reaching the goal of bilingualism, which is a necessary goal for minority children. First it presents several types of programmes, and then it goes on to compare them in terms of factors which are necessary as preconditions for succeeding in making children bilingual. The analysis shows that most European and Europeanized countries do not organize the education of minority children so that they will succeed in becoming bilingual.

The last section before the conclusion examines who has been blamed for the failure, the children themselves (and their parents, their group and their culture) or the linguicist societies — and the conclusions are not especially flattering for us. At the same time I hope that they will be provocative enough for the reader to start to examine her/his own society and its linguicism.

## Monolingualism or Multilingualism?

The large majority of the countries in the world are *de facto multilingual* (in the sense that several languages are spoken natively inside their borders, like Nigeria, with over 500 languages, or India with over 1,600 mother tongues claimed by its people). It is inevitable that most countries should be multilingual: the number of independent countries is less than 200, while the number of languages spoken in the world probably is between 4,000 and 5,000, depending on how a language is defined.

An example of a *monolingual* country (where only one language is spoken natively) is Iceland, with its 240,000 inhabitants. There are no indigenous minorities and no immigrants. Even people who come to stay because they are married to Icelanders mostly learn Icelandic, and their children become native speakers of Icelandic (even if some of them hopefully become native speakers of another language in addition to Icelandic). But this type of monolingual country is an exception in our world.

Just like countries, individuals can be monolingual or bi- and multilingual. A monolingual is a person who 'knows' only one language, whatever that means. Obviously almost everybody, excluding very small children, knows at least a few words of other languages, but they would not call themselves multilingual because of that. Maybe it is easiest to define a monolingual in a negative way: a monolingual is a person who is NOT bi- or multilingual. We shall define bilingualism later in the chapter. There are more multilinguals than monolinguals in the world. Monolingual people are thus a minority in the world, but many of them belong to a very powerful minority, namely the minority which has been able to function in all situations through the medium of their mother tongue, and who have therefore never been forced to learn another language. The majority of multilinguals are multilingual *not* because they thought that

multilingualism was so desirable that they consciously wanted to become multilingual. It is rather because all those people whose mother tongues have no official rights in their country have been *forced* to learn other languages in addition to their own. But since they have been forced precisely because of their powerless status (= they have not been able to demand official rights for their own language), this means that they as a group have less power than monolinguals. Reagan does not need to know any of the languages spoken in the USA except English, while native Americans and Chicanas need to learn English in addition to their mother tongues.

But perhaps those who are monolingual in the present world need not learn other languages because their mother tongues (English, Chinese, Russian, French, etc.) are so much better and so much more developed than other languages? Perhaps 'smaller' languages are small because they are in fact somehow more primitive? From a *linguistic* point of view all languages spoken natively by a group of people have equal worth. All are logical, cognitively complex and capable of expressing any thoughts, provided enough resources are devoted to cultivation (creation of new lexical items, among other things). There is no such thing as 'primitive languages'. On linguistic grounds *all languages could have the same rights*, the same possibility of being learned fully, developed and used in all situations by their speakers. But in practice we know that this is far from the case. Different languages have different political rights, not depending on any inherent linguistic characteristics, but on the power relationships between the speakers of those languages.

The political rights or lack of rights of any language cannot be deduced from linguistic considerations. They are part of the societal conditions of the country concerned, and can only be understood in their historical context, by studying the forces which have led to the present sociopolitical division of power and resources in the societies concerned.

This is also true of cultural attitudes towards monolingualism and multilingualism. These vary on a continuum: at one end monolingualism is seen as a desirable norm; at the other end multilingualism is seen as the normal state of affairs. Granted the number of languages in the world, most countries and people should, of course, be closer to the multilingualism end of the continuum in their attitudes, and in fact most countries might be placed there. But there are some very powerful exceptions, namely most European countries and, especially, most Europeanized countries. It seems that the extreme monolingualist ideology is very strong in Europeanized countries, those countries which have been colonized by European settlers to such an extent that a virtual extinction of the indigenous populations has been attempted, either 'only' physically (like parts of Australia, for instance Tasmania, or some parts of Latin America) or both physically and linguistically/ culturally (North America, New Zealand, Australia). Likewise, this strong monolingual ideology also prevails in most former imperial European countries which are the sources of the languages of the former colonizers (Britain, France, etc.).

These negative attitudes towards multilingualism pertain both in relation to official multilingualism in a country (which is seen as divisive for the nation) and to individual multilingualism. Being bilingual has in several countries, especially the United States, been used almost as a synonym for being poor, stupid and uneducated. And it is true that coming from a linguistic minority in a monolingually oriented country has often meant misery and non-education.

For an *individual*, monolingualism almost inevitably means *monoculturalism* and *monoculism*, being able to see things with one pair of glasses only and having a poorly developed capacity to see things from another person's or group's point of view. It mostly means knowing not more than one culture from the inside, and therefore lacking relativity.

For a *country*, official monolingualism in the majority of cases means that *all the minorities are oppressed and their linguistic human rights are violated.*

To me monolingualism, both individual and societal, is not so much a linguistic phenomenon (even if it has to do with language). It is rather a question of a psychological state, backed up by political power. Monolingualism is a psychological island. It is an ideological cramp. It is an illness, a disease which should be eradicated as soon as possible, because it is dangerous for world peace. It is a reflection of *linguicism*.

## Linguicism

Linguicism is akin to the other negative -isms: racism, classism, sexism, ageism. Linguicism can be defined as *ideologies and structures which are used to legitimate, effectuate and reproduce an unequal division of power and resources (both material and non-material) between groups which are defined on the basis of language (on the basis of their mother tongues).*

D.P. Pattanayak, the Director of the Central Institute of Indian Languages, says in a powerful article (1986) that the Western way of looking at multilingualism is something like this: a country should ideally be monolingual. If it is officially bilingual, that is a pity but one can live with it. If it has three or more languages, it is underdeveloped and barbaric. In order to become civilized, it should strive towards becoming monolingual.

But if there are many more languages than countries, and if many countries decide to be officially monolingual, what happens to all the other languages and to their speakers? Should the speakers of these languages become monolingual, too? And if so, in which language should they become monolingual, their own or the language that the power elite in the country has decided should be THE language of that country? The last alternative would mean that thousands of languages would become extinct. Or should the speakers of other languages become bilingual? If so, what is the best way of becoming bilingual for a minority language speaker? Specifically, in which language should the minority child be taught, predominantly in her own language, or predominantly in the majority language, in order to become a competent bilingual?

The controversy about this, both about the *goal* (monolingualism or multilingualism) and about the *means* (operationalized as mother tongue medium education or second/foreign language medium education) is the main topic of this chapter. While we go along, we shall examine both the goals and the means in order to see the extent to which they reflect linguicism.

We could tentatively present the positions in Europe and Europeanized countries in the following, extremely simplified way:

*Minorities* (like many non-European and non-Europeanized countries) think that genuine multilingualism is a perfectly normal and desirable state. It is possible and desirable to have multilingualism as the linguistic goal in the education of all children. Mother tongue medium education is often a good way to bilingualism/multilingualism for minorities. Learning one's mother tongue is a human right which does not need any further legitimation.

*Majorities*[2] think that monolingualism in the majority language is the normal and desirable state. Societal multilingualism is divisive and should not be a goal. If individual multilingualism has to be accepted, the emphasis should be on the learning of the majority language. If mother tongue medium education for minorities has to be accepted, the only legitimation for it is that it leads to increased proficiency in the majority language.

## The Goal of Education for Linguistic Minority Children

If you want to have your fair share of the power and the resources (both material and nonmaterial) of your native country, you have to be able to take part in the democratic processes in your country. You have to be able to negotiate, try to influence, to have a voice. The main instrument for doing that is language. You must be able to communicate with your fellow citizens, in order to be able to influence your own situation, to be a subject in your life, not an object to be handled by others. Language is the main instrument for communication. If you live in a country with speakers of many different languages, you have to share at least one language with the others, in order for a democratic process to be possible. And if the language most widely spoken by your fellow citizens (either because it is the mother tongue of the majority, or because the power elite[3] has decided that that will be the *lingua franca*) is NOT your mother tongue, you belong to a *linguistic minority* in your country. That means that *you have to become (at least) bilingual in order to participate*.

In a democratic country, it should be the duty of the school system to give every child, regardless of linguistic background, the same chance to participate in the democratic process. If this requires that (at least) some children (i.e. the linguistic minority children) become bilingual or multilingual, then it should be the duty of the educational system to make them bilingual/multilingual, as individuals (as opposed to the *country* being multilingual).

If Western attitudes really are inclined towards monolingualism (and I find no convincing arguments to refute Pattanayak's analysis), what are the chances that European and Europeanized countries will come up with good solutions to questions about the education of minority children, solutions which would promote multilingualism? Slight, as I see it.

Monolingualism does *not* prevent *some* knowledge of other languages, provided these are 'modern' and 'European' and have been learned at school as part of becoming 'educated'. If monolingualism (with *some* knowledge of other languages) is the explicitly or at least implicitly desirable and accepted societal norm, there is an inherent conflict between supporting that norm, and organizing minority (or majority) education so that it would lead to high levels of bi- or multilingualism.

But this conflict is seldom discussed openly. In fact, most European countries have at least some passages in their declarations of goals for the education of minorities which refer to bi- or multilingualism. Mostly it is discussed as a societal phenomenon ('Britain is multilingual'), and here it means only that several languages are spoken in a country. This is often only stating a fact, not declaring a wish ('OK, there *are* several languages spoken in this country, and since we cannot really do much about it, we had better accept it and try to see if there is anything positive in it'). Bilingualism/multilingualism is seldom declared as a *goal* for the educational system. If it is, then the language learning *emphasis is put on the learning of the majority language* (L2 = language two, the second or foreign language) *by the minority children*. The part of their bilingualism which has to do with the *minority language* (L1 = the first language, the mother tongue), again states the fact, but does not declare a wish ('OK, they do speak that minority language, but obviously they need to learn L2, English/German/Dutch etc.: that is the most important thing in their education. If learning English makes them bilingual, then the goal of education must be to make them bilingual, because they *have* to learn English').

It thus seems that both minorities and majorities agree that minority children should be given the opportunity to learn the majority language in school. But they disagree about the learning of the minority mother tongue. Many minorities think that their mother tongues should have the same rights, also in schools, as majority people's mother tongues do. Majorities act as if minority mother tongues were of less value (cultural linguicism), and emphasize educational efforts geared towards the learning of the majority language (institutional linguicism).

## Definitions of Mother Tongue

Before we can continue our discussion, we have to define what a mother tongue is. This gives us

**Table 1** Definitions of the mother tongue

| Criterion | Definition |
|---|---|
| Origin | the language(s) one learned first |
| Competence | the language(s) one knows best |
| Function | the language(s) one uses most |
| Identification | |
| (a) internal | the language(s) one identifies with |
| (b) external | the language(s) one is identified as a native speaker of by others |

a better opportunity to assess whether minority and majority mother tongues have the same rights or whether majority mother tongues are given more institutional support (institutions in the abstract sense of laws and regulations, and in the concrete sense of day care centres, schools, etc.).

There are several different ways of defining a mother tongue. I use four different criteria for the definitions: Origin, Competence, Function and Identification (see Table 1).

I have three theses about the definitions:
(1) The same person can have different mother tongues, depending on which definition is used.
(2) A person's mother tongue can change during her lifetime, even several times, according to all other definitions except the definition by origin.
(3) The mother tongue definitions can be organized hierarchically according to the degree of linguistic human rights awareness of a society.

I am a good example of the first thesis myself. My mother tongue is Swedish according to the definition by origin, because both my bilingual parents spoke it to me when I was a baby. But I am bilingual in Finnish and Swedish according to the same definition (see Table 2) because I myself used both languages side by side from the very beginning. My mother tongue is Finnish according to the definition by competence; I feel that it is the language I know best (even if I know Swedish, too, just as well as any monolingual Swedish academic). My mother tongue would be English (or possibly English and Danish) according to the definition by function (I speak mostly English — in addition to three other languages — at home, and read and write English more than other languages, and I live in Denmark). And according to all identification definitions I have two mother tongues, Finnish and Finland Swed-

ish. This also illustrates the second thesis, because both English and Danish have come into the picture through emigration and marriage, i.e. changes.

The third thesis about the definitions is the most interesting one from the point of view of linguicism. According to my view, the definition by *function* is the *most primitive* one ('this Turkish child speaks German/Dutch/Danish/English all day long at the day care centre/in school, much more than Turkish, she even uses German with siblings, so German/Dutch/Danish/English must be the child's mother tongue'). Use of this definition does not consider the fact that most minority children are *forced* to use an L2 because there are no facilities in their mother tongue. The children and their parents have not themselves been given a chance to choose freely, from among existing alternatives, which language they would like to use in day care and school. This definition is, explicitly or implicitly, used in educational institutions in many European immigration countries.

When the degree of awareness rises a bit, the next definition, also pretty primitive, is used, namely the definition by *competence* ('the Turkish children could not even count in their so-called mother tongue' says a well-known linguist, implying that Swedish, in which the children had been taught how to count, was their mother tongue, because they knew it better than Turkish). Use of this definition fails to consider that a poor proficiency in the original mother tongue is a result of not having been offered the opportunity to use and learn the original mother tongue well enough in those institutional settings where the children spent most of their day (day care centres, schools, organized after-school activities). A poor competence in the original mother tongue (which is a result of the neglect of the mother tongue in institutions earlier on, i.e. a result of earlier oppression) is then often used to legitimize additional oppression. The child is labelled as a majority language speaker, or she is denied teaching in the original mother tongue on the grounds that she does not know it well enough or because she knows the majority language better.

Use of a combination of definitions by *origin* and *identification* shows the highest degree of linguistic human rights awareness: *the mother tongue is the language one has learned first and identifies with*.

Use of a definition of function or competence in educational institutions when defining a minority child's mother tongue reflects cultural and institutional linguicism. It can be open (the agent does not try to hide it), conscious (the agent knows about it), visible (it is easy for non-agents to detect) and actively action-oriented (as opposed to merely attitudinal). All this is typical of the early phases of the history of minority education, as described in the later sections of this chapter. Or it can be hidden, unconscious, invisible and passive (lack of support rather than active opposition), typical of the later phases of minority education development. Those countries which have developed the more sophisticated, culturally (rather than biologically) oriented forms of racism (ethnicism — see Mullard, 1985b), typically also exhibit this more sophisticated form of linguicism, a linguicism which blames the victim in subtle ways, by colonizing her consciousness.

## Results of Institutional and Cultural Linguicism for Minority Mother Tongues

The above recommended mother tongue definition implies that the language identified with is the original mother tongue, the language learned first. But in a society with institutional and cultural linguicism and discrimination, not all minority children are allowed to identify positively with their original mother tongues and cultures.

Many minority children are being forced to feel ashamed of their mother tongues, their parents, their origins, their group and their culture. Many of them, especially in countries where the racism is more subtle, not so openly expressed, take over the negative views which the majority society has of the minority groups, their languages and cultures. Many disown their parents and their own group and language. They shift identity 'voluntarily', and *want* to be German, Dutch, American, British, Swedish, etc.

Often this does not work either. The child's new majority identity is not accepted by everybody. This is generally expressed more openly in the years after the minority youngsters reach puberty, and it is more common with youngsters who do not look like the stereotype of what a 'real' German, Dutch, Swede, Norwegian, etc. person 'should' look like, and/or with youngsters whose accent does not sound 'native'. The minority youngster then often hears: 'You are not one of us, you are not a real Swede/American/Dutch/German/Dane, etc. you are a Finnish devil/a Turkshit/a damn Paki, etc'.

The child has then 'voluntarily' disowned her original identity, but the new identity is not accepted by all the people from the majority group either. There is a conflict between the internal and the external identification. The youngster is not accepted, at least not unconditionally, by the majority group, with which she has been forced to identify (but whose language and culture she has not been given the opportunity to learn 'fully': see Cummins, 1984). At the same time the road back to her own group is often closed too, not only psychologically (= she does not *want* to identify with the 'dirty Turks' or 'aggressive silent Finns'), but often also linguistically and culturally. The child no longer knows (or has never had the chance to learn) the original mother tongue 'properly'. Nor does she have all the components of cultural competence in the original culture (Phillipson & Skutnabb-Kangas, 1983).

## Declaration of Children's Linguistic Human Rights

In order to avoid this type of situation, all those institutions, educational and otherwise, which now function in the way described above *vis-à-vis* minority children and their mother tongues, should be changed. Majority cultures, which now degrade minority children's languages and cultures, should be changed. In order to make the demands for change more concrete, we need a *declaration of children's linguistic human rights*.

### The declaration of children's linguistic human rights

(1) Every child should have the right to identify positively with her original mother tongue(s) and have her identification accepted and respected by others.

(2) Every child should have the right to learn the mother tongue(s) fully.

(3) Every child should have the right to choose

when she wants to use the mother tongue(s) in all official situations (Skutnabb-Kangas, 1986: 160).

Not to live up to these demands for minority children is linguicist. If Dutch, West German, Swedish, British, etc. day care centres and schools, actively or through passivity and lack of positive action, prevent minority children from being able to identify positively with their mother tongues, then they function in a linguicist way. If in the same vein they prevent minority children from learning their mother tongues fully and from using them in all official situations, including day care centres and schools, then these institutions also function in a linguicist way. If the education of minority children is not discussed in these terms, i.e. if the Swedes, Norwegians, Dutch, Germans, etc. are not even aware of or deny the fact that they are suppressing minority children's basic human rights every day, then the Dutch, German, Swedish, British, etc. cultures are linguicist *vis-à-vis* minority children and their languages.

All the demands formulated in the declaration of children's linguistic human rights are met to a very large extent in relation to majority children. Nobody questions their right to identify positively with their mother tongue, to learn it fully or to use it in official situations, for instance in schools. For majority children these rights are so self-evident that they may never think of them as human rights. Some people might think that it cannot be a human right to use one's mother tongue in all official situations, for instance. But even if one did not accept that the rights in the declaration are legitimate human rights, there is no way of denying the fact that majority and minority mother tongues do not enjoy the same rights in the educational systems of most European and Europeanized countries. Groups defined on the basis of their mother tongues thus have unequal access to educational resources, i.e. these educational systems reflect linguicism.

## Definitions of Bilingualism

Above we claimed that the majorities are mostly interested in the part of the bilingualism goal which has to do with the learning of the majority language by minority children. The mother tongues of the minority children are tolerated as parts of the curriculum only if the teaching of them leads to a better proficiency in the majority language. The minorities themselves, partly as a result of this, have to put a strong emphasis on the learning of the mother tongue as a linguistic human right. But the minorities do, of course, want their children to learn the majority languages fully too. We want our children to become bilingual, not monolingual or strongly dominant in either of the two languages. One of the confusing facts has been that many majority educational authorities claim that they want our children to become bilingual too. But when this claim is analysed, it transpires that the *definitions* used by majorities and minorities of bilingualism as the educational goal are different. That is one of the reasons why it is imperative to define 'bilingual' every time the term is being used. There are literally hundreds of definitions. In Table 2 I organize them according to the same criteria which I used in the mother tongue definitions, and give a sample.

When majority educational authorities talk about bilingualism as a goal for the education of minority children, they seem to mean either a non-demanding competence definition (for instance 2d or 2e) or the most general function definition (uses two languages). We minorities would rather like to use a combination of 2, 3 and 4, a definition which makes sure that the speaker has the chance to learn and use *both* languages at a very high level and to identify positively with both. Again we see that the definitions used by the majority authorities confirm the picture of linguicism: there are almost no demands made on the minority child's competence in her mother tongue.

My own definition is specifically planned to suit immigrant and indigenous minority children. The goal of minority education should be to make the children bilingual according to this definition:

> 'A speaker is bilingual who is able to function in two (or more) languages, either in monolingual or bilingual communities, in accordance with the sociocultural demands made on an individual's communicative and cognitive competence by these communities and by the individual herself, at the same level as native speakers, and who is able positively to identify with both (or all) language groups (and cultures) or parts of them.' (Skutnabb-Kangas, 1984: 90)

The implications of this definition for the educational system are far-reaching, and should be compared with the implications of less

**Table 2** Definitions of bilingualism

| Criterion | Definition |
|---|---|
| | A speaker is bilingual who: |
| 1. Origin | (a) has learned two languages in the family from native speakers from the beginning |
| | (b) has used two languages in parallel as means of communication from the beginning |
| 2. Competence | (a) has complete mastery[4] of two languages |
| | (b) has native-like control of two languages |
| | (c) has equal mastery of two languages |
| | (d) can produce complete meaningful utterances in the other language |
| | (e) has at least some knowledge and control of the grammatical structure of the other language |
| | (f) has come into contact with another language |
| 3. Function | (a) uses (or can use) two languages (in most situations) (in accordance with her own wishes and the demands of the community) |
| 4. Identification | |
| internal | (a) identifies herself as bilingual/with two languages and/or two cultures (or parts of them) |
| external | (b) is identified by others as bilingual/as a native speaker of two languages |

Skutnabb-Kangas, 1984: 91

demanding definitions (for more detail see Skutnabb-Kangas, 1984).

In the next section we turn to an examination of concrete educational programmes, in order to see to what extent there is a mismatch between the goals and the means in the education of minority students. If the educational systems are organized to give minority students a fair chance of becoming bilingual and succeeding in school, then the claims of linguicism are unfounded. If, on the other hand, the education is organized to prevent minority children from gaining access to the instruments (here operationalized in terms of high levels of bilingualism and a 'good' education) for claiming their fair share of power and resources, and if the mother tongue (minority or majority language) plays a decisive part in the division of children into those who do and those who do not gain such access, then the educational system functions in a linguicist way.

## Comparing the Success of Educational Programmes in Different Countries in Reaching the Goal of Bilingualism

Some of the educational programmes for minority and/or majority children achieve a *high*

*degree of success* (HDS) in making the children bilingual and giving them a fair chance of good school achievement (see Table 3). Others show a *low degree of success* (LDS): many children do not learn any of the languages at the same level as monolinguals, or they become strongly dominant in one of the languages, i.e. they fail to become bilingual. They also show, as a group, low levels of achievement in schools, often massive failure. One of the most frequently discussed factors in explaining the difference between the two groups is *which of the two languages has been used as the medium of education* (ME). Paradoxically, instruction through the medium of a mother tongue can lead to either HDS or LDS. Likewise, instruction through the medium of a second language can also lead to either HDS or LDS. In order to understand this we must look both at societal factors which determine what type of programme is chosen for different groups, and at cognitive, pedagogical, linguistic and sociological factors which determine the outcome of the instruction. It becomes abundantly clear from the analysis that 'which language should a child be instructed in, L1 or L2, in order to become bilingual?' poses the question in a simplistic and misleading way. The question should rather be: '*under which conditions* does instruction in L1 or L2, respectively, lead to high levels of bilingualism?'

I will analyse different types of educational programmes in very concrete terms, in order to highlight the decisive factors, under four main headings: *segregation, mother tongue maintenance* (or language shelter), *submersion* and *immersion* programmes. In three instances it is necessary to treat separately the programmes meant for minorities and majorities. For each programme, I assess the degree of success (high or low), the medium of education (L1 or L2) and the linguistic and societal goals of the programme. The classification of the goals builds more on factual results achieved than on declarations of intention, and may therefore not always tally with the officially declared goals. Some of the discussion that follows is also found in Phillipson, Skutnabb-Kangas & Africa (1986).

My example of a *segregation* model for a *majority* population (in this case a powerless majority) is the Bantu education now given at the elementary level to Namibians in nine different L1s, in Namibia. Namibia is still illegally occupied by South Africa, despite the efforts of the United Nations (manifested in several declarations) to end this state of affairs. (To a certain extent also the education for Blacks in South Africa is of the same kind.) Segregation programmes produce poor results, meaning scholastic failure for the majority of those who start school (and many do not), and low levels of cognitive/academic proficiency (see Cummins, 1984) in both languages. This fits with the linguistic goal, dominance in L1, and the societal goal, perpetuation of apartheid.

My example of *segregation* for a *minority* is the education of migrant Turks in Bavaria, West Germany, through the medium of Turkish, again with low levels of success. The linguistic goal is dominance in Turkish. The societal goal is to prepare the migrant pupils for forced repatriation when their parents' labour is no longer needed or when they themselves become 'too expensive' or 'too troublesome' for West Germany (for instance when resisting assimilation and racism by political or other means).

In contrast to segregation, mother tongue (MT) maintenance programmes which also use the children's mother tongues as ME, show high levels of success — because the linguistic goals (bilingualism) and societal goals (equity and integration) are different. An example of *mainte-*

*nance* for a *majority* is the MT-medium education given in the Soviet republic of Uzbekistan to the seven main language groups, including the dominant group, the Uzbeks. Since the main groups are all in the same position educationally, with the same rights, they are here treated as together forming a majority. In Uzbekistan, where only a tiny elite was literate 70 years ago when the country was still under feudal conditions, all children now complete at least 10 years of education. The main groups have the right to education through the medium of their own languages, with Russian or another Uzbekian language as a second language.

Examples of *maintenance* for *minorities* are the Finnish-medium classes for the Finnish migrant population in Sweden (or Spanish-medium classes for the Chicana population in the USA), both still rare. The first three cohorts of Finnish youngsters who have gone through the whole comprehensive school (nine years) in Finnish in Botkyrka, a suburb of Stockholm, continue their education in upper secondary schools in the more academic streams to a somewhat greater extent than Swedish youngsters from the same schools (Hagman & Lahdenperä, this volume).

An example of *submersion*[5] for a *majority* is education through the medium of a former colonial language in many African countries, for instance Zambia (Chishimba, 1984). For the vast majority of the population the results are poor, both academically and linguistically (Africa, 1980). The linguistic goal achieved is dominance in English for the elite, and, for the masses, dominance in their mother tongues (which the school does nothing to develop) and limited proficiency in English.

*Submersion* programmes for *minorities* are still by far the most common way of educating both indigenous and immigrant minorities in most countries in the world. Even in Sweden, where we have come a long way, some 80% of the immigrant children are educated this way, through the medium of Swedish, regardless of the fact that *all immigrant organizations in every Scandinavian country demand mother tongue medium education*. Most migrants, for instance in the UK and West Germany (except Turks in Bavaria who are in segregation programmes and some Greek and other migrants in maintenance programmes), undergo submersion, resulting in dominance in the majority language at the expense of the mother tongue, and poor school achievement. Societally this means assimilation for some (de-

**Table 3**

| | L1 | | | | L2 | | |
| --- | --- | --- | --- | --- | --- | --- | --- |
| | Segregation: LDS | | Maintenance: HDS | | Submersion: LDS | | Immersion: HDS |
| | Bantu | Turks | Uzbekistan | Finns, Chicanas | Zambia | W. Europe minorities | Canada |
| *Organizational factors* | | | | | | | |
| 1 Alternative programmes available | - | - | + | + | - | - | + |
| 2 Pupils equally placed *vis-à-vis* knowledge of ME | + | + | + | - | - | - | + |
| 3 Bilingual (B), trained (T) teachers | B | B or T | BT | BT | B | T | BT |
| 4 Bilingual materials (e.g. dictionaries) available | - | + | + | + | - | - | + |
| 5 Cultural content of materials appropriate for pupils | - | - | + | + | - | - | + |
| *Learner-related affective factors* | | | | | | | |
| 6 Low level of anxiety (supportive, non-authoritarian) | - | - | + | + | - | - | + |
| 7 High internal motivation (not forced to use L2, understands & sympathetic with objectives, responsible for own learning) | - | - | + | + | - | - | + |
| 8 High self-confidence (fair chance to succeed, high teacher expectations) | - | - | + | + | - | - | + |
| *L1-related linguistic, cognitive, pedagogical and social factors* | | | | | | | |
| 9 Adequate linguistic development in L1 (L1 taught well (W), badly (B) or not at all in school) | B | B | W | W | - | - | W |
| 10 Enough relevant, cognitively demanding subject matter provided | - ? | + ? | + | + | - ? | - ? | + |
| 11 Opportunity to develop L1 outside school in linguistically demanding formal contexts | +? | - | + | - | + | - | + |
| 12 L2-teaching supports (+) or harms (-) L1-development | + | + | + | + | -? | - | + |
| *L2-related linguistic, cognitive, pedagogical and social factors* | | | | | | | |
| 13 Adequate linguistic development in L2 (L2 taught well (W), badly (B) or not at all in school) | B | B | W | W | B | B | W |
| 14 L2 input adapted to pupils' L2 level | + | + | + | + | -? | - | + |
| 15 Opportunity to practise L2 in peer group contexts | - | - | + | + ? | - | - | - |
| 16 Exposure to native speaker L2 use in linguistically demanding formal contexts | - | + | + | + | - | + | + |

LDS = low degree of success
HDS = high degree of success

pending on whether the country in question allows assimilation or not) and marginalization for the many. It should, perhaps, also be added that *transitional programmes*[6] belong to the submersion type, too; they are simply a version of submersion which is a bit more sophisticated than direct submersion (see my typology in Skutnabb-Kangas, 1984: 125–133).

By contrast, Canadian *immersion*[7] programmes, in which English speaking *majority* children are educated through the medium of an L2 (mostly French, but several other languages are also in operation: see Lambert & Taylor, 1982), lead to high levels of bilingualism and success at school (Swain & Lapkin, 1982). The societal goals include linguistic and cultural enrichment for the power majority, and increased employment prospects and other benefits for an elite. As is clear from the definition of immersion programmes, the concept cannot, by definition, be applied to minorities .

To summarize so far, in all HDS contexts the *linguistic goal* has been *bilingualism,* and the *societal goal* has been a *positive* one for the group concerned. In all LDS contexts, the *linguistic goal* has been *dominance in one of the languages,* either L1 or L2, *NOT* bilingualism. The other language (non-ME) has been neglected or taught badly. The *societal goal* has been to *keep the group* (or at least most of them) *in a powerless subordinate position.*

Next we turn to how the programmes are organized, in order to see the extent to which they create optimal conditions for efficient L2-learning and bilingualism. The preconditions for learning L2 effectively and for becoming bilingual have been grouped into four categories, called *organizational* factors, *learner-related affective* factors, and *linguistic, cognitive, pedagogical and social L1-related and L2-related* factors, respectively. These factors are chosen to reflect the present views in different disciplines in relation to important or necessary preconditions for L2-learning and bilingualism .

## How Do Different Programmes Support L2-learning and Bilingualism?

We start with *organizational factors. Alternative programmes* (Table 3, factor 1) are available only in the HDS programmes, i.e. in maintenance and immersion contexts. These programmes are optional. An Uzbek or Tadjik in the USSR, a Finn in Sweden or a Chicana in the USA who wants education through the medium of Russian, Swedish or English (instead of Uzbek, Tadjik, Finnish or Spanish, respectively), can opt for that. An English-speaking Canadian child can choose between English-medium education or a French-medium immersion programme. By contrast, children in segregation or submersion programmes have no choice. Either alternatives do not even exist, as in most submersion programmes, or, if they do, children in segregation or submersion programmes are precluded from them administratively or economically.

Factor 2 covers whether there are *in the same class both native speakers of the medium of education (ME) and pupils for whom the ME is an L2.* This is a normal situation in submersion programmes, disadvantaging the L2-*learners.* In Zambia, the pupils' class background and geographical location (urban or rural) has a decisive influence on their prior knowledge of English. In all the other programmes pupils are, in relation to prior familiarity with the ME, on an equal footing in that initially either they all know the language of instruction (segregation and maintenance) or none of them do (immersion).

The third factor shows that the HDS programmes have teachers who are *both bilingual and well trained.* For instance, in immersion programmes, the teacher understands everything that the English-speaking children say in English, even if she herself speaks only French to the children. Thus the children can communicate all their needs to the teacher initially in their L 1, and only later start doing so in L2 when they feel confident enough. The LDS programmes have either well trained monolingual teachers who do not understand their pupils' mother tongues (submersion for minorities) or else the training of the teachers is inadequate, even if they are to some extent bilingual (for instance segregation, and submersion for majorities in Zambia). We consider, though, that a bilingual (mostly meaning minority group) teacher without any training is usually a better choice than a monolingual well trained teacher. This is especially so in second language contexts, where the pupil hears L2 outside school anyway. Especially in relation to small children, it is close to criminal, real psychological torture, to use monolingual teachers who do not understand what the child has to say in her mother tongue. Not giving minority teachers a good training, adjusted to the conditions in the receiving country, is one of the reflections of the institutional racism in the Western countries. At the same time it protects the employment prospects of majority teachers, and makes minority children's failure in schools look like the children's fault, instead of the deficiency of the school system which it of course is.

Factor 4 shows that most of the LDS programmes lack *bilingual materials*. The materials actually used (Factor 5) in them are imported or racist or both, thus imposing alien cultural values.

The *learner-related affective factors* suggest that a supportive learning environment and non-authoritarian teaching reduce *anxiety* (6). *Internal motivation* (7) is increased when the pupil is not *forced* to use L2, and can start producing L2 utterances only when she feels ready for it. Again this stresses the importance of bilingual teachers, because the child is forced to use L2 if the teacher does not understand the child's L1. High motivation is also related to an understanding of and sympathy with the educational objectives and to sharing in responsibility for one's own learning (which is difficult without bilingual materials). *High self-confidence* (8) is related to whether learners have a real chance of succeeding in school, and to favourable teacher expectations. One of the conditions for this is that the teacher accepts and values the child's mother tongue and cultural group, and is sympathetic with the parents' way of thinking, even though the teacher might have a different class background from the parents. There is a positive correlation between a plus-rating on these three factors (low anxiety, high motivation and high self-confidence) and the successful programmes.

The final two sets cover *linguistic, cognitive, pedagogical and social language-related factors. Linguistic development in L1* (9) is inadequate when the MT is taught badly, as in most segregation programmes (which should not be blamed on the teachers!) or not at all, as in most submersion programmes. It should also be mentioned that a couple of hours a week of mother tongue instruction for a minority child is more therapeutic cosmetics than language teaching.

Enough *relevant cognitively demanding subject matter* (10) to promote the common underlying proficiency for all languages (CALP: see Cummins, 1984; Skutnabb-Kangas, 1984) is provided in the HDS programmes. This is done through the medium of L1 in maintenance and through L2 in immersion (where it is made sure that the children understand, and where it has been shown that they can transfer the knowledge: see Swain & Lapkin, 1982). The input may satisfy this criterion in some segregation programmes, because the pupils at least understand the in-

struction. In submersion, when both language and subject matter are unfamiliar, it is less likely (for details see Skutnabb-Kangas, 1984). If the child learns how to use language as an effective instrument for thinking and problem solving in one language (by gaining a lot of relevant knowledge and using it), this capacity can also be transferred to other languages.

In addition to L1-development in school, pupils also need the *opportunity to develop their MTs outside school in linguistically demanding formal contexts* (11). Otherwise they are restricted to being able to discuss everyday things in informal settings only. This opportunity exists at least to a certain extent for all indigenous groups, but not for immigrants. Some groups may therefore be able to compensate for inadequate school provision outside the school setting. A more general factor which influences whether the language learning situation is additive (Lambert, 1975: you *add* a new language to your existing linguistic repertoire, without losing your mother tongue) or subtractive (another language replaces the mother tongue) is the degree to which *L2-teaching supports or harms L1-development* (12). Only submersion programmes threaten the MTs in this way.

*Linguistic development in L2* (13) is inadequate when the L2 is badly taught, as it is in all the LDS programmes. A teacher, monolingual in L2, can never be a really good L2 teacher! A good L2 teacher knows both languages.

Also relevant is the degree to which *L2 input is adapted to pupils' L2 level* (14). It is difficult to adapt the input in this way in immigrant submersion contexts, because the difference in the pupils' proficiency in the same class is too great. The task is relatively more feasible when no pupils are native speakers of the ME, as in Zambia.

Absence of the *opportunity to practise the L2 in peer group contexts outside school* (15) may be due to practicalities (immersion children do not meet many L2 children), to sheer racism (Turkish children are often avoided by German children), or to a shortage of L2 native speakers, as in Zambia, or as in Bantu education, where institutionalized racism and apartheid aggravate the situation.

*Exposure to native speaker L2 use in linguistically demanding formal contexts* (16) depends on the existence of L2 institutions staffed by native L2 speakers. Turks in West Germany cannot escape exposure to native German, whereas Zambians are exposed to a range of non-native Englishes, some of them appropriate regional models, some of them interlanguages (= languages spoken by learners of English) (but see Kachru, 1986).[8]

As we can see from the chart (Table 3), there is a clear difference between the programmes in that the HDS programmes with bilingualism as the linguistic goal and with positive societal goals have organized the teaching so that many of the preconditions for efficient L2 learning and bilingualism are met. The LDS programmes do so to a much lesser extent.

This comparison also functions as a validation of the way we attributed goals to the different programmes — otherwise it might have been claimed that we first looked at the results and then attributed positive goals to the HDS programmes and negative goals to the LDS programmes. Likewise, the comparison validates our claims about linguicism.

We can see that the situation for those who would want to organize minority children's education properly is tricky in those countries where the exploitation of a minority (or a powerless majority, as in Namibia) is open and brutal. Measures which under different, less oppressive conditions would be positive (like mother tongue medium education) can in the hands of an oppressive regime become instruments for segregation and apartheid.

We can also draw a conclusion by taking an example from the European situation. As long as West Germany uses Turkey as its Bantustan, from which it fetches workers (whose childhood and education costs have been paid by their parents and the Turkish society) when it needs them, and sends them back when it no longer needs them or when they become old, sick or unemployed, it seems difficult to do much by changing things in the schools in West Germany. Still, at the same time as progressive people work for the political changes needed in order to give minorities human conditions in West Germany, preparation for change is needed in schools, too. It is necessarily a defensive strategy, a defensive line of argumentation, that must be used, as long as societal conditions do not allow the type of offensive strategies we use in Scandinavia, and as long as the results of using an offensive strategy might be misused so as to strengthen the segregation.

We migrants in the Scandinavian countries, especially those of us who come from the other Scandinavian countries, *cannot be thrown out*, and that provides a different basis for our work. The defensive strategy, necessary in openly linguicist countries like West Germany, thus involves using arguments to legitimize the minority mother tongue in schools, which emphasize its instrumental value in learning the majority language. The offensive strategy used in Scandinavia emphasizes the human rights argument for legitimizing the minority mother tongues. The defensive line of argumentation may later on function as a negative boomerang, because the argument itself is linguicist. But choice of argument to be used is determined by the stage at which the society in question finds itself in the historical development of minority education.

In the final section we shall look at these stages. Who is to blame, according to the analyses on which different measures are based? Whose fault is it thought to be that minority children experience difficulties in school? Is it the child who is deficient, or is the society that controls the school 'deficient', i.e. linguicist and racist'?

## Deficient Children or Deficient Schools and Societies?

We shall chart stages in the development of minority education in different countries. This is partly based on a report by Stacy Churchill for OECD, Centre for Educational Research and Innovation (CERI) (see Churchill, 1985). The readers are invited to look at the measures in their own countries and communities and try to place them in the scheme. What has been done, based on what problem definition, and with what goal? Table 4 summarizes the development.

When minority children experience problems in school, a *reason for the problems* is diagnosed, explicitly or implicitly. Then *measures* are suggested and taken to alleviate the problems. Behind the measures one can also discern an opinion about the *future of the minorities*: are these going to (be allowed to) maintain their languages and cultures, or are they going to disappear fast, or in some generations, to be assimilated into the majority? If they are not going to be assimilated immediately, is this seen as good and positive or bad and divisive for the society?

The first four phases in the development which most countries seem to be going through are based on *deficit theories*. There is *something wrong with the minority child* (1, L2-related handicap: the child does not know enough of the majority language), *the minority parents* (2, socially conditioned handicap: the parents are working class), *the whole minority group* (3, culturally conditioned

**Table 4**

| Reason for problems | Measure | Goal |
|---|---|---|
| *Deficit theories* | | |
| 1  Linguistic L2-related handicap, learning deficit (the child does not master L2 well enough) | More teaching of MaL (auxiliary teaching, ESL, introductory classes etc); compensatory | MI is to become MaL-speaking as fast as possible |
| 2  Social handicap, socially linked learning deficit (the child's parents come from lowest social classes) | More social and pedagogical help (aids, tutors, psychologists, social workers, career advisers etc); in addition to measure 1; compensatory | Same as 1 |
| 3  Cultural handicap, culturally linked learning deficit (the child has a 'different' cultural background; the child has low self-confidence; the child is discriminated against | Inform MI-children about MA-culture/about their own culture; inform all children about MI-cultures/start multicultural/intercultural educational programmes; eliminate discrimination/racism in teaching materials; attitudinal courses for teachers; in addition to measures 1 and 2; compensatory | MiL in the family 1-2 generations; MI-children need help to appreciate MI-culture (until they become MaL-speaking) |
| 4  Linguistic L1-related handicap, learning deficit because of L1 deprivation (the child does not know her own L properly and has therefore poor grounding for the learning of L2 CALP) (the child loses content while learning L2) | Teaching of L1 as subject; elementary education through the medium of L1 with as fast a transition to L2-medium as possible. MiL has no intrinsic value, it is therapeutic; compensatory (more self-confidence, better co-operation with home, gives better basis for MaL-learning, functions as bridge for transmission of content during L2-learning); in addition to measures 1 and 3 | Same as 3 |
| *Enrichment theories* | | |
| 5  High levels of bilingualism beneficial for the individual but difficult to attain, demands much work and energy. The primary goal is to learn MaL properly; it is a prerequisite for equal opportunity | Teaching through the medium of MiL for several years inside MA-school; obligatory teaching of MaL; transition to MaL-medium teaching after elementary education | MiL is allowed to be maintained for private use; bilingualism necessary; MiL is allowed to exist (in a diglossic situation) as long as demographic basis exists |
| 6  Bilingualism enhances development. If problems arise, the causes are similar to those of monolingual children; some problems may be caused by racism/discrimination | Separate, equal school systems for MI and MA children, L1 is medium for both and L2 obligatory (or possible to study) for both. Positive discrimination of the M1 economically (smaller units allowed) | Existence of minorities is enriching for the whole society. MiL has (at least some) official status and its use is encouraged, also for MaL-children |

MI = minority; MiL = minority language; MA = majority; MaL = majority language.

handicap: the child's cultural background is 'different'), *or all of these* (4, L1-related handicap: the child does not know her own language and culture properly, and this leaves her without a firm basis for L2-learning, and gives her poor self-confidence). To a small extent there may also be something lacking in majority *individuals* (not systems), peers and teachers who may discriminate, because they have not had enough information.

In these four phases it is envisaged that the minority should become majority-language-speaking fast (1, 2). But as long as the children still speak their original mother tongue, the school should help them to appreciate it (3, 4). The main measures depend on which specific handicap the child is thought to suffer from. It seems that the measures from earlier phases are continued when the school system moves to the next phase.

Different European countries seem to show a somewhat different course of development. In Scandinavia, especially Sweden, we have focused much on the language handicaps (1 and especially 4). This has been mainly because of us Finns. We are the largest immigrant group in Sweden, and our social structure and cultural traits are relatively close to those of Sweden, partly as a result of the 650 years of colonization by Sweden. We Finns differ from the Swedes mainly in relation to language. Swedish is Indo-European, Northern Germanic, Finnish is Finno-Ugric, not related at all. The United Kingdom/Queendom has focused on cultural differences (3), in addition to the L2-related handicap (1), and the mother tongue deprivation discussions have barely started. West Germany has focused more on the social handicap explanations (2), in addition to cultural and linguistic L2-related handicaps, especially in relation to the largest migrant minority group, people from Turkey.

When one looks at the measures on a pan-European level, most energy just now is being spent on measures based on the later phases in the cultural deficiency explanation. The interculturalism seen in government declarations and invading all European teacher in-service training courses and new curricula is important to analyse because it still represents deficiency models, even if the package in which it is served (ethnicism and linguicism) is much more appetizing than was the old 'racism-based-on-biological-differences'.

It is also important to note that many of the measures, taken on the basis of the different

explanations of reasons for problems, may be needed in many ways. It is good for minority children to have additional tuition in L2 and to learn more about their own culture, and it is useful that majority children and teachers learn something about minority cultures. And it is, as we have shown, necessary for minority children to develop their mother tongues in MT-medium programmes. But it is the *basis* for these measures which is wrong. All of them, even the mother tongue deprivation model, see the *child* as deficient and lacking, and try to compensate for the 'deficiencies', in order for the child to change to fit the school. It is still considered to be a deficiency in European schools to have another mother tongue and cultural background than the majority of the pupils and not to be middle class (and a boy).

The *enrichment theories* start from the conception that schools should be adapted to the children, not vice versa. The child's mother tongue and cultural and social background should be a positive starting point for the school. The existence of minorities is seen as costly but enriching for societies, and bilingualism/biculturalism is seen as beneficial and stimulating for the child. If minority children experience problems in school, these may be due to the extra work involved (5) or, in the last phase (6), either to similar reasons as for monolingual children or to these and racism, linguicism and discrimination. Only the last phase implies *transformative* change (see Mullard, 1985a); all the others are more or less liberal/reformist. And it is only the last phase which can start to combat linguicism.

The only labour immigrant minority in the world which has come to the first enrichment phase is Finns in Sweden. I am disregarding both (1) temporarily immigrated elites, NATO officers, diplomats, oil experts, international business-women and civil servants, etc., and (2) labour migrants who have set up their own schools at their own expense, without financial support from the receiving country. We are thus talking about education inside the ordinary state-supported educational system.

Very few minorities in the world have come to phase 6, if we think of minorities in terms of numbers. It is indicative that the best protected educational rights among this type of numerical minorities are enjoyed by present or former power minorities (such as white South Africans, a present power minority, or Swedish-speakers in Finland, a former power minority, descendants of former colonizers). It is thus indicative of the importance of political factors that until now not many countries have accepted the existence of minorities as an enrichment, unless these minorities have or have had the power to dictate the conditions. In some situations where there are equal minorities on both sides of the border (German-speakers in Denmark, Danish-speakers in Germany), this has been achieved. Some minorities in socialist countries have also succeeded. Many of these, for instance Yugoslavia, do organize the education of minorities in ways where the non-socialist countries have much to learn (see Bugarski (forthcoming); Göncz (forthcoming); Institute for Ethnic Studies, Ljubljana, 1985; Lük Necak, 1985; Mikes, 1984; Petrovic & Blagojevic, 1985). The USSR has done the same (see Drobizheva, 1986; Grigulevich & Kozlov (eds), 1981; Guboglo, 1986). Some minorities in a few Third World countries have come far, too, for instance in India (Ekka, 1984; Pattanayak, 1981). And some of the well-organized labour migrant minorities might succeed, too, if we know what we are doing and why. There is a wealth of international experience to share, because the linguicism is the same.

## Conclusion

Trying to summarize extremely complicated matters in a short paper necessarily entails huge overgeneralizations, and the argumentation is to some extent crude shorthand (for a more detailed exposition see my *Bilingualism or Not: The Education of Minorities* (1984, 378 pages). A few general remarks in conclusion are of necessity even more shorthand.

High levels of bilingualism/biculturalism benefit every child, but for minority children bilingualism is a necessity. It is possible to achieve, if the main principle is followed which seems to hold across different situations: *support via all institutional measures the language which is otherwise less likely to develop in the cognitively demanding decontextualized register.*

This language which otherwise does not get the chance, is for the minority children their mother tongue, and for power majorities (such as English-speakers in Canada) a minority language. These are the 'easy' cases. But what about the others?

If several minorities together form the majority, the choice of ME should reflect the power relations between the minority groups and the group whose language they want to learn as their second language. The weaker the minority groups, the stronger the emphasis on their own language. But being educated through the medium of one's own language and wanting to become bilingual necessitates either much contact with that second language *and* good teaching in it, given by bilingual well-trained teachers (as in the Uzbekistan case), or, if there is little contact with the second language (as in Zambia where there is little contact with native English-speakers), extremely good teaching in that language (which Zambia does not have). The absolute degrading of African languages during the colonial period and through neo-colonial economic politics and its concomitant ideology has produced a colonized consciousness, where the African languages are in a weak position (and need all the support schools can give), even when the former colonial power is no longer physically present with armies (see Angula, 1984; Kalema, 1980, 1985; Mateene, 1980a and b, 1985a and b; Phillipson, 1986).

Very few educational programmes in Europe for migrant minorities try to make the children bilingual, even if many claim that they do. They practise linguicism, as we have shown. But why do they do that? If we as linguists tell them that all languages are of equal worth, and make them aware of the problems, might they not change? If we tell them how minority children should be educated in order for them to reach high levels of bilingualism and to achieve at school, would they not organize education accordingly?[9] Is it not a question of lack of information? The answer is a simple no.

Western industrial countries will need cheap labour at home in the future, too. The shitwork still needs to be done by somebody in Western countries.[10] The Third World produces much of the raw materials, food, clothing and equipment that we use. The exploitation of those countries now just takes different, more invisible forms than slavery and colonization, but it is at least equally severe. But we cannot export all of our cleaning, cooking, sweeping, public transport and washing up, or our sick and old, to be taken care of in the Third World, as easily as we export capital. Therefore, the industrial world needs to educate the children of the migrants, the great-grandchildren of the slaves from the colonies, for these jobs. Therefore, minority education needs to be racist and linguicist, in order to force the great-grandchildren of the slaves to continue to take the shitwork. In this it has succeeded.

Why so much fuss about language, then, if all these things are decided politically, anyway? — if what is best for a child linguistically, cognitively, pedagogically and socially does not count? — if language, in addition to that, can mislead our engagement so that we don't see how it is used in the interculturalism celebration to fool us, to prevent us from seeing the same old racism in its cultural clothes, in the assimilationist ethnicism? — and if power is all that matters anyway?

For three reasons, at least:

- we need our language for analysis. Without a thorough analysis we struggle in the dark;
- we need our language for solidarity, both with our contemporaries, and across generations;
- we need bilinguals as mediators. Those who are bi-something (bilingual, bidialectal, bicultural) have been forced to look at two different languages, dialects, cultures *from the inside*. It is easier for us bilinguals to *understand both parties*.

In a world at five to twelve ( = on the verge of self-destruction) what is needed is *not* monolingual technical idiots (white, middle-class, male) who can make the missile and push the button. They are people who have never been forced to and who are probably not able to see matters from the inside from somebody else's point of view. You can obviously not discuss with a missile, but a real bilingual/bicultural might be able to mediate before the button is released, provided she has the instruments for analysis, and the solidarity.

It may be time for linguists also to realize that linguicism is not a bunch of ill-willed, misinformed individuals. It is not a question of information, but of power structure. Obviously, it is our job as linguists to produce information, but unless we know whose questions we ask in our research and why, we may unknowingly provide arguments for supporting linguicism and racism, especially the hidden, unconscious, invisible kind, which is the most difficult one to detect and to fight. A poster I have on my study door has, as a part of the devastating and beautiful picture by Malaquias Montoya, a text by G. R. Castillo: 'One day the apolitical intellectuals of my country will be interrogated by the simplest of our people'. Researchers are some sort of intellectuals, too, aren't we?

## Notes

1. Previously published in Phillipson, Robert and Skutnabb-Kangas, Tove, 1986, *Linguicism Rules in Education*, Roskilde, Roskilde University Centre, Institute VI, 42–72. Thanks to Eduardo Hernández-Chávez, Kahombo Mateene, Chris Mullard, D. P. Pattanayak, Markku Peura and Robert Phillipson for inspiring discussions and insights. Of course, none of them is responsible for the results. Thanks to Robert, too, for helping to nativize the language.
2. When using terms minority/majority, I define them in terms of power relationships, not (entirely) in terms of numbers. If 'majority' is used to denote a numerically strong but politically weak group (like Blacks in South Africa), this is marked by calling them a powerless majority, implying that they have the capacity to become a 'real' majority, i.e. to gain access to their fair share of power, which would be 'more' than the power of the numerical minorities, among them the white power-minority. But using labels like 'majority' and 'minority' is unsatisfactory from another point of view, too: it obscures the class differences both between and, especially, within these groups, and makes them appear much more homogeneous than they are. The enormous heterogeneity of both 'majorities' and 'mi-

norities' should be constantly borne in mind. Within each group there are contradictory and conflicting views, and this is one source of change in society.
3. Terms like 'power elites' are often used in vague ways, as synonymous with 'ruling class' or 'decision-makers'. The vagueness makes it difficult to distinguish between groups in power in less and more democratic political systems. Giddens (1973: 118–127) has an illuminating discussion of the differences, from the 'strongest case' of a 'ruling class' to the 'weakest', i.e. most democratic, with 'leadership groups'. All of these groups can decide about the official language or the language of instruction. The decisions tend to be more beneficial for minorities in the 'weaker' formations.
4. 'Mastery', of course, has sexist connotations, in addition to its (for me) negative class connotations. Many of the words many of us use unawares every day are living examples of the hidden, unconscious sexism, racism and classism in our societies. There are many good candidates even in this paper, and where they have been unavoidable (because explanations would be too long) I have at least tried to mark my distance (for instance when calling French,

English and German 'modern' 'European' languages).

5. A submersion, or sink-or-swim programme, is a programme where linguistic minority children with a low-status mother tongue are forced to accept instruction through the medium of a foreign majority language with high status, in classes where some children are native speakers of the language of instruction, where the teacher does not understand the mother tongue of the minority children, and where the majority language constitutes a threat to their mother tongue — a subtractive language learning situation.

6. A *transitional programme* is a programme where linguistic minority children with a low-status mother tongue are instructed through the medium of their mother tongue for a few years and where their mother tongue has no intrinsic value, only an instrumental value. It is used only in order for the children to learn the majority language better, and in order to give them some subject matter knowledge while they are learning the majority language. As soon as they can function in the majority language orally, they are transferred to a majority language medium programme. A transitional programme is a more sophisticated version of submersion programmes, a more 'humane' way of assimilating.

7. An *immersion* programme is a programme where linguistic majority children with a high-status mother tongue voluntarily choose (among existing alternatives) to be instructed through the medium of a foreign (minority) language, in classes with majority children with the same mother tongue only, where the teacher is bilingual so that the children in the beginning can use their own language, and where their mother tongue is in no danger of not developing or of being replaced by the language of instruction — an additive language learning situation.

8. The worldwide spread of English has led to local variants becoming established, first in North America, later in Third World countries. There is now an increasing tendency to regard such 'nativized' forms as Indian English or West African English as authentic local norms. Native speakers of these variants represent the norm (Kachru, 1986) even in situations where they may have English as their second language. Thus 'exposure to native speaker language' may be a more varied concept than the one implicit in the text (see also Phillipson, 1986).

9. You can often hear school administrators say that they would like to adhere to some of the principles referred to in this chapter, and indeed instruct minority children through the medium of their mother tongues. But it just so happens that they have 49 different languages in one single school (a situation which is not unusual), and therefore they can do nothing. It is impossible to justify that one group gets such instruction, when the 48 others do not. This is, with due respect to the practical difficulties involved, a false argument. There are many innovative ways of solving most of the problems, *if the political will exists* (small classes, age-integrated classes, bussing, firm long-term planning which guarantees instruction through the medium of certain languages at certain places for a long time so that people with those mother tongues can move to where they know there will be instruction, co-operation across school district (and even country) borders, summer camps, guaranteeing young minority people teacher jobs in advance if they promise to undergo training, etc., etc.). In most cases practical arguments are used to mask the real arguments, and the issue of principle is avoided.

10. It is sometimes claimed that there is a high correlation between the percentage of women on the labour market and the percentage of foreigners in the lower sectors of the dual labour market. Simplified: if domestic women go out to work and do not do the shitwork, foreigners have to be imported to do it, because domestic men refuse to do it. Good counter-examples are Finland and Saudi Arabia. In Finland most women are gainfully employed (around 48% of the total workforce is female) but there is virtually no migrant labour. In Saudi Arabia there are very few domestic women working outside their homes, but there is a big migrant labour force. Likewise, the welfare state is sometimes blamed: when people do not take care of their children, the sick and the old at home any longer, the new work thus created goes to migrants. Again, Finland and Saudi Arabia are counter-examples: Finland manages with the welfare state and without migrants, Saudi Arabia does not, regardless of the presence of migrants. Both arguments are parts of the conservative ideology, refusing to admit the function of migrants for capitalist societies.

### References

Africa, H. (1980) Language in education in a multilingual state: a case study of the role of English in the educational system of Zambia. PhD Dissertation, Toronto: University of Toronto.

Angula, N. (1984) English as a medium of communication for Namibia: Trends and possibilities. In Commonwealth Secretariat & SWAPO (1984), pp. 9–12.

Bugarski, R. (forthcoming) Language policy and language planning in Yugoslavia. To appear in French in J. Maurais (ed.) *L'aménagement linguistique comparé*. Quebec & Paris: Conseil de la langue française, le Robert.

Calvet, L.J. (1974) *Linguistique et Colonialisme*. Petit Traité de Glottophagie. Paris: Petite Bibliothèque Payot.

Chishimba, M.M. (1984) Language policy and education in Zambia. *International Education Journal* 1 (2), 151–180.

Churchill, S. (1985) *The Education of Linguistic and Cultural Minorities in the OECD Countries*. Clevedon: Multilingual Matters.

Commonwealth Secretariat & SWAPO (1984) English language programme for Namibians. Seminar Report, Lusaka, 19–27 October 1983.

Cummins, J. (1984) *Bilingualism and Special Education: Issues in Assessment and Pedagogy*. Clevedon: Multilingual Matters.

Drobizheva, L. (1986) Social and psychological aspects of inter-ethnic relations in the USSR. In Y. V. Arutiunian (ed.) *Multilingualism: Aspects of Interpersonal and Intergroup Communication in Pluricultural Societies*. Moscow: Institute of Ethnography of the Academy of Sciences of the USSR, pp. 19–31.

Ekka, F. (1984) Status of minority languages in the schools of India. *International Education Journal* 1 (1) 1–19.

Giddens, A. (1973) *The Class Structure of the Advanced Societies*. London: Hutchinson.

Grigulevich, I.R. and Kozlov, S.Ya. (eds) (1981) *Ethnocultural Processes and National Problems in the Modern World*. Moscow: Progress Publishers .

Göncz, L. (forthcoming) Psychological studies of bilingualism in Vojvodina. In *Yugoslavian General Linguistics*.

Guboglo, M. (1986) Language and communication in Soviet society. In Y. V. Arutiunian (ed.) *Multilingualism: Aspects of Interpersonal and Intergroup Communication in Pluricultural Societies*. Moscow: Institute of Ethnography of the Academy of Sciences of the USSR, pp. 3–18.

Institute for Ethnic Studies (Ljubljana) (1985) Some Yugoslav experiences in the achievement of the equality of the nations and nationalities in the field of education. Paper presented at the National Seminar on Education in Multicultural Societies, Ljubljana, 15–17 October.

Kachru, B.B. (1986) *The Alchemy of English. The Spread, Functions and Models of Non-native Englishes*. Oxford: Pergamon Press.

Kalema, J. (1980) Report on functions and activities of the OAU Inter-African Bureau of Languages. In K. Mateene and J. Kalema (eds), pp. 1–8.

— (1985) Introduction. In K. Mateene, J. Kalema and B. Chomba (eds), pp. 1–6.

Lambert, W. (1975) Culture and language as factors in learning and education. In A. Wolfgang (ed.).

Lambert, W. and Taylor, D. (1982) Language in the education of ethnic minority immigrants: Issues, problems and methods. Paper presented to Conference on Education of Ethnic Minority Immigrants, Miami.

Lük Necak, A. (1985) Education in multicultural societies and its social implications. Paper presented at the National seminar on Education in multicultural societies, Ljubljana, 15–17 October.

Mateene, K. (1980a) Introduction. In K. Mateene and J. Kalema (eds), pp. vi–vii.

— (1980b) Failure in the obligatory use of European languages in Africa and the advantages of a policy of linguistic independence. In K. Mateene and J. Kalema (eds), pp. 9–41.

— (1985a) Colonial languages as compulsory means of domination, and indigenous languages as necessary factors of liberation and development. In K. Mateene, J. Kalema and B. Chomba (eds), pp. 60–69.

— (1985b) Reconsideration of the official status of colonial languages in Africa. In K. Mateene, J. Kalema and B. Chomba (eds), pp. 18–28.

Mateene, K. and Kalema, J. (eds) (1980) *Reconsideration of African Linguistic Policies*. Kampala: OAU Bureau of Languages, OAU/BIL Publication 3.

Mateene, K., Kalema, J. and Chomba, B. (eds) (1985) *Linguistic Liberation and Unity of Africa*. Kampala: OAU Bureau of Languages, OAU/BIL Publication 6.

Mikes, M. (1984) Instruction in the mother tongue in Yugoslavia. *Prospects* XIV (1), 121–131.

Mullard, C. (1985a) Racism, ethnicism and etharchy or not? The principles of progressive control and transformative change. In T. Skutnabb-Kangas and J. Cummins (eds) *Minority Education: From Shame to Struggle*. Clevedon: Multilingual Matters, Chap 17. Originally presented as a plenary paper at the International Symposium on Minority Languages in Academic Research and Educational Policy, Sandbjerg Slot, Denmark, April 1985.

— (1985b) *Race, Power and Resistance*. London: Routledge and Kegan Paul.

Pattanayak, D.P. (1981) *Multilingualism and Mother Tongue Education*. Delhi: Oxford University Press.

— (1986) Educational use of the mother tongue. In B. Spolsky (ed.), pp. 5–15.

Petrovic, R. and Blagojevic, M. (1985) The educational structure of ethnic groups in Yugoslavia. Paper presented at the National seminar on Education in Multicultural Societies, Ljubljana, 15–17 October.

Phillipson, R. (1986) The rule of English. In R. Phillipson and T. Skutnabb-Kangas.

Phillipson, R. and Skutnabb-Kangas, T. (1983) Cultilingualism: Papers in cultural and communicative (in)competence. *ROLIG-papir 28*, Roskilde Universitetscenter.

— (1986) *Linguicism Rules in Education* (3 volumes). Roskilde University Centre, Institute VI: Roskilde.

Phillipson, R., Skutnabb-Kangas, T. and Africa, H. (1986) Namibian educational language planning: English for liberation or neocolonialism? In B. Spolsky (ed.), pp. 77–95.

Skutnabb-Kangas, T. (1984) *Bilingualism or Not: The Education of Minorities*. Clevedon: Multilingual Matters.

— (1986) Who wants to change what and why: Conflicting paradigms in minorlty education research. In B. Spolsky (ed), pp. 153–81.

Spolsky, B. (ed.) (1986) *Language and Education in Multilingual Settings*. Clevedon: Multilingual Matters.

Swain, M. and Lapkin, S. (1982) *Evaluating Bilingual Education: A Canadian Case Study*. Clevedon: Multingual Matters.

Wolfgang, A. (ed.) (1975) *Education of Immigrant Students*. Toronto: Ontario Institute for Studies in Education.

## Questions

(1) Define Linguicism. Explain the difference between linguicism that is open, conscious, visible and action-oriented, and linguicism that is hidden, unconscious, invisible and passive. What do the two forms of linguicism say about the developmental stage which a society might be in? Where would you place your country, region or community?

(2) According to Skutnabb-Kangas, what is the consequence for a country that is officially monolingual or a person who is monolingual? Keeping in mind Stubbs' objection to the territoriality principle, what is the consequence for a country like Belgium that is officially bilingual according to the territoriality principle? Is there a difference between a country that is officially monolingual and one which is officially bilingual according to the territoriality principle? How does this relate to linguicism?

(3) Study the definitions for mother tongue given by Skutnabb-Kangas in Table 1. If you are bilingual, define your own mother tongue according to the four criteria. Then write an essay discussing how your mother tongue has changed through your lifetime. Identify the events that have taken place in your life to account for the change. If you are not bilingual, find someone who is, and answer this question.

(4) Make a chart containing the four types of bilingual education given by Skutnabb-Kangas (that is, segregation, submersion, mother tongue maintenance and immersion). In the chart, for each type of bilingual education:
  (a) give a definition;
  (b) give an example;

    (c) say whether the type leads to monolingualism, subtractive bilingualism or additive bilingualism;

    (d) indicate which of the organizational, affective, first language and second language factors that make bilingual education programs successful are present in each type.

    (e) indicate whether the type is weak or strong according to the definition by Baker in '*Foundations of Bilingual Education and Bilingualism,*' Chapter 11.

    (f) say whether the type is available in your local school district.

(5) Explain the difference between teaching a language as a subject and using a language as a medium of education (what Skutnabb-Kangas calls ME). Also indicate what is the preferred way of using a second language in:

    (a) transitional bilingual education;

    (b) maintenance bilingual education;

    (c) two-way dual language education;

    (d) foreign language (FL) classes;

    (e) second language (SL) classes;

    (f) immersion classes;

    (g) structured immersion or sheltered SL classes.

(You may want to refer to '*Foundations of Bilingual Education and Bilingualism,*' Chapter 11, in order to expand on this question.)

(6) Define the following theories that have been adopted by different societies, at different times, for their language minority educational policy:

A. Deficit Theories

    (i) L2 related handicap.

    (ii) Socially conditioned handicap.

    (iii) Culturally conditioned handicap.

    (iv) L1 related handicap.

B. Enrichment Theories

    (v) Benefit to individual

    (vi) Benefit to society

Then place your country as it is today in a specific stage, justifying your position by referring to the different educational policies followed. Can you give historical examples of policy that suggest that your country has gone through different stages? Do you think that your country's policy in the future will move in the direction of benefits to society? Is the country likely to follow a deficit or an enrichment approach in the future?

(7) According to Skutnabb-Kangas, the main principle to follow for bilingualism should be: 'support via all institutional measures the language which is otherwise less likely to develop in the cognitively demanding decontextualized register.' If the school in your local community were to do this, what would it do? How would it change?

(8) According to Skutnabb-Kangas, why is it that few countries organize education for minorities so that they achieve highly in school and reach high levels of bilingualism?

## Activities

(1) Find out the indigenous languages spoken in the following European countries, traditionally seen by some as being monolingual:

    (a) Britain;

(b) Spain;

(c) France;

(d) Netherlands;

(e) Italy.

Refer to policies that protect minority languages in these countries, if those are available. Make a table with the languages, the policy and a short quote from the policy.

(2) Ask five educators in one school what 'bilingual' means to them. Then ask them how the term 'bilingual' is used in their school. Then read the definitions of bilingualism provided by Skutnabb-Kangas. Find out which definitions are acceptable to them. Record their answers on an answer sheet with three columns: one for their definition, one for the school's definition, one for the Skutnabb-Kangas definitions that are acceptable. Make sure to record on top of the answer sheet the characteristics of the school in question (example: size, public or private, urban or suburban, large language minority population or large language majority population, socio-economic profile of the school). Different groups might interview educators in schools that have different characteristics. Share the groups' answers. Make a chart with the class's results.

(3) Observe a classroom with a linguistically heterogeneous group. This may be a two-way dual language program or a submersion program with second language classes. Give a sociolinguistic profile of the classroom. Then record any instances of:

(a) accommodation by teacher;

(b) accommodation by students;

(c) miscommunication or lack of communication.

Share with the teacher the instances that you have recorded. Ask for her understanding and interpretation of what was going on, and her evaluation of how effective was the particular strategy. Write an essay to describe and evaluate this conversation.

(4) Observe a bilingual student who is proficient in two languages for a day. Note down language use at home, in the classroom, and in the playground. Record your observations on a record sheet designed by you or the class. Then write an essay summarizing the differences in language use in different domains.

(5) Interview an adult who learned one language first, but no longer feels competent in that language. Find out why language shift happened, how the person feels about the shift, how the shift in language has affected the person's identity, and how others, both speakers of the first language and the second language, view the person. Tape and transcribe the interview. Write down your perceptions and explanations of the language shift.

(6) Read the Declaration of Children's Linguistic Human Rights to at least ten persons with different characteristics and ask them for their reaction. Make sure you record their age, sex, level of education, profession, ethnicity and languages they speak. Make a chart showing the varying characteristics of the ten people you interviewed and their answers. Then summarize your findings in an essay.

(7) Identify a two-way dual language program (or similar) in your vicinity. Interview both a language minority and a language majority child who are receiving dual language instruction in mixed groups. Find out how each feels when the medium of instruction is not their mother tongue. Are there differences between the language majority child

and the language minority child? Record their answers. Then write an essay summarizing the differences.

(8) Interview a monolingual teacher about the bilingual teachers in their school. Record her personal beliefs, ideas and characteristics. Find out how she feels about the employment of bilingual teachers and whether preferential treatment should be given in their employment, their value with language minority children and, in general, their teaching competences and their training. Then ask her about what she needs to know in her school about bilingualism, bilingual education and the language and culture of ethnolinguistic minorities. Tape and transcribe the interview.

(9) Visit a bilingual classroom. Survey the resource material available in the minority language. On a recording sheet, write the title, the amount of each title available, the subject, where published and in which language. What language dominates in terms of available resource material? Is there any material that is bilingual, that is, written in both the majority and the minority language? Observe the class for a day. Who uses the material in the minority language and how is it used? Who uses the bilingual material and how is it used? Record your answers.

## Further Reading

For more on different types of bilingual education, see:

Fishman, Joshua A. and Lovas, John (1972) Bilingual education in a sociolinguistic perspective. In Bernard Spolsky (ed.) *The Language Education of Minority Children* (pp.83–93). Rowley, MA: Newbury House.

Hornberger, Nancy (1991) Extending enrichment bilingual education: Revisiting typologies and redirecting policy. In Ofelia García (ed.) *Bilingual Education: Focusschrift in Honor of Joshua A. Fishman* (pp.215–34). Amsterdam: John Benjamins.

Mackey, William (1970) A typology of bilingual education. *Foreign Language Annals* 3, 596–608.

For more on bilingual education models and policy in Europe, see especially:

Baetens Beardsmore, Hugo (ed.) *European Models of Bilingual Education.* Clevedon: Multilingual Matters.

For bilingual education policy in Southeast Asia, see especially:

Jones, Gary M. and Ozóg, A. Conrad K. (eds) *Bilingualism and National Development.* Clevedon: Multilingual Matters.

Readers interested in international bilingual education policy should consult:

Paulston, Christina B. (ed.) (1988) *International Handbook of Bilingualism and Bilingual Education.* New York: Greenwood Press.

# Bilingual Education and Anti-Racist Education

## Jim Cummins

For more than a decade, controversy about the appropriateness and effectiveness of bilingual education has been a major focus of public debate in the US. However, despite considerable recent research, confusion and disagreement persist among educators, politicians and the general public, both about whether bilingual education programs actually succeed in promoting educational equity for language minority students and also whether such programs are consistent with US social values.

I argue in this article that the debate on bilingual education must be considered in a political context for two reasons: first, the research findings on the effects of bilingual education are both abundant and clear; the common perception that research is either largely unavailable and/or inadequate is a myth generated by strong vested interests. The second reason for examining closely the political context of the issue is that the educational changes required to reverse the pattern of language minority group school failure are essentially *political* changes because they involve changes in the power relations between dominant and dominated groups — specifically, in the ways that educators, as representatives of dominant group institutions, relate to the language minority students and their communities.

Those against bilingual education maintain that such programs are a threat to national unity and ineffective in teaching English to language minority students since the primary language, rather than English, is used for a considerable amount of instruction in the early grades. Many opponents of bilingual education argue that if children are deficient in English, then they need instruction in English, not their native language. Unless minority students are immersed in Eng- lish at school, the reasoning goes, they will not learn English, and thus they will be unable to participate in the US mainstream.

From a historical point of view, the concerns about bilingual education being against US interests and a potential catalyst for separatist tendencies are somewhat ironic in view of the fact that the education of Mexican Americans in the Southwest was openly dedicated until the late 1960s to *separating* Mexican American students from the US mainstream by segregated schooling (conducted exclusively in English). In Texas, for example, the judgement of the court in the United States versus the State of Texas case documented the 'pervasive, intentional discrimination throughout most of this century' against Mexican American students (a charge that was not contested by the State of Texas in the trial) and noted that:

> ...the long history of prejudice and depriva-
> tion remains a significant obstacle to equal
> educational opportunity for these children.
> The deep sense of inferiority, cultural isola-
> tion, and acceptance of failure, instilled in a
> people by generations of subjugation, cannot
> be eradicated merely by integrating the
> schools and repealing the 'no Spanish' stat-
> utes. (Civil Action No. 5281 Memorandum
> Opinion, January 1981)

When we look at the data on the academic achievement of language minority students, a striking pattern emerges. The groups that tend to experience the most severe underachievement are those that have experienced subjugation and discrimination for several generations, namely, Latinos (with the exception of some groups of Cuban students), Native Americans and African Americans. The same trend emerges in international studies.[1]

The variation among groups, all of whom experience a home–school language shift, suggests that the language difference between home and school is not the crucial factor in explaining group underachievement. This conclusion, contrary to the usual rationale for bilingual programs, is strengthened by the fact that Latino students who speak English at home tend to perform just as poorly (when social class is taken into account) as those who speak Spanish at home.[2] This suggests that a rationale focusing on linguistic rather than social factors is oversimplified.

If the language difference between home and school is not the critical factor in explaining language minority students' school failure (as both the 'pro' and 'anti' bilingual education groups have assumed), then what is? Several investigators have argued that status and power relations between majority and minority groups constitute the source of minority students' underachievement, with linguistic and other factors playing an important, but secondary or intervening role.[3] School failure tends to occur among minority groups that have experienced persistent racism and who have been denied opportunities to validate their cultural and linguistic traditions. (Ogbu terms such groups 'caste minorities,' while I have discussed their 'dominated' status in relation to the dominant group.[4]) The dominated group, regarded as inherently inferior by the dominant group, is denied access to high-status positions and language minority students are disempowered in very much the same way that their communities are disempowered by institutions. It is not difficult to see how this educational disabling process has operated in the past. Where

educators defined their role only as teaching English and 'Americanizing' students, many language minority students were punished for speaking their language in the school, they were made to feel ashamed about their cultural background, their parents were excluded from meaningful participation in children's education, and students' low verbal IQ's (in English, their weaker language) were viewed as the cause of their academic difficulties. Massive over-representation of language minority students in classes for the retarded resulted.[5]

## Educators as Advocates

According to this analysis reversing the pattern of language minority students' school failure requires educators to redefine their roles in order to empower rather than disable students. Educators must become advocates for the promotion of language minority students' linguistic talents. They must actively involve the parents in their children's education and institute assessment procedures that view the student's present academic performance as a function of the educational and social context in which the child has developed.[6]

In short, reversing the pattern of language minority students' underachievement involves much more than just some initial instruction in the students' first language or more effective teaching of English. Even though policy-makers and educators see a linguistic problem involving only the learning of English, very clear data have been available for more than 20 years that social and historical causes — rather than linguistic causes — are central.

---

'It was a nice summer day in Rumania. The wind blew over the trees and the sun was shining when my father and I began to talk about life. He asked me about trying a new life in the United States...

...For me now, a bilingual education is the most important thing in my life. In this program all students get special help. The teachers introduce us to general notions about the correct writing, reading and especially speaking. We feel like a family, and I feel too like a part of it.

I learned something about other cultures, their traditions and new ways of doing things.

Now, with my English I feel like a woman and a half because I came here five months ago and already I am feeling and talking like in my own language. I have new ideas and more inspiration. That's because I took my heart in my teeth and I tried.

I'm the master of my future; I have it in my own hands.

To me bilingual education can be a bridge between my old and my new culture and can change the world around me.

For the teachers who help us in this program I say a hot THANK YOU for all they do for me and for everybody.'

(Teodora Tastaman, Reading High School, Reading, Pennsylvania, Grade 10. From National Association for Bilingual Education *Newsletter* 7 (4), 1984.)

## Are Bilingual Programs Effective?

Much of the recent political opposition to bilingual education draws on the results of the literature survey carried out by Baker and de Kanter.[7] They set up criteria for methodological adequacy that resulted in the exclusion of several studies hitherto regarded as strong evidence for the effectiveness of bilingual education.[8] They concluded on the basis of the evidence *they* regarded as acceptable that 'there is no firm empirical evidence that TBE [transitional bilingual education] is uniquely effective in raising language minority students' performance in English or non-language subject areas' and thus exclusive reliance should not be placed on TBE in federal policy decisions. They suggest that what they term 'structured immersion' is a promising alternative to TBE. By 'structured immersion,' Baker and de Kanter mean a program similar to the Canadian French immersion programs in which the students' second language is used as the major medium of instruction.

The Baker and de Kanter report has been strongly criticized by proponents of bilingual education on methodological grounds (e.g. the criteria for inclusion/exclusion of studies) as well as for misleading and unwarranted conclusions.[9] A recent analysis of the same group of studies, which used considerably more sophisticated methodological techniques than the Baker and de Kanter review, reached a very different conclusion:

> When statistical controls for methodological inadequacies were employed, participation in bilingual education programs consistently produced small to moderate differences favoring bilingual education for tests of reading, language skills, mathematics, and total achievement when the tests were in English, and for reading, language, and mathematics, writing, social studies, listening comprehension, and attitudes toward school or self when tests were in other languages. (p. 269)[10]

## Bilingual Programs Can Work

In-depth studies of bilingual programs that have explicitly attempted to develop full bilingualism among Latino students and to involve Latino parents in promoting their children's education report dramatic gains in students' academic performance.[11] These studies demonstrate that bilingual programs can be highly

effective in reversing the pattern of language minority students' academic failure.

These studies also refute the assumptions underlying the call for 'English immersion' programs since they show an *inverse* relationship between the amount of English in the program and students' achievement in English. This is precisely what is predicted by the 'interdependence principle,' which states that transfer of underlying academic skills across languages will occur provided there is sufficient environmental exposure to the second language and children are motivated to acquire that language.[12] Thus instruction in Spanish will develop not just Spanish academic skills but also the underlying conceptual foundation for academic skills development in English.

Virtually all the evaluation findings from bilingual education programs in North America, Europe, Africa and Asia support the interdependence principle; they show either no relationship or an inverse relationship between exposure to the majority language in school and achievement in that language. Thus, it is difficult to understand the frequent claim that research data on bilingual education are lacking; rather, what has been lacking is a rational process of examining the research data in relation to the predictions derived from theory.[13]

This conclusion is supported by preliminary results from a large-scale comparative evaluation of immersion and bilingual education programs.[14] The results support the interdependence principle and also suggest that the call for English immersion programs is more strongly based on political than on pedagogical considerations. The study in question involves about 4,000 students and is being carried out for the US Department of Education by SRA Technologies Inc. The early results were reported in *Education Week* (April 23, 1986) as follows:

> English immersion, an instructional alternative that is popular among critics of bilingual education, has fared poorly in the US Education Department's first large-scale evaluation of the method, according to early results... Limited-English proficient students in bilingual programs consistently outperformed 'immersion strategy' students in reading, language-arts, and mathematics tests conducted in both English and Spanish... Especially perplexing to the SRA researchers was the poor English-language

performance of the immersion students, who had received the most English-language instruction. Moreover, the larger the native-language component of their schooling, the better the students performed in English... Researchers determined that the immersion classes used English 90 per cent of the time, compared with 67 per cent in the early exit bilingual programs and 33 per cent in the late-exit bilingual programs. Overall test scores from five school districts showed an inverse relation between English-language exposure and English-language proficiency among kindergarten and 1st graders.

It is important to note that no claim is being made here regarding the general effectiveness of 'bilingual education.' The crucial element in reversing language minority students' school failure is *not* the language of instruction but the extent to which educators work to reverse — rather than perpetuate — the subtle, and often not so subtle, institutionalized racism of the society as a whole. In other words, bilingual education becomes effective only when it becomes anti-racist education. Strong promotion of students' primary language can be an important component in empowering language minority students but it is certainly not sufficient in itself. In addition, educators must develop a relationship of collaboration and partnership with language minority communities and the pedagogy must permit students to become active generators of their own knowledge. (I discussed this intervention framework more fully in 'Empowering Minority Students: A Framework for Intervention,' *Harvard Educational Review*, 56, 1986.)

## Conclusion

It is perhaps naive to expect the policy debate on bilingual education to be any more rational than debates on other politically volatile issues. Nevertheless, it is sobering to realize the extent to which two patently inadequate 'conventional wisdoms' have dominated the debate for almost 15 years despite the fact that each is clearly refuted by massive amounts of research and evidence. The usual rationale for bilingual programs is that children cannot learn in a language they do not understand and therefore some initial native language instruction is necessary to overcome the effects of a home–school language shift. This 'linguistic mismatch' assumption is refuted by the success of many language minority students under conditions of a home–school language shift and also by the results of French immersion programs in Canada in which children from the English-speaking majority group are taught largely through French in the early grades with no adverse effects.

The opposing conventional wisdom, however, fares no better. The 'insufficient exposure' explanation of language minority students' difficulties in English academic skills assumes that there is a direct relationship between the amount of exposure to English and students' achievement in that language. We have seen that this assumption is refuted by the results of virtually all evaluations of bilingual programs, including the results of French immersion programs for language majority students, which show no relationship between amount of exposure to English and achievement in English. As predicted by the interdependence principle, the data clearly show that instruction through the minority language entails no loss to the development of academic skills in the majority language.

In view of the overwhelming evidence against the 'insufficient exposure' theory, it is legitimate to ask what function such arguments serve. Although spurious, these arguments have served to emasculate many bilingual education programs, leading to the implementation of relatively ineffective 'quick-exit' models rather than the considerably more effective programs aimed at biliteracy. And because such quick-exit bilingual programs usually do not require or encourage any personal or institutional role re-definitions on the part of educators, institutionalized racism in the schools is preserved. In fact, it is probably preserved even more effectively because there is the appearance of change to meet 'the needs' of language minority students.

In this society, it is necessary to obscure contradictions between the rhetoric of equality and the reality of domination, and both quick-exit bilingual programs and immersion programs serve that function very well. It is for this reason that the two conventional wisdoms upon which these programs are based (the 'linguistic mismatch' and 'insufficient exposure' assumptions) have persisted and become almost immune from critical scrutiny despite their patent inadequacy. Effective anti-racist bilingual programs will continue to be vehemently resisted by the dominant group regardless of the research evidence in their favor. This resistance is entirely predictable because effective bilingual programs will threaten the power of the dominant group.

'Two years ago in Seattle, I got off a plane. In front of me was a whole new world. I wondered if I would survive in this world, a world where the people, the language and the whole environment were different than mine. I had a question in my mind about what my future was going to be.

I found myself as a deaf person in a strange world. I started to go to school and participated in the bilingual program where I would learn both English and my own language. Bilingual education brought back my hearing. It helped me to survive in the new world. It helped my family adapt to the new environment. The bilingual program introduced me to American people and taught me their way of life and their language. It brightened up my future. It helped me to climb up the 'vocabulary ladder' to show the Americans that I was not a useless person, no matter what country I came from. It supplied me with a good education and a better chance to achieve my goals. It assisted me in looking forward into my future in America. I knew that I could do and be whatever I wanted.'

(Mai Nguyen-Huynh, Cleveland Magnet School of Science, Cleveland, Ohio, Grade 6. From National Association for Bilingual Education *Newsletter* 7 (4), 1984.)

## Notes

1. Cummins, J. (1984) *Bilingualism and Special Education: Issues in Assessment and Pedagogy*. Clevedon: Multilingual Matters.
   National Assessment of Educational Progress (1983) *Students from Homes in Which English Is Not the Dominant Language: Who Are They and How Well Do They Read?* N. 11-R-50. Denver: Education Commission of the States.
   Ogbu, J.U. (1978) *Minority Education and Caste*. New York: Academic Press.
2. National Assessment of Educational Progress, op. cit.
3. Cummins, J. (1984) *Bilingualism and Special Education: Issues in Assessment and Pedagogy*, op. cit.
   Cummins, J. (1986) Empowering minority students: A framework for intervention. *Harvard Educational Review* 66, 18–36.
   Fishman, J. (1976) *Bilingual Education: An International Sociological Perspective*. Rowley, MA: Newbury House.
   Ogbu, J.U. op. cit.
   Paulston, C.B. (1980) *Bilingual Education: Theories and Issues*. Rowley, MA: Newbury House.
4. Cummins, J (1986) Empowering minority students: A framework for intervention. op. cit.
   Ogbu, J.U. op. cit.
5. Mercer, J. (1973) *Labelling the Mentally Retarded*. Berkeley, CA: University of California Press.
6. Cummins, J. (1986) Empowering minority students: A framework for intervention. op. cit.
7. Baker, K.A. and A.A. de Kanter (1981) *Effectiveness of Bilingual Education: A Review of the Literature*. Washington, DC: Office of Planning and Budget, US Department of Education.
8. Egan, L.A. and R. Goldsmith (1981) Bilingual–bicultural education: The Colorado success story. *NABE News*, January.

Modiano, N. (1968) National or mother tongue language in beginning reading: A comparative study. *Research in the Teaching of English* 2, 32–43.
Rosier, P. and W. Holm (1980) *The Rock Point Experience: A Longitudinal Study of a Navajo School*. Washington, DC: Center for Applied Linguistics.
9. Campbell, R.N. and T.C. Gray (1981) Critique of the US Department of Education report on effectiveness of bilingual education: Review of literature (mimeo). Washington, DC: Center for Applied Linguistics.
10. Willig, A.C. (1985) A meta-analysis of selected studies on the effectiveness of bilingual education. *Review of Educational Research* 55, 269–317.
11. California State Department of Education (1985) *Case Studies in Bilingual Education: First Year Report*. Federal Grant #G008303723.
    Campos, J. and B. Keatinge (1984) The Carpinteria pre school program: Title VII second year evaluation report. Report submitted to the Department of Health, Education and Welfare, Office of Education, Washington, DC.
12. Cummins, J. (1979) Linguistic interdependence and the educational development of bilingual children. *Review of Educational Research* 49, 222–51.
    Cummins, J. (1984) *Bilingualism and Special Education: Issues in Assessment and Pedagogy* op. cit.
13. Cummins, J. (1984) *Bilingualism and Special Education: Issues in Assessment and Pedagogy* op. cit.
    Cummins, J (1986) Empowering minority students: A framework for intervention. op. cit.
14. Crawford, J. (1986) Immersion method is faring poorly in bilingual study. *Education Week*, April 23, 5, No. 30, 1, 10.

## Questions

(1) Why does Cummins say it is ironic that there has been so much concern about bilingual education often separating Latino students? Can you think of examples where ethno-linguistic groups are separated from different groups for education and there is no opposition? What is the difference between having a group forcibly segregate another group for education, and having a group establish separate educational facilities for itself? What are the advantages and disadvantages of separating groups for education? What occurs in your local school?

(2) Define the Interdependence principle. How does it explain the failure of English immersion programs in the United States for language minority children? Also say how Interdependence relates to the Common Underlying Proficiency, also discussed by Skutnabb-Kangas, this volume. (You may want to read *'Foundations of Bilingual Education and Bilingualism,'* Chapter 9, for more on this.)

(3) Bilingual education is usually considered a form of 'multicultural education' (what in Europe is often called 'intercultural education'). But not all bilingual programs are anti-racist. Cummins, for example, says that 'bilingual education becomes effective only when it becomes anti-racist education' and that 'effective bilingual programs will threaten the power of the dominant group.' What is the difference between multicultural and anti-racist education? What do bilingual educators have to do to transform bilingual practices into anti-racist ones? What types of bilingual education programs could be truly anti-racist and threaten the power of the dominant group? Why are these not the most prevalent types of bilingual programs? (For more on the distinction between multicultural education and anti-racist education, see the list of further reading, especially, Cummins, 1988.)

(4) Define the two 'conventional wisdoms' on the education of language minorities that are responsible for the prevalence of transitional bilingual education programs today:
   (a) The linguistic mismatch hypothesis, leading to the initial use of the native language in instruction.
   (b) The insufficient exposure hypothesis, leading to a quick exit from transitional bilingual education programs.
   In a column to the right of the definition, state how that conventional wisdom has been refuted by research. Then summarize the reasons Cummins gives why the two 'conventional wisdoms' continue to be used.

## Activities

(1) Visit a school with special education classes. Survey the classes for language minority representation. Find out if language minority students are over-represented in those classes compared to the total population in the school. Make a graph of your results. Interview the teacher of each class. Find out whether any bilingual instruction and/or services are available to language minority students in special education. Record your answers.

(2) Go to the library and find the Baker and de Kanter report. Write a detailed summary of its findings. What do you think? (See *'Foundations of Bilingual Education and Bilingualism,'* Chapter 12, for the context of this report and for references.)

(3) Visit a bilingual program for one day. Observe varying anti-racist practices (or their absence) in at least one classroom. Observe practices in the administration's office and

in other offices in the school (e.g. that of the psychologist, the speech therapist, the bilingual coordinator, etc.). Also observe practices in the lunchroom and in the playground. Record all your observations. Then write an essay of why you can or cannot consider this bilingual program an anti-racist one. Refer to specific practices you observed or things that were directly told to you.

(4) Find a parent who has taken her child out of a transitional bilingual education program in the United States and one who has insisted that her child be kept in bilingual classrooms. Interview both of them. Question them on their beliefs and motives. Tape and transcribe both interviews and share the results with the class.

## Further Reading

Readings following Casanova's article (this book) are also relevant to this policy discussion. Another interesting article by Cummins that questions multicultural practices and places bilingual education within an anti-racist framework is:

From multicultural to anti-racist education: An analysis of programmes and policies in Ontario. In Skutnabb-Kangas, Tove and Cummins, Jim (eds) (1988) *Minority Education: From Shame to Struggle* (pp. 127–57). Clevedon: Multilingual Matters.

For more on multicultural education see especially:

Banks, J.A. and Lynch, J. (eds) (1986) *Multicultural Education in Western Societies*. London: Holt, Rinehart and Winston.

For more on anti-racist education, see the following:

Brandt, G.L. (1986) *The Realization of Anti-racist Teaching*. London: Falmer Press.

Cole, Michael (1986) Teaching and learning about racism: A critique of multicultural education in Britain. In S. Modgil, G.K. Verma, K. Mallick and C. Modgil (eds) *Multicultural Education* (pp. 123–48). London: The Falmer Press.

Mullard, Chris (1984) *Anti-Racist Education: The Three O's*. National Association for Multi-racial Education.

# Realities of Teaching in a Multiethnic School

## David Corson

### Introduction: Confronting the Legacies of the Past

Current policies in many countries, favouring the recognition of the rights of children from cultural minorities and their differential treatment in schools, are new phenomena which do not mesh easily with traditional nineteenth century monolingual and monocultural education and with the training and philosophies of many teachers. Although there is a wealth of historical precedent to overcome in some countries, major changes are beginning to occur in national attitudes to minorities and a climate of opinion favouring the more open and tolerant treatment of minorities is becoming more common, even across those countries that once tried to offer the world a veneer of cultural and ideological unity. A demand by minorities for recognition of their rights seems a major factor in the elimination of several totalitarian regimes, as witnessed in 1989–90. Elsewhere cultural diversity is gradually becoming more a cause for celebration and is actively promoted through national policies on languages (Lo Bianco, 1987) and through multicultural policies (Canadian Multiculturalism Act, 1988) As part of this development, new attitudes in education systems to minority languages and cultures are evident in many places, although rather reactionary attempts are still sometimes made to understate social and cultural diversity and to keep schools at a distance from the issues (see for example Britain's Swann Report (DES, 1985), Kingman Report (DES, 1988) and Bourne & Cameron's discussion of both (1988)).

This welcome change in social values presents problems of a new kind for the management of modern schools. For many schools in some societies the problems have always existed, and they have always been addressed by schools to vary-ing degrees. Elsewhere the problems seem new, although they may have their roots in long-term injustices. Moreover, policy makers are beginning to accept that large-scale national policies are rarely efficient in dealing with school problems arising from widespread multiethnicity. Because of the specificity of the problems and the uniqueness of the diverse school contexts that teachers find themselves working in, policy makers are increasingly asking schools themselves to make efforts to understand the realities of their own unique situations and to discover solutions to their own unique problems. The starting point that some identify is to understand the realities of the cultural community immediately beyond the school's boundaries.

### Discovering Contextual Realities: The School's Cultural Community

Because they have worked for many years with the children of a community, staff in a community's schools sometimes assume that they are experts on the local context. This may be a false assumption: the community reality may be very different from the commonsense impressions that teachers have formed. Teachers who are not members of the local social network, who travel into the community each day and draw their conclusions about it from the filtered impressions that they receive from their students and from the caricatured descriptions that often circulate in the staffrooms of schools, may be highly biased in their assessments of the school's sociocultural context. Sometimes teachers are so affected by their own acute sense of failure with children from certain backgrounds, or by their apparent success with others, that they perceive the backgrounds that failing children come from with a prejudiced or ironic view: they see those backgrounds as a deficit environment that is lacking some ingredient necessary for the children to succeed in school.

A large part of the answer to a school's difficulties in providing for culturally different children might be found in the results of careful research conducted outside the school into the cultural background of the children concerned. Policy changes might follow, leading to thoughtful adjustments to school organisation and pedagogy in accord with any cultural differences in approaches to learning and to schooling itself that might be found in the research (Corson, 1990a). In a highly pluralist school, community surveys may be essential before working policies can be drawn up. This kind of accurate surveying is a job for experts; it is expensive and time-consuming. Furthermore there are many pitfalls in collecting large-scale data about culture and language in a multiethnic context. An alternative approach is possible. School-based researchers, who rely on their colleagues for advice or who use expert but unpaid local informants, can do a great deal to create a knowledge base for policy and planning at school level. This small-scale approach to community research can go on alongside research into the realities of the school itself.

## Discovering and Addressing the Realities of the Multiethnic School Itself

This section looks at two component factors in the school's multiethnic reality: the attitudes and professional knowledge that teachers possess about the languages and cultures of the school; and the linguistic and cultural diversity of the children themselves. The section concludes by recommending that the one comprehensive method for coping with the many unique problems that these factors can introduce into a school is for the staff to develop coherent policies that deliberately set out to solve the multiethnic school's problems.

As part of developing these policies, administrators and teachers first need to make themselves familiar with any background information touching on the problems that the future policies address. Usually some school-based research is needed to gain this expertise, and this means that teachers, as school policy makers, need to become familiar with some basic approaches to small-scale research. Professional development activities may be needed to provide training in small-scale research methods suited to the institution and its context. Professional development in research methods is a form of training that asks

teachers to take the expertise in assessment and evaluation, that they already hold, a little further: to see school-based research as a way of solving the school's learning problems in the same way as good pupil assessment and evaluation is an aid in solving individual pupil learning problems.

### Teacher attitudes and professional knowledge about the languages and cultures of the school

Like everyone else, teachers are prone to the influence of prejudiced attitudes and stereotypes. But because of the real power that teachers have over the lives of children, they are in a unique position to put their stereotypes to work, sometimes with harmful effect. Stereotypes provide much of the content of the 'social categories' that we hold; they can encourage us to make distinctions in rank, order and value which can be very inequitable in a context where multiethnic groups are meeting and mingling. Hewstone & Giles (1986) offer four statements about stereotypes. In summary these are that:

- stereotyping stems from illusory correlations between people's group membership and their psychological attributes and traits;
- stereotypes influence the way information is processed about the members of groups (i.e. more favourable information is remembered about in-groups and more unfavourable information is remembered about out-groups);
- stereotypes create expectancies about other people and the holders of stereotypes often search for information and behaviours in others that will confirm those expectancies;
- stereotypes constrain their holders' patterns of communication and promote communication which confirms the stereotypes held (i.e. they create self-fulfilling prophecies).

Achievement in schools may seem to depend very much on objective criteria. However, when teachers judge a pupil's cultural background against the yardstick of their own categories about what constitutes 'quality' in educational performance, that cultural background can become an inaccurate indicator of children's educational potential. The matter is made worse if there are other indicators that reinforce teacher prejudices: such as children's dislike of schoolwork, lack of parental interest in the school, or evidence of disadvantage in the children's dress or appearance. Expectations can be adjusted accordingly. It is known that the teacher's expectations of children's potential can influence academic success and children's true potential can be overlooked or reduced in effect. This view is especially supported by Rosenthal & Jacobson's 1968 study *Pygmalion in the Classroom.* Verma & Bagley (1975) cite the 'considerable amount of research', since the 'Pygmalion effect' was identified, that indicates that the average teacher has different perceptions and expectations of poor and minority group children, which lead to different treatment and depressed performances on the part of such children. Prejudices and stereotypes, then, can affect the life chances of all groups when those groups are obviously different in some way from dominant groups. Clearly it is a responsibility of the school to try to minimise the impact of those prejudices and stereotypes wherever they might distort just arrangements for education. One way of dealing with this common problem is to conduct frank and open discussions among staff in a professional development exercise designed to uncover stereotypes and to counter their influence.

As a method of fact gathering about staff attitudes and current school procedures, Maybin (1985: 97) suggests a checklist of questions for use at the school level. This list could be extended to cover other issues of ethnicity as well. It was compiled by school inspectors and circulated in Inner London Education Authority schools:

- Are all staff aware of the language and dialect repertoires of the pupils in the school?
- Do staff recognise that pupils' ability to use language effectively has an important impact on their view of themselves, and therefore on their confidence as learners?
- Do staff accept the validity of all pupils' spoken abilities, and use these as a basis for developing their skills in reading and writing?
- Are staff knowledgeable about what is meant by 'dialect', and do they have a positive approach to dialects other than standard? How is this reflected in the way in which they assess pupils' written work?
- Are staff knowledgeable about the mother tongues which their pupils speak, and do they see these as a potential or real strength in the school?
- Does the school acknowledge and support pupils' bilingualism and promote an interest in their language among all pupils'?
- Is there a satisfactory system within the school for identifying pupils who need help with English as their second language, for

providing this help and for monitoring their progress?

- Are the teaching resources for English as a second language sufficient to meet the needs of the pupils in the school, and are they organised so that pupils have access to them in a range of subject areas?
- Do teachers make positive attempts to draw out the experience of pupils who as yet are not entirely confident in expressing themselves in English?
- Has progress been made in responding to the issue of language diversity through the language policy and practice of the whole school?

A checklist modelled on this one could provide a set of discussion questions for use among staff before more detailed information about teacher attitudes is collected.

## The linguistic and cultural diversity of the children

A wise starting point for inquiring into children's language diversity is to make sure that parents and children understand what the inquiry is all about: what sort of information is needed; why is it needed; who is going to have access to it; how long will the information be kept? It is also important that those organising research in this area are familiar with fundamental theoretical issues: how is the kind of language that children use affected by different 'contexts of situation' and by serving different 'functions of language'? Teachers need to know a lot about language and about research methods before they can gather reliable information about language use; again school-based in-service work may be needed to build this expertise. The questions below are preliminary ones aimed at providing the data on which initial planning in a multiethnic school can be based. This is a summary of a more complete questionnaire that is provided elsewhere, along with a description of the basic research methods for obtaining this information (Corson, 1990a):

- What do you know about the languages represented in your school?
- How is the use of community languages promoted in your school?
- What provisions are made for the formal learning of community languages?
- Where there are formal language classes, how are they organised?

- How does your school support community efforts at language maintenance?

Raising the school's awareness of pupils' cultural diversity and its implications for the school's operations is perhaps the central activity of professional development in multiethnic schools. The questions below, for school staff and policy makers to consider, again are only introductory ones. However, collated responses to these questions will give key background information about the realities of teaching in a multiethnic school:

- What different cultures are represented within your school?
- How is this diversity reflected in the character of the school?
- How does the school give value to the special experiences that culturally different children can offer?
- How do children and staff learn about important cultural practices of the cultures represented in the school?
- What are the provisions for staff, children and community to work together?
- What are the different perceptions of educational and social success in the cultures represented in your school?
- How does your school presently respond to overt racist behaviour among staff and children (name calling, denigratory comments about other cultures, physical assaults, stereotyping, deliberate mispronunciation of names, etc.)?

### Policy making at school level

As mentioned, schools with difficult multiethnic decisions to make will find that they can be helped by designing a policy for handling each important inter-ethnic issue. This policy approach may be essential in providing a fair education where many different minorities in small numbers are present in single schools. Elsewhere I write about policy making at school level (Corson, 1988a,b; 1990a,b; 1991) giving particular attention to 'language policies across the curriculum', citing these as central to school administration, and suggesting that they offer models for other types of policy making such as 'studies in work across the curriculum', 'science and technology across the curriculum', etc. 'Language policies across the curriculum' are viewed as an integral and necessary part of the administrative and curriculum practices of modern schools (DES, 1989), yet relatively few schools

anywhere have seriously tackled the problem of introducing them. One reason for this is that until recently schools in many places did not consider themselves very autonomous institutions; they accepted direction and control in decision-making, in important curriculum areas, from outside bodies within the wider educational system. Another reason is that schools as organisations are only now beginning to recognise the close link between the organisational arrangements that they create and the style and quality of the curriculum that they provide for children. The way to bind the two areas of administration and curriculum together more closely may be for schools to operate through closely negotiated policies designed to address the unique needs of the school, its clients, and its social and cultural context.

A policy sets out guidelines that provide a framework for action in achieving some purpose on a substantive issue. This suggests that not all issues in schools need a policy, but only those of substance and importance. Most multiethnic issues in schools fall into this category of being substantial and important. We do need policies in modern schools to set out our considered responses to issues that involve beliefs or values or philosophy: things like providing assistance to a wide range of children with special curriculum needs, for the allocation of scarce resources needed by teachers in developing their curriculum programme, for the use of facilities, for integrating the help of parents and the community into the school, and so on. The one policy that reaches across all of these and many other areas is a language policy that sees language as the central instrument in learning and as the most accessible pedagogy available to teachers across the curriculum. A language policy across the curriculum is not a 'simple' policy however; to appreciate its complexity it may be useful to think of it as a bundle of policies, each one addressing a substantive language-related issue for the school in its social and cultural context.

Consistent, thoroughly negotiated and wide ranging policies of the kind outlined above seem to provide a vehicle for protecting ethnic minority rights in schools, provided that schools themselves are adequately and equitably funded to begin with. The idea that schools, in response to their social and cultural context, should decide their own modes of operation, their goals (within certain limits) and their curriculum (again within certain limits) is an attractive one; it is certainly consistent with prominent contemporary theories about individual and community rights when they are related to the policy process in education (Diorio, 1986). In particular a language policy across the curriculum can be extended to embrace all of the issues that I raise in this article, because this kind of policy is really a 'policy for learning' in the school. It needs to cover many aspects of the organisation and management of the school: such as staff development, the supervision of minority language teachers, school-based research, support and advisory services, the role of parents, participation of minority groups in school governance, the avoidance of racial discrimination, bilingualism and first language maintenance, and second language teaching. It needs to cover many aspects of teacher approaches to language use: such as cultural awareness, providing for 'special case' ethnically different children, attitudes to language use, and gender, language and the curriculum. Of course it also needs to cover the full curriculum itself: addressing such areas as oral language use, reading across the curriculum, watching and moving, language awareness, and assessing language and learning proficiency. A multiethnic school with a commonly agreed, regularly revised and operating document of this kind, might be a long way down the road to true effectiveness.

Modern schools, seeking to reduce the social distance between themselves and the cultural communities from which their students are drawn, are trying to extend participation in policy making to parents and others as well. Although in modern democracies parents and community members are increasingly better placed to influence a school's programme, there is often very strong reluctance on the part of parents to participate very much in school governance. In advanced industrial societies parents Willingly concede authority to professionals (Murphy, 1980). It will take persistence on the school's part to overcome this reluctance to participate. At the same time it will take strength of purpose not to cater simply for the needs and interests of the politically active in preference to the apathetic, of the rich in preference to the poor, or of the culturally similar in preference to the culturally different. The implementation of a language policy, for example, will need to be explained carefully to parents and to those critics of a school who tend to demand product rather than process from its curriculum. This will pose a serious difficulty in those communities where parents perceive schools as existing expressly to reproduce a particular cultural bias or to maintain a social status quo. In New Zealand, for example, the phenomenon of 'white flight' has been noticed in some multiethnic schools where new 'policies' of biculturalism have been introduced by administrators without the latter communicating and negotiating those policies with the many parents whose backgrounds are narrowly monocultural. Many parents have withdrawn their children from the schools and sent them elsewhere. A wise policy about policy making will mention ingenious but practical ways in which parents can be involved in the design of policies or at least ways that they can be kept informed about the stages in policy development. If this is to be more than tokenism, the goals and organisational reality of the school will need to be communicated over a long period to the community, beginning in small ways but extending deliberately and purposefully until regular two-way communication becomes commonplace and natural. A well thought out policy may be needed for just this task alone, providing a bridge to other developments.

## Meeting the Language Needs of Children in Multiethnic Schools

This section discusses the two major approaches to providing language instruction for children in multiethnic schools: bilingual schooling; and school organisation for second language teaching (SLT). My discussion covers practices that are already operating successfully in pluralist schools. It is important not to make hasty generalisations about approaches in this area, however, since children's language needs are unique and severe educational disadvantages for individuals can go unnoticed. Some examples will illustrate this latter point: In some places difficult and often intractable problems exist in planning bilingual education for those children whose mother tongue is a regional variety of a national language, as may be the case for Italian-born Australian or British children (Tosi, 1984; Bettoni, 1985). How can bilingual studies proceed in Italian and English for these children if neither English nor Italian is the children's true mother tongue? Elsewhere social dialects of a language pose problems of a related kind: in the USA many Hispanic students come from very low-income family backgrounds, live in segregated neighbourhoods, and consequently speak a form of vernacular Spanish which is far removed from the literary Spanish which bilingual teachers usually possess (Valdes *et al.*, 1981). More common, in highly pluralist societies, are schools and classes that include too great a diversity of minority students to allow any form of genuine bilingual schooling to proceed: SLT is the best that can be reasonably provided. Only research at the single school level, coupled with access to outside consultants and the incorporation of decisions into a language policy across the curriculum, can offer solutions to problems that have this degree of specificity.

As presently practised, bilingual schooling is most commonly provided when the clients are present in large numbers in a class or school. Approaches to SLT, on the other hand, provide for individual special cases in a classroom and for small groups of linguistically different children. For these latter children additional individualised provisions may be needed to maintain the mother tongue, to introduce the majority language thoroughly, and to provide cultural studies activities as a bridge between the cultures of the two languages: peer tutoring techniques, parent help and withdrawal teaching by culturally similar adults are commonly used in this supplementary way.

### Bilingual schooling

There has been a radical change in attitude and approach to bilingualism in education as our information about the links between language, culture, self-identity, thinking prowess and educational success has grown. Maintaining the minority mother tongue is said by many to develop a desirable form of cultural diversity in societies, to promote ethnic identity, to lead to social adaptability, to add to the psychological security of the child, and to develop linguistic awareness (Crystal, 1987). What is the evidence for the many favourable claims that are made about the effectiveness of bilingual schooling?

Evidence is appearing in many places. In the Netherlands, for example, a bilingual maintenance approach to the education of minority children is favoured because it is found to be as effective in promoting majority language learning as other assimilation and transition approaches and actually requires less time to be devoted to the teaching and learning of the majority tongue (Vallen & Stijnen, 1987). In the UK the MOTET project in Bradford (Fitzpatrick, 1987) assessed the effects of bilingual education

in a one-year experimental programme with infant children whose home language was Panjabi. The class programme aimed to preserve a 'parity of esteem' between English and Panjabi by allotting equal time and space to each language across the curriculum. The study concluded that there were no negative effects from bilingual education. Instead there were the positive effects of mother tongue maintenance as well as a level of progress in English that was equivalent to a matched control group who had not received a bilingual programme. Again in the Netherlands, programmes in Leyden and Enschede (Appel, 1988) for the primary age children of Turkish and Moroccan immigrant workers suggest that minority language teaching for children from these backgrounds has no negative educational or social effects. In short these programmes achieve only good results. Moorfield (1987) reviews programmes over the last twenty years in Mexico, the USA, Sweden and Canada where children began school speaking a minority language or dialect and where that language was used as the main or only medium of instruction. Later for all these children there was a gradual transition to instruction in both the minority and the majority language. Academic progress achieved in each case was much better than in those programmes where minority language children were taught entirely in the majority language. Student self-esteem, pride in their cultural background and group solidarity were also enhanced in each case. In other settings, where the needs for bilingualism and biliteracy are so obvious that the question of their desirability is never even raised, initial and advanced literacy in two languages becomes possible; 'real' bilingualism becomes a natural and necessary acquisition for all children (Garcia and Otheguy, 1987). Cummins & Swain (1986) provide a guide to the research in bilingual education currently taking place in Canada. The authors contradict many of the prejudiced views that have been widely held about bilingualism and education:

- they offer strong evidence that quality bilingual programmes have been influential in developing language skills and in contributing to broader academic achievement;
- they suggest that in some respects older learners have advantages over younger ones;
- they report evidence that lower ability children also benefit from immersion programmes;
- they conclude that a quality bilingual pro-

gramme will support and aid development in the first language.

While it is possible to draw a favourable conclusion from the bilingual research as a whole to link quality bilingual schooling with cognitive advantages for the learner, Baker (1988) advises us not to overestimate these advantages, especially in relation to everyday mental functioning. On the other hand there is good evidence to suggest that bilinguals are superior to monolinguals on divergent thinking tests; bilinguals have some advantage in their analytical orientation to language; bilinguals also show some increased social sensitivity in situations requiring verbal communication; and bilinguals may have advantages in cognitive clarity and in analytical functioning. What, then, are the favoured organisational arrangements for providing bilingual instruction multiethnic schools?

The study 'Learning English through Bilingual Instruction' carried out by Wong Fillmore in the USA examined effective instructional practices in developing the English academic language skills of Hispanic and Chinese minority language students (Chamot, 1988). Four major instructional factors were significant:

- high quality teaching, including clear lesson organisation, directions and explanations, appropriate aids, attention to higher level skills, and opportunities for oral activities;
- high quality instructional language, including clarity, coherence, use of contexts, paraphrasing, responding to student feedback, and discussion of grammar and vocabulary;
- effective classroom management with stress on academic rather than on non-academic activities;
- provision of equal opportunities for the practice of English.

Effective classrooms in these studies displayed a balance of teacher-directed and individualised activities. In bilingual classrooms students profited most when the languages were presented separately without translations. Notable differences appeared in the learning orientations of the Chinese and the Hispanic students, with the latter gaining most from interaction with their peers and the former learning most in structured and fairly quiet classrooms.

Also in the USA a long-term comparison of three approaches to bilingual schooling for Hispanic children has been undertaken. The three approaches are:

- immersion strategy, in which content subjects are taught through simplified English;
- early-exit or short-term transitional bilingual programmes of 2 to 3 years;
- late-exit or long-term transitional bilingual programmes of 5 to 6 years.

Comparisons found long-term bilingual programmes to be most effective in promoting progress in both Spanish and English and that immersion programmes promoted a greater use of English by students in school itself (Chamot, 1988). Elsewhere in the USA, Spanish-dominant children attending schools in California (Compos & Keatinge, 1988) benefited both academically and in their English language acquisition by having their mother tongue used as the language of instruction in the early junior school years.

Some important variable factors in bilingual programmes have been identified in multiethnic schools. Level of mother tongue language development, at the outset of programmes, is one of these variable factors. Following ideas first expressed by the Finnish researchers, Toukomaa and Skutnabb-Kangas, Canadian researchers Cummins & Swain (1986) put forward their 'threshold hypothesis': one aspect of this hypothesis is that there may be threshold levels of language competence which bilingual children must attain in their first language in order to avoid cognitive disadvantages and to allow the potentially beneficial aspects of becoming bilingual to influence cognitive functioning. Theoretical information of this kind is essential for language planning in bilingualism at the school level.

Elsewhere Cummins & Swain provide evidence to show that there are aspects of language proficiency that are common to both first and second languages, aspects that are interdependent. This evidence allows us to understand why *less* instruction in the second language often results in higher second language proficiency scores for minority students, while for majority language students *more* instruction in the second language results in higher second language proficiency scores. They also present research evidence suggesting that in some aspects of second language learning older learners are more efficient learners. They go on to offer ideas in programme planning for bilingual proficiency. From Cummins & Swain's discussion three key points can be made about bilingualism and schooling:

- a high level of proficiency in both languages

is likely to be an intellectual advantage to children in all subjects across the curriculum, when compared with their monolingual classmates;

- in social situations where there is likely to be serious erosion of the first (minority) language, there is a need for the development and maintenance of that language if intellectual performance is not to suffer;
- high level second language proficiency depends on well-developed first language proficiency.

Putting these three points together we can conclude that children from linguistic minority groups generally profit from bilingual programmes in which their first language plays the major role, because this lays a language foundation which cannot otherwise be guaranteed. This conclusion contrasts with the findings for children from dominant majority language groups who benefit from bilingual programmes in which the second language is used most frequently (Appel & Muysken, 1987). In the latter case a firm foundation in the first language is guaranteed by the fact that it is the language of wider communication in the society.

The third point above, that learning a second language well depends on developing prior proficiency in the first, is broadly consistent with the findings of educators in the USSR, whose experience in these matters may outstrip experiences elsewhere (McLaughlin, 1986). Research in Germany too (Rehbein, 1984) suggests strong links between high level development in conceptual information and discourse strategies in the first language on the one hand and second language development on the other.

Because their language is not the language of wider communication, many indigenous or new settler minority children in many countries may arrive in schools with their first language relatively under-developed in certain contexts, styles and functions of use. Their grasp of the majority language may be limited to a small range of functions as well, often passively related to television viewing and the like. For these children intensive early exposure to the majority language may result in low achievement in that language, as well as a decline in mother tongue proficiency. Bilingual programmes in the minority language are essential if widespread and discriminatory school failure and its attendant social costs are to be avoided.

A second important variable factor in bilingual programmes for minority children is age of acquisition of the second language. Very young children (under five), given the necessary environment, acquire a second language quickly and seem to pick up two languages simultaneously without much difficulty. Although most theorists agree that there is some advantage in a very early start in second language learning, the causes and the nature of that advantage are far from clear. The situation becomes more complex for older children. Skutnabb-Kangas and Toukomaa in Sweden (Skutnabb-Kangas, 1981) found that Finnish children moving to Sweden and learning Swedish early in their school careers lost much of their proficiency in Finnish; others who moved later (at ten years) maintained a level of Finnish very close to their age mates in Finland while also acquiring proficiency in Swedish. Even allowing, as Harley (1986) suggests, that different social influences might have influenced the younger children's academic performance, arriving as they did so young in a new culture where they were negatively stereotyped, it is the case that similarly adverse social factors often affect young language learners in a new culture: the age-related results of the Swedish study are significant, whether we explain them in purely linguistic or in sociocultural terms as well. Support for this view comes from Canadian studies of immigrant Japanese children, and there is evidence from the Netherlands and Indo-China too that older children manage to maintain and develop cognitive and academic skills in their first language to a greater extent than younger immigrant children (Cummins *et al.*, 1984) and children between nine and twelve years also make more rapid progress in academic aspects of their second language than do children between five and eight years (Appel & Muysken, 1987).

In summary, it seems very important that the child's first language (i.e. minority language) be given maximum attention up to the stage of middle schooling so that skill in using it to manipulate abstractions develops and also so that it can be used to perform the cognitive operations necessary for acquiring the second language. This is not happening in many places, notably in most public school systems in the USA, in Australasia and in the UK. Nor is it happening in radically different places like Hong Kong, where English-medium schools, in an overwhelmingly Cantonese-speaking city, seem to adversely affect many Cantonese mother tongue students' educational attainment (Yu & Atkinson, 1988). At the same time, in learning the majority language as a second language, it would seem that older SL learners up to the age of early adolescence at least have a cognitive advantage over younger ones when educated in school settings on academic SL tasks that are context-reduced (e.g. abstract and difficult) (Harley, 1986). Combining these two conclusions, there seems to be a strong argument for deferring formal bilingual programmes until quite late in schooling and concentrating instead on minority mother tongue development. Certainly the value of beginning formal second language education should not be considered as a separate issue from the learner's first language development.

Other influences on children's performances in bilingual programmes are beginning to emerge. Two of these are the respective roles of high ability and level of family affluence on results. Baker (1988) summarises the scanty evidence that is available: children from low-income backgrounds and of average or below average ability may all be successful in bilingual schooling. This tentative conclusion also extends to schools that are sited in exclusively low-income communities and to children of below average reasoning ability. Moreover, while the evidence in favour of bilingual programmes for children with learning difficulties is less conclusive, there are promising indications at least that second language immersion does no harm for special education pupils (Bruck, 1985).

Motivation to learn or retain is another variable of influence. For children in some bilingual communities there is an important interaction between the motivation to use the majority language, which they receive from the social setting, and their age level. Social pressures can pull adolescent students, in particular, towards a use of the dominant language (to the extent that they can use it) and these pressures may frustrate attempts in school to use the minority language for instruction. Wald (1984) reports language preferences among early adolescent Hispanic children in the USA. In some cases the preference for English existed even when the children had far greater conversational ability in Spanish. This is a complex issue for the sociology of language use, and our knowledge in the area of age and language solidarity is only beginning to develop.

### School organisation for second language teaching (SLT)

As part of a coherent language policy, and depending on their SL needs and school capacities, multiethnic schools often provide more than one of the following options in meeting their unique set of language problems. Each of these sixteen approaches has been used or is in use somewhere in a multiethnic school. In most contexts several methods operate alongside one another, each one addressing different language problems and providing for the unique needs of those minority children whose numbers may not be large enough to permit viable bilingual teaching. Elsewhere (Corson, 1990a) I elaborate on each of the organisational arrangements listed below:

(1)  reception units;
(2)  integrated and cooperative teaching;
(3)  paired teaching;
(4)  parallel teaching and programming;
(5)  withdrawal teaching;
(6)  SL extension;
(7)  correspondence school enrolment;
(8)  peer support systems;
(9)  enrolment in SL evening classes;
(10) curriculum planning for first language support;
(11) curriculum planning for the development of study skills;
(12) familiarisation programmes;
(13) language support across the curriculum;
(14) incidental teaching;
(15) rotation teaching;
(16) special purpose teaching.

Sometimes other patterns of organisation and planning are possible or necessary. Sometimes people from indigenous cultures or from other cultures that are very different from the majority culture prefer arrangements that differ from those provided for the children of immigrants coming from cultures rather similar to the dominant one. Following the wishes of groups in the parent community itself, the school may need to make different types of arrangement reflecting cultural preferences. For example: a dispersal of the minority group into classes mixed with majority language students (analogous to the 'mainstreaming' of special education pupils in some countries) is preferred by some groups of Pacific Island immigrants in New Zealand and by some Panjabi-speaking groups in the UK. These people prefer to take the responsibility themselves, outside the school, for passing on their own culture and they want nothing more from the school than that it give their children full access to the dominant culture and the majority language. Others ask that their children be concentrated in separate groups, at least for some of the time, so that the culture can be preserved. Among the Inuit native people of Canada the episodic teaching of highly dispersed small groups by itinerant teachers is common and quite practical. Elsewhere there is a recognition of pupil preferences in grouping, especially of the wishes of older children. Some balance, then, needs to be maintained between school, pupil and parent preferences in these matters.

The effective organisation of SL programmes does not end with simple language provisions. At least three other issues need to be addressed in a school policy where cultural pluralism is part of the social context: how is the school to approach the cultural features of minority groups; what is the 'official' attitude of the school to the minority cultures; and what place can members of the minority culture have in school governance? In the next section I describe a school setting where great attention has been paid to the school community's multiethnic nature and where the school has been re-shaped accordingly.

## The Reality of a Multiethnic School

It is possible to modify and build on the foundations of contemporary schooling to make the school more organic to its cultural community. In a few places school principals and their colleagues have begun to change things in a planned way, and with good effect (McPherson & Corson, 1989; Corson, 1990a). Drawing on interviews with teachers and other adults in a school's community, Cazden (1989) reports a case study of one contemporary inner-city school: Richmond Road School in Auckland, New Zealand.

In this case study, over many years a Maori school principal purposefully communicated a vision to his staff, based on his own professional expertise, his insights into cultural questions, and his understanding of 'how children thought, and how they saw the world'. Richmond Road School in 1989 had 269 students, of whom 21 per cent were Samoan, 20 per cent were European New Zealanders, 18 per cent were Maori, 34 per cent were other Polynesian, and 7 per cent were Indian and others. Even after the Principal's death, the school has demonstrated its capacity to be a 'self-sustaining system' by taking on the task of reform and improvement that is necessary to keep a worthwhile system operating. How is Richmond Road different?

In contrast to the isolation of teachers in single-cell classroom schools, Richmond Road teachers work in a setting of intense collectivity. Children and staff interact in complex organizational 'systems', as they are always referred to: vertical/family groupings of children; non-hierarchical relationships among the staff; curriculum materials that are created by teacher teams at the school and rotate around the school for use by all; and monitoring systems for continuous updating of information on children's progress. (Cazden, 1989: 11)

For his vertical grouping system the Principal borrowed the example offered by non-graded country schools. It is often claimed that small rural schools offer a most desirable form of elementary education of which former teachers and students alike have happy memories. At Richmond Road four *ropu* (vertical groups) operate in shared or separate spaces, one of them including a Samoan bilingual group, another a Maori bilingual group, and a third the ESL language unit for non-English speaking newcomers to New Zealand. Each *ropu* includes children from the entire age range, from five-year-old new entrants to eleven-year-olds. Children stay in the same *ropu* for their entire primary schooling, working with one home-group teacher in frequently changing vertical home groups of 16–20 pupils. Also attached to the school are Maori and Samoan immersion culture/language pre-schools: *Te Kohanga Reo* and *A'oga Fa'a Samoa* (Maori and Samoan 'language nests'). The two dual immersion bilingual units operating in two of the primary school *ropu* receive the graduates from these pre-school language nests, provided parents agree. During half of each morning and every other afternoon, the teachers in these units speak only Maori or Samoan and the children are encouraged to do likewise.

Paired teaching and reciprocal instruction is common in this school. The provisional authority possessed by the Principal, based in his specialist cultural and administrative knowledge, forms a model for provisional authority among all the school community members: 'whoever has knowledge teaches'. As a result the official hierarchy of ascribed statuses has much less meaning. For example, although *Nga kaiarahi reo* (the language leaders/assistants) have no formal professional training, they function as full teachers in virtue of their undoubted expertise and on-the-job training. Again, the school's caretaker (janitor) is involved in the educational work of the school as a valued colleague, supporting children and staff, respected by parents, and a friend to all the children. Parents too contribute their special knowledge and 'the front door is always open'. The school is organic to its community.

In this system of organisation the obvious stress on communal activity for the students is extended in other directions too: the bonds of participation between people are promoted at various levels. The vertical grouping of the *ropu* makes cooperative curriculum and resource development by teachers possible. Organized into five curriculum groups, that deliberately cut across the *ropu* teaching teams, teachers collaborate in making 'focus resources' for school-wide topics that follow a multi-year plan, so that all minority groups are assured of exposure to each topic. Each team makes materials at ten reading levels for use in four learning modes: 'teacher'/ child; cooperative; collaborative; and independent. Each teacher is responsible for making a number of different items. When ready, materials are presented to colleagues during staff meetings and then they are rotated throughout the school, staying in each *ropu* for fixed periods. Clearly, as well as collaboration, there is efficiency and effectiveness here. One staff member remarks: 'think if you'd prepared that quality of work all by yourself for your class...it'd be impossible to do that, for the amount of quality you get back. You get a greater range of ideas too...' (Cazden, 1989: 28). Like the school itself, curriculum materials are matched to the community the school serves and target the needs of the students.

Richmond Road is also a learning community for adults: they learn about teaching, about other cultures and about themselves. A stress by the Principal on workshops and conferences, on contact with up-to-date theory, and on worthwhile staff meeting discussions, encourages staff to share and explore their own and each other's cultural and class backgrounds (which are as diverse as the children's). By working together themselves, teachers learn about collaborative techniques for learning and this offers a sound model for the students: 'I think that's why the children work together here, because they can see us working together' (Cazden, 1989: 11). It is plain that the overtly competitive nature of regular schooling is missing from this environment. The self-esteem of the pupils, including their growing sense of pride, their sense of who he or she is, and their sense of involvement in a worthwhile community, is put ahead of their academic performance. Yet the environment for academic development does not seem to suffer as a result. Cazden sets Richmond Road against a recent US report on 'effective schools' (Bryk & Driscoll, 1988) and finds that that report's essential features are matched 'amazingly well' at Richmond Road:

- shared values, especially about the purpose of the institution, what students should learn, and how teachers and students should behave;
- a common agenda of activities that provide opportunities for interaction and link students, faculty and administration to the school's traditions;
- and a distinctive pattern of social relationships that embody an ethos of caring (from Cazden, 1989: 1–2).

## Conclusion

Great advantages can come from well-run multiethnic schools, not just for the institution of education itself. Where the minority community has a major hand in policy making and in the schooling process, the entire programme of schooling is directed towards elevating the status of the community and questioning the role of schooling in that process. Language questions become subsumed under much more important issues, among which language is only an all-pervading and sometimes distracting factor (García & Otheguy, 1987). When minority language maintenance is initiated in a community and when minority culture values influence the organisation of schooling, the minority members of that community become the experts: they are the advisers and real controllers of the education programme; their values shape the educational outcomes. Local political mobilisation with real purpose can begin to occur. Community attitudes are laid bare and discussed. Local people receive formal training as teachers. Parents participate in the activities of the school to a greater degree and they acquire skills that were previously not their own. All of these things, and many more, contribute to the elevation of local minority groups. Political consciousness awakens where perhaps previously there was none. And the language of the minorities becomes available as a recognised political voice at the same time as their political will begins to assert itself.

It is likely that multiethnic schools controlled and run by remote bureaucracies and staffed by teachers whose culture is not the culture of the local community get in the way of all this. When majority culture educators look at minority children they tend to focus on what those children lack, and usually what they see is the absence of a high level proficiency in the majority language and knowledge of the majority culture. This lack becomes the focus of the schooling that they offer those children. It is a commonplace for observers of educational reform to claim that policies of compensatory, multicultural and anti-racist education, imposed from afar, make little difference to educational inequality. It is likely that only a local community can really decide what is necessary. When communities themselves are in charge of education, when they themselves have the respect and the dignity that goes with deciding the future of their offspring, they themselves come to see education in a much broader way. They begin to ask each other about the best way to educate their children and about what might be wrong with the conventional processes of schooling that they are familiar with.

## References

Appel, R. (1988) The language education of immigrant workers' children in the Netherlands. In Skutnabb-Kangas and Cummins, op. cit. (pp. 57–78).

Appel, R. and Muysken, P. (1987) *Language Contact and Bilingualism*. London: Edward Arnold.

Baker, C. (988) *Key Issues in Bilingualism and Bilingual Education*. Clevedon: Multilingual Matters.

Bettoni, C. 1985) *Tra Lingue Dialetto e Inglese*. Leichhardt: FILEF Italo-Australian Publications.

Bourne, J. and Cameron, D. (1988) No common ground: Kingman, grammar and the nation — A linguistic and historical perspective on The Kingman Report. *Language and Education* 2 (3), 147–60.

Bruck, M. 1985) Consequences of transfer out of early French immersion programs. *Applied Psycholinguistics* 6, 39–61.

Bryk, A. S. and Driscoll, M. E. (1988) *The High School as Community: Contextual Influences and Consequences for Students and Teachers*. Madison, WI: National Center on Effective Schools.

Campos, S. and Keatinge, H. (1988) The Carpinteria language minority student experience from theory, to practice, to success. In Skutnabb-Kangas and Cummins, op. cit. (pp. 299–307).

Canadian Multiculturalism Act (July 1988). Ottawa: Canadian Government Publishing Centre.

Cazden, C. (1989) Richmond Road: A multilingual/multicultural primary school in Auckland, New Zealand. *Language and Education* 3 (3), 143–66.

Chamot, A. (1988) Bilingualism in education and bilingual education: The state of the art in the United States. *Journal of Multilingual and Multicultural Development* 9 (1), 11–35.

Corson, D. J. (1988a) Work in progress: Language policy across the curriculum (LPAC). *Language and Education* 2 (1), 61–3.

— (1988b) *Education for Work: Background to Policy and Curriculum*. Palmerston North: The Dunmore Press.

— (1990a) *Language Policy Across the Curriculum*. Clevedon: Multilingual Matters.

— (1990b) Applying a social epistemology to school level policy making. *British Journal of Educational Studies* 38 (3), 259–76.

— (1991) School language policies. In *Encyclopedia of Language and Linguistics*. Oxford: Pergamon and University of Aberdeen Press.

Crystal, D. (1987) *The Cambridge Encyclopedia of Language*. Cambridge: Cambridge University Press.

Cummins, J. *et al.* (1984) Linguistic interdependence among Japanese and Vietnamese immigrant students. In Rivera, ed., op. cit., 1984a.

Cummins, J. and Swain, M. (1986) *Bilingualism in Education: Aspects of Theory, Research and Practice*. London: Longman.

Department of Education and Science (DES) (1985) *Education for All: Report of the Committee of Inquiry into the Education of Children from Ethnic Minority Groups* (The Swann Report). London: HMSO.

— (1988) *Report of the Committee of Inquiry into the Teaching of English Language* (The Kingman Report). London: HMSO.

— (1989) *English for Ages 5–16* (The Cox Report). London: HMSO.

Diorio, J. A. (1986) Rights, equality and the ethics of school policy. *Curriculum Inquiry* 16 (2), 147–78.

Fitzpatrick, F. (1987) *The Open Door*. Clevedon: Multilingual Matters.

García, O. and Otheguy, R. (1987) The bilingual education of Cuban-American children in Dade County's ethnic schools. *Language and Education* 1 (2), 83–95.

Harley, B. (1986) *Age in Second Language Acquisition*. Clevedon: Multilingual Matters.

Hewstone, M. and Giles, H. (1986) Social groups and social stereotypes in intergroup communication. In Gudykunst, W., ed., *Intergroup Communication*. London: Edward Arnold.

Hirsh, W. (1987) *Living Languages*. Auckland: Heinemann.

Lo Bianco, J. (1987) *National Policy on Languages*. Canberra: Australian Government Printing Service.

McPherson, J. and Corson, D. J. (1989) *Language Policy Across the Curriculum: Eight Case Studies of School Based Policy Development*. Wellington: Ministry of Education.

Maybin, J. (1985) Working towards a school language policy. In *Every Child's Language: An In-Service Pack for Primary Teachers* (pp. 95–108). Clevedon: Open University and Multilingual Matters.

McLaughlin, B. (1986) Multilingual education: Theory east and west. In Spolsky, op. cit. (pp. 32–52).

Moorfield, J. (1987) Implications for schools of research findings in bilingual education. In Hirsh, op. cit. (pp. 31–43).

Murphy, J. (1980) School administrators besieged: A look at Australian and American education. *American Journal of Education* 89 (Nov.), 1–26.

Rehbein, J. (1984) *Diskurs und Verstehen: Zur Rolle der Muttersprache bei der Textverarbeitung in der Zweitsprache*. Hamburg: University of Hamburg.

Rivera, C. (ed.) (1984a) *Communicative Competence Approaches to Language Proficiency Assessment: Research and Application*. Clevedon: Multilingual Matters.

— (1984b) *Language Proficiency and Academic Achievement*. Clevedon: Multilingual Matters.

Rosenthal, R. and Jacobson, L. (1968) *Pygmalion in the Classroom*. New York: Holt, Rinehart and Winston.

Skutnabb-Kangas, T. (1981) *Bilingualism or Not: The Education of Minorities*. Clevedon: Multilingual Matters.

Skutnabb-Kangas, T. and Cummins, J. (1988) *Minority Education: From Shame to Struggle*. Clevedon: Multilingual Matters.

Spolsky, B. (1986) *Language and Education in Multilingual Settings*. Clevedon: Multilingual Matters.

Tosi, A. (1984) *Immigration and Bilingual Education*. Oxford: Pergamon.

Valdes, G., Lozano, A. and Garcia-Moya, R. (eds) (1981) *Teaching Spanish to the Hispanic Bilingual: Issues, Aims and Methods*. New York: Teachers College Press.

Vallen, T. and Stijnen, S. (1987) Language and educational success of indigenous and non-indigenous minority students in the Netherlands. *Language and Education* 1 (2), 109–24.

Verma, G. and Bagley, C. (1975) *Race and Education Across Cultures*. London: Heinemann.

Wald, B. (1984) A sociolinguistic perspective on Cummins' current framework for relating language proficiency to academic achievement. In Rivera, pp. 55–70 (op. cit.), 1984b.

Yu, V. and Atkinson, P. (1988) An investigation of the language difficulties experienced by Hong Kong secondary school students in English-medium schools. *Journal of Multilingual and Multicultural Development* 9 (4), 267–84.

## Questions

(1) What is a 'language policy across the curriculum'? Does your local school have such a policy? How does this differ from language policy as discussed by Stubbs?

(2) What is the difference between schools that are bilingual and those that are organized for second language teaching (SLT)? What are the differences in the students, personnel, instruction, services and philosophy? Are there political differences?

(3) Define the 'threshold hypothesis' (You may also want to refer to '*Foundations of Bilingual Education and Bilingualism*,' Chapter 10.) Then rate the bilingual education program most likely to take the language minority student beyond the second threshold so as to reap

the cognitive advantages of bilingualism, using a scale where 1 = 'absolutely not', 2 = 'possible', 3 = 'likely':

(a) submersion;
(b) submersion with withdrawal second language classes;
(c) structured immersion;
(d) early exit transitional;
(e) late exit transitional;
(f) maintenance;
(g) two-way dual language.

Make a chart to display your results.

(4) Describe the planning and implementation of a language policy across the curriculum in the Richmond Road school in Auckland, New Zealand. Has there been any such planning in your local school?

## Activities

(1) Prepare a short questionnaire to give to at least ten teachers in a particular school about:
(a) the languages and cultures of the school;
(b) their attitudes towards them;
(c) their professional knowledge of them;
You may refer to the checklists provided in the article to prepare your questionnaire. Remember to record the teachers' characteristics. Tabulate the responses. Write an essay of the results and of any relationship you may have found between teacher characteristics and their attitude and knowledge.

(2) Observe a second language classroom for one day. Record your observations of how the four major instructional factors identified by Wong Fillmore are present or absent in this classroom. On a scale where 1 = 'absent', 2 = 'somewhat present', 3 = 'highly present', rate the classroom on each of the four factors. Then total the results and discuss how effective is this classroom.
Different groups may visit different types of second language classrooms. For instance, some might visit a withdrawal (or pull-out) second language class, others the second language component of a bilingual class, a structured immersion class, the English part of a two-way dual language class or a submersion class. Compare your results.

(3) Interview a principal/head in a school with which you are familiar. Find out the extent to which the principal is knowledgeable of the community's culture and languages, of the use to which these are put in the school. What are the attitudes of the principal toward the inclusion of the community's culture and languages? Tape and transcribe your interview.

(4) After selecting a school, survey the immediate community of the school asking for ethnicity, country of birth, length of residency in the country, language spoken at home and proficiency in the majority language of members of that community. With that information, draw a 'Language Policy across the Curriculum' for the school. Indicate what additional resources the school would need in order to implement the policy.

(5) Interview three parents of different ethnolinguistic minorities. Find out how they differ in their preference for educating their children and their interest in bilingualism. Record the interview on an answer sheet. Different groups might select different social characteristics for the parents, such as social class, educational level, gender, settlement history,

caste minorities or immigrants. (See Cummins (1986), this volume, for a review of this categorization by Ogbu. You may also want to refer to '*Foundations of Bilingual Education and Bilingualism*,' Chapter 17.)

(6) Interview four persons who have learned a second language as follows:
   (a) before the age of five;
   (b) five to eight;
   (c) nine to twelve;
   (d) over twelve.

Ask them about the way they learned the language, their motivation, their experiences and their attitudes. Record their answers. Then write an essay comparing the four subjects. Do you think there's an optimal age for second language acquisition?

# A Spanish-English Dual-Language Program in New York City

## Sidney H. Morison

Outside Public School (PS) 84 on West 92nd Street in New York City a student-made sign at the entrance reads Welcome and Bienvenidos, while inside one sees Salida, Oficina, Salon de Medico, and other official signs in Spanish — alongside their English counterparts. Letters and notices to parents, in two languages, line the counter in the main office, where a bilingual secretary registers children, answers the phone, types official notices, and generally organizes the school from behind her desk. She speaks Spanish and English interchangeably, as the need or desire arises, and no one pays particular notice. Although Spanish is not the dominant language of the school, it is commonplace to hear it spoken throughout the building, among children, teachers, paraprofessionals, parents, and custodial staff and even on the public-address system.

In front of the auditorium, there is a large, colorful, Mexican piñata hanging from the ceiling, looking down upon murals and other displays done by children, which depict recent events like the Olympic games they had been following on television and *el metamorfasis de la mariposa* ('the metamorphosis of the butterfly'), which so many children had observed in their classrooms. Most of the writing here, now, is in Spanish, by children in the dual-language (DL) program. The auditorium was the scene on 13 January 1989 of a press conference in which New York State Commissioner of Education Thomas Sobol announced the New York State Board of Regents' proposal to raise the cutoff level on the Language Assessment Battery, which defines children with limited English proficiency (LEP).[1] By raising the cutoff, the state extends its support of bilingual education, providing children whose first language is other than English more time in the program.

PS 84 is not a bilingual school, but Spanish is clearly a viable language here. It is used socially without censure and officially in all school–home communications. There are, after all, Hispanic children in all our classes, representing 53 percent of the total student population. More important, Spanish enjoys status equal with that of English as a language of instruction in our program. This structural commitment not only moves us closer to our goal of bilingualism — an ideal held since the first bilingual classes were established at PS 84 in 1970 — but also represents a significant step in reversing the view of bilingual education as remedial.

### The Dual-Language Program: Structure and Goals

During the 1988–89 school year, there were 9 classes in the DL program out of a total of 25 — not including special education. The classes are organized in three levels: (1) early childhood, consisting of two kindergartens and three mixed first–second grades; (2) middle grades, consisting of two mixed third–fourths; and (3) upper grades, consisting of one fifth-grade class and one sixth. Each kindergarten class is limited to 25 students, while the other early-childhood and middle grades are capped at 28. The program is voluntary, open to both Hispanic and non-Hispanic children, and a conscious effort is made to balance the number of Spanish-dominant and English-dominant children in each class. Within a class, there is no grouping by language levels; rather, teachers arrange and encourage mixed linguistic groupings for both social and cognitive activities. Effort is also made to maintain a sizable immigrant Spanish population so that the program does not become a second-language program for middle-class children.

Early childhood classes are self-contained, meaning that each has its own room and teacher.

They are, however, part of a community of classes on a corridor — along with monolingual classes — where interaction is encouraged. All early-childhood teachers share similar concerns and are responsible for helping children learn to read, write, and socialize. Consequently, there are collaborations of all kinds, including trips, curriculum projects, sharing, and joint planning that cut across programs. DL teachers, however, have a specific, shared commitment to affirm Spanish as a language of instruction and to protect it from falling into disuse. They implement this commitment by speaking English one day and Spanish the next, alternating in this way throughout the year, agreeing not to switch languages on a Spanish day and avoiding the temptation of repeating in one language what they did the previous day in the other language.

In the middle grades, a different model is used. Here, each teacher has her own room and the two classes alternate daily between them. Class A begins with English-speaking teacher A on Monday, then goes to Spanish-speaking teacher B on Tuesday, again to teacher A on Wednesday and so on, while class B begins the alternating schedule with teacher B. At the end of every ten-day period, each class has seen each teacher five times. It is essential, in this model, for the two teachers to work as a team since each must get to know as many as 56 children. Consequently, curriculum is a shared responsibility, based mainly on the teachers' strengths and interests. Topics are not repeated from one room to another; one teacher may focus mainly on mathematics, for example, the other on creative writing, and social studies topics may be divided. While there is bound to be overlapping, teachers — through ongoing meetings — make certain their coverage is complementary rather than repetitious.

The two upper-grade DL classes are part of a fifth–sixth-grade minischool, which functions as a unit in a partially departmentalized program. Taking into consideration certain special needs of this age group beyond language, teachers work closely together to provide an intimate small-group setting for six classes. Children receive the benefit of teacher specialization, and at the same time they are involved in mixed-group projects that include chorus, architecture, and environmental studies in connection with cultural institutions. Within this setting, special programming was arranged to maintain continuity within the DL program. The teacher of the fifth-grade DL class is the designated Spanish speaker and sees only the DL classes — on alternate days — for major subjects. In other words, the sixth-grade DL class — or the fifth-grade one — will see her, on alternate days, for social studies and some math but will see non-DL teachers in the minischool on the other days for science, art, and other subjects.

As a result of this arrangement, upper-grade students are immersed in Spanish about 35 percent of the time, slightly less than children in the other grades. But this is not a major concern. We are convinced that the actual time spent in Spanish is not as critical as the structure that separates the two languages, be it self-contained classes or some form of team teaching. Strict separation, with no switching, is really the linchpin of the program, providing necessary support for Spanish, the minority language, while adding to its status as a language of instruction.

Neither English nor Spanish is taught. At the risk of oversimplifying, I believe the situation to be thus: children learn language as a by-product, through use. The primary aim of the DL program is academic growth. Bilingualism and biliteracy are, of course, expected outcomes but are, in a sense, secondary since the acquisition of a second language is never separated from substantive material. Children are not given a differentiated curriculum based on language dominance. Rather, language dominance is used only to balance classes, and all children are exposed to the same curriculum.

In addition to academic growth and bilingualism, the third goal of the program is the support of minority-language children. This has been a goal of our bilingual program since its inception in 1970 and is still an important rationale today. An immersion bilingual program without specific minority-language and cultural support could lead to loss of the first language for the minority-language child as he or she learns English. The majority-language child, on the other hand, adds a second language, since English, as the dominant language in the society, is not likely to suffer.

## History of the Dual-language Program

The DL program at PS 84 was inaugurated in the fall of 1984, after 15 years of struggle and growth that represented our attempts to build a school more responsive to children and their families. The years of the late 1960s, which mark my beginnings with the school, were times of great political turmoil during which minority parents all over New York City were demanding community control of schools in the wake of the system's failure to educate their children adequately. They were also years in which Hispanic parents in the city echoed demands by language minorities across the country for bilingual education. At PS 84, a political movement of parents, supported by interested teachers, forced the removal of an unsympathetic administration, selected a principal of their choosing, and pressed for educational reform that viewed the child as central.

They called upon Professor Lillian Weber, of City College in New York City, an authority on open education and the British infant school, to provide on-site training and support for teachers. Weber helped them to organize and work with heterogeneous classes and to include the children's own experience and language as both content and support for their learning. She advocated decentralizing the school into smaller, corridor communities, in which teachers could share and plan together; where children of different classes could mix; and where parents and other adults, such as student teachers and paraprofessionals, could be included.[2]

In this context of inclusion, children whose first language was Spanish were encouraged to use it, and, by 1970, the school's bilingual–bicultural program was established. We had to overcome, however, the results of a tracking system that had effectively segregated Hispanic and black children and placed them in low-functioning and special-education classes. At the time, the school's population was about 40 percent Hispanic, 30 percent black, and 30 percent white. By eliminating the low-functioning and special-education classes and organizing heterogeneously, we sought to demonstrate our belief in equality and the richness of diversity. Within each class, teachers stressed the use of colloquial Spanish and the sharing of Spanish folk customs. The few Hispanic paraprofessionals assigned to the school at the time were encouraged to use their bilingualism in working with children, and Hispanic parents were invited into the classroom.

In 1970, two Hispanic bilingual teachers were hired — the first ever at the school — and the school's first bilingual classes were organized. We sent letters to parents, describing our intentions, indicating the voluntary nature of the program, and encouraging the participation of non-Hispanic children. The following year, as the demand for space increased, two more bilingual teachers were hired. The decade of the 1970s also saw a deepening of the involvement of Hispanic parents in education, as well as a deepening of our own efforts to encourage that involvement. Our total Hispanic population had increased to 47 percent, and we had grown to eight bilingual classes by 1978. We had acquired more bilingual staff as the result of an aggressive search: eight teachers, a coordinator, a guidance counselor, a bilingual secretary, several bilingual paraprofessionals, and three bilingual trainees from a Board of Education program whom we later hired as teachers. Our home–school correspondence was being written in two languages, and Spanish was even used on the public-address system. From 1972 to 1977, two Hispanic parents were presidents of the parent–teacher association, and from 1974 to 1979 two of our school's Hispanic parents chaired the district's community school board.

With teachers from Puerto Rico, Cuba, the Dominican Republic, Colombia, and Spain, the heritage of our children was well represented, and Spanish was spoken freely throughout the building. Once-quiet children were now speaking; walls were covered with pictures and stories of Latin American countries. The smell of Spanish food frequently filled the air, and Latin music and dance were popular. Practically invisible prior to 1971, Spanish parents were in classrooms — invited by teachers — sharing stories, recipes, or crafts, organizing fiestas, and going on class trips. For many of the poorer parents, the traditional barrier between school and home was down, and they could even see, in certain teachers, possibilities for their own children's futures.

Although non-Hispanic children were included in the DL program from the beginning, classes remained predominantly Hispanic, causing some concern. We wanted to avoid any sort of program isolation. Consequently, in the interest of heterogeneity and wider exposure to native English speakers, bilingual classes were integrated into every corridor community, a move that also had the effect of helping establish Spanish language and culture school wide. Within the classes, which contained Spanish-dominant, English-dominant, and balanced bilingual children, teaching practices developed in a rather pragmatic fashion, as teachers responded to the most immediate needs or pressures.

In the early grades, prior to 1984 the teacher spoke English, with Spanish translation, as she introduced new topics or did daily routines with the entire class. She formed reading groups according to language levels, however. Children learned to read in their dominant language and were switched to the second language at the teacher's discretion. Even while they were supported in their first language, however, through reading, general communication, and understanding curriculum content, second-language development was encouraged in many ways, both formal and informal. For example, there was a good deal of small-group activity — like playing with blocks, housekeeping, caring for and feeding animals, painting murals, and hands-on exploration of mathematical materials such as color rods and pattern blocks — in which language levels and ability were mixed. This was the basic structure of all early-childhood classes for the purpose of language development in general, and it was certainly indicated for bilingual classes as well. Another daily activity was story reading. Here, the teacher read to the class, alternating daily between Spanish-language and English-language stories. Socially, through small-group activity, recess, song, dance, holiday celebrations, and trips, both English and Spanish were used liberally. As the year progressed, teachers would also begin responding in a child's second language to questions the child asked in his or her first language. For example, when a child asked, '¿Quiero ir al baño?' the teacher would respond, 'You want to go to the bathroom?' In this manner, children also began to speak about other classroom routines and activities as well.

In the middle grades, teachers were concerned mainly with reading in English, since annual standardized reading tests influenced promotion, and LEP students who were in a bilingual program more than one year had to be tested in English regardless of their readiness. Teachers continued the practice of the early grades, of separating Spanish and English writing for display on walls inside and outside the classrooms, and they were mandated to teach major subject areas in Spanish to LEP students. But the pressure of testing continued to cause switching of languages and emphasis on English skills. As Spanish-dominant children moved into English, they seemed to fare well academically but appeared to lose their Spanish or, at best, use it less. English dominant children, on the other hand, were far from becoming bilingual or biliterate. As 1930 approached, teachers and administrators questioned more and more what we were doing. After nearly ten years, the goal of English competency was being achieved and

there was certainly a schoolwide awareness of and appreciation for Spanish language and culture, but it was clear we were not producing bilingual children as we had hoped. Consequently, during the early 1980s, our bilingual coordinator and I visited and researched existing immersion programs. In 1983, we invited Ricardo Otheguy, professor at City College, to consult with us.

Discussions were open and fruitful. Professor Otheguy was immediately impressed with the ease with which our teachers spoke and he likened the group to a college faculty. A shared, positive view of the program as non-remedial was also impressive, but it was evident from the beginning that we did not have a clear linguistic pedagogy. To be sure, the teachers were not beginners, and there were elements in our program that proved to be important to what was subsequently developed. For example, separation of languages was not a new idea for us, nor was the support of Spanish language and culture. But certain notions that had always determined our teaching practice had to be dispelled as our meetings progressed. Teaching to the tests had always been a major determinant, along with the idea that the language of instruction had to be immediately understood in order for students to absorb the curriculum, even if that meant switching from one language to the other within a lesson.

Otheguy was clear and relentless in his efforts to move us beyond these limitations. After he got us to state without reservation that our goal was to produce truly bilingual children, we moved to the notion of separation of languages that included protection of the minority language. It is always easier, he pointed out, for a person to switch to the dominant language when given the choice, and there will be a certain period of struggling to understand for many children. But if a bilingual outcome is the goal, a teacher must make a conscious effort to stay in the native language. Research indicating that children in bilingual classes that separated languages scored higher in both English and Spanish than children in bilingual classes that mixed languages was encouraging. We were further encouraged by the notion that English, as a majority language, is acquired naturally by children living in the United States. Spanish, on the other hand, has to be nurtured, developed, and protected.

## Implementation

Nevertheless, as we began the first year of implementation of the DL program in September

1984, fears remained that confusion would develop in children learning to read and that subject matter would be lost to those struggling to understand the language being used. As a result, there was frequent switching or concurrent mixing of languages at the beginning, as teachers acted on their fears rather than on theory. It took time before they were able to observe that the children adapted and did not share the same uncertainties. Reading and writing, in both languages, developed — albeit unevenly — as predicted and, toward the end of the first year in kindergarten, children understood everything the teacher was saying.

Struggling to understand the second language appears to be a transitional problem with virtually no casualties. Children entering the program in kindergarten or first grade may indeed be confused or bewildered for a time, but they are not without support from their parents, teachers, and classmates. All parents are forewarned to expect a difficult period and reassure their children, while teachers try to provide challenging curricular activities that provoke the need or desire to communicate This works well in our informal, activity centered classrooms, where children work cooperatively and the flow of language is continuous. Teachers skillfully exploit this social and cognitive setting by seeing that groups are as linguistically heterogeneous as possible. They also establish daily whole-class activities that are designed to build vocabulary and develop concepts. These activities include taking attendance, keeping the calendar, and discussing the weather and the daily schedules. Lunchtime is another rich source of language development and vocabulary building, in an informal, relaxed setting, with teachers eating with their classes in a family-style service.

Children themselves are extremely sensitive and develop great compassion for one another, since one group needs help on English days and another on Spanish days. Those who are or become bilingual often assume the role of translator, helping others even without being asked. In the immersion context, children also seem to be more attentive than we remember them being before the DL program began, searching for cues in the context of what is being talked about in the reactions of other children or in the speaker's body language. In the previous setting, where teachers often resorted to translations, children often tuned out the less familiar language and simply waited for explanations in their first language.

As time passes, so does any initial discomfort, and evidence of growth in different aspects of language development emerge. Communication, which at first relies heavily on nonverbal cues and the occasional help of self-appointed translators, is slowly replaced by mixtures of gesture, vocalizations, and a blend of Spanish and English words. In the early grades, children spontaneously use words or phrases in their second language, often without being aware of the language of the day. An English speaker's first Spanish word, for example, may be 'presente' on a day when the teacher calls the roll in English. In the middle grades, it is common to see a child who has just had a breakthrough in reading in his or her first language spurt ahead in second-language reading a week or two later. Older children have been writing plays and poetry in two languages with the help of a poet-consultant from the Teachers and Writers Collaborative; and comprehension, in reading as well as oral language, develops steadily at every grade level. As children use their second language more frequently, there seems to be less blending of the two, and accents seem to be universally quite authentic.

The question of whether or not children will become confused learning to read in two languages simultaneously is no longer even discussed. After five years of experience, it is taken for granted that learning to read is one process. Each class library has collections in both Spanish and English, and the teacher reads to the children every day. The children eagerly follow along, especially when big books are used.[3] The teacher also records experiences so that children can see their words being put into print. The children also write little books of their own, on letters of the alphabet, colors, collective stories, and so on. In the beginning, second-language reading lags behind, but that is expected and no pressure is applied to hasten the balance.

Development in writing takes a similar, uneven course. Though children write every day, their second-language output is quite meager at first. A single word or a picture might be all a child can do. But in time, pictures are labeled and words extended to phrases or sentences. Children are resourceful, once they are motivated, in finding the written words they need.

Just as it took time to overcome fears and doubts in language pedagogy, it also took time to work out problems of organization, personnel, and administration. During the first five years, we tried self-contained classes and team approaches, in which first teachers and then children alternated between rooms; and we tried different teams until we found the best combinations. Curriculum responsibilities needed to be clarified, as did methods of reporting to parents, assigning homework, and teacher–parent communications. Schedules were frequently changed — even schoolwide — to accommodate special activities, common preparation periods, or meetings.

Meetings between teachers are essential to the program's success just as they are to the successful functioning of the school. At PS 84, teachers talk informally over coffee in the mornings, during their preparation times, at lunch, or after school; and they come to formal meetings at any time, provided discussions have to do with children, curriculum, teaching practice, or important school issues. They do this, l believe, because they are treated like professionals, with certain decision-making powers, supported in their efforts to improve what they do, and because the quality of the meetings is generally intellectually stimulating.[4]

DL meetings are no exception. Discussions at these meetings have included theories of language acquisition, teaching methods and appropriate books, and observations of children and children's use of language in different settings. The teachers are always self-critical and willing to discuss what they are doing in light of their own school experiences, in which, in most cases, their mother tongue was not supported, and are able to use those reflections to gain insight into current practice. Frequently, meetings are held in Spanish, which teachers have come to enjoy since it adds to the status of the language in school. It adds, too, along with their teaching, to the improvement of their own command of Spanish.

Until June 1988, the person responsible for planning and organizing department meetings had been Ruth Swinney, our former program coordinator, who played a critical role in the program's growth and development. As a former teacher, she was able to provide close technical support in the classroom and, through her love of literature, help teachers develop class libraries of outstanding children's literature in Spanish, by Latin American and Spanish authors. Swinney also established annual, paid summer training institutes for DL teachers and was an important link between the school and the New York State Education Department, whose Bilingual Office, under the direction of Carmen Perez-Hogan, has provided

funding for the past three years. In September 1988, Swinney was appointed the district's director of DL programs, in which capacity she supervises DL programs starting up in other schools.

## Plans for the Future

Since its beginning in 1984, the DL program has grown, as of September 1989 from 7 classes to 11 of a total of 28 classes in the school, and the demand for seats far exceeds what is available. As a result of word of mouth and other publicity, we are inundated with requests for information and tours, especially from white middle-class parents who are attracted by the enrichment offered by such a program. We are, however, expanding very cautiously, trying to recruit and train teachers and trying to maintain a balanced population, by which we mean having at least half the children be from immigrant Hispanic families. We are also trying to maintain equal numbers of Spanish- and English-dominant speakers. It is interesting that in the middle and upper grades some of the monolingual teachers have expressed interest in teaming with bilingual colleagues, as another way of expanding the program. Collegial relationships already exist between the monolingual and bilingual teachers, as a result of working together on the same grades; and though all the DL teachers are currently bilingual, that is not a necessary condition since languages are separated in instruction.

Even as the demand for more classes from kindergarten through sixth grade has grown, so, too, has the demand for a continuation program into grades seven and eight. Parents want both advanced literacy in two languages and a continuation of the PS 84 school environment. With the help of the district program director, a DL middle school has been designed and approved by the Community School Board for opening in September 1990. The DL Academy, as it is referred to, will accept children from PS 84's program and eventually from other programs in the district.

The DL program continues to grow, albeit cautiously, looking forward to a middle-grade extension in 1990–91. Expansion will most likely include monolingual teachers in the near future and continued teacher training, incorporating teachers in other DL classes that are just starting up.

## Notes

1. William G. Blair (1989) New York Widens Bilingual Studies. *New York Times*, 15 Jan.
2. For a more detailed account see Sidney H. Morison (1974) Decentralization 5 Years On: A Principal's View. *Urban Review* 7 (1), 197–206, July.
3. Big books are approximately 14" x 18" versions of familiar children's stories. They encourage reading along and choral reading. Children find them extremely attractive and love to browse through them and read their normal-size counterparts.
4. Sidney H. Morison (1981) The school as an intellectual community, Pt. 1. *Principal* 60 (5), 37–38 (Jan. 1981). Ibid., pt. 2, 60 (5), 54–55 (May 1981).

## Questions

(1) Morison tells us that PS 84 has a 'Dual Language Program.' Describe the structure of this type of bilingual education at PS 84? Why and how does it reverse the view of bilingual education as 'remedial'? What is the place of a minority language (in this case Spanish) in the school? How does the structure of PS 84 differ from the 'two-way bilingual program' at Coral Way? (See Lyons, this volume, or Mackey and Beebe (1977), for more on Coral Way.)

(2) Morison talks of the New York State Board of Regents' action to raise the cutoff level on the Language Assessment Battery (LAB) by which children exit transitional bilingual classrooms. Based on reading Cummins, Skutnabb-Kangas and Corson (in this book), what is the theoretical basis for this decision? What type of transitional bilingual education program, as discussed in Corson, does the New York State Board of Regents attempt to support by raising the cutoff level? How is the program at PS 84 different?

(3) Explain, by means of a diagram, the difference in structure of the following at PS 84:
(a) early childhood classes (kindergarten, 1st, 2nd);
(b) middle grades (3rd, 4th);
(c) upper grades (5th, 6th).
What are the reasons for this structural difference?

(4) What does Morison mean when he says that 'Neither English nor Spanish is taught'? In this respect, how is the dual language program different from foreign language instruction for the majority and ESL teaching for the minority?

(5) The chapter by Skutnabb-Kangas mentioned (as one of the organizational factors responsible for success) that 'pupils should be equally placed with regards to their knowledge of the medium of instruction.' How does this relate to PS 84? On what grounds have dual language programs argued their viability regarding this factor? What do you think?
Describe a two-way program organized in such a way that the organizational factor above is taken into account, at least in the beginning. (You may want to refer to Baetens Beardsmore, this volume, to expand on this, or refer again to the Coral Way School.)

(6) Describe the practices of teaching to read and write in two languages at PS 84. How do these practices differ from those used to teach literacy in a school with which you are familiar?

(7) Morison says that white middle-class parents are interested in registering their children in dual language programs. What does this say about interest in Spanish–English bilingualism in the United States among non-Latinos? Do you agree or disagree and why?

## Activities

(1) Share with a principal in a school with which you are familiar some of Morison's quotes regarding the education of Latino children. Find out how the principal differs from Morison with regards to bilingualism in education. Tape and transcribe the interview.

(2) Compare the structure of PS 84 to that of a school with which you are familiar that has a large number of language minority students. What are the differences in support toward the minority language(s), curriculum, teacher attitudes and parental involvement?

(3) Interview five monolingual majority language parents in your community. Find out their interest in bilingualism for their children. In particular, ask them which non-English language would they want their children to learn and why? Then ask them about their support for:

   (a) Schools that would develop their children's bilingualism.

   (b) Schools that would maintain the mother tongue of language minority students and develop their bilingualism.

   Record their answers on an answer sheet. Then write an essay integrating your findings.

   Groups might interview parents with different characteristics; for example, white vs. non-white, professionals versus non-professionals, older vs. younger, mothers vs. fathers. Share the findings with each other, compare and discuss similarities and differences.

(6) Select one of the case studies of structuring schools given below as Further Reading. After reading that account, write an essay comparing the structure of that school with PS 84.


## Further Reading

For early interesting accounts of the structure of different kinds of bilingual programs, see:

Cohen, Andrew D. (1975) *A Sociolinguistic Approach to Bilingual Education.* Rowley, MA: Newbury House.

Lambert, Wallace and Tucker, Gary (1972) *Bilingual Education of Children: The St Lambert Experiment.* Rowley, MA: Newbury House.

Mackey, William F. (1972) *Bilingual Education in a Binational School.* Rowley, MA: Newbury House.

Mackey, William F. and Beebe, Von Nieda (1977) *Bilingual Schools for a Bicultural Community: Miami's Adaptation to the Cuban Refugees.* Rowley, MA: Newbury House.

For more recent accounts of structuring bilingual schools, see especially,

Byram, Michael (1986) *Minority Education and Ethnic Survival: Case Study of a German School in Denmark.* Clevedon: Multilingual Matters.

Hornberger, Nancy (1988) *Bilingual Education and Language Maintenance: A Southern Peruvian Quechua Case.* Dordrecht, Holland: Foris Publications.

Holm, Agnes and Holm, Wayne (1990) Rock Point, a Navajo way to go to school: A valediction. *Annals of the American Academy of Political and Social Science* 508, 170–84.

Pung Guthrie, Grace (1985) *A School Divided: An Ethnography of Bilingual Education in a Chinese Community.* Hillsdale: Lawrence Earlbaum Associates.

For more on two-way dual language programs or what also has recently been called two-way bilingual/immersion, see especially:

Lindholm, Kathryn, J. (1992) Two-way bilingual/immersion education: Theory, conceptual issues, and pedagogical implications. In R. V. Padilla and A. Benavides (eds) *Critical Perspectives on Bilingual Education Research.* Tucson, AZ: Bilingual Review Press.

# The Bilingual Education of Cuban-American Children in Dade County's Ethnic Schools

## Ofelia García and Ricardo Otheguy

### Introduction

Children who speak languages other than English in the United States come mostly from working-class homes or from the homes of the poor, and they almost always attend public schools. It is therefore in public schools where one usually finds programmes addressing the educational needs of these children, and also in public schools where one finds most discussion of the precise forms those programmes should take. The most salient characteristic of these public school programmes is, of course, the use of the child's home language. Consequently, the most intense aspect of the discussion centres on the manner and the extent of use to which this language should be put.

A much less familiar context for discussion of the role of languages other than English is the private school. In the United States, private schools that make extensive use of another language are frequently high-tuition, elite schools for children who may speak languages other than English but who usually are not either working class or poor. New York's Lycée Français, which makes extensive use of French, and Miami's Loyola School, which makes extensive use of Spanish, are examples that come readily to mind.

But private, low-tuition schools for the children of working-class linguistic minorities do exist in the United States (Fishman, 1980a, b, 1982, 1985; García, 1987). The approach these schools take to the use of languages other than English is very different from that of public schools or of elite private schools. It is an approach that holds important lessons for anyone interested in language learning, or in the education of American language-minority children in any setting.

This paper presents the results of an ethnographic study of such private but low-tuition, non-elite schools in Dade County, Florida.[1] (Dade County comprises the adjoining cities of Miami and Hialeah, as well as surrounding areas, all of which contain large Hispanic populations, mostly from Cuba or of Cuban background, but from other parts of the Spanish-speaking world too.) These schools make extensive use of Spanish and are run mostly by and for Cubans.

We report on the basis of field-work conducted in seven ethnic schools.[2] Our methodology was not defined a priori. We knew that these schools would be suspicious of North American researchers, but we were confident that our Cuban identity and our knowledge of the Spanish language would gain us access to the schools. We initially contacted administrators of all the Cuban non-elite schools in Dade County. The administrators of ten schools granted us intensive interviews. In seven of the ten schools we were most welcomed. In these we were able to extend our study to include intensive interviews with teachers and shorter, informal interviews with other staff, parents and children. We were also invited to observe classrooms, lunchrooms, playgrounds and administrative offices. Our observations included not only structured classroom situations, but also recess, lunch and dismissal. In order to supplement the information given to us by administrators and teachers, school documents were also studied.

The schools in our study are attended in a very few cases by the children of the Cuban poor of Dade County, but mostly by the children of Cuban factory workers, office clerks, store salesmen, warehouse employees, hospital workers, banktellers, small shopkeepers, mechanics, construction workers, secretaries, and bus drivers, with only a handful of children of doctors, lawyers, and other professionals — in short, Hispanic children from the same socio-economic background as those who attend public schools in Dade County itself or in other urban centres throughout the United States. Dade County also has two high-tuition, elite private schools that make extensive use of Spanish and are attended by the children of the Cuban and other Hispanic professional and upper-middle-classes and the wealthy, but they are not the subject of this study. For the convenience of the reader, we will distinguish between these two types of schools by reserving the term 'ethnic schools' for the low-tuition, non-elite schools of our study.

In approaching these ethnic schools it is useful to keep in mind the questions that guide discussion of the education of language-minority children from these same socio-economic backgrounds in public schools. These questions frame the discourse of bilingual education policy in the United States and provide the intellectual baseline from which we started our study, although, significantly, not that at which we ended it. The questions are the same for all linguistic minorities, but since our study is about Hispanics we will refer them only to this group. They are the following:

- Should schools maintain and develop Spanish? Should all Hispanic children receive instruction in two languages or should Spanish be used only with those not proficient in English?
- How does one determine language dominance and is there a difference in the curriculum for Spanish dominant children and English dominant children?
- How much instruction in English as a second language should children receive and when should it stop?
- Which language should initial reading be in? When should reading in the second language start?

The first of these questions has been argued vehemently by educators, sociologists and politicians (For an analysis of the public debate in the US press, see Cummins, 1982). The US federal government only supports temporary programmes of bilingual instruction for children who do not speak English. In fact, recent federal guidelines state that bilingual education programmes that 'mainstream' children into English-only classes 'as quickly as possible' are more likely than others to receive federal funding

(Crawford, 1986). Some critics oppose the 'maintenance approach' in bilingual education on the grounds that it leads to social and political divisiveness (Glazer, 1981). Others argue that 'maintenance programmes' hinder the development of English (Rodriguez, 1982). Yet, many educators and researchers claim that language minority children would benefit from an education that develops their native languages even after they have acquired English (Cummins, 1979; Fishman, 1976; MacDonald *et al.*, 1982; Otheguy, 1982). The language minority community, specifically the Hispanic community, has also vehemently supported programmes of instruction in which Spanish is developed (Attinasi, 1979, 1985; Cole, 1983).

Likewise, determining the language dominance of children has been a very important question in bilingual programmes in public schools. Educational officials worry about the right test to determine which is a bilingual Hispanic child's primary language, since only Spanish dominant children participate in bilingual programmes. Whereas Lado (1961) favours discreet point testing, Brière (1972) and Oller (1979) prefer general communication tests. Recently, more ethnographic approaches to testing language dominance have become popular (Bennett & Slaughter, 1983; Philips, 1983; Saville-Troike, 1983).

In keeping with the spirit of these temporary and transitional bilingual programmes, the public school approach to teaching English as a Second Language is also most often compensatory and remedial. Although most bilingual programmes in the United States include pull-out ESL classes, researchers argue for more integrated English language instruction (Krashen, 1981; Terrell, 1981). Moreover, English instruction in these programmes often ends quickly and abruptly as children are 'mainstreamed'. Yet Cummins (1981) has argued that it takes children five to seven years to develop appropriate decontextualised language skills in a second language.

Finally, in most transitional bilingual programmes in the United States initial reading is taught in the native language. This view follows the UNESCO principle (1953) and is supported by Modiano (1973) and Rosier (1977), among others. Recently, however, many educators have argued that first-language and second-language reading can be developed simultaneously (Barrera, 1983; Goodman, Goodman & Flores, 1979).

A most important characteristic of the ethnic

schools we studied is their widespread reputation as successful schools where Cuban-American children do well academically, while at the same time becoming fully bilingual and biliterate. This reputation is all the more remarkable when compared with the reputation of public schools attended by the same type of children. (With some justification, though with a fair measure of exaggeration too, most public schools in the United States are held to provide Hispanic and other language-minority children with little opportunity for academic success.) We found no standardised test scores to document the greater success of the ethnic schools, as none were available. Yet, administrators teachers, parents, and the surrounding Cuban-American community all agreed that Cuban-American children did better academically, and that they learned better Spanish, better manners, and better values in these than in the public schools.

Typical comments we recorded were the following. 'La preparación que da X es muy superior a la de la escuela pública, ya que es enseñanza tipo Cuba' ('X school prepares children far better than the public school since it is a Cuban type of education'), said one mother we interviewed. 'Aquí nuestros niños progresan porque es como si estuvieran en un sistema educativo latinoamericano' ('Here, our children make it because it is just as if they were in a Latin American educational system'), told us another mother.

There was widespread conviction that the curricula in these ethnic schools was more academically rigorous than that of the public school. Our informants also unanimously claimed that the public schools did not enforce discipline standards. 'En las escuelas públicas los niños no están fiscalizados. Aquí sí.' ('In public schools children are not supervised. But here, yes'), told us an administrator using the Spanish 'fiscalizados' for the more common US Spanish 'supervisados'. Concerning the teaching of Spanish, one principal shared with us: 'No hay comparación. Aquí se enseña español de verdad. En la escuela pública nada mas que se enseña a leer palabras, mientras que aquí se les enseña a los niños la gramática y las conjugaciones' ('There is no comparison. Here we teach real Spanish. In public schools they teach you only to read words, whereas here we teach children grammar and conjugations'). The sense that the education, both in English and Spanish, that these schools provide is superior to that of public schools was

gathered from all the interviews with administrators, teachers, and parents.

Although Cuban-American children fare better in Dade County's public schools than other Hispanics in public schools in the United States, they do indeed experience greater failure than Anglo students. This is often the result of the impatience of the educational system with their English language development. For example, after the 1980 Mariel influx of Cubans into Dade schools, the percentage of Hispanic students not promoted significantly exceeded the statistically probable failure rate (Bilingual/Foreign Language Education, p. 5). In contrast to the public schools, the ethnic schools never confuse children's academic ability with linguistic proficiency. Often children who speak English poorly are the best students. Cuban parents intuitively know that their children will be given a better chance in these schools, at the same time that they will be provided with strict discipline and academic rigour.

Public schools are also regarded (and here with no exaggeration) as operating in most cases within a widely publicised and well developed plan to insure that language-minority children do not become biliterate, or even bilingual (Fishman, 1980a; Gaarder, 1977; Otheguy & Otto, 1980; Otheguy, 1982). This amounts to recognising that, with some exceptions, in most public school settings the four questions outlined above receive a straightforward answer by those in actual authority, such as principals and programme supervisors. They are debated only by people outside the public schools, and by people in public schools who hold less authority and control, such as classroom teachers.

Actual practice in public schools results from the resolution of tensions between groups with competing answers to these four questions, yielding considerable variation from school to school. Still, it is an accurate generalisation that most public school bilingual programmes in the United States are fiercely transitional, having as their only goal the quick mainstreaming of children into regular, English-monolingual classes. Use of Spanish or other minority languages in most public school bilingual programmes is only for children who speak no English, and only for as long as this condition lasts. Rarely are Hispanics who speak English included. Most of these programmes aim to produce English-monolingual children and use the native language only as a temporary expedient until it can be set aside and forgotten by children who, in the best of cases, learn to read and write only in English.

Since these public school bilingual programmes for Hispanic children are often staffed by Hispanics, the approaches just described and the contrast we are about to establish with the approach taken in the ethnic schools of Dade County cannot be solely attributed to differences in the ethnic backgrounds of the educators involved. It is true that many Hispanics in public schools are considerably more interested in developing Spanish than are the authorities, but even among Hispanics educators in public schools one finds beliefs and practices that fit the description we have sketched.

As we shall see, our description of public schools could not be applied to the ethnic schools of Dade County. In taking a totally different tack with children of the same background, these ethnic schools give us a useful context in which to ponder questions of educational language policy.

## The Schools

Although we observed much variation among the different ethnic schools with regard to teaching style and curricular practices, the socio-educational climate was remarkably similar from school to school. There are three factors that characterise the seven schools we studied: (a) their working class nature; (b) the Cuban character of the staff, the children and the ambiance; and (c) the presence of Spanish as the social, though not necessarily the instructional, language of the schools.

### Working class schools

These are schools with modest tuition fees ranging from $60 to $90 a month for ten months. (As a basis of comparison for readers for whom these figures may not be meaningful, this is identical to the range of tuition charged by the other large non-public but also non-elite school system in the United States, namely the Roman Catholic parochial school system.) All ten schools were located either in the Little Havana section of Miami, or in Hialeah, both predominantly Cuban working-class neighbourhoods. The schools opened as early as 6:30 a.m. and closed as late as 6:00 p.m. The optional extended school hours are meant to attract, and indeed do attract, many children of working mothers.

### Cuban schools

The ethnic character of these schools was also without question. The principals, the teachers, the students, and the socio-cultural ambiance of the schools were strikingly Cuban. The principals and the owners were all Cuban born. With one exception, none of the principals had ever had any experience in US public schools. They had been owners or teachers of a school in Cuba, usually one that had the same name as the one now in Dade County. Twenty-five years ago, the schools in Cuba also served mostly the children of working class families (in some cases the parents of current students!) and was located far from the affluent neighbourhoods, in most cases in the provinces and not in Havana.

In contrast to the two elite Hispanic schools of Dade County that we are familiar with (Belén Jesuit School and Loyola School, only the first of which is a Roman Catholic school, despite the names), these working class Cuban schools are staffed mostly by Cuban teachers who in most cases were born, raised and educated in pre-Castro Cuba. Most of these teachers we met were highly professional and skilled in their academic areas, although they spoke accented English. There was also a small, but growing number of younger Cuban-American teachers, raised and educated in Dade County. There were very few native-born American Anglophone teachers, and they were usually the instructors of non-academic subjects such as Gym, Music and Art. We found that even these few Anglo teachers were deeply familiar with Cuban culture and values, and had some knowledge of Spanish.

Again in contrast to the elite Belén and Loyola (whose student body includes many Hispanics from other than Cuban background, and Anglo Americans), the students in these schools were mostly Cuban-American children. All of the ten schools reported that between 80 and 90 % of their children were of Cuban parents, with a small number of other Hispanic children and an even smaller number of Anglophone (usually Black) children. The Cuban-American children came to school speaking Spanish only. We observed that the younger children spoke Spanish exclusively to each other in hallways and playgrounds. But beginning with third-graders we observed English as the language of socialisation both in the classroom and in the playground.

The sociocultural ambiance of the schools was most strikingly Cuban. Cuban flags, emblems, and busts of Jose Martí, the famous Cuban patriot and writer, were proudly portrayed in the schools. The Cuban national anthem was sung, along with the Star-Spangled Banner, in every school assembly. Although eight of these 10 schools claimed to be non-denominational, voluntary Roman Catholic religious instruction was offered, including a voluntary, but in fact school-wide, First Holy Communion programme in the month of May for first-graders, all in line with traditional Cuban religious customs.

It is also clear that the schools go to great lengths to conform to the sociopolitical values of the exiled Cuban community. Cuba in these schools does not mean today's Cuba but 'la Cuba de ayer,' and signs of a pre-Castro Cuba, now outdated by about a quarter century, are prevalent everywhere. An aged and yellowed photograph of the school that bore the same name back in Cuba usually hangs in the school's entrance. Cuban History and Geography are taught from a pre-Castro perspective. The Cuban map found in many classrooms shows administrative divisions into Cuban provinces that ceased to exist 25 years ago. While one may question the pedagogical soundness of this anachronistic approach to the social studies, it is nevertheless striking the respect these schools have for the values of the community they serve, as well as the continuity they provide for the community's social and behavioural norms. The schools reinforce and continue the ways, styles, values, and mores that prevail in the homes of the barrios of Little Havana and Hialeah.

### Spanish in the schools

The transmission of Cuban traditions and values took place in Spanish, the language of power and prestige within these ethnic schools. It was clear to us from the very beginning that Spanish was the *social* language of the school. It belonged naturally there: it was the language of the janitor, the secretary, the teachers; it was the language in which children were spoken to by employees in the hallways and by the Principal in the office; it was clearly the language of authority.

Oddly enough, however, Spanish in these schools seems to be more absent from the curriculum than in public school bilingual programmes. In fact, we were told by all the administrators, except one, that *these are not bilingual schools!* Whereas bilingual programmes in public schools teach some subjects in Spanish, most subjects in these schools are taught in English by a Cuban teacher. Only Cuban History and Geography, and Roman Catholic religion, are taught in Spanish. Full literacy in English according to familiar

American standards is expected and, as we could see, obtained.

In this climate of instructional use of English by Cuban teachers, development of Spanish was nevertheless central. Spanish was taught, we were told, as a 'first language' by a specialised and different teacher. Everyone stressed that there was no such thing as Spanish as a second language. Literacy in Spanish according to monolingual Cuban standards was expected of all children, and indeed obtained. The texts used to develop Spanish literacy are most often those that were used in Cuba 25 years ago for Spanish monolingual children, and no concessions or adaptations are made to children who, after all, use English as their intragenerational language after the third grade.

It seems to us that the success of these ethnic schools in developing biliteracy stems from the more prestigious status accorded to Spanish in comparison to what happens in public schools. However, successful biliteracy is also a product of a compartmentalised curriculum that protects the minority language (Fishman, 1980a; García, 1983; Legarreta, 1979; Wong-Fillmore, 1982). These Cuban schools do not see Spanish in competition with English; in fact they are more likely to see English in competition with Spanish. Principals and teachers know that English, as the majority language, is acquired naturally by children living in the United States. It is Spanish, they believe, that has to be nurtured, developed, and protected.

### Our Findings

The most significant finding of our study is that the four questions outlined above as basic to the study of public bilingual education were completely useless and inapplicable to the ethnic schools we were investigating. The very heart of public bilingual education discourse made no sense to those to whom we spoke. Philosophical and curricular questions which provoke heated arguments in public bilingual education circles were non-questions in these ethnic community schools. We think that the irrelevance of these core bilingual education questions to these archetypical bilingual schools holds important lessons that are worth spelling out. (For a similar observation about a bilingual programme in a community-controlled public school, see Mac-Donald *et al.*, 1982: 220.)

As has been pointed out, most public schools offer bilingual instruction only until children are proficient in English. Then children are 'main-streamed' into 'regular monolingual' classrooms. Naturally then, there is considerable debate about when this exit decision should be made and on what basis to make it. The question of whether bilingual programmes should be transitional or should maintain the native language is also a natural one to debate in a public school setting where the transitional approach holds sway and proponents of maintenance are viewed with at best amused indulgence and at worst suspicion.

But these issues are not relevant at all to the people we interviewed. These community educators were only concerned about the best possible way of educating their own children. None of the ethnic schools focused solely on bilingualism or monolingualism as a goal. In fact, *there was remarkably little interest in language questions.* 'El melting pot es irrevocable' ('The melting pot is irrevocable') told us one administrator who became impatient with our questions dealing with the effects of non-English language maintenance on social cohesiveness. Yet, this same administrator felt that the only conceivable way of educating language minority children in a language majority environment was to use both languages. 'El español se enseña aquí como un first language' ('Spanish is taught as a first language'), he told us with the English code-switching that is characteristic of most United States Spanish. For these Cuban teachers this *was* mainstream education, and there was nothing remarkable or 'irregular' about it.

Bilingualism and biliteracy are important resources of the language minority community. 'El español sólo debe ser para el Latino' ('Spanish should be only for Latinos') claimed one teacher who considered bilingualism to be the Cuban's biggest asset. Thus it is with a naturalness that, if anything, is disturbed only by fierce ethnic pride that literacy in the minority language is expected, just as proficiency in, say, Mathematics is expected.

The curricular questions that take up so much of our time in public bilingual education were likewise dismissed. Most Hispanic children in public bilingual education programmes have been classified as 'Spanish Dominant' or 'Limited English Proficient' (LEP). Such children are perceived by public school educators to be deficient and in need of remediation. In the transitional bilingual classrooms of most public schools, in fact, the native language is used mostly to teach English. In addition, these LEP children receive supplementary English-as-a-Second-Language (ESL) instruction in pull-out programmes.

The concept of whether children were Spanish or English dominant did not prove to be useful in our discussions in Dade County. None of the professionals that we interviewed made any use of that categorisation of children, and in many cases had not even heard of it. Even after we explained to them the concept of language dominance and its importance in public bilingual education, they still dismissed it. They were only able to report that children entering first grade usually spoke only Spanish and that three or four years later they were completely bilingual. When pressed to tell us whether those bilingual children were Spanish-dominant or English-dominant, they unanimously repeated the answer that the first administrator had given us: 'Pues, hablan los dos idiomas' ('Well, they speak both languages').

Although all teachers and administrators we interviewed were unable to answer our question on dominance directly, they frequently referred to the children's language use. One teacher told us: 'Ellos hablan español pero se pelean en inglés' ('They speak in Spanish but they fight in English'). A Spanish monolingual secretary told us: 'Ellos hablan español con nosotros y hablan inglés cuando no quieren que los mayores entiendan. Entre ellos a veces mezclan' ('They speak Spanish with us and English when they don't want the adults to understand. They sometimes switch languages when speaking to each other'). In schools where Spanish literacy is taught and expected, educators seem to have a more natural attitude toward children's use of two languages. The teachers expect them to speak, read and write Spanish well. They do not expect them, however, to use Spanish as if they lived in a monolingual context where only one language was available to them.

The concept of language dominance is not useful in these schools because no curricular decisions are based on it. There is no remediation or special programme when children arrive not speaking the majority language. This condition is regarded as normal and known to change naturally in the course of the next four years. Bilingualism and biliteracy are expected of all. Furthermore, both the minority and the majority language are equally valued. This stands in sharp contrast to most public bilingual school programmes where Spanish-dominant tends to be synonymous with inferior, whereas English dominant means superior. Bilingualism and biliteracy is again the ideal expectation of all students in these ethnic schools.

The role of the ESL specialist is also controversial in public bilingual education circles. As we have mentioned, most public school bilingual programmes have an ESL pull-out class for children who have just arrived in the United States. English classes fall under the rubric of remediation for students who are behind in certain areas, in this case in the area of English proficiency. We wanted to know what special remedial classes existed in the Dade County ethnic schools for those children that are Spanish monolingual (a group comprised of all their five-year-olds, and, to different degrees, of most of their six- and seven-year-olds). It soon became obvious to us that these ethnic educators' philosophy about language made these remedial classes irrelevant.

In sharp contrast to most public school authorities, these educators were not suspicious about the use of Spanish in the classroom. Furthermore, they did not doubt that children living in the United States would learn English, the majority language. They took a relaxed, natural approach to teach and develop the English language. They focused not on the structure of English, as most traditional ESL classes at the elementary level do, but instead used English as an instrument of communication. For this reason, English was used to teach most content. At the same time, the bilingualism of the teacher and the children was used as an instructional resource. Spanish was often used to help a child gather meaning from something said in English that he didn't understand. English was developed precisely by using Spanish as a meaning-giving resource

We observed the same disregard for curricular issues that are central to public bilingual education on the question of the language of initial reading. Most public bilingual programmes introduce reading in the child's native language (Goodman, Goodman & Flores, 1979), as the rather dubious proposition is accepted as dogma that the child cannot be taught to read in a language that he 'does not understand', nor can be taught to read in two languages simultaneously. Therefore initial reading instruction for Hispanics in public school bilingual programmes must be in Spanish. However, in most of these programmes the native language is used, even at these early stages, only as a tool to teach English and only as an insignificant and soon to be discarded stopping point on the way to the real prize, which is reading in English. Hispanic children rarely become literate in Spanish in

public schools, and seldom read much of anything in Spanish after the early grades (Barrera, 1983).

In the ethnic schools we studied in Dade County, monolingual Spanish speaking children in the first grade were most often taught to read in both languages at the same time. Reading was seen as *one* process of learning to gather meaning from print, a notion, by the way, that is as familiar to researchers on bilingualism as it is foreign to public school bilingual programmes. This practice — born of the natural and common sense approach taken, not from familiarity with the conceptualisation of bilingual reading that would support it — is possible only because of the sustained, unsuspicious and resourceful use of Spanish on the part of the teacher in order to give meaning to the students' reading. English literacy is, as is English language proficiency, a result of the creative and effective use of Spanish in the classroom. Spanish literacy is also expected and developed in its own right.

## Ethnic Schools for Language Minority Children

As we thought about why our four initial questions for this study had failed, we realised that we too had framed our original conception of the education of Hispanic children in the United States within what one might call the majority context, that is, the intellectual and pedagogical context within which most US-born, white, English-speaking educators frame their thinking about the education of linguistic minorities.

When majority educators look at the education of Hispanic children in the United States, they focus on their linguistic deficits. The fact that some Hispanic children don't speak English tends to obscure all other educational matters. Discussions about the education of these children begin and end with the issue of the English language, of how they lack it, and how best to give it to them. Making these children proficient in English is often presented as the most important question faced by the public schools they attend; sadly, it is often the only educational question regarding these children that these schools tend to face, and one for which they provide in most cases a patently unsatisfactory answer.

However, when Hispanic parents and educators in control of the education of their own children think about the educational process, they ask different kinds of questions. They ask questions about the best way to educate their children, about pedagogy, instructional strategies and teaching methods, about curriculum and materials. We asked them about language, they told us about education. They were interested in telling us about their use of a given textbook or of a given method in Math and Reading instruction. Some shared with us their new Science or Social Studies curricula. Administrators pulled out charts of school organisation, and teachers showed us lesson plans and units. Hispanic educators question the educational process itself, and not the role of the minority language or the minority child in the majority school. Spanish naturally belongs in ethnic schools that are controlled, staffed and run by the Hispanic community, so there is no need to question its role in the educational process. The Hispanic children attending these schools are not in any way unusual. They do not walk into the school to discover that they already need remediation. They are not inferior to majority children or deficient. They are not even different from other children in the school or from the educators. They *are* the children. They most often match the look, speech, behaviour, and values of the educators and the authorities of the school.

The ethnic schools of Dade County should force us to take a new look at bilingual education programmes in public schools, which we continue to be committed to developing and strengthening. But there is a need to look at the education of Hispanic children in public school bilingual programmes from the perspective gained by studying schools where the community itself is in control of the education of their own children.

Those of us in the public schools need to learn from these educators that substantive high expec-

tations do matter; that bilingualism and biliteracy are obtainable if one holds both children and teachers unequivocally responsible for obtaining it; that initial literacy in two languages is possible and doesn't have to be limited to Spanish; that advanced literacy in two languages is possible and doesn't have to be limited to English; that in US society all children acquire English naturally and that therefore English acquisition should not be the main focus of education; that parents and community do matter for education; that when they are in control, even if some of their ideas may at times be foolish or unsophisticated, the results are ultimately superior; that the context of a child's home culture is essential, even if it should occasionally seem silly or anachronistic; and that continuity with the intellectual and social climate of the home is of paramount importance if the school is to help children develop and foster their intellectual and social growth.

## Notes

1. A much shorter version of this paper was read before the 14th Annual Meeting of the North Dakota Study Group on Evaluation, sponsored by the Johnson Foundation at the Foundation's Wingspread house in Racine, Wisconsin. A much larger study on Dade County, encompassing both private and public schools as well as a detailed discussion of sociocultural factors that affect the education of Hispanics is available in García & Otheguy (1986).

2. Our sample included the following schools: Edison, Inter-American, Jose Martí, Lavernia, La Luz, Pan American, and La Progresiva. We gratefully acknowledge the assistance of those in these schools who gave us so much of their time.

## References

Attinasi, J. (1979) Language attitudes in a New York Puerto Rican Community. In R. Padilla (ed.) *Bilingual Education and Public Policy in the United States*. Ypsilanti, MI: Eastern Michigan University.

— (1985) Hispanics attitudes in Northwest Indiana and New York. In L. Elías-Olivares (ed.) *Spanish Language Use and Public Life in the United States*. New York: Walter de Gruyter & Co.

Barrera, R. B. (1983) Bilingual reading in the primary grades: Some questions about questionable views and practices. In T. Escobedo (ed.) *Early Childhood Bilingual Education: A*

*Hispanic Perspective*. New York: Teachers College Press.

Bennett, Adrian and Slaughter, Helen (1983) A sociolinguistic discourse approach to the description of the communicative competence of linguistic minority children. In Charlene Rivera (ed.) *An Ethnographic/Sociolinguistic Approach to Language Proficiency Assessment*. Clevedon: Multilingual Matters.

*Bilingual. Foreign Language Education. July 1982 Status Report*. Bureau of Education, Dade County.

Brière E. J. (1972) Are we really measuring proficiency with our foreign language tests? In B. Spolsky (ed.) *The Language Education of Minority Children*. Rowley, MA: Newbury House.

Cole, S. (1983) Attitudes towards bilingual education among Hispanics and a nationwide sample. Center for the Social Sciences at Columbia University, Preprint Series.

Crawford, J. (1986) Mainstreaming is factor in bilingual grant awards official says. *Education Week*.

Cummins, J. (1979) Linguistic interdependence and the educational development of bilingual children. *Review of Educational Research* 49, 222–51.

— (1981) The role of primary language development in promoting educational success for language minority students. In *Schooling and Language Minority Students: A Theoretical Framework*. Los Angeles: Evaluation, Dissemination and Assessment Center.

— (1982) *War of Words: Bilingual Education and the Search for American Identity* (Report to the Ford Foundation). Toronto: Ontario Institute for Studies in Education.

Fishman, J. A. (1976) *Bilingual Education. An International Sociological Perspective*. Rowley, MA: Newbury House.

— (1980a) Minority language maintenance and the ethnic mother tongue school. *Modern Language Journal* 64, 167–73.

— (1980b) Ethnocultural dimensionals in the acquisition and retention of biliteracy. *Basic Writing* 3 (1), 48–60.

— (1982) Language-related ethnic community schools in the USA: A catalog of school-in-society language resources. In *Non-English Language Resources of the United States* (A Preliminary Return Visit). Final Report to NIE.

— (1985) *The Rise and Fall of the Ethnic Revival in the United States*. The Hague: Mouton.

Gaarder, B.A. (1977) *Bilingual Schooling and the Survival of Spanish in the United States*. Rowley, MA: Newbury House.

García, Ofelia (1983) Sociolinguistics and language planning in bilingual education for Hispanics in the United States. *International Journal of the Sociology of Language* 44, 43–54.

— (1987) The education of biliterate and bicultural children in ethnic schools in the United States. In *The Spencer Fellows Series*. The National Academy of Education.

García, Ofelia and Otheguy, Ricardo (1986) The masters of survival send their children to school. *Bilingual Review/Revista Bilingue* No. 1 (January–April).

Glazer, N. (1981) Pluralism and ethnicity. In M. Ridge (ed.) *The New Bilingualism. An American Dilemma*. Los Angeles: The University of Southern California Press.

Goodman, K., Goodman, Y. and Flores, B. (1979) *Reading in the Bilingual Classroorm: Literacy and Biliteracy*. Rosslyn, VA: National Clearinghouse for Bilingual Education.

Krashen, S. (1981) *Second Language Acquisition and Second Language Learning*. London: Pergamon.

Lado, R. (1961) *Language Testing*. London: Longmans, Green.

Legarreta, D. (1979) The effects of program models on language acquisition by Spanish speaking children. *TESOL Quarterly* 13, 521–34.

MacDonald, B., Adelman, C., Kushner, S. and Walker, R. (1982) *Bread and Dreams. A Case Study of Bilingual Schooling in the USA*. University of East Anglia, Norwich, UK: Centre for Applied Research in Education (CARE).

Modiano, N. (1973) *Indian Education in the Chiapas Highlands*. New York: Holt, Rinehart and Winston.

Oller, J. W., Jr. (1979) *Language Tests at School*. London: Longman.

Otheguy, R. (1982) Thinking about bilingual education: A critical appraisal. *Harvard Educational Review* 52, 301–14.

Otheguy, R. and Otto, R. (1980) The myth of static maintenance in bilingual education. *Modern Language Journal* 64, 350–57.

Philips, S.U. (1983) An ethnographic approach to bilingual language proficiency assessment. In C. Rivera (ed.) *An Ethnographic/Sociolinguistic Approach to Language Proficiency Assessment*. Clevedon: Multilingual Matters.

Rodriguez, R. (1982) *Hunger of Memory: The Education of Richard Rodriguez*. Boston: David R. Godine

Rosier, P. (1977) A comparative study of two approaches of introducing initial reading to Navajo children: The direct method and the native language method. Unpublished PhD Dissertation, Northern Arizona University, Flagstaff.

Saville-Troike, M. (1983) An anthropological linguistic perspective on uses of ethnography in bilingual language proficiency assessment. In C. Rivera (ed.) *An Ethnographic/Sociolinguistic Approach to Language Proficiency Assessment*. Clevedon: Multilingual Matters.

Terrell, T. (1981) The natural approach in bilingual education. In California State Department of Education, *Schooling and Language Minority Students: A Rheoretical Framework*. Los Angeles:

Evaluation, Dissemination and Assessment Center.

UNESCO (1953) The use of vernacular languages in education. *Monographs on Fundamental Education* No. 8. Paris: UNESCO.

Wong-Fillmore, L. (1982) Instructional language as linguistic input: Second language learning in classrooms. In L. C. Wilkinson (ed.) *Communicating in the Classroom*. New York: Academic Press.

## Questions

(1) Explain why each of the four initial research questions were not relevant in the ethnic schools in this study. What is the lesson learned? What is the difference in the approach taken in the education of Latino children in public schools and their education in ethnic schools?

(2) Give examples of how (a) Cuban culture (as it exists in the United States) and (b) the Spanish language is present in the Cuban schools visited.

## Activities

(1) Visit an all-day school or supplementary school in which an ethnic language is taught and which is controlled by the ethnic community. Then visit a public school in which the same ethnic language is taught. Report on the differences found in school structure, teaching approach, use of the ethnic language, administrators, educators, students and community.

(2) Select a specific ethnolinguistic group. Through interviews with ethnic leaders and others, make a Resource List of places that teach the language. Telephone or visit these places and obtain information on when classes meet, age group, admission requirements, tuition, etc. Complete the resource list with this information. Create an overall copy of the resource list by pooling findings from the class. Make copies and disseminate the overall resource lists drawn up for different ethnolinguistic groups by your classmates.

(3) In a school with which you are familiar, interview the principal and at least five teachers with the four questions posed by García and Otheguy. Record their answers. Then write an essay explaining how their answers differ from the ones given to García and Otheguy, and the reasons for the differences.

## Further Reading

For more on the role of the ethnic mother tongue school in the United States, see especially:

Fishman, Joshua A. (1980) Minority language maintenance and the ethnic mother tongue school. *Modern Language Journal* 64, 167–73.

# Empowering Minority Students: A Framework for Intervention

## Jim Cummins

During the past twenty years educators in the United States have implemented a series of costly reforms aimed at reversing the pattern of school failure among minority students. These have included compensatory programs at the pre-school level, myriad forms of bilingual education programs, the hiring of additional aides and remedial personnel, and the institution of safeguards against discriminatory assessment procedures. Yet the dropout rate among Mexican-American and mainland Puerto Rican students remains between 40 and 50 percent compared to 14 percent for whites and 25 percent for blacks (Jusenius & Duarte, 1982). Similarly, almost a decade after the passage of the nondiscriminatory assessment provision of PL94-142[1] we find Hispanic students in Texas over-represented by a factor of 300 percent in the 'learning disabilities' category (Ortiz & Yates, 1983).

I have suggested that a major reason previous attempts at educational reform have been unsuccessful is that the relationships between teachers and students and between schools and communities have remained essentially unchanged. The required changes involve *personal redefinitions* of the way classroom teachers interact with the children and communities they serve. In other words, legislative and policy reforms may be necessary conditions for effective change, but they are not sufficient. Implementation of change is dependent upon the extent to which educators, both collectively and individually, redefine their roles with respect to minority students and communities.

The purpose of this paper is to propose a theoretical framework for examining the types of personal and institutional redefinitions that are required to reverse the pattern of minority student failure. The framework is based on a series of hypotheses regarding the nature of minority students' educational difficulties. These hypotheses, in turn, lead to predictions regarding the probable effectiveness, or ineffectiveness, of various interventions directed at reversing minority students' school failure.

The framework assigns a central role to three inclusive sets of interactions or power relations: (1) the classroom interactions between teachers and students, (2) relationships between schools and minority communities, and (3) the intergroup power relations within the society as a whole. It assumes that the social organization and bureaucratic constraints within the school reflect not only broader policy and societal factors but also the extent to which *individual educators* accept or challenge the social organization of the school in relation to minority students and communities. Thus, this analysis sketches directions for change for policy-makers at all levels of the educational hierarchy and, in particular, for those working directly with minority students and communities.

### The Policy Context

Research data from the United States, Canada, and Europe vary on the extent to which minority students experience academic failure (for reviews, see Cummins, 1984; Ogbu, 1978). For example, in the United States, Hispanic (with the exception of some groups of Cuban students), Native American, and black students do poorly in school compared to most groups of Asian-American (and white) students. In Canada, Franco-Ontarian students in English language programs have tended to perform considerably less well academically than immigrant minority groups (Cummins, 1984), while the same pattern characterizes Finnish students in Sweden (Skutnabb-Kangas, 1984).

The major task of theory and policy is to explain

the pattern of school success and failure among minority students. This task applies both to students whose home language and culture differ from those of the school and wider society (language minority students) and to students whose home language is a version of English but whose cultural background is significantly different from that of the school and wider society, such as many black and Hispanic students from English language backgrounds. With respect to language-minority students, recent policy changes in the United States have been based on the assumption that a major cause of students' educational difficulty is the switch between the language of the home and the language of the school. Thus, the apparently plausible assumption that students cannot learn in a language they do not understand gave rise in the late sixties and early seventies to bilingual education programs in which students' home language was used in addition to English as an initial medium of school instruction (Schneider, 1976).

Bilingual programs, however, have met with both strong support and vehement opposition. The debate regarding policy has revolved around two intuitively appealing assumptions. Those who favor bilingual education argue that children cannot learn in a language they do not understand, and, therefore, L1 (first language) instruction is necessary to counteract the negative effects of a home/school linguistic mismatch. The opposition contends that bilingual education is illogical in its implication that less English instruction will lead to more English achievement. It makes more sense, the opponents argue, to provide language-minority students with maximum exposure to English.

Despite the apparent plausibility of each assumption, these two conventional wisdoms (the 'linguistic mismatch' and 'insufficient exposure' hypotheses) are each patently inadequate. The argument that language minority students fail primarily as a result of a home/school language switch is refuted by the success of many minority students whose instruction has been totally through a second language. Similarly, research in Canada has documented the effectiveness of 'French immersion programs' in which English background (majority language) students are instructed largely through French in the early grades as a means of developing fluent bilingualism. In spite of the home/school language switch, students' first language (English) skills develop as well as those of students whose instruction has been totally through English. The fact that the first language has high status and is strongly reinforced in the wider society is usually seen as an important factor in the success of these immersion programs.[2]

The opposing 'insufficient exposure' hypothesis, however, fares no better with respect to the research evidence. In fact, the results of virtually every bilingual program that has been evaluated during the past fifty years show either no relationship or a negative relationship between amount of school exposure to the majority language and academic achievement in that language (Baker & de Kanter, 1981; Cummins, 1983a, 1984; Skutnabb-Kangas, 1984). Evaluations of immersion programs for majority students show that students perform as well in English academic skills as comparison groups despite considerably less exposure to English in school. Exactly the same result is obtained for minority students. Promotion of the minority language entails no loss in the development of English academic skills. In other words, language minority students instructed through the minority language (for example, Spanish) for all or part of the school day perform as well in English academic skills as comparable students instructed totally through English.

These results have been interpreted in terms of the 'interdependence hypothesis,' which proposes that to the extent that instruction through a minority language is effective in developing academic proficiency in the minority language, transfer of this proficiency to the majority language will occur given adequate exposure and motivation to learn the majority language (Cummins, 1979, 1983a, 1984). The interdependence hypothesis is supported by a large body of research from bilingual program evaluations, studies of language use in the home, immigrant student language learning, correlational studies of L1–L2 (second language) relationships, and experimental studies of bilingual information processing (for reviews, see Cummins, 1984; McLaughlin, 1985).

It is not surprising that the two conventional wisdoms inadequately account for the research data, since each involves only a one-dimensional linguistic explanation. The variability of minority students' academic performance under different social and educational conditions indicates that many complex, interrelated factors are at work (Ogbu, 1978; Wong-Fillmore, 1983). In particular, sociological and anthropological research suggests that status and power relations between groups are an important part of any comprehensive account of minority students' school failure (Fishman, 1976; Ogbu, 1978; Paulston, 1980). In addition, a variety of factors related to educational quality and cultural mismatch also appear to be important in mediating minority students' academic progress (Wong-Fillmore, 1983). These factors have been integrated into the design of a theoretical framework that suggests the changes required to reverse minority student failure.

## A Theoretical Framework

The central tenet of the framework is that students from 'dominated' societal groups are 'empowered' or 'disabled' as a direct result of their interactions with educators in the schools. These interactions are mediated by the implicit or explicit role definitions that educators assume in relation to four institutional characteristics of schools. These characteristics reflect the extent to which (1) minority students' language and culture are incorporated into the school program; (2) minority community participation is encouraged as an integral component of children's education; (3) the pedagogy promotes intrinsic motivation on the part of students to use language actively in order to generate their own knowledge; and (4) professionals involved in assessment become advocates for minority students rather than legitimizing the location of the 'problem' in the students. For each of these dimensions of school organization the role definitions of educators can be described in terms of a continuum, with one end promoting the empowerment of students and the other contributing to the disabling of students.

The three sets of relationships analyzed in the present framework—majority/minority societal group relations, school/minority community relations, educator/minority student relations — are chosen on the basis of hypotheses regarding the relative ineffectiveness of previous educational reforms and the directions required to reverse minority group school failure. Each of these relationships will be discussed in detail.

## Intergroup Power Relations

When the patterns of minority student school failure are examined from an international perspective, it becomes evident that power and status relations between minority and majority groups exert a major influence on school performance. An example frequently given is the academic failure of Finnish students in Sweden, where they are a low-status group, compared to their success in Australia, where they are regarded as a high-status group (Troike, 1978). Similarly, Ogbu (1978) reports that the outcast Burakumin perform poorly in Japan but as well as other Japanese students in the United States.

Theorists have explained these findings using several constructs. Cummins (1984), for example, discusses the 'bicultural ambivalence' (or lack of cultural identification) of students in relation to both the home and school cultures. Ogbu (1978) discusses the 'caste' status of minorities that fail academically and ascribes their failure to economic and social discrimination combined with the internalization of the inferior status attributed to them by the dominant group. Feuerstein (1979) attributes academic failure to the disruption of inter-generational transmission processes caused by the alienation of a group from its own culture. In all three conceptions, widespread school failure does not occur in minority groups that are positively oriented towards both their own and the dominant culture, that do not perceive themselves as inferior to the dominant group, and that are not alienated from their own cultural values.

Within the present framework, the *dominant* group controls the institutions and reward systems within society; the *dominated* group (Mullard, 1985) is regarded as inherently inferior by the dominant group and denied access to high-status positions within the institutional structure of the society. As described by Ogbu (1978), the dominated status of a minority group exposes them to conditions that predispose children to school failure even before they come to school. These conditions include limited parental access to economic and educational resources, ambivalence toward cultural transmission and primary language use in the home, and interactional styles that may not prepare students for typical teacher/student interaction patterns in school (Heath, 1983; Wong-Fillmore, 1983). Bicultural ambivalence and less effective cultural transmission among dominated groups are frequently associated with a historical pattern of colonization and subordination by the dominant group. This pattern, for example, characterizes Franco-Ontarian students in Canada, Finns in Sweden, and Hispanic, Native, and black groups in the United States.

Different patterns among other societal groups can clearly be distinguished (Ogbu & Matute-Bianchi, in press). Detailed analysis of patterns of intergroup relations go beyond the scope of this paper. However, it is important to note that the minority groups characterized by widespread school failure tend overwhelmingly to be in a dominated relationship to the majority group.[3]

### Empowerment of students

Students who are empowered by their school experiences develop the ability, confidence, and motivation to succeed academically. They participate competently in instruction as a result of having developed a confident cultural identity as well as appropriate school-based knowledge and interactional structures (Cummins, 1983b; Tikunoff, 1983). Students who are disempowered or 'disabled' by their school experiences do not develop this type of cognitive/academic and social/emotional foundation. Thus, student empowerment is regarded as both a mediating construct influencing academic performance and as an outcome variable itself.[4]

Although conceptually the cognitive/academic and social/emotional (identity related) factors are distinct, the data suggest that they are extremely difficult to separate in the case of minority students who are 'at risk' academically. For example, data from both Sweden and the United States suggest that minority students who immigrate relatively late (about ten years of age) often appear to have better academic prospects than students of similar socioeconomic status born in the host country (Cummins, 1984; Skutnabb-Kangas, 1984). Is this because their L1 cognitive/academic skills on arrival provide a better foundation for L2 cognitive/academic skills acquisition, or alternatively, because they have not experienced devaluation of their identity in the societal institutions, namely schools of the host country, as has been the case of students born in that setting?

Similarly, the most successful bilingual programs appear to be those that emphasize and use the students' L1 (for reviews, see Cummins, 1983a, 1984). Is this success due to better promotion of L1 cognitive/academic skills or to the reinforcement of cultural identity provided by an intensive L1 program? By the same token, is the failure of many minority students in English-only immersion programs a function of cognitive/academic difficulties or of students' ambivalence about the value of their cultural identity (Cohen & Swain, 1976)?

These questions are clearly difficult to answer; the point to be made, however, is that for minority students who have traditionally experienced school failure, there is sufficient overlap in the impact of cognitive/academic and identity factors to justify incorporating these two dimensions within the notion of 'student empowerment,' while recognizing that under some conditions each dimension may be affected in different ways.

### Schools and power

Minority students are disabled or disempowered by schools in very much the same way that their communities are disempowered by interactions with societal institutions. Since equality of opportunity is believed to be a given, it is assumed that individuals are responsible for their own failure and are, therefore, made to feel that they have failed because of their own inferiority, despite the best efforts of dominant-group institutions and individuals to help them (Skutnabb-Kangas, 1984). This analysis implies that minority students will succeed educationally to the extent that the patterns of interaction in school reverse those that prevail in the society at large.

Four structural elements in the organization of schooling contribute to the extent to which minority students are empowered or disabled. As outlined in Figure 1, these elements include the incorporation of minority students' culture and language, inclusion of minority communities in the education of their children, pedagogical assumptions and practices operating in the classroom, and the assessment of minority students.

### Cultural/linguistic incorporation

Considerable research data suggest that, for dominated minorities, the extent to which students' language and culture are incorporated into the school program constitutes a significant predictor of academic success (Campos & Keatinge, 1984; Cummins, 1983a; Rosier & Holm, 1980). As outlined earlier, students' school success appears to reflect both the more solid cognitive/academic foundation developed through intensive L1 instruction and the reinforcement of their cultural identity.

Included under incorporation of minority group cultural features is the adjustment of instructional patterns to take account of culturally conditioned learning styles. The Kamehameha Early Education Program in Hawaii provides strong evidence of the importance of this type of cultural incorporation. When reading instruction was changed to permit stu-

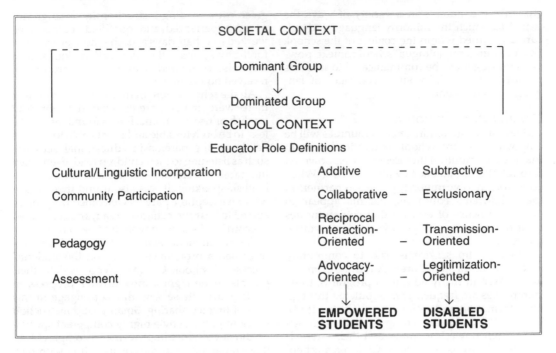

**Figure 1** Empowerment of minority students: A theoretical framework

dents to collaborate in discussing and interpreting texts, dramatic improvements were found in both reading and verbal intellectual abilities (Au & Jordan, 1981).

An important issue to consider at this point is why superficially plausible but patently inadequate assumptions, such as the 'insufficient exposure' hypothesis, continue to dominate the policy debate when virtually all the evidence suggests that incorporation of minority students' language and culture into the school program will at least not impede academic progress. In other words, what social function do such arguments serve? Within the context of the present framework, it is suggested that a major reason for the vehement resistance to bilingual programs is that the incorporation of minority languages and cultures into the school program confers status and power (jobs, for example) on the minority group. Consequently, such programs contravene the established pattern of dominant/dominated group relations. Within democratic societies, however, contradictions between the rhetoric of equality and the reality of domination must be obscured. Thus, conventional wisdoms such as the insufficient exposure hypothesis become

immune from critical scrutiny, and incompatible evidence is either ignored or dismissed.

Educators' role definitions in relation to the incorporation of minority students' language and culture can be characterized along an 'additive–subtractive' dimension.[5] Educators who see their role as adding a second language and cultural affiliation to their students' repertoire are likely to empower students more than those who see their role as replacing or subtracting students' primary language and culture. In addition to the personal and future employment advantages of proficiency in two languages, there is considerable, though not conclusive, evidence that subtle educational advantages result from continued development of both languages among bilingual students. Enhanced metalinguistic development, for example, is frequently found in association with additive bilingualism (Hakuta & Diaz, 1985; McLaughlin, 1984).

It should be noted that an additive orientation does not require the actual teaching of the minority language. In many cases a minority language class may not be possible for reasons such as low concentration of particular groups of minority students. Educators, however, communicate to students and parents in a variety of ways the extent to which the minority language and culture are valued within the context of the school. Even within a monolingual school context, powerful messages can be communicated to students regarding the validity and advantages of language development.

### Community participation

Students from dominated communities will be empowered in the school context to the extent that the communities themselves are empowered through their interactions with the school. When educators involve minority parents as partners in their children's education, parents appear to develop a sense of efficacy that communicates itself to children, with positive academic consequences.

Although lip service is paid to community involvement through Parent Advisory Committees (PAC)[6] in many education programs, these committees are frequently manipulated through misinformation and intimidation (Curtis, 1984). The result is that parents from dominated groups retain their powerless status, and their internalized inferiority is reinforced. Children's school failure can then be attributed to the combined effects of parental illiteracy and lack of interest in their children's education. In reality, most parents of minority students have high aspirations for their children and want to be involved in promoting their academic progress (Wong-Fillmore, 1983). However, they often do not know how to help their children academically, and they are excluded from participation by the school. In fact, even their interaction through L1 with their children in the home is frequently regarded by educators as contributing to academic difficulties (Cummins, 1984).

Dramatic changes in children's academic progress can be realized when educators take the initiative to change this exclusionary pattern to one of collaboration. The Haringey project in Britain illustrates just how powerful the effects of simple interventions can be (Tizard, Schofield & Hewison, 1982). In order to assess the effects of parental involvement in the teaching of reading, the researchers established a project in the London borough of Haringey whereby all children in two primary level experimental classes in two different schools read to their parents at home on a regular basis. The reading progress of these children was compared with that of children in two classes in two different schools who were

given extra reading instruction in small groups by an experienced and qualified teacher who worked four half-days at each school every week for the two years of the intervention. Both groups were also compared with a control group that received no treatment.

All the schools were in multi-ethnic areas, and there were many parents who did not read English or use it at home. It was found, nevertheless, to be both feasible and practicable to involve nearly all the parents in educational activities such as listening to their children read, even when the parents were non-literate and largely non-English-speaking. It was also found that, almost without exception, parents welcomed the project, agreed to hear their children read, and completed a record card showing what had been read.

The researchers report that parental involvement had a pronounced effect on the students' success in school. Children who read to their parents made significantly greater progress in reading than those who did not engage in this type of literacy sharing. Small-group instruction in reading, given by a highly competent specialist, did not produce improvements comparable to those obtained from the collaboration with parents. In contrast to the home collaboration program, the benefits of extra reading instruction were least apparent for initially low-achieving children.

In addition, the collaboration between teachers and parents was effective for children of all initial levels of performance, including those who, at the beginning of the study, were failing in learning to read. Teachers reported that the children showed an increased interest in school learning and were better behaved. Those teachers involved in the home collaboration found the work with parents worthwhile, and they continued to involve parents with subsequent classes after the experiment was concluded. It is interesting to note that teachers of the control classes also adopted the home collaboration program after the two-year experimental period.

The Haringey project is one example of school/community relations; there are others. The essential point, however, is that the teacher's role in such relations can be characterized along a *collaborative-exclusionary* dimension. Teachers operating at the collaborative end of the continuum actively encourage minority parents to participate in promoting their children's academic progress both in the home and through involvement in classroom activities. A collaborative orientation may require a willingness on the part of the teacher to work closely with mother-tongue teachers or aides in order to communicate effectively, in a non-condescending way, with minority parents. Teachers with an exclusionary orientation, on the other hand, tend to regard teaching as *their* job and are likely to view collaboration with minority parents as either irrelevant or detrimental to children's progress.

## Pedagogy

Several investigators have suggested that many 'learning disabilities' are pedagogically induced in that children designated 'at risk' frequently receive intensive instruction which confines them to a passive role and induces a form of 'learned helplessness' (Beers & Beers, 1980; Coles, 1978; Cummins, 1984). This process is illustrated in a micro-ethnographic study of four-teen reading lessons given to West Indian Creole-speakers of English in Toronto, Canada (Ramphal, 1983). It was found that teachers' constant correction of students' miscues pre-vented students from focusing on the meaning of what they were reading. Moreover, the constant corrections fostered dependent behavior because students knew that whenever they paused at a word the teacher would automatically pro-nounce it for them. One student was interrupted so often in one of the lessons that he was able to read only one sentence, consisting of three words, uninterrupted. In contrast to a pattern of class-room interaction which promotes instructional dependence, teaching that empowers will aim to liberate students from instruction by encourag-ing them to become active generators of their knowledge. As Graves (1983) has demonstrated, this type of active knowledge generation can occur when, for example, children create and publish their own books within the classroom.

Two major pedagogical orientations can be distinguished. These differ in the extent to which the teacher retains exclusive control over class-room interaction as opposed to sharing some of this control with students. The dominant instruc-tional model in North American schools has been termed a transmission model (Barnes, 1976; Wells, 1982). This model incorporates essentially the same assumptions about teaching and learn-ing that Freire (1970, 1973) has termed a 'banking' model of education. This transmission model will be contrasted with a 'reciprocal interaction' model of pedagogy.

The basic premise of the transmission model is

that the teacher's task is to impart knowledge or skills that she or he possesses to students who do not yet have these skills. This implies that the teacher initiates and controls the interaction, constantly orienting it towards the achievement of instructional objectives. For example, in first- and second-language programs that stress pat-tern repetition, the teacher presents the materials, models the language patterns, asks questions, and provides feedback to students about the correctness of their response. The curriculum in these types of programs focuses on the internal structure of the language or subject matter. Con-sequently, it frequently focuses predominantly on surface features of language or literacy such as handwriting, spelling, and decoding, and empha-sizes correct recall of content taught by means of highly structured drills and workbook exercises. It has been argued that a transmission model of teaching contravenes central principles of lan-guage and literacy acquisition and that a model allowing for reciprocal interaction among stu-dents and teachers represents a more appropriate alternative (Cummins, 1984; Wells, 1982).[7]

A central tenet of the reciprocal interaction model is that 'talking and writing are means to learning' (Bullock Report, 1975: 50). The use of this model in teaching requires a genuine dia-logue between student and teacher in both oral and written modalities, guidance and facilitation rather than control of student learning by the teacher, and the encouragement of student–student talk in a collaborative learning context. This model emphasizes the development of higher level cognitive skills rather than just factual recall, and meaningful language use by students rather than the correction of surface forms. Language use and development are con-sciously integrated with all curricular content rather than taught as isolated subjects, and tasks are presented to students in ways that generate intrinsic rather than extrinsic motivation. In short, pedagogical approaches that empower students encourage them to assume greater con-trol over setting their own learning goals and to collaborate actively with each other in achieving these goals.

The development of a sense of efficacy and inner direction in the classroom is especially important for students from dominated groups whose experiences so often orient them in the opposite direction. Wong-Fillmore (1983) has reported that Hispanic students learned consid-erably more English in classrooms that provided opportunities for reciprocal interaction with teachers and peers. Ample opportunities for expressive writing appear to be particularly significant in promoting a sense of academic efficacy among minority students (Cummins, Aguilar, Bascunan, Fiorucci, Sanaoui, & Basman, in press). As expressed by Daiute (1985):

> Children who learn early that writing is not simply an exercise gain a sense of power that gives them confidence to write — and write a lot... Beginning writers who are confident that they have something to say or that they can find out what they need to know can even overcome some limits of training or development. Writers who don't feel that what they say matters have an additional burden that no skills training can help them overcome. (pp. 5–6)

The implications for students from dominated groups are obvious. Too often the instruction they receive convinces them that what they have to say is irrelevant or wrong. The failure of this method of instruction is then taken as an indication that the minority student is of low ability, a verdict frequently confirmed by subsequent assessment procedures.

## Assessment

Historically, assessment has played the role of legitimizing the disabling of minority students. In some cases assessment itself may play the primary role, but more often it has been used to locate the 'problem' within the minority student, thereby screening from critical scrutiny the subtractive nature of the school program, the exclusionary orientation of teachers towards minority communities, and transmission models of teaching that inhibit students from active participation in learning.

This process is virtually inevitable when the conceptual base for assessment is purely psycho-educational. If the psychologist's task is to discover the causes of a minority student's academic difficulties and the only tools at his or her disposal are psychological tests (in either L1 or L2), then it is hardly surprising that the child's difficulties will be attributed to psychological dysfunctions. The myth of bilingual handicaps that still influences educational policy was generated in exactly this way during the 1920s and 1930s.

Recent studies suggest that despite the appearance of change brought about by PL 94-142, the underlying structure of assessment processes has remained essentially intact. Mehan, Hertweck & Meihls (in press), for example, report that psychologists continued to test children until they 'found' the disability that could be invoked to 'explain' the student's apparent academic difficulties. Diagnosis and placement were influenced frequently by factors related to bureaucratic procedures and funding requirements rather than to students' academic performance in the classroom. Rueda & Mercer (1985) have also shown that designation of minority students as 'learning disabled' as compared to 'language impaired' was strongly influenced by whether a psychologist or a speech pathologist was on the placement committee. In other words, with respect to students' actual behavior, the label was essentially arbitrary. An analysis of more than four hundred psychological assessments of minority students revealed that although no diagnostic conclusions were logically possible in the majority of assessments, psychologists were most reluctant to admit this fact to teachers and parents (Cummins, 1984). In short, the data suggest that the structure within which psychological assessment takes place orients the psychologist to locate the cause of the academic problem within the minority student.

An alternative role definition for psychologists or special educators can be termed an 'advocacy' or 'delegitimization' role.[8] In this case, their task must be to delegitimize the traditional function of psychological assessment in the educational disabling of minority students by becoming advocates for the child in scrutinizing critically the societal and educational context within which the child has developed (Cazden, 1985). This involves locating the pathology within the societal power relations between dominant and dominated groups, in the reflection of these power relations between school and communities, and in the mental and cultural disabling of minority students that takes place in classrooms. These conditions are a more probable cause of the 300 percent over-representation of Texas Hispanic students in the learning disabled category than any intrinsic processing deficit unique to Hispanic children. The training of psychologists and special educators does not prepare them for this advocacy or delegitimization role. From the present perspective, however, it must be emphasized that discriminatory assessment is carried out by well-intentioned individuals who, rather than challenging a socio-educational system that tends to disable minority students, have accepted a role definition and an educational structure that makes discriminatory assessment virtually inevitable.[9]

## Empowering Minority Students: The Carpinteria Example

The Spanish-only preschool program of the Carpenteria School District, near Santa Barbara, California, is one of the few programs in the United States that explicitly incorporates the major elements hypothesized in previous sections to empower minority students. Spanish is the exclusive language of instruction, there is a strong community involvement component, and the program is characterized by a coherent philosophy of promoting conceptual development through meaningful linguistic interaction.

The proposal to implement an intensive Spanish-only preschool program in this region was derived from district findings showing that a large majority of the Spanish-speaking students entering kindergarten each year lacked adequate skills to succeed in the kindergarten program. On the School Readiness Inventory, a district-wide screening measure administered to all incoming kindergarten students, Spanish-speaking students tended to average about eight points lower than English-speaking students (approximately 14.5 compared to 23.0, averaged over four years from 1979 to 1982) despite the fact that the test was administered in students' dominant language. A score of 20 or better was viewed by the district as predicting a successful kindergarten year for the child. Prior to the implementation of the experimental program, the Spanish-background children attended a bilingual preschool program — operated either by Head Start or the Community Day Care Center — in which both English and Spanish were used concurrently but with strong emphasis on the development of English skills. According to the district kindergarten teachers, children who had attended these programs often mixed English and Spanish into a 'Spanglish.'

The major goal of the experimental Spanish-only preschool program was to bring Spanish-dominant children entering kindergarten up to a level of readiness for school similar to that attained by English-speaking children in the community. The project also sought to make parents of the program participants aware of their role as the child's first teacher and to encourage them to provide specific types of experiences for their children in the home.

The preschool program itself involved the integration of language with a large variety of concrete and literacy-related experiences. As summarized in the evaluation report: 'The development of language skills in Spanish was foremost in the planning and attention given to every facet of the pre-school day. Language was used constantly for conversing, learning new ideas, concepts and vocabulary, thinking creatively, and problem-solving to give the children the opportunity to develop their language skills in Spanish to as high a degree as possible within the structure of the pre-school day' (Campos & Keatinge, 1984: 17).

Participation in the program was on a voluntary basis and students were screened only for age and Spanish-language dominance. Family characteristics of students in the experimental program were typical of other Spanish-speaking families in the community; more than 90 percent were of low socioeconomic status, and the majority worked in agriculture and had an average educational level of about sixth grade.

The program proved to be highly successful in developing students' readiness skills, as evidenced by the average score of 21.6 obtained by the 1982–83 incoming kindergarten students who had been in the program, compared to the score of 23.2 obtained by English-speaking students. A score of 14.6 was obtained by Spanish speaking students who experienced the regular bilingual preschool program. In 1983–84 the scores of these three groups were 23.3, 23.4, and 16.0, respectively. In other words, the gap between English- background and Spanish-background children in the Spanish-only preschool had disappeared; however, a considerable gap remained for Spanish-background students for whom English was the focus of preschool instruction.

Of special interest is the performance of the experimental program students on the English and Spanish versions of the Bilingual Syntax Measure (BSM), a test of oral syntactic development (Hernandez-Chavez, Burt, & Dulay, 1976). Despite the fact that they experienced an exclusively Spanish preschool program, these students performed better than the other Spanish-speaking students in English (and Spanish) on entry to kindergarten in 1982 and at a similar level in 1983. On entrance to grade one in 1983, the gap had widened considerably, with almost five times as many of the experimental-program students performing at level 5 (fluent English) compared to the other Spanish-background students (47 percent vs. 10 percent) (Campos & Keatinge, 1984).

The evaluation report suggests that:

> although project participants were exposed to less *total* English, they, because of their enhanced first language skill and concept knowledge were better able to comprehend the English they were exposed to. This seems to be borne out by comments made by kindergarten teachers in the District about project participants. They are making comments like, 'Project participants appear more aware of what is happening around them in the classroom,' 'They are able to focus on the task at hand better' and 'They demonstrate greater self-confidence in learning situations.' All of these traits would tend to enhance the language acquisition process. (Campos & Keatinge, 1984: 41)

Campos and Keatinge (1984) also emphasize the consequences of the preschool program for parental participation in their children's education. They note that, according to the school officials, 'the parents of project participants are much more) aware of and involved in their child's school experience than non-participant parents of Spanish speakers. This is seen as having a positive impact on the future success of the project participants — the greater the involvement of parents, the greater the chances of success of the child' (p. 41).

The major relevance of these findings for educators and policy-makers derives from their demonstration that educational programs *can* succeed in preventing the academic failure experienced by many minority students. The corollary is that failure to provide this type of program constitutes the disabling of minority students by the school system. For example, among the students who did not experience the experimental preschool program, the typical pattern of low levels of academic readiness and limited proficiency in both languages was observed. These are the students who are likely to be referred for psychological assessment early in their school careers. This assessment will typically legitimize the inadequate educational provision by attributing students' difficulties to some vacuous category, such as learning disability. By contrast, students who experienced a preschool program in which (a) their cultural identity was reinforced, (b) there was active collaboration with parents, and (c) meaningful use of language was inte-

grated into every aspect of daily activities were developing high levels of conceptual and linguistic skills in *both* languages.

## Conclusion

In this article I have proposed a theoretical framework for examining minority students' academic failure and for predicting the effects of educational interventions. Within this framework the educational failure of minority students is analyzed as a function of the extent to which schools reflect or counteract the power relations that exist within the broader society. Specifically, language-minority students' educational progress is strongly influenced by the extent to which individual educators become advocates for the promotion of students' linguistic talents, actively encourage community participation in developing students' academic and cultural resources, and implement pedagogical approaches that succeed in liberating students from instructional dependence.

The educator/student interactions characteristic of the disabling end of the proposed continua reflect the typical patterns of interaction that dominated societal groups have experienced in relation to dominant groups. The intrinsic value of the group is usually denied, and 'objective' evidence is accumulated to demonstrate the group's 'inferiority.' This inferior status is then used as a justification for excluding the group from activities and occupations that entail societal rewards.

In a similar way, the disabling of students is frequently rationalized on the basis of students' 'needs.' For example, minority students need maximum exposure to English in both the school and home; thus, parents must be told not to interact with children in their mother tongue. Similarly, minority children need a highly structured drill-oriented program in order to maximize time spent on tasks to compensate for their deficient preschool experiences. Minority students also need a comprehensive diagnostic/prescriptive assessment in order to identify the nature of their 'problem' and possible remedial interventions.

This analysis suggests a major reason for the relative lack of success of the various educational bandwagons that have characterized the North American crusade against underachievement during the past twenty years. The individual role definitions of educators and the institutional role definitions of schools have remained largely unchanged despite 'new and improved' programs and policies. These programs and policies, despite their cost, have simply added a new veneer to the outward facade of the structure that disables minority students. The lip service paid to initial L1 instruction, community involvement, and nondiscriminatory assessment, together with the emphasis on improved teaching techniques, have succeeded primarily in deflecting attention from the attitudes and orientation of educators who interact on a daily basis with minority students. It is in these interactions that students are disabled. In the absence of individual and collective educator role redefinitions, schools will continue to reproduce, in these interactions, the power relations that characterize the wider society and make minority students' academic failure inevitable.

To educators genuinely concerned about alleviating the educational difficulties of minority students and responding to their needs, this conclusion may appear overly bleak. I believe, however, that it is realistic and optimistic, as directions for change are clearly indicated rather than obscured by the overlay of costly reforms that leave the underlying disabling structure essentially intact. Given the societal commitment to maintaining the dominant/dominated power relationships, we can predict that educational changes threatening this structure will be fiercely resisted. This is in fact the case for each of the four structural dimensions discussed earlier.[10]

In order to reverse the pattern of widespread minority group educational failure, educators and policy-makers are faced with both a personal and a political challenge. Personally, they must redefine their roles within the classroom, the community, and the broader society so that these role definitions result in interactions that empower rather than disable students. Politically, they must attempt to persuade colleagues and decision-makers — such as school boards and the public that elects them — of the importance of redefining institutional goals so that the schools transform society by empowering minority students rather than reflect society by disabling them.

## Acknowledgements

Discussions at the Symposium on 'Minority Languages in Academic Research and Educational Policy' held in Sandbjerg Slot, Denmark, April 1985, contributed to the ideas in the paper. I would like to express my appreciation to the participants at the Symposium and to Safder Alladina, Jan Curtis, David Dolson, Norm Gold, Monica Heller, Dennis Parker, Verity Saifullah Khan, and Tove Skutnabb-Kangas for comments on earlier drafts. I would also like to acknowledge the financial support of the Social Sciences and Humanities Research Council (Grant No. 431-79-0003) which made possible participation in the Sandbjerg Slot symposium.

### Notes

1. The Education of All Handicapped Children Act of 1975 (Public Law 94-142) guarantees to all handicapped children in the United States the right to a free public education, to an individualized education program (IEP), to due process, to education in the least segregated environment, and to assessment procedures that are multidimensional and non-culturally discriminatory.
2. For a discussion of the implications of Canadian French immersion programs for the education of minority students, see California State Department of Education (1984).
3. Ogbu (1978), for example, has distinguished between 'caste,' 'immigrant,' and 'autonomous' minority groups. Caste groups are similar to what has been termed 'dominated' groups in the present framework and are the only category of minority groups that tends to fail academically. Immigrant groups have

usually come voluntarily to the host society for economic reasons and, unlike caste minorities, have not internalized negative attributions of the dominant group. Ogbu gives Chinese and Japanese groups as examples of 'immigrant' minorities. The cultural resources that permit some minority groups to resist discrimination and internalization of negative attributions are still a matter of debate and speculation (for a recent treatment, see Ogbu & Bianchi, in press). The final category distinguished by Ogbu is that of 'autonomous' groups who hold a distinct cultural identity but who are not subordinated economically or politically to the dominant group (for example, Jews and Mormons in the United States). Failure to take account of these differences among minority groups both in patterns of academic performance and socio-historical relationships to the dominant group has contributed to the confused state of policy-making with respect to language minority students. The bilingual education policy, for example, has been based on the implicit assumption that the linguistic mismatch hypothesis was valid for all language minority students, and, consequently, the same types of intervention were necessary and appropriate for all students. Clearly, this assumption is open to question.

4. There is no contradiction in postulating student empowerment as both a mediating and an outcome variable. For example, cognitive abilities clearly have the same status in that they contribute to students' school success and can also be regarded as an outcome of schooling.

5. The terms 'additive' and 'subtractive' bilingualism were coined by Lambert (1975) to refer to the proficient bilingualism associated with positive cognitive outcomes on the one hand, and the limited bilingualism often associated with negative outcomes on the other.

6. PACs were established in some states to provide an institutional structure for minority parent involvement in educational decision making with respect to bilingual programs. In California, for example, a majority of PAC members for any state-funded program was required to be from the program target group. The school plan for use of program funds required signed PAC approval.

7. This 'reciprocal interaction' model incorporates proposals about the relation between language and learning made by a variety of investigators, most notably in the Bullock Report (1975), and by Barnes (1976), Lindfors (1980), and Wells (1982). Its application with respect to the promotion of literacy conforms closely to psycholinguistic approaches to reading (Goodman & Goodman, 1977; Holdaway, 1979; Smith, 1978) and to the recent emphasis on encouraging expressive writing from the earliest grades (Chomsky, 1981; Giaccobe, 1982; Graves, 1983; Temple, Nathan & Burris, 1982). Students' microcomputing networks such as the *Computer Chronicles Newswire* (Mehan, Miller-Souviney & Riel, 1984) represent a particularly promising application of reciprocal interaction model of pedagogy.

8. See Mullard (1985) for a detailed discussion of delegitimization strategies in antiracist education.

9. Clearly, the presence of processing difficulties that are rooted in neurological causes is not being denied for either monolingual or bilingual children. However, in the case of children from dominated minorities, the proportion of disabilities that are neurological in origin is likely to represent only a small fraction of those that derive from educational and social conditions.

10. Although for pedagogy the resistance to sharing control with students goes beyond majority/minority group relations, the same elements are present. If the curriculum is not predetermined and presequenced, and the students are generating their own knowledge in a critical and creative way, then the reproduction of the societal structure cannot be guaranteed — hence the reluctance to liberate students from instructional dependence.

## References

Au, K.H. and Jordan, C. (1981) Teaching reading to Hawaiian children: Finding a culturally appropriate solution. In H. Trueba, G. P. Guthrie and K.H. Au (eds) *Culture and the Bilingual Classroom. Studies in Classroom Ethnography* (pp. 139–52). Rowley, MA: Newbury House.

Baker, K.A. and de Kanter, A.A. (1981) *Effectiveness of Bilingual Education. A Review of the Literature.* Washington, DC: US Department of Education, Office of Planning and Budget.

Barnes, D. (1976) *From Communication to Curriculum.* New York: Penguin.

Beers, C.S. and Beers, J.W. (1980) Early identification of learning disabilities: Facts and fallacies. *Elementary School Journal* 81, 67–76.

Bethell, T. (1979) Against bilingual education. *Harper's*, February, pp. 30–3.

Bullock Report (1975) *A Language for Life* (Report of the Committee of Inquiry Appointed by the Secretary of State for Education and Science under the Chairmanship of Sir Alan Bullock). London: HMSO.

California State Department of Education (1984) *Studies on Immersion Education: A Collection for United States Educators.* Sacramento: Author.

Campos, J. and Keatinge, B. (1984) *The Carpinteria Preschool Program: Title VII Second Year Evaluation Report.* Washington, DC: Department of Education.

Cazden, C.B. (1985) The ESL teacher as advocate.

Plenary presentation to the TESOL Conference, April, New York.

Chomsky, C. (1981) Write now, read later. In C. Cazden (ed.) *Language in Early Childhood Education* (2nd edn, pp. 141–49). Washington, DC: National Association for the Education of Young Children.

Cohen, A.D. and Swain, M. (1976) Bilingual education: The immersion model in the North American context. In J.E. Alatis and K. Twaddell (eds) *English as a Second Language in Bilingual Education* (pp. 55–64). Washington, DC: TESOL.

Coles, G.S. (1978) The learning disabilities test battery: Empirical and social issues. *Harvard Educational Review* 48, 313–40.

Cummins, J. (1979) Linguistic interdependence and the educational development of bilingual children. *Review of Educational Research* 49, 222–51.

— (1983a) *Heritage Language Education: A Literature Review*. Toronto: Ministry of Education.

— (1983b) Functional language proficiency in context: Classroom participation as an interactive process. In W.J. Tikunoff (ed.) *Compatibility of the SBIS Features with Other Research on Instruction for LEP Students* (pp. 109–31). San Francisco: Far West Laboratory.

— (1984) *Bilingualism and Special Education: Issues in Assessment and Pedagogy*. Clevedon: Multilingual Matters.

Cummins, J., Aguilar, M., Bascunan, L., Fiorucci, S., Sanaoui, R. and Basman, S. (in press) *Literacy Development in Heritage Language Programs*. Toronto: National Heritage Language Resource Unit.

Curtis, J. (1984) Bilingual education in Calistoga: Not a happy ending. Report submitted to the Instituto de Lengua y Cultura, Elmira, NY.

Daiute, C. (1985) *Writing and Computers*. Reading, MA: Addison-Wesley.

Feuerstein, R. (1979) *The Dynamic Assessment of Retarded Performers: The Learning Potential Assessment Device, Theory, Instruments, and Techniques*. Baltimore: University Park Press.

Fishman, J. (1976) *Bilingual Education: An International Sociological Perspective*. Rowley, MA: Newbury House.

Freire, P. (1970) *Pedagogy of the Oppressed*. New York: Seabury.

— (1973) *Education for Critical Consciousness*. New York: Seabury.

Giacobbe, M.E. (1982) Who says children can't write the first week? In R.D. Walshe (ed.) *Donald Graves in Australia. 'Children Want to Write'* (pp. 99–103). Exeter, NH: Heinemann Educational Books.

Goodman, K. S. and Goodman, Y.M. (1977) Learning about psycholinguistic processes by analyzing oral reading. *Harvard Educational Review* 47, 317–33.

Graves, D.H. (1983) *Writing: Teachers and Children at Work*. Exeter, NH: Heinemann Educational Books.

Hakuta, K. and Diaz, R.M. (1985) The relationship between degree of bilingualism and cognitive ability: A critical discussion and some new longitudinal data. In K.E. Nelson (ed.) *Children's Language* (Vol. 5, pp. 319–345). Hillsdale, NJ: Erlbaum.

Heath, S.B. (1983) *Ways with Words*. Cambridge: Cambridge University Press.

Hernandez-Chavez, E., Burt, M. and Dulay, H. (1976) *The Bilingual Syntax Measure*. New York: The Psychological Corporation.

Holdaway, D. (1979) *The Foundations of Literacy*. Sydney, Australia: Ashton Scholastic.

Jusenius, C. and Duarte, V.L. (1982) *Hispanics and Jobs: Barriers to Progress*. Washington, DC: National Commission for Employment Policy.

Lambert, W.E. (1975) Culture and language as factors in learning and education. In A. Wolfgang (ed.) *Education of Immigrant Students* (pp. 55–83). Toronto: OISE.

Lindfors, J. W. (1980) *Children's Language and Learning*. Englewood Cliffs, NJ: Prentice-Hall.

McLaughlin, B. (1984) Early bilingualism: Methodological and theoretical issues. In M. Paradis and Y. Lebrun (eds) *Early Bilingualism and Child Development* (pp. 19–46). Lisse: Swets & Zeitlinger.

— (1985) *Second Language Acquisition in Childhood, Vol. 2. School-age Children*. Hillsdale, NJ: Erlbaum.

Mehan, H., Hertweck, A. and Meihls, J. L. (in press) *Handicapping the Handicapped: Decision Making in Students' Educational Careers*. Palo Alto: Stanford University.

Mehan, H., Miller-Souviney, B. and Riel, M. M. (1984) Research currents: Knowledge of text editing and control of literacy skills. *Language Arts* 65, 154–9.

Mullard, C. (1985) The social dynamic of migrant groups: From progressive to transformative policy in education. Paper presented at the OECD Conference on Educational Policies and the Minority Social Groups, January, Paris.

Ogbu, J.U. (1978) *Minority Education and Caste*. New York: Academic Press.

Ogbu, J.U. and Matute-Bianchi, M.E. (in press) Understanding sociocultural factors: Knowledge, identity and school adjustment. In California State Department of Education (ed.) *Sociocultural Factors and Minority Student Achievement*. Sacramento: Author.

Ortiz, A.A. and Yates, J.R. (1983) Incidence of exceptionality among Hispanics: Implications for manpower planning. *NABE Journal* 7, 41–54.

Paulston, C.B. (1980) *Bilingual Education. Theories and Issues*. Rowley, MA: Newbury House.

Ramphal, D.K. (1983) An analysis of reading instruction of West Indian Creole-speaking students. Unpublished doctoral dissertation, Ontario Institute for Studies in Education.

Rosier, P. and Holm, W. (1980) *The Rock Point Experience: A Longitudinal Study of a Navajo School*. Washington, DC: Center for Applied Linguistics.

Rueda, R. and Mercer, J.R. (1985) Predictive analysis of decision making with language minority handicapped children. Paper presented at the BUENO Center 3rd Annual Symposium on Bilingual Education, June, Denver.

Schneider, S.G. (1976) *Revolution, Reaction or Reform: The 1974 Bilingual Education Act*. New York: Las Americas.

Skutnabb-Kangas, T. (1984) *Bilingualism or Not:*

*The Education of Minorities*. Clevedon: Multilingual Matters.

Smith, F. (1978) *Understanding Reading* (2nd edn). New York: Holt, Rinehart & Winston.

Temple, C.A., Nathan, R.G. and Burris, N.A. (1982) *The Beginnings of Writing*. Boston: Allyn & Bacon.

Tikunoff, W.J. (1983) Five significant bilingual instructional features. In W. J. Tikunoff (ed.) *Compatibility of the SBIS Features with Other Research on Instruction for LEP Students* (pp. 5–18). San Francisco: Far West Laboratory.

Tizard, J., Schofield, W.N. and Hewison, J. (1982) Collaboration between teachers and parents in assisting children's reading. *British Journal of Educational Psychology* 52, 1–15.

Troike, R. (1978) Research evidence for the effectiveness of bilingual education. *NABE Journal* 3, 13–24.

Wells, G. (1982) Language, learning and the curriculum. In G. Wells (ed.) *Language, Learning and Education* (pp. 205–26). Bristol: Centre for the Study of Language and Communication, University of Bristol.

Wong-Fillmore, L. (1983) The language learner as an individual: Implications of research on individual differences for the ESL teacher. In M.A. Clarke and J. Handscombe (eds) *On TESOL '82: Pacific Pespectives on Language Learning and Teaching* (pp. 157–71). Washington, DC: TESOL.

## Questions

(1) Explain the following three theories that attempt to explain why students of particular ethnolinguistic backgrounds fail academically:
   (a) bicultural ambivalence;
   (b) being a caste minority;
   (c) disruption of intergenerational transmission.
   (You may wish to consult '*Foundations of Bilingual Education and Bilingualism,*' Chapter 13, for more explanations on the underachievement of language minorities.)
   What do you think of these theories? Do you know of examples that fit each of the theories? Do you know of counter-examples?

(2) Make a list of the four structural elements for empowerment of language minority students, according to Cummins. In a second column, explain how each of these features is present in the Carpenteria pre-school program. In a third column, apply each of these features to what you know about PS 84 and the ethnic schools in Dade County. Indicate which features are present and how.

(3) Give examples from your experience (either as a student or as a teacher) of a transmission model of education and a reciprocal interaction model. Describe in detail and

evaluate each model's purpose and effectiveness. Why does Cummins says that most transmission models induce a 'learned helplessness'?

Reflect on your own experience to answer these questions:

(a) Who are the teachers most likely to use a transmission model of education? Who are the students most likely to receive a transmission model of education?

(b) Who are the teachers most likely to use a reciprocal interaction model of education? Who are the students most likely to receive a reciprocal interaction model of education?

(4) What exactly is the 'advocacy' or 'delegitimization' role that Cummins asks psychologists or special educators to undertake? Give details of the assessment process in a school with which you are familiar. How would you evaluate whether assessment is advocacy-oriented or legitimization-oriented?

## Activities

(1) Read Freire (1971) listed under Further Reading. Make a poster portraying 'banking education' or what Cummins calls the 'transmission-oriented model of pedagogy' and then 'problem-posing education' or what Cummins calls the 'reciprocal interaction model of pedagogy.' Display all the students' posters. Select the best to be displayed throughout the semester.

(2) In groups, for a specified learning objective, design a lesson using 'transmission oriented instruction,' and one using 'reciprocal interaction instruction.' Try them out. (You may role-play in your class.) Have students evaluate their effectiveness.

(3) Select two classrooms at the same grade level. One should be in a public school that serves large groups of language minority students. The other should preferably be in a private school with a mostly majority population. Compare the two classrooms as to:

(a) community participation;

(b) pedagogy;

(c) assessment: academic, psychological and linguistic.

Make a chart to summarize your results.

(4) Find out what is the United States PL 94-142. Observe a special education classroom. Then ask the teacher whether she agrees with Cummins that 'the underlying structure of assessment processes has remained essentially intact.' Why does she agree or disagree? Prepare a report to share with the class.

## Further Reading

Freire, P. (1971) *Pedagogy of the Oppressed*. New York: Herder and Herder.

Lucas, T., Henze, R. and Donato, R. (1990) Promoting the success of Latino language-minority students: An exploratory study of six High Schools *Harvard Educational Review* 60 (3), 315–40.

For more sources on what has come to be known as 'critical pedagogy,' see Further Reading following Ada (a chapter later in this book).

# The Canadian Second Language Immersion Program

## Fred Genesee

Canada is a relatively young nation, founded in 1867, with a population of approximately 25 million citizens who inhabit a territory that is second in size only to the USSR. The country has a federal form of government consisting of ten provincial legislatures, two territorial legislatures, and one national parliament located in Ottawa. Political power is highly decentralized, with the provincial government holding considerable legislative and political power in certain jurisdictions, including, for example, education, health care, and municipal affairs, and the federal government holding powers in other jurisdictions.

There are three founding groups — Native peoples (including the Inuit or Eskimos and Indians), the French, and the English. These groups differ greatly with respect to their population size, geographical distribution, and social and economic power. It is not certain when the Native people arrived in North America, although it was probably during prehistoric times and possibly during the last Great Ice Age. The Inuit have traditionally inhabited the northern regions, and the Indians the more southern parts of the country. Since confederation in 1867, the Native peoples have comprised a small and diminishing percentage of the total Canadian population (see Table 1, and Barnaby (1988)). They have no separate, elected political representation; they vote in elections in the same way as other Canadian citizens. Matters of special relevance to them are dealt with by the Federal Department of Indian and Northern Affairs.

Canadians of British and French origin constitute by far the largest ethnic groups in Canada, with those of British origin being more numerous (40 percent) than those of French origin (27 percent). French and English Canadians are unequally distributed across the country. This is most notable in the case of French Canadians who reside mainly in Quebec, northern New Brunswick, the eastern border of Ontario, and southern Manitoba. English Canadians constitute a large percentage of the population in all regions of the country with the one exception of Quebec where they make up only 17 to 20 percent of the population. It is clear from Table 1 that even Canadians of British or French origin are slowly diminishing in numerical importance as a result of a rise in the number of non-English, non-French immigrants. It is estimated that there are some seventy-eight different cultural groups in Canada. They constitute approximately 33 percent of the total population.

The historical and social significance of French and English along with the growing importance and recognition of ethnic diversity in Canada are two of the most salient features of Canadian culture. Indeed, in contrast to the notion of a cultural 'melting pot' in the United States, Canada has been characterized as an 'ethnic mosaic'. In recognition of these characteristics of Canadian society, the federal government has adopted official policies of bilingualism and multiculturalism. According to the Official Languages Act, passed in 1969:

> The English and French languages are the official languages of Canada for all purposes of the Parliament and Government of Canada, and possess and enjoy equality of status and equal rights and privileges as to their use in all the institutions of the Parliament and Government of Canada (Section 2).

This means that Canadians have access to services provided by the federal Parliament or government in English or in French anywhere in Canada. The Act does not require that all Cana-

**Table 1** Ethnic origin of the Canadian population, 1901 to 1971

| Origin | 1901 (%) | 1921 (%) | 1941 (%) | 1961 (%) | 1971 (%) |
|---|---|---|---|---|---|
| British | 57.0 | 55.4 | 49.7 | 43.8 | 44.6 |
| French | 30.7 | 27.9 | 30.3 | 30.4 | 28.7 |
| Indian and Eskimo | 2.4 | 1.3 | 1.1 | 1.2 | 1.3 |
| German | 5.8 | 3.4 | 4.0 | 5.8 | 6.1 |
| Italian | 0.2 | 0.8 | 1.0 | 2.5 | 3.4 |
| Dutch | 0.6 | 1.3 | 1.9 | 2.4 | 1.9 |
| Polish | 0.1 | 0.6 | 1.5 | 1.8 | 1.4 |
| Scandinavian | 0.6 | 1.9 | 2.1 | 2.1 | 1.8 |
| Ukrainian | 0.1 | 1.2 | 2.7 | 2.6 | 2.2 |
| Other | 2.5 | 6.2 | 5.7 | 7.4 | 8.6 |
| TOTAL | 100.0 | 100.0 | 100.0 | 100.0 | 100.0 |

*Source*: Report of the Royal Commission on Bilingualism and Biculturalism, Book IV, p. 248.

dians be bilingual, but rather only that government employees dispensing federal government services are required to be bilingual. This type of bilingualism is referred to as institutional bilingualism.

The multiculturalism policy adopted in 1971 is designed:

> to encourage and assist within the framework of Canada's official languages policy and in the spirit of existing human rights codes, the full realization of the multicultural nature of Canadian society through programs which promote the preservation and sharing of ethnocultural heritages and which facilitate mutual appreciation and understanding among all Canadians.

Part of the multiculturalism program is concerned with the maintenance and development of heritage languages, including languages other than French, English, or Native peoples' languages. This is a relatively recent aspect of multiculturalism, and to date relatively little has been accomplished (for reviews of this work see Cummins, 1983; and O'Bryan, Reitz & Kuplowska, 1976).

The remainder of this chapter will focus on French–English bilingualism and particularly on bilingual education programs oriented toward teaching English-speaking children French. Reference will also be made to bilingual programs that teach nonofficial languages, such as Hebrew and Ukrainian, to English-speaking children. In general, then, the focus will be on bilingual

education for majority English-language children. The reader is referred to Chapter 7 in this volume for a review of educational programs designed for Inuit and Indian children.

## A Brief Sociolinguistic History of English–French Relations

Like many parts of the New World, Canada was settled and governed by different European nations during its early development. The first colonization of Canada was undertaken by the French beginning with Jacques Cartier's landing in Canada in 1534. French control gave way to British control in 1763 when the British defeated the French at the Battle of the Plains of Abraham near Quebec City (Cook, Saywell & Ricker, 1977). French Canadian culture was deeply rooted in North America at the time of the British conquest. Thus, it resisted the assimilationist effects of British legislation and immigration policy which would have eroded the vitality of a less entrenched ethnolinguistic group.

The British North America Act of 1867 legally constituted the Canadian confederation, which at the time consisted of Ontario, Quebec, New Brunswick, and Nova Scotia. Analogous to the American Declaration of Independence, the BNA Act, as it is usually referred to, affirmed Canada's linguistic duality only in Quebec, where the use of both the French and English languages was required in the Parliament and Courts of the province. It was not until 1969, with the passage of the Official Languages Act, as described earlier, that both languages were actually accorded status as official languages nationwide. According to Canadian bilingualism policy, federal government services throughout the country must be made available in both French and English. This policy does not apply to services provided by Canada's ten provincial governments or the two territorial governments in the Yukon and the Northwest Territories. At the provincial level, only one province, New Brunswick, also recognizes French and English as official languages. The remaining nine provinces are monolingual, with eight recognizing English and one, the Province of Quebec, recognizing French as the official language. Despite the lack of official status for both English and French in most of the provinces, certain provincial government services are now available in both languages in most provinces. There is an increasing move in this direction. The official language policies of the provincial governments tend to reflect their respective constituencies. Thus, the one officially bilingual province, New Brunswick, has a sizable percentage of both French-speaking and English-speaking residents; Quebec, which recognizes French as the only official language, is inhabited predominantly by French-speaking residents; and the remaining eight provinces, which all recognize English as the official provincial language, have predominantly English-speaking residents.

Notwithstanding regional differences in the prevalence of English and French, in general the English and French languages are important features of Canadian life. Consequently, competence in both English and French is an important means of communication in Canadian political, cultural, and economic affairs, and bilingual competence is often associated with tangible and/or intangible rewards. The reward value associated with English–French bilingualism is enhanced by the international status and utility of English and French, be it in diplomatic, economic, or cultural spheres. Notwithstanding the historical importance of the French and English cultures in the early development of Canada, the federal government recognizes neither as official cultures. As already noted, Canada has adopted an official policy of multiculturalism which recognizes the legitimacy and value of all cultures represented among its citizenry.

## The Quiet Revolution

Despite its historical importance during the early colonization and subsequent development of Canada; despite its contemporary status as an official national language; despite its demographic significance as the native language of approximately 25 percent of the Canadian population; and despite even its international status as a major world language, French has until recently been the disadvantaged partner in Canadian confederation.[1] This has been true to a large extent even in the Province of Quebec where the vast majority of the population speak French as a native language (viz., some 80 percent in a total population of 6 million); indeed, many Quebecers speak only French. Evidence of the inferior status of French can be found in at least three areas: (1) legislation, (2) patterns of language use, and (3) language attitudes.

### Legislation and the French language

As has already been noted, French is recognized as an official language by only two of Canada's ten provinces (namely, Quebec and New Brunswick) and by neither territorial government. While the eight 'English provinces' do not presently recognize French as an official provincial language, they do not forbid its use. The legislative picture was not always so tolerant. The use of French, particularly in public schools, has been forbidden by law in certain provinces at certain periods during the years since confederation. For example, in 1890 the government of the Province of Manitoba revoked an earlier law requiring the use of French in the provincial Parliament and permitting its use in public schools. Students caught using French in school by the authorities could be physically punished. The 1890 law has since been repealed, and political efforts are being made to restore French to its original status. According to the new Canadian Charter of Rights and Freedoms (1982), public education will be available in all provinces in both official languages, where numbers warrant.

### Patterns of language use

Widespread daily use of French, except in communication with official federal government agencies, is limited to the provinces of Quebec and New Brunswick and to other specific regions with sizable French-speaking communities (e.g. the Ontario–Quebec border, Northern Alberta, and parts of Ontario). Even in these areas, however, English often predominates over French as the lingua franca. This is particularly true in public settings and in business and commerce. In an extensive study of the language of work in Quebec in 1972, J. D. Gendron notes that:

In the province of Quebec itself, French remains basically a marginal language, since non-French-speaking persons have little need of it and many French-speaking people use English as much as and sometimes more than their mother tongue for important work. This applies even though Quebec's French-speaking people constitute a vast majority both in the labor force and in the overall population. (p. 108)

This means that 'in interrelationships in mixed conversation groups, English-speaking persons concede much less to French than do French-speaking persons to English' (p. 93). Thus, 'the burden of bilingualism is unequally distributed between French- and English-speaking people, both as regards the degree of competence in the other language and the language demands on a worker during the course of his career' (p. 94).

### Language attitudes

Perhaps no other single piece of evidence attests to the disadvantaged or inferior status that the French language has had relative to the English language than the results of a study carried out by Lambert, Hodgson, Gardner & Fillenbaum (1960). In what has become a classic study in the social psychology of language, Lambert and his colleagues asked groups of English and French Canadians in Montreal to listen to and give their impressions of people speaking either French or English. Unknown to the listeners, they were actually hearing the same perfectly bilingual individuals on separate occasions, sometimes speaking French and sometimes English. Analyses of the listener's reactions to the speakers indicated that they were much more favorable toward the English 'guises' than toward the French 'guises'. In other words, the same speakers were perceived significantly differently when heard using each of their two languages — it is as if they were two different people. Furthermore, it was found that not only did English Canadians form more favorable impressions of the English guises than the French guises, evidence of in-group favoritism, but so did French Canadians. That is, even the French Canadian subjects perceived the speakers more favorably when they spoke in English than when they spoke in French, even though this meant denigrating members of their own ethnolinguistic group.

Subsequent research has substantiated these findings (d'Anglejan & Tucker, 1973) and further indicates that the tendency for French Canadians to denigrate members of their own group is not manifest by children before the age of twelve but emerges around adolescence (Anisfeld & Lambert, 1964) and thus appears to be a socially learned phenomenon (see Day, 1982, for a recent review of similar research). Lambert has interpreted these results to mean that language can act as an important symbol of ethnolinguistic group membership, and that members of ethnic minority groups may internalize the negative stereotypes of their group that members of the majority group often have.

Discontent over these linguistic and cultural inequities had been developing for some time, particularly in Quebec. Early attempts by the French-speaking community to arrive at a more equitable relationship with the English community through negotiation had been largely unsuccessful. Repeatedly faced with an apparent lack of responsiveness on the part of the English community to their concerns, French-speaking Quebecers began to make vocal and public demands for change. This culminated in the early 1960s with concerted political, social, and, in some cases, militant actions to bring about change. There were, for example, mass demonstrations against public institutions that would or could not communicate with French-speaking Quebecers in French. The social unrest manifested during this period has come to be called the Quiet Revolution.

During the last twenty years, some Quebec politicians have called for separation from the rest of Canada. A political party whose avowed intentions are to seek Quebec's separation from Canada was elected as the provincial government in 1976. One of the most important pieces of legislation which this government passed after taking office was a law declaring French the only official language of the province. This law then assures the linguistic rights of the majority French-speaking citizens of Quebec. Some analysts believe that a 1978 referendum by this same government seeking support for Quebec's separation from Canada failed because of the reassurance that this law gave the French population that their language would be respected and safeguarded.

### The St Lambert Experiment: A Community Experiment in Social Change

At the same time that the French community in

Quebec was expressing dissatisfaction with inequities in the language situation, some English-speaking Quebecers began to grow more concerned about English–French relations. More specifically there was an emerging awareness in the English community, precipitated by events of the Quiet Revolution, that French was becoming an important language of communication in most spheres of life in Quebec and, concomitantly, that English alone would no longer assure social and economic success in the province. The coexistence of French and English Canadians has been characterized by Canadian novelist Hugh MacLennan (1945) as *two solitudes*, an apt metaphor in this and many other communities inhabited by people of different linguistic and cultural backgrounds. Faced with the evolving importance of French as the main working language of Quebec and with an increasing dissatisfaction with the linguistic barriers that separated English and French Canadians, a concerned group of English-speaking parents in the small suburban community of St Lambert, outside of Montreal, began to meet informally in the early 1960s to discuss the situation (Lambert & Tucker, 1972).

They felt that their incompetence in French contributed to, and indeed was attributable in part to, the two solitudes that effectively prevented them from learning French informally from their French-speaking neighbors. They felt that their inability to communicate in French was also attributable to inadequate methods of second-language instruction in English schools. At that time, French was taught for relatively short periods each day (twenty to thirty minutes) by teachers who were usually native English-speakers with competence in French-as-a-second-language that varied from excellent to poor. There was an emphasis on teaching vocabulary and grammar rules and on using pattern practice drills based on then popular audiolingual techniques. This approach was common to many second-language programs throughout North America which retain some of the same characteristics even to this day. Unlike second-language instruction in other parts of North America, however, second-language instruction in Quebec began in elementary school and continued systematically until the end of secondary school. This is still true, and it has become customary to varying degrees in the other Canadian provinces.

Despite twelve years of second-language instruction, however, students graduating from the public schools of Quebec were inadequately prepared to deal with the demands of using a second language in diverse real-life situations. As one of the group of twelve St Lambert parents who spearheaded interest in alternative methods of second-language instruction pointed out:

> Children were graduating from English Protestant schools in this province with little more knowledge of French than their parents had had, despite claims that the programs had been considerably improved over the years. Their knowledge was not perceptibly superior to that of graduates from the English provinces of Canada and was not sufficient to enable the students to communicate with their French-Canadian neighbors. The parents felt their children were being short-changed and should have the opportunity to become 'bilingual' within the school system, since it was so difficult to achieve this skill outside of school. (Melikoff in Lambert & Tucker, 1972: 220)

Most of the St Lambert parents who participated in these discussions could attest to the failure of second-language instruction, using their own experiences as evidence.

In their search for better methods of second-language instruction for their children, the St Lambert Bilingual School Study Group, as they came to call themselves, sought the assistance and advice of experts within their community. In particular, they consulted with Dr Wallace E. Lambert of the Psychology Department, McGill University, who had conducted research on social psychological and cognitive aspects of bilingualism, and with Dr Wilder Penfield of the Montreal Neurological Institute, McGill, who had conducted research on brain mechanisms underlying language functions. The involvement of these two scholars was indeed fortunate because not only did they give their overall support to the parents' project, but their professional advice shaped the new program in some important ways.

The efforts of the St Lambert group finally succeeded, with the school district agreeing to set up an experimental kindergarten immersion class in September 1965, some two years after their first meetings. In her description of events leading up to 1965, Olga Melikof notes that school officials did not accept the experimental class because of any conviction that it was a worthwhile educational experiment, but rather because public pressure on them was too great to ignore. She characterizes the official school district attitude as follows: 'You asked for it, if it doesn't work, it's not our fault' (p. 227). 'At no time would the Board undertake to accept the experiment for more than a year at a time' (p. 233). Despite a lack of official support from the school authorities, parents were surprisingly enthusiastic — registration for the experimental kindergarten class 'opened one spring day at 1 p.m., and by 1:05 p.m. the quota of 26 children was reached' (p. 226).

The process of community involvement that has just been described has been repeated many times since the first immersion class was opened in St Lambert in 1965. The introduction of French immersion programs in most school districts elsewhere in Quebec and Canada has been instigated and promoted by local community groups, along with the assistance of individual school district officials and researchers. Official support has customarily been lukewarm at the outset. Parents have continued to play an important role in the evolution of immersion programs, as evidenced by the establishment of Canadian Parents for French, a voluntary, nonprofit association of English-speaking parents who seek to improve the quality of second-language instruction in public schools across Canada.

It was in the educational system, and in French immersion in particular, that the St Lambert parents sought a response to important sociolinguistic changes that were taking place around them. Moreover, it was through educational innovation that they also sought to bring about social change within their own communities. Improved French-second-language learning was not intended to be the sole goal of immersion. Rather, it was intended to be an intermediate goal leading to improved relationships between English and French Quebecers and thus ultimately to a breaking down of the two solitudes that had become unacceptable.

## St Lambert: An Experiment in Bilingual Education

The St Lambert French immersion program that was inaugurated in September 1965 was designed to achieve the following primary goals:

(1) To provide the participating children with functional competence in both written and spoken aspects of French.

(2) To promote and maintain normal levels of English-language development.

(3) To ensure achievement in academic subjects commensurate with the students' ability and grade level.

(4) To instill in the students an understanding and appreciation of French Canadians, their language and culture, without detracting in any way from the students' identity with and appreciation for English Canadian culture. These goals are shared by most immersion programs across Canada in essentially the same form.

The program in St Lambert was an *early total* immersion program. That is, all curriculum instruction, beginning in kindergarten (five years of age) and continuing through the primary grades, was taught through French, although it is common for the children themselves to use English with one another and the teacher during kindergarten. (See Figure 1 for a schematic summary of the early total immersion program.) At first, French was to be used as the only medium of instruction until the end of grade three; this was later altered so that only kindergarten and grade one were taught entirely in French. When English was introduced into the curriculum, it was used to teach English-language arts, for approximately one hour per day. Instruction through English was subsequently expanded in successive grades to include other subjects, such as math or science. By grade six, or the end of elementary school, 60 percent of the curriculum was taught in English and 40 percent in French. This was usually implemented by teaching through English during the morning and through French during the afternoon of each day and always with native speakers of English and French, respectively. This basic pattern is characteristic of many current early total immersion programs, although there are, of course, variations among programs. For example, early immersion programs offered elsewhere delay the introduction of English until grade three or even grade four or limit the amount of exposure to English once it is introduced (see Genesee, 1983, for a review). Some important variations will be discussed in a later section of this chapter. Follow-up to the early immersion years is often provided at the secondary school level by offering a number of selected courses in French. These may be either language arts or other subject courses such as geography or history. The particular courses and number of such courses that students take at

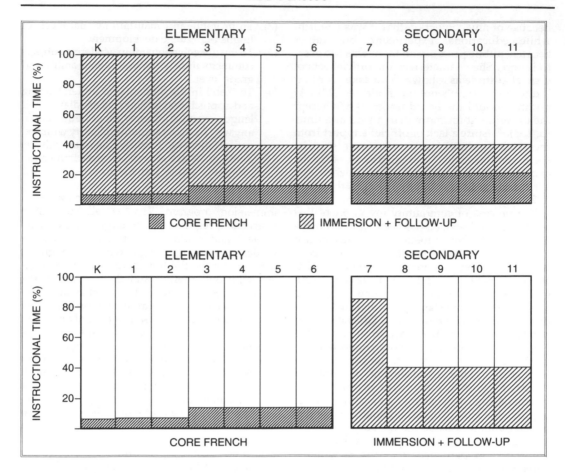

**Figure 1** Schematic representation of an early total immersion and one-year-late immersion program

this level are a matter of individual student choice.

The most distinctive feature of the St Lambert immersion program was its use of the second language to teach regular academic subjects, such as mathematics, science, and social studies, in addition to language arts. This is one of the distinctive characteristics of all immersion programs. Immersion teachers teach regular school subjects using French much as they would if their pupils were native speakers of the language. The same subject matter is never taught in the same school year using both English and French. Formal instruction in the grammatical rules of French is presented in the French-language arts class, which constitutes a large part of the primary grades, as does English in the case of a regular English program. Clearly, however, the

children are not native speakers, and so the teachers emphasize oral–aural communication skills during kindergarten and the first half of grade one. Reading, writing, and other literacy skills are introduced slowly and only when it is felt that the children have acquired the corresponding oral/aural language skills. The children are not required to use French with the teacher or with one another until the second half of grade one. In fact, the children commonly use English among themselves and with the teacher during this stage.

Generally, immersion programs are designed to create the same kinds of conditions that occur during first-language learning; namely, there is an emphasis on creating a desire by the student to learn the language in order to engage in meaningful and interesting communication

(Macnamara, 1973; Terrell, 1981). Thus, language learning in immersion is incidental to learning about mathematics, the sciences, the community, and one another. This stands in sharp contrast to more traditional methods of second-language instruction where the emphasis is on the conscious learning of the elements and rules of language for their own sake. Moreover, the immersion program is designed to allow the student to apply his or her 'natural language learning' or cognitive abilities as a means of learning the language. It is now generally accepted that first-language acquisition in children is a systematic process that reflects the child's active cognitive attempts to formulate linguistic rules that correspond to adult competence in the language. This process is called creative construction (Dulay & Burt, 1978; Slobin, 1973). According to this conceptualization, opportunities to communicate in the language are advantageous for learning, and 'errors' are a normal and important part of the learning process. The immersion approach permits the learner to progress according to his or her own rate and style, again in much the same way that first-language learners do (Bloom, Hood & Lightbown, 1974; Nelson, 1981).

Another distinctive pedagogical feature of the Canadian immersion program is the use of monolingual language models and 'linguistic territories' within the school. The French teachers in the immersion programs present themselves to the students as monolingual French speakers, even though in most cases these teachers are very competent in English. The French teachers in kindergarten and grade one especially must know enough English to understand the students whose comments are initially all in English. Many of the students learn about their French teachers' bilinguality only in the later grades when they overhear them using English with an English teacher. The classrooms in which French and English instruction are presented are kept as distinct as possible. This means that the children usually change classrooms for the French and English parts of the school day once English is introduced into the curriculum. An explicit rule to use French in the French classroom and with the French teachers is established. These two strategies — the use of monolingual second-language teacher models and the establishment of French territories within the school — have been adopted and are observed very conscientiously in order to facilitate the students'

second-language learning by encouraging, indeed requiring, their use of the second language. Otherwise, there would be a natural tendency for the students to use English, their stronger language.

## The Spread of Immersion: The Present Situation

Since the St Lambert experiment began, immersion has expanded dramatically. Immersion programs are now available in several different forms, in a variety of languages, and in all Canadian provinces and the territories. The number of students enrolled in immersion increased from approximately 17,763 in 1976 to 102,168 in 1982 (Stern, 1984). Participation in immersion programs is voluntary, and to date the majority of programs serve children from 'middle-class' socioeconomic backgrounds. The alternative forms of immersion currently available differ primarily with respect to the grade level(s) during which the second language is used as a major medium of curriculum instruction. Differentiations are often made between (1) early, (2) delayed, and (3) late immersion. A secondary basis of differentiation is made according to the amount of instruction provided in the second language (viz., total versus partial) and/or the number of years during which the second language is used as a major medium of instruction. Excluded from this rough taxonomy are (1) second-language programs in which the second language is used for teaching language arts only and one non-language subject and (2) programs in which the second language is never used to teach at least 50 percent of the curriculum during any school year. These latter types of programs would generally be regarded as enriched second-language programs.

### Early immersion

There are two main types of early immersion: total and partial. The early total immersion program has already been described in the section on the St Lambert Experiment and is schematically represented in Figure 1. The early partial immersion program differs in that less than 100 percent of curriculum instruction during the primary grades (kindergarten, one, two, and three) is presented through the second language. The most common formula is 50 percent French/50 percent English. The amount of French instruction in early partial immersion programs tends to remain constant throughout the elementary grades, in contrast to total immersion programs in which the French component decreases. Another difference between these two types of immersion is the sequencing of literacy instruction. In total immersion programs, literacy training in the native language occurs after literacy training in the second language has begun. In partial immersion programs, literacy training tends to occur in both languages simultaneously from grade one on.

Among early total immersion alternatives, the main variation involves the grade level at which English instruction is introduced — it may be grade two, as in St Lambert, grade three, or grade four. Another variation among early total immersion options is the amount of instruction presented through English once it is introduced into the curriculum. In some cases, English exposure increases quickly, for example, from 20 percent in grade three to 60 percent in grade five. In other cases, it increases very slowly (for example, remaining stable at 20 percent during grades three, four, and five).

### Delayed immersion

Immersion programs that postpone use of the second language as a major medium of instruction until the middle elementary grades (i.e. four or five) are classified here as delayed. These programs usually offer a core second-language course of twenty to forty-five minutes a day in the primary grades prior to the immersion component which may be of one or two years duration (see Cziko, Holobow & Lambert, 1977, for an example). This may then be followed by partial immersion until the end of elementary school, during which language arts and other subject material are taught through the second language. In the delayed immersion, option training in first-language literacy precedes training in second-language literacy.

### Late immersion

Late immersion programs postpone intensive use of the second language until the end of elementary school or the beginning of secondary school (Figure 1). In *one-year* late immersion programs, all or most of the curriculum, except English-language arts, is taught through the second language for one year (see, for example, Genesee, Polich & Stanley, 1977). In *two-year* late immersion programs, this schedule is repeated for two consecutive years (see Genesee 1981). Late immersion programs may be preceded by

core second-language instruction throughout the elementary grades, or they may be preceded by special preparatory second-language courses one or two years immediately prior to immersion (see Swain, 1978). Most late immersion options — one-year/two-year and with/without prior core second-language instruction — are usually followed in the higher grades by advanced second-language arts courses and, in some cases, by selected nonlanguage courses, such as geograpyy that are taught through the second language.

### Double immersion

By far the most common alternative forms of immersion, as just described, involve the use of a single second language. Genesee and Lambert have investigated variations of immersion for majority English-speaking children in which two nonnative languages (French and Hebrew) are used as major media of curriculum instruction during the elementary grades (see Genesee & Lambert, 1983). French and Hebrew were selected as immersion languages in the programs in question because both have sociocultural significance for the participants but for different reasons. On the one hand, French, being one of the official languages of Canada, has social and economic relevance to these children and their families on a day-to-day basis. In this regard, the Hebrew–French double immersion programs are the same as the St Lambert program and other French immersion programs for majority-language children in Canada. On the other hand, Hebrew is valued because of its religious and cultural significance and because of its increasing nonsectarian importance as a national language of Israel. In this respect, the Hebrew–French double immersion programs differ from French-only immersion in being heritage language or language revitalization programs. The underlying principles or both programs are nevertheless the same, and, in particular, their success is predicated on the participation of children who are members of the majority language group.

In one type of double immersion program studied by Genesee and Lambert, English-speaking children from Montreal received all their curriculum instruction during the primary grades in French and Hebrew. The French curriculum comprised language arts, mathematics, science, and social studies. The Hebrew curriculum comprised language arts, history, and religious and cultural studies. Native French- and

Hebrew-speaking teachers were used to teach each curriculum. English was not introduced until grade three in the case of one school and grade four in the case of another. We have referred to this alternative as *early double immersion*. In contrast, in another double immersion program English along with French and Hebrew were used as media of instruction from kindergarten on. This program alternative has been referred to as *delayed double immersion* because the amount of exposure to French increased systematically from five hours per week in grade one to twelve hours per week in grades five and six. Instruction through English decreased somewhat from twelve hours per week in grade one to nine hours per week in grade six as a result. Exposure to Hebrew changed insignificantly.

These programs are described in some detail here because they represent effective and feasible models of multilingual/multicultural education of possible interest to ethnolinguislic groups who are interested in revitalizing heritage language and at the same time wish to acquire competence in an additional second language of some local or national relevance. Examples other than Hebrew–French immersion for English children come to mind. For example, Ukrainian Canadians in western Canada might wish to have their children, who in most cases have become Anglicized, acquire competence in Ukrainian while also learning Canada's other official language, French.

## Research Findings

The extension of immersion programs to all the Canadian provinces and its evolution to include alternative forms is attributable in no small measure to the research component that has accompanied the development of immersion from the beginning. Several large-scale longitudinal evaluations have been set up in a number of Canadian centers to monitor the effectiveness of immersion programs in these locations. They include the Protestant School Board of Greater Montreal evaluations (Genesee, 1983), the Bilingual Education Project, OISE (Swain & Lapkin, 1982), the Ottawa Board of Education Project (Stern *et al.*, 1976), and the British Columbia French Project (Shapson & Day, 1980), as well as the St Lambert Experiment (Lambert & Tucker, 1972). The results of these evaluations provide a comprehensive and reliable indication of the linguistic and academic outcomes of immersion. The findings reviewed here pertain to students

from middle socioeconomic backgrounds because they constitute the majority of participants (see Genesee, 1976b, for a discussion if the suitability of immersion for all children).

In brief, assessment of the English literacy skills (e.g. reading, spelling, writing) of early total immersion students has revealed that during the primary grades when no instruction in English is provided, they are usually behind their peers who have been in an all-English program. This is not surprising in view of the students' lack of training in English literacy. What is surprising is their ability to take English-language tests and complete them reasonably well despite a lack of such training. Quite likely, this is possible because the immersion students are able to transfer skills they have been taught in French to English, a language they already know well in its aural and oral forms. In other words, they do not have to learn to read and write in English from the beginning once they have acquired these skills in French. During the same grades, early total immersion students demonstrate no deficits in listening comprehension, aural decoding, or oral communication. A study by Genesee, Tucker & Lambert (1975) found that in interpersonal communication early total immersion students were more sensitive to the communicative needs of their listeners than were nonimmersion students. The lag in English literacy that the immersion students experience during the primary grades is eliminated as soon as English-language instruction is introduced into the curriculum. Evaluation of different immersion variants has shown that this catch-up occurs at the end of one year of having received English-language arts instruction whether English is delayed until grades two, three, or four. This has also been found to be the case in double immersion programs (Genesee & Lambert 1983). Furthermore, follow-up assessments in higher grades have revealed that there are no long-term advantages to introducing English instruction into the curriculum earlier (e.g. grade two) rather than later (e.g. grade four). Genesee & Lambert (1983) found that the use of English as a medium of instruction from kindergarten on in double immersion programs appears to inhibit second-language acquisition. Typically, early partial immersion programs, which use English 50 percent of the time and French 50 percent of the time, result in equivalent levels of English-language development as early total immersion programs. It has been found that students in delayed and late immersion programs also develop normal levels of English-language proficiency and experience no lags whatsoever.

The expansion of immersion programs shortly after their inauguration in 1965 raised concerns about the effectiveness of such an approach for children with low levels of academic or intellectual ability and for children who had relatively low levels of English-language development. In a series of studies, Genesee (1978) examined the English-language development of immersion students with low academic ability in comparison with that of similar students in all-English programs. Academic ability was assessed using IQ tests. He found that below-average students in immersion achieved the same levels of proficiency in English reading, spelling, vocabulary, and writing as below-average students in the English program. In other words, below-average students were not handicapped by the immersion experience as many had expected. M. Bruck (1982) has reported similar results for immersion children who were considered 'language disabled' in English in comparison with similarly disabled children in the English stream.

Immersion students have been shown to achieve higher levels of proficiency in all aspects of French, including reading, writing, listening comprehension, and oral communication, than students receiving core French-language instruction. This is to be expected in view of the considerably greater exposure to French provided by immersion. Research by Genesee (1976a) has found that below-average students in early immersion programs cannot be distinguished from their above-average peers by native French-speaking evaluators who are asked to subjectively assess their oral production and listening comprehension skills. In contrast, above-average immersion students usually outperform below-average students on tests that assess literacy and academic achievement, for example, reading comprehension and mathematics. Comparisons of the French-language proficiency of immersion students with that of native French-speaking students has indicated that immersion students achieve very high levels of communicative ability but that their proficiency is not native-like even by the end of six or seven years.

The results of academic achievement testing have shown that immersion students achieve the same levels of academic proficiency in math and science, for example, as English control students who have been receiving all academic instruction in English.

Finally, investigations regarding some of the social psychological aspects of immersion indicate that the participating students develop the same identity with and positive attitudes toward the English Canadian culture and language as do students attending English-language programs (Genesee, 1984). The attitudes of immersion students toward French Canadians tend to be more positive than those of nonimmersion students during the early years of the program and then come to resemble those of their nonimmersion compatriots in later years. It is possible that lack of ongoing contact with French Canadians may account for this developmental shift. Immersion students generally indicate a willingness to use French when called upon to do so. Students in Montreal, for example, report using French in face-to-face encounters much more often than do nonimmersion students. At the same time, there is evidence that immersion students do not actively seek out contact with French Canadians or opportunities to use French. They also express reservations about using French at the expense of English. It seems quite likely that some of these feelings stem from conflicts between French and English Canadians in society at large. Notwithstanding such reservations and conflict, immersion students express positive attitudes toward learning French in the immersion programs. Many of their comments indicate that they are in favor of more French, especially during the follow-up years. In contrast, nonimmersion students express relatively negative attitudes toward their French program and toward learning French in general.

Taken together, these findings indicate that immersion programs are suitable for children with diverse learning and language characteristics provided they are members of a majority language group, such as English Canadians. The suitability of immersion programs for children from minority language groups is an open question, subject to empirical investigation. In a review of research on the effectiveness of immersion programs for all children, Genesee (1976b) concluded that 'the results from the existing research are generally inconclusive on the suitability of...immersion for minority group children' (p. 510). Only one study pertinent to this issue was available at that time. There has been no research progress since then. Proponents of second-language immersion programs for majority English-speaking children have generally doubted their applicability for children from minority language backgrounds who do not enjoy the same individual or social respect that English speakers in North America enjoy (Hernández-Chávez, 1984). In Canada, English immersion programs for French speaking Canadians have not been recommended because this form of education poses a wide-scale threat to French in North America. That is, too much English too soon could undermine the vitality of French. The important point here is that the implementation of specific forms of bilingual education must take into account the sociocultural context in which schooling takes place.

## Summary

Immersion programs were first instituted in the Province of Quebec, Canada, in the mid-1960s. They were developed in reaction to particular sociocultural events in the province at the time, and they were designed to respond to the needs and characteristics of a specific group of children. Since the original St Lambert project, immersion has become a relatively widespread and commonplace form of education in the Canadian public school system. The results of numerous longitudinal scientific evaluations have consistently indicated that majority English-language children participating in these programs do not experience any long-term deficits in native-language development or academic achievement. At the same time, they achieve functional competence in the second language that is markedly better than that of students in core second-language programs. Although not truly native-like in all aspects, the second-language skills of immersion students are rated very highly even by native speakers of the language. Since immersion programs in Canada are optional, these results necessarily pertain to students who have chosen or whose parents have chosen on their behalf to attend the program instead of regular English schools.

The documented success or the Canadian immersion programs depends on a combination of pedagogical practices, as outlined earlier, as well as certain sociocultural conditions. The major sociocultural conditions include the following: (1) the participating children speak the language of the majority in North America, that is, English; (2) educational, teaching, and administrative personnel working in immersion programs value and support, directly or indirectly, the children's home language and culture; (3) the participating children and their parents similarly value their home language and culture and do not wish to forsake either; and (4) acquisition of the second language is regarded by all concerned as a positive addition to the child's repertoire of skills. Thus, the success of immersion is more than simply a question of when to use students' first and second languages for instructional purposes. It is equally dependent on an understanding of the sociocultural conditions in which the students are raised and educated.

Interest in immersion from both pedagogical and linguistic perspectives continues as researchers continue to explore the suitability of immersion for all children. Genesee and Lambert, for example, are currently examining its effectiveness for black as well as white children from inner-city neighborhoods in US school districts. Previous research has focused largely on middle-class, white children. An experimental early total immersion program in Mohawk, an Amerindian language, is currently underway for Indian children who do not speak Mohawk but rather have learned English as a native language. A systematic evaluation of this project is planned by Genesee and Lambert as well. Researchers are beginning to address important issues concerning teaching approaches in immersion classes (Swain, 1984) and the relationship between intergroup relations in society at large and relations between English and French Canadian teachers in immersion schools (Cleghorn & Genesee, 1984). The findings from these studies will help to expand our already rich understanding of the immersion approach to bilingual education.

## Note

1. Discussion of the social and political events that preceded the emergence of French immersion in 1965 focuses on issues pertaining to language and English–French relations. This coverage is necessarily simplified and is not intended to reflect a complete or unbiased interpretation of history.

## Bibliography

Anisfield, E. and Lambert, W.E. (1964) Evaluational reactions of bilingual and monolingual children to spoken languages. *Journal of Abnormal and Social Psychology* 69, 89–97.

Barnaby, A. (1988) Chapter 7 in Christina Bratt

Paulston (ed.) *International Handbook of Bilingualism and Bilingual Education*. New York: Greenwood Press.

Bloom, L. M., Hood, L. M. and Lightbown, P. (1974) Imitation in language development: If, when, and why. *Cognitive Psychology* 6, 380–420.

Brown, R. C., Cazden, C. and Bellugi, U. (1970) The child's grammar from I to III. In R. Brown (ed.) *Psycholinguistics*. New York: Free Press, pp. 100–54.

Bruck, M. (1981) Language impaired children: Performance in an additive bilingual education program. *Applied Linguistics* 3, 45–60.

Cleghorn, A. and Genesee, F. (1984) *Languages in Contact: An Ethnographic Study of Interaction in an Immersion School*. Montreal: Psychology Department, McGill University .

Cook, R., Saywell, J. and Ricker, J. (1977) *Canada: A Modern Study*. Toronto: Clarke, Irwin and Co.

Cummins, J. (ed.) (1983) *Heritage Language Education: Issues and Directions*. Ottawa: Ministry of Supply and Services.

Cziko, G. A., Holobow, N. and Lambert, W.E. (1977) *A Comparison of Three Elementary School Alternatives for Learning French: Children at Grades Four and Five*. Montreal: Department of Psychology, McGill University.

d'Anglejan, A. and Tucker, G.R. (1973) Sociolinguistic correlates of speech style in Quebec. In R. W. Shuy and R. W. Fasold (eds) *Language Attitudes: Current Trends and Prospects*. Washington, DC: Georgetown University Press, pp. 1–27.

Day, R. R. (1982) Children's attitudes toward language. In E. B. Ryan and H. Giles (eds) *Attitudes Toward Language Variation: Social and Applied Contexts*. London: Edward Arnold, pp. 116–31.

Dulay, H. and Burt, M. (1978) Some remarks on creativity in language acquisition. In W. C. Ritchie (ed.) *Second Language Acquisition Research: Issues and Implications*. New York: Academic Press, pp. 65–89.

Gendron, J. D. (1972) *Commission of Inquiry on the Position of the French Language and on Language Rights in Quebec: Language at Work*. Quebec: L'editeur officiel du Quebec.

Genesee, F. (1976a) The role of intelligence in second language learning. *Language Learning* 26, 267–80.

— (1976b) The suitability of immersion programs for all children. *Canadian Modern Language Review* 32, 494–515.

— (1978) A longitudinal evaluation of all early immersion school program. *Canadian Journal of Education* 3, 31–50.

— (1981) A comparison of early and late second language learning. *Canadian Journal of Behavioral Sciences* 13, 115–25.

— (1983) Bilingual education of majority language children: The immersion experiments in review. *Applied Psycholinguistics* 4, 1–46.

— (in press) Beyond bilingualism: Social psychological studies of French immersion programs in Canada. *Canadian Journal of Behavioral Science*.

Genesee, F. and Lambert, W.E. (1983) Trilingual education for majority language children. *Child Development* 54, 105–14.

Genesee, F., Polich, E. and Stanley, M.H. (1977) An experimental French immersion program at the secondary school level — 1969 to 1974. *Canadian Modern Language Review* 33, 318–32.

Genesee, F., Rogers, P. and Holobow, N. (1983) The social psychology of second language learning: Another point of view. *Language Learning* 33, 209–24.

Genesee, F., Tucker, G. R. and Lambert, W.E. (1975) Communication skills of bilingual children. *Child Development* 46, 1010–14.

Hernández-Chávez, E. (1984) The inadequacy of English immersion education as an educational approach for language minority students in the United States. In *Studies on Immersion Education: A Collection for US Educators*. Sacramento, CA: California State Department of Education, pp. 144–81.

Lambert, W. E., Hodgson, R.C. Gardner, R.C. and Fillenbaum, S. (1960) Evaluational reactions to spoken languages. *Journal of Abnormal and Social Psychology* 60, 44–51 .

Lambert, W. and Tucker, R. (1972) *Bilingual Education of Children: The St Lambert Experiment*. Rowley, MA: Newbury House.

MacLennan, H. (1945) *Two Solitudes*. Montreal: Duell, Sloan and Pearce.

Macnamara, J. (1973) Nurseries, streets, and classrooms. *Modern Language Journal* 57, 250–4.

Melikoff, O. (1972) Appendix A: Parents as change agents in education. In W. Lambert and R. Tucker (eds) *Bilingual Education of Children: The St Lambert Experiment*. Rowley, MA: Newbury House.

Nelson, K. (1981) Individual differences in language development: Implications for development and language. *Developmental Psychology* 17, 170–87.

O'Bryan, K. G., Reitz, J.G. and Kuplowska, O. (eds) (1976) *Non-official Languages: A Study in*

*Canadian Multiculturalism.* Ottawa: Ministry of Supply and Services, Canada.

Shapson, S. M. and Day, E. (1980) *Longitudinal Evaluation of the Early Entry Immersion Program in Coquitlam School District: Report to the End of Year 6.* Burnaby, BC: Faculty of Education, Simon Fraser University.

Slobin, D.I. (1973) Cognitive prerequisites for the development of grammar. In C.A. Ferguson and D.I. Slobin (eds) *Studies in Child Language and Development.* New York: Holt, Rinehart and Winston, pp. 175–280.

Stern, M.H. (1984) The immersion phenomenon. *Language and Society.* Ottawa: Ministry of Supply and Services, pp. 4–7.

Swain, M. (1978) French immersion: Early, late or partial? *Canadian Modern Language Review* 4, 577–85.

— (1984) *19th Report of the Activities of the Modern Language Centre.* Toronto: Ontario Institute for Studies in Education.

Swain, M. and Lapkin, S. (1982) *Evaluating Bilingual Education: A Canadian Case Study.* Clevedon: Multilingual Matters.

Terrell, T.D. (1981) The natural approach in bilingual education. In *Schooling and Language Minority Students: A Theoretical Framework.* Developed by the California State Department of Education, Office of Bilingual Bicultural Education. Los Angeles: California State University Evaluation, Dissemination, and Assessment Center, pp. 117–46.

## Questions

(1) Describe the present sociolinguistic situation of Canada. Identify the three founding groups and their socio-historical differences in population size, geographical distribution, social and economic power. Also define 'heritage languages.' Define the official language policy of the central government and several provinces in Canada.

(2) Genesee refers to the 'quiet revolution' of French. What does he mean? Describe the historical events of this 'quiet revolution.'

(3) Give the history of the French immersion programs and in particular of the St Lambert French immersion program. Define linguistic goals, parental involvement, use of second language, use of first language, approaches to language learning, teacher characteristics and classroom structure. How does this differ from the structure of a bilingual school with which you are familiar? How does this differ from submersion education and structured immersion programs for language minority students in the United States?

(4) What is the difference between early immersion, delayed immersion and late immersion? What is the difference between total immersion and partial immersion? What are the justifications for these different forms of immersion?

(5) Describe the findings of early total immersion programs for Anglophone students with regard to:
   (a) students' English literacy;
   (b) students' English oracy;
   (c) students' French literacy;
   (d) students' French oracy;
   (e) students' academic achievement in math and science;
   (f) students' attitudes toward the minority.
   What can you conclude from these results? If these programs have been so successful for Anglophone students in Quebec, why are they not recommended for Francophone students in Quebec nor for Latino students in the United States?

(6) What are double immersion programs? What are delayed double immersion programs? Why are they significant in Canada? Could these double immersion programs

also be considered a heritage language program or a language revitalization program? Why or why not?

## Activities

(1) Make a poster in which you portray the Canadian ethnic mosaic. Find out as much as you can about linguistic heterogeneity in Canada today before you work on your mosaic. Display the posters. Select the best for permanent display.

(2) Conduct a newspaper search to trace Canadian language policy since this article appeared. What have been the changes in Canada and Quebec? How would you evaluate the situation in Canada today?

(3) Set up a 'matched guise' experiment in which the *same* bilingual person is asked to read a passage first in a majority language, then in a minority language. Tell the five listeners that they will hear *two* different persons. Then ask them to rate the speaker on the following characteristics, using a scale where 1 = 'Low', 2 = 'Average', 3 = 'High.'

    (a) IQ;
    (b) financial prosperity;
    (c) 'good looks;'
    (d) personality;
    (e) confidence;
    (f) social class status;
    (g) academic achievement;
    (h) trustworthiness;
    (i) friendliness;
    (j) happiness.

Share your results with the class. What can you conclude from your findings? How do they differ from those of Lambert described in the article?

(4) Ask a majority and a minority person to make a list of generally held stereotypes about the ethnolinguistic group to which the minority person belongs. Compare both lists. Bring them to class and share with others. Compile an integrated list.

(5) Write a play script that would reflect the metaphor 'two solitudes' in relation to two ethnolinguistic groups with which you are familiar. Choose the best script in the class and perform the play for other students.

(6) Role-play Anglophone people in Quebec in the early 1960s trying to get a French immersion program started. Enact different situations; for example, talking to the educational authorities, to language specialists, amongst themselves, with French speakers, at home with their spouses and their children.

(7) Research whether there are any immersion programs for the language majority in your area. If there are, make a Resource List with their location, requirements, tuition, size, languages, etc. If there is only one, describe it in detail. If there is no such schools, ask administrators in three schools how students learn languages other than the majority one and whether the program is successful. Then tell them about immersion programs, and ask them how they feel about them. Record their answers.

## Further Reading

For more on immersion education and its implications for the United States, see:

*Studies on Immersion Education: A Collection for United States Educators* (1984). Sacramento: California: California State Department of Education.
For how other countries have implemented immersion programs, see especially:
Artigal, Josep Maria (1993) Catalan and Basque immersion programs. In Hugo Baetens Beardsmore (ed.) *European Models of Bilingual Education* (pp. 30–53). Clevedon: Multilingual Matters.

# Heritage Language Teaching in Canadian Schools

## Jim Cummins

The dramatic increase in ethnic and linguistic diversity in Canada's cities during the past 25 years has given rise to intense debate among virtually all sectors of society — policy makers, educators and the general public — about appropriate ways of educating students whose mother tongue is other than English or French. A major issue has been the extent to which the public school system should play a role in supporting the continued development of children's mother tongues (usually termed 'heritage languages' in Canada).[1] While ethnocultural communities have strongly pressed the case for the teaching of heritage languages within the public school system, these demands have outraged those who see heritage languages as having no place within the Canadian mainstream. I will first outline the demographic and political context within which the debate about heritage language teaching is taking place and then review the major issues of contention in the debate.

### The Demographic Context

Approximately one-third of the Canadian population is of an ethnic origin other than Anglo/Celtic or French (termed 'ethnocultural' in this paper). This proportion is likely to rise significantly in view of dramatic increases in immigration levels in recent years. Immigrants to Canada numbered 84,302 in 1985 but have increased steadily during the past six years to a current (1991) projected level of 220,000, with projections of 250,000 annually from 1992 through to 1996. These increases have been implemented as part of the federal (Conservative) government strategy to combat the combined effects of low birth rates and a rapidly ageing population.

Within the schools of major urban centres, linguistic and cultural diversity have increased substantially in recent years. For example, in Toronto and Vancouver, more than half the school population comes from a non-English-speaking background. In Quebec, the large immigrant populations in some Montreal schools are seen by some politicians and commentators as a serious threat to the survival of the cultural integrity of the province (Cummins & Danesi, 1990). The demographic trends clearly indicate that cultural and linguistic diversity in urban schools will continue to increase. In other words, students from non-English-speaking (or, in Quebec, non-French-speaking) backgrounds will increasingly become the mainstream population in urban schools, a fact that has enormous implications for the education system at all levels. For example, to this point, teacher education programmes have taken relatively little account of the implications of diversity (Henley & Young, 1989) but this situation is likely to change as the needs of the field become more apparent.

### The Policy Context

Federal policy with respect to heritage language teaching takes place within the context of Canada's national policy of multiculturalism, proclaimed by then-Prime Minister Trudeau in October 1971. One outcome of this policy was the commissioning of the *Non-Official Languages Study* (O'Bryan et al., 1976) which found substantial support among ethnocultural communities across the country for heritage language teaching within the public school system. A parallel study, the *Majority Attitudes Study* (Berry et al., 1977) found some lukewarm support for the policy of multiculturalism among anglophone and francophone Canadians but significant opposition to the use of public moneys to support the teaching of heritage languages.

Despite the ambivalence of many anglophone

and francophone Canadians, the federal government initiated the Cultural Enrichment Program in 1977. This programme provided some very modest support (approximately 10% of the operating costs of supplementary schools, usually conducted on Saturday mornings) directly to ethnocultural communities for the teaching of heritage languages. This support was eliminated in 1990 (as part of a more general fiscal belt-tightening) but the federal government emphasized that it was simply changing priorities for heritage language support rather than diminishing its commitment to heritage languages. The major federal initiative in this area in recent years has been the establishment of the National Heritage Languages Institute in Edmonton, Alberta, which is expected to start operations in late 1991.

Because education is under provincial jurisdiction, the Canadian federal government cannot provide support directly to school systems for the teaching of heritage languages. Most provincial governments, however, operate programmes designed to encourage the teaching of heritage languages. The most extensive of these provincial programmes has been Ontario's *Heritage Language Program* (HLP). Announced in the spring of 1977 (shortly before a provincial election was called), the HLP provides funding to school systems for 2 hours per week of heritage language instruction. School systems are mandated to implement a programme in response to a request from community groups who can supply a minimum of 25 students interested in studying a particular language. Currently, more than 60 languages are taught to almost 100,000 students in the HLP. A central aspect of the HLP is that the instruction must take place outside the regular five-hour school day. This allows for three basic options, namely, at weekends, after the regular school day, or integrated into a school day extended by half-an-hour. This latter option has been highly controversial within the Toronto Board of Education, occasioning a teacher work-to-rule for several months during the early 1980s.

In Quebec, the *Programme d'Enseignement des Langues d'Origine* (PELO) was also introduced in 1977. This programme is established on generally similar lines to the Ontario HLP but on a considerably smaller scale. In 1989–90 14 languages were taught to 5,886 students in the programme. The Quebec government initially took responsibility for the development of programmes of study and curriculum guides at the elementary level for Greek, Italian, Portuguese and Spanish.

Subsequently, the Ministry delegated the responsibility to school boards who wished to offer courses in other languages. While it is possible for school boards to offer the language within the regular school day, this happens only rarely with most courses being offered for 30 minutes daily during the lunch break or before or after school.

Within the Prairie provinces of Manitoba, Saskatchewan, and Alberta, provincial governments are generally very supportive of heritage language teaching, partly because of the relatively high proportion of the populations of these provinces that are of ethnocultural backgrounds and the fact that, unlike Ontario, there has been relatively little controversy surrounding the teaching of heritage languages. In these three provinces, bilingual programmes involving 50% of the instruction through a heritage language are in operation, although the numbers of students involved are relatively small. The two most common languages taught in these bilingual programmes are Ukrainian and German, although in Edmonton programmes involving Hebrew, Yiddish, Chinese (Mandarin), Arabic and Polish are also in operation. A variety of heritage languages are also taught as subjects within the school systems and by community groups with financial support from the provincial governments.

## Controversial Issues

In contrast to bilingual programmes in the USA and some European countries which have been implemented primarily to remediate perceived problems in minority students' academic development, heritage language programmes in Canada share what Joshua Fishman (1976) has labelled an 'enrichment' rationale. The major goal is to promote proficiency in the heritage language, leading ultimately to bilingualism or trilingualism. By contrast, remedial or compensatory programmes may employ the heritage language as a temporary medium of instruction but the goal is usually monolingualism in the majority language.

In terms of the three orientations to language planning distinguished by Ruiz (1988), remedial programmes clearly fall into the 'language-as-problem' category (the problem being minority students' low academic achievement) whereas the Canadian heritage language programmes share aspects of the 'language-as-right' and 'language-as-resource' orientations. Ethnocultural communities have argued that government support for heritage teaching is a right in view of federal and provincial multicultural policies and they have also emphasized that heritage languages represent both an individual and a national resource that entails considerable economic and diplomatic benefits for the country as a whole.

A survey of school boards carried out by the Canadian Education Association (1991: 47–48) indicated that 'satisfaction with the heritage languages programs runs high in almost every school board surveyed'. Among the advantage cited by teachers, parents and students were the following:

(a) positive attitude and pride in one's self and one's background;
(b) better integration of the child into school and society;
(c) increased acceptance and tolerance of other peoples and cultures;
(d) increased cognitive and affective development;
(e) facility in learning other languages;
(f) increased job opportunities;
(g) stronger links between parent and school;
(h) ability to meet community needs.

Disadvantages cited by boards of education were far fewer than advantages. According to the Canadian Education Association report, most boards mentioned primarily administrative difficulties connected to scheduling, classroom space, class size, etc., as well as shortages of appropriate teaching materials in the target language.

In support of some of the positive outcomes noted by boards of education, a considerable number of studies suggest that continued development of two languages, and the attainment of literacy in both, entail educational benefits for minority students (see Cummins & Danesi, 1990 for a review). A recent Canadian example (Swain & Lapkin, 1991) examined the influence of heritage language proficiency on the learning of additional languages. The study involved more than 300 grade 8 students in the Metropolitan Toronto Separate (Roman Catholic) School Board French–English bilingual programme. The programme starts at the grade 5 level and entails teaching 50% of the time through each language. Students also have the opportunity to study a heritage language outside regular school hours. Swain & Lapkin compared four groups of students on various measures of French proficiency: those who had no knowledge of a heritage language (HL); those with some knowledge but no literacy skills in the HL; those with HL literacy skills but who mentioned no active use of HL literacy; and finally those who understand and use the HL in the written mode. The first group had parents with higher educational and occupa-

tional status than the other three groups who did not differ in this regard.

Highly significant differences in favour of those students with HL literacy skills were found on both written and oral measures of French. There was also a trend for students from Romance language backgrounds to perform better in oral aspects of French but the differences between Romance and non-Romance language background students were not highly significant. The authors conclude that there is transfer of knowledge and learning processes across languages and development of first language literacy entails concrete benefits for students' acquisition of subsequent languages. In short, the research data suggest that there is considerable validity to the claim that promoting heritage language proficiency may enhance the educational development of the individual child. Multilingual skills are clearly also of potential benefit to the country as a whole in view of the increasing cross-cultural contact in both domestic and international spheres.

These probable benefits, however, are not significant enough to quell the considerable opposition to the use of 'taxpayers' money' for the teaching of heritage languages. This opposition was vehement in some parts of the country throughout the late 1970s and 1980s. The case for the opposition is succinctly put in a submission to the Toronto Board of Education in 1982 (cited in Johnson, 1982):

> Many people of diverse backgrounds fear balkanization of school communities, loss of time for core curriculum subjects, undue pressure on children, disruption in school programming and staffing, inadequate preparation for eventual employment, and indeed, a dramatic shift of direction in Canadian society.

The latter point appears to be at the heart of the debate. At issue are very different perspectives on the nature of Canadian society and how it should respond to demographic changes that are radically increasing the extent of linguistic and cultural diversity. While the dominant anglophone and francophone groups generally are strongly in favour of learning the other official language, they see few benefits to promoting heritage languages for themselves, for Canadian society as a whole, or for children from ethno- cultural backgrounds. The educational focus for such children should be on acquiring English and becoming Canadian rather than on erecting linguistic and cultural barriers between them and their Canadian peers. In short, whereas advocates of heritage language teaching stress the value of bilingual and multilingual skills for the individual and society as a whole, opponents see heritage languages as socially divisive, excessively costly, and educationally retrograde in view of minority children's need to succeed academically in the school language.

What is being contested in the debate is the nature of Canadian identity and the perceived self-interest of different sectors of Canadian society. For almost 20 years, multicultural policies remained almost immune from sustained criticism, and in fact, have been viewed as an important component of the Canadian identity (Troper, 1979). During the 1970s and 1980s, it became commonplace for Canadian politicians (from parties of both the political left and right) to sing the praises of the Canadian 'mosaic' as opposed to the American 'melting pot'. However, as diversity increases and traditional symbols of national identity are being modified to conform with the statutes of the Canadian Charter of Rights and Freedoms, the multiculturalism policy itself has come under critical scrutiny.[2] Policies with respect to heritage language teaching will clearly be affected by the outcomes of this broader debate. However, at this point, heritage language programmes in most provinces are beyond the experimental stage and are likely to remain relatively stable in view of the political pitfalls for any government that might want to significantly increase or reduce support.

## Notes

1. The term 'heritage language' usually refers to all languages other than the aboriginal languages of First Nations peoples and the 'official' Canadian languages (English and French). A variety of other terms have been used in Canada to refer to heritage languages: for example, 'ethnic', 'minority', 'ancestral', 'third', and 'non-official' have all been used at different times and in different provinces. The term used in Quebec is 'langues d'origine'. The term 'community languages', commonly used in Australia, Britain, and New Zealand, is rarely used in the Canadian context. A number of Canadian proponents of heritage language teaching have expressed misgivings about the term because 'heritage' connotes learning about past traditions rather than acquiring language skills that have significance for children's overall educational and personal development. In the Toronto Board of Education the term 'modern languages' is used partly in an attempt to defuse the strong emotional reactions that the term 'heritage languages' evokes.

2. Examples of the kind of issue that have been debated at a national level are the appropriateness of Christian prayers within public schools and the right of Sikhs within the Royal Canadian Mounted Police to wear turbans.

## References

Berry, J.W., Kalin, R. and Taylor, D.M. (1977) *Multiculturalism and Ethnic Attitudes in Canada*. Ottawa: Ministry of Supply and Services Canada.

Canadian Education Association (1991) *Heritage Language Programs in Canadian School Boards*. Toronto: Canadian Education Association.

Cummins, J. and Danesi, M. (1990) *Heritage Languages: The Development and Denial of Canada's Linguistic Resources*. Toronto: Our Schools, Our Selves/Garamond.

Fishman, J. (1976) Bilingual education: What and why? In J.E. Alatis and K. Twaddell (eds) *English as a Second Language in Bilingual Education*. Washington, DC: TESOL, pp. 263–272.

Henley, R. and Young, J. (1989) Multicultural teacher education, Part 4: Revitalizing faculties of education. *Multiculturalism* 12 (3), 40–41.

Johnson, W. (1982) Creating a nation of tongues. *Toronto Globe and Mail*, 26 June.

O'Bryan, K. G., Reitz, J. and Kuplowska, O. (1976) *The Non-Official Languages Study*. Ottawa: Supply and Services Canada.

Ruiz, R. (1988) Orientations in language planning. In S.L. McKay and S.C. Wong (eds) *Language Diversity: Problem or Resource*. New York: Newbury House, pp. 3–25.

Swain, M. and Lapkin, S. (1991) Heritage language children in an English–French bilingual program. *Canadian Modern Language Review* 47 (4), 635–41.

Troper, H. (1979) An uncertain past: Reflections on the history of multiculturalism. *TESL Talk* 10 (3), 7–15.

## Questions

(1) Canada refers to 'heritage languages.' Britain, Australia and New Zealand talk about 'community languages.' In the United States, the preferred term is 'ethnic languages,' although, as Cummins says, official institutions might refer to all of these as 'modern' languages or 'foreign' languages. Discuss what the difference in terminology connotes. Which term do you prefer, for which language, and why?

(2) Describe Ontario's Heritage Language Program and Quebec's Programme d'Enseignement des Langues d'Origine (later entitled Programme d'Enseignement des Langues et des Cultures d'Origine). Do you know if a similar program exists in your community? If so, describe its goals and structure.

(3) Contrast the enrichment rationale of Canadian heritage language programs with the remedial or compensatory rationale of the United States transitional bilingual education programs. What are some of the advantages of heritage language programs as identified by teachers, parents and students? What would be the equivalent of those programs in the United States?

(4) What were the results of the Swain and Lapkin (1991) study concerning the influence of heritage language proficiency on the learning of additional languages? What are the implications of these results?

## Activities

(1) Ask the following two questions of at least twenty-five language minority people. Then survey twenty-five language majority adults. Tabulate the answers and arrive at percentages. On a poster board, make a bar graph or a pie chart with your comparative results:

  (a) 'Do you think public funds ought to be used to teach heritage languages/ethnic languages in public schools? Why or why not?'

  (b) 'Do you think public funds ought to be used to teach foreign languages in public schools? Why or why not? If yes, which languages should be taught? To whom? For how long? How?'

(2) Cummins reports that many dominant Anglophone and Francophone groups in Canada see heritage language teaching as 'socially divisive, excessively costly, and educationally retrograde.' Interview at least five language majority speakers and read them Cummins' quote. Find out if they agree or disagree, and why. Record their answers.

## Further Reading

For more on heritage language programs in Canada, see:

> Danesi, Marcel, McLeod, Keith and Morris, Sonia (eds) (1993) *Heritage Languages and Education: The Canadian Experience.* Oakville, Ontario: Mosaic Press.

See also:

> Cummins, Jim and Danesi, Marcel (1990) *Heritage Languages: The Development and Denial of Canada's Linguistic Resources.* Toronto: Published jointly by Our Schools/Our Selves Educational Foundation and the Garamond Press.

# European Models of Bilingual Education: Practice, Theory and Development

## Hugo Baetens Beardsmore

### Introduction

The rapidly growing momentum of European integration has led to an increase in investment in the promotion of linguistic skills via education, spearheaded by initiatives emanating from the Commission of the European Communities. These initiatives are likely to influence both linguistic and more general education throughout Western Europe.

The Commission of the European Communities intervenes on a supranational level among the 12 member states of the EEC by means of a series of directives and programmes affecting language and education under the acronyms ERASMUS and LINGUA. The ERASMUS programme is designed to bring about collaboration amongst universities situated in different countries. The goal of ERASMUS is to encourage European integration by enabling students to spend a part of their studies in a university of a different member state; by the end of the century it is hoped that no students, whatever their discipline, will be able to obtain a degree without having spent a part of their study period abroad. The budget investment for 1990–1995 is 200 million ecu or approximately 220 million US dollars.

The nature of ERASMUS programmes varies enormously, based on negotiations between different universities according to their specific needs. One of the most ambitious programmes is between the universities of London and Paris where, in the law departments, second year students from both institutions exchange places so that the second year French students spend a year in London while their British counterparts spend a year in Paris.

ERASMUS programmes have implications for language acquisition, since, as the London–Paris law department exchanges imply, not only do the students involved get training in the opposite country's legal systems but they also get taught through the medium of a different language, considerably enhancing their linguistic capacities and international job prospects. In cases where minor languages are involved extra subsidies are available from the EEC for students to spend a preparatory linguistic training period in the country they move to on the exchange programme.

The general educational implications are self-evident. Students get confronted with a new culture and language in their host institutions, develop a greater awareness of European diversity and European commonalities, there is cross-fertilisation of teaching ideas and methodologies, a restructuring and rethinking of programmes and an impetus to innovation and adaptation, both on the institutional and individual levels.

The LINGUA programme is aimed at developing linguistic competence at secondary school level. The EEC is encouraging the learning of three languages for all pupils in secondary education, irrespective of academic orientation. Choice of languages is left open among the nine official languages of the member states so as not to impose a major language on the diversified populations that make up Europe.

Its flexibility allows, for example, the autonomous region of Catalonia in Spain to promote Catalan as the first language, Castilian as the language of inter-Spanish communication, and French or English as a language of wider communication. The LINGUA programme intervenes financially to promote language learning in professional and technical education, language learning in businesses and enterprises and inter-university collaboration on language teacher-training; the budget available for 1990–1995 is 200 million ecu or approximately 220 million dollars. The EEC also intends to set up a European Academy of foreign language teaching.

The inspiration for both ERASMUS and LINGUA has evolved from an awareness of the need to respect the linguistic and cultural heterogeneity of the Europe of tomorrow and to enhance communication across linguistic borders, without imposing a unique lingua franca which would be unacceptable to certain member states, or privileging certain linguistic communities either traditionally predisposed towards multilingualism (like the smaller nations) or reticent towards it (like Britain and France). Inspiration has also been taken from some of the multilingual education programmes of the type I intend to describe below.

I shall describe three successful European models of multilingual education, destined for very different populations, and compare them with the Canadian immersion model, for the simple reason that the latter is the best documented and therefore more widely known. In so doing I will try to extract significant features that account for success, according to the circumstances. The models are:

(1) The trilingual education system applied to the entire school population of the Grand Duchy of Luxembourg.

(2) Multilingual education as developed in the network of European Schools situated in different European cities.

(3) The Foyer Project, developed in Brussels to enable immigrant populations to benefit from mainstream education in a bilingual city.

In all three cases a minimum of three languages are involved, which makes them more complex than standard Canadian immersion. My aim is to show how even complex language learning environments can cope with bilingualism in education while at the same time to warn against the adoption of any single model, no matter how well-tried, without the necessary modifications to specific local circumstances. This is because far too often well documented success stories, like Canadian immersion, have been taken over as a blue-print in circumstances where they do not satisfy local needs, merely because the research background has proved their effectiveness in the context for which they were developed.

## Trilingual Education in the Grand Duchy of Luxembourg

The Grand Duchy of Luxembourg represents a unique example of a western nation where the entire school population undergoes developed education transiting through three different languages as medium of instruction (for details, cf. Baetens Beardsmore & Lebrun, 1991).

The Luxemburger is monolingual by birth and becomes trilingual through education. This achievement is a complex, long-term process. In nursery schools and the first year of primary education Luxemburger is the sole medium of instruction but is progressively replaced by German. German is taught as a subject during the first year of primary school and by the end of Grade 6 the transition to the exclusive use of German as a medium must be completed. In Grade 2 of primary school French is introduced as a subject in preparation for its use as a medium in secondary education. In the first 3 Grades of secondary education most classes are taught through the medium of German, except for the French language and mathematics, which are now taught through the medium of French. The further the pupil progresses in secondary education the more subjects are taught through the medium of French, with German gradually disappearing as a medium, except for language classes. This complex system operates on the principle of introducing the child to schooling by means of the home L1, rapid transition to a genetically related L2, German, and a gradual transition to a genetically unrelated L3, French.

Throughout the programme German and French are the focus of attention as a subject matter in parallel to their being used as a medium of instruction, which may well have implications for the quality of the outcome in terms of productive accuracy. Figure 1 indicates the number of contact hours per language for the entire curriculum in Luxembourg for children following the standard programme from age 6–18.

For illustrative purposes Table 1 indicates the amount of time in the secondary standard curriculum devoted to each language, expressed in percentages. As such it reflects the step-wise nature of the transition from one major language of instruction to another and is merely a continuation of a similar transition in primary education, but where the shift occurs from Luxemburger to German. Variations in percentages in Table 1 depend on course options selected by pupils but whatever the options at least one fifth of the time

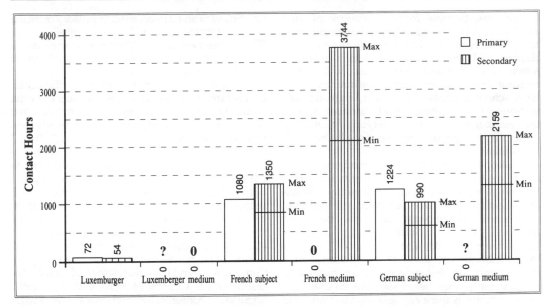

**Figure 1** Hours of language exposure during school career in Luxembourg schools

in school is devoted to the study of languages as a subject, a very different picture from standard Canadian immersion programmes where apparently very little time is devoted to the study of the languages *per se*.

Of all pupils who completed the standard secondary school programme in the 1985–1986 school year 70% succeeded in final examinations leading to higher education, indicating that trilingual education can have a high success rate, irrespective of social class, selection, or other variables so often considered as conducive to success (Fishman, 1977). This model is unique in that it proves that trilingual education can work for an entire school population. Moreover, since all university studies have to be followed in a

country other than the Grand Duchy itself, there being no full university in Luxembourg, linguistic standards must be sufficiently high for students to be able to pursue their studies in a foreign country.

## Multilingual Education in European Schools

The trilingual education system used in the Grand Duchy of Luxembourg was adapted by a far more complex system upon the foundation of the European School network in 1958. These schools have been described in detail elsewhere (Baetens Beardsmore & Swain, 1985; Baetens Beardsmore & Kohls, 1988), so that here I shall merely outline their characteristics.

**Table 1** Amount of time in the standard secondary curriculum devoted to each language, expressed in percentages

| Language | Grades | | | | | | |
|---|---|---|---|---|---|---|---|
| | 1 | 2 | 3 | 4 | 5 | 6 | 7 |
| Luxembourg subject | 3% | – | – | – | – | – | – |
| Luxembourg medium | – | – | – | – | – | – | – |
| German subject | 13% | 13% | 10% | 10-13% | 10-13% | 10% | 0-17% |
| German medium | 50% | 36% | 36% | 0-13% | 0-13% | 0-20% | 0-27% |
| French subject | 20% | 20% | 15% | 13-16% | 10-16% | 10-16% | 0-17% |
| French medium | 13% | 10-30% | 26% | 40-60% | 40-60% | 43-70% | 38-83% |
| Other languages | May use French, German or the target languages | | | | | | |

European Schools form a network of nine establishments situated in five different countries and intended primarily for the education of the children of European civil servants. The largest school is in Brussels, with about 3000 pupils ranging from kindergarten to secondary level. Each school consists of different linguistic sub-sections covering the nine official languages of the member states, where everyone follows the same programme, irrespective of the language of instruction.

A European School is not an elite school, though it tends to have this reputation. Priority is given to European civil service children, but each school has an obligation to take in others if space is available, with particular emphasis on those from less favoured groups, including the handicapped (*Schola Europaea*, 1988). The programme is controlled by intra-governmental instances, education is free, though non civil service children may pay a small subsidy, there is no selection on entry, no streaming, nor is there any specialisation until the fourth year of secondary education.

The principles behind European Schools can be summarised as follows:

(1) The child's distinct national, cultural, religious and linguistic identity should be maintained, underlining the significance of instruction in the L1 .

(2) Throughout schooling, all children must acquire a thorough knowledge of an L2 (to be selected from English, French or German) through which they will be able to learn content matter and be prepared to take examinations through the medium of both L1 and L2.

(3) The higher the child progresses in the school the more lessons are taught via the medium of a second or third language.

(4) The programme is designed to promote linguistic and cultural pluralism rather than assimilation so that all children are obliged to take on a second and third language, with no linguistic discrimination in favour of speakers of a major language like English or French.

(5) From primary school onwards, communal lessons are taught to members of different sub-sections brought together for integration purposes. In the primary section these communal lessons are known as European Hours. The further the children progress in the programme the more lessons are taught to mixed groups from different sub-sections.

(6) Study of an L3 becomes compulsory from the third grade of secondary education.

(7) All teachers are qualified native speakers of the language they use as a medium of instruction.

A pupil who progresses through the entire programme will receive L2 as a subject over the whole 12-year syllabus, giving a total of 1,100 hours of formal language instruction, in addition to lessons taught via the medium of an L2. The L3 programme consists of a minimum of 360 hours of core language instruction in addition to optional courses in which the L3 is the medium of instruction. Since the founding of the schools success rates on university entrance examinations have been approximately 90%, indicating that the strong language commitment has no detrimental effects on academic achievement.

Moreover, the Commission of the European Communities and the Council for Cultural Cooperation of the Council of Europe, in May 1990, organised a conference aimed to examine to what extent experience gained in European School type education could be extended to the general population by examining the use of an L2 as a working language for non-language subjects and the creation of special bilingual or international language sections, indicating the faith and confidence in the model.

## The Foyer Project in Brussels

This project is a unique Belgian initiative aimed at producing bicultural children with trilingual competence (for details, cf. Bryan & Leman, 1990). The Belgian capital of Brussels has an official bilingual status where schools are divided into Dutch or French-medium establishments but where children are required to receive the second national language from the age of seven onwards for a minimum of three and a maximum of five lessons per week. Given that 24% of the population of Brussels is of immigrant origin, that 50% of new-born children are of foreign origin and that in certain areas these immigrants make up 80–90% of the kindergarten and primary school population, there is a serious education problem for those who do not have Dutch or French as their primary language.

To help these children fit into the mainstream educational system five schools have been involved in the Foyer Project, each working with a specific minority population in a different Dutch-medium school. The outside environment of the city is predominantly French so that the primary language of socialisation of the children involved may be, but is not necessarily, French. The home language may be a dialect variant of a standard language, e.g. Sicilian for the Italian group, Moroccan Arabic for the Moroccans. The school language is Dutch, while French becomes compulsory under legislation for Brussels from the age of seven onwards.

The Foyer Project begins with a three year kindergarten period in which the minority group spends 50% of the time as a separate group and 50% of the time with the mainstream children. In the first year of primary school the minority group is separate for 60% of the time for lessons in the ethnic language and culture and mathematics, spends 30% of the time as a separate group learning Dutch and 10% of the time integrated with the mainstream children. In the second year of primary school 50% of the time is spent as a separate ethno-cultural group for language and culture, 20% as a separate group for Dutch lessons and 30% for integrated lessons with the mainstream group, including mathematics lessons. From the third year onwards 90% of the time is spent with the mainstream group using Dutch while the minority language is taught for three to four hours per week separately. French lessons are taught with the mainstream group according to the legal requirement.

Certain characteristics identify the Foyer Project. The immigrant population is fixed at slightly lower than the Dutch-language population so as to avoid the displacement of Dutch as the medium in which the school operates. This is necessary because Dutch is a minority language in Brussels and could easily be displaced by French, or even the immigrant language, if numbers were not controlled. Immigrant languages are taught by native-speaker teachers and literacy skills are taught in the ethnic language first. The schools require strong parental involvement and make efforts to integrate scholastic and extra-curricular activities with an aim to providing intercultural exchanges between the groups involved.

Results from the project are encouraging, though given the experimental nature of the enterprise it is too early yet to predict the final outcome. There are no data available on the effects of this trilingual development on success in secondary school to date as the cohorts have not yet moved up sufficiently.

## Comparisons Between Different Models

Although one must be extremely prudent in making comparative assessments of the outcome of different bilingual education systems, given the multiplicity of diverging variables that need to be taken into consideration, it can be useful to examine results in support of claims about success.

Table 2 provides a comparative overview of results on French as an L2 as attained on a series of standardised tests by 13-year-old pupils in the Luxembourg trilingual system, the European School multilingual system and a Canadian immersion programme. When the tests were taken the Luxembourg pupils had received approximately 1400 contact hours with French both as a subject and a medium of instruction, European School pupils had received approximately 1300 hours of French as a subject and a medium, while Canadian immersion children had received about 4450 contact hours, primarily of French as a medium. The similarity of scores obtained across the three models of education reveals how diverging programmes can attain comparable results. What is significant in the interpretation of such results is an analysis of the factors that have contributed to them, in spite of such variations in programmes.

For the manifest success of Luxembourg, European School and Canadian immersion models (and as far as can be judged, of the Foyer Project)

**Table 2** Achievement scores on three standardised tests for the Grand Duchy of Luxembourg (Lux.), the European School (ES) and Canadian immersion pupils

|  | Lux. (n= 179) | Stand. dev. | ES (n = 80) | Stand. dev. | Canada (n = 80) | Stand. dev. |
|---|---|---|---|---|---|---|
| Total class contact hours | 1450 | – | 1325 | – | 4450 | |
| Written comprehension (max. = 22) | 15.26 | 3.4 | 15.6 | 2.9 | 14.6 | 4.2 |
| Auditory comprehension (max. = 22) | 14.84 | 3.5 | 17.7 | 3 | 14.9 | 3.7 |
| Cloze (max. = 44) | 21.3 | 4.3 | 21.95 | 4.8 | 19.9 | 4.3 |

requires careful analysis lest they be misappropriated for application in totally different contexts serving totally different populations, as has been the warning about immersion programmes imported from Canada into the United States (Hernández-Chávas, 1984).

Such an analysis can hopefully bring to light a set of minimal criteria which are potentially conducive to the effective promotion of bilingual education in most contexts, to which must be added the specific criteria peculiar to any given population in a particular environment. Indeed, this is what the theoretical discussions of bilingualism in education have attempted to unravel, as reflected in the macrological analyses produced by Spolsky, Green & Read, 1974; Fishman, 1976, 1977; Cummins, 1984; Baetens Beardsmore, 1992).

An analysis of the level of language competence achieved by the end of the European School programme among 17+ year olds (Housen & Baetens Beardsmore, 1987) led us to consider what the theoretical explanations were for the ultimate attainment. This study forms part of a series on the model in question, including an examination of the nature of European Hours given in primary school (unpublished), an investigation comparing Canadian immersion results with European School results achieved by 13+ year-olds (Baetens Beardsmore & Swain, 1985) a study comparing achievement on French as an L2 and French as an L3 among 13+ and 14+ year-olds (unpublished) and a comparative study of results on English and French as an L2 among 13+ year-olds in a European School, where these were not part of the wider, out-of-school environment (unpublished). In all cases, it became apparent that the success of the schools could be accounted for by a combination of curricular and extra-curricular factors.

In any adaptation of a particular model of bilingual education it is important to bear these two types of factor in mind. Success in bilingual education depends in part on the extent to which the languages involved are dependent on school instruction alone, as is the case with Canadian immersion programmes, and one must bear in mind Fishman's (1977: 102) comment that 'School use of language is just not enough'. In cases where a particular language in a bilingual programme is primarily school dependent expectancy levels for ultimate attainment must be realistically adjusted. A comparison between some of the factors that distinguish the models developed in Europe

from Canadian immersion programmes clearly reveals why similar levels of achievement were attained by 13+ year-olds who had received highly disproportionate classroom contact hours with the target language.

In educational contexts there are some factors which the school can control and others which it cannot. For example, the research indicates that the most significant differences between the populations tested related to the pupils' self-motivated use of the L2; pupils in a European School initiate peer-group interaction in the L2 whereas immersion pupils do not. However, the structure of the European School programme makes it necessary for linguistically mixed groups to use a common L2 as a medium of communication. Since immersion children come from homogeneous English backgrounds it is only natural for them to communicate amongst themselves in English and not the L2. In the European School investigated the L2, French, serves as a lingua franca for cross-linguistic communication. In Canada there is no need for a lingua franca because of the homogeneous background of the pupils. In both cases this is a factor outside the schools' control. In the European School investigated there are considerable native-speakers of the L2 with whom communication can take place at peer-group level, whereas in Canada there are no native-speakers of French available for peer-group interaction. The European School can control this factor via the curriculum whereas an immersion programme cannot. A factor outside the control of both types of school is the nature of the out-of-school environment. For pupils from the Brussels European School French tends to be used at least sometimes and often more with friends outside school and between classes, and is used most or all of the time with Francophones in the community. In immersion cases there are no native-speakers available for the use of French outside the classroom.

Although French as an L2 is not essential as a lingua franca in the Luxembourg case, the fact that this language is widely used in the out-of-school environment and prevalent in media and official instances, means that similar factors beyond the control of the school also intervene in influencing the linguistic climate in and around the schools which help to determine proficiency. The same is true for the Foyer Project, where the out-of-school French environment provides ample stimulus for the use of the language to compensate for the limited classroom contact hours, while the proportion of time devoted to Dutch and the first language varies as proficiency develops.

## Theoretical Considerations

To explain success in bilingual education Cummins (1979, 1981, 1984) posited three conceptual arguments. The first is the *Threshold Level Hypothesis*, which assumes that if bilingual children attain only a low level of proficiency in either of their languages, their interaction with the environment is likely to be impoverished, thereby hindering intellectual growth. If children attain a high threshold level of proficiency in one or two languages, this will positively influence the potential for intellectual growth and lead to beneficial aspects of becoming bilingual.

Cummins' second hypothesis suggests that there is a close relationship between proficiency in L1 and L2 for the development of literacy-related aspects of language usage; this is known as the *Common Underlying Proficiency*, which assumes that adequate and sufficient instruction in one language will enable the transfer of sub-skills to another language, provided there is enough exposure to this L2 in the school and the environment and sufficient motivation to learn it.

The third hypothesis distinguishes between *Context-Embedded, Cognitively Undemanding* linguistic activity, and *Context-Reduced, Cognitively Demanding* linguistic activity. The former reflects the lower threshold level and is typical of conversational interaction, whereas the latter requires a much higher level of proficiency necessary for handling content matter through the medium of a different language.

In Luxembourg, the European Schools, and as far as can be judged from early results from the Foyer Project, these factors are reflected in the nature of the programmes. Although the L2 is introduced in a core language programme from early stages in education, it is not until the L1 has been solidly established that the L2 becomes a partial medium of instruction. In Luxembourg the switch is rapid, whereas in European Schools and the Foyer Project it is more progressive. The common underlying proficiency between L1 and L2 allows for the transfer of literacy-related sub-skills requisite for academic progress in two, and later three, languages in all the systems, including Canadian immersion. There is also a gradual but steady transition from context-embedded, cognitively undemanding activities in L2 to cognitively-demanding, context reduced

activities of the type necessary for examinations through other languages than the L1.

In his controversial hypotheses on language acquisition and language learning, Krashen (1981, 1982) developed the *Comprehensible Input* model to reflect what he felt to be the most significant factor in determining progress. This hypothesis suggests that acquisition progresses through a series of distinct stages where the pupil moves from one step to the next by processing the input provided. According to Krashen, for efficient progress the input must contain lexis and structures already acquired, labelled $i$, together with some language not yet acquired and a little beyond the current level of proficiency, giving $i + 1$. According to Krashen, the non-acquired $+ 1$ element can be inferred from contextual, paralinguistic and general knowledged cues embedded in the message. This input must be intrinsically interesting and relevant by appealing to the acquirer's tastes and imagination and must be provided in sufficient quantity.

Swain (1985) argued that comprehensible input, or $i + 1$ alone, is insufficient for the acquisition of high levels of L2 proficiency, based on results obtained on Canadian Grade 6 immersion pupils. The children concerned had received French comprehensible input for almost seven years, and although they had reached good levels in certain aspects of French, they were appreciably different from native-speakers, particularly in activities requiring high levels of grammatical knowledge. The subjects performed satisfactorily on subject-matter tests and therefore must have understood what was taught through the L2. This suggests that it is not input alone that is important in L2 acquisition. With immersion pupils, input is derived mainly from listening to teacher talk, so the less than native-like grammatical competence can only be accounted for by the inadequacy of the input hypothesis. On the other hand, Swain claims that *output* fulfils a vital role in the process of L2 acquisition in that it enables the acquirer to apply the available linguistic resources in a meaningful way. This pushes the acquirer toward the delivery of a message that is conveyed as precisely, coherently and appropriately as possible, enabling experimentation with target language structures by trial and error.

In Luxembourg, in European Schools and in the Foyer Project in Brussels, the nature of the environment, in school and outside school, pushes the speaker in the active use of the L2. In the three systems, unlike the Canadian experience, exposure to the L2 is not restricted to the classroom and output is fostered by two-way interactional exchanges in which meaning is actively negotiated.

Although the above theoretical constructs go a long way to explaining the nature of the outcome of the four models discussed they fail to give sufficient emphasis to the social and psychological aspects of language acquisition contexts. These are felt to be of particular significance in a bilingual education system, since they may well be decisive in determining to what extent a learner makes use of the potential for Cummins' hypotheses to operate in cases where the programme takes his parameters into account. Similarly, there may well be sufficient opportunities for both input and output to have effect yet these opportunities may not be taken up, or else may be modified by other factors.

This possibility was taken into account in the study of the European School by Housen & Baetens Beardsmore (1987) when it was noticed that there was differentiated ability in L1, L2, L3 and L4 amongst the pupils investigated which would not be explained in terms of the highly satisfactory test-score results. One case was that of an English pupil with French as an L2 who revealed signs of backsliding in the second language, another that of a Dutch girl who had higher proficiency in her L4, Italian, than her L3, English, in spite of the fact that she had greater classroom contact hours with English, significant opportunities for input and output, and a genetic similarity between her L1, Dutch, and her L3, English, all of which should have led to different predictions.

Schumann's (1978, 1986) *Acculturation Model* provided the framework of interpretation to account for levels of achievement in the different languages. According to Schumann, acquisition depends on the degree to which the learner acculturates to the target language group. This he bases on the broad concepts of social and psychological distance. Social distance depends on the following seven factors which determine whether the target language acquisition context is good or bad for affecting social distance.

(1) *Social dominance pattern.* The learner's group can be dominant, non-dominant, or subordinate in relation to the target language group. If it is dominant or subordinate, social distance will prevail, inter-group contact will be limited, and target language acquisition inhibited; if it is non-dominant, social dis-

tance will be minimal and target language acquisition fostered.

(2) *Integration strategies.* These can lead to (a) assimilation to the target language group's life style and values, (b) adaptation, which partly preserves original culture patterns and partly adopts those of the target language group, or (c) preservation, which rejects the target language group's values. Social distance is fostered by preservation and minimised by assimilation.

(3) *Degree of enclosure.* This factor refers to the structural aspects of integration and involves such things as endogamy, institutional separation, and associational clustering. Sharing of social, religious and cultural institutions decreases the degree of enclosure thereby fostering intergroup contacts and the acquisition of the target language.

(4) *Cohesiveness and size of the learner's group.* The larger and more cohesive the learner's group is, the more likely intragroup contacts will outweigh intergroup contacts, thus increasing social distance and hindering target language acquisition.

(5) *Congruence.* The more similar the two group's cultures are, the more likely integration will be facilitated and consequently social distance reduced.

(6) *Intended length of residence.* The longer the learner intends to reside in the target language area, the more inclined he or she will be to seek contacts with the target language group and the smaller the social distance will be.

(7) *Attitudes.* Favourable attitudes improve both the quality and the quantity of contacts between the learner and the target language group and facilitate the acquisition process. Unfavourable attitudes may have the opposite effect.

Together with the above sociological factors the following three psychological factors also come into play, according to Schumann.

(1) *Language shock, culture shock, culture stress.* These refer to the degree of anxiety engendered by expressing oneself in a weaker language, and the ease or difficulty with which one assimilates the cultural attributes borne by the other language. The greater these are felt, the greater the psychological distance from the acquisition of the target language.

(2) *Ego-permeability.* This refers to the permeability of an individual's ego boundaries and

comes about by lowering the inhibitions felt in speaking the weaker language.

(3) *Motivation.* This can be integrative or instrumental. Schumann feels that integrative motivation minimizes psychological distance and increases opportunities to interact in the target language.

When the above criteria of social and psychological distance were applied to an analysis of the pupils in the European School, where the curriculum clearly took into account Cummins' hypotheses, Krashen's $i + 1$ input hypothesis, Swain's output hypothesis, and where there were ample opportunities for peer-group interaction both inside and outside the school, an explanation was found as to why the Dutch girl's L4 was higher than her L3 and why the English boy's L2 showed signs of backsliding. In both cases the pupil's individual profile reflected degrees of social distance from the target languages which coincided with levels of proficiency. The English boy's reactions towards the French language community showed signs of increasing rejection with age, accounting for his backsliding, in spite of good test scores. The Dutch girl was indifferent to all things English but strongly attracted to the Italian environment in her school, explaining her activation of opportunities to promote her competence in Italian. Standardised test score results were good for all the languages involved with both subjects, yet it was Schumann's acculturation model which brought out the more subtle differences and explanations which accounted for the real nature of their proficiency.

A final hypothesis which encompasses all of the earlier mentioned parameters is related to the perception the pupil has of the language learning effort. Acquiring a second language to a substantial level of competence is a long-term process where the rewards of satisfactory ability and ease of interaction are often postponed. Core language lessons often attempt to overcome such postponement by the use of artificial techniques, whereby minimal interaction can be achieved within the limits of each lesson (particularly in the functional notional syllabus as promoted by the Council of Europe cf. Yalden, 1983). Bilingual education is far more successful on this count, however, by the fact that the languages involved are perceived as *immediately pertinent* by the recipients, in circumstances which are as near natural as is possible. Although it is not natural, in Canadian immersion programmes, for homogeneous English-speaking pupils to interact informally in the L2, the fact that the whole of the classroom experience is conducted in French and that subject-matter is also taught through this language means that French is immediately pertinent, at least within the limits of the classroom. In a European School, and to a slightly lesser extent in Luxembourg and in the Foyer setting, the L2 is needed for both curricular and extra-curricular activities, inside school and outside. In such cases it is believed that immediate pertinence is perceived in a way which works backwards to generate spontaneous output, by which further input is received, producing circular reinforcement.

## Conclusions

If one attempts to summarise the major features which represent minimal conditions for a successful bilingual education programme, then the following elements require consideration.

No single model of bilingual education is universally applicable and no single existing model should be transplanted to a totally different context (Mackey, 1972). As Spolsky, Green & Read (1974) have pointed out, a bilingual programme depends on three types of factors, situational, operational and outcomes. On the situational level it is necessary to analyse the context in which bilingual education operates (i.e. the population, its status, size, resources, aspirations, etc.). On the operational level it is necessary to analyse the factors involved in the interaction of the school with the surrounding community. On the outcomes level it is necessary to appraise realistically what the goals of a given programme can achieve and be cautious about the myth of the 'perfect bilingual'.

Comparisons between different models reveal how different paths can lead to high levels of proficiency, that such proficiency is tempered by contextual variables more so than by programme variables, and that the former play a considerable role in determining ultimate achievement. These contextual variables are only partially within the control of the school or the programme designer but are decisive in determining the nature and outcomes of any programme.

All models share features in common. They all illustrate the significance of Cummins' hypotheses, the role of input and output and the notion of immediate pertinence. Research into the European School model has also revealed to what extent social and psychological distance play a decisive role in activating output.

Apart from the contextual variables relating to the out-of-school environment and the population make-up within each programme, which the school cannot manipulate, what significant variables appear to affect success?

Canadian research reveals how unrealistic it is to expect homogeneous English-speaking peers to interact in the L2 in self-initiated peer negotiation outside the formal classroom. This feature appears significant in determining the productive proficiency in oral communication in the target language, if the output hypothesis plays the important role which research leads us to believe. Indeed, the speed with which English has displaced the other languages in Singapore as the common lingua franca would lend substance to the argument that the school alone cannot produce high levels of proficiency, since in Singapore cross-ethnic interaction, being conducted in English, lends immediate pertinence to the task of acquiring English and stimulates self-initiated peer negotiation, as attested by Gupta (cf. this conference) in her observation of kindergarten classes. Hence Canadian immersion results reflect high levels of receptive competence in the L2 and realistically adjust expectancy levels on productive proficiency to take into account those features of linguistic ability that cannot reasonably be produced by an education system alone. The message to the educational planner, then, is not to expect bilingual education to produce native-like competence in two languages if the contextual variables do not allow for this to develop. Examination criteria must be adjusted and clearly specify levels of dual-language proficiency on the outcome level accordingly, as has been done in the Canadian context.

Other points which the models share are the following. All four models are characterised by highly proficient teachers in the target language. European Schools only use native-speakers as teachers, Luxembourg's teachers all receive their qualifications in the countries of the language which they use, where they acquire native-like competence. Foyer project teachers are native-speakers of the immigrant language or of Dutch, near-native speakers of French. Canadian immersion teachers are native-speakers or highly competent bilinguals. All the models consider this teacher proficiency a significant feature when high levels of bilingualism are the goal. Unfortunately, in many cases where bilingual education is provided level of teacher proficiency is not always commensurate with the goals of the programme.

Parental involvement in and understanding of the specificity of bilingual education is strongly encouraged in the models outlined. This is because bilingual education may require parents to receive reassurance about progress in cases where part of the curriculum is being taught through a language the parents do not know. Canadian immersion requires strong parental support, since it is voluntary, and parents are briefed on the nature of bilingual development so as to allay fears they may have about their children's linguistic and scholastic progress. Luxembourg parents are familiar with the system, having gone through it themselves. The Foyer project encourages parental participation and contacts to create racial harmony, as does the European School system.

Although literacy need not be taught through the first language, as is the case in Canadian immersion, the European models all begin literacy in the first language, since this appears an easier solution for the transfer of skills to the second language.

A major difference between Canada and the European programmes, however, is that the target language is taught as a subject, prior to its introduction as a medium. Moreover, the second language as a subject is continued in parallel to its use as a medium throughout the education process. It is felt that this parallelism helps to account for the higher rates of accuracy in written and spoken productive competence in Europe, as revealed by interviews with pupils from the Canadian, European School and Luxembourg models.

This point is of even greater significance in cases where homogeneous school populations and a lack of stimulus in the target language from the outside environment imply that peer inter- action cannot take place with native speakers. The difference between programmes where an L2 is taught merely as a subject in core-language lessons and truly bilingual education where the L2 is used as a medium is that in the latter the core language lessons have more immediate pertinence. Each language as a subject lesson can be perceived as of potential use for the language as a medium lesson, so that they are of greater relevance in the linguistic market place of the school. The short-term pay-off is apparent to the pupil, whereas in core language lessons the pay-off is often so long-term that the pupil loses sight of the goal in the years of effort required to attain sufficient competence to be able to do anything realistically with the language. Hence, the motivational variable, so often called upon as the answer to acquiring language proficiency, is automatically built in to properly developed, long-term bilingual education. Socio-cultural factors are stronger than linguistic factors in bilingual development, and in cases where bilingualism forms part of educational development it is these socio-cultural factors that require manipulation within the constraints of the situational context of the school.

## References

Baetens Beardsmore, H. (1992) Bilingual education. In J. Lynch, C. Modgil and S. Modgil (eds) *Cultural Diversity and the Schools: Consensus and Controversy* Vol. I (pp. 173–83). London: Falmer Press.

Baetens Beardsmore, H. and Swain, M. (1985) Designing bilingual education: Aspects of immersion and 'European School' models. *Journal of Multilingual and Multicultural Development* 6 (1), 1–15.

Baetens Beardsmore, H. and Kohls, J. (1988) Immediate pertinence in the acquisition of multilingual proficiency: The European schools. *The Canadian Modern Language Review* 44 (4), 680–701.

Baetens Beardsmore, H. and Lebrun, N. (1991) Trilingual education in the Grand Duchy of Luxembourg. In O. García (ed.) *Focusschrift in Honor of Joshua Fishman* (pp. 107–20). Amsterdam/Philadelphia: Benjamins.

Byram, M. and Leman, J. (1990) *Bicultural and Trilingual Education*. Clevedon: Multilingual Matters.

Cummins, J. (1979) Linguistic interdependence and the educational development of bilingual children. *Review of Educational Research* 49, 221–51.

— (1981) The role of primary language development in promoting education success for language minority students. In *Schooling and Language Minority Students: A Theoretical Framework* (pp. 3–49). Los Angeles: Evaluation, Assessment and Dissemination Center.

— (1984) *Bilingualism and Special Education: Issues in Assessment and Pedagogy*. Clevedon: Multilingual Matters.

Fishman, J. (1976) *Bilingual Education: An International Sociological Perspective*. Rowley: Newbury House.

— (1977) The sociology of bilingual education. In B. Spolsky and R. Cooper (eds) *Frontiers of Bilingual Education* (pp. 94–105). Rowley: Newbury House.

Gupta, A. (1991) English in the playground in the Singapore schools. Paper presented at the International Conference on Bilingualism and National Development: Current Perspectives and Future Trends (BAND91), Brunei Darussalam, 9–12 December 1991.

Hernández-Chávez, E. (1984) The inadequacy of English immersion education as an educational approach for language minority students in the United States. In *Studies on Immersion Education: A Collection for United States Educators* (pp. 144–83). Los Angeles: Evaluation, Assessment and Dissemination Center.

Housen, A. and Baetens Beardsmore, H. (1987) Curricular and extra-curricular factors in multilingual education. *Studies in Second Language Acquisition* 9, 83–102.

Krashen, S. (1981) *Second Language Acquisition and Second Language Learning*. Oxford: Pergamon Press.

— (1982) *Principles and Practice in Second Language Acquisition*. Oxford: Pergamon Press.

Mackey, W. (1972) A typology of bilingual education. In J. Fishman (ed.) *Advances in the Sociology of Language* Vol. II (pp. 413–32). The Hague: Mouton.

*Schola Europeae* (1988) No 101.

Schumann, J. (1978) The acculturation model for second language acquisition. In R. Gringas (ed.) *Second Language Aquisition and Foreign Language Teaching* (pp. 27–50). Washington: Center for Applied Linguistics.

— (1986) Research on the acculturation model for second language acquisition. *Journal of Multilingual and Multicultural Development* 7 (5), 379–92.

Spolsky, B., Green, J. and Read, J. (1974) A model for the description, analysis and perhaps evaluation of bilingual education. In *Navajo Reading Study Progress Report 23*. Albuquerque: University of New Mexico.

Swain, M. (1985) Communicative competence: Some roles of comprehensible input and comprehensible output in its development. In S. Gass and C. Madden (eds) *Input in Second Language Acquisition* (pp. 235–53). Rowley: Newbury House.

Yalden, J. (1983) *The Communicative Syllabus: Evolution, Design and Implementation*. Oxford: Pergamon Press.

## Questions

(1) What is the goal of programs of the EEC such as ERASMUS and LINGUA? Describe each. How are these programs different from those available to advance in a second language in your community?

(2) Make a chart that explains the trilingual education system in the Grand Duchy of Luxembourg. How is Luxemburger maintained despite its formal absence from the curriculum by the end of primary education? How does the use and teaching of language in Luxembourg schools differ from that at PS 84 and in Canadian French immersion programs? Where would you put Luxembourg's program in the typology of bilingual education? (The typology is presented after the Lyons article at the start of this book.)

(3) Describe a typical school in the European Schools Movement. List each of their principles. In different columns put a plus sign or minus sign to indicate whether the principle exists in:
   (a)  Transitional bilingual education programs in the US.
   (b)  Two-way dual language programs as at PS 84.
   (c)  Ethnic schools as those in Dade County.
   (d)  Canadian French immersion schools.
   (e)  Luxembourg's trilingual education system.
   (f)  The Foyer Project in Brussels.
   Which programs are more similar in structure? How do the others differ?

(4) Study Table 2. Compare the contact hours devoted to French in Luxembourg, the European School, and French Canadian immersion schools. Then explain the results of the written comprehension, auditory comprehension and cloze tests. To what factor does Baetens Beardsmore attribute the difference? Do you agree or disagree, and why?

(5) In the three educational contexts presented in this paper, the following theoretical constructs were taken into account:
   (a)  Cummins' threshold hypothesis.
   (b)  Cummins' common underlying proficiency.
   (c)  Cummins' idea of a move from context-embedded, cognitively undemanding activities, to cognitively-demanding, context-reduced activities.
   (d)  Krashen's comprehensible input.
   (e)  Swain's ideas on output.
   Briefly define each and say how they have been used in Luxembourg, the European Schools and the Foyer Project.

(6) List the seven social factors and three psychological factors given by Schumann to determine the social and psychological distance that affects second language acquisition. From your experience as a second language learner, which social and psychological factors were most pertinent to you? (If you haven't experienced second language learning, interview someone else.)

(7) What is the most important overall characteristics of teachers in all models of bilingual education? Are they bilingual teachers in the sense that they teach both languages? How does this differ from the typical bilingual teacher in the United States? What are the advantages of bilingual teachers who teach only one language to make students bilingual? Are there disadvantages? Why or why not?

## Activities

(1) Select two different language minority groups with which you are familiar. Make a table showing how each of the factors apply to them, using the following scale:

| | | | |
|---|---|---|---|
| Social Dominance | Subordinate=1 | Dominant=2 | Non-dominant=3 |
| Integration | Preservation=1 | Adaptation=2 | Assimilation=3 |
| Enclosure | High=1 | Average=2 | Low=3 |
| Cohesiveness/Size | High=1 | Average=2 | Low=3 |
| Congruence | Low=1 | Average=2 | High=3 |
| Intended Length Residence | Short=1 | Average=2 | Long=3 |
| Attitudes | Unfavorable=1 | Neutral=2 | Favorable=3 |

Add up the scores and compare them. Find out which ethnolinguistic group has the least social distance to the language majority group (highest score) and thus the greatest prospects for second language acquisition. Do you agree with this? Why or why not? Compare your results.

(2) Select two different language learners. Make a table showing how each of the factors apply to them, using the following scale:

| | | | |
|---|---|---|---|
| Language and Culture Shock | High=1 | Average=2 | Low=3 |
| Ego-Permeability | Low=1 | Average=2 | High=3 |
| Motivation | None=1 | Instrumental=2 | Integrative=3 |

Find out which language learner has the least psychological distance from the majority group and thus the greatest prospects for second language acquisition. Do you agree with this? Why or why not? Compare your results.

(3) Visit a school that teaches a second language to language majority students. Find out if the language is taught as a subject (core language lessons), used as a medium of instruction, or both. How would you evaluate their second language program given what you know about second language acquisition.

(4) Observe a second language class for language majority students to determine how the teacher relies on comprehensible input and/or output for second language acquisition. Evaluate the language learning material used. Find out if the syllabus follows any of the traditional second language approaches. (For more background on this, see *'Foundations of Bilingual Education and Bilingualism,'* Chapter 14.) Report back to the class.

# Bilingual Education in Wales

## Colin Baker

### Introduction

To understand the current philosophy, policy provision and practice of bilingual education in Wales, it is essential to contrast the fate of the Welsh language this century with the growth of bilingual education in Wales. This reveals the opposite movement of language decay and the continuing development of bilingual education. The growth in bilingual education is viewed as a gentle revolution away from a formal education system where the Welsh language as a subject, and especially as a medium of instruction, was rarely visible in the curriculum. Thus the chapter commences by briefly portraying the historical context of modern bilingual education in Wales. The recent growth and present composition of bilingual education indicates a reversal from Anglicised education. Welsh has increasingly become a medium throughout the curriculum and is increasingly being used in formal examinations, an important indicator of the currency and market value of Welsh. While the statistics of the growth of bilingual education provide clear evidence of a gentle revolution, they do not convey the movement as having vision, ideas and drive from within and without. Therefore, the chapter proceeds to show how institutional growth of bilingual education has been supported by a wide variety of agencies, voluntary movements, initiatives and commitments. In conclusion, the chapter briefly examines the extent to which the growth of education has contributed to the balance sheet of the fortunes of the Welsh language.

### The Welsh Language and Bilingual Education

If the fate of Welsh medium education had followed the fate of the Welsh language in the last 100 years, it would have shown a pattern of decline and diminution. Rather than paralleling the decline of the language, Welsh medium education has recently grown and flourished. This is the paradox which this chapter initially seeks to portray.

The growth of Welsh medium education in relation to the decline in the absolute number of Welsh speakers and their relative numerical dominance in the population can be illustrated by two sets of figures. First, the following graph (see Figure 1) provides evidence from Census data (1891 to 1991) of the decline in the absolute number and percentage distribution of Welsh speakers in the population of Wales.

The following graph (see Figure 2) provides a second set of data revealing a positive relationship between year and the increase in numbers of Designated Bilingual Schools. Such Designated Bilingual Schools have been established in mainly urban, English-speaking areas. They contain pupils from Welsh-speaking homes and from English language backgrounds; a mixture of 'heritage language' and 'immersion' children. Apart from the Designated Bilingual Schools, the revolution in the place of Welsh in education is also found in 'natural' Welsh schools, that is, schools in predominantly Welsh speaking areas where the main medium of instruction is Welsh.

It is clear from these two figures that bilingual schooling has not reflected Welsh language Census trends. On the contrary, the possibility of a reaction to language trends is one major explanation of the development of bilingual education. In this sense, bilingual education has become a main engineer of attempted language reversal.

If a reaction thesis is tenable, the immediate question is the cause of the reaction. Locating and defining the origins of the development of bilingual education can never rest with simple influences. The development is likely to be the result of complex educational, political, economic and social factors. Reactions to developing transport systems and mass communication systems, industrialisation and urbanisation, in-migration

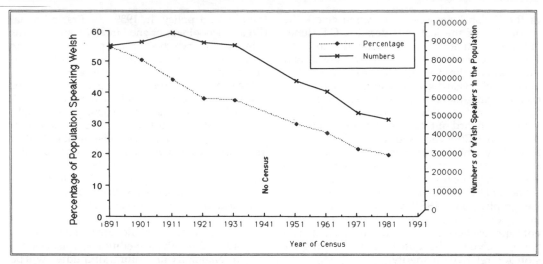

**Figure 1** Welsh speakers in the population of Wales

and out-migration, the growth of mass media and a decline in religious attendance may each have an effect. The growth of nationalistic political consciousness, a reaction to the authoritarian imposition of the English language and Anglophone culture are similarly important external effects on the development of Welsh bilingual education. That is, the development of bilingual education in Wales is not a purely educationally derived phenomenon. It does not develop from simple arguments about the educational virtues of bilingual education. Rather, such growth is both an action and reaction in the general growth

of consciousness about the virtues of preserving an indigenous language and culture. Such growth cannot be viewed in simple, functional terms. Conflicts with authority, protests, non-violent but militant action all have been a part of the equation of change.

**The Gentle Revolution**

The growth of bilingual schools is one major indicator of a gentle revolution that has occurred in schools in Wales in the last four decades. That a revolution and not evolution has occurred is demonstrated by brief illustrations of the position

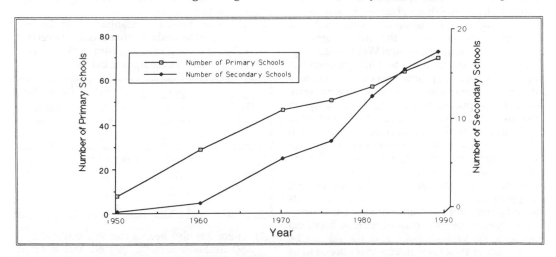

**Figure 2** The increase in Designated Bilingual Schools by year

of the Welsh language in education before the revolution of the last four decades. G.E. Jones (1982) notes that in the years following the 1889 Welsh Intermediate Education Act, Welsh had little status in the eyes of school headteachers and was 'widely regarded as an inferior language and certainly an unnecessary one; it was of no help in "getting on" … [a] low-status irrelevancy' (p. 18). When the Board of Education produced a report on 'Welsh in Education and Life' (1927), of the 135 secondary schools surveyed, in none was Welsh the everyday language of the school and no Welsh language textbooks were available for the school or Higher Certificate stages in History and Geography (Jones, 1982). Upward social mobility often dominated the ideas and priorities of parents and teachers, and thus the English language was perceived as the route to vocational progression and relative prosperity.

It is worthy of note that, despite a gentle revolution in bilingual education in Wales, problems identified in the first two decades of the century (by The Report on Welsh in Education and Life, 1927) as surrounding the indigenous language, are still issues of debate today in Wales and many minority language European contexts: the comparative economic and utilitarian value of Welsh and English, examination syllabuses and the expectations of higher education constraining the implementation of a full Welsh cultural curriculum, the apathy of certain groups of Welsh speakers to their own language and culture, the presence of monolingual English speakers in the Welsh speaking heartlands, the 'brain-drain' of Welsh speakers (especially teachers) to England, the unequal distribution and availability of media in the two languages, debates about literary, classical Welsh and living, colloquial Welsh, concerns that bilingualism has negative effects on 'intelligence' and school attainment, debates about the value of a minority language as opposed to fostering major European languages, the role of the organic community in the health of the Welsh language, debates as to the relative power of government in Cardiff and London, and the depopulation of small 'Welsh' villages (Board of Education, 1927). L'histoire, qu'est-ce autre chose qu'une analyse du présent, puisque c'est dans le passé que l'on trouve les éléments dont est formé le présent? (attributed to Durkheim).

The beginning of the revolution in bilingual education in Wales cannot and should not be dated. Before structural change there needs to be change in public opinions or in dominant philosophy and policy. In 1939, the first bilingual (Welsh) school was opened in Aberystwyth, this being a primary school in the private sector. As Edwards (1984) noted, 'Despite scornful opposition from Welsh as well as non-Welsh speakers, it thrived and in time became the pattern for many similar primary bilingual schools (5–11 years old), all of which were subsequently established and supported by local education authorities' (p. 250). The establishment in 1956 of Ysgol Glan Clwyd as the first designated bilingual secondary school marks the beginnings of secondary school change in Welsh education.

The current statistics (Welsh Office, 'Statistics of Education', 1976–1990) show that:

(1) Approximately one in every four primary school children in Wales are mostly or partly taught through the medium of Welsh. Under the National Curriculum, all children will be taught Welsh as a first or a second language. Thus, from Welsh being excluded from the curriculum in the early decades of this century, it has now become virtually compulsory in schools throughout Wales.

(2) There are 417 Welsh-speaking (bilingual) primary schools and 42 Welsh-speaking (bilingual) secondary schools in Wales. In terms of the total number of schools, this is respectively 24.1% of primary schools and 17.7% of secondary schools. A Welsh-speaking (bilingual) school is currently defined under the 1988 Education Reform Act as a school where a half or more subjects (other than English and Welsh) are taught wholly or partly in Welsh.

(3) There has been a substantial rise in the percentage of secondary schools offering certain subjects through the medium of Welsh. This is illustrated in the figures below:

|        | Maths  | French    | PE/Games |
|--------|--------|-----------|----------|
| 1979   | 6.1%   | 6.1%      | 6.6%     |
| 1990   | 17.7%  | 14.3%     | 17.3%    |
| Change | +11.6% | +8.4%     | +10.7%   |
|        | Physics | Chemistry |          |
| 1982   | 7.1%   | 3.7%      |          |
| 1990   | 9.5%   | 9.1%      |          |
| Change | +2.4%  | +5.4%     |          |

(4) There has also been a rise in the number of examination subjects offered and entered. The figures below (see Figure 3) concern

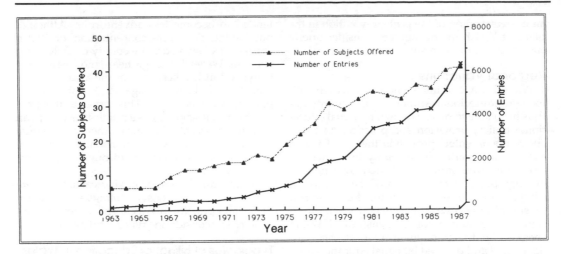

**Figure 3** Examination subjects offered through the medium of Welsh. Note: In 1988, with the introduction of the General Certificate of Secondary Education, 71 subjects were offered through the medium of Welsh. The number of entries was 8886.

Welsh medium subjects offered to 16 year olds (at the Ordinary level) .

From the small acorn planted some four decades ago, still young but sturdy oak trees have developed. In the last decade, the central girth of those trees has expanded, with an increasing percentage of pupils being taught Welsh as a first or second language. That the seeds of change are slowly being planted elsewhere in the system is evident from the increasing number of secondary schools using Welsh as a medium of transmission in the curriculum. Particular growth has recently occurred in the Mathematics and Science curriculum. History, Geography and Religious Education have been 'natural' subjects for Welsh-medium teaching due to their obvious Welsh cultural links, relative lack of problems with terminology and a partial availability of suitable curriculum material. Since the inception of bilingual secondary education, these tended to be the first subjects taught in Welsh. For opposite reasons, Maths and Science have tended to be among the last subjects to use Welsh as the medium of communication.

One of the best and clearest indicators of growth in bilingual education is the linear increase in 'Ordinary' level subjects (taken at the age of 16) offered through the medium of Welsh and the take-up by pupils and schools of these exams. In a quarter of a century, both 'Ordinary' level entries and subjects in Welsh increased by more than sixfold. This statistic is important

because such examinations are prime symbols of the currency value of bilingual education as perceived by pupils, parents and employers. The market-value of Welsh-medium examinations appears both to have risen in recent years and is currently regarded as a desirable commodity. Such examinations are also good reflectors of the status of Welsh-medium courses in schools. Such status has both grown and is yet to peak. However, one Achilles heel of bilingual education in Wales has been post-school bilingual provision. Higher education and further education have sometimes failed to keep pace with changes in bilingual education. This can decrease the intrinsic value of Welsh-medium examinations. A related problem has been to retain bilingually educated pupils within the Welsh higher education system. Many pupils from bilingual secondary education exert their freedom of choice of University by selecting a University or College in England. While this provides evidence that bilingual education does not impede the ability to participate and compete favourably with monolingually educated pupils, it also causes anxiety that Welsh speakers will emigrate permanently to England, thereby reducing the stock of able Welsh speakers working in Wales.

It is important to view the growth of bilingual education as not occurring in a vacuum. Such growth has been promoted and sustained by a wide and complexly interacting variety of formal and informal support systems. It is important for an understanding of the gentle revolution in the place of Welsh in education to consider briefly such support mechanisms.

## Regional Variations

Wales is divided into eight counties each with its own Educational Authority. Each county has thus been able to devise its own bilingual educational policy, provision and practice. As Baker (1985) documented, growth in the use of Welsh has not only varied from county to county but also cannot be simply explained by language demographics. A comparison of the counties of Clwyd and West Glamorgan, for example, reveals differences of language policy and provision not accounted for by densities of Welsh speakers in the population. One of the most developed and detailed bilingual education policies derives from the county of Gwynedd which contains substantial heartland areas of Welsh-speakers. This county's policy is to develop the ability of pupils and students so that they can be full members of the bilingual society of which they are a part (Gwynedd County Council, 1986). All pupils are expected to become thoroughly bilingual, to be able to speak, read and write fluently and confidently in both English and Welsh by the age of eleven.

In a response to in-migrant monolingual English pupils, the county of Gwynedd created Language Reception Centres in the mid 1980s to aid the transition of such children into bilingual classrooms. In-migrant children spend about 14 weeks in such a Centre before transferring to mainstream schools. The activity of the Centre is focused on Welsh language communicative competence. This is in contrast to the situation in major cities of England where Reception Centres for non-English speaking in-migrants has been abandoned to maximise early integration. The important difference is that in England the now discredited Reception Centres were for minority ethnic groups. In Wales, the Reception Centres are for majority language speakers (English) in the context of preserving a minority language (Welsh). The county of Gwynedd has also been one of the bodies ensuring that developments in Computer Based Learning have been translated into Welsh (and created in Welsh) to give the Information Technology revolution a Welsh dimension (Humphreys, 1987, 1988).

In comparison with Gwynedd, developments in bilingual education in the county of Clwyd were early in the gentle revolution and have since tended to become less adventurous. Although not having the same concentration of Welsh speakers as Gwynedd, the county of Dyfed also contains Welsh language heartland areas. Like Gwynedd, it has been one of the areas where a recent small backlash against Welsh-medium education has occurred. This serves to illustrate that bilingual schooling is a political as well as an educational event. The development of bilingual education regionally and nationally cannot be properly understood except through the political economy.

Overall, this discussion has indicated that there are regional variations in bilingual education policy and practice in Wales. This is now further explored by considering types of bilingual school.

## Typologies of Bilingual Education in Wales

There exists a wide variety of bilingual educational provision in Wales. For example, in some primary schools in the North-West of Wales, all, or almost all the curriculum is delivered through the medium of Welsh. Such schools tend to be in heartland areas where a large percentage (e.g. over 70%) of the population is Welsh speaking. The philosophy of such schools is that children need to have their education in the minority language; there being enough opportunities to learn English in the community, through the mass media and when experiencing Anglo-American culture that particularly dominates the teenage years. These schools will mostly be populated by first language Welsh speakers. However, a varying proportion (e.g. 5% to 30%) of each class will be from English-speaking homes. In some areas, such children will be recent in-migrants into rural areas. It is rare to find a class full of first language Welsh speakers.

At the other end of the language dimension there are schools in predominantly English speaking areas of Wales (e.g. Gwent, Pembroke, border areas with England) where Welsh is taught as a second language in primary and secondary schools for half an hour or so per day. Such second language teaching produces relatively few fluent Welsh speaking children. In between basically monolingual Welsh and monolingual English schools in Wales, there is the widest variety of practice of bilingual education. The kaleidoscopic variety of bilingual educational practice in Wales makes the production of a simple typology inherently dangerous. The balance of first language Welsh and first language English children in a classroom varies considerably as does the amount of Welsh-medium teaching. Such wide variations occur due to such factors as the language skills of available teachers, Local Education Authority policy, and the preferences of Headteachers and Governors of individual schools. The language of the hidden curriculum and the playground can differ from the language of the formal and pastoral curriculum and the managerial language of the classroom. A Welsh-medium school usually contains a mixture of first language Welsh pupils, relatively fluent second language Welsh speakers, plus those whose out-of-school language is English (i.e. 'immersion' pupils). While lessons may be mostly in Welsh, there will sometimes be dual-language episodes between teachers and pupils as well as English-only conversations between pupils.

## The Official Typology

The Government (Welsh Office) categorisation of bilingual education in Wales can be summarised as follows:

(1) Primary schools having classes where Welsh is the sole or the main medium of instruction of first and second language pupils.
(2) Primary schools having classes of first and second language pupils where some of the teaching is through the medium of Welsh.
(3) Primary schools having classes of second language pupils where some of the teaching is through the medium of Welsh.
(4) Primary schools having classes where Welsh is taught as a second language but not used as a teaching medium.
(5) Secondary schools where Welsh is taught as both a first and second language.
(6) Secondary schools where Welsh is taught as a first language only.
(7) Secondary schools where Welsh is taught as a second language only.
(8) Schools where Welsh is not taught at all.

This official typology does not take into account the variations among schools in the range of subjects which are available through the medium of Welsh, through the medium of English and sometimes available (in secondary schools) through both languages.

Apart from the official typology, various other typologies exist (e.g. Faculty of Education, Aberystwyth, 1988). Two counties in Wales have, for policy-making and practical purposes, established categorisations of bilingual schools. The county of Dyfed divides its primary schools into three categories: schools in traditionally Welsh heartland areas where Welsh is to be the dominant language of the curriculum; bilingual schools where the use of Welsh and English in the curriculum will vary according to demand and resources; and schools with English as the language of the classroom and Welsh is taught as a second language.

The county of Gwynedd has developed a sixfold model of its bilingual secondary schools, as follows:

### Schools initially established to provide bilingual education

Such schools contain a mixture of first language Welsh speakers and those from partly or mostly English language backgrounds who have elected to take their education through the medium of Welsh. These schools normally exist in an area where there is an alternative English-medium school. All the staff are bilingual and a substantial part of the curriculum is taken through the medium of Welsh. At least 70% of the curriculum (from the age of 11 to 16) will be through the medium of Welsh. However terminology is taught bilingually (e.g. in Science, Maths, 'Control, Design and Technology', Geography, Civics). At the same time, such schools provide for those less fluent in Welsh. While seeking to improve their Welsh competence, a typical pattern is for such pupils to take 30% of their curriculum through the medium of Welsh, 20% through the medium of English and 50% in classes where both languages are used side by side. The culture of the school will aim to be dominantly Welsh.

### Schools of over 600 children in Welsh areas

Such schools contain children from a wide range of language backgrounds: from first language Welsh speakers to varying levels of fluency and literacy in Welsh and to recent English-only in-migrants. Such schools serve nearly all the secondary children in the catchment area. All teachers are bilingual. In terms of language contact time, up to four types of provision may be found within a school. First, for fluent Welsh speakers and writers, 70% or more of the curriculum taken in Welsh. Second, for those less fluent but still capable enough to follow subjects in Welsh, 50% of the curriculum may be through the medium of Welsh. Third, for those whose Welsh is still developing, 30% of the curriculum is taken in Welsh. Fourth, separate provision may need to be provided for recent in-migrants. In practice, classes may need to operate bilingually. Because the schools contain a wide variety of Welsh language competence, bilingual presentations (oral and written resources) may exist alongside individual, pupil-centred learning strategies.

### Schools of over 600 children in linguistically mixed catchment areas

Such schools exist in areas that were formally predominantly Welsh but are now Anglicised. There are similarities with the second type (see above). The differences are in the teaching staff not all speaking Welsh and in the specification of the percentage of Welsh in the curriculum. Those who are less fluent in Welsh may either take around 30% of their subjects in Welsh with some subjects being taught bilingually. Alternatively, those with lower ability in Welsh may take around 20% of the 'practical' curriculum in Welsh to strengthen their second language. When such pupils reach the fourth year in Secondary schooling (about 14 years old), English-medium teaching tends to prevail as examination syllabuses determine method and medium of teaching.

### Schools of under 600 in Welsh speaking catchment areas

Such schools are found in small towns and rural heartland areas, often being the only choice for parents. The small size of such schools constrains choice of language teaching medium. While teachers will all be bilingual, teaching is at two levels: for fluent Welsh speakers and writers, 70% or more of the curriculum taken in Welsh; for Welsh learners an attempt is made to immerse them in Welsh in the first two years so that a substantial number of subjects may be taken through the medium of Welsh afterwards. Special arrangements are promised for in-migrants (e.g. transport to neighbouring English-medium provision).

### Schools of under 600 pupils in linguistically mixed areas

Such schools are located in Anglicised areas where there is no close alternative state schooling. First language Welsh speakers form a minority of the intake of such schools. Not all teachers will be Welsh speaking; some that are Welsh speaking may not be linguistically competent enough to teach in Welsh. Where possible, 'separate class' provision is made for fluent Welsh speakers with

70% or more of the curriculum delivered through Welsh. For the less fluent, around 30% of the curriculum is expected to be provided in Welsh, increasing to around 50% for those close to fluency in Welsh. Practical necessities mean that classes sometimes operate bilingually to cater for different levels of competence in Welsh. The language balance of the classroom, the availability of suitable and up-to-date learning materials and the preferred teaching style of an individual teacher are some of the major determinants of how policy is interpreted and finely tuned in the classroom. In the movement from a philosophy of bilingual education through the layers of politics, policy, planning, provision and practice, adjustments and departures naturally occur.

### Large schools with very few first language Welsh speakers

Such schools of over 1000 pupils exist in urban, relatively densely populated, Anglicised areas. Almost all pupils speak English as a first language but have been taught Welsh as a second language in the Primary school. A substantial proportion of teachers in the school will not be able to teach in Welsh. English-medium lessons prevail with the expressed Gwynedd ideal being for 20% of the curriculum being in Welsh or delivered bilingually. Fluent Welsh speakers are requested to receive 30% of the curriculum in Welsh. The County policy for such schools with regard to administration and organisation reveals the missionary approach:

> In order to nurture a new tradition in the early years, the schools in this Model need to reflect Welshness in their administration and organisation. The co-operation of the staff will be all important in order to support the lead given by the school's headteacher. A clear policy on the model of using Welsh and English in the school's administration and organisation is required. This policy should give direction on use of noticeboards, signs, memoranda, letters, information for teachers, morning services, publications, reports, organisation and discipline. (Gwynedd County Council, 1986: 29)

No existing typology of bilingual education in Wales captures the full kaleidoscope of colours that exist. The existing categorisations also lack empirical backing. It is a straightforward procedure to collect information on bilingual schools in Wales which can be statistically analysed (cluster analysis) to produce empirically based categorisations. Simple, neat, unidimensional models could then be replaced by a more sophisticated, complex and grounded classification of bilingual education. Such a categorisation would need to show that the formal subject curriculum, the pastoral and classroom management curriculum and not least, the hidden curriculum, have complex bilingual dimensions with considerable variation from school to school. Such a categorisation is also needed to reflect recent government reforms in the curriculum. It is such reforms that are now considered.

## The National Curriculum and Bilingual Education in Wales

The 1988 Education Reform Act divides up curriculum subjects into core and foundation subjects. The core subjects are Mathematics, English and Science. The foundation subjects are History, Geography, Technology, Music, Art, Physical Education and a modern foreign language such as French and German. The place of Welsh as a core or foundation subject varies according to type of school. In a Welsh speaking school, Welsh becomes a core subject. In all other schools in Wales, with a very small number of exemptions, Welsh becomes a foundation subject. Thus the National Curriculum recently instituted in England and Wales tends to raise the status of the Welsh language in the Principality by Welsh becoming a compulsory subject for almost all pupils from 5 to 16 years of age. The national assessment which occurs at the ages of 7, 11, 14 and 16 is also being made available through the medium of Welsh. This contrasts with community languages in England (e.g. Bengali, Urdu, Punjabi, Chinese, Greek, Turkish) for which there is no provision in the National Curriculum for such languages as a teaching medium. Such languages can only be introduced as a modern language into the secondary curriculum so long as a European modern language is also taught to these pupils. Assessment materials are not available in these Community languages.

One major problem in the delivery of Welsh as a teaching medium and as a second language in the National Curriculum is the shortage of Welsh speaking teachers. For example, in the 1989 Secondary School Staffing Survey (Welsh Office Statistics of Education, 1990), 20.8% of teachers in Wales were categorised as fluent in oral and written Welsh. Another 30.1% rated themselves

as having limited Welsh. Therefore, imaginative solutions have been proposed and implemented to enable monolingual English teachers to teach Welsh as a second language in the classroom. A recent innovatory project is entitled Parablu. Parablu is a series of 48 sequentially structured television programmes directly usable in the classroom. An accompanying resource pack includes a bilingually produced teacher handbook, audio tapes (songs and language practice), graded reading books and musical scores. Parablu is designed for teachers who are not Welsh speakers or who are learners of Welsh and have no experience of teaching Welsh as a second language. With approximately 2000 videos and well over a 1000 resource packs sold to primary schools in Wales, Parablu is currently targeted at the 5–7 year old age group, but is also being used for ages beyond this group. The videos integrate education and entertainment in a lively way having been produced by a major independent television company in Wales (HTV). Parablu centres on the activities of a group of touring actors who live in a caravan and put on shows for children. In the family atmosphere of the caravan, language about meals, daily living and retiring to bed can be enacted using simple vocabulary and concepts. The actors and actresses put on plays and performances. This leads to various activities such as dancing, games and jokes. More importantly, it leads to rehearsing, the learning of parts and coaching, providing an opportunity for repetition and consolidation in second language learning.

## The Role of School Inspectors

Not only at the visible and formal level, but also in an informal manner, Her Majesty's Inspectors of Education (HMI) in Wales have supported and influenced the post-War bilingual education movement from the early Primary bilingual education beginnings to the recent compulsory publication of their inspections of schools. For example, such publications contain implicit assumptions of the cross-curricula validity of the use of the indigenous language, perceptive and considered advice for the progressive evolution of bilingualism throughout the school, not just in the formal curriculum, but also in the culture and ethos of the school. It is easy to underestimate the legitimisation process effected by HMI on the growth of bilingual education in the last two or three decades. Baker (1985) and Rawkins (1987) have argued that Welsh language policy lacks integration, cohesion and synthesis, laying blame with the government's piecemeal and reactive approaches to language planning. However, specifically in terms of Welsh language education, central government agencies have played neither a neutral nor an uninterested role. Particularly through HMI (though not ignoring the role of civil servants and politicians), central policy has often been positive to change. While it is popular and probably psychologically and strategically necessary to claim that not enough is being achieved in education in Wales to preserve the heritage language, there is evidence that central policy has frequently encouraged developments in bilingual education.

Alongside HMI's needs to be added the contribution of Local Education Authority Advisers to developments in bilingual education. These local education officers inspect and advise schools within their region and often have influence in the determination of local provision and policy. In the counties of Wales, such Advisers have made key contributions at various levels of the county system: policy, planning, provision, and not least at the sharp ends of educational politics and classroom practice.

### The Role of Parents

Despite such official support, without the pressure, enthusiasm, commitment and interest in bilingual education of groups of parents and teachers, it is unlikely that bilingual education would have begun or advanced as it has. While local authority officers in Flintshire were of paramount influence in the opening of Ysgol Glan Clwyd in 1956, the growth of Designated Bilingual Schools in South Wales owes much to parental endeavour. Through the activity of Rhieni Dros Addysg Gymraeg (Parents for Welsh Medium Education) and through informal networks of local parents and language activists, Local Education Authorities (often as a reaction to sustained pressure and persuasion) have responded to market preferences. Such parental groups have naturally contained Welsh speaking parents who wish the language to be reproduced in their children with the essential help of formal education. However, the pressure for such bilingual schooling has also come from non-Welsh speaking parents. Merfyn Griffiths, headteacher of such a Designated Bilingual school (Ysgol Gyfun Llanhari) commented that, in 1986,

there are Welsh-medium schools, at both primary and secondary levels, where over 90% of the pupils come from homes where the language is not spoken. By now it is non-Welsh-speaking parents and learners who are often the most ardent advocates of Welsh medium education and who apply most pressure on local education authorities to establish more Welsh-medium schools. Without their support, faith and enthusiasm, further progress will not be possible. (p. 5)

The willingness and enthusiasm of non-Welsh speaking parents to opt for bilingual education, particularly where there is a choice of school, is a positive feature of recent trends. Such enthusiasm tends to have regional variations. Growth rates in pupil admissions are evident in Mid Glamorgan, for example, whereas in much of North Wales there has been a comparative lack of growth.

### Motivations

Motivations for choosing bilingual education in Wales (where there is a choice of English-medium or bilingual education) are often discussed, but rarely researched. While Khleif (1980) suggests a naked economic motive (i.e. the Welsh language increasing opportunities for entry and promotion in the jobs market), such attributions are both simplistic and ill-founded, as Reynolds (1982) has rightly noted. The researches of Bush *et al.* (1984) and Davies (1986) have indicated that motivations within a person can be varied and complex. Integrative motivations as well as instrumental orientations frequently exist and co-exist. Parents and pupils alike are often positive to the Welsh language, not only for its utilitarian value, but also for cultural, affiliative and social reasons (Baker, 1988 & 1992).

Part of the motivation of parents opting for bilingual education is likely to be the perceived success of the target school. Popular belief tends to be that Designated Bilingual schools in particular, are more successful than their Anglicised counterparts. The meagre statistics available to support or refute this claim (e.g. external examination results) while used by supporters, require other differences between schools (e.g. social class composition, material resources) to be taken into account in such a comparison (Baker, 1991).

### School Ethos

The perceived success of bilingual schools can never be demonstrated solely by hard statistical indicators. Part of the reputation of the schools, whether real or mythical, is in terms of more indefinable qualities such as ethos, esprit de corps and purposefulness. A contrastive, research-based analysis of bilingual schools suggests that such perceived success is partly, if not largely, based on the relatively greater commitment and dedication of the teachers (and pupils) in such schools (Roberts, 1985). One function of the school, to promote the Welsh language and culture, appears to provide teachers with increased motivation, commitment and sense of direction. This research finding allows an essential notion to be added to an analysis of the development of bilingual education. Apart from central and Local Education Authority policy and provision, bilingual education is ultimately dependent for its success on grounded activity in classrooms. Any history of the growth of bilingual education needs to take into account the growth in reputation, particularly of Designated Bilingual Schools, such that perceived success has itself been a contributory and direct cause of expansion. Such perceived success derives from pioneering Headteachers and a great many devoted and committed teachers.

However, the commitment of many Welsh medium teachers which has contributed to the perceived success of Designated Bilingual Schools is a factor causing current concern. The supply of Welsh speaking teachers is likely to be outstripped by the demand, despite bursaries to attract recruits. In many curricula areas under the National Curriculum, a shortage of Welsh speaking teachers threatens at the least, to stem the growth of bilingual education in the different types of school. A mere supply of teachers is a low baseline to achieve; a supply of good quality teachers is an important, and in a long-term view, a possibly more important issue.

On a more positive note, curricula support for teachers in Wales has been a remarkable part of the growth of bilingual education. As reviews by Webster (1982), Prys Owen (1985), I.W. Williams (1987), T.P. Jones (1987) H.G. Roberts (1987) and G.E. Humphreys (1988) show well, the provision of curricula materials across most ages, subjects and ability levels has lent considerable support to the growth from acorns to blossoming trees. In the progression from a complete dearth of Welsh language material in the 1950s (Ministry of Education, 1953) to the still insufficient but eminently improved availability three decades later (T.P. Jones, 1987), various institutions have played important innovatory and supportive roles by

commissioning, funding or publishing. Such institutional support of the curriculum is now considered.

## Institutional Support

One major institution in the creation of curriculum materials has been the Schools Council Committee in Wales (later called the Schools Curriculum Development Committee in Wales) (B. Jones, 1986). This body established 'Gorwelion' to facilitate the teaching of Welsh as a first language in secondary schools, and the Bilingual Education Project to satisfy the needs of second language pupils with above average proficiency in Welsh entering secondary schools. The development of major resources at the Primary level (e.g. the language materials of Cyfres y Ddraig, Cynllun y Porth), Special Education level (Cynllun y Canllaw) as well as at the secondary level depended much on innovatory, pioneering educationists who worked on those projects with visible success in dissemination and take-up.

Alongside the major input by the Schools Council for the Development of the Curriculum in Wales, bilingual education has also flourished due to the contribution of Welsh language resources from the central Cardiff-based Welsh Joint Education Committee. Through its Welsh Language and Culture Committee, the Publications Advisory Panel, and not least by its willingness to provide examinations in any subject through the medium of Welsh, the WJEC has provided a central co-ordinating function in an educational system in Wales that is more often noted for its county variations in policy and provision. One example of the WJEC's contribution has been the Welsh Textbook Scheme, with its principle of guaranteed sales. With increased help from the Specific Grant terms of the 1980 Education Act, the WJEC has maintained an oversight of the cross-curricula provision of Welsh readers and Welsh textbooks. Despite such co-ordinated activity, T.P. Jones (1987) still finds 'that the need for Welsh curricular materials is probably as acute now as it has ever been because of the increasing awareness among parents of the value of Welsh medium education, coupled with the necessity to keep up to date with contemporary pedagogic innovations' (p. 25). Such a task faces the recently constituted Committee for the Development of Welsh Medium Education, with its advisory supervision of the overall development of bilingual education in Wales.

Other institutions have also supported the

development of bilingual education. The University Colleges at Bangor and Aberystwyth and the teacher training Colleges at Carmarthen and Bangor have increasingly responded to the need to provide teacher-education at initial and in-service levels for Welsh medium school teachers. Aberystwyth's contribution through the Welsh Textbooks Project, the co-ordinating work of its Resources Centre, publication of 'Cyfres Mathemateg Cambria' and a comprehensive catalogue of Welsh medium educational resources has been complemented by Bangor's contribution to Welsh medium Science, Religious Education (through the Welsh National Centre for Religious Education) and Special Education. As Owen's (1985) survey of Welsh medium resources found, there are needs for further resources across the curriculum (e.g. Modern Languages, Drama, Music), for updating material to fit recent movements and evolution within all subjects, and for a response to the demands of the National Curriculum.

## Educational Research

The provision of Welsh medium curriculum resources has followed the provision of Welsh-medium education and imperfectly helped to sustain such expansion. In contrast, it is dubious whether educational research, however widely defined, has played much more than a minimal role in this expansion. As Reynolds' (1982) seminal 'state of the art' paper and Baker's books (1985, 1988) revealed, research into bilingual education in Wales has been meagre. The paradox is that, up to the 1960s, Wales had an international reputation for research into bilingualism (e.g. Saer, 1923; Barke & Parry-Williams, 1938; Smith, 1923; W.R. Jones, 1966). Such research, however, cast doubt on bilingual education, connecting bilinguals with 'mental confusion' and relatively lower school achievement compared to monolinguals (J.L. Williams, 1960). At the time of expansion of bilingual education in Wales, foundational educational research in Wales generally failed to respond. There are exceptions, the most notable being the Attitudes and Attainment research of Sharp *et al.* (1973), and the evaluation of the Schools Council Bilingual Project (Dodson, 1985).

The overall failure of research to respond to the expansion of bilingual education in Wales needs to be traced to a variety of interacting factors such as lack of personnel, decreasing financial support of educational research, and foundational research being given decreasing priority. An initiative to reverse this trend has been the institution of the Committee for the Development of Welsh Medium Education and the remit of three geographically separate agencies (Aberystwyth, Bangor, Cardiff) to engage in both research and curriculum development activity. If this political manoeuvre is to become translated into activity that is genuinely supportive of, and responsive to long term bilingual education in Wales, one or more Centres will need to engage in research and not just circulate curriculum materials.

The failure of research to support bilingual education in Wales is to be contrasted with the success of research in supporting the various Canadian immersion and heritage language programmes that have blossomed since the 1960s (see Baker, 1988). Evaluations of these experiments in bilingual education and research on the cognitive advantages of balanced bilingualism, by outcome and not by intention, provided the positive publicity for such education to expand rapidly. If objective evaluations, for example of Designated Bilingual Schools, had demonstrated their relative success, it is not unlikely that doubting Welsh-speakers and agnostic monolingual English-speakers would have increasingly chosen this form of education. With current protests (e.g. in Gwynedd and Dyfed) regarding Welsh medium education and repeated threats of court action, the failure of educational research in Wales to address bilingual issues is starkly illuminated.

## Conclusions: The Balance Sheet

Bilingual education derives its *raison d'être* not only from a concern to save the Welsh language from further diminution, but also from educational, economic, social, cultural and political reasons. Perceived success in public examinations, the beliefs of some in the extra commitment of bilingual teachers and relatively pleasant ethos of such bilingual schools, the utilitarian hopes that Welsh language skills will enhance job opportunities (a remarkable reversal of nineteenth century and early twentieth century beliefs in the lack of economic value of Welsh for employment and mobility), and the concern to preserve a variety of Welsh cultural forms, are some of the reasons for the continuing growth of bilingual education. Indeed, the rationale of such schools needs increasingly to be built on the *varied and multiple* advantages of bilingual education.

The growth of the bilingual education movement has also needed to contend with a variety of constraints, particularly a decentralised decision making system allowing for wide county by county variation. A similar constraint may occur in the future with the recent reforms in terms of the local management of schools and an imposed National Curriculum. A combination of local school management and a compulsory curriculum will be crucial issues in the future health and development of bilingual education.

If the relationship between the Welsh language and bilingual education can be artificially isolated, bilingual education in Wales has gathered momentum and strength due to its relationship with the plight of the Welsh language. If there is such a strong relationship, a key question is how bilingual education has contributed to the fate of the language. Initially such a question must be framed in a wider collage of positive and negative effects. In the balance sheet of the fate of the Welsh language this century, there are factors possibly connected with the downward trend revealed in Census figures: the in-migration of English monolinguals, the emigration of Welsh speakers, mass communications, information technology, increased communication links (e.g. railways, roads, air travel), tourism, urbanisation and industrialisation, decline in religious attendance and the influence of Anglo-American culture. There are also factors other than bilingual education which need placing on the credit side of the balance sheet; for example, Mudiad Ysgolion Meithrin (Welsh Medium Nursery School Movement), Yr Urdd (The Welsh League of Youth — a strong and well organised national youth organisation), language activists in a variety of public, private and 'pressure group' organisations, and figure-heads among politicians, administrators and educationists who have promoted policy and provoked publicity.

The central question is whether the Welsh language would have any chance of survival without the growth of formal primary and bilingual secondary education in Wales. It appears likely that, despite all the elements on the credit side of the balance sheet, without such growth in

bilingual education, the Welsh language would have almost no chance of survival as a living language of the people. Simply stated, without the growth of bilingual education, there is good reason to believe the Welsh language would not survive. Yet, the danger is in placing too much reliance on formal bilingual education as the salvation of the heritage language. In a minor sense, this reflects the half-truth of a famous Welsh writer, Saunders Lewis, who argued that bilingualism is the chief killer of the Welsh language. This view is that bilingualism is a half-way house on the road to majority language monolingualism. It is a debatable point whether there needs to be heritage language education rather than 'balanced' bilingual education to achieve 'balanced' bilingualism in children. Informal influences within school and pervading Anglicising influences out of school (e.g. TV, 'pop' culture, the information technology revolution) soon provide skills in the majority language and enculturation into English and American value-systems (Baker, 1992). In a major sense, bilingual education alone cannot reverse language trends. There needs to be other support mechanisms for the language, from cradle to grave, from high culture to lowly kerbstone. To live, a language needs an economic basis. For children to leave bilingual education and find the Welsh language has no market value will only, in time, create language disaffection and decay. There is also the current danger of Welsh becoming the language of the school, and English the language of the street, screen and shop. Rather than Welsh being a school-only phenomenon, it needs to penetrate an individual's whole way of life, and be present in everyday active, participatory culture.

In the balance sheet of the Welsh language, bilingual education in Wales is a crucial investment. Bilingual education cannot by itself guarantee a final profit balance. At the same time, without the growth of bilingual education, it is likely the Welsh Nation would soon have become bankrupt in its heritage language and culture.

### References

Baker, C. (1985) *Aspects of Bilingualism in Wales.* Clevedon: Multilingual Matters.
— (1988) *Key Issues in Bilingualism and Bilingual Education.* Clevedon: Multilingual Matters.
— (1991) The effectiveness of bilingual education. *Journal of Multilingual and Multicultural Development* 11 (4), 269–77.

— (1992) *Attitudes and Language.* Clevedon: Multilingual Matters.
Barke, E.M. and Parry-Williams, D.E. (1938) A further study of comparative intelligence of children in certain bilingual and monolingual schools in South Wales. *British Journal of Educational Psychology* 8, 63–7.

Board of Education (1927) *Welsh in Education and Life*. London: HMSO.

Bush, E., Atkinson, P. and Read, M. (1984) A minority choice: Welsh medium education in an Anglicised area — Parents characteristics and motives. *Polygot* 5, Fiche 1 (April).

Davies, J.P. (1986) Dadansoddiad o Nodau Graddedig Ar Gyfer Oedolion Sy'n Dysgu'r Gymraeg fel Ail Iaith. Unpublished PhD thesis, University of Wales.

Dodson, C.J. (1985) Schools council project on bilingual education (Secondary Schools) 1974–1978: Methodology. In C.J. Dodson (ed.) *Bilingual Education: Evaluation, Assessment and Methodology*. Cardiff: University of Wales Press.

Edwards, D.G. (1984) Welsh-medium education. *Journal of Multilingual and Multicultural Development* 5 (3&4), 249–57.

Faculty of Education, University of Wales Aberystwyth (1988) *Report on Secondary Education in Rural Wales*. University of Wales, Aberystwyth: Faculty of Education.

Griffiths, M. (1986) Introduction. In M. Griffiths (ed.) *The Welsh Language in Education*. Cardiff: WJEC.

Gwynedd County Council (1986) *Language Policy*. Caernarfon: Gwynedd County Council.

Humphreys, G.E. (1987) Polisi Iaith Awdurdod Addysg Gwynedd — Adolygu a Gweithredu ym 1986. *Education for Development* 10 (3), 7–23.

— (1988) *Bilingual Education in Wales. Facing the Future with Confidence*. Newport: National Eisteddfod Publications.

Jones, B. (1986) The work of the schools council in Wales 1964–1984. In M. Griffiths (ed.) *The Welsh Language in Education*. Cardiff: WJEC.

Jones, G.E. (1982) *Controls and Conflicts in Welsh Secondary Education 1889–1944*. Cardiff: University of Wales Press.

Jones, T.P. (1987) Thirty years of progress. A brief outline of the development of Welsh language teaching materials. *Education for Development* 10 (3), 24–39.

Jones, W.R. (1966) *Bilingualism in Welsh Education*. Cardiff: University of Wales Press.

Khleif, B.B. (1980) *Language, Ethnicity and Education in Wales*. New York: Mouton.

Ministry of Education (1953) *The Place of Welsh and English in the Schools of Wales*. London: HMSO.

Owen, P. (1985) *Welsh Language Exploratory Survey*. Cardiff: School Curriculum Development Committee.

Rawkins, P.M. (1987) The politics of benign neglect: Education, public policy, and the mediation of linguistic conflict in Wales. *International Journal of the Sociology of Language* 66, 27–48.

Reynolds, D. (1982) A state of ignorance? *Education for Development* 7 (2), 4–35.

Roberts, C. (1985) Teaching and learning commitment in bilingual schools. Unpublished PhD thesis, University of Wales.

Roberts, H.G. (1987) Microelectronics — the Welsh connection. *Education for Development* 10 (3), 55–62.

Saer, D.J. (1923) The effects of bilingualism on intelligence. *British Journal of Psychology* 14, 25–38.

Sharp, D., Thomas, B., Price, E., Francis, G. and Davies, I. (1973) *Attitudes to Welsh and English in the Schools of Wales*. Basingstoke/Cardiff: Macmillan/University of Wales Press.

Smith, F. (1923) Bilingualism and mental development. *British Journal of Psychology* 13, 271–82.

Webster, J.R. (1982) Education in Wales. In L. Cohen, J. Thomas and L. Manion (eds) *Educational Research and Development in Britain 1970–1980*. Slough: NFER-Nelson.

Welsh Office (1976–1990) *Statistics of Education in Wales*. Cardiff: Welsh Office.

Williams, I.W. (1987) Mathematics and science: The final frontier for bilingual education. *Education for Development* 10 (3), 40–54.

Williams, J.L. (1960) Comments on articles by Mr D.G. Lewis and Mr W.R. Jones. *British Journal of Educational Psychology* 30, 271–2.

## Questions

(1) Explain what Baker means by the 'gentle revolution' in Wales. Discuss how it was similar or different from the 'quiet revolution' in Quebec described by Genesee.

(2) What have been the major changes in the use of Welsh in schools in Wales from the early 20th century to the present?

What are the reasons given by Baker for the growth in bilingual schools in Wales. List the categories of bilingual programs offered by the Welsh Office. Where do they fit with regards to the bilingual education typology presented after the Lyons article at the start of this book?

(3) What are the Language Reception Centres in Gwynedd? How do they operate? How do they differ from those in England?

Do you think Language Reception Centres are a good idea? Why or why not? Are there any in your community?

(4) Describe the difference between bilingual teaching in Welsh schools and the following with respect to language use and teacher characteristics:

(a) Transitional bilingual education in the US.

(b) Dual language programs in the US.

(c) French Canadian immersion programs.

(d) European Schools.

Explain why you think language alternation in the transitional bilingual classroom in the United States most often leads to shift to the majority language, whereas the same does not occur in Wales. Do you think language alternation is a good practice in bilingual education for your community? Why or why not?

(5) Describe the role of parents, both language majority and language minority, in the Welsh 'gentle revolution.' How does this compare to the situation in PS 84, in St Lambert, and in a bilingual program in your community?

(6) The chapter uses terms from 'economics' to portray the Welsh language, such as 'the currency and market value of Welsh,' 'the balance sheet,' 'crucial investment,' 'profit balance,' 'naked economic motive,' 'bankrupt.' How important is the relationship between a minority language and the economy in the salvation and maintenance of that language? Are there any economic benefits to speaking the minority language in your area? If yes, what are they?

## Activities

(1) Through research in a library, find out more about another European context (other than Wales) in which a minority language is used. Write a brief profile of that language and include its use in education. Then compare that sociolinguistic profile to what exists in your country.

(2) One Welsh emblem is the dragon. Draw a dragon with six flames coming out of the mouth. Inside the different flames, write in six key factors in fighting for language survival. The Welsh colors are red and green. Use red to highlight your 'flames of survival.'

(3) Select a school in which there are a large number of recently arrived students. Find out what kinds of provisions are made for them and the services they receive. Find out if the community has a special school or special classes for them. Make a report to class.

# Allocating Two Languages as a Key Feature of a Bilingual Methodology

## Rodolfo Jacobson

### Introduction

Bilingual methodology as a technical construct concerning how to teach children whose first language is not English has been grossly misunderstood by approaching it from the vantage points of either ethnic culture or lexical competency in the non-English language. Even though the knowledge of and the familiarity with both are important components of bilingual teacher training, they do not represent *per se* the core of bilingual methodology. As a matter of fact, a multicultural approach should underlie any viable educational method in the United States and the mastery of specialized terms needed for the teaching of mathematics or science or social studies is obviously a prerequisite of any sound instructional approach regardless of the language or languages of instruction. If the bilingual method is not justifiable on cultural nor lexical grounds, then on what grounds is it justifiable?

The author's recent research has gathered convincing evidence that it is the distributional pattern chosen for a given bilingual program that determines the method. In other words, the manner how the two languages are being allocated is ultimately indicative of the bilingual method being used. To elaborate on the above, the author proposes to describe the range of language distributional options available to the bilingual teacher and to briefly comment on his recent research findings that demonstrated the viability of some of these options.

### Broad Categories of Language Distribution and Their Rationales

It is obvious that two languages must be used as media of instruction if a bilingual focus is to be maintained in an educational program. Bilingual educators have usually insisted on the separation of the two languages, one of which is English and

the other, the child's vernacular. By strictly separating the languages, the teacher avoids, it is argued, cross-contamination, thus making it easier for the child to acquire a new linguistic system as he/she internalizes a given lesson. This viewpoint was felt to be so self-evident that no research was ever conducted to support this argument. At the bottom of all this lies a rather poor conception of what a young mind is capable of, i.e. the child's incapability of sorting out language data belonging to two different sources and assigning them to two systems. Children in multilingual settings have been shown to possess unusual talents that allow them to become, not only bilinguals, but polyglots regardless of how they have been exposed to the various linguistic sources. To be sure, language separation is one way of approaching the child's learning through two languages allowing him/her to become bilingual by means of two monolingual processes in which he/she associates one language with some experiences and the other language with others.

The insistence on language separation for bilingual programs has generated, by the very nature of this dogma, the opposition to the concurrent use of two languages. Again, it was felt that the inappropriateness of the concurrent use was so self-evident that no research had to be conducted to prove this fact. As language separation would lead to the uncontaminated acquisition of either language, the concurrent use of both languages would lead to confusion, mixing and highly accented speech patterns in the target language. Whether this latter argument could actually be upheld, should have been supported by hard data but, unfortunately, no research project in the past has ever explored this issue. More recently, however, data seem to suggest that certain forms of concurrent use can be as successful as are certain forms of language separation.

The notion of bilingual instruction can be expanded to mean instruction of bilingual children where 'bilingual' is interpreted as home-language-dominant and limited-English-proficient. Teaching such children in their weaker language (English) has recently been viewed as a means of upgrading their skills in the target language. Research in a different setting (Canada) has lately become available and educators in the United States are using in some programs the target language with children of other-language backgrounds without seriously analyzing these experiments in terms of (1) the similarities and differences between the two settings and (2) the degree of transferability of the Canadian design. Regardless of these concerns, it appears that some bilingual educators have become fascinated with the fact that *some* children can learn a second language well when they are exposed to it most or even all of the time, in particular when school subjects are being taught through that medium.

Three broad language distribution categories and their rationales have here been discussed. However, it has been noted that serious research evaluating the merits of each distributional category is still scarce. As a first step toward a clearer understanding of language distribution, one may wish to examine which subcategories of distributional patterns may lend themselves to begin gathering the methodological data that are so urgently needed.

## Sub-categories of Language Distributional Patterns

The two languages of a bilingual program can be separated on the basis of four criteria, i.e. *topic, person, time* and *place*. By topic we mean content or school subjects, such as deciding which language should become the medium of instruction for, say, one-half of the academic subjects and which language, for the other half. Such a decision could be content-free or content-sensitive. The former would involve a random split between school subjects in order to assign one language as a medium of instruction to one set and the other to the remaining set. The latter would involve the assignment of one language to those subjects that seem to be more appropriately taught in that language and that of the other language to the remainder of subjects for the very same reason. The content-sensitive topic-oriented language separation approach presents the difficulty of having to support the notion that one linguistic system is good, say, to

teach social studies but not math or science and the other system, to teach math or science but not social studies. Whichever approach is followed it will lead to a design where the languages are separated by topic.

The separation of the two languages by person, in turn, requires the presence in the classroom of two persons, one of whom communicates consistently in English and the other, in the child's vernacular. Two teachers using a team approach, a teacher and an aide, a teacher and an interchangeable set of volunteer parents could all implement such a design. Children would soon become conditioned to the fact that a given language is chosen according to the person whom they address. The staff's normative behavior would eliminate for the child the need of assessing a particular communicative event first before engaging in a language choice event.

The time factor is probably easiest to control by posting a classroom schedule that calls for the use of English, say, in the mornings and that of the child's home language after lunch. Other time distribution on a regular or sporadic basis can be agreed on by posting signs at the door indicating which language would be used on a given day. The Alternate Day Approach used in the Philippines and described in the professional literature (G.R. Tucker, 1970: 281–300) is an example of the latter language separation approach on the basis of time.

The physical location (Cohen, 1975: 104–6) where a class is taught may serve as another consistent cue for the child to know whether English is the medium of communication or whether the home language, say, Spanish is expected. Where different rooms for these language-controlled activities are unavailable, activity centers can serve the same purpose of serving as an easy cue for the child to respond to.

The artificiality of language separation based on any of these criteria is obvious as in a real life situation neither topic nor person nor time nor place are easily controlled. Furthermore, the separation that can so be controlled, is uncontrollable within the mind. The child has only one mind where to internalize whichever information he/she has been exposed to. Unless such a mind is properly disciplined, there will always remain the risk of confusion or cross-contamination.

The two languages can also be used concurrently to ensure that the teacher's information is fully comprehended regardless of any lacunae in the target language that may still exist. How this is done may be crucial for both types of learning, the acquisition of language and that of factual knowledge. Again, four ways of language distribution in the learning of content can be identified. The teacher may randomly switch from one language to the other disregarding any principle of unilingual consistency within a sentence or between several sentences of the same thought group. Such a code-switching behavior is frequently observed in some situations in informal dialogs among bilingual ethnics and its use in school settings — controversial as it may appear — would simplify the decoding process for those children who have been exposed to this kind of verbal behavior. However, if the development of language is to go hand in hand with the acquisition of factual knowledge, caution with such a flipflopping procedure may be in order. On the other hand, the teacher may consistently alternate between the two languages by saying everything twice, in English and in the child's vernacular, in a way that reminds us of the consecutive interpretation used during court cases when defendants do not speak the language of the court. It has been argued that the translation into the child's vernacular of everything that is being taught may prevent him/her from ever developing the kind of English language proficiency that must be one of the objectives of a sound bilingual program. Unfortunately no research data are available to support the fears concerning the use of flipflopping or concurrent translation in the classroom.

Thirdly, one may preview a school unit in the child's vernacular and teach it in depth in English. The reverse is equally possible: the unit is taught in English and then reviewed in the child's vernacular. The child who tries to gain his/her factual knowledge from the preview–review portions of the lesson may internalize a watered-down version of the topic, unless he/she makes a strong effort to use these portions only to fill in the gaps caused by his/her incomplete knowledge of English when the in-depth version of the lesson was presented.

An innovative model of teaching concurrently in the two languages has recently been proposed where a highly structured approach to code-switching is introduced. Here, the switching is only teacher-initiated, the alternation occurs mainly between thought groups and only when the teacher can justify it on several grounds and, finally, this dual language use is consciously incorporated in the lesson in response to certain cues that the teacher wishes to acknowledge.

Some of the concerns that bilingual educators have upheld in regard to the concurrent use of two languages seem to be addressed here, i.e. there is no intra-sentential code-switching, the alternation is not random but purposeful, the use of both languages is fully balanced and the structure of the lesson does not encourage the child to tune out whilst his/her weaker language is spoken. Jacobson (1978, 1979a, 1979b, 1981a, 1981b, 1982, 1983a, 1983b, 1983c, 1985, 1988) who had been developing the *New Concurrent Approach* since 1975 tested it in a Federal project from 1981–84 (see below), thus being one of the very few who gathered hard data on specific methodological options in bilingual education.

The use of the target language — here, English — in teaching the child whose mother tongue differs from the school language can be carried out in two ways, similar in certain aspects but different in others. The similarity consists in the use of the target language as a medium of instruction. The difference, in turn, resides in such facts as (1) whether or not children are starting out alike with a zero level background in the target language, (2) whether or not they are members of the middle class with positive self-identity, (3) whether or not the teachers are balanced bilinguals who accept the children's language when necessary even though they may avoid its use in their own responses and (4) whether or not the further development of the mother tongue is of concern and provisions are made to that effect, in order not to alienate the children from their home environment and their culture. The choice between immersion and submersion seems to be a subtle one based on the notions of additive as opposed to subtractive bilingualism and the role of the self-image in the language acquisitional process. On the other hand, both are language distributional practices that merit serious considerations when bilingual methodology is at issue.

Ten subcategories of language distributional patterns have been discussed on a somewhat theoretical plane. Figure 1 shows the relationship of these subcategories to the broader categories considered above.

It may now be pertinent to offer some actual examples of these subcategories, so that the nature of these options is understood more fully.

## Bilingual Methods Illustrated

The difference between the various language distributional practices can best be appreciated if

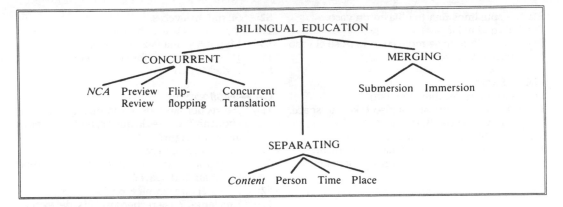

**Figure 1** Subcategories of language distributional patterns

the content is kept stable and only the languages are selected variably to illustrate the methods discussed in the preceding section. The vernacular used in the example shall be Spanish and the objective of the lesson will be to review a science lesson concerning 'Air with regard to Weight and Space', and to recall an experiment demonstrating the fact that air has weight and takes up space. Depending on the method chosen, a portion of the cited lesson might be as follows:

### LSA — Time

April 22 — Today English is spoken
T:    Do you remember what we have been learning about air? What have we learned about air and weight?
S1:   ...that air has weight.
T:    Very good; and what have we learned about air and space?
S2:   ...that air takes up space.
T:    Excellent. And do you remember the experiment that we did the other day with the cup and the paper napkin?
S3:   We put a napkin on a cup with water and the paper did not get wet.
T:    Very good. And who can tell me why the paper did not get wet when I turned the cup upside down?
S4:   ...because the air in the cup did not let the water through.

April 23 — Hoy se habla español
T:    Se recuerdan Uds., Clase, ¿qué aprendimos acerca del aire? ¿Qué aprendimos acerca del aire y del peso del aire?
S1:   ...que el aire pesa.
T:    Muy bien y ¿qué aprendimos acerca del aire y del espacio que ocupa el aire?

S2:   ...que el aire ocupa espacio.
T:    Excelente. Y ¿se recuerdan del experimento que hicimos el otro día con el vaso y la toallita de papel?
S3:   Pusimos una toallita encima de un vaso con agua y el papel no se mojó.
T:    Muy bien. Y ¿quien me puede decir por qué no se mojó el papel cuando puse el vaso boca abajo?
S4:   ...porque el aire en el vaso no dejó pasar el agua.

### LSA — Place

The English Room (or Activity Center)
T:    We have learned that air has weight but what have we learned about air and space?
S1:   Air takes up space.
T:    Good. And who remembers the experiment that we did the other day with the paper cup?
S2:   I do. We put a napkin on a cup with water.
T:    Right. And what happened?
S3:   The paper did not get wet.
T:    Why?
S4:   ...because the air did not let the water through.
El quarto español (o el centro de actividades en español)
T:    ¿Que estudiamos hoy aqui?
S1:   Ciencias.
T:    Entonces ¿estudiamos lo mismo que tuvimos en el otro cuarto?
S2:   No, allá fué 'science.'
T:    Muy bien, Clase, aquí es ciencias porque hablamos en español. ¿Se recuerdan del experimento que hicimos entonces con un vaso de cartón y una toallita de papel?

**S3:** Sí, pusimos una toallita en un vaso.
**T:** Y ¿qué más?
**S4:** La toallita no se mojó cuando puso el vaso boca abajo.

### LSA — Person

The Classroom Teacher (English)
**T:** Air has weight and it also takes up space. Did you know that, class?
**S1:** Yes, Miss, like in the experiment.
**T:** Who else remembers that experiment?
**S2:** I do. We put a napkin on a paper cup.
**T:** And…
**S3:** The paper did not get wet.
**T:** Why?
**S4:** …because of the air in the cup.
**T:** Very good. Mrs Gomez will now review that lesson a bit more.

La asistente de la maestra (Español)
**A:** ¿Qué me pueden decir del aire?
**S1:** …que el aire pesa.
**A:** Bien, y ¿qué más?
**S2:** …que ocupa espacio
**A:** Muy bien. Y ¿que hizo Mrs Jones con el vaso?
**S3:** Lo puso boca abajo.
**A:** ¿Sí? Y ¿por qué?
**S4:** Para ver si el agua mojaba el papel.

### LSA — Topic

Science
**T:** Do you remember what we have been learning about air? What have we learned about air and weight?
**S1:** …that air has weight.
**T:** Very good; and what have we learned about air and space?
**S2:** …that air takes up space.
**T:** Excellent. And do you remember the experiment that we did the other day with the cup and the paper napkin?
**S3:** We put a napkin on a cup with water and the paper did not get wet.
**T:** Very good. And who can tell me why the paper did not get wet when I turned the cup upside down?
**S4:** …because the air in the cup did not let the water through.

Estudios sociales
**T:** ¿Quién sabe que es lo que hace el cartero?
**Sa:** Es un señor que trae las cartas y los paquetes.
**T:** Muy bien y ¿tu has recibido una carta alguna vez?

**S2:** Si, muchas veces.
**T:** Y ¿quienés te escribieron?
**S3:** Mi papá y una vez, mi abuelo.
**T:** ¿De dónde te escribió tu abuelo?
**S4:** …de Mexico.

### CA — Flipflopping

**T:** ¿Se recuerdan Uds. de lo que aprendimos about air? ¿Qué es lo que aprendimos about air and weight?
**S1:** … que el aire pesa.
**T:** Muy bien. And what have we learned about air and space?
**S2:** …que el aire ocupa espacio.
**T:** Excelente. Y ¿se recuerdan Uds. del experimento que hicimos el otro diá? The one with the cup and the paper napkin.
**S3:** We put a napkin on a cup con agua y el papel no se mojó.
**T:** Y ¿quién me dice why the paper did not get wet?
**S4:** …porque the air in the cup did not let the water through.

### CA — Preview/Review

**T:** Hoy vamos a repasar la lección del aire que estudiamos ayer. Dijimos que el aire pesa y que ocupa espacio, ¿se recuerdan?
**S1:** Si, señora Jones, y también hicimos un experimento que me gustó mucho.
**T:** Muy bien. Entonces vamos a ver que es que recordamos. Air has weight. That is very important, class. And what did we say about space?
**S2:** Air takes up space.
**T:** Yes and we showed that in our experiment with the paper cup. What else did we use in the experiment?
**S3:** A kleenex.
**T:** Yes, we used a paper napkin.
**S4:** And water.
**T:** We put some water in the cup and then we covered it with a napkin. Did the water spill when we turned the cup?
**S5:** No, the air did not let it through.

### CA — Translation

**T:** We learned yesterday that air has weight. Ayer dijimos que el aire pesa. And what have we learned about air and space? Y ¿qué aprendimos acerca del aire y el espacio?
**S1:** …que el aire ocupa espacio.
**T:** You are right, air takes up space. And we

also did an experiment. ¿No se recuerdan del experimento que hicimos?

**S2:** Si, con un vaso de cartón.

**T:** Did we use anything else besides the paper cup? ¿Qué más usamos?

**S3:** Una toallita de papel.

**S4:** Y le pusimos agua al vaso.

**T:** You are right, we put some water in the cup and then, we covered it all up with a napkin. And what did I do then? ¿Qué hice yo entonces?

**S5:** Ud. puso el vaso boca abajo.

**T:** Yes, I turned the cup upside down. And did the napkin get wet? ¿Se mojó la toallita de papel?

**S6:** No, se quedó sequita.

**T:** ¿Por qué? But why?

**S7:** Because of the air.

### CA — NCA

**T:** Do you remember what we have been learning about air? What have we learned about air and weight?

**S1:** ...that air has weight.

**T:** Very good. And what have we learned about air and space?

**S2:** ...that air takes up space.

**T:** Very good. ¿Se recuerdan del experimento que hicimos el otro día con el vaso y la toallita de papel? ¿Me pueden decir lo que hicimos?

**S3:** Pusimos una toallita encima de un vaso y no se mojó el papel.

**T:** Muy bien. Who can tell me now why the paper didn't get wet?

**S4:** ...because the air in the cup didn't let the water into the napkin.

**T:** Muy bien. Tú sí pusiste atención. El papel no se mojó porque el aire ocupa espacio y no permite que entre el agua.

### MA — Immersion

**T:** Do you remember what we have been learning about air?

**S1:** Air? Oh, aire.

**T:** Yes, air and weight.

**S1:** ...que el aire pesa.

**T:** Yes, air has weight.

**S1:** Air has weight.

**T:** What about air and space?

**S2:** Air ocupa espacio.

**T:** Yes, air takes up space. Who remembers the experiment that we did the other day?

**S3:** With the cup and the napkin?

**T:** Yes, we covered a cup with a napkin. Was there some water in the cup?

**S4:** Yes, water.

**T:** And what happened when I turned the cup over? Did the napkin get wet?

**S5:** No, no se mojó.

**T:** It did not get wet because the air in the cup took up space.

### MA — Submersion

**T:** Do you remember what we have been learning about air?

**S1:** El aire pesa.

**T:** We don't want to speak Spanish, do we? Air has weight.

**S1:** Air has weight.

**T:** What about space?

**S2:** Espacio. Si, ocupa espacio.

**T:** Say: it takes up space.

**S2:** It takes up space.

**T:** Good. We only want to speak English in class. Now tell me about the experiment.

**S3:** With the cup and the napkin.

**T:** Did we put water into the cup?

**S4:** Yes.

**T:** And did we cover it with the napkin?

**S5:** No se mojó.

**T:** It did not get wet when I turned it over.

The discussion of the preceding sections makes it unnecessary to elaborate on these examples. They merely serve the purpose of illustrating the theoretical aspects alluded to above. A decision concerning which method works can not be made on speculative grounds. A series of research projects must be designed in order to gather data as to what works in bilingual education. Only the surface of such a reseach agenda has been scratched by conducting the Title VII Demonstration Project in Bilingual Instructional Methodology (1981–84) in San Antonio. The following section will briefly describe which methodological options have been explored in the cited project, what special issues have been addressed and which findings have emerged.

### Title VII Demonstration Project in Bilingual Methodology

Two of the language distributional patterns described above were chosen as a basis for a Federal project in bilingual methodology. Its objective was to demonstrate the relative effectiveness of a language separation model (LSA — by school subjects) as compared to a concurrent model (NCA) by implementing over three years (1981–84) a carefully conceived design in two local schools. Indian Creek Elementary was selected as the site for the LSA Model and Sky Harbour Elementary for the NCA Model. Children of limited English language proficiency (LEP) were identified to participate in the Project with the understanding that they would not be exited prior to the completion of the Project in order to produce longitudinal data on bilingual methodology. Two Project classrooms operated in each school, hereby allowing the participating children to progress from grades K and L during the first year to grades 2 and 3 during the final year. The teaching staff consisted of four bilingual teachers and four bilingual aides so that each grade had the necessary personnel to implement the sophisticated design. A program coordinator and a project director were responsible, not only for its faithful implementation but also for the required staff development, in particular in the area of the less familiar NCA Model. The parent involvement component provided an opportunity to make the experiment relevant to the community as the social context for this program was deemed to be of crucial importance. Finally, a rigorous evaluation component served the purpose of monitoring the children's academic achievement and also of globally assessing the extent to which the Project achieved the overall objectives stated in the proposal.

In addition to the central objective of the Project, that of demonstrating the effectiveness of two bilingual approaches, several special issues emerged and were also addressed. A discussion of these issues is beyond the scope of the present study but the listing of the topics that were researched as the Project was progressing may be in order:

(1) *The bilingual readiness program for level K* whose objective was to firmly establish Spanish as one of the language media to be used in the classroom.

(2) The attention to *affective factors with emphasis on a classroom climate* favorable to bicultural–bilingual performances.

(3) *The role of the first language* as medium through which cognitive skills can best be acquired.

(4) *The communicative competence in bilingual settings* as a means of developing appropriate verbal interaction.

(5) *The control of language choice* in order to promote the skills of language alternation as a function of person, place and topic.

(6) *The bilingual continuum* as a way of assessing children's degree of bilinguality in order to allow the teacher to strive for greater bilingual balance in their verbal behavior.

The findings of the Project have confirmed the viability of two bilingual methods, the LSA — topic and the NCA models. Both language goals were achieved as the children became proficient in English and developed their mother tongue to a degree that allowed them to learn through either language. The unproven hypothesis that children will mix the languages when taught in a language alternation mode was rejected, at least when the latter is, as in NCA, a carefully structured concurrent approach. All Project teachers predicted at the end of the last year that the participating children would not experience any learning problem in future years just because the medium of instruction would have shifted to English only. Having acquired in their home language the necessary cognitive skills to achieve academically and having transferred them to the school language as the latter became firmly established, the children began to display their academic potentials in various content areas. No significant difference emerged between groups regardless of whether the languages were separated or used concurrently. However, some trends emerged suggesting that mathematical skills were favored when languages were used concurrently but other skills were favored when languages were separated. The Project as a whole showed the effectiveness of a design that combines demonstration and research components as the results of several research tasks could be utilized and the effectiveness of the upgraded approach be demonstrated at once in a realistic setting. In this way, the earlier cited 'special issues' yielded valuable responses to crucial research questions and these responses, in turn, could then be incorporated into the normal routine of a bilingual classroom.

## Conclusion

Of ten language distributional patterns only two (LSA by school subject and NCA) have been researched and been found to be viable methods for a bilingual program. The replication of the experiment is of course necessary to substantiate the claim that the two approaches are equally valid and should be implemented on a larger scale. The other eight bilingual options described above, in turn, have not yet been researched and attempts should be made to explore the degree of viability of each. Based upon the results of future research projects, teachers should be able to select the language distributional pattern that adjusts itself best to their personality and their teaching strategies and, by the same token, presents itself as the best possible means to reach limited English speaking children in order to bring about the academic achievement necessary for their success in an ever more demandingsociety.

### References

Cohen, A. (1975) *A Sociolinguistic Approach to Bilingual Education.* Rowley, MA: Newbury House.

Jacobson, R. (1978) Codeswitching in South Texas: Sociolinguistic consideration and pedagogical applications. *LASSO Journal* 3.1.

— (1979a) Beyond ESL: The teaching of content other than language arts in bilingual education. In R. Bauman and J. Sherzer (eds) *Working Papers in Sociolinguistics.* Austin, TX: Southwest Educational Development Laboratory.

— (1979b) Can bilingual teaching techniques reflect bilingual community behavior? A study in ethnoculture and its relationship to some amendments contained in the New Bilingual Education Act. In R. Padilla (ed.) *Ethnoperspectives in Bilingual Education. Vol. 1: Bilingual Educational and Public Policy in the United States.* Ypsilanti, MI: Eastern Michigan University Press.

— (1981a) Can and should the Laredo experiment be duplicated elsewhere? The applicability of the concurrent approach in other communities. In P.G. Gonzales (ed.) *Proceeding, Eighth Annual International Bilingual Bicultural Education Conference, Seattle, Washington.* Rosslyn, VA: National Clearinghouse for Bilingual Education.

— (1981b) The implementation of a bilingual instruction model: The new concurrent approach. In R.V. Padilla (ed.) *Ethnoperspectives in Bilingual Education Research. Vol. 3: Bilingual Education Technology.* Ypsilanti, MI: Eastern Michigan University Press.

— (1982) The role of the vernacular in transitional bilingual education. In B. Hartford, A. Valdman and C.R. Foster (eds) *Issues in International Bilingual Education: The Role of the Vernacular.* New York: Plenum Press.

— (1983a) Promoting concept and language development in the classroom. In S.S. Seidner (ed.) *Issues of Language Assessment (II Language Assessment Institute Proceedings).* Rosslyn, VA: National Clearinghouse for Bilingual Education .

— (1983b) Intersentential codeswitching: An educationally justifiable strategy. ERIC ED 231 221.

— (1983c) Can two languages be acquired concurrently? Recent developments in bilingual methodology. In H.B. Altman and M. McLure (eds) *Dimension: Language 1982.* Louisville, KY: University of Louisville Press.

— (1985) Uncovering the covert bilingual: How to retrieve the hidden home language. In E. Garcia and R. Padilla (eds) *Advances in Bilingual Education Research.* Tucson, AZ: University of Arizona Press.

— (1988) A new design for the qualitative assessment of children's language choice. *Sociolinguistics* 17.1.

Tucker, G.R. (1970) An alternate day approach to bilingual education. In J.E. Alatis (ed.) *Bilingualism and Language Contact.* GURT, 1979. Washington, DC: Georgetown University Press.

## Questions

(1) Read the definitions and examples given by Jacobson of the ten language distribution patterns in bilingual classrooms. Make a chart to display the definitions and give a brief explanation.

(2) Jacobson, for this study, gives the following definition of bilingual: 'home-language-dominant and limited-English proficient.' What does this tell you about the bilingual instructional program that he discusses? Will such programs be enrichment-oriented, as were the heritage language programs discussed by Cummins, or remedial or compensatory?

What type of bilingual programs existed in the two schools where Jacobson studied the difference between the language separation model and the new concurrent approach? Would the language distribution pattern make a difference when the goal is other than language shift? Why or why not?

Do you think there should be a difference in a language distribution pattern between the mother tongue class, the second language class with second language learners, and the second language class with bilinguals? What would you prefer for each? Why? Is there ever room for both language separation and concurrent use? When? How?

(3) Two-way dual language programs in the United States generally separate languages, whereas in Welsh bilingual programs, as described by Baker, more concurrent use is made of the two languages. How do Welsh bilingual programs on the one hand, and two-way dual language programs and transitional bilingual education programs in the United States on the other hand, differ with regard to the sociolinguistic situation of the two languages? How do they differ in linguistic goals? Can the sociolinguistic situation of the languages, as well as the linguistic goal of the program, affect the language distribution in bilingual classrooms? Why or why not?

## Activities

(1) Jacobson identifies the following four types of concurrent use of two languages:
   (a)  Random switching or 'flipflopping.'
   (b)  Saying everything twice or 'concurrent translation.'
   (c)  A short preview in one language, followed by a deeper 'review' in the second language.
   (d)  A 'highly structured approach to code-switching' or the New Concurrent Approach (NCA).

Work in pairs or small groups. After selecting a specific curriculum objective for a particular grade level, develop ten minutes of a lesson using one of the types of concurrent use. (Make sure that different groups are working on different types of concurrent use.) Present the lesson to the class. Have the class evaluate the effectiveness of each type of concurrent use.

(2) Tape and transcribe at least one half-hour of instruction from any of the following settings:
   (a)  A second language class with a large number of students who are second language learners and speak the same first language as the teacher.
   (b)  A bilingual class where instruction is taking place in the students' mother tongue.
   (c)  A two-way dual language program in which there are linguistically heterogeneous groups.
   (d)  An immersion class in a second language.

Analyze the language use in the classroom. If two languages are used (by either students or teacher), say when, why and how. If they are strictly separated (by either students or teacher), say when, why and how. Share the transcript with the teacher of the class. How does the actual use of language(s) differ from the teacher's perception of how the language is used?

Whenever possible, different groups should tape different settings so that comparisons can be made.

## Further Reading

For more on language use in bilingual classrooms, see especially:

Legarreta, Dorothy (1977) Language choice in bilingual classrooms. *TESOL Quarterly* 1, 9–16.

Wong Fillmore, Lilly, Ammon, P., McLaughlin, B. and Ammon, M. (1985) Learning English through bilingual instruction. Final report submitted to the National Institute of Education, Berkeley, CA: University of California.

# Creating Successful Learning Contexts for Bilingual Literacy

## Nancy H. Hornberger

The Philadelphia School District, like other large urban school districts in the United States, serves an increasingly bilingual school population. Of the district's nearly 200,000 students in 1989, approximately 9 percent were Hispanic and 3 percent Southeast Asian.[1] The two elementary schools reported on here, each with about one thousand students, have concentrated language-minority populations: the Potter Thomas School, grades K-5, counts approximately 78 percent of its students as Hispanic (of which the vast majority are Puerto Rican); the Henry C. Lea School, grades K-8, counts about 37 percent of its students as Southeast Asian (of which the vast majority are Cambodian).[2] As these and other schools seek to serve linguistically and culturally diverse student populations, teachers are confronted with a complex teaching challenge.

Such a challenge requires: not one uniform solution but a repertoire of possibilities and alternatives. This article seeks to open up some of those alternatives by focusing on two teachers, in very different contexts, who appear to be successfully creating learning contexts for biliteracy — a new term designating bilingual literacy.

The two classrooms, a fourth/fifth grade at Potter Thomas and a fourth grade at Lea, are situated in widely disparate communities, within different types of programs, and the particular languages involved contrast in a number of ways thought to be relevant to the development of biliteracy; yet in both classes, language-minority children appear to be successfully becoming biliterate. This article asks what the teachers do that permit this.[3]

Many of the things these two teachers do could simply be characterized as 'good teaching' anywhere, not just for linguistic-minority children, and not just for biliteracy. However, although good teaching in these classrooms may look a lot like good teaching anywhere, it actually reflects sensitivity to a wide range of factors unique to these classrooms. Specifically, then, I will try to identify the things these teachers do that go beyond good teaching to be good teaching for bilingual literacy.

Lee Shulman has argued that pedagogical excellence must be defined by a model that goes beyond a set of globally effective teaching skills considered without reference to the adequacy or accuracy of the content being taught, the classroom context, characteristics of the students, and the accomplishment of purposes not assessed on standardized tests.[4] I will try here to contribute to our understanding of pedagogical excellence by providing a description of the content- and context-specific ways these two elementary teachers teach for linguistic-minority children's biliterate development. Here, the content is the children's second language and literacy; and the context will be discussed in terms of four themes drawn from the literatures on bilingualism, literacy, second- and foreign-language teaching, and the teaching of reading and writing, and which identify critical aspects of contexts for teaching for biliteracy: motivation, purpose, text, and interaction.[5]

The description focuses not only on the similarities but also on the differences in the ways these teachers teach. Significantly for a discussion of biliterate development, one classroom uses both of the children's languages as media of instruction, while the other uses only their second language. As a 'believer' in bilingual education and the value of students' being able to develop and apply their first-language literacy skills in their acquisition of second-language literacy, I was perplexed over the fact that the Cambodian children appeared to be thriving despite the fact that they were not receiving any instruction in

176

their first language. Clearly, however, they are also involved in biliterate development, because they read and write in their first language at home and in their community. I therefore also ask what the things are that the teacher in the monolingual instructional setting does for students' biliterate development that appear to compensate for the lack of first-language instruction in school.

The term *biliteracy* refers to any and all instances in which communication occurs in two (or more) languages in or around written material. An individual, a situation, and a society can all be biliterate: Each one would be an instance of biliteracy. I have recently argued that every instance of biliteracy is situated along a series of continua that define biliterate contexts (the micro–macro, oral–literate, and monolingual– bilingual continua), individual biliterate development (the reception–production, oral language–written language, and first language–second language transfer continua), and biliterate media (the simultaneous–successive exposure, similar–dissimilar structures, and convergent–divergent scripts continua).[6] The more the contexts of the individuals' learning allow them to draw on all points of the continua, the greater are the chances for their full biliterate development. Here, a learning context for biliteracy is taken to be successful to the degree that it allows children to draw on the three continua of biliterate development, that is, on both oral and written, receptive and productive, and first- and second-language skills, at any point in time.

## Contexts and Media of Biliteracy

The Puerto Rican community of North Philadelphia and the Cambodian community of West Philadelphia differ in a number of ways, most of which can be aptly summarized by John Ogbu's argument concerning the variability among minority groups in school performance and the persistence of problems created by cultural differences for some minority groups — the involuntary minorities.[7] The Puerto Rican pattern of immigration tends to be a cyclical one in which the mainland community is constantly receiving new arrivals from the island and in which individuals may alternate island and mainland residence during their lifetimes; the Cambodian pattern is one of once-for-all refugee immigration. While long-term contact with their homeland and the development of a sense of identity in opposition to the dominant culture have led to the creation of institutions in the Puerto Rican community that foster and

strengthen the maintenance of Spanish language and literacy, in the Cambodian community no such institutions have (yet) evolved.[8]

The program at Potter Thomas School has been since 1969 a two-way maintenance bilingual program in Spanish and English: Spanish-speaking children learn English while maintaining their Spanish (the *Latino* stream), and English-speaking children learn Spanish while maintaining their English (the *Anglo* stream). This program, which belongs to the enrichment model of bilingual education, is unique in Philadelphia and rare in the United States.[9] In it, both languages are developed beginning in kindergarten and through fifth grade at the school, and both languages and literacies are used for subject matter instruction. In contrast, the program at Lea School, which has arisen over the last decade in response to the influx of Southeast Asian children into the school, pays no explicit attention to the Cambodian children's first language and literacy, but rather mainstreams them into their second language by means of a pull-out ESOL (English for Speakers of Other Languages) program.[10]

The two classrooms described here contrast sharply in terms of their populations. While the *Anglo* and *Latino* streams, the Spanish and English reading cycle structure, and the bilingual teaching staff at the Potter Thomas School yield up classrooms that are relatively homogeneous as to linguistic and cultural background, the classrooms at Lea School are linguistically and culturally more heterogeneous. M. López, who came to mainland United States from Puerto Rico at age eight, teaches reading to classes of approximately twenty-five students, all of Puerto Rican background. In contrast, L. McKinney, a third-generation Italian immigrant, teaches reading to approximately twenty-eight students, of whom eleven are Southeast Asian (nine Cambodian, one Vietnamese, one Vietnamese-Laotian), sixteen African-American, and one Ethiopian.

Though community, program, and classroom contexts differ for the two teachers, they share the context of the various policies and guidelines that govern all public schools in the district. Grade assignment guidelines that assign children to grade by age regardless of level of English or achievement mean that both teachers' classes encompass a wide range of English and academic abilities. City-wide and state-mandated testing has consequences for students' promotion to the next grade and their participation in Chapter 1 and TELLS programs.[11] Grading guidelines dictate that a student reading below grade level cannot receive a grade higher than C and those reading on grade level cannot receive a grade higher than B. The standardized curriculum assigns goals and objectives for every curriculum area, for every grade, for every school in the district. Both the standardized curriculum and the grading guidelines create indirect pressure for schools and teachers to use basal reading series for reading instruction, and in fact, in both these cases, the teachers feel that they really have no autonomous choice about the basals.

The foregoing paragraphs describe differences and similarities between the two classrooms across the three continua of biliterate contexts: macro–micro, oral–literate, and monolingual–bilingual. As for the continua of biliterate media, the two classrooms differ on all three. The Spanish language and its writing system are relatively similar to English: Both are Indo-European languages and both use the Roman alphabet. In contrast, the structure of the Khmer language (especially in terms of its phonology, syllable structure, and syntax) and its script, which is derived from Sanskrit, are markedly different from English. Furthermore, whereas the Puerto Rican children in Potter Thomas School are acquiring literacy in both languages simultaneously, those Cambodian children at Lea School who are acquiring Khmer literacy are most likely doing so before or after English literacy, rather than simultaneously with it.

The classrooms are alike, then, in that the linguistic minority children in them are developing biliteracy. They differ, however, in the degree to which the linguistic minority community and the school program support the maintenance of bilingual literacy, the students and teacher share linguistic and cultural backgrounds, and the two languages and scripts are similar or divergent and simultaneously or successively acquired by the students.

## Learning Contexts for Biliterate Development

What do the two teachers do to create successful learning contexts for their students' biliterate development? Four themes identifying critical aspects of contexts for teaching for biliteracy — motivation, purpose, text, and interaction — must be considered to answer this question.

## Motivation

Both teachers make membership in the class-room community desirable through affective and experiential bonds while at the same time maintaining the successful execution of literacy tasks as the criterion for membership. In both classrooms, the teachers explicitly include themselves in the community; for example, they share personal anecdotes with their students and hold themselves accountable to them for their own absences.

Yet the basis for the classroom community is entirely different in the two classrooms. López builds on a shared cultural background with her class in ways that are often times probably not even apparent. For example, she brings four stuffed dolls to school one day because they are so appealing to her; she sets them up at the front of the room, and in response to students' requests and on condition of their completing their assignments, lets them borrow the dolls for brief periods in order to, as she tells me, 'help them be children; they're too grown up.' Both the open display of tenderness and affection and the motherly concern for the children are expressions of the warm human caring that particularly characterizes Puerto Ricans.

McKinney does not share a common cultural and linguistic background with her students, but makes up for that by creating classroom-based shared experiences. One way she does this is the annual camp trip she and another teacher take their classes on for three days in May. Throughout the year, she refers frequently to the future camp trip, linking class activities to what they will do, see, and experience at camp — for example, camp buildings and natural features were the reference points for a map lesson in social studies. The students participate in a candy sale to raise money for the trip. Students who present consistent behavior problems are warned, and, if necessary, excluded from the trip. She works conscientiously, often with the help of the home–school coordinator, to convince parents that their children will benefit from the trip and be well supervised, and is genuinely sorry that each year there are a few parents who will not give permission for their children (usually girls) to go. Furthermore, she makes every effort to assure that no child will be excluded because of lack of ability to pay the $30 contribution asked of each child (toward a $50 per child cost).

Another way she creates classroom-based shared experience is the games in which she participates with the students. One of the most popular is a panel game modeled on a television quiz show. The panel game exemplifies both important aspects of membership in the communities these teachers create. Not only is membership made desirable through affective/experiential bonds, but membership is made dependent on the successful execution of literacy tasks. The questions used in the game are comprehensive review questions composed by the teacher and covering social studies, math, and language arts lessons from the preceding weeks.

Aside from creating a desirable, literacy-based classroom community, the other major way these teachers build their students' motivation is through taking an interest in and holding accountable each individual as an individual. This individual attention to each student's ability, activities, and current status achieves the double purpose of demonstrating the teacher's concern for that student and at the same time making clear her expectation that each and every student participate fully.

In these two classrooms, this good teaching practice requires the teachers to be attentive to specific community, program, and classroom characteristics. For López, this requires accommodation to the high classroom population turnover rate that is a concomitant of the cyclical immigration pattern mentioned earlier: Aside from the new students the school registers at the beginning of each year, many more arrive and leave during the school year. For the 1986–1987 school year, for example, records show 198 admits and 235 dismissals for Potter Thomas School.[12] At the classroom level, this means that students come and go throughout the year. For example, one student arrives in early March for his first day in López's class; he has just come to Philadelphia from Puerto Rico and knows neither English nor the routines of an American classroom. López finds him a place and a desk, introduces him to the class and has students introduce themselves to him, points out to him the two other students who arrived from Puerto Rico during the year, and explains to him about the activity students are working on at that moment, journal writing. That day, and every day thereafter, she tries to bear in mind his particular linguistic and cultural needs, even while attending as well to the needs of all her other students.

For McKinney, this attention to individuals requires keeping track of which ESOL students have been pulled out for which ESOL class at which time. For example, she arranges for ESOL children in her class to be excused from ESOL to attend the special Settlement Music School assembly program with the rest of their classmates; or for them to copy an outline from the board, to make up a social studies test, and to go down and get their library books, all missed because of ESOL. This configuration is further complicated by the fact that different segments of both ESOL and non-ESOL students are also regrouped for Chapter 1 and TELLS instruction apart from the rest of the class at different times during the week.

At its best, the teacher's ability to focus on individuals makes it possible for each individual to experience a coherent learning activity in the context of a group lesson. Consider the experience of one student as McKinney works with her group using *Increasing Comprehension*.[13] When the students take turns reading aloud, this girl reads the second paragraph. After all three paragraphs have been read, McKinney asks which sentence in each paragraph is similar to the 'main idea sentence' given in the exercises. The student volunteers at her paragraph, 'I got it,' and reads, 'It is its lung that makes this one-foot-long fish different from other fish' from the story, to justify 'It is its lung that makes the walking catfish different' as the sentence expressing the paragraph's main idea. Despite the fact that several student turns intervened between her original reading and her answer to the main idea question, she has the opportunity to successfully answer the question relating to the paragraph she originally read. Her experience epitomizes the way motivation works in these classrooms: As an individual she is held accountable and given opportunity to successfully execute the literacy task; and as a member of the classroom community she values, she wants to do so.

## Purpose

These two teachers establish both broadly social and more narrowly task-focused purposes for their students' biliterate development. As to broad social purpose, there is a contrast between the two teachers in their approach to the students' non-English linguistic and cultural identities. López feels her identity to be primarily American, despite having spent her early childhood in Puerto Rico, and having attended Spanish church and studied Spanish in high school in mainland United States; she attributes this American identity in part to the fact that she never lived in a Hispanic neighborhood and her father did not allow Spanish to be spoken at home. Nevertheless, regardless of her own sense of identity, she explicitly states that the important thing at Potter Thomas is for the teacher to accept students where they are — whether they prefer Spanish or English, or want to identify with the Puerto Rican or the American culture. That is, she leaves open the option for maintenance of either or both languages and cultures by her students. Her bilingual/bicultural maintenance approach is congruent with the school's two-way maintenance bilingual education program and the community's institutional support for literacy and culture in Spanish as well as English.

In contrast, McKinney notes that although she does not want the Cambodian children to lose their culture, she sees it happening, just as it happened in her own family's history. While she is appreciative of linguistic and cultural diversity, she tends to see it as a contribution to a 'mix.' She is cognizant of unique aspects of the Cambodians' language and culture — for example, an American-born student gives evidence of his teacher's awareness when, on being frustrated because a Cambodian child keeps saying 'wolleyball' instead of 'volleyball,' he finally remembers that his teacher told him they do not have *v* in their language.

Although McKinney is aware of their different language and culture, at the same time she intentionally mixes Southeast Asian and non-Southeast Asian students at their work tables and does not seem enthusiastic about the Cambodians' using their language in class. She says that last year her all-Cambodian pre-primer group would at times speak Khmer among themselves — at which she would admonish them, 'Hey, wait a minute! I don't know what you're saying.' Her tolerant assimilation approach is congruent with the school's pull-out ESOL/mainstream program and the community's relative lack of institutional support for literacy in Khmer.

At the level of task-focused purpose, the two classrooms are quite similar in many ways. In both classrooms, tasks are clearly defined, teacher correction is focused on the task and includes teacher acknowledgement of her own mistakes, and the teacher continuously adapts the definition of the task to the immediate situation. All of these are good teaching practices. What is of interest here, however, is the ways in which the teachers' task definitions, corrections, and adaptations reflect responsiveness to the particular configuration of biliterate contexts, media, and development in any

one situation in their classrooms, and the contrasts between the two classrooms.

For example, López corrects a child for using English during Spanish reading, not because she cannot understand but because the present task (Spanish vocabulary introduction) requires the use of Spanish. At other moments of the same lesson, the teacher encourages use of one language to aid development of the other (see Interaction discussion below).

In McKinney's classroom, where Cambodian children are becoming literate in their second language without recourse to their first, it is significant that her corrections of students' oral reading and of their writing emphasizes meaning rather than phonological or grammatical form (her approach to her students' use of black English vernacular is similar). For example, one student reads a paragraph from *Increasing Comprehension* fluently, but substitutes 'Joe's' for 'Joseph's' and 'train track' for 'railroad track.' McKinney does not correct these, and the child goes on to answer the multiple-choice comprehension question correctly. Three students get full credit on their homework sentences despite grammatical errors such as: 'I am skater with my sister'; 'I'm reading a book call Peter Pan'; 'The winner has win again.'

Such instances are consistent with McKinney's expressed approach to student writing. In correcting written work, she says, she looks for complete sentences and for answering the question, but does not pay too much attention to spelling; for creative writing, especially, she prefers not to grade at all since it is not done for grammar or spelling, but for the expression of ideas.

This emphasis on meaning over form is also reflected in her adaptation of tasks to the situation. In a lesson based on a reading about Native Americans, she adapts to the ambiguity in an exercise involving fill-in-the-blank sentences followed by a word-search puzzle: As she notices that in more than one case the sentence can be meaningfully filled by more than one word, she tells the class she will accept an answer if it makes sense, even if it is not the one she is looking for, but that they should be aware that they may not find that word on the word search.

In López's classroom, the bilingual maintenance purpose is reflected in attention to the allocation of use of the two languages. In McKinney's classroom the tolerant assimilation purpose is reflected in greater attention to the meanings expressed by the children than to the form in which they express them.

## Text

As noted above, both teachers feel constrained to use basal reading series. Such texts can be used in narrow and limiting ways; yet these teachers not only use them in more open and challenging ways, but they also seek to expose their students to genres in addition to those in the basal readers and workbooks .

For example, López reads aloud a short biography of Luis Muñóz Marin to her class, one of several short biographies she reads over the course of the year.[14] Her room, as well as the Potter Thomas School library, is stocked with books in both Spanish and English, for students to read and do book reports on.

While the variety in López's classroom derives primarily from exposure to both first- and second-language texts, in McKinney's classroom it derives primarily from a wide exposure to both oral and written texts, and both receptive and productive interaction. She says, 'Reading is very important to me, and I want the kids to feel that reading is enjoyable, not just a burden.' There are a lot of books and magazines in this classroom, including a well-stocked and well-organized library, complete with card catalog, designated librarians, and borrowing rules. The library collection encompasses fantasy, adventure, biography, and social studies and science reference works.

Every day in the twenty-five minutes between recess and lunchtime, McKinney reads aloud to the class. During this time, she reads books of her own choice that she liked as a child or that she has found to be good, such as *The Lion, the Witch, and the Wardrobe* by C.S. Lewis. To a certain degree, she follows the sequence of genres indicated in the district curriculum guide, but her main goal is for the children to 'like being read to.' There are variations on the story time. Sometimes she will read a story brought in by a student (e.g. *The Lost Prince, A Droid Adventure*). Toward the end of the year, the students themselves each choose, practice, and read a story to their classmates.

She gives the students an opportunity to gauge their oral reading of a story in their reading group at least once during the year, by taping and playing back their reading. 'I explain in the beginning that this is...a learning tool, that it's something that we're not making fun of each other. We all sound pretty bad when it comes

down to it... But you want to really be able to say, "What is it that I have done wrong?" And somebody else might be able to pick something up that you didn't, and, ...it's what we call constructive criticism.'

Each year, basal readers are put aside for a couple of weeks and the children read booklength stories. McKinney tries to 'bring out...what an author puts into writing a book...and that language is very important. Like in the *Ghost of Windy Hill* [by Clyde Robert Bulla], we point out all the dark language that's in the story, and events that are leading up to, foreshadowing (I'm a frustrated English major). Why is this person in the story? Why did this happen? And why didn't the author tell you this?... So it's a great way to — like a short story is hard to get children to get into it as much.'

In writing, students explore a variety of genres, including autobiography, personal letters, poems, and fantasy stories. In providing for her students' exposure to a wide range of genres and to opportunities to listen, discuss, read aloud and silently, and write across those genres, McKinney is cognizant of the fact that different students in her class are at different points along the continua of biliterate development. For example, she notes that the written work of one student is much better than her oral reading or her speaking, which are barely intelligible. The writing sometimes takes her by surprise, she says, because it does not seem the student could have understood so well.

In López's class, there is not such a variety of oral and written texts and receptive and productive interaction as in McKinney's class; the variety of genres lies instead along the first language-second language continuum. It seems that, because of the interconnectedness of the developmental continua of biliteracy, a particularly rich environment along one or two of the continua may make up for poverty with respect to another.[15]

## Interaction

In both classes, interaction with and around texts is characterized by opportunities for a range of participant structures; the activation of prior knowledge; and the development of strategies for signaling understanding of text, analyzing features of text, and reasoning about text.[16] All of these are good teaching practices. Yet, differences between the two classrooms in their interactions around text point to options that go beyond what is simply good teaching to what is good teaching for biliterate development.

Small-group peer interaction occurs differently in the two classrooms. In López's classroom, there is a complex desk arrangement that yields approximately four group areas of seven to eight desks each (in either two rows or a three-sided rectangle), as well as some individually situated desks; and there are at least three different seating patterns for the children, one each for Spanish reading, English reading, and homeroom periods. Within these groups, when the students are not working with the teacher, there is a certain amount of peer interaction, which seems to be neither encouraged nor discouraged by the teacher. Both the students' initiation of peer interaction and the teacher's permission of it seem to me to be congruent with a culture that values social relationships and mutual support and cooperation.

This is somewhat different from the peer interaction in McKinney's class, which appears to be both planned and tightly controlled. The children are seated at nine work-table areas (created by pushing four desks together) and do a minimum of moving around. Rather, the teacher comes to them when she wants to work with, for example, a reading group made up of two or three adjacent work tables. She encourages the children to interact with the others at their work table, and distinguishes between 'busy noise,' which is directed noise, evidence that students are working, and 'noisy noise,' which is not. Yet she also specifies when such interaction should and should not occur. Thirty minutes into the children's writing of fantasies, she tells them, 'Let someone at your table read your story and see if they understand it.' On another occasion, she tells three students, 'Sometimes you girls help each other and that's OK sometimes, but sometimes you have to get it yourself.'

The two teachers differ as well in the degree to which they emphasize classroom-based or community-based prior knowledge. López does of course draw on concepts developed or topics discussed in previous lessons in the course of any particular lesson, but far more characteristic are her frequent appeals to students' knowledge from outside the class or the school. For example, during Spanish reading, she draws the students out on whether they like and how they prepare *pulpo* (octopus, apparently a favorite Puerto Rican delicacy) in order to introduce the word *marino* (marine); in a discussion of President Reagan's overnight decision to send American soldiers to Honduras, she includes a student's volunteered news that his *tio* (uncle) was called to go; and she clarifies the name of a stone, *yunque*, by identifying it as the same name as the mountain in Puerto Rico. During English reading, too, she draws on students' community-based knowledge: in order to define *sift*, she elaborates on 'Mom' making a cake and on preparing rice for cooking by sifting out the stones; to *define* ancestors, she provides a brief exposition of the source of the three ancestral heritages — European, Indian, and African — that make up Puerto Rico; and in discussing *interview*, she encourages a discussion of the interviews several of the students had had a few weeks earlier to go to Conwell Middle Magnet School next year.

An area of prior knowledge that in a sense represents a combination of classroom-based and community-based knowledge is the students' knowledge of the other language, and López frequently draws on this. Direct translation is a convenient means of rapid identification: In reviewing English vocabulary, at the word *ledge*, she asks, 'What's the Spanish for that?' and a student replies *lecho*. Similarly, she assists the students to draw on school–community language resources when their own knowledge falls short; indeed, she models this strategy for them. In compiling a list of the capitals, languages, and nationalities of the South American countries, she is uncertain of the name in Spanish for Bolivian and Paraguayan nationalities, and sends a student to ask one of the Spanish teachers for these terms. A corollary to this explicit drawing on community language resources is the acceptance of both languages in the communication of information. When the Spanish reading class needs to refer to a map, and the map happens to be in English, that is not seen as an obstacle to the communication of the necessary information — in this case, identification of the oceans, continents, and countries. The children bring with them a wealth of knowledge from their experience at home and in the community, and their knowledge of two languages, and she takes advantage of her shared linguistic/cultural background to exploit that wealth.

In contrast, McKinney is not able to exploit a common reservoir of community-based knowledge, but compensates for that by emphasizing the students' classroom-based prior knowledge. She does of course draw on their experience outside the classroom and school. Far more characteristic, however, are her frequent appeals, usually through display questions, to students' knowledge from previous lessons or shared class experiences. She may encourage students to connect across stories: A story about Pablo Picasso includes a picture of his painting *Harlequin* and she reminds the full group of an earlier story they read about a harlequin. She may seek connections across reading groups as well — after the full group composes a new stanza for the poem 'Over in the Meadow,' she jokes with the rhymes group that this stanza is 'almost as good as the one you did, Rhymes.'[17] She draws on shared class experience in discussing vocabulary: For the word *exhibit*, she refers to class trips to the Academy of Natural Science, the zoo, and the art museum; for *meadow* and *camper*, she ties discussion to their future camp trip; and for *germ*, she discusses the flu going around the class and school.

Perhaps most representative of her activation/reinforcement of students' classroom-based prior knowledge are her 'remember' statements: 'Remember I said English is hard because when you learn a rule, you have to learn five more that have broken it'; 'Remember I want you to get a little more independent. Read the directions yourselves'; 'Remember we talked about the main sentence in the paragraph in our workbooks? What sentence usually tells us what the main idea of the paragraph is?' Indeed, McKinney insists that remembering is the sign of learning: 'You learn something, you remember it. If you learn something and forget it, you haven't really learned it.'

Finally, the two teachers differ in their approach to the development of students' strategies for interacting with text. Both teachers encourage their students to signal understanding through such moves as defining word meanings, identifying the main idea in paragraphs, and following a story line as it unfolds; to analyze features of the texts they read, ranging from minimal units such as letters, sounds, morphemes, or words to sentence-level features such as punctuation and complete thoughts to discourse-level features such as title information, the structure of paragraphs, main characters, author's purpose, and genre; and to reason about the texts they read by exploring alternative interpretations and expressions in text and by inferring, guessing, and predicting from text. The teachers seek to develop these strategies by pointing out features or giving definitions and rules, or asking the students to do so. Yet there is a difference in the way the two

teachers do this. Whereas López's approach is characterized by helping her students 'connect and transfer' across languages, McKinney's is characterized by her insistence on precision at all times.

When I asked López about her approach to teaching reading and writing, she said, 'I don't know any name for it, but I think of it as just adding to the pile. I try to get the kids to connect and transfer. I've noticed, I guess, language is language; the skills are almost the same; for example, prefixes outlines.' Here, 'adding to the pile' refers to drawing on and building on prior knowledge, while 'connect and transfer' refers to helping students make explicit connections across their two languages.

Thus, López encourages her students to signal understanding through translation. We have already seen how students sometimes define words through translation into the other language. She also encourages students to analyze features across languages. As one student unsuccessfully looks up *disolvieron* (they dissolved [it]) in the dictionary, she elicits from the class the fact that one needs to take off the suffix to get the root word, and makes an explicit connection between analyzing suffixes in Spanish and in English. Finally, she encourages students to reason across languages. For example, she explains the difference between fact ('I can see it, hear it, touch it') and opinion ('I think') and has students judge whether particular sentences express fact or opinion, assigning this kind of task for both Spanish and English.

McKinney encourages students to signal understanding, analyze features of text, and reason about text in very similar ways, but whereas López emphasizes the connections between two languages, McKinney emphasizes precision in one. As children signal understanding by giving definitions or answering comprehension questions, their answers must be precise. For example, McKinney does not accept 'to sweep' as a definition of 'broom' because 'it tells me what you can do with it, but it doesn't tell me what it is'; nor 'a screw' as a definition of 'tool' because 'it is a type of tool, but not a definition.' The following interchange exemplifies both the type of question and the type of response expected as she guides students toward being able to signal understanding of a story as it unfolds:

**McKinney:** In chapter 6, Mr. Arden gets very angry with Bob. Why?

**Sophorn:** He goes into Mr. Arden's library.

**McKinney:** Why did Bob go in?
**Sreysean:** He wanted to read a book.
**McKinney:** No.
**Noeun:** He wanted to find out what was in back.
**McKinney:** No.
**Sophorn:** The door was open.
**McKinney:** Yes.

The same precision is required in analyzing features of text. *Spoon* is not acceptable as a word with the same sound pattern as *room*; 'apostrophe s' is not acceptable as the mark of contractions and possessives since 'there's not always an s'; and a definition of a homonym as 'same word, different meaning,' clarified as 'same spelling, different meaning,' is not acceptable since 'the important thing is "sound the same," even though they're spelt [sic] differently in most cases.' Complete sentences are often required in oral answers ('Who was the man that was responsible? Try to answer me with a good sentence.'), and always in students' written work.

Finally, she requires precision as students reason about text. She guides them toward precision in their reasoning about alternative word meanings: Not only a book, but also a person can be 'firm'; the suffix '-er' can be used to compare things (e.g., 'bigger') as well as to mean 'one who does'; 'center' means not only 'the middle' but also 'building,' as in 'health center'; and you cannot always tell the meaning of compound words by taking them apart — for example, though 'a blueberry is a berry that is blue, a strawberry is not a berry that is straw.'

As students choose, in succession, each of the five sentences of the following paragraph as the main idea, she guides them toward the correct response (sentence 2), but at the same time does not deny the 'main ideaness' of their responses, since in this case all the sentences seem to carry only part of the main idea:

> Most zoos keep the animals in special pens, or fenced-in areas. But there is another kind of zoo. This kind of zoo lets the animals go free and puts the people in cages! These zoos put all the animals in a big park. The visitors can see the animals from their car or from a bus or train.

As she guides students to infer, guess, or predict from text, the goal of precision remains whether they are inferring at the level of grammar, vocabulary, or discourse

Look at these words [it's, its]. One's a contraction, one's a possessive. Remember I told you there are some possessives that don't use an apostrophe — pronouns; so which one of these is the contraction? You should know the answer from what I just said.

I'm not going to tell you what 'flummoxed' means, you'll have to figure it out from the story. [After reading the story 'The Woman Who Flummoxed the Fairies' to the class, she guides students through some of the of the things that the woman did, to elicit the meaning 'tricked' for 'flummoxed.']

In the following dialogue, McKinney guides Tyjae and the other students to infer exactly why Bob, the character in the story they are reading, justifies continuing to work for a man whom he has begun to suspect of doing something illegal.

**McKinney:** Why does Bob say, 'Oh, he's rich, he won't break the law'? Can't rich people break the law?
**Tyjae:** Rich people can do anything they want to cause they have money .
**McKlnney:** Sometimes it can seem that way… Does Bob want the job? Why? [She elicits the idea that he wants to keep the job because he is making good money, and therefore does not want to admit that there might be something wrong.] So in a way, Bob is trying to make himself feel good.

## Good Teaching for Biliteracy

The two elementary teachers reported on here adapt their teaching for their students' biliterate development, and, specifically, for the particular biliterate contexts and media of their program, school, community, and school district. Both teachers have found ways to create successful learning contexts for biliteracy for the students in their classrooms, but these contexts are both similar and different.

Both teachers build motivation in their students by creating a classroom community in which membership is made desirable through affective/experiential bonds and simultaneously is dependent on the successful execution of literacy tasks. Yet, whereas López builds those bonds on a shared linguistic and cultural background with her students, McKinney builds them by creating classroom-based shared experience. Both teachers take an interest in and hold accountable each individual in the classroom community. For López, this requires accommodation to a high classroom population turnover while for McKinney it requires accommodation to a complex multilayered pull-out structure.

Both teachers build meaningful purpose in their students by keeping them focused on literacy tasks that are clearly defined and suited to the immediate situation, and at the same time embody a broad social purpose that is congruent with the program and community context. Yet whereas López, the Potter Thomas two-way maintenance program, and the Puerto Rican community share a broad bilingual/bicultural maintenance purpose, reflected in, attention to the allocation of use of the two languages in literacy tasks, McKinney, the Lea School ESOL pull-out program, and the Cambodian community share a broadly tolerant assimilationist purpose, reflected in more attention to meaning than form in literacy tasks.

Both teachers build their students' exposure to a variety of texts. Yet whereas the strength of López's approach is the inclusion of both first- and second-language texts, the strength of McKinney's is the inclusion of opportunity for oral and written, receptive and productive interaction with a wide range of genres.

Both teachers build students' interaction with text by taking advantage of a variety of participant structures, drawing on students' prior knowledge, and developing students' strategies for signaling understanding of text, analyzing features of text, and reasoning about text. López allows small-group peer interaction to occur spontaneously and asystematically as a natural outgrowth of shared cultural values, emphasizes her students' community-based prior knowledge, and seeks to help her students to 'connect and transfer' strategies across languages. McKinney structures small-group peer interaction more carefully, emphasizes her students' classroom-based prior knowledge, and builds her students' strategy use by insistence on precision at all times.

Michèle Foster has recently noted that 'we have little empirical evidence that documents what takes place when teachers and students share a common cultural background which positively affects classroom interaction.'[18] Patricia Nichols

has suggested that while it is undoubtedly true that 'teachers teach from within their own cultural traditions,' it is also possible for teachers to adopt a '"double perspective" ...which requires [them] to understand...the limitations of their own cultural perspectives and to appreciate separate ways of understanding and shaping the world.'[19]

López's teaching provides evidence of the positive effects that a shared linguistic and cultural background can bring to the teaching of bilingual literacy. On the other hand, McKinney's teaching seems to exemplify a double perspective that allows space for Cambodian children to draw on their own linguistic and cultural backgrounds within a learning context that is situated squarely in a second language and culture.

Both teachers have found ways to build their students' biliterate development. The differences between the two teachers' approaches point primarily to the degree to which community-based knowledge and experience, the development of students' first-language literacy, and goals for bilingual/bicultural maintenance are incorporated into the students' learning. These are not negligible differences. Nevertheless, it seems to me that in the highly complex, increasingly multicultural environments in which our schools are situated, we will need to allow for the greatest possible range of approaches for teaching for biliteracy, among them both of those discussed here.

## Acknowledgement

I want to thank M. López and L. McKinney, the two teachers who not only permitted but welcomed me into their classrooms and shared with me both the successes and the difficulties of their teaching, as well as the School District of Philadelphia and the principals of the Lea and Potter Thomas schools, John Grelis and Felicita Melendez, who consented to the study. I am also grateful for a National Academy of Education Spencer Fellowship, which enabled me to devote full time to this research during 1989, and for the Dean's Fellowships, the Literacy Research Center, and the Research Fund, all of the Graduate School of Education, University of Pennsylvania, which provided support for graduate students to work with me on the project.

## Notes

1. Dale Mezzacappa (1989) Fallout clouds school board appointments. *The Philadelphia Inquirer*, October 9, pp. B1–2.

2. School District of Philadelphia. *Superintendent's Management Information Center* (Philadelphia: Philadelphia School District Office of

Research and Evaluation, 1987–88), pp. 114–15, 376–77. Report No. 8818.

3. Data for the paper come from a long-term comparative ethnographic study on school–community literacy in two languages, beginning in February 1987. All quoted material is from tapes or field notes unless otherwise indicated. The classrooms described were the focus of intensive observation by the author during spring 1988 and spring 1989. Criteria for determining the success of the learning contexts in these two classrooms include my own observation over time of the students' oral and written performance in literacy tasks, the students' progress in reading level through the school year, and school-wide (and in one case, district-wide) recognition of the teachers' excellence. Attention here is explicitly on the teachers, although evidence of the efficacy of their approaches is in the children's responses; and on their teaching of reading, writing, spelling, and language arts, though many of the characteristics of this teaching are observable in their teaching of math, science, and social studies content areas as well.

4. Lee S. Shulman (1987) Knowledge and teaching: Foundations of the new reform. *Harvard Educational Review* 57 (1), 1–22.

5. Nancy H. Hornberger, 'Teaching for biliteracy: What do TESOL and reading tell us about it?' (unpublished manuscript).

6. Nancy H. Hornberger (1989) Continua of biliteracy. *Review of Educational Research* 59 (3), 271–96.

7. John U. Ogbu (1987) Variability in minority school performance: A problem in search of an explanation. *Anthropology and Education Quarterly* 18 (4), 312–34.

8. See Cheri L. Micheau (1990) Ethnic identity and ethnic maintenance in the Puerto Rican community of Philadelphia (PhD diss., University of Pennsylvania) for a description of some of the institutions in the Puerto Rican community.

9. See Nancy H. Hornberger (in press) Extending enrichment bilingual education: Revisiting typologies and redirecting policy (In Ofelia García (ed.) *Festschrift for Joshua A. Fishman, Volume 1. Focus on Bilingual Education.* Philadelphia: John Benjamins Publishers), for a discussion of the enrichment model of bilingual education and the Potter Thomas program as a representative of it.

10. Joel Hardman, 'Learning and coping in the shadow of ESOL' (Working Paper in Education, University of Pennsylvania), discusses some problems ESOL creates for language minority students.

11. Chapter 1 refers to Chapter 1 of the Education Consolidation and Improvement Act of 1981, revised from Title I of the Elementary and Secondary Education Act of 1965; and specifically to the Chapter 1 Local Educational Agency Grant program that provides financial assistance for supplemental, remedial instruction for educationally deprived students in school districts with high concentrations of low-income students. TELLS (Testing Essential Literacy and Learning Skills) is the state-wide testing program initiated in the Commonwealth of Pennsylvania in the 1980s. Both of these programs provide for supplementary instruction for children whose test scores fall below a certain level.

12. School District of Philadelphia *Superintendent's Management Information Center*, p. 377.

13. Alvin Kravitz and Dan Dramer (1978) *Increasing Comprehension* (pp. 8–9). Cleveland: Modern Curriculum Press: Skill Booster Series.

14. She reads from Kenneth Kieszak (1977) *Puntos Criticos: Una Colección de Biografias Cortas.* New York: Globe Books.

15. Shirley Brice Heath argues a similar point in 'Sociocultural contexts of language development' in *Beyond Language: Social and Cultural Factors in Schooling Language Minority Students*, ed. Bilingual Education Office, California State Department of Education (Los Angeles: Evaluation, Dissemination, and Assessment Center, California State University, 1986), pp. 143–86 (especially p. 144).

16. On participant structures, see Susan U. Philips, *The Invisible Culture: Communication in Classroom and Community on the Warm Springs Indian Reservation* (New York: Longman, 1983). On prior knowledge, see Richard C. Anderson, Rand J. Spiro and Mark C. Anderson (1978) Schemata as scaffolding for the representation of information in connected discourse, *American Educational Research Journal* 15 (3), 433–40. On strategies, see Susan L. Lytle (1982) Exploring comprehension study: A style of twelfth grade readers' transactions with text (PhD diss., University of Pennsylvania).

17. The full group is reading *Full Circle* and the rhymes group, *Rhymes and Reasons*, levels 3.2 and 4.1, respectively, of the Macmillan series. While I am aware that the use of basal readers and reading groups is a debated and controversial practice, it is also a tenacious one. See Robert E. Slavin (1987) Ability

groupingand student achievement in elementary schools: A best-evidence synthesis, *Review of Educational Research* 57 (3), 293–336, for a thorough treatment of the issue. It is not my intention here to discuss the relative merits of this practice as against other possible ways of organizing reading instruction, but only to document the kinds of interactions these teachers work toward in these groups and in the other interactional structures in their classrooms.

18. Michèle Foster (1989) 'It's Cookin' Now': A performance analysis of the speech events of a black teacher in an urban community college. *Language in Society* 18 (1), 2.

19. Patricia C . Nichols (1989) Storytelling in Carolina: Continuities and contrasts. *Anthropology and Education Quarterly* 20 (3), 232.

## Questions

(1) What type of schools does Hornberger use for her case study? Do the schools differ with regard to language aims? How? Where would you place these schools in the bilingual education typology? (The typology is presented after the Lyons article at the start of this book.) In which ways is the Thomas Potter School (what Hornberger calls a 'two-way maintenance bilingual program') different from PS 84 (a 'classical' example of a contemporary 'two-way dual language')? In which ways is the Thomas Potter School different from the Coral Way School, the original 'two-way bilingual education program'? What can you conclude? How are the different linguistic aims in Thomas Potter and Lea related to fostering biliteracy?

(2) Draw comparisons between Puerto Ricans and Cambodians on the following: migration history, mother tongue, role of the mother tongue in the United States, size of group, kind of group (according to the Ogbu typology) and literacy history. Then explain the pattern of biliteracy development of Cambodian children and that of Puerto Ricans. What explains such differences?

(3) In a table with three columns, provide a summarizing profile of how López, McKinney, and a teacher you know (this teacher might be you) differ in their strategies and 'contexts' for biliteracy. Break up the table into four sections and provide examples of how the following is accomplished:

A. Motivation

  (a) Increasing membership in the classroom community.

  (b) Being attentive to specific community, program, and classroom characteristics.

  (c) Taking an interest and holding accountable each individual.

B. Purpose

  (a) Social purpose.

  (b) Task-focused purposes.

C. Text

  (a) Use of basal readers.

  (b) Exposure to other genres.

D. Interaction

  (a) Structure of peer interaction.

  (b) Structure of teacher–student interaction.

  (c) Strategies for interacting with text:

    (i) classroom-based or community-based activation of prior knowledge;

    (ii) signaling understanding of text;

    (iii) analyzing features of text;

    (iv) reasoning about text.

## Activities

(1) Using the table produced in Question 3 (above), discuss in small groups what are the top priorities in 'creating successful learning contexts for bilingual literacy.' Rank them and make a final list of the first five to ten priorities after having the class's consensus. Then observe a bilingual classroom where biliteracy is valued. First identify the bilingual classroom observed as to its type of bilingual education and, if in the United States, whether it receives 'Chapter 1' funds or not. Use your list as a checklist of points to observe. Share your results with the teacher of the class. Report your finding to the class.

(2) In the library, research the sociolinguistic situation of the different Latino groups in the United States and of the different Asian groups. Refer to their migration history, their socio-demographic characteristics, their geographic concentration, their language use and proficiency, and their prospects for language maintenance or language shift. (One importance source for this information is McKay, Sandra Lee and Wong, Sau-ling Cynthia (eds) (1988) *Language Diversity: Problem or Resource? A Social and Educational Perspective on Language Minorities in the United States*. Cambridge: Newbury House Publishers.)

(3) Make an inventory of all the texts used in the teaching of biliteracy in a bilingual classroom. Identify their language and language variety(ies) used, genres, country where published, richness and variety of content, richness of language, quality of printing, quality of illustrations, ethnic content, bicultural and/or multicultural content and gender content. Compare the list of texts to teach literacy in the majority language with that to teach literacy in the minority language. Are basal readers used? Then observe at least one lesson in each language. How are the texts used? How would you evaluate their use?

(4) Make a diagram of a classroom in which there is relatively much peer interaction. Tape an instance of what you consider to be 'busy noise.' Then another instance of 'noisy noise.' Play it back to your class. Ask them to write an essay on how each kind of noise makes them feel.

(5) Collect an instance of a particular student's writing in the following genres: an autobiography, a personal letter, a poem and a fantasy story. Evaluate the students' writing across genres. Where is the student most efficient as a writer, what strategies are used, and why?

(6) Record a bilingual student reading both in the majority language and the minority language. Make a 'miscue analysis' of the readings. Ensure that the selection read has approximate equal difficulty. Then select a short passage in the majority language and one in the minority language and prepare cloze passages. Have the student complete the cloze. Report the results of the miscue analysis and the cloze tests to the class. (For more on 'reading miscue,' you may follow guidelines given by Goodman, Yetta, Watson, D.J. and Burke, C.L. (1987) *Reading Miscue Inventory: Alternative Procedures*. New York: Richard D. Owen. Guidelines for both 'miscue analysis' and 'cloze tests' are excellently explained in Southgate, Vera, Arnold, Helen and Johnson, Sandra (1981) *Extending Beginning Reading*. London: Heinemann Educational Books.)

## Further Reading

An early and incisive treatment of biliteracy is available in:
   Goodman, Kenneth, Goodman, Yetta and Flores, Barbara (1979) *Reading in the Bilingual*

*Classroom: Literacy and Biliteracy*. Rosslyn, VA: National Clearinghouse for Bilingual Education.

An excellent questioning of traditional practices is,

Barrera, Rosalinda (1983) Bilingual reading in the primary grades: Some questions about questionable views and practices. In Theresa H. Escobedo (ed.) *Early Childhood Bilingual Education: A Hispanic Perspective* (pp. 164–84). New York: Teachers College.

For a more comprehensive look at biliteracy practices (English/Spanish) in classrooms, see especially:

Ada, A.F. (1987) *A Children's Literature-based Whole Language Approach to Creative Reading and Writing*. Northvale, NJ: Santillana.

Pérez, Bertha and Torres-Guzmán, María (1992) *Learning in Two Worlds: An Integrated Spanish/English Biliteracy Approach*. New York: Longman.

Specifically for writing practices in bilingual programs, see especially;

Edelsky, Carole (1986) *Writing in a Bilingual Program: Había una Vez*. Norwood, NJ: Ablex.

# Relating Experience and Text: Socially Constituted Reading Activity[1]

## Concha Delgado-Gaitán

### Introduction

Educational problems related to the literacy skills of linguistic minority children have generated much research in the area of sociocultural influences on learning, particularly the contextual and interactional factors in inferring meaning from text. Researchers concerned with text comprehension have moved ethnographic approaches into the forefront of literacy research (Au & Jordan, 1981; Au & Kawakami, 1984; Díaz, Moll & Mehan, 1986; Erickson, 1984; Gilmore, 1983; Heath, 1983; Moll & Díaz, 1987; Scheffelin & Cochran-Smith, 1984; Scollon & Scollon, 1984; Tannen, 1982; Tharp & Gallimore, 1988; Trueba, 1984). Central to this research is the meaning of literacy acquisition as a phenomenon taking place in specific social and cultural environments by means of social interaction (Tharp & Gallimore, in press).

Social interactions provide the principal vehicle by which learning and development occur. Children's cognitive skills develop according to the level and amount of interaction with adults or peers in learning environments of which classroom literacy activities are a part. According to Tharp & Gallimore (1988), children's learning is measured by the distance between their ability to perform a task independently and the level attained with the assistance of more knowledgeable others. This constitutes Vygotsky's (1978) notion of the zone of proximal development which requires teacher involvement in order to provide children with the appropriate practice to move them through their respective zone, a perspective also advanced by Díaz, Moll & Mehan (1986), Moll & Díaz (1987), Tharp & Gallimore (1988), Erickson (1982), Scribner & Cole (1981), and Wertsch (1985). Children internalize what they learn from the adult or peer and are then able to perform independently in their

problem-solving tasks. Text-related content and the means to deal with it are thus learned through socially constructed behavior in which the teacher, each student and peers, have definite roles (Cook-Gumperz, 1986; Erickson, 1984).

This study supports the theoretical premise that the learning is socially constructed through meaningful interaction. Teacher interaction with the Spanish-speaking novice readers in this third-grade classroom shows how Spanish-speaking students respond to the teacher's instructional strategies in their effort to comprehend their reading text. In this study, 'novice' refers to students who are beginning readers, and does not necessarily imply 'low' ability. It is the researcher's contention that students exhibit high or low reading performance not as a result of static traits of fixed intelligence; rather they perform according to the level of expectations and the level and quality of teacher interaction in a socially constituted activity. The teacher, however, has labeled the novice readers as 'low' readers in contrast with high readers who, according to the teacher, are 'better' readers.

### The Study

Classroom literacy activities provided the primary unit of analysis and thus an explanation for the term 'literacy' is required. This term is useless unless we clarify its significance to the people who use it. In this study, the focus is on text comprehension in relation to the children's sociocultural experience of literacy and the way children appear competent in the social context in which their reading ability is evaluated. This definition emerged as the study progressed and the categories were identified.

Three major questions guided the research: (1) How are daily classroom reading lessons organized in the novice reading group? (2) What conditions constrain or enhance student participation in the reading lesson? (3) What conditions change novice students' performance in literacy activities?

### Literacy in Mrs Cota's third-grade

Mrs Cota's third grade class in Marina School was selected as the research site. In this bilingual class, the students were placed in high and low Spanish-speaking reading groups. On the first day of school, Mrs Cota assessed all of her students according to their reading ability in order to place them in a group with other students of similar ability. Students remained in those same groups through the school year. The advanced reading groups scored at a mean of 79% on the Spanish Comprehensive Tests of Basic Skills, while the mean score for the low readers was 30% and those students relegated to the low reading groups read at least one full year below their respective grade level.

Of particular concern to Mrs Cota were the Spanish-speaking novice readers. Mrs Cota believed that the seven Spanish speaking students in the novice reading group did not comprehend the text they read. She also believed that they were behind in reading since they had not yet learned to read well in Spanish and they still had to transition to English reading. The teacher's behavior toward the novice group conformed with her belief that these students had to be treated 'very strictly' because that was the best way for them to 'catch-up' with the skills of advanced readers.

### Method

The principal unit of analysis was the classroom reading lesson. Over a three month period, observations of the low-reading group were conducted three times during their reading lesson. Fieldnotes, audio and video recording were used to collect data. Teacher and student interviews were also collected.

Following the micro-ethnographic observations and interviews, an intervention was designed to implement a literacy activity based on the premise of the 'Experience–Text–Relationship' (ETR), reading lesson, an alternative structure for learning to comprehend text. The ETR literacy technique designed in the Kamehameha Early Education Program (KEEP) (Au, 1979) provided a context in which Hawaiian students who were traditionally low in reading skills could utilize their native experience as a basis for discussing the reading text stories. The intervention in reading was initially implemented by me; later I trained the teacher to conduct the experimental lesson based on the ETR approach.

Methodologically, the concept of intervening in the setting as part of ethnographic data collection has been discussed by Trueba (1979) and Moll & Díaz (1987) as an ethnographic pedagogy. Essentially, ethnographic research leads to specific experimental practices such as the introduction of the ETR method which in turn redirect ethnographic inquiry by clarifying areas for additional data collection.

The classroom literacy activity data will be discussed in two major categories, the structure and organization of the reading lesson and the content interaction between the teacher and the students.

### The daily reading lesson

The teacher typically used the 'round robin reading circle' for reading instruction. Mrs Cota called the students to sit around the table for reading in their textbooks and written tasks in their workbooks Reading lessons were conducted in Spanish because students were limited English speakers. The teacher stood facing the students to tell them that they would be talking about the 'point of the story'. Before the story was discussed, the teacher flashed cards with the new words to the students and called on different students individually to read a word.

Following this initial exercise, the teacher asked the students to read and answer two specific questions which related to the point of the story. The students read individually and silently. The teacher allowed a twenty-minute period for the students to read the assigned number of pages. Before the teacher even began to ask questions, the students often raised their hands to volunteer an answer as if they were going to ask a question. The teacher usually ignored the hands; sometimes she reminded the students that no questions had been asked and to please lower their hands. The teacher then posed questions about the reading.

The following example is one lesson presented by Mrs Cota to the novice group. It illustrates that the students may not have understood the question posed by the teacher. When called upon to respond, students called out an answer, attempting to demonstrate knowledge. The teacher, however, viewed their answers as incorrect, and considered them as evidence of a comprehension problem.

*Text 1*

[Seven students sat in their reading group. The teacher spent the first fifteen minutes of the lesson drilling the students on new vocabulary words to be found in the story. First she flashed each word to the entire group and told them to repeat it after her. New words included, *cerca* 'near', *montaña* 'mountain', and *encontró* 'came across'. After several rounds of repeating the words as a group, the teacher flashed a card to each student around the table and they repeated the word. Then, she asked each student to go up to the board; she dictated each word and they wrote it. If they misspelled it, she asked the group to help them spell it correctly. As instructed by the teacher, the students began to read their story about the coyote and the mountain. The teacher then asked questions about the fable they had read. ]

**T:**   *¿Por dónde andaba el coyote tan simpático que era pero tan s-o-s-p-e-c-h-o-s-o?*
(Said the teacher in a low, deep voice and she squinted her eyes to convey suspicion.)
(Where was the coyote wandering? He was so charming but so s-u-s-p-i-c-i-o-u-s.)
[All hands wave enthusiastically, and T. calls on student B.]

**B:**   *¿Por la montaña?*
(By the mountain?)

**T:**   *Pues cerca de la montaña. ¿Verdad? ¿Y, qué hacía el Coyote ese día?*
(Well near the mountain. Right? And what was the coyote doing on that day?)
[All hands wave enthusiastically, and T. calls on S.]

**S:**   *¿Buscando comida?*
(Looking for food?)

**T:**   *Sí, y ¿que sé encontro?*
(Yes, and what did she find?)
[All hands wave enthusiastically, and T. calls on students G.]

**Group:**   *¿Un lobo?*
        (A wolf?)

**T:**   *No, no es lobo. ¿Es, qué? ¿Qué es?*
(No, it's not a wolf. It's a what, what is it?)

**G:**   *!Yo sé, yo sé, yo sé!*
(I know, l know, I know!)

**T:**   *Mario.*

**M:**   *Es una zorra.*
(It's a fox.)

**T:**   *Sí una zorra. ¿Y qué quería hacer la zorra?*
(Yes, it's a fox and what did the fox want to do?)

[All hands wave anxiously, and T. calls on G.]

**G:**   *Quería comer.*
(It wanted to eat.)

**T:**   *No. ¿Quién sabe?*
(No. Who knows?)
[All hands wave anxiously, and T. calls on H.]

**H:**   *No quería dejarse del coyote?*
(It didn't want to give in to the coyote?)

**T:**   *No. A ver, ¿quién se acuerda?*
(No, let's see who remembers?)
[All hands wave anxiously, and T. calls on M. Another student, B. puts his hand down and opens his book to a page and reads it silently while the others are anxiously trying to answer a question. ]

**M:**   *¿Quería comerse al coyote?*
(It wanted to eat the coyote?)

**T:**   *No, ustedes no están pensando. Piensen en que queriá hacer la zorra antes de encontrarse con el coyote.*
(No, you're not thinking. Think about what the fox was doing before he ran into the coyote.)

**Group:**   [All hands go up anxiously.) *!Yo sé, yo sé, yo sé!*
(I know, I know, I know!)
[And the teacher calls on student B, who meanwhile has been leafing through his book looking for the section to which the T. referred in her question.]

**B:**   *La zorra iba caminando cerca de la montaña pensando como iba a conseguir el ramo de uvas que veía en los altos de la montaña.*
(The fox was walking near the mountain thinking about how he was going to get a bunch of grapes that was hanging from the mountain.)

**T:**   *Exacto. Muy bien eso iba pensando la zorra.*
(Exactly. Very good, that's what the fox was thinking.)

[The teacher spent about half an hour on this part of the discussion which represented the first one-forth of the fable. She then stopped and told the students that they would continue on the following day. She assigned workbook exercises in which the students to match a word in the story with the correct meaning.]

Mrs Cota's questions to the students emphasized surface structure, not meaning. The teacher initially allowed for turn taking so that most of the students were getting a chance to respond to one of her questions. The pattern changed when she noticed that the students did not remember exactly what the fox wanted to do before meeting up with the coyote. She began looking for a student who she thought might have a correct response. When the teacher asked *¿Quién sabe?* 'Who knows?' the students recognized that the teacher was searching for a specific point and their hands waved enthusiastically. At that point the students were prepared to answer the teacher's question with any fact that they recalled about the story. The students' behavior showed that their goal was the need to please the teacher not to comprehend text. This explains why the students' statements were framed as questions, expressing uncertainty that their answers matched the questions.

Student B realized that he could find the answer in the book. Thus, while the teacher searched for someone to answer, he re-read the section that answered the question, displaying appropriate strategic behavior. He did not rely on his memory to guess at the answer. Nevertheless, the teacher either missed or ignored that part where student B re-read the section in the story.

The teacher's questions were based on recall only, not inference, which did not encourage interaction among the students or between the teacher and the students. Her questions largely ignored the students' previous knowledge (Au & Kawakami, 1984). The teacher concerned herself with the students getting all parts of the story correct. She believed that the most effective way of testing comprehension meant asking direct 'right and wrong' questions which all students were expected to answer easily.

The teacher's goal of getting precise answers to her questions actually interfered with her clarification questions. For example, she asked *¿Qué queriá hacer la zorra?* 'What did the fox want to do?' She then rejected two answers by G. and H. which were correct, according to the story, but did not refer to the exact place in the story that she had in mind. Furthermore, she failed to clarify exactly what part of the story she was referring to until M. said, *¿Quería comerse al coyote?* 'It wanted to eat the coyote?' It occurred to her that the students might be guessing, and it was then that she re-framed her question and gave them more clues about where the fox was before meeting up with the coyote. One of the important things to notice is that the group spent an inordinate amount of time constructing these small details of only one-fourth of the fable without any discussion as to the meaning of these facts.

Text 1 shows that this teacher equated comprehension with memorization and memorization with learning. She concentrated on getting the students to recall the storyline in sequence. She assumed that children had to be drilled on vocabulary words before they could understand the text and that comprehension comprised a list of facts linked together. Her assumptions reflect the notion of one correct meaning of text, not various socially constructed meanings largely based on sociocultural experience which children bring into the reading lesson. Her emphasis on memorization created difficulties. Some students memorize better than others. Possibly what we see here is that those students who do not memorize as quickly learn differently, but the fact that they may not memorize as quickly as others does not qualify them as slow learners. It should be noted that despite the insistence on a single route to comprehension, the teacher's interaction style conveyed a sincere and pleasant attitude toward the children. The students responded well to her strict but kind manner. She teased during the lesson by exaggerating a character. Clearly she was interested in helping the students learn.

### Effective Teaching of Comprehension — Phase 1: Redefining Comprehension

Hawaiian children's low comprehension and reading achievement demanded reorganization of reading lessons in the KEEP classrooms (Au, 1979; Au & Jordan, 1981). The major innovation stressed the importance of learning comprehension by building linkages between the students' experience and new information in the text (Brown *et al.*, 1983; Calfee *et al.*, 1981; Flavell *et al.*, 1981; Griffin & Cole, 1984). The traditional lesson presented by Mrs Cota had three phases, a drill on vocabulary, an introduction to the reading, and a discussion about the story. The KEEP lessons fundamentally increased the role of discussion before and after reading. KEEP referred to the lesson as a three-fold model, Experience, Text, and Relationship (ETR). Elements of the KEEP ETR program include:

(a) the cultural compatibility through the use of the Hawaiian 'talk story' discourse;

(b) the use of previous experience as a basis for understanding text: and

(c) teacher/student questioning strategies at interaction based on the Vygotskian notion of assisted performance.

These comprehension strategies have enhanced

the reading performance of Hawaiian students (Au & Kawakami, 1984; Calfee *et al.*, 1981; Tharp & Gallimore, 1988). This model became the basis for the ethnographic pedagogy which I carried out in this third grade class with Spanish-speaking students.

After intensive observation of Mrs Cota's third-grade literacy lessons, it became apparent that the novice Spanish-speaking students needed a great deal of special attention. Mrs Cota asked me if I could work with these students to help them during the school day. I constructed a plan for developing comprehension based on the analysis of the observational data and the ETR model by working with each student individually. This took the form of a pedagogy designed to examine the problem of comprehension as perceived by the teacher. The sessions alternated in two different formats. In one format, the students read a story which they had not read previously from their assigned book. In the second one, they read from a book of their choice.

In each case the procedure was as follows. The students were asked if they had previous knowledge about the subject. In most cases, they did. This led to an open discussion between the researcher and the student with the child taking the lead in the discussion. I assisted them in organizing the content into a sequence they understood. They answered questions about their own version of the story pertaining to 'characters', 'sequence of events', 'analysis', 'interpretation', 'feelings', 'opinions', and 'predictions'. In answer to the question, 'What was the most important part of this story to you?' the students consistently shared a part of emotional significance to them. For example, one student's personal story was about his mischievous dog in Mexico and a series of comical events involving his dog. By describing these events, the student lessened the hurt he felt at leaving his dog, a treasured companion, behind in Mexico.

During the literacy activity, the pace was usually fast and lively as the students regaled me with their stories. Following these questions, the students were asked to read the story either in the text or library book; they were reminded that this was also a story like the one they had just told me about a similar topic. They read it silently and were asked to request assistance on any words they did not know or on any part they did not understand. Students frequently asked for help on words but not on comprehending any part of the story. After reading the story, they re-told it

in their own words. Most of the time the students were able to relate the story in proper order with the correct characters as they appeared in the text. Using the students' cues, I proceeded to ask more analytical questions about the story and related it to the characters. For example, questions were asked that made the students look at how one character related to another or how one part of the story related to another, i.e. 'What part of the story was funniest to you?' The students made comparisons and contrasts and expressed freely their opinions and beliefs about the stories they read. Except for some more analytical questions such as, 'How would another pet like a cat behave differently than your dog?' little prompting or probing was ever necessary in this part of the session.

In more advanced sessions, toward the end of the school year, I asked the students to write their personal stories instead of telling them to me orally. I reviewed their stories with them in a format similar to their oral stories. This process required longer periods of time and often required more than one session. The students began to understand that their written stories were just like those in the books. For example, one student commented, *Yo sé este fin del cuento en mi libro — Es como el cuento que escribí aquí.* (He pointed to his journal). 'I know where the ending is in the story in my book. It's like the one in the story I wrote'. This helped them to demystify the stories in the textbook and to begin seeing how it was possible for them to put their own words in some form that made sense. The students were expected to form complete sentences as much as possible such that when they re-read their own story, it would read smoothly. The students included words from the text that they found difficult even though these words were never listed as potential new items in the text. The words that the students found difficult were often not the same ones that the textbook writers envisioned and included in the 'new vocabulary word list' in the story.

In summary, the experience phase included four principal elements:
(1) It introduced meaning to the students' reading through exploring their own experience.
(2) Students reconstructed the structure of a textbook story after they learned how to reconstruct their own story verbally. Through appropriate prompts from the researcher, this relationship could be characterized by a triangle showing connections between the student, a more competent other and the text.

(3) Students discussed formal relationships between experience and the text to amplify understanding of text-related features of the story such as characters, storyline, and meaning of story.

(4) As they had done for their personal stories, students answered analytical questions about the textbook stories and determined their overall meanings.

### Reconfiguring the reading group — Phase II

Group reading comprehension lessons were devised by the researcher based on three factors found to be significant in the individual sessions with the students. These features included (a) maximizing teacher/student interaction; (b) utilizing students' personal experience to reconstruct the sequence of text; and (c) generating comparative relationships between text and personal experience to construct high level analytical questions. The approach varied somewhat from the Experience Text Relationship (ETR) process conducted by Au & Kawakami (1984). That is, I did not move the students from their experience to the text and then draw relationships between the two. Rather, I first listened to the students' experiences; then we discussed the relationship to the text; and then, they read the text. This approach had, however, the Vygotskian theoretical perspective in common.

The following is an example of a group reading lesson within the framework of the ethnographic pedagogy.

[Seven children sat and listened to the story read orally by the researcher. The story dealt with animals that performed in the circus and a special type of animal found by a little boy, who trained an ant to dance. ]

**R:** *¿Qué es un circo?*
(What's a circus?)

**S1:** *¿A dónde va uno a ver animales?*
(Where one goes to see animals?)

**T:** *¿Quienes de ustedes han ido al circo?*
(Who has been to the circus?)

**Group:** *!Yo fui! !Yo fui!*
(I went! I went!)

**T:** *Si, pues parece que algunos de ustedes han ido [al circo] y otros todavía no tienen esa oportunidad pero ojalá una vez pueden ir. Los que no han ido al circo personalmente, pueden saber mucho del circo porque a la mejor conocen a alguien que fue al circo o han visto un circo en libros o la televisión.*
(Yes, well it looks like some of you have been

[to the circus] and others have not yet had that opportunity but hopefully you'll be able to do so. The ones who have not been to the circus personally, you may know a great deal about the circus because you may know someone who has been to a circus or maybe you've seen one in books or on television.

**S2:** *Sí, yo vi un circo grandote en un cine.*
(Yes I saw a big circus in a movie.)

**T:** *¿Cuáles animales se encuentran?*
(Which animals do you find?)

**S2:** *Son grandes.*
(They're big.)

**S3:** *Hay elefantes y changos, y caballos y muchos otros.*
(There are elephants and monkeys and horses and lots of others.)

**T:** *¿Qué piensan los demás sobre lo que dice S3? ¿Cuáles otros animales se encuentran en el circo? Me gustaría que también se hablaran uno con otro. Por ejemplo, S2 puede dirijir sus comentarios a S3 no solo tienen que dirijirse a mi.*
(What do the rest of you think about what S3 said? Which animals do you find in the circus? I would like you to talk to each other too. For example, S2 can ask questions or make comments directly to S3 not just to me.)

**S4:** [Looked at the teacher then at looked at S3] *Yo creo que hay otros animales en el circo como una vez yo vi unos leones y tigres.*
(I think that there are other animals in the circus like one time I saw some lions and tigers.)

[The lesson continued until the researcher had discussed what roles the circus animals performed and what the boy in the story found in the circus that was different from what was typically found there.

The lesson exemplified here began with a group activity that posed a question which the group collectively had to negotiate and discuss. The researcher's question forced them to think about a personal experience. 'Have you ever been to the circus? Some of you have and others have not'. The message was that if you had not been to the circus, there were other ways to know about it. It was then possible to participate in the discussion because they had many sources of knowledge .

Following a brief discussion among the students, they shared their findings and were then told to read their story silently. The task was to find out what unusual animal the boy in the story had found in the circus. The students were also reminded that they could assist each other with unfamiliar words and with any parts that were difficult for them. The students were left alone to read with each other for a while. When the students were through with the short story, the focus of the discussion was determined by the students' interest. The researcher provided a sequence of questions to the students which were framed according to their previous comments. An effort was made to have the students use the facts they recalled about the text to arrive at a higher level analysis about the text. The following is an account of a part of the literacy event.

*Text 2*

**CD:**  *¿Se sorprendieron por algo que pasó en el cuento?*
(Were you surprised by any part of the story?)

**S1:**  *!Yo sé! !Yo sé!*
(I know! I know!)

**S2:**  *Las hormigas.*
(The ants.)

**S3:**  *Brincaban y bailaban. Que curiosas.*
(They jumped and danced, how cute.)

**S4:**  *Y había osos también, grandotes.*
(And there were bears too, big ones.)

**CD:**  *¿Y por qué es raro ver a hormiguitas en un circo?*
(Why is it strange to see ants in a circus?)
[Pause for a few seconds and then the hands went up.]

**S3:**  *¿Por qué son chiquitas?*
(Because they are small.)

**CD:**  *¿Por qué es tan raro que las hormiguitas chiquitas bailen?*
(Why is it so strange that the small ants dance?)

**S1:**  *Por que bailaban y casi nunca se ven hormiguitas bailando.*
(Because you never see ants dancing.)

**CD:**  *Entonces, ¿cómo es que había hormiguitas en este circo?*
(Then how did the ants get in the circus?)

**S2:**  *Yo sé, es que a unos niños los llevaron allí y les enseñaron a bailar.*
(I know the children took them there and taught them to dance.)

**CD:**  *¿Creen ustedes que es possible enseñar a las hormiguitas bailar?*
(Do you think it's possible to teach ants to dance?)

[The students continued to interact with the adult and with each other. With the exception of two factual questions, the rest were more open ended interpretive level questions.]

The attempt was to focus less on isolated facts of the story and to make the students interact with each other and the teacher at a level that allowed them to use the interactive context, their cultural knowledge, and their interpretive skills to comprehend text. The questions illustrated a responsive teaching approach based on a conversational exchange that built on the students' proceeding utterances.

### Transformation of reading comprehension lesson

Four major points of contrast emerged between the ethnographic pedagogy process and the instructional observations of the teacher completed prior to the training on the ethnographic pedagogy procedure:

(1)  In the traditional literacy event, the teacher interacted with one individual student at a time. In contrast, the variation of the Experience–Text–Relationship approach provided a context in which all students encouraged to participate not only with teachers but also with peers. It encouraged students to listen to each other because discussion was based on students' comments.

(2)  The intent of the questions about the text also differed. In the traditional approach, the teacher generally tested for recall while the scaffolding approach to inquiry had as its purpose a comprehension process that combined existing knowledge with new knowledge from text to achieve a synthesis.

(3)  The types of questions differed in that the traditional approach to comprehension often limited the level of questions to memorization, whereas the scaffolding approach relied on comments generated by use of advance cognitive organizers to respond to questions about the text.

(4)  The use of literacy tools (listening, reading, writing) in the traditional approach is restricted primarily to individualized reading with minimal writing done often only in workbooks. The sociocultural literacy process integrated listening, reading and writing for the purpose of understanding the synthesis between previous and new knowledge .

Discussion about the students' experience as it related to their assigned text affected their knowledge acquisition level. The students relegated to a 'low' reading group were only low from the standpoint that they had not been taught how to read meaningfully. The ethnographic pedagogy transformed the inequity in the instructional practices to opportunities in the structional process in two specific ways. First, students became meaningfully engaged in literacy activities when there was a relationship made between their personal knowledge and the written text. This suggests that these students learn experientially. Second, the organization of interaction provided the students the opportunity to interact meaningfully with the teacher and peers. This occurred when the teacher tailored the questions to the students' comments and built on the level of difficulty which accommodated their cognitive development. This interactive context demonstrated that learning occurred in social interaction with others who were knowledgeable and can mediate the process. Scholars hold that literacy is best learned when such interaction relates to real life (Tharp & Gallimore, 1988; Vygotsky, 1978; Wertsch, 1985). In order for children to make sense of text, they must be provided with the opportunity to use their sociocultural experience to interact with the text, as they were in the interventions described here.

## Conclusion and Implications

The processes of acquiring literacy and sociocultural knowledge are intimately related. When the teacher isolated the text from the student's experience, the lesson created a skewed representation of the student's ability. In this study, students demonstrated increased comprehension when the social setting was varied and reorganized. Their comprehension was enhanced when the interactive context in which they were engaged built new knowledge from previous experience.

This study illustrated a pedagogical approach based on an interactive theory of reading comprehension. Its primary claim is that both the ability to comprehend text and the very content of literacy are learned through socially constructed behavior, not through rehearsal of facts isolated from the reader's own experience. This claim implies that educators need to look beyond conveniently packaged reading programs that reduce reading to simplistic, mechanistic decoding techniques and consider how children's experiences relate to their literacy acquisition.

Additional research is crucial in the area of literacy and Spanish-speaking Mexican students. This study uncovered the need to look beyond just the language issues in teaching literacy. Educators must begin to maximize literacy acquisition through changing patterns of teacher/student interaction as well as interaction between peers. Micro-ethnographic methods combined with a design for more adaptive pedagogy can provide a vehicle to understand how children learn reading comprehension.

### Note

1. I am especially grateful to Roberto Rueda for his comments on an earlier version of this paper and to the editors of this book for their assistance.

### References

Au, K.H. (1979) Using the experience–text–relationship method with minority children. *The Reading Teacher* 32, 677–9.

Au, K.H. and Jordan, C. (1981) Teaching reading to Hawaiian children: Finding a culturally appropriate solution. In H.T. Trueba, G.P. Guthrie and K.H. Au (eds) *Culture in the Bilingual Classroom: Studies in Classroom Ethnography* (pp. 139–152). Rowley, MA: Newbury House.

Au, K.H. and Kawakami, A. (1984) Vygotskian perspective on discussion process in small-group reading lessons. In P.L. Peterson, L.C. Wilkinson and M. Hallinan (eds.) *The Social Context of Instruction: Group Organization and Group Processes* (pp. 209–25). New York: Academic Press.

Briggs, P. and Underwood, G. (1982) Phonological coding in good and poor readers. *Journal of Experimental Child Psychology* 34, 93–112.

Brown, A.L., Bransford, J.D., Ferrara, R.A. and Campione, J.C. (1983) Learning, remembering, and understanding. In J.H. Flavell and E.M. Markman (eds) *Handbook of Child Psychology. Vol. 3, Cognitive Development* (4th edn) (pp. 77–166). New York: Wiley & Sons.

Calfee, R.C. and Piontkowski, D.C. (1981) The reading diary: Acquisition of decoding. *Reading Research Quarterly* 16, 346–76.

Calfee, R.C., Cazden, C.B., Duran, R.P., Griffin, M., Martus, M. and Willis, H.D. (1981) Designing reading instructions for cultural minorities: The case of the Kamehameha Early Education Program. Report on the KEEP program. Honolulu, HI.

Carpenter, P.A. and Just, M.A. (1986) Cognitive

process in reading. In *Reading Comprehension from Research to Practice* (pp. 11–30). Hillsdale, NJ: Lawrence Erlbaum Associates.

Cook-Gumperz, J.(1986) *The Social Construction of Literacy*. Cambridge: Cambridge University Press.

Delgado-Gaitán, C. (in press) Adult literacy: New directions for Mexican immigrants. In S. Goldman and H.T. Trueba (eds.) *Becoming Literate in English as a Second Language: Advances in Research and Theory*. Norwood, NJ: Ablex.

Díaz, E., Moll, L. and Mehan, H. (1986) Socio-cultural resources in instruction: A context-specific approach. In California State Department Bilingual Education Office (ed.) *Beyond Language: Social and Cultural Factors in Schooling Language Minority Students* (pp. 187–230). Los Angeles, CA: Evaluation, Dissemination and Assessment Center.

Erickson, F. (1984) School literacy, reasoning, and civility: An anthropologist's perspective. *Review of Educational Research* 54, 525–46.

Flavell, J.H., Speer, J.R. Green, F.L. and August, D.L. (1981) The development of comprehension monitoring and knowledge about communication. *Monograph of the Society of Research in Child Development No. 192*, 46.

Gilmore, P. (1983) Spelling Mississippi: Recontextualizing a literacy related speech event. *Anthropology and Education Quarterly* 14, 235–55.

Griffin, P. and Cole, M. (1984) Current activity for the future: The zo-ped. In B. Rogoff and J. Wertsch (eds) *Children's Learning in Zone of Proximal Development* (pp. 45–64). San Francisco, CA: Jossey-Bass, Inc.

Heath, S.B. (1983) *Ways With Words*. Cambridge: Cambridge University Press.

Moll, L. and Díaz, S. (1987) Change as a goal of educational research. *Anthropology and Education Quarterly* 18, 300–11.

Schieffelin, B. and Cochran-Smith, C. (1984) Learning to read culturally: Literacy before schooling. In H. Goelman, A. Oberg and F. Smith (eds) *Awakening to Literacy* (pp. 3–23). London: Heinemann Educational Books.

Scollon, R. and Scollon, S. (1984) 'Looking it up and boiling it down!' Abstracts in Athbaskan children's story retellings. In D. Tannen. (ed.) *Coherence in Spoken and Written Discourse* (pp. 173–95). Norwood, NJ: Ablex.

Tannen, D. (ed.) (1982) *Spoken and Written Language*. Norwood, NJ: Ablex.

Tharp, G.R. and Gallimore, R. (1988) *Rousing Minds to Life: Teaching, Learning, and Schooling in Social Context*. Cambridge, MA: Cambridge University Press.

Trueba, H.T. (1979) Ethnographic research in bilingual education. *Proceedings of the Workshop on Language Policy* (pp. 65–69). University of Illinois, Division of Applied Linguistics.

— (1984) The forms, functions and values of literacy: Reading for survival. *NABE Journal* 9, 21–39.

Vygotsky, L.S. (1978) *Mind in Society*. Cambridge, MA: Harvard University Press.

Weisner, T. and Gallimore, R. (1985) The convergence of ecocultural and activity theory. Paper read at the annual meetings of the American Psychological Association, Washington, DC, December,1985.

## Questions

(1) Explain the concept of 'ethnographic pedagogy' within the context of ethnography. What was the ethnographic pedagogy that Delgado-Gaitán carried out in the third-grade class with regard to comprehension and grouping? Then, in two columns, contrast, by giving examples, the daily reading lessons of the teacher prior to training in 'ethnographic pedagogy,' and afterwards. Make sure you make reference to student interaction, teachers' questioning techniques, teachers' goals in a student's comprehension of text, and use of listening, reading and writing.

(2) Explain what Delgado-Gaitán means by 'learning is socially constructed through meaningful interaction.' Reflect on your own learning. Do you agree or disagree? Can you give an example of something you didn't learn until you were able to construct it through meaningful interaction? What are the consequences for instruction of this concept?

## Activities

(1) Read Vygotsky's (1978) *Mind in Society*. Cambridge, MA: Harvard University Press. Summarize his concepts of 'zone of proximal development' and 'assisted performance.' What are the consequences of those concepts for instruction?

(2) Tape for at least twenty minutes the questioning that is part of a reading class. Then transcribe it. Analyze the transcription. How does the teachers' questions differ from those of Mrs Cota?

(3) Observe a reading lesson in a specific classroom. Describe practices, including grouping, texts, questions, peer interaction, role of listening, reading, speaking and writing. Do children's experiences relate to their literacy acquisition? How do the practices in this classroom differ from those found in Mrs Cota's class after the 'ethnographic pedagogy'? Do different reading groups receive different reading instruction? Have students assigned to a 'low' reading group been taught to read meaningfully?

(4) Develop a plan of a reading lesson for adults using the 'ethnographic pedagogy procedure' described in this chapter. Role-play with you as the teacher. Ask students to evaluate the lesson. Did it work? Did it work as well for everybody, for some groups better than others? Discuss.

(5) In the United States, three definitions of 'literacy' have been greatly debated. Define 'functional literacy' (Kozol, 1985), 'cultural literacy' (especially the 'prescriptivist' view of Hirsch, 1987) and 'critical literacy' (Freire, 1970; Freire & Macedo, 1987). You may choose to read the original sources given below. An integrated short essay that provides the answer is: McLaren, Peter (1988) Culture or canon? Critical pedagogy and the politics of literacy. *Harvard Educational Review* 58, 213–34. How do you evaluate the three definitions of 'literacy' given above?

## Further Reading

For classical treatments on reading and literacy, see especially:

Smith, Frank (1978) *Reading Without Nonsense*. New York: Teachers College Press.

Stubbs, Michael (1980) *Language and Literacy: The Sociolinguistics of Reading and Writing*. London: Routledge.

For functional literacy, see:

Kozol, Jonathan (1985) *Illiterate America*. New York: Anchor Press/Doubleday.

For cultural literacy, see especially:

Hirsch, E.D. (1987) *Cultural Literacy: What Every American Needs to Know*. New York: Houghton Mifflin.

For critical literacy, see especially:

Freire, Paulo and Macedo, Donaldo (1987) *Literacy: Reading the Word and the World*. South Hudley, MA: Bergin and Garvey.

# A Process Approach to Literacy Using Dialogue Journals and Literature Logs with Second Language Learners

## María de la Luz Reyes

The current literature on classroom-based research reveals that the constructivist view of learning and knowledge has greatly influenced classroom practices (Hiebert & Fisher, 1990). One manifestation of that view in literacy instruction is in the shift from skills-based to process instruction, with Whole Language and writing process as two prime examples. Many positive benefits of the use of these instructional philosophies are being reported (Goodman, 1986, 1989; Harste, 1989; Newman, 1985; Short & Burke, 1989; Smith, 1986). The literature in this area purports that the use of the process approach to literacy enables young writers to be in control of the writing task and assists them in communicating their ideas effectively (Atwell, 1987; Calkins, 1986; Graves, 1983). The belief is that through immersion in writing with a focus on process rather than product, students show marked improvement in grammar, spelling, sentence structure, vocabulary development, and writing fluency, as well as a sense of audience and voice (Atwell, 1984, 1987; Calkins, 1986; Graves, 1985).

The way that teachers translate the philosophies underlying process approaches and how they implement those conceptual phenomena, however, may take many different forms. A classroom teacher's version of a particular philosophy may vary significantly from what its creators and advocates intended. The result is that as a practice becomes popular and widespread, its efficacy is evaluated not according to the ideal, but in terms of what its new advocates implement as their own 'reality.' Many of these advocates are teachers who earnestly attempt to remain faithful to the philosophy, who learn, become informed, and then actually implement those practices in ordinary classrooms where

numerous variables and environmental factors may yield different results. This article examines the implementation of such a process approach to literacy in a bilingual education class where two popular writing genres, dialogue journals and literature logs, were used with a group of Hispanic students with limited English proficiency.

## Dialogue Journals and Literature Logs

Dialogue journals and literature logs are two popular methods for promoting reading and writing in classrooms organized around a process approach to literacy. These tools are frequently cited as effective means of initiating students into writing (Langer, in press; McGettigan, 1987; Staton, 1980), assisting them in gaining writing fluency, and bridging the reading and writing connection (Graves, 1985). Although there are personal journals that require no response, dialogue journals are a form of written communication between the student and the teacher about topics that either party wishes to discuss. The on-going dialogue presumably allows student and teacher to communicate and to construct a mutually interesting reading text (Staton, 1980). Dialogue journals are said to be successful because students are free to select their own topics, determine the amount of writing, ask questions, and seek academic or personal help in a nonthreatening, nongraded context. Success with this medium is also attributed to the fact that teachers are able to concentrate on individual needs, validate students' interests, praise their efforts, get to know them better, and focus on meaning.

Literature logs share some similar features with dialogue journals. Like dialogue journals, they provide an outlet for students' informal but personal writing. The literature log is the child's written response to some thing she or he has read. Although literature logs do not necessarily require a response by the teacher, some teachers do comment on what students are reading and share their own reflections on books they read (Atwell, 1984). The potential benefits of reading followed by a written reflection include opportunities for students to think about books, read more critically, use the author's writing as a model for their own, and relate better to characters or events. Written reflections can help students think through content better, question it, or compare it to their own experiences.

Literature logs differ from dialogue journals in several ways. First, they require written talk about what students read. In some process classes, students select the books they read; in other cases, they respond to read aloud books selected by the teacher or a recommended reading list. The students' entries in a literature log require that they complete certain tasks: read a book, comprehend what is read, and select important or interesting things from the book in order to provide a personal reaction. Unlike dialogue journals where the student's experiences are the source of the writing, the springboard for writing in literature logs is someone else's experiences. So although the literature log may be informal, it is more similar to a school task than a journal. There is often a grade, or requirement attached to completing the task, making literature logs some kind of evaluative measure of a student's academic performance.

Holistic process approaches to literacy using literature logs and dialogue journals have been reported to be effective with mainstream students at virtually every grade level (Atwell, 1982, 1984, 1987; Calkins, 1986; Emig, 1971; Graves, 1983, 1985; Staton, 1980; Staton, Shuy, Peyton, & Reed, 1988). This literature, however, makes no mention of students' writing in languages other than English, or how students' writing might compare in their first and second language. The focus of this article is to examine the effectiveness of a process approach to literacy using these two writing genres to determine whether Hispanic students derive similar benefits as those reported for mainstream students. What is reported here is part of a larger descriptive writing study based on classroom observations and interviews designed to examine the development of Hispanic students' first and second language writing fluency. This article addresses the following questions:

(1) How does the construction of meaning differ in native (Spanish) and English (L2) using dialogue journals and literature logs?
(2) What features of written discourse: topic choice, codeswitching, sensitivity to audience, writer's voice, grammatical structures, and spelling indicate marked improvement using dialogue journals and literature logs?

## The Study

### Rivera Middle School

The study was conducted at Rivera Middle School located in a large urban school district in the Southwest where the school administration supported a Spanish/English bilingual program. At the time of the study the School District's policy for bilingual education called for Whole Language as the preferred approach for literacy instruction, with English to Speaker of Other Languages (ESOL) as the official medium of instruction for reading and writing. Content area classes (math, science, social studies) were to be conducted in Spanish. Thus, textbooks for the content areas were available in Spanish and in English. In keeping with the School District's policies and the spirit of a Whole Language approach, however, there were no language texts or basals used for language arts. Literature books, the majority of which were in English, served as the base for instruction. Conversations and interviews with the principal and the bilingual teachers at the school site confirmed that District's policies were interpreted as mandates. To ensure implementation of these policies, the District's Bilingual Education Program provided summer workshop and sponsored attendance at institutes, and talks on Whole Language and writing process conducted by well-known proponents (e.g. Donald Graves, Frank Smith, Andrea Butler, Kenneth Goodman).

The attendance area of Rivera Middle School included a large low-to-middle income Mexican-origin Hispanic community. For the academic year in which the data were collected, the total student population was comprised of approximately 550 sixth, seventh and eighth graders of whom 73 percent were Hispanic. All students were divided into 'teams' for instructional purposes. There were several teams within the school, each with a distinct name. Most teams received traditional English-only instruction. The 6th, 7th and 8th grade students enrolled in bilingual classes received Spanish and English instruction and comprised the 'Toltec' team. This team was subdivided into nine classes grouped homogeneously by English language proficiency. The 7th and 8th graders attended mixed classes, but the 6th graders were taught separately.

Nine bilingual teachers served as faculty for the Toltec team and met weekly for planning and problem-solving. The bilingual 6th grade class was selected for this study for the following reasons: (a) The language arts teachers who interacted with this class were *fully* Spanish/English bilinguals, that is, they could speak, read and write both languages; (b) they expressed a commitment to writing process on a frequent, ongoing basis; (c) they reportedly embraced Whole Language philosophy; and (d) they permitted some writing in Spanish and English.

### Participants

Ten students from this bilingual class were selected as case studies. These students kept both a dialogue journal and a literature log. Five boys and five girls with a median age of 12.1 years comprised the sample. Five were born in Mexico, four in the United States, and one in Guatemala. All ten spoke Spanish as their first language and resided in homes where Spanish was the primary language. Under *Lau Guidelines* (1975) which specify language categories for bilingual instruction, seven students were classified under category 'B' (predominantly speak a language other than English and entitled to bilingual services), three were classified under category 'C' (bilingual). According to these Guidelines, students in category 'C' are entitled to bilingual services if their achievement scores are below grade level.

The main teacher involved in the study had been trained at a Whole Language Institute, and throughout the academic year prior to and during the study attended ongoing Saturday inservices from Whole Language consultants, some from Arizona who had been trained and influenced by the Goodmans and their protegés.

### Procedures

Entries in the interactive journals and literature logs were collected from October to May for all students. This represents a total of 357 writing samples. The journal data analyzed represent 261 samples of students' writing, with an average of 26 entries per student. The data from the literature logs represent 96 pages of student writing with an average of 9.6 entries per student. The total number of entries varied considerably by dialogue journal or literature log because early in the year students were encouraged to write in their journals daily and many of them did so; in contrast, the literature log requirements called for one entry per week. The number of log entries was also limited because the writing was dependent on completion of some amount of prior reading, and many students changed books before completing them.

Students were followed and observed for four intensive days followed by weekly observations throughout the year to determine the various kinds of writing they were engaged in during typical school days. Fieldnotes were taken on the social context of the writing, e.g. the medium of instruction used, student–teacher interaction, how literacy events were organized, how tasks were assigned, and materials used. The two language arts teachers for this group were interviewed on audio tape to determine their philosophy of writing, their expectations, goals and objectives, their attitudes toward literacy in Spanish and English, their understanding of the writing process, and other pertinent issues related to the teaching of writing. Informal interviews were also conducted with other subject area teachers, the special education specialist, the bilingual counselor, bilingual aides, and the school principal to get a better understanding of the school and classroom organization, school climate, and general philosophy about teaching language minority students.

### Language Arts Classes

Language arts activities for this group were conducted by two teachers although Mrs Sands was the one in charge of the dialogue journals and literature logs for the ten focal children in this study. Twenty minutes for writing in dialogue journals was set aside daily. Spanish and English were permitted and encouraged for these journals, but there was an unspoken understanding between the teacher and the students that writing in the literature logs was clearly to be in English. Individual, small group, and peer writing conferences and mini lessons were conducted daily in English. The majority of the available library books were in English and other instruction was mainly in English although Mrs Sands did not hesitate to explain or elaborate in Spanish when needed for clarification.

Another language arts teacher who strongly supported a process approach to literacy directed a twenty minute Reading Enrichment period, scheduled before lunch, where she often read aloud Spanish or English stories. The few available Spanish texts, published in Spain, contained unfamiliar vocabulary and archaic Spanish expressions that often elicited comments like, 'What does *that* mean?' 'That's stupid,' or 'I don't understand!' Other activities in the Reading Enrichment included poetry, free writing, and the writing of a biography as an end of the year project. Spanish and English were equally acceptable in writing assignments in the Reading Enrichment period where no grade was attached to the work. In practice, the unwritten rule seemed to be that if no grade was required for a class or activity, it was not viewed as falling under the ESOL directive, allowing more latitude for use of primary language.

### Analysis of data

The researcher and two assistants coded and analyzed the data for: emerging themes/topics (e.g. family, cultural events, school-related incidents) and how these themes affected length and complexity of writing; language used by student (Spanish/L1 or English/L2) and language used by teacher in written responses; codeswitching (alternation of L1 and L2 language codes in writing) including conditions which elicited alternation of languages; positive and negative self-concepts and attitudes toward school; and writing skills, i.e. spelling inventions and grammatical structures.

### Findings

Three general findings emerged. One indicated that limited English speakers can and do attempt to write in English *before* they have complete control over the oral and written system of the second language. Other writing research conducted with second language learners (Hayes & Bahruth, 1985; Edelsky, 1986; Hudelson, 1984; Staton, 1980; Ursúa, 1987) found similar results. A second finding suggested that while limited English speaking students may write in English, the development of complex ideas and the construction of meaning may suffer considerably. This was especially evident in the dialogue journals. The third finding indicated that the implementation of literature logs without the appropriate cultural and linguistic modifications used in the dialogue journals contributed to their lack of success. Observations and evidence from the dialogue journals provided ample evidence

that the true spirit of Whole Language was being implemented. The teacher was generally flexible in accepting and using Spanish and English and in providing assisted performance to students who needed it. The context for dialogue journals was relaxed, friendly, and open, accommodating individual needs and interests. In contrast, the implementation of the literature logs was rigid, business-like, inauthentic in restricting bilinguals to reading and writing in English, and unaccommodating to students' needs. Overall, the findings suggest that writing is negatively affected when the topic is imposed, when students have no personal interest or find no relevance in the topic, and when they are not assisted in contextualizing a given writing situation in their own terms. These are consistent with other studies on first language writers which have found that mediation and scaffolding is a key ingredient for student success (Applebee *et al.*, 1984; Langer, 1986; Langer & Applebee, 1986).

To illustrate these findings, I will first compare the dialogue journals and the literature logs with respect to the writing features listed above. Second, I will use typical, unedited, examples from the dialogue journals to show factors that contributed to students' relative success in controlling the writing task, and in developing fluency, writer's voice, and sensitivity to audience. And last, I will illustrate how this particular manner of implementing literature logs in a process classroom prevented all but one student from approximating the quality of written reflections characteristic of young writers in other studies (Atwell, 1984, 1987; Graves, 1983, 1985).

### Topics

Four common topics emerged in the journals. In order of importance, they were: nuclear and extended family; culturally specific object, event, or place; personal interaction with teacher (inquiring about teacher's personal life, health); and school-related incidents (loss of books, supplies, socials, other classes, academic problems). All ten students were able to write longer, more detailed entries when the topic centered around their families or was culturally relevant. Many of the entries initiated by students related events or incidents about family members. They included feelings and opinions. These topics seemed to capitalize on students' 'expertise,' making communication with the teacher relatively easy and nonthreatening. The importance of their families came across strongly. One student who was an adopted child wrote:

> My stepmother is very nice to me and she loves me very much just as my real mom. My father is in Durango. My father is very nice to me he give me money when I visit him. He called yesterday. My stepmother is married to man who works at T. Toys. He is the manager. Almost every week he brings toys to me and his daughter. Because he got divorce. His daughter's name is B.T. B.T comes every week to visit his father. She likes me very much.

In contrast, school-related topics tended to be shorter and more functional in nature (e.g. 'Where can I get another notebook?'). They rarely included elaboration. This was true for all students.

Students' responses in the literature logs were largely devoid of personal accounts or feelings. The typical literature log entry was short and provided a one-line synopsis of the story, e.g. 'I'm reading (*book title*). It is about (*character*) who does XYZ. It is a good book. I like it.' Students did not elaborate on characters or events. Other responses included brief answers to teacher's questions about their books, e.g. 'Yes, I'm finished [with the book] and that's sad because she got sick and died.' The third kind of response in the logs consisted of short explanations about lost, misplaced, or exchanged books. In general there was little substance in the literature log entries. Although the longest entries in the dialogue journals and the literature log did not vary significantly, the writing in the journals indicated better control over the construction of meaning.

### Students' and teacher's language choice

With respect to students' language output, four out of ten students initiated their first journal entries in Spanish while the other six initiated them in English. The native language writers generally continued writing in Spanish unless the teacher exhorted them to use English. In the literature logs, only one student initiated entries in Spanish. When Mrs Sands responded to her in English, she switched to English, and from then on, wrote *only* in English. In the dialogue journals, however, Mrs Sands matched the language output of the students.

Although codeswitching is the norm of oral discourse in many Hispanic communities and was a common occurrence in the verbal interaction between the teacher and these students, the instances of codeswitching in *written form* were quite infrequent. When they did occur, they occurred under the following conditions:
- when a culturally specific word was needed to clarify something, e.g. We ate 'menudo' (a type of Mexican soup);
- when an expression was learned in a specific language, e.g. '¡Sangre Preciosa de Jesucristo!' (Precious Blood of Jesus!); 'fuimos al party' (we went to the party);
- when emphasis was desired, e.g. 'Hello, how are you? Como está?' (in the same line);
- when the writer wanted to convey confidential information or a more personal message, e.g. 'Maestra, cree usted que...' (Teacher, do you think that...); or
- when the writer lacked the English equivalent term, or the word was not readily available, e.g. 'She let me manejar (drive) the car.'

These bilingual students, like those in Edelsky's (1986) study, seemed to understand the conventions of using English, rather than codeswitching, for academic or school related tasks.

### Positive and negative self-concepts

The feelings and attitudes projected by the students about themselves and about school in the dialogue journals and literature logs differed considerably. In the dialogue journals, entries reflected both positive and negative feelings about school and self. One girl often wrote about how she enjoyed school. The following reflects her interest in school:

> I would like to go to college because I would like to be a Stewardess. Because when we went to Guatemala I sou them ladies passing the food and I liked it.

A boy wrote back in response to the teacher's query:

> Yes I do like this school, its great. Well I miss my old school. I like it to, like I like this school... I had one best friend, his name was Jose... We were the best students in the class room. We were the best on math, science, reading, art, story, and doing speling (sic) test.

These entries contradict the persistent myth that most Hispanic students suffer from a poor academic self-concept.

In the literature logs, however, the feelings

projected, even by those who felt confident in the journals, were overwhelmingly negative. Eight out of ten frequently wrote that they disliked reading. Several actually wrote, 'I hate reading.' Some masked their inadequacies with reading and hinted at having problems by saying, 'The book is too boring and too long' or 'Please tell me [about the book] so I now [know] it is a little about. Tell me a little please.' A few students worried considerably about their grades for the literature log, an issue that was not of concern in the dialogue journals.

A strong emotional attachment and respect for the teacher was evident in both journals and literature logs. The students looked forward to the teacher's responses so much that they felt personally slighted when she did not respond to them. The students' family situation could have contributed to this attachment. Most of them were members of large families where the attention of parents had to be shared among several other siblings. One student was an adopted child. One talked about his father in Mexico, and another one lived with his grandmother, but reported that his mother was in another state. Some typical responses that indicated their need for the teacher's attention were:

CJ:     Mrs how come your didn't write back to me now you behind in my journal two days make that 3 days.

MR:     Please write back.

JS:     I missed you.

BM:     You're my favorite teacher.

In the journals, Mrs Sands often reciprocated the affection, e.g. 'I missed you, too, honey.' But in the literature logs, this attachment got some students in trouble. In one case, a student gave a one-line summary of a story in her literature log and at the bottom of the page she wrote, 'Write back soon.' Right next to it she printed in a vertical line, 'SWEET TEACHER.' Part of Mrs Sands' response included a firm reminder: 'The Log is not a place for cute pictures and word pictures. It is a businesslike diary of what you are reading. You also must record the book and pages you have read at the back of your journal.' Some students were confused about the rules governing social and personal interaction in the two written discourse forms.

### Writing skills

An interesting and significant finding from both the dialogue journals and the literature logs

was that even over time, the students did not attend to correct form. The work of Atwell (1984, 1987), Graves (1985) and others implies that exposure to the teacher's model of conventional form in the journals, increased reading and writing opportunities, writing conferences, and mini lessons help students learn and apply correct form. This was not the case in this study. Despite the fact that Mrs Sands conducted daily writing conferences with individual students, peer conferences, and mini lessons in which she focused on specific errors that students were committing in their writing, modeled correct form (she underlined book titles, indented paragraphs, and used the students' own inventive spellings in conventional form) the students did not adopt the correct forms. Unless Mrs Sands explicitly, and individually called their attention to the incorrect form in writing *in the journal or log* (which she rarely did), the students ignored repeated errors. Siddle's (1986) research on various kinds of interventions for black students in a process writing class also found, for example, that peer conferencing with other black students had little effect on improving writing form. Students continued to make the same writing errors. In the case of Siddle's black students, as in the case of these bilingual students, explicit attention to some aspect of conventional writing form made the biggest positive change.

### Writing in dialogue journals

Students showed better control of their journal writing when the topics were self-selected, culturally relevant, familiar, personal, or important to them than when topics were imposed by the teacher. Additionally, the five students who preferred to write in Spanish, and were allowed to do so, wrote more complex ideas and longer, more fluent entries in their native language than in English, especially when they were free of worry over grades. The following writing protocols illustrate the differences by comparing a student's (Sara) writing on a self-selected topic and a teacher selected topic, and her English and Spanish writing. Sara's journal writing is a typical example of how self-selected topics, cultural relevance and language choice contributed to these bilingual students' writing fluency and development of complex ideas. Their voice was confident and their writing sensitive to their audience (the teacher). In the first example below Sara initiates writing on the topic of brujerías (witchcraft):

Maestra perdoneme porque no le escribi su carta pero you perdi la carta. Mestra usted gre en brujerias. You si. Porque las brujas an quedrido hacerle brujerias a mi mama.

(Teacher forgive me for not writing you a letter but I lost the letter. Teacher do you believe in brujerías [witchcraft]. I do. Because the witches have wanted to cast spells on my mother.)

Some traditional Hispanic families, like Sara's, still use 'curanderas' (healers) to perform certain healing rituals like 'el mal ojo,' literally 'the bad eye' — a general ailment believed to be caused by someone who admires or covets something in someone else's person, but does not touch it or obtain it. In this case, Sara appeared to be quite concerned with the topic and the potential harm that could come to her mother. An interview with Mrs Sands revealed an awareness of this cultural dimension, so she showed no surprise at the topic but chose to respond with interest, matching Sara's language output in Spanish:

Es muy, muy interestante lo que dices... Me cuentas mas de las brujerías que le han hecho a tu mamá? (What you say is very, very interesting... Can you tell me more about the brujerías that have been done to your mother')

The teacher's interest appeared to give Sara a nod of approval to explain the reason for her fears. By matching Sara's language output the teacher also validated Spanish (Sara's L1) as a legitimate vehicle for communication at school. Freedom to use Spanish seemed to contribute to Sara's success in communicating her ideas. The work of Diaz, Moll & Mehan (1986) and Reyes (1987) also revealed that use of the students' primary language in examining students' understanding of a topic contributed to improved academic performance in reading. Mrs Sands reported that at the outset of the journal writing, she made a special effort to match the language output of each student in order to encourage him or her to write.

Sara's second entry on this topic explains that a woman had come to her house asking for her mother's clothes — apparently in an attempt to cast a spell on her. Her grandmother, however, had refused to give the woman anything. Again, Mrs Sands responded with interest, encouraging

Sara to continue pursuing the topic of her choice. Sara is allowed to write in Spanish, but in an attempt to increase her receptive reading skills in English, Mrs Sands began using a combination of English and Spanish in her responses to Sara:

That sounds very spooky to me. I think you're right, though, when you say that 'la señora quería hacerle brujerías pero abuelita no se creía (the lady wanted to cast spells but grandmother did not believe her). When one really believes in some of those things they become dangerous.

Sara, however, chose to continue in Spanish, writing in detail about an incident where a witch allegedly cast a spell on someone:

Querida Mrs Sands,
Mi mama me platico Endonde vivia antes con mi abuelita que en segida de la casa que vivian vivian una senora que tenia un hijo. Un dia una bruja se dio un caldo para que se lo comiera el esposo pero el hijo miro el caldo y se lo comio y la bruja le iso una brujeria y el se fue al hospital para ver que tenia malo porque le dolia la pansa. Entonces dijeron que no tenia nada. En tonses la mama fue con una bruja para ver si lo alludapa pero dijo que otra bruja le iso una brujeria y ella dijo que tenia que peliarla para que ella le quite la brujeria. Y tenia que pelia a la otra bruja.

(My mother told me that when she lived with my grandmother next to her house lived a woman who had a son. One day a witch gave her some soup for the husband to eat the son saw the soup and he ate it and the witch cast a spell on him and he went to the hospital to see why he was sick because his belly hurt. Then they told him that nothing was wrong with him. Then the mother went to another witch to see if she could help her but she said that another witch had cast the spell and she would have to fight her to remove the spell. And she had to fight the other witch.)

Her concern for possible harm to her family continued for about two weeks. She wrote about it almost daily. She was curious and interested in the topic of 'brujerías' and was able to express her concerns and elaborate incidents in detail. Although she did not always write complete sentences, Sara demonstrated knowledge of correct form in complex and complex-compound sentences (e.g. 'Mother told me that when she lived with my grandmother next to her lived a woman who had a son,' and 'Then they told him that nothing was wrong with him'). Her vocabulary was adequate, and she showed competency in using the present, past, preterit, present progressive, future, and subjunctive tenses. Throughout these entries Sara's voice comes across confidently. She appears to be absorbed in constructing meaning and exploring her topic. Her writing is fluent and reasonably lengthy (about 3/4 page). She is clearly aware of the teacher as her audience, and she exhibits common inventive spellings in Spanish (e.g. confusion with the soft 'c' and 's' in writing 'disia' [used to say] for 'decia'). The evidence is strong that Sara is confident and in control of the writing task.

When Mrs Sands suggested that Sara drop the topic of 'brujerías,' Sara began to lose control of the writing task. When I inquired about the change of topic she indicated that in retrospect she feared that Sara was too focused on witchcraft, and so she tried to redirect her attention to something else. The following shows how the length and quality of Sara's writing suffered as a result:

> Dear Sara,
> Dejamos de hablar sobre esas cosas porque me estan asustando. Puedes decirnos cuentos espantosos el dí 31 de oct. Ok?

> (Let's stop talking about these things because they are scaring me. You can tell ghost stories on October 31st, Ok?

Sara responded obediently with *two* words:

> Si maestra. (Yes teacher.)

Hereafter, Sara began to reduce her writing to two or three lines. Soon, she stopped writing in her journal altogether. Desperate to start the dialogue between them again, Mrs Sands made another suggestion: to write in English:

> Dear Sara,
> I have an idea. Why don't you write in English and I will write in Spanish. Así podemos practicar los dos idiomas (that way we can practice both languages). Ok?...

Sara responded *in English* but came across tongue-tied. She seemed to be unable to sustain any complex ideas. Apologizing for her inadequacies, she wrote:

> I dont now very good the English. If I dont now how to write soting in English I will write in Espanish.

In contrast to her earlier, more lengthy entries, Sara now appeared to focus on form and succeeded in writing one or two grammatically correct sentences but with little meaning. For over a month her writing consisted of two or three line entries *in English*. Those entries indicate loss of authority in her voice and no initiation of personal topics. Her writing was reduced to brief responses to the teacher's questions.

For Sara, as well as the other students, dialogue journals allowed them an opportunity to write on a consistent basis without worry over grades. When they chose their language, initiated their own topics, expressed their opinions, and communicated personally with the teacher, they produced more interesting and complex ideas. Although their mechanical writing skills did not appear to improve, they were more successful in communicating their ideas.

### Writing in literature logs

Unlike students in the research literature on writing, the bilingual students in this study were not successful at writing in their literature logs. Only one student was able to come close to providing a personal reaction to a character or an event in a literature book similar to the mature and sophisticated responses of the students described in Atwell's (1984), Calkins' (1983), or Graves' (1983, 1985) classroom-based writing research studies. A close analysis of the writing protocols (Figures 1–5) of Marisa indicates a very interesting pattern that I believe contributed to her relative success with the task of writing about what she was reading. In Figure 1 Marisa begins with a personal greeting, 'Dear Miss Sands Hi.' Although this is not a letter, this stylistic device seems to serve as an 'ice breaker' helping Marisa get started with her writing. In the second part of the protocol, Marisa engages in some social interaction with the teacher as she asks, 'So what did you do for thanksgiving?' This gives her a chance to talk about a recent event (Thanksgiving dinner) still on her mind. Because of the close bond she feels for the teacher. Marisa seems to have a need to socialize with her before getting on to the task of reporting what she read. In the

Nov. 29
Dear Miss S.                                    Personal greeting
Hi
So what did you do for thancks giving I at
with my family and my ant and uncul we ate    Social interaction
turcky and ham corn, machpatatas saled,
fruit, Jello cack. But we at 2 turcks.
Well my Book the Best frend fight in tell      Response to book
[until] thair [they] blid [bleed?] thay tell
abaut what thay did in the fight
P.S. what is your book about                    Personal closing

**Figure 1** Student's Entry A in literature log

third part of the protocol, Marisa provides a response to the book she is reading, but like her classmates, she writes a mere two-line summary of the story. There is no elaboration, personal reflection, or internal response that comes from identification with the characters or events.

In a departure from her insistence on treating the literature log as a 'business-like diary,' Mrs Sands responds to Entry A as in Figure 2.

In Figure 2, Mrs Sands matches the pattern of Marisa's writing protocol. She, too, starts off with a personal greeting, 'Dear Marisa' and follows it with a social repartee, listing all the various 'yummy' Foods that were part of her Thanksgiv-

ing dinner. She then moves on to her own response to her book, *A Separate Peace*, but she doesn't just take a turn telling about what she read; instead, she does two things that seem to enable Marisa to move beyond a one-line response. First, she comments on Marisa's book, providing her own internal response to the friendship between the characters. Second, perhaps from information in the journal about Marisa's close friendship with Angela, the teacher uses an analogy to help Marisa relate to the characters; that is, she compares Marisa's friendship with Angela: 'It would be like your trying to make your friend Angela into an ath-

Dear Marisa,                                    Personal Greeting
My family and I just stayed at home.
We ate turkey, dressing, cranberry sauce,
mashed potatoes, sweet potatoes, vegetables  Social interaction
and pumpkin pie. It was yummy, but now I'm
back to lighter goods!
    I'm still reading *A Separate Peace* and
really not enjoying it much. I just keep
waiting for it to get better and it doesn't. The  Teacher's response to her book
two friends in the story continue to be        and student's book
friends in spite of an accident one of them
has, but I am beginning to think that they
are both trying to live their lives through
each other. It would be like your trying to
make your friend Angela into an athlete        *Assisted performance:*
because you weren't good at sports and her     Teacher uses analogy to help
trying to make a good math student out of you  student relate to characters
because you weren't good at math. It's a little
crazy to think about it that way but that is the
direction in which my thoughts are going.
    Do you think best friends sometimes         Poses compelling question for
fight more than other people do?                student
    Mrs S.

**Figure 2** Teacher's response to literature log Entry A

lete...and her trying to make a good math student out of you...' This provides a relevant social context for Marisa to understand the struggle between the two friends in the story. Lastly, the teacher ends her response by posing a question of potential interest to Marisa: 'Do you think that best friends sometimes fight more than other people do?' In doing these two things the teacher has aimed at what Vygotsky (1978) calls the 'zone of proximal development' (the level of performance that a student is capable of reaching with some assistance). This assisted performance on the part of Mrs Sands produces the response observed in Figure 3. In Figure 3, Marisa's literature entry starts with a personal greeting followed by some social interaction, but this time the social interaction is brief. Marisa moves quickly to a personal reaction to Mrs Sands' earlier question about whether best friends fight. 'Best friends don't fight, that is why they are best friends,' Marisa argues. Then she uses an example of herself and her best friend to justify her opinion: 'I have not had any little fight with Angela. She is my best friend.' Her argument, although not totally logical at this point and based on her limited experiences, still allows Marisa to move beyond the level of literal comprehension. She uses her own personal experience to reflect upon the topic of friendship and reaches some conclusion about it. Marisa's internal response becomes the central focus of her writing. In addition to this personal reflection, there is evidence that Marisa is generating hypotheses about capitalizing book titles, but is unclear about the rules. She makes the wrong prediction and capitalizes the words 'book' and 'best' each time she uses them. This error, like

children's generalization errors in spoken discourse (e.g. 'foots'), marks a stage of growth for the writer. Again, Marisa ends with a personalized, informal closing, 'Well, I better let you go... P.S. wright back soon!' The closing is used as a polite way to end the writing, to take leave.

In Figure 4, Mrs Sands follows the same pattern beginning with some social interaction and then some comments on her own book, but is brief, allowing Marisa to take center stage. The written protocol in Figure 5 includes some social interaction similar to the two previous ones, but now Marisa is more successful in formulating a personal reaction about her reading.

In examining Spanish/English bilingual classrooms, Cazden's study (cited in Fox & Allen, 1983) noted that Hispanic children and their bilingual Hispanic teacher engaged in a period of social interaction which included using terms of endearment, touching, hugging, and inquiring about each other's families before settling down to academic work. The personal greetings and the social interaction in Marisa's writing protocols seem to have served the same purpose, enabling her to feel a sense of security before engaging in the more 'risky' task of learning, especially in a second language. This last protocol shows Marisa involved in making meaning and 'straining against her level of competence' (Bartholomae, 1980). From a strict conventional standpoint this writing protocol might still be judged unfavorably because it contains many errors in conventional form. The words, 'large' and 'lovely,' for example, are spelled correctly when they are first introduced, but are misspelled when they are used the second and third time in the same entry. These errors do not indicate that

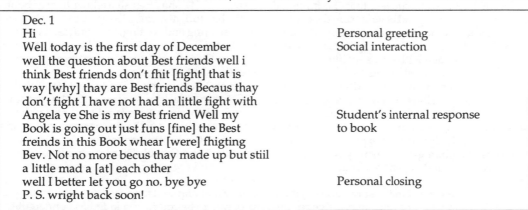

Dec. 1
Hi                                                    Personal greeting
Well today is the first day of December               Social interaction
well the question about Best friends well i
think Best friends don't fhit [fight] that is
way [why] thay are Best friends Becaus thay
don't fight I have not had an little fight with
Angela ye She is my Best friend Well my               Student's internal response
Book is going out just funs [fine] the Best           to book
freinds in this Book whear [were] fhigting
Bev. Not no more becus thay made up but stiil
a little mad a [at] each other
well I better let you go no. bye bye                   Personal closing
P. S. wright back soon!

**Figure 3** Student's Entry B in literature log

```
12-1
Dear Marisa,                                    Personal greeting
It sounds as though you and Angela
have a wonderful friendship. Maybe there        Social interaction
are just all kinds of friendships.
A Separate Peace is not much better             Teacher's response to book
and I'm almost through!
```

**Figure 4** Teacher's response to Entry B in literature log

```
Dec. 6
Dear Miss S.                                    Personal greeting
Hi
Well I have rad 8 page it was about this gril.
hear name [is] Angie thay call her 'Large and
Lovely' beacus she is 160 pouds very large but
thay just tiss [tease] her about her beaing     Student's internal response to book
[being] lovly sometimes she is scared to look
in the mirre beacus she would see some
thing very larg
well I don't thinck it is verv rice beacus thay
call her large and Lovly
well how is your book going out well I better
let you go Bye
P.S. good luck with your book                   Personal closing
wright hear [here] miss.
```

**Figure 5** Student's Entry C in literature log

Marisa cannot spell; she obviously spelled them correctly in the second line. The spelling errors do suggest that Marisa is more engaged in constructing meaning and, in the context of her confrontation with the process of composing, is focused solely on communicating her ideas.

## Discussion

The overall results suggest that the bilingual students in this study did benefit from the process approach to literacy in increased opportunities for writing, but they did not reap its full benefits. A process approach with the use of literature logs provided positive elements of instruction: increased exposure to whole literature rather than abridged versions in basal readers, exposure to good writing models, and increased opportunities for reading and writing. Yet, despite the fact that students had increased exposure to writing activities, they had great difficulty writing more reflective (critique-like) entries in their literature logs.

What went wrong? On the surface, everything seemed to be ideal for producing positive results: The teacher was fluent in English and Spanish,

sensitive and informed about Hispanic culture, made home visits to learn more about the students, was affectionate and caring, and was also knowledgeable and fully absorbed in, and committed to, Whole Language/writing process techniques. She kept up to date with the writings of Atwell, Graves, Calkins, Butler, Smith, Goodman, and others. She was an avid reader, and like Atwell (1984), she often shared her love of books with the students. She tried to turn the students on to reading and writing, but confessed to being frustrated in the realization that her students were not benefiting from the process approach in the way she had anticipated.

Several factors appear to have contributed to the students' lack of success with the literature logs. Some of these are related to district policies, and some to the way the teacher interpreted and managed the process approach. A major factor was that the School District's policies undermined the very program they were mandating. Although it may have been unintentional, the policy that required language arts in the bilingual program to be conducted *in English* undercut the teacher's attempts to implement the true spirit of

Whole Language and the intent of bilingual education, both of which allow for the use of native languages as a medium of instruction. The District policy violated the essence of both instructional philosophies.

In examining the teacher's role, it appears that despite the fact that she understood both bilingual education and Whole Language theories, two factors prevented her from making the needed changes that would have provided her students with more effective, appropriate, and relevant literacy activities. The first factor was a deeply rooted attitude that limited English speakers must be moved to English usage as quickly as possible or they may not learn English well. This was clearly reinforced by the District's policies, and also by the attitude of other teachers in the program (revealed in the interviews) who were more concerned with teaching English than developing literacy. Mrs Sands herself acknowledged that she gave more priority to English writing. This was evidenced in logs and sometimes in subtle or explicit requests (as in the case of Sara) that students write in English. The poor quality of the responses in the literature logs revealed that while limited English proficiency allowed students access to the gist of the stories, the lack of teacher mediation prevented them from enjoying the richness of details and from making a connection between their own lives and those of the book characters. There was ample evidence in the dialogue journals and logs that the students either did not comprehend, or could not produce *in English* what they did comprehend. Since English was the only acceptable writing medium for the literature logs, this may have exacerbated the students' inability to express themselves fluently. This teacher, as well as the others in the program, were really juggling two opposing values. While they accepted the fact that younger monolingual English speakers use invented spelling (personal code) to focus on writing ideas, in practice, they were reluctant to allow bilingual students to write in Spanish (primary code) to develop fluency before switching to English.

A second factor was the decontextualization of the literature logs combined with a kind of hesitancy on the part of the teacher to intervene directly in assisting students in the task of selecting books and in monitoring their actual reading. Since her visits to the students' homes had revealed the absence of print materials, it seems reasonable to conclude that the students were not familiar with the range of available options, especially in English trade books. Many students started books, found them too long or too difficult, and simply gave up reading them. They often reported not knowing what books to choose or that they were bored with them. But despite the fact that students showed insecurity in making these choices by themselves, the teacher seemed reluctant to impose her own expertise and simply directed them to find another one. I believe that the students' calls for assistance went unheeded not because the teacher was insensitive or did not understand the importance of mediation. Evidence from the dialogue journals, for example, reveals that she frequently assisted students' understanding by anticipating problems. Often she restated phrases in Spanish so the student could grasp the full meaning, e.g. 'I'm on the road to recovery (Me estoy mejorando).' She also provided excellent models of her own reflective writing, but most students did not benefit from that exposure. I believe that the teacher failed to provide appropriate mediation partly because the zealous training she received and her desire to remain faithful to what and how she was taught led her to a distrust of her own teaching. In the interviews she hinted that she expected the process approach to work exactly as she had read it and learned it: 'The kids are not responding like they're supposed to.' Mrs Sands' hesitancy to make appropriate instructional changes appeared to have been based on a naive assumption that implementation of a program as-she-learned-it would be effective for her students. She reported, for example, that the consultants in Whole Language and process writing never discussed any cultural or linguistic modifications of these approaches for non-native English speaking students despite the fact that many of the teachers in training were assigned to bilingual classrooms. For Mrs Sands, as for other novices, the failure to consider the need for modifications that are linguistically or culturally appropriate strongly implies that programs work equally well with all students, regardless of backgrounds. In this case, Mrs Sands appeared to be unable to distinguish between real and superficial features of Whole Language and responded as if scaffolding of reading and writing activities and use of primary language were a violation of the process approach.

This practice of introducing the superficial features of popular instructional programs without appropriate changes explains, at least in part, why the process approach did not fully benefit these bilingual students. What is often ignored in program implementation is the fact that students who do not belong to the 'culture of power' may not always understand the rules of classroom discourse (Delpit, 1986, 1988). The high regard that Hispanics hold for teachers as authority figures in the classroom (Macias, 1989; Delgado-Gaitán, 1987), for example, suggests that they rely upon, and expect direct instructional intervention from the teacher. They look for it. In the literature logs and dialogue journals they sought the teacher's assistance (e.g. 'Please tell me a little bit about the book'). The absence of direct mediation in reading and writing tasks may have created dissonance for these bilingual students who found themselves in an environment where the role of the teacher faded into the background. This, together with their personal attachment to the teacher and their need for social interaction before moving on to school tasks were often sources of confusion for the students because the rules for engaging in social interaction and for written discourse were not always clear. In defining the literature logs as 'business-like diaries,' the teacher may have removed the very thing (social interaction) that assisted the students in finding relevance and authenticity in this particular writing task. Dialogue journals permitted the students to situate the task in familiar, culturally relevant contexts and provided writing practice with authentic tasks (Brown, Collins & Duguid, 1989; Tharp & Gallimore, 1989). In contrast, the literature log task made it difficult for bilingual students to view the task as authentic when it was stripped of social context and relied on an understanding of characters and events in unmediated cultural contexts.

The lack of success with a process approach to literacy found in this study does not suggest abandoning process approaches. Nor does it suggest strict adhering to direct instruction — a return to what I call 'drill, grill, and kill.' Rather,

it suggests that administrators, consultants and teachers should give thoughtful consideration to the implementation of popular instructional approaches in light of the cultural, social, and linguistic needs of the learners. The unique needs of learners should be taken into account. For example, to increase Hispanic students' chances of success with Whole Language and process approaches to literacy, teachers should think about modifying the approach to include: on-going opportunities to read and write in Spanish and English; instruction in strategies for book selection; exposure to and availability of age-appropriate, interesting, and quality literature from both cultures; multiple copies of the same books to increase a student's opportunities for checking his or her comprehension with others reading the same book; and increased, guided opportunities to discuss the contents of the books in the student's preferred language to assist him or her in making connections with books and finding authenticity in the task *before* attempting to write in literature logs. Thinking about Vygotsky's (1978) 'zone of proximal development' and the kinds of things that teachers should do to help students reach their potential might help teachers adapt the writing process so that instruction 'allows students to experience the possibilities for contextualizing a given writing situation in their own terms, terms that would allow them to initiate and participate in the process by which they and their subject are transformed' (Bartholomae, 1979: 89). If a process approach to literacy is to benefit *all* students, it must consider each learner's unique needs.

## Acknowledgements

This study was partially supported by small grants from the IMPART PROGRAM, Office of the Associate Vice Chancellor for Faculty Affairs, and the PRESIDENT'S FUND, Office of the Vice President for Human Resources, University of Colorado, Boulder.

## References

Applebee, A.N., Langer, J.A., Durst, R.K., Butler-Nalin, K., Marshall, J.D. and Newell, C. E. (1984) *Contexts for Learning to Write: Studies of Secondary School Instruction.* Norwood, NJ: Ablex.

Atwell, N. (1982) Class-based writing research: Teachers learn from students. English Journal, 70, 84–87.

— (1984) Writing and reading literature from the inside out. *Language Arts* 61, 240–52.

— (1987) *In the Middle: Writing, Reading, and Learning with Adolescents.* Portsmouth, NH: Boynton/Cook.

Bartholomae, D. (1979) Teaching basic writing: An alternative to basic skills. *Journal of Basic Writing* 2 (2), 85–109.

— (1980) The study of error. *College Composition and Communication* 31, 253–69.

Brown, J.S., Collins, A. and Duguid, P. (1989) Situated cognition and the culture of learning. *Educational Researcher* 18 (1), 32–42.

Calkins, L. (1983) *Lessons from a Child: On the Teaching and Learning of Writing*. Portsmouth, NH: Heinemann.

— (1986) *The Art of Teaching Writing*. Portsmouth, NH: Heinemann.

Delgado-Gaitán, C. (1987) Mexican adult literacy: New directions for immigrants. In S.R. Goldman and H.T. Trueba (eds) *Becoming Literate in English as a Second Language* (pp. 9–32). Norwood, NJ: Ablex.

Delpit, L. D. (1986) Skills and other dilemmas of a progressive black educator. *Harvard Educational Review* 56, 379–85.

— (1988) The silenced dialogue: Power and pedagogy in educating other people's children. *Harvard Educational Review* 58, 280–98.

Diaz, S., Moll, L. C. and Mehan, H. (1986) Sociocultural resources in instruction: A context-specific approach. In *Beyond Language: Social and Cultural Factors in Schooling Language Minority Students*. Los Angeles, CA: Evaluation, Dissemination and Assessment Center, California State University.

Edelsky, C. (1986) *Writing in a Bilingual Program: Habia una Vez*. Norwood, NJ: Ablex .

Emig, J. (1971) *The Composing Process of Twelfth Graders* (NCTE Research Report No. 13). Urbana, IL: National Council of Teachers of English.

Fox, S.E. and Allen, V. (1983) *The Language Arts: An Integrated Approach*. New York: Holt, Rinehart and Winston.

Goodman, K. (1986) *What's Whole in Whole Language?* Portsmouth, NH: Heinemann.

— (1989) Whole-language research: Foundations and development. *The Elementary School Journal* 90 (2), 207–21.

Graves, D. H. (1983) *Writing: Teachers and Children at Work*. Portsmouth, NH: Heinemann.

— (1985) The reader's audience. In J. Hansen, T. Newkirk and D. Graves (eds) *Breaking Ground: Teachers Relate Reading and Writing in the Elementary School* (pp. 193–99). Portsmouth, NH: Heinemann.

Harste, J. (1989) Commentary. The future of whole language. *The Elementary School Journal* 90 (2), 243–9.

Hayes, C.W. and Bahruth, R. (1985) Querer es poder. In J. Hansen, T. Newkirk and D. Graves (eds) *Breaking Ground: Teachers Relate Reading and Writing in the Elementary School* (pp. 97–108). Portsmouth, NH: Heinemann.

Hiebert, E.H. and Fisher, C. (1990) Whole language: Three themes for the future. *Educational Leadership* 47 (6), 62–3.

Hudelson, S. (1984) Kan yu ret an rayt en ingles: Children become literate in English as a second language. *TESOL Quarterly* 18, 221–38.

Langer, J. (1986) A sociocognitive perspective on literacy. In J. Langer (ed.) *Language, Literacy, and Culture: Issues of Society and Schooling*. Norwood, NJ: Ablex.

— (in press) Literate thinking and literacy instruction. In E.H. Hiebert (ed.) *Literacy for a Diverse Society: Perspectives, Programs and Policies*. New York: Teachers College Press.

Langer, J. and Applebee, A.N. (1986) Reading and writing instruction: Toward a theory of teaching and learning. In E. Z. Rothkofp (ed.) *Review of Research in Education* (Vol. 13). Washington, DC: American Educational Research Association.

Lau Guidelines (1975) *Lau v. Nichols*. 414 US 563 (1974).

Macias, J. (1989) Transnational educational anthropology: The case of immigrant Mexican students. Paper presented at annual meeting of the American Educational Research Association, March, San Francisco, CA.

McGettigan, K. (1987) Dialogue journal: An initiation into writing. *Reading, Writing, and Learning Disabilities* 3 (4), 321–32.

Moll, L.C. and Diaz, S. (1983) Bilingual communication skills in classroom contexts. Final Report (NIE-G-80-0155). Washington, DC: National Institute of Education.

Newman, J. (1985) Insights from recent reading and writing research and their implications for developing whole language curriculum. In J. Newman (ed.) *Whole Language Theory in Use* (pp. 7–36). Portsmouth, NH: Heinemann.

Reyes, M. de la Luz. (1987) Comprehension of content area passages: A study of Spanish/English readers in third and fourth grade. In S.R. Goldman and H.T. Trueba (eds) *Becoming Literate in English as a Second Language* (pp. 107–26). Norwood, NJ: Ablex.

Short, K.G. and Burke, C.L. (1989) New potentials for teacher education: Teaching and learning as inquiry. *The Elementary School Journal* 90 (2), 193–206.

Siddle, E.V. (1986) A critical assessment of the natural process approach to teaching writing. Unpublished qualifying paper, Harvard University.

Smith, F. (1986) *Insult to Intelligence*. New York: Arbor House.

Staton, J. (1980) Writing and counseling: Using a dialogue journal. *Language Arts* 57, 514–18.

Staton, J., Shuy, R., Peyton, J.K. and Reed, L. (1988) *Dialogue Journal Communication: Classroom, Linguistic, Social and Cognitive Views*. Norwood, NJ: Ablex.

Tharp, R.G. and Gallimore, R. (1989) *Rousing Minds to Life*. Cambridge, MA: Cambridge University Press.

Ursúa, C. (1987) You stopped too soon: Second language children composing and revising. *TESOL Quarterly* 21, 277–304.

Vygotsky, L.S. (1978) *Mind and Society: The Development of Higher Psychological Process* (M. Cole, V. John-Steiner, S. Scribner and E. Souberman (Eds and Trans.)). Cambridge, MA: Harvard University Press.

## Questions

(1) Reyes focuses mainly on two process instruction activities: dialogue journals and literature logs. Explain what they are. In a second column indicate whether these activities are used in a classroom (or classrooms) with which you are familiar. In what way does implementation differ in those classrooms from the ones described by Reyes?

(2) Indicate practices in the Language Arts classes that Reyes describes which favor English over Spanish. Be specific in your answer.

(3) Process instruction has quickly spread throughout the English-speaking world, first in New Zealand, Australia, Britain and Canada, and later on in the United States. Define process instruction and list other terms that are used interchangeably. What consequences may be derived from the historical origins of process instruction for biliteracy? Reflect on the chapter by Morison. Was process instruction present at PS 84 both for English and Spanish? How was this accomplished? Why do you think language minority students are successful at PS 84 and not entirely so in the classrooms studied by Reyes? Be specific in your answer.

(4) Summarize the reasons for the success of dialogue journals over literature logs in the classrooms studied by Reyes.

(5) Reyes (1992; see related reading later), speaking about programs that use whole language and writing process, says 'these seemingly successful programs are not producing the same rate of success for linguistically different students as for native English speakers.' Are skills-based literacy programs producing the same rate of success? Why or why not? According to Reyes, what are the dangers in too little correction for language minority students in process instruction? Why is error correction an important issue for language learners? How could the Vygotskian concept of 'assisted performance' (for more on this reread Delgado-Gaitán, this volume) alleviate this need of process instruction for language minority students? What is the difference between the teacher as a 'mediator' and as a 'facilitator'? What is some of the 'scaffolding' that language minority students sometimes need?

## Activities

(1) Visit a school where biliteracy is important. Make a video-tape of a literacy lesson in English and one in the non-English language. Show it to the class and write an essay comparing both practices. If possible, different groups should visit schools for different ethnolinguistic communities, with differences in script, directionality, etc. Reflect on

how the structure of language itself may affect literacy practices. How is meaning constructed in the two literacy classes?

(2) Read Delpit, Lisa (1988) The silenced dialogue: Power and pedagogy in educating other people's children. *Harvard Educational Review* 58 (3), 280–98. What is her main point? How do you feel about it? How do her views relate to Reyes'? Do you think there has been enough dialogue about process instruction in the teaching of language minority students in bilingual instruction? Why or why not?

(3) Research other highly structured, skills-oriented reading programs, such as DISTAR. Find out how they are used. Report to class on how such programs work.

(4) Visit a classroom with a large number of language minority students. Describe their literacy practices, both in English and, if available, in a non-English language. Then visit another classroom at the same grade level where there are few language minority students (possibly a private school). Describe their literacy practices. Contrast the difference between the two. If possible, make a video-tape to share with the class.

(5) Make an inventory of children's literature and children's authors in a specific bilingual classroom. First compare the availability of texts in English and the LOTE, their quality, their content, and the differences in their classroom use. Are there any bilingual texts? How are those used? Then analyze the children's literature books in English. Find examples that are ethnocentric.

(6) Ask five language minority students who are bilingual to write a short story in their mother tongue about a fictional young character who lives in the old country. A week later, ask the same five students to write the same short story, this time using English. Compare stories. What are the differences in structure, lexicon and message? What could these differences be attributed to? How much of the other culture do you think can be transmitted through English? What consequences does this have for instruction?

(7) Interview three types of parents: a language majority parent, a language minority parent who was schooled in the United States, and a language minority parent who has recently arrived. Ask them about their expectation of the teacher's responsibility in providing direct instruction (teacher-centered classroom, structured and planned instruction, error correction vs. student-centered classrooms, mediated instruction, focus on meaning). Summarize the results of the interviews. What can you conclude?

(8) How is it possible for an English-monolingual teacher to use the LOTE resources of her students in a linguistically heterogeneous class? Describe specific practices. What are the consequences of these practices for both language minority and language majority students?

## Further Reading

For more on this topic by Reyes, see:

> Reyes, María de la Luz (1992) Challenging venerable assumptions: Literacy instruction for linguistically different students. *Harvard Educational Review* 62, 427–46.

For more on whole language curricula and its implementation, see especially:

> Goodman, Kenneth, Smith, E. Brooks, Meredith, Robert and Goodman, Yetta (1987) *Language and Thinking in School: A Whole Language Curriculum.* New York: Richard C. Owen.

# Combining Language and Content for Second-Language Students

Donna Christian, George Spanos, Joann Crandall, Carmen Simich-Dudgeon and Karen Willetts

Many students are faced with the daily challenge of learning through a language other than their mother tongue, whether through English as a second language (ESL) or foreign language immersion settings. They need to develop the required language skills for participating in all aspects of schooling while they strive to keep pace with other students in content mastery as well. Many educators have found that combining language and content instruction can be an effective way of helping these students progress toward both goals.

In this chapter, we explore the integration of language and content and suggest some specific strategies for teachers to use in the classroom. Such integration may be twofold:

(1) *Content material is incorporated into language classes.* Material from academic content areas provides practice in using specific terminology, types of reading passages, required writing styles (e.g. science lab reports), and cognitive thinking skills. This type of instruction, referred to as content-based language instruction, prepares the students for the academic demands that subject area classes impose.

(2) *Accommodation is made for the students' limited language proficiency in content classes.* This occurs through the adaptation of language and materials and the presentation of information that is more comprehensible to these students. This type of instruction, referred to as language-sensitive, or 'sheltered,' content instruction, assists these students in their pursuit of academic success.

The following discussion illustrates both approaches and considers how they can be implemented in a variety of settings. We focus on the situation of language minority students learning English as a second language, but it will become clear that the same principles apply to English-speaking students learning other languages as well.

## A Language-sensitive Content Class

In an intermediate school located in the Chinatown of a major metropolitan city, ninth-grade students are seated in groups of four or five at round wooden tables, conversing in a mixture of Mandarin and Cantonese, with a sprinkling of English. The instructor enters and begins to distribute the contents of a large brown bag. The students continue to chatter in Chinese, their interest piqued by the paper towels, soup-sized plastic bowls, rolls of masking tape, and pennies that she lays out in the middle of the wooden tables.

Speaking in English, the instructor tells each group to choose a student as recorder. Once the students have done this, she asks the recorder to jot down the following instructions:

(1) Tape the penny to the middle of a plastic bowl.
(2) Fill another bowl with water.
(3) Place the bowl with the penny in the middle of the table.
(4) Look at the penny and move back until you can no longer see the penny. Stay still.
(5) Choose one student to fill the penny bowl with water from the other bowl.
(6) The rest of you stay where you are. Observe what happens. Discuss this with your group.
(7) Tell your recorder to write down what you have observed.

When the teacher says 'Begin,' the resulting scene is tumultuous, as students start to order one

216

another to carry out the directions in a combination of English and Chinese. Naturally, there are a few hitches — for example, spilled water and students falling off their chairs as they attempt to position their bodies to make the pennies disappear. The teacher calmly moves from group to group to ask questions like 'What step are you on?' or 'What happens to the pennies when you put water in the bowl?'

Once all the groups have completed the seven steps, the instructor reconvenes the class. When she asks for volunteers to report on what happened, eager students vie with each other for the opportunity to speak. It is interesting to note that the students' conversations have now shifted to English and that the reports are surprisingly fluent.

With about 15 minutes left, the teacher asks the students to explain in writing why they think the pennies seemed to move as water was added to the bowls. Several students begin referring to their science textbooks, specifically to the section that deals with refraction, or the bending of light. At this point, it becomes clear that the goal of the lesson is to present a scientific principle, namely, that light bends when it moves from one medium to another medium at an angle; but the class has been conducted according to well-established language teaching principles as well. The result is that students were actively communicating in small groups using oral and listening skills to discover the scientific principles involved in the exercise.

## A Content-based English as a Second Language Class

In our first example, a science teacher used language learning methods and techniques in what we call language-sensitive content instruction, enabling the instructor to facilitate both content learning and language acquisition for limited-English-proficient (LEP) students. Next, we have a chance to look in on a second-grade ESL classroom.

Large sheets of paper are taped around the room with the following headings: 'My name is ____,' 'I live in ____,' 'I eat ____,' 'I wear ____,' and 'I am ____.' Small groups of students are huddled around pictures and books about various animals — lions, panda bears, whales, jaguars, buffalo, kangaroos. Each group is engaged in research, finding the answers to the questions: 'Where does a (lion) live?' 'What kinds of food does a (panda bear) eat?' 'What kind of covering does a (whale) have?' 'What word best describes a (kangaroo)?'

One student in each group is leading the discussion; another is recording the group's decisions. In one group, a student suggests that the panda lives in the zoo. Another agrees, but wants to know in what country. They look through the books and magazines until they find a map that shows where the panda lives. The recorder writes 'China' on their sheet. They come across a picture of a panda eating bamboo. They decide to write bamboo in the 'I eat ___' column. A lively discussion begins when they try to find one word to describe the panda. They know pandas look 'cuddly,' but they also know that pandas can be 'fierce.' Another group chose the jaguar. They are filling in the chart on the bulletin board, listing the jaguar's home as 'South America' and the animal's covering as 'fur.'

After the groups complete their work and present their findings to the class, the teacher asks them to talk about the similarities and differences among these animals. She poses questions such as 'How are these animals the same?' Finally, she asks them: 'How many pandas are living?' 'How many jaguars?' The students conclude that these animals are all in danger of extinction.

It is easy to see how this content-enriched ESL class differs from the traditional ESL class. Although the students are learning English language skills — listening, speaking, reading, and writing — and getting practice in using particular grammatical patterns (*wh*-questions) and new vocabulary, the class also does much more: It builds on academic content (e.g. characteristics of animals) and develops academic language skills (such as classification and comparing/contrasting), which assist them to function more effectively in a mainstream academic classroom.

## Integrating Language and Content Instruction

The focus of many language classrooms today is on the development of oral communication skills in order to help students talk about themselves, relate to their peers and teachers, and function appropriately in the language. This development of interpersonal communicative skills is important, but it is not enough. We also need to provide students with meaningful content-area instruction and contexts upon which to base their language skills.

Students who speak English as a second language need to master more than conversational skills in order to do academic work in English. They must also be able to use English to read science books, do math word problems, or reflect upon and evaluate history lessons. These latter skills, referred to as Cognitive Academic Language Proficiency (CALP) by Cummins (1981), take longer to develop (five to seven years) than interpersonal communicative skills (or BICS — Basic Interpersonal Communication Skills). Both facets of language proficiency can and should be developed together. By using academic content as a basis for language lessons, teachers can focus attention on higher-order thinking skills such as analyzing, synthesizing, or predicting, and can provide students with the appropriate language labels and conventions for participating in content classes.

As we have seen earlier, this approach is not limited to the language classroom. All teachers can make content instruction more meaningful by using hands-on approaches that relate math and science, for example, to real-life activities. Our first example presented a language-sensitive content classroom where a science teacher used language teaching methods and techniques to facilitate both content learning and language acquisition for LEP students. Students get needed support after transition if the mainstream or content teacher uses a language-sensitive approach in the classroom. Further, research suggests that second-language learning is facilitated when the learner is taught using meaningful input, when new information is presented and linked to already known information, and when the learning environment is relaxed and motivating (Krashen & Terrell, 1983).

### Integrating language and content in bilingual education

Whereas the focus in the sections above has been on language minority students in ESL and English language content classes, content-based instruction is also a 'natural' for bilingual education. In bilingual education programs, content-area instruction may be delivered in two languages. Theoretically, students are taught content in their first language while they develop skills in English. However, bilingual students need to study the same curriculum and acquire the same knowledge as their English-speaking counterparts. Using academic content as the basis for ESL instruction can help the students toward that goal. Although we may expect skills and knowledge to transfer from the native language to English, there are inevitably alternative vocabulary, structures, and conventions that the students need

to learn to become 'academically bilingual.' Content-based ESL instruction can provide the context for such language development.

### Foreign language programs

Students learning languages other than English, either in foreign language classrooms or in two-way bilingual programs, can also benefit from the combination of language and content instruction. In foreign language immersion classrooms, for example, two educational goals exist side by side: the learning of another language and the acquisition of content knowledge and basic skills. Students receive all instruction in a language that is not native to them. By integrating language and content, we can work toward both educational goals at the same time. In fact, it is important that this be done so that academic language skills are developed during the process. When a social studies unit in French is presented to native English speakers, relevant vocabulary, grammatical structures, and language functions can be systematically treated so that both the content and the language are taught.

We can use this approach in traditional foreign language classes as well. In a German class that meets twice a week, for example, lessons can revolve around topics taught in content classes. A unit from the music class on great composers could be adapted for the German class, or a geography class could be reviewed by focusing on the topography of Europe. New content can also be introduced, especially when relevant to the language and culture under study.

### Two-way bilingual programs

In two-way bilingual programs, where language minority students and English-speaking students come together for instruction in both languages, the needs of both groups are served by integrating language and content. In a program using Spanish and English as languages of instruction, for example, lessons that incorporate English and math instruction for the Spanish speaker, and science and Spanish for the English speaker, provide language and concept development for both groups.

## How to Combine Language and Content

Language and content-area instruction can be integrated in one lesson or unit, or the approach can form the basis for an entire curriculum. Even though the extent of implementation may vary widely, the underlying principles and procedures remain the same. In fact, teachers may start with one lesson or unit and later pool resources with other teachers to develop a whole curriculum from this approach.

(1) *Develop one lesson*. To plan a single lesson, teachers can take an objective from a content-area curriculum, such as science, and think about what language students need in order to be able to accomplish that objective. The language development goals should include specific vocabulary items as well as grammatical structures and language functions (such as requesting information or defining) that are important for the lesson. Naturally, the level of proficiency of students will need to be considered. Once the content and language objectives of the lesson have been identified, activities that will accomplish both can be planned. The sample lessons (in Appendix A) provide models for developing an integrated lesson. The plans include the following kinds of information, which should be taken into consideration when planning a lesson:

- grade level
- language level
- subject area
- topic
- key content competencies
- core vocabulary
- thinking skills
- language skills
- literacy skills
- study skills
- materials needed
- extension activities
- assessment

Close cooperation between language and content-area teachers is especially helpful in the planning stages, and ongoing collaboration is desirable.

(2) *Develop a unit in one academic area*. This level provides a more sustained effort than a single lesson, but the approach is the same. A unit in math, social studies, science, or any other content area can be adapted in this way. For example, a unit on word problems in math is ideal for integration with language objectives (think of the practice on English comparatives that could be incorporated, based on phrases like 'greater than,' 'faster than,' and so on). Again, content objectives need to be examined to determine what

language structures and functions can be taught or reinforced at the same time.

The advantage of developing a series of lessons is that it then becomes possible to spiral the language being taught, building from one lesson to the next. In other words, a particular structure can be introduced in one lesson, then reinforced and expanded in later lessons in the unit.

(3) *Develop a content-based ESL or sheltered English curriculum*. This is, of course, the most ambitious project to undertake. In most school systems, teams of teachers regularly collaborate on curriculum development, either informally or at the request of the school district. Such teams could be made up of teachers who have tried combining language and content instruction in their classes so that they can pool resources and experience. As mentioned above, the collaboration of content area and ESL teachers is particularly effective.

Naturally, a curriculum should reflect local needs. Requirements for content-area topics need to be considered, as well as the choice of a format best suited to the local population. A totally integrated curriculum for LEP students combines language instruction with all content areas. Alternatives include content-enriched English language instruction and language-sensitive content classes, such as sheltered English classes for LEP students. For example, an ESL curriculum might be developed in conjunction with the social studies strand or reflect selected topics across a number of content areas. In a bilingual program, the content-enriched ESL class might reinforce concepts taught in the native language. In an ESL pullout situation, the curriculum would reinforce concepts presented in English in a mainstream classroom, where LEP students might number only a few among a class of native speakers of English. In a self-contained classroom, the ESL curriculum could provide the entire social studies component for a group of LEP students.

Whether a single lesson or a whole curriculum, teachers can integrate language and content area instruction in ways that make learning each one more effective. Although some careful preparation is needed in advance to plan the lessons, it is well worth the effort. For further reading on combining language and content for second-language students, see Appendix B.

### References

Cummins, J. (1981) The role of primary language development in promoting educational success for language minority students. In *Schooling and Language Minority Students: A* *Theoretical Framework.* Sacramento, CA: California State Department of Education.

Krashen, S. and Terrell, T (1983) *The Natural Approach.* San Francisco, CA: Alemany.

## Appendix A: Strategies for Integrating Language and Content

### Social studies

(Developed by Melissa King, Stephen Matthiesen, and Joseph Bellino)

*Purpose*: This strategy introduces and reviews important events, people, dates, and concepts in the social studies content area using color-coded sentence strips. As constituents of sentences are manipulated, content information is presented and the following language foci are addressed:

- develop sentence structure and vocabulary;
- review *wh*-questions;
- promote oral language proficiency and the transition to reading/writing.

*Language Level*: Beginning to Intermediate.

*Educational Level*: Grade one or higher.

*Materials*:

- Strips of colored paper and colored cards.
- Colored markers.
- Pocket chart (optional) for visual display.
- Magnetic tape (optional) for display of cards/sentences on magnetic chalkboard or thumbtacks for display on bulletin board.

*The Basic Approach*: This strategy involves the use of color-coded sentence strips to present content information and develop a variety of language skills.

*Step 1. Prepare the following materials:*

- color-coded sentence strips with content information that is to be focus of lesson(s);
- color-coded *wh*-question cards that correspond to specific sentence parts on the colored strips;
- color-coded word cards that contain key words/phrases from the target sentences.

Example:

| Cortez | went from Cuba | to Mexico | in 1519 | to look for gold |
|--------|----------------|-----------|---------|------------------|
| blue | red | green | purple | orange |
| Who | from Where | Where | When | Why |
| blue | red | green | purple | orange |

*Step 2. Introduce content information on 'World Explorers' to students by*

(a) breaking target sentences into constituent parts:
- build up sentence constituent by constituent;
- tape or tack strips to board as they are added;
- have students repeat or read constituents as they are added;

(b) eliciting appropriate responses to *wh*-questions about the content:
- ask questions about each constituent as it is added, then
- review by asking basic questions and alternate forms (such as 'What country did he come from?') after complete sentence developed.

(c) eliciting appropriate *wh*-questions to correspond with given content information:
- point to the answer and have students supply the question.

(d) distributing question cards and word cards to students for physical response drills:
- have student with question card stand up and ask, then student with appropriate answer stand up and answer.

(e) distributing word cards to students so they can reconstruct target sentences by standing up in correct order.

*Step 3. Encourage student–student interaction with color-coded cards and sentence strips. Have students pair up to practice with each other.*

*Step 4. Move from oral practice into writing activities:*

(a) have students write appropriate content information or *wh*-question following an oral cue;

(b) have students write target sentences when given a word or phrase as an oral stimulus;

(c) have students create new sentences (following the structural pattern) when given additional content information.

*Extension*: Model other similar sentences for an oral and/or written review, for example:

(1) Cabot went from England to America in 1497 to find a trade route.
(2) Cartier went from France to Canada in 1534 to find a trade route.

This strategy could easily be adapted to other social studies units as well as other content-area subjects.

### Using physical response strategies: Art

(Developed by Carolyn Andrade, Carol Ann Pesola, and Donna Christian)

*Purpose*: A major difficulty in teaching language to beginners is how to get started and how to facilitate the early stages of language learning. The use of physical response strategies can be an effective way to approach this problem, particularly in immersion settings. In this technique, teachers use only the target language, and students are expected to respond physically but not verbally. In other words, students demonstrate understanding through means other than oral production. The approach shares its conceptual underpinnings with those of the 'total physical response' (TPR) and 'natural' approaches.

The physical response orientation has a number of advantages for early language learning. It involves processes that resemble natural language acquisition, by developing comprehension and involving action responses, and it reduces the level of anxiety in the new language situation. In the classroom, the approach further has the advantage of pairing mental processing with action, which may lead to greater retention, and all students are able to participate. For young children, this involvement orientation is especially important, as is the fact that no reading or writing skills are required (although they may be developed).

Integrating language and content instruction using physical response strategies can be particularly effective in art, music, and physical education classes. Concepts appropriate to the age levels of students can be taught, and the content lends itself well to physical rather than verbal responses from the students. The teacher's language can be geared, in variety and complexity, to the language level of the students, while still allowing the teacher to promote concept learning.

The following activities suggest ways in which physical response activities can facilitate the learning of language and basic concepts in art. The lessons are designed for beginning language learners (in a foreign language or ESL context) in various elementary grades.

*The Basic Approach:*
*Step 1: Planning;*
- set language and content goals for the lesson
- determine the vocabulary needed for the lesson;
- break down the lesson/task into steps:
  teacher: language + gestures + context
  student: physical responses
- define sequence of activities;
- identify and gather materials needed.

*Step 2. Conducting the lesson*
- teach vocabulary using visuals, movement, and demonstration; use familiar commands (put, take, and so on) and allow for lots of manipulation of vocabulary through novel commands (new combinations of familiar command structures with new vocabulary);
- introduce and practice concepts through sequenced activities, with teacher using language, gesture, and demonstrations, and students responding with action, first as a group and then in smaller groups or individually;
- combine and reinforce concepts, continue practice.

*Step 3. Ending the lesson*
- end with a quiet activity to calm students down before the next class; because of the active nature of this approach, it is important to provide the students with a 'cool-down' or quiet time before moving on to the next activity; a good example is a short story (told orally or read).

*Sample Lesson*
*Objective*: basic shapes and colors (making a mobile).
*Language Level*: Beginning (ESL or foreign language).
*Educational Level*: Elementary.
*Materials*:
- Colored paper in at least five colors
- Objects to trace basic shapes (rectangle, square, circle, triangle)
- Pencils
- Scissors
- String
- Wooden sticks (approximately 18–24 inches long)

*Activities*:

(1) Setting the stage: demonstrate/teach vocabulary (a) action verbs: put, take, cut, draw, make, find (b) colors: red, blue, yellow, green, black, white (c) shapes: square, rectangle, circle, triangle.

(2) Demonstrate tracing shapes and cutting them from paper of different colors. Have children cut out pieces of various shapes in various colors: (i) Find a circle; draw a circle on the red paper; cut out the circle. (ii) Make a square on the blue paper, cut it out. (iii)Put the box (rectangle) on the yellow paper; draw the rectangle; cut out the rectangle. (iv) Make a green triangle. Then let children cut out shapes and colors as they choose.

(3) Once children have a number of shapes cut out, practice sorting and naming the shapes and colors. Get children moving around as they sort. (i) Put all the triangles together. Who has a red triangle? If you have a red triangle, stand up. Put all the red triangles on the table and sit down. (ii) Who has a black rectangle? Put the black rectangles by the window. (iii) Put all the blue pieces together. Take the blue squares to the blackboard. Continue sorting, then redistribute shapes so that each child has at least 2 of each shape in different colors.

(4) Demonstrate gluing strings of different lengths to shapes and tying them to the wooden sticks, more or less evenly spaced. Allow children time to design arrangements of shapes to their liking. With older children, two sticks may be crossed and nailed together to make a more complex mobile.

(5) Hang children's work around room and use at later times to practice shapes and colors in follow-up activities.

## Appendix B: Further Reading

The following articles and books provide additional information about integrating language and content instruction.

Cantoni-Harvey, G. (1987) *Content-area Language Instruction: Approaches and Strategies*. Reading, MA: Addison-Wesley.

Chamot, A. and O'Malley, M. (1986) *A Cognitive Academic Language Learning Approach: An ESL Content-based Curriculum*. Silver Spring, MD: National Clearinghouse for Bilingual Education.

Crandall, J. A. (ed.) (1987) *ESL Through Content-area Instruction*. Englewood Cliffs, NJ: Prentice-Hall Regents.

Crandall J. A., Dale, T., Rhodes, N. and Spanos, G. (1989) *English Skills for Algebra*. Englewood Cliffs, NJ: Prentice-Hall Regents.

Crandall, J. A., Spanos, G., Christian, D., Sunich-Dudgeon, C. and Willetts, K. (1988) *Combining Language and Content Instruction for Language Minority Students*. Silver Spring, MD: National Clearinghouse for Bilingual Education.

Cuevas, G. (1984) Mathematics learning in English as a second language. *Journal for Research in Mathematics Education* 15, 134–44.

Curtain, H. and Pesola, C. (1988) *Languages and Children: Making the Match*. Reading, MA: Addison-Wesley.

Evans, R. (1986) *Learning English Through Subject Areas: The Topic Approach to ESL*. Victoria, Australia: Ministry of Education, Curriculum Branch (Schools Division).

Krashen, S. and Terrell, T. (1983) *The Natural Approach*. San Francisco: Alemany.

Mohan, B. (1986) *Language and Content*. Reading, MA: Addison-Wesley.

Northcutt, L. and Watson, D. (1986) *SET: Sheltered English Teaching Handbook*. Carlsbad, CA: Northcutt, Watson, Gonzales.

Penfield, J. (1987) ESL: The regular classroom teacher's perspective. *TESOL Quarterly* 2 (1), 21–39.

Short, D., Crandall, J. and Christian, D. (1989) *How to Integrate Language and Content Instruction: A Training Manual* (CLEAR Educational Report No. 15). Los Angeles: University of California, Center for Language Education and Research.

Snow, M. A. and Brinton, D. M. (1988) *The Adjunct Model of Language Instruction: Integrating Language and Content at the University* (CLEAR Technical Report No. 8). Los Angeles: University of California, Center for Language Education and Research.

Spanos, G., Rhodes, N., Dale, T. and Crandall, J. A. (1988) Linguistic features of mathematical problem-solving: Insights and applications. In R. Cocking and J. Mestre (eds) *Linguistic and Cultural Influences on Learning Mathematics* (pp. 221–40). Hillsdale, NJ: Lawrence Erlbaum.

Willetts, K. (ed.) (1986) *Integrating Language and Content Instruction* (CLEAR Educational Report #5). Los Angeles: University of California, Center for Language Education and Research.

Willetts, K. and Crandall, J. A. (1986) Content-based language instruction. *ERIC/CLL News Bulletin* 9 (2). (Washington, DC: Center for Applied Linguistics).

## Questions

(1) The authors propose two strategies for the integration of language and content:
   (a) 'content-based language instruction';
   (b) 'language-sensitive content instruction' or 'sheltered content instruction.'
   Define each. Can they work in tandem? When are these strategies useful? When are they dangerous? Is language and content integration equally useful when a language minority child is learning a second language as when a language majority child is learning a foreign language? Why or why not? Use the Additive and Subtractive distinction to frame an answer.

(2) Contrast the language-sensitive science lesson for language minority students described in the article with a typical science lesson in a high school with which you are familiar. What are the differences? Then contrast the content-based ESL class described in the article with a typical one in the same school. What are the differences?

(3) How do these strategies relate to different language aims in different types of bilingual education? Do teachers in your area have a choice of strategy?

## Activities

(1) Briefly describe physical response strategies in teaching a second language and its advantages. (You may want to read more on Asher's Total Physical Response.) Now plan a second language lesson using this strategy that also integrates content. You may model it after the Art lesson that appears in Appendix A. Role-play it to the class with one of you being the teacher.

(2) Develop a language-sensitive lesson in a content area. As the article suggests, consider the following: grade and language level, subject area, topic, core vocabulary, materials and human resources needed, skills, concepts, knowledge, thinking processes and attitudes engendered, extension activities and assessment. You may model your lesson after the Social Studies lesson that appears in Appendix A.

(3) Try out the penny and bowl activity described in the article with a class of second language learners. Record what happens with students' language use. Tape and transcribe it for analysis. Present your analysis to the class.

(4) Prepare a public oral presentation on the arguments for integration of language and content. Some in the class should take the position of opposing bilingual education, while others should role play being supporters of bilingualism as a goal. If your role is to oppose bilingualism, make sure you show how integration of language and content can be used to expedite the shift to the majority language. If your role is to support bilingualism and biliteracy, be specific about when this integration is dangerous and when it can be useful. Have a student panel evaluate who was most convincing.

## Further Reading

For more on integrating language and content instruction see especially;

Faltis, Christian (1993) *Joinfostering: Adapting Teaching Strategies for the Multilingual Classroom* (Chapter 4). New York: Macmillan Publishing Co.

# Language Education in Bilingual Acadia: An Experiment in Redressing the Balance

## William Francis Mackey

### Acadia

Although it is not a state and no longer a colony, Acadia remains a unique, dynamic territorial and cultural entity. As an important colony of France, it included all of what is today the three Canadian Maritime provinces of Nova Scotia, Prince Edward Island and New Brunswick, east of a line between Campbellton and Calais, embracing all the lands between the Bay of Fundy and the Bay des Chaleurs.

By mid-18th century it had become a pawn in the great colonial wars between the French and British empires. In 1755, the English, in an effort to consolidate their gains in America took the drastic step of deporting the entire Acadian population of 13,000 to far-away lands in Europe, but mostly to other American colonies as far distant as the Gulf of Mexico. The cultural history of the Acadians has always been one of contact and accommodation, even before the tragedy of the great diaspora immortalized in American literature by Longfellow's epic 'Evangeline'.

Spearheaded by some 3,000 escapees, the Acadians gradually returned to their idyllic homeland, only to find that the fertile lands were now occupied by English settlers whose population had already grown from a nucleus of some 14,000 refugees fleeing the excesses of the American Revolution (the so-called United Empire Loyalists) strengthened by mostly Protestant newcomers from England, Scotland and Ireland who held title under grants from the British Crown. The returning Acadians had to settle for the less fertile coastal and forested regions to the North and East. But they were not joined by other settlers from France, since that country had by then ceded the entire area to Britain, according to the terms of the Treaty of 1763.

It was only generations later that they were joined in that sparsely populated tongue of land between Maine and Quebec, where the St. John River forms the international boundary between the USA and Canada, by an influx of Quebecers, to form the very French-speaking independent-minded self-styled Republic of Madawaska whose inhabitants (the Brayons) are famous for their buckwheat flapjacks. Nearby Grand Falls, with its yearly international potato festival, calls itself 'the potato capital of the world' rivaling PEI (Prince Edward Island) a.k.a. Spud Island.

Today, Acadia as a territorial and extra-territorial ethnic reality embraces dynamic communities in all the Canadian Maritime provinces, with the bulk of the population centered in New Brunswick where its quarter million French speakers makes up a third of the population concentrated in a crescent-shaped area following the coastline from the Nova Scotia border to the northernmost tip of Maine (see Figure 1). Within this area the degree of bilingualism of the population ranges from nil to practically equilingual, depending largely on the percentage of mother-tongue English speakers in the immediate area. If, for easy identification, we rename these areas by the names of their leading cities, we get a distribution arranged in ascending degree of contact which looks something like this: Edmundston (4% English mother-tongue), Bathurst (15%), Buctouche (20%), Campbellton (35%), Grand Falls (55%), Moncton (60%), Chatham-Newcastle (70%), Fredericton (93%), St. John (99%)

### Language in Education in Acadia

In all these areas, until the middle of this century, the French speaking population was schooled largely in English, while tirelessly trying to negotiate the right to their own schools in their own language. By mid-century the Acadians had won this right, but only in New Brunswick; the others were under the jurisdiction of other prov-

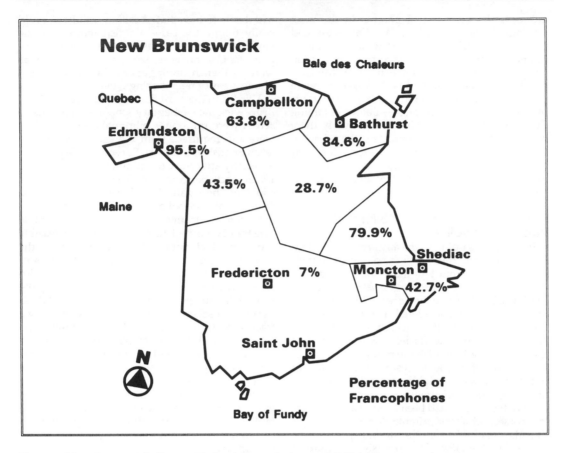

**Figure 1** New Brunswick (*Source*: Federal Commissioner of Official Languages)

inces. For more than a generation the New Brunswick Acadians have even had their own educational system with schools at all levels including a university and several community colleges. The schools are governed within the Ministry of Education by a quasi-autonomous parallel division operating exclusively in French.

Consequently French has become the dominant language of education to such an extent that, in some areas, parents and especially grandparents remark that the children are much less bilingual than they were. The question of bilinguality became crucial after 1969 when the New Brunswick Official Languages Act led to the requirement that applicants for many of the government post be fluent in both languages.

This requirement coupled with its counterpart at the federal level and bilingual policies in other areas created a strong demand for some sort of bilingual education. In this context, throughout the other part of the province with its population of some 700,000 English-speakers, parents also became dissatisfied with the level of bilingualism which schools had provided their children, who had been allowed to study French simply as a school subject. Following the example of their Montreal cousins, they too in desperation began organizing classes in which all subjects were taught in the second language, the so-called immersion programs which by then were becoming increasingly popular from coast to coast. By 1990 more than 15% of the entire English-speaking school population of New Brunswick, about triple the national average, was doing its schooling in French. Much of this was financed with the help of a federal program for the promotion of bilingualism.

The apparent success of these programs

attracted the attention of parents in the most unilingual French-speaking Acadian areas and they had their school boards emulate their Anglophone counterparts by requesting immersion programs entirely in English. The Ministry pointed out however that such programs were precisely what their parents and grandparents had fought against so long — before obtaining their own entirely French schools. Surely there must be other ways of improving the bilingual skills of their children without sacrificing their French schools of which they were so justly proud, by reverting to the old ways of an all-English education.

## Restoring the Balance of Bilingualism through Schooling

It was at this point, in the autumn of 1984, that I was called in to meet with the parents and their school board, in one of the most isolated and most unilingual French-speaking districts in the Madawaska-Restigouche area, to see what options could be considered. Having been long involved in linguistic research in all parts of Acadia since the mid-forties, I well understood the dilemma with which the parents were faced. It was one of trying to restore the balance of bilingualism without taking away from the level of mother-tongue competence achieved in school.

Since the parents had been looking at the advantages of second language immersion in Anglophone Canada, this had to be the starting point of the discussion. A review of the extensive literature on immersion (some 400 titles) showed that one of its most remarkable achievements was in the high levels of comprehension of the second language. This to me was not surprising since the Anglophone children in immersion programs spend most of their class time hearing or reading French.

A second consideration was the great difference between the Anglophone population in Montreal and the Acadian population in the nature and degree of language contact outside the school. While uniformly low in the Anglophone areas, Acadian contact with the second language ranged from low to all-pervasive, not only between regions as had been pointed out, but also between individuals and families who had become more and more mobile. Any program which failed to take this difference into account could hardly reach the bilingual potential of the population!

In the areas of intense contact, mostly towns which were more than 50% English-speaking, it

had been found that Acadian children could easily follow the same English mother-tongue language arts program as their Anglophone compatriots. Contrariwise, some of the other areas were as French unilingual as the most Francophone areas of neighboring Quebec.

Thirdly, in the most Francophone areas of New Brunswick the elementary school teachers themselves were no longer bilingual, although they were still required, from the early years on, to teach English as a subject. For some time past, but especially after the Communities Equality Act of 1981, teachers from the Anglophone districts could not be legally transferred to teach in the Francophone school districts, or vice versa.

Within the framework of these considerable constraints we had to come up with a feasible program which supplied the best models of the second language simultaneously to learners of differing levels of bilingual competence and different degrees of motivation for learning the second language. If English were maintained simply as a school subject it could occupy only a fraction of the time devoted to it in an immersion program. And we had to point out that in 100 minutes a week in less than 40 weeks, the parents could not reasonably expect a miracle. But they could expect that during this limited period, their children might obtain as much direct contact with the new language as one would during a comparable period in either an immersion program or in a conventional second language course — and perhaps more.

We could, ourselves, confirm this, thanks to some 20 years (1965–1985) of direct classroom observation, analysis, measurement and experimentation, including a review of many other studies in this area of research (Mackey 1965–1990). In our studies, we had tried to measure the extent to which each of some 30 types of learning and teaching in the classroom correlated with the students' ability to speak the second language. The results had been published as part of our center's research collection and were readily available. What concerned us here were the cost–benefit time-on-task aspects (Mackey *et al.*, 1987). Those who learn something, so it seems, do so not on account of the method but in spite of it (Huot, 1988).

In the last analysis, it had become quite evident that no matter what method was used, the benefit obtained from the average speaking lesson was hardly proportional to the investment in learning time and teaching energy. And this was neither the fault of the teacher nor that of the learner. It was the inherent inefficiency of the system. Whether the lesson tended toward one extreme or the other in language behavior the results were certainly not impressive.

If the teacher did all the talking, the students had no speaking practice; if the learners did all or most of the talking, most of the utterances that impressed themselves on the learner's mind were in some way not correct. The most efficient lessons generated few correct utterances per hour of contact. You could have six correct utterances produced by a single student, and the rest of the class having said little or nothing at all. This is not surprising if you have 30 or more learners to share the talking time.

One of the reasons for the silences and mistakes was that the young learners were required to perform before their peers under pressure of time by speaking a language they did not know or had imperfectly absorbed. Some, because of individual learning styles and personality traits, performed better than others. This might have been because no single method can accommodate the infinite variations of the human brain — no two of which seem to learn in exactly the same way, since processing of the same stimulus is differently distributed between cerebral hemispheres as to both type and degree (Trocmé, 1982, 1985). But it could not be said that in this context each learner acquired the language to the best of his or her capacity within the time allotted. If we were to offer an option to this type of teaching, it had to be something other than a new textbook or method. It had to be based on the rectification of observed deficiencies in the system, and consequently on a different rationale. The rationale was to include the following: (1) Give individual learners time to absorb the language you expect them to use; (2) let each advance according to individual capacities and interest; (3) make maximal individual use of the time available.

It would also have to be different from traditional teaching in respects other than an immediate comprehension objective. It would need to have the following features:

- Graded content and staged skills.
- Interest individualized through variety of choice.
- Self-paced and not class-placed.
- Self-motivation and not teacher-motivation.
- Self-reliance and not teacher-reliance.
- High quality input and not simply peer-input.
- Maximum exposure per classroom hour.

It had to be realistic, operational, effective, affordable and compatible with school schedules. These were the features we set out to develop.

After a year of planning, materials acquisition, development and dry-runs, we came up with a program of staged multimedia self-directed second language acquisition.

## Multimedia Self-Directed Second Language Acquisition

Although the staging of the skills became quite elaborate, it followed the general order of listening, reading, listening–speaking and reading–writing. For materials, we literally considered everything on the world market, including a lot of excellent out-of-print or out-of-stock material — books, tapes, videos and software. This material was computer-analysed for language level and difficulty, graded and re-graded into levels, and within each level into menus each containing a selection of material of roughly the same degree of difficulty. For each menu the aim was to supply the most abundant selection possible, so as to give to each learner the maximum freedom of choice according to interest and ability. From the beginning all texts were accompanied with a corresponding audio cassette. After picking an interesting text, each young learner (aged eight and up) through individual headphone and independently of others, was free to listen and look, listen and read, listen only or read only, for as long or as little, as fast or as slow, as each found it necessary or still interesting. There was no language teaching (Mackey, 1987).

Instead there was a self-directed program with the following characteristics:

- The first was emphasis on language learning and direct contact with the new language. This contrasted with teacher-based methods in which language lessons, indeed languages, are processed by the teacher before learners obtain direct access to the language.
- The second characteristic was based on the idea that the learners, even small children, should take responsibility for their own learning. Individualization was therefore unavoidable. It consequently became necessary to make sure that the classroom environment was conducive to learning. Needed was a climate of free, relaxed, indeed effortless learning, and elimination of such negative elements as: (1) competition, (2) intimidation and authoritarianism, (3) conditioning of pupils to be dependent.

- Thirdly, each skill and skill combination was progressively introduced, i.e. staged. Once introduced it was both maintained as an independent skill, transformed and linked with other skills. Work on each skill proceeded according to steps related to other sub-skills.
- Fourthly, use of now widespread and generally available technology. The technology, not teachers, handled the repetitive and physically exhaustive work. The technology took the wear and tear, while permitting (1) individualization and (2) the transmission of the most interesting recorded productions.

Most of the hundreds of illustrated books at the learner's disposal were appended to accompanying audio-cassettes that the children could listen to as they read. The sources included ESL materials, language arts and social studies materials, library books and magazines. Types of books covered:

- story-line illustrated readers;
- illustrated non-fiction;
- textbooks in which only parts were selected;
- illustrated dictionaries;
- 'giant-size' readers;
- in-house photocopied materials.

Video was introduced after the initial reading/listening stage. The learners were in front of the television between two and three times a week. Currently there are some 300 episodes and/or individual video titles in the program. The video programs include TV-Ontario and the Canadian National Film Board productions as well as such series as 'The Secret Garden', 'The DeGrassi Kids' and 'Anne of Green Gables'. Most video is narrative in nature. The focus is on the subject matter, not on the new language itself.

From the very start, learners, including small school children, were expected to organize their own work. They chose their materials, and kept track of the work they had done. For this purpose, learners used individualized control sheets.

After four years of experimentation, field observations lead to expected and some unexpected findings, notably that children can learn a second language in the absence of trained specialized second language teaching staff or native speakers; that the approach lends itself to heterogeneous groupings of learners. It is possible to speculate from this that it is certainly conceivable to have pupils of different chronological ages; from different school grade levels; and having vastly different language proficiency — ranging from beginners to bilinguals — in the same program; — that is, studying together at the same time in the same room.

Other observations: Large classes were no problem. In 1990, we combined Grades 7, 8 and 9 — three classes of 30 learners each. Schools report a marked reduction in discipline problems in the experimental classes. Anyone, including parents and outsiders, can visit classes at any time without disturbing the work of the learners. Teachers report increasing requests for more books to read.

Once they got used to the approach, teachers were almost unanimously supportive and relaxed. Their main concern was not being able to assess regularly the children's learning — that is, to give tests and to correct work. In general, the teachers seemed to take pride in their project classes. ESL specialists were especially supportive.

Main problems encountered: (1) periodic internal evaluation is the biggest concern at the local level; (2) ongoing equipment repair, especially headsets; (3) as the approach is quite different from traditional classroom experience and orthodox teaching, there are people who are skeptical about its effectiveness; it is a controversial project; (4) a silent period worries people; (5) development is a time consuming activity. It takes time on the part of the Department to put together the components and the materials; (6) it requires keeping a lot of material in order within the classroom, as well as on order within the Department.

Since this was such a revolutionary concept of classroom learning, the Education Ministry did not decide to adopt it without some thoroughgoing and rigorous experimentation supplying hard evidence on its comparative effectiveness.

The Evaluation and Measurement Department of the Education Ministry who were given this task saw to it that the experimental design, the measurement and the evaluation be done independently of the designers and implementers of the new program. To this end, they commissioned an ongoing, long-term external evaluation from outside the province, from a research center that had not previously heard of the project and had had nothing to do with its development. It was the TESL Center at Concordia University in Montreal that was given this task, with an initial three-year mandate. The researchers succeeded in developing a powerful and rigorous experimental design comprising not only the school but also the community, including measurements of previous and ongoing out-of-class exposure to the two languages coupled with pretests to establish comparable control groups in varying contexts. Over a three-year period, volumes of test results were accumulated in addition to term tests and final post-tests. The results after the first three years were reported by the director of the research team, Patsy Lightbown (1988 and forthcoming). They proved good enough to convince the Ministry to continue the experiment, to expand it and to extend it to the higher grades.

By 1990, in more than a hundred classrooms and control groups, there were some three thousand learners from Grade 3 to Grade 12 in most Acadian areas of the province involved in this new self-learning program. At the same time, some exploratory experimentation had been under way to extend the program through Grade 12 and the end of secondary school. Requests for information were so numerous that in 1989 the Ministry decided to put out a brochure in English and in French describing the structure and development of the new program (Ministère de l'Education, 1990).[1]

## Implications for Bilingualism and Education

Should this multimedia self-directed language acquisition program prove to be a viable option, it might have implications for those areas where bilingual education has as yet remained unfeasible, or for plurilingual classrooms, or for classes with learners at different levels, or for schools without qualified native teachers, or for individuals who learn better when free from regimentation. In school rooms where learners have been put into groups not of their own making, the overriding motif has often become one of conformity and compliance at the expense of learning and the individual pursuit of knowledge. There may be

some wider implications. For our model is not one of transmission and control. It is rather an individual growth model as opposed to a production one. It is analogous to letting trees grow as opposed to manufacturing them, to gardening as opposed to food production, to culture as opposed to technique. It is a holistic approach rather than an analytic one. In a growth model, if the soil (context) is rich enough, many things happen at the same time at different levels within the same individual. Like the work of the artisan with the apprentice, the outcome is what counts. Problems are solved in context as they arise. You learn as you go. It is essentially product-oriented. Contrariwise, a production model has to be process-oriented. It requires conformity and specialization, uniformity and compliance. One learns to do one thing in one way at one time. That is why it is better suited to technology than it is to culture, more appropriate for techniques requiring the control of behavior then it is for the multivariate activities related to language and free expression. Often the need for compliance is achieved at the expense of learning. Operating within the hierarchical structure of public education our program has so far succeeded in reducing the use of learning as a tool for the control of behavior.

### Note

1. This brochure, 'An Experiment in Staged Self-Directed Language Acquisition' (English), 'Projet expérimental d'auto-acquisition par étapes de la langue seconde: programme multimédia d'anglais' (French), is available from: Ministère de l'Education du Nouveau Brunswick, Box 6000, Fredericton, N-B. E3B 5H1, Canada.

### References

Huot, D. (1988) *Etude comparative de différents modes d'enseignement/apprentissage d'une language seconde; Aspects de l'intégration des pédagogies des langues maternelle et seconde pour un public adulte.* Berne: Peter Lang.

Lightbown, P. (forthcoming) Can they do it themselves? A comprehension-based ESL course for young children. *Proceedings of a Conference on Comprehension-based Language Teaching, Ottawa, 11-13 May, 1989.*

Lightbown, P. and Halter, R.H. (1988) *Evaluation of ESL Learning in Regular and Experimental Programs in Four New Brunswick School Districts.*

Vol. 1: 1985–1986/1986/1987; Vol. 2: 1987–1988. Montreal: Concordia University TESL Centre.

Mackey, W.F. (1987) Is language teaching a waste of time? Epilgue to Mackey *et al.*

Mackey, W.F., Loveless, G., Louisy, P. and Heechung, V. (1987) *Polychronometric Techniques in Behaviour Analysis: Language Teaching* (ICRB Publication B-163). Quebec: International Center for Research on Bilingualism.

Ministère de l'Education du Nouveau-Brunswick (1990) *An Experiment in Staged Self-directed Language Acquisition.* New Brunswick.

Trocmé, Helène (1982) La conscientisation de l'appren-
    ant dans l'apprentissage d'une langue étrangère.
    *Revue de Phonétique Appliquée* 161–63, 253–67.

— (1985) Brain research and human learning.
    *Revue de Phonétique Appliquée* 73–75, 303–
    15.

## Questions

(1) Who are the Acadians and what was Acadia? Locate where the region is today on a map.

(2) Mackey tell us that in an effort to develop the bilingualism of their children in the 1970s, Anglophones in New Brunswick started organizing immersion programs in French. But immersion programs were not suitable to develop the bilingualism of the Francophone Acadians in the more French-speaking areas of New Brunswick because, as Mackey says, the parents were 'trying to restore the balance of bilingualism without taking away from the level of mother-tongue competence achieved in school.' Explain what Mackey means by that statement and why immersion programs were not indicated.

(3) As an alternative to immersion, Mackey proposed a 'program of staged multimedia self-directed second language acquisition.' List the main features of the program, including rationale, features, emphases and materials used.
    What are the advantages of this program? How effective has it been? What have been the problems it has encountered?
    Could a program such as this work in your community? Why or why not?

(4) Explain what Mackey means when he says that the self-directed language acquisition program is 'not one of transmission and control' and that it has 'succeeded in reducing the use of learning as a tool for the control of behavior'? How does this relate to Freire's concept of 'critical pedagogy' or to the 'reciprocal interaction-oriented pedagogy' proposed by Cummins?

## Activities

(1) Read Longfellow's *Evangeline*. Find other literary treatments of hardships experienced by another ethnolinguistic group. Make an oral report to your class on the tragedy of the Acadian diaspora and on the other literary work you read.

(2) Try to find out about a self-directed learning program in your area. Describe how it operates, and what teachers' and students' attitudes toward the program are. In particular, find out if language minority students have different attitudes from language majority students towards this self-directed learning. Also, find out if there are differences in outcome between language majority and language minority students.

# Cooperative Learning: Instructing Limited-English-Proficient Students in Heterogenous Classes

## Evelyn Jacob and Beverly Mattson

A major educational challenge is to help students with limited English proficiency to achieve academically and to develop the language skills necessary to successfully function in classrooms. Schools face a special challenge when students comprise diverse language groups at varying levels of English proficiency. How can these diverse needs be met?

In this chapter we discuss cooperative learning methods as a solution to the dilemma faced by teachers with heterogeneous classrooms that include limited-English-proficient (LEP) students. These heterogeneous classes may include students at different grade levels, from different language backgrounds, or with different levels of English language proficiency. We draw on theory, research, and interviews we conducted with teachers across the country.

### What is Cooperative Learning?

In cooperative learning students work together in small groups — two to six members — that are positively interdependent (Kagan, 1986). Positive interdependence means that the achievement of any team member contributes to the rewards of all.

Cooperative learning involves two primary features: cooperative task structures and cooperative reward structures. Cooperative task structures are those in which two or more individuals 'are allowed, encouraged, or required to work together on some task' (Slavin, 1983: 5). This contrasts with independent task structures, where mutual assistance is impossible or forbidden. Cooperative reward structures are those in which two or more individuals are 'in a situation where the task related efforts of any individual helps others to be rewarded' (Slavin, 1983: 4). This

contrasts with competitive or individualistic reward structures. In competitive reward structures, one person's success is another's failure, while in individualistic reward structures, one person's performance has no influence on another's reward.

Cooperative learning methods contrast with both whole class methods and with small group methods. Whole class teaching methods usually involve neither cooperative task structure nor cooperative reward structure. Instead, students usually are required to work alone with either a competitive or an individualistic reward system. Learning in small groups is not necessarily cooperative. Although small group methods may employ a cooperative task structure in which students work together on some task or project, the reward structure may be competitive or individualistic.

### Types of Cooperative Learning

While all cooperative learning methods share cooperative task and reward structures, there are various types of cooperative learning methods. Kagan (1985a) divides cooperative learning methods between those that apply across various subject areas and grade levels and those that apply only to specific subject matter and grade levels. Cooperative learning methods that can be applied across subject areas and grade levels include the following (see Kagan, 1985a, 1985b, 1986).

#### Peer practice

In this approach, group members drill and assist one another in learning predetermined content (for example, vocabulary words or math facts) with the aim of bringing each to his or her highest level. In some instances, the group members cooperate to compete against other groups. Examples of peer practice methods are Student Teams Achievement Divisions (STAD) and Teams-Games-Tournaments (TGT) (Slavin, 1986).

### Jigsaw

In this approach, all groups are given the same task — for example, mastering a learning unit or document. Within a 'home' group each member is given primary responsibility for a unique part of the unit or document. Each student works with members from other home groups who have responsibility for the same content. After working in these 'expert' groups, the students return to their home groups to teach them the material in which they are expert. Students are then evaluated on their mastery of the entire unit. Examples are original Jigsaw and Jigsaw II (Aronson, Blaney, Stephan, Sikes & Snapp, 1978; Slavin, 1986).

### Cooperative Projects

In the Cooperative Projects approach, students work to produce a group project that they may have selected from several options. Usually, individuals within each group make a unique contribution to the group's efforts. In addition, groups frequently make unique contributions to the class as a whole without overt between-group competition. Examples of cooperative project methods are Group Investigation (Sharan & Hertz-Lazarowitz, 1979) and Co-op Co-op (Kagan, 1985a, 1985b).

### Learning Together

Learning Together is a framework for applying cooperative learning principles (Johnson & Johnson, 1975; Johnson, Johnson, Holubec & Roy, 1984). It does not have a specific method of organization but outlines decisions teachers need to make to apply cooperative learning. It emphasizes positive interdependence among students, individual accountability, and students' use of collaborative skills.

There also are several curriculum-specific approaches that vary widely in their organization. *Finding Out/Descubrimiento* is a science and math curriculum for Spanish-English bilingual students in grades two and three (DeAvila, Duncan & Navarrete, 1987). Team Assisted Individualization (TAI) is a math program for grades two through seven (Slavin, 1985). Rotation

Science Centers (RSC) is a science curriculum for grade three and upward (Kagan, 1985a). Cooperative Integrated Reading and Composition (CIRC) is a reading and writing program for grades three and four (Slavin, 1986). While TAI, RSC, and CIRC can be used with LEP students, these materials are only available in English.

## Cooperative Learning and LEP Students

To learn more about how cooperative learning methods are used with LEP students, we interviewed 17 teachers and 12 school administrators across the United States. These persons self-identified or were identified by others in response to announcements in newsletters indicating our interest in interviewing individuals who were experienced in using cooperative learning methods with LEP students. We conducted open-ended telephone interviews, asking teachers about their use of cooperative learning methods and asking administrators about the implementation of cooperative learning in their districts or schools.

We found that only recently have cooperative learning methods been explicitly used with LEP students. Moreover, while the approach has been implemented by districts for LEP students in a few states (California and Oregon), in the rest of the country the approach has been implemented primarily by individual teachers.

Individual teachers used cooperative learning most often where English was the language of instruction and the language of communication among the students. The classes frequently were ESL or sheltered English classes with LEP students representing a variety of language backgrounds, or they were self-contained regular curriculum classes with both native English speakers and LEP students.

All classes were characterized by considerable student heterogeneity. The number of different ethnolinguistic groups per teacher ranged from 2 to 13, with an average of 6 groups. Moreover, teachers typically had more than one grade level in their classes and a wide range of levels of English proficiency. In some classes there were native English speakers as well as LEP students.

Cooperative learning methods were used in all grade levels, from pre-kindergarten through adult education. While English and language arts were the most frequent subjects in which cooperative learning methods were used, they were also used in other academic and nonacademic subjects.

## Effects of Cooperative Learning Methods

Teachers were enthusiastic in their support of cooperative learning methods. Almost all of the teachers we interviewed reported increases in their students' English language proficiency. Most reported improvement in academic achievement or student learning and in social relations among students. Several teachers also mentioned psychological benefits for individual students.

### English proficiency

Teachers reported that students increased their English vocabulary and usage, and that students 'blossomed out' and were more confident in English. In addition, teachers felt that cooperative learning promoted spontaneous conversations among students and provided students more learning opportunities in English. These positive evaluations are exemplified through one teacher's written evaluation of one of her lessons that used a peer practice approach: 'I was astonished by the amount of dedication to task, the ease of instruction on the part of the [tutors] and the concentration and total attention of the [tutees]... I could not believe the amount of English paraphrasing I heard.'

Some teachers also mentioned that students' contributions to discussions in classes had increased. For example, one teacher said that students talked more, expressed more ideas in class, and generally contributed more to discussions.

The teachers' reports are consistent with current theory and research. Cooperative learning provides opportunities for face-to-face interaction among students around school tasks, which theory suggests is important for second-language acquisition (Krashen, 1981). Research indicates that cooperative learning methods resulted in greater improvement in English proficiency than traditional whole class methods (Bejarano, 1987; DeAvila & Duncan, 1977, as reported in Cohen, 1986; Sharan *et al.*, 1985).

### Academic achievement

Three-fourths of the teachers reported that cooperative learning had a positive effect on students' academic achievement. Generally, teachers felt that students were performing better on class work and on quizzes. In particular, they stated that they had observed a higher quality of student learning, that students had greater reten-

tion and consolidation of material, and that students learned more from each other.

The teachers' reports are substantiated by research. There is strong and consistent evidence that cooperative learning raises the academic achievement of students in general (Slavin, 1983). Moreover, there is strong evidence, although from a limited number of studies, that cooperative learning raises the academic achievement of ethnic minority students (Lucker, Rosenfield, Sikes & Aronson, 1976; Slavin, 1977; Slavin & Oickle, 1981).

### Social relations

In reporting better social relationships among students, teachers noted more praise and supportive comments among students (rather than put-downs or sharp criticisms), closer group feelings, and less competition. Teachers also commented on the benefits of cooperative learning for relationships between native English-speaking students and LEP students. They reported changes in attitudes toward minority students and cultural awareness as well as increases in cross-cultural help and cooperation.

Again the literature supports the teachers' reports. Cooperation promotes greater interpersonal attraction among heterogeneous individuals than do interpersonal competition and individualistic efforts (Johnson, Johnson & Maruyama, 1983).

### Psychological adjustment

Several teachers mentioned affective benefits for individual students, such as improved motivation, positive attitudes toward classes and school, and increased self-esteem and self-confidence. Teachers also reported less absenteeism and fewer discipline problems.

Although this topic has been less thoroughly researched than the previous ones, the literature lends support to the teachers' comments. Johnson, Johnson & Maruyama (1983) conclude that cooperative learning situations seem to promote higher levels of self-esteem than do competitive and individualistic situations.

## Difficulties in Using Cooperative Learning

Some teachers we interviewed commented about the difficulties they experienced in implementing cooperative learning methods. The changes in the teacher's role and the social structure of the class required by cooperative learning methods involved some readjustment for many teachers. They also felt that cooperative learning methods require more teacher time in planning, preparation, and implementation in the initial stages. Some teachers reported difficulties in trying to use cooperative learning methods within the confines of class and school schedules without commercially available materials.

Several teachers also commented on problems in forming and maintaining the groups. They said that organizing heterogeneous groups by gender, ethnic group, achievement level, and level of English language proficiency can be complicated. Maintaining groups often requires much effort by teachers because of clashes in students' personalities within groups or because of the need to integrate students who are 'loners' or non-English speakers.

## Training and Support Needed

Teachers made suggestions concerning the training and information needed to implement cooperative learning methods with LEP students. They said that training should be longer than the typical one to three days of workshops, and that the instructors should use cooperative learning methods to present the workshops. The teachers wanted explicit help in integrating cooperative learning methods with language acquisition theory and research. They wanted to know how to implement cooperative learning methods in a way that follows principles of effective instruction for LEP students. The teachers also suggested that presentations of cooperative learning methods should include specific examples of lessons under each approach and explanations of similarities and differences among the approaches. Further, they wanted to know how to adapt cooperative learning methods for students of different cultural backgrounds and different levels of English proficiency, for different kinds of content or activities, and for different kinds of class schedules. Finally, they were interested in learning about commercially available materials and about ways to teach group process skills to their students.

Teachers felt that successful implementation of cooperative learning requires ongoing training and support after they begin implementing the methods. This could include coaching, support group meetings, and networking with others using the methods. They felt it was important to realize that successful implementation takes a commitment of time and resources, especially at the beginning, to develop activities.

Support from building- and district-level administrators is also crucial (Ellis, 1987). An innovation such as cooperative learning is most likely to Work when administrators provide support such as released time, encouragement, and validation (Ellis, 1987). Moreover, administrators need to understand cooperative learning methods in order to provide helpful and valid evaluations. These suggestions are consistent with the general literature on training (Joyce & Showers, 1982).

## Deciding Which Cooperative Learning Method to Use

Cooperative learning methods can be used in any type of program and with a wide variety of academic and nonacademic subjects. Teachers need not select just *one* method. Many teachers use more than one approach with their students. The specific methods selected will depend on a teacher's instructional goals — both for subject matter and for communication experiences in English. Teachers may also take into account their objectives for the development of students' collaborative skills; the ages, ethnicity, and levels of English proficiency of their students; the time allotted to a unit; and the daily schedule for an activity.

### Subject matter instructional goals

Peer practice methods appear best suited for learning basic skills and information. Jigsaw methods are useful for mastering text, while cooperative project approaches are useful for analytic and creative thinking. Learning Together emphasizes the development of interpersonal and group skills (see Kagan, 1985a).

### Communication goals

In peer practice approaches, students assume roles of tutor and tutee, with much of the interaction focused around drill and practice. In Jigsaw approaches, students may assume the additional roles of expert consultant or team leader. Interactions in Jigsaw may include expert presentations, discussion and analysis among experts, and tutoring. In cooperative project approaches, students' roles are expanded further to include investigator and resource gatherer. Interactions may become more complex and may include planning, decision making, critical analysis and synthesis, and creativity (see Kagan, 1985b).

## Implementing Cooperative Learning

After selecting an appropriate method, teachers need to prepare the necessary materials and arrange the room to facilitate cooperative group work. This might involve developing study sheets and quiz sheets for peer practice approaches, or dividing up a text assignment into parts for a Jigsaw approach. Rearranging the furniture may include placing tables and chairs in circles, clusters, or pairs in discrete areas around the room. There should also be areas in which students can store their in-process projects.

Teachers need to divide the class into groups of two to six members, depending on the cooperative learning method chosen. Teachers generally use one of two methods: teacher-selected assignments or random assignments. With teacher-selected assignments, most approaches suggest that groups be heterogeneous with regard to factors such as ability, gender, native language, and English language proficiency.

Initially, teachers should establish guidelines on how groups will function. For example, students might be told that each group member should assist other members of the group with understanding the material or completing the project.

After explaining the task and desired behaviors, teachers need to monitor and intervene in groups, both for the accomplishment of academic tasks and for desired collaborative behavior. In some instances, teachers may need to assist students in resolving group difficulties.

After the groups have finished their work, they can be evaluated on task performance and on the way the groups functioned. Some teachers lead discussions about students' perceptions of the groups' processes and functioning.

## Conclusion

The practical experience of teachers and administrators suggests that cooperative learning methods are an important approach in heterogeneous classes of LEP students. For successful implementation and long-term use, training teachers to use cooperative learning methods needs to be carried out over a long period of time, with intervening help and support from colleagues and administrators.

### References

Aronson, E., Blaney, N., Stephan, C., Sikes, J. and Snapp, M. (1978) *The Jigsaw Classroom*. Beverly Hills, CA: Sage.

Bejarano, Y. (1987). A cooperative small-group methodology in the language classroom. *TESOL Quarterly* 21, 483–504.

Cohen, E. G. (1986) *Designing Groupwork: Strategies for the Heterogeneous Classroom*. New York: Teachers College Press.

DeAvila, E.A., Duncan, S.E. and Navarrete, C.J. (1987) *Finding Out/Descubrimiento: Teacher's Resource Guide*. Northvale, NJ: Santillana.

Ellis, S. (1987) Introducing cooperative learning groups: A district-wide effort. Paper presented at the annual meeting of the American Educational Research Association, Washington, DC.

Johnson, D.W. and Johnson, R. (1975) *Learning Together and Alone: Cooperation, Competition, and Individualization*. Englewood Cliffs, NJ: Prentice-Hall.

Johnson, D.W., Johnson, R., Holubec, E.J. and Roy, P. (1984) *Circles of Learning: Cooperation in the Classroom*. Alexandria, VA: Association for Supervision and Curriculum Development.

Johnson, D.W., Johnson, R.T. and Maruyama, G. (1983) Interdependence and interpersonal attraction among heterogeneous and homogeneous individuals: A theoretical formulation and a meta-analysis of research. *Review of Educational Research* 53, 5–54.

Joyce, B. and Showers, B. (1982) The coaching of teaching. *Educational Leadership* 40 (1), 4–10.

Kagan, S. (1985a) *Cooperative Learning Resouces for Teachers*. Riverside: University of California, Printing and Reprographics.

— (1985b) Dimensions of cooperative classroom structures. In R. Slavin *et al.* (eds) *Learning to Cooperate, Cooperating to Learn* (pp. 67–96). New York: Plenum.

— (1986) Cooperative learning and sociocultural factors in schooling. In Bilingual Education Office, California State Department of Education *Beyond Language: Social and Cultural Factors in Schooling Language Minority Students* (pp. 231–98). Los Angeles: California State University, Evaluation, Dissemination and Assessment Center.

Krashen, S. (1981) *Second Language Acquisition and Second Language Learning*. Oxford: Pergamon.

Lucker, G., Rosenfield, D., Sikes, J. and Aronson, E. (1976) Performance in the interdependent classroom: A field study. *American Educational Research Journal* 13, 115–23.

Sharan, S. and Hertz-Lazarowitz, R. (1979) A group-investigation method of cooperative learning in the classroom. In S. Sharan, P. Hare, C. D. Webb and R. Hertz-Lazarowitz (eds) *Co-

*operation in Education* (pp. 14–46). Provo, UT: Brigham Young University Press.

Sharan, S., Kussell, P., Hertz-Lazarowitz, R., Bejarano, Y., Raviv, S. and Sharan, Y. (1985) Cooperative learning effects on ethnic relations and achievement in Israeli junior high school classrooms. In R. Slavin *et al.* (eds) *Learning to Cooperate, Cooperating to Learn* (pp. 313–44). New York: Plenum.

Slavin, R. (1977) *Student Learning Team Techniques: Narrowing the Achievement Gap Between the Races* (Report No. 228). Baltimore, MD: Johns Hopkins University, Center for Social Organization of the Schools.

— (1983) *Cooperative Learning*. New York: Longman.

— (1985) Team-assisted individualization: Combining cooperative learning and individualized instruction in mathematics. In R. Slavin *et al.* (eds) *Learning to Cooperate, Cooperating to Learn* (pp. 177–209). New York: Plenum.

— (1986) *Using Student Team Learning: The Johns Hopkins Team Learning Project*. Baltimore, MD: Johns Hopkins University, Center for Research on Elementary and Middle Schools.

Slavin, R. and Oickle, E. (1981) Effects of cooperative learning teams on student achievement and race relations: Treatment by race interactions. *Sociology of Education* 54, 174–180.

## Questions

(1) What is cooperative learning and what does being positively interdependent mean? How does it differ from whole class and and small group activity? Define the following cooperative learning methods:
  (a) Peer practice.
  (b) Jigsaw.
  (c) Cooperative projects.
  (d) Learning together.

(2) Describe how cooperative learning in the second language classroom can be useful with linguistically heterogeneous students. List the students' outcomes that Jacob and Mattson found with cooperative learning methods. Are cooperative learning methods also useful in second language classrooms with a linguistically homogeneous population? Explain how and why.

(3) Is cooperative learning equally useful in all content instruction? Is it equally useful in primary, secondary and tertiary education? What do you think?

## Activities

(1) Reflect on your experiences with cooperative learning (either as a student or a teacher) and describe them briefly. Make ten statements about such experiences (making sure that you define yourself as a student or a teacher). Compile a list of the ten statements that best describe students' experiences with cooperative learning. Then compile another list for teachers' experiences.

(2) Find out more about any of the following cooperative learning methods: Student Teams Achievement Division (STAD), Teams-Games-Tournaments (TGT), Jigsaw and Jigsaw II, Group Investigation, Co-op Co-op, Finding Out/Descubrimiento, Team Assisted Individualization (TAI), Rotation Science Centers (RSC), Cooperative Integrated Reading and Composition (CIRC). Plan a lesson using one of the cooperative learning methods above. Role-play a fifteen-minute session with you as the teacher. Then evaluate the experience.

(3) Observe a classroom in which the teacher is relatively an expert in using cooperative learning. Describe the room arrangement, the material used, the arrangement of materials and the grouping of students. What training has the teacher received? What support is available to her?

# Creative Education for Bilingual Teachers

## Alma Flor Ada

Schools today, and teachers in particular, are under a great deal of criticism. Bilingual teachers, caught between the accepted practices they are required to follow and the sound theories and research that contradict those practices, are especially vulnerable to attack. Most bilingual teachers were not educated in bilingual programs, nor have they had the experience of teaching in bilingual schools that receive full societal support. In many instances they themselves have been victims of language oppression and racism; thus, in order to empower their students to overcome conditions of domination and oppression, they must first be empowered themselves. This paper, based on reflections of bilingual teachers in US schools, will analyze the nature of the teacher training process and propose elements of an empowering process for training bilingual teachers.

All teachers must contend with the uncertainties arising from the lack of societal support for their profession, but the situation is doubly difficult for bilingual teachers.[1] Education in general is often criticized, but its critics talk of improvement, not of elimination. Bilingual education, on the other hand, faces opposition from a large proportion of the population, who would willingly do away with it.

Criticism of bilingual education comes from a variety of sources. Under the pervasive influence of the misused 'melting pot' metaphor, some opponents fear that bilingual education will promote divisiveness among the general population. They see the maintenance of home languages as un-American. Other opponents, often members of language minority communities themselves, fear that participation in bilingual education will segregate and ostracize children and will jeopardize their future societal success.

### Subtractive versus Additive Bilingualism

The fear that home-language maintenance will hinder the acquisition of English is not borne out by research. Achieving high-language proficiency in English does not preclude maintaining proficiency in the mother tongue. Despite its widespread acceptance, the subtractive model of bilingualism, in which mastery of the second language is achieved at the expense of proficiency in the first, need not be the framework on which bilingual education rests. Additive bilingualism, in which a second language is acquired while maintaining and continuing to develop the first, is a healthy and viable alternative to subtractive bilingualism (Cummins, 1981, 1986; Dolson, 1985; Lambert & Tucker, 1972; Skutnabb-Kangas, 1984).

The benefits of additive bilingualism are many. Peal & Lambert's (1962) classic study suggested that having a dual repertoire to label and organize reality fosters students' cognitive flexibility. Since then, most research shows that bilingualism contributes positively to the cognitive, linguistic, and psychosocial development of children. Other, more subtle, advantages have been found; for example, enhanced metalinguistic development frequently correlates with bilingualism (for reviews, see Cummins, 1986; Dolson, 1985).

A major benefit, so obvious that it is frequently ignored, is the knowledge of two languages. There is a bitter irony in the fact that an English-speaking student may earn college credit for learning to speak another language, while a language minority child is encouraged not to use, and therefore lose, the same skill.

In addition to preserving a valuable skill, encouraging the maintenance and development of the home language can foster a bilingual student's identity and self esteem, which tend to correlate with academic success. While it is difficult to determine whether the greater success of students in bilingual programs that emphasize the use of the first language is due to better promotion of cognitive/academic skills in the

237

first language or to the reinforcement of cultural identity provided by the intensive use of the home language, Cummins (1986) states that 'considerable research data suggest that, for dominated minorities, the extent to which students' language and culture are incorporated into the school program constitutes a significant predictor of academic success' (p. 25).

Finally, it should be noted that the maintenance of the home language strengthens family and community ties. Home language maintenance enhances communication between generations. When students are encouraged to forget the language of their families and communities, they may lose access to their heritage. Frequently heard comments along the lines of, 'my parents made it without bilingual education,' disregard the significant changes that have taken place in society, and fail to take into account the grief of immigrants whose sacrifices and efforts are rewarded by estrangement from their grandchildren, with whom communication is limited, at best.

## Beyond the Use of Two Languages

I believe the views of Freire (1982a, 1982b) and Aronowitz & Giroux (1985) are correct: schools do hold out the possibility of critical analysis and reconstruction of social reality through meaningful dialogue between teachers and students, by a process termed 'transformative education.' In this paper I refer to that transformative education process, which differs from the traditional reproductive education, as *creative education*.[2] Through creative education, students learn to under stand and appreciate themselves, to use that understanding as a means of valuing the diversity of others, to reflect critically upon their experiences so that these can be a source of growth, and to respond creatively to the world around them. If bilingual students are to have an opportunity to validate their own language and culture — acknowledging both the difficulties faced by their ethnic groups and the possibilities open to them for effecting change and for making positive contributions to society — they must be participants in creative education. Only then will students and teachers be able to reclaim bilingualism as an asset for both individuals and society.[3]

Proponents of bilingual education suggest that the communicative and critical thinking skills that will empower students can best be developed, in the case of dominated minorities, through the utilization of the child's first language (Ada & de Olave, 1986; Cummins, 1986; Skutnabb-Kangas, 1984). These reasoning processes, once developed in the home language, are transferable to the second language, along with learning skills and academic content. Most important, the child's experience with success — a result of an additive approach that builds upon the child's existing knowledge — will create a positive attitude towards learning which will also be transferable to the second language.

However, if creative education is to be viable, teachers themselves must be empowered. Unfortunately, many teacher education programs seem designed to train teachers to accept social realities rather than to question them. Teachers are trained to conform to a mechanistic definition of their role rather than to recognize it as involving a relationship between human beings, with a possibility of growth for both teachers and students. As a result, teachers frequently find themselves trapped in a series of ritualistic activities — taking attendance, maintaining order, creating and following lesson plans, testing and reporting test results — with little opportunity to step back from the reality in which they are immersed in order to analyze it critically and become true agents of transformation. In short, if a creative education is to be brought about, teachers must experience it themselves.

## Bilingual Teachers' Unheard Voices

Before something like creative education is introduced to teachers, it is important to know what those teachers' experiences have been. In order to listen to the voices of bilingual teachers, I engaged in dialogue with four groups of them and discussed the problems they face daily and the ways in which teacher education programs might better address those problems. In all, thirty-eight participants contributed to these reflections.[4]

All the participants welcomed the opportunity to discuss their teacher education. When first asked what their education had given or not given them, they were extremely enthusiastic about engaging in dialogue. Typical comments were quite broad: 'We would need a year to discuss everything my teacher education failed to give me'; or 'We could write a whole book about what my teacher education didn't provide.' Yet, despite the promise of critical reflection that those initial statements held out, when the participants were asked to describe their education, they responded with a series of limited observations:

'I wasn't given any preparation for class management'; 'We were not told anything about all the bureaucratic requirements, all the forms we would have to fill out'; and 'I needed to know how to handle A/V equipment.'

As the dialogue came closer to tackling the issues and social realities they faced in their daily lives as teachers, the participants began to look at their experiences in a comprehensive way. As they realized the impact of having been led to look at their profession as a sequence of unrelated tasks, rather than as a vital life project that has impact on society, the teachers expressed recurrent themes of isolation, powerlessness, and insecurity. This realization emerged out of a broad criticism of their teacher-training programs and generated myriad questions that troubled these teachers: If children really benefit from learning in their mother tongue, why should we put a ceiling on how much first-language instruction they receive? What varieties of the home language are acceptable in the classroom? How much of their cultural heritage do children need in order to develop self-esteem? Should education be neutral, free from political implications? Will children not have a better chance of survival if they are taught to be 'good Americans' rather than to question the ethics of the country they live in? How will children fare if they are exposed to creative education and helped to develop as critical thinkers for a brief period, and then later forced to return to a traditional style of education?

Although these questions were raised out of concern for the children, the questions by no means applied only to them. The questions had to do as well with the teachers' own identities, their ideologies and beliefs, their use of language, their culture, and the social realities that surrounded them. The concerns they expressed about the children reflected their own concerns about themselves as teachers in schools that often devalue their work because they are members of cultural groups that are often socially invisible.

## Isolation

The absence of support for bilingual education in the society at large reinforces the perception of many bilingual teachers that support is flagging within their own schools. Administrators and monolingual teachers, while applying pressure to have language minority students mainstreamed as soon as possible, often attack bilingual teachers

for the lack of success of those very children who have been prematurely required to perform in a language whose mastery threshold they have not yet reached (Cummins, 1981).

The importance of peer support was mentioned in every group discussion. The mistaken perception of bilingual education as non-prestigious makes peer support networks among bilingual teachers a necessity. One, in suggesting that teacher education programs should encourage future teachers to develop such support mechanisms, said that 'especially in non-prestigious areas like bilingual education, it is imperative to receive affirmation from one's peers.' The lack of peer support — and their being 'locked' in classrooms with little interaction with the rest of the school, the district, and the community — results in a feeling of isolation among teachers in general, and bilingual teachers in particular.

All the groups agreed on the need for interaction with parents and community so as to involve them in the educational process. One teacher suggested that teacher education programs should include inservices from community leaders. Another pointed out that the need is twofold: to involve the community in the educational process and to get teachers involved in community action. A third teacher suggested that teacher education programs should include a form of internship in community projects so that teachers might gain a holistic view of the community and become involved in wider societal issues. In addition, all the groups saw education and teaching as political activities, and they considered it desirable for teachers to be politically aware.

## Sense of Inadequacy in Language Mastery

Since language performance plays a major role in the perception that others have of us and thus may affect our personal and professional success, feeling inadequate in the use of language is a painful experience. Bilingual teachers may feel inadequate in their language ability because of several factors. Those teachers whose mother tongue is English may not have had the opportunity to acquire full mastery of a second language — a sad reflection on our limited and deficient foreign language teaching. Members of language minorities who chose to become bilingual teachers may also have been victims of language oppression as children, when they were scolded or punished in school for using their home language. Therefore it should not be surprising that many bilingual teachers lack confidence in their literacy skills. Yet if these individuals can acknowledge that the language inadequacy they experience stems from deeply rooted institutionalized oppression and is highlighted by the one-teacher model, they will be better able to understand what their students may be going through.[5] Instead of reproducing a negative outcome, these teachers' past experiences can serve as a positive, constructive example. However, in order to free teachers from feelings of inadequacy, we must examine the reasons for language limitations and then discuss ways to overcome them.

Future bilingual teachers would benefit from an opportunity to live, study, and, perhaps, teach in a country where the language they will be teaching is spoken. Spending a few months in such an environment might be an ideal way to recapture, or to master, their language. This exposure might be beneficial in other ways as well. A successful bilingual teacher in one of the groups said the most valuable part of her teacher training had been the incentive it provided for her to visit and teach in Peru and Mexico. Observing different life styles, interacting with people in other countries, and having to teach under conditions very different from those she had always known gave her greater flexibility and creativity. She stated that she could better innovate because of her first-hand knowledge of diverse situations, and she derives strength from her experiences in unfamiliar places; she also feels the need to adopt a critical outlook because she has a new perception of the sociopolitical reality of the children who come to her classroom.

## Powerlessness

The lack of opportunity to explore conflicting issues in a psychologically-safe climate often leads to denial, defensiveness, and, most especially, powerlessness. Indeed, powerlessness was one of the recurring themes in all four discussion groups. Although the participants felt at first that their powerlessness stemmed from isolation and feelings of inadequacy, further examination revealed that the deeper causes were the interactive forces between the schools, the community, and the larger society.

The participants recognized that parents ought to be involved in the educational process because they are genuinely concerned about their children's education. For the most part, however,

adequate mechanisms are not in place to facilitate real parent participation. Since parents are often perceived by the school authorities as uneducated and ineffective, they are given a limited role in decision making. In addition, parents sometimes withdraw their support of bilingual programs by choosing to take their children out of them or by discouraging the use of the home language. This lack of support increases the frustration felt by teachers. It is not widely understood by the teachers that parents withdraw support because they have internalized the negative view towards bilingual education that is widespread in society.

## Uncertainty Regarding Cultural Identity

To their feelings of powerlessness and language inadequacy many bilingual teachers add their own conflicts regarding their identity. In spite of the fact that the American society claims to respect the ideals of equality, diversity, and inclusion, the reality for language minority people has been inequality, the push for conformity to one standard, and exclusion. One of the greatest contradictions confronting minorities is that society urges them to become mainstream and thereby abandon their language and cultural traditions, but even after they assume the views and behavior of the majority culture in hope of increased acceptance, they often continue to be victimized by the same forces that compelled their conformity.

In the case of some Hispanics, the question of self-identity is doubly complicated. As one teacher explained: 'One of the great puzzlements of my childhood was hearing my barrio cousins and friends say in school that they were Spaniards, not Mexicans. Because my father used to tell stories about how cruel and blood thirsty the Spaniards had been and how they had destroyed the Indian civilizations, I could not believe that any of my classmates would want to call themselves Spaniards. To this day I am troubled by the fact that my home language is Spanish.' This painful experience — of having a mixed heritage in which one represents the dominator and the other the dominated — is not uncommon among Hispanics. It is an unresolved issue felt throughout Latin America. Every one of us who has Spanish-speaking parents or grandparents in this hemisphere is a *mestizo*, either ethnically or culturally.

Guillén (1972) proposes a solution in a powerfully poetic image. By accepting his mixed heritage, he manages to unite the shadows of his two grandparents, the Spanish warrior and the African slave.[6] Such an acceptance would help us to keep in mind past inequities and the valuable lessons the knowledge of these past inequities provides. This knowledge would allow us to accept ourselves as a whole and give us the strength to struggle against present-day oppressors, who obviously are not the Spaniards of today.

In any case, these are issues that need to be addressed during the creative education process, since they strongly affect the Hispanic teacher's sense of identity and thus limit the ability to model self-worth for children.

## The Need to Integrate Theory and Experience

The participants saw the need for teacher education programs to integrate solid theory and ample experience in a mutually supportive manner. Many of them described their own educational experience as highly mechanistic. According to one teacher, 'All we were told was how to set goals and objectives and how to write lesson plans. I wrote more than a hundred lesson plans, but I knew nothing about the classroom.' Another teacher's complaint was that 'all courses dealt with the ideal student, as if all students would be alike. We never heard anything about the students as real individuals.' A third teacher said, 'They gave us seminar syndrome. We never had the opportunity to experiment and explore. Now we do the same thing with our students. A lot of teaching goes on, but very little learning.'

This brings us to the most crucial issue. Participants in all groups said that although they were very much concerned about the need to develop critical thinking in their students, they wanted to learn how to empower themselves first. The strongest criticism of teacher education was directed at the discrepancy between what the faculty in the schools of education taught and what they practiced. One participant expressed the shared complaint in this way: 'They preached to us to teach creatively, but we were never allowed any creativity. They encouraged us to be good communicators, but the classes they taught were deadly. There was some lip service paid to the need for encouraging children to think, but we were expected to memorize and repeat.'

Creative education recognizes that the process of learning is more than the accumulation of information. Some teachers came to this recognition on their own. One teacher said, 'My teacher training wasn't great; the content was too remote. But I did get something — I learned myself. I learned how to learn, how to develop learning skills, how to organize my own learning style, and this has been the most useful thing for me.' In discussing what a creative teacher education program should provide, another teacher commented, 'It would offer the opportunity to look inside, to find their own biases, to learn not to be afraid of sharing intimacies and their own experiences. Students may not learn content, but they learn the teacher; they learn how to emulate the teacher. It is important to provide opportunities to validate the teacher's self-integrity.'

## Summary

In order to provide creative education for language minority children, bilingual teachers themselves need to experience the liberating forces of this type of education. Teachers need to be validated as human beings, as conscientious, creative, intellectual human beings. They need the power that comes from communicating effectively, both orally and in writing, and the power that is built on solidarity. They need to understand the societal forces that have influenced their cultural and linguistic identity so that they can stop passively accepting their circumstances and become not only agents of their own transformation but also leaders in the world around them.

## Acknowledgements

Discussions at the First Working Conference on Critical Pedagogy held at the University of Massachusetts, Amherst, in February 1986, motivated me to write this paper. I would like to express my appreciation to the participants at this conference. I would also like to thank Paulo Freire, Tove Skutnabb-Kangas, Jim Cummins, Ellen Herda, and Dennis Parker, as well as my students in the Multi cultural Program, University of San Francisco, for their enriching dialogue. This paper benefited from the insightful comments of my daughter Rosalma Zubizarreta and my editor and friend, Bernice Randall.

## Notes

1. Schools in the United States are currently perceived, as noted with considerable insight by Giroux (1986), as instruments of societal reproduction. As such, they are attacked by conservatives and radicals alike — by conservatives for failing to produce adequately trained workers for an increasingly complex technological economy; by radicals for legitimizing the prevailing societal value of the dominant corporate order and perpetuating the existing gender, racial, and class inequalities.

2. For an application of creative methodology to a language arts curriculum, see Ada & de Olave (1986).

3. The positive value of bilingualism increases as the country moves from an industrial society to a technological/informational one. It is indeed paradoxical that precisely when the country most needs communication skills in order to export its technology to the rest of the world, we should see the appearance of an 'English-only initiative' aimed at discouraging the maintenance and development of such skills.

4. The first group comprised bilingual teachers working with migrant children in the Parajo Valley School District, Watsonville, California; the second group were bilingual teachers in a number of communities between Santa Cruz and Salinas, California; the third group were bilingual teachers from the San Francisco Bay area; the fourth group included principals, counselors, and teacher educators, as well as teachers. Not all those in group four are engaged in bilingual education, but they all work with minority populations in various areas in California. All members of groups two and three are pursuing a Master of Education degree; those in group four are doctoral students. Although approximately 50 percent of them received their teacher education in California, the institutions they attended vary greatly (University of California at Davis, Berkeley, Santa Cruz, and Los Angeles; San Jose State University; Stanford University, University of Southern California). The others studied in Ohio, Michigan, New York, Massachusetts, Florida, and elsewhere.

5. The elite bilingual schools found in other countries, which include American schools abroad, use a two-teacher model of education. In a single classroom, each of two teachers provides instruction for half the day, speaking only in his or her native language and thus motivating the children to become proficient in that language. In that system, the children, not the teacher, are expected to become fully bilingual. In contrast, the one-teacher model, which is followed in most bilingual programs in the United States, requires a single teacher to teach all subjects in both languages. Yet, few teachers are equally proficient in both languages, precisely because there has not been a tradition of additive bilingual education in this country.

6. In the poem *Balada de los dos abuelos*, Guillén writes: 'Sombras que solo yo veo,/ me escoltan mis dos abuelos./.../Yo los junto./.../Los dos se abrazan./Los dos suspiran. Los dos/las fuertes cabe zas alzan,/los dos del mismo tamaño,/bajo las estrellas altas;/los dos del mismo tamaño,/ansia negra y ansia blanca;/los dos del mismo tamaño,/gritan, sueñan, lloran, cantan./Sueñan, lloran, cantan./ Lloran, cantan./¡Cantan!'

## References

Ada, A F. and de Olave, M. de P. (1986) *Hagamos Caminos*. Reading, MA: Addison Wesley.

Aronowitz, S. and Giroux, H.A. (1985) *Education under Siege*. South Hadley, MA: Bergin & Garvey.

Cummins, J. (1981) The role of primary language development in promoting educational success for language minority students. In Office of Bilingual Education (ed.) *Schooling and Language Minority Students. A Theoretical Framework*. Los Angeles: California State University.

— (1986) Empowering minority students: A framework for intervention. *Harvard Educational Review* 56, 18–36.

Dolson, D. (1985) The effects of Spanish home language use on the scholastic performance of Hispanic pupils. *Journal of Multilingual and Multicultural Development* 6 (2), 135–55.

Freire, P. (1982a) *Education for Critical Consciousness*. New York: Continuum.

— (1982b) *Pedagogy of the Oppressed*. New York: Continuum.

Giroux, H.A. (1986) Radical pedagogy and the politics of student voice. Unpublished manuscript.

Guillén, N. (1972) Balada de los dos abuelos. In *Abra Poetica: 1920–1958.* Havanna: Instituto Cubano del Libro, pp. 137–9.

Lambert. W. and Tucker, R. (1972) *Bilingual Education of Children. The St Lambert Experiment.* Rowley, MA: Newbury House.

Peal, E. and Lambert, W. (1962) The relation of bilingualism to intelligence. *Psychological Monographs* 75, 1–23.

Skutnabb-Kangas, T. (1984) *Bilingualism or Not: The Education of Minorities.* Clevedon: Multilingual Matters.

## Questions

(1)  Define traditional reproductive education. Then define what Ada calls 'creative education' or 'transformative education.' Identify related terms (refer to those by Freire, Cummins, Skutnabb-Kangas, Reyes). Define these other terms and draw distinctions between them and what Ada calls 'creative education.' How is 'creative education' related to what is called 'critical pedagogy' and 'feminist pedagogy'? (See below for more sources to answer this part of the question.) Why is creative education particularly important for female bilingual teachers?

(2)  What is the difference between viewing teaching as 'a sequence of unrelated tasks, rather than as a vital life project that has impact on society'? How do you view teaching? How do you think your teacher-training program views teaching? List the courses you have taken in your teacher-training program. In a second column, say whether the course has focused on a sequence of unrelated tasks, a project that has an impact on society, or both.

(3)  Compare the following quote by a teacher in Ada's study with your own teacher training. How is it the same? How is it different?: 'They preached to us to teach creatively, but we were never allowed any creativity. They encouraged us to be good communicators, but the classes they taught were deadly. There was some lip service paid to the need for encouraging children to think, but we were expected to memorize and repeat.'

## Activities

(1)  Bilingual teachers regularly told Ada of having the following feelings:
    (a)  isolation;
    (b)  sense of inadequacy in language mastery;
    (c)  powerlessness;
    (d)  uncertainty regarding cultural identity;
    (e)  need to integrate theory and experience.
    If you are a teacher now, reflect on your teaching experience and whether you have experienced the feelings shared by Ada's teachers. Write an essay in which you state what your feelings are for each of the above, and give specific instances that have brought on those feelings. If you are not teaching now, interview a teacher and relate her experience.

(2)  Read more on 'critical pedagogy' also known as 'a pedagogy of critique and possibility,' 'a pedagogy of student voice,' 'the pedagogy of empowerment,' 'radical pedagogy,' 'a pedagogy for radical democracy,' and 'a pedagogy of possibility.' Choose from the list in Further Reading. Write an essay summarizing what you learned and how it applies to bilingual education.

(3)  Read more on 'feminist pedagogy.' Write an essay that differentiates between 'critical

pedagogy' and 'feminist pedagogy.' Make sure you say how the two are related, and how 'feminist pedagogy' relates to bilingual education.

(4) If you can read Spanish, look up Nicolás Guillén's poem, *'Balada de los dos abuelos.'* Share it with the class. If you cannot read Spanish, find a poem about the differences within oneself. (These differences could be racial, ethnic, cultural, linguistic, social, religious.) Then write a poem about your own 'mestizaje.'

(5) Imagine that the opening speaker in a debate argued that empowerment and 'creative education' should not be given to language minorities because it would allow them to use that power for their own enhancement and would weaken the political and economic stability of the country. Prepare a reply and deliver it in front of your class.

(6) Develop a course on 'creative education' and 'critical pedagogy' for a bilingual teacher-training curriculum. Make sure the course is designed not only to increase critical thinking in the students themselves, but also to help teachers introduce critical thinking into classrooms. Make a list of readings and activities in which you would engage the students.

## Further Reading

For more on critical pedagogy, see especially:

Freire, Paulo (1970) *Pedagogy of the Oppressed*. New York: Seabury Press.

Freire, Paulo (1985) *The Politics of Education*. South Hadley, MA: Bergin and Garvey.

Freire, Paulo and Shor, Ira (1987) *A Pedagogy for Liberation*. London: Macmillan.

Giroux, Henry A. (1986) Radical pedagogy and the politics of student voice. *Interchange* 17, 48–69.

Giroux, Henry A. (1988) *Teachers as Intellectuals: Toward a Critical Pedagogy of Learning*. Granby, MA: Bergin and Garvey.

Shor, Ira and Freire, Paulo (1987) What is the 'Dialogical Method' of teaching? *Journal of Education* 169, 11–31.

For more on 'feminist pedagogy' and the difference with 'critical pedagogy,' see especially:

Maher, Frances (1987) Toward a richer theory of feminist pedagogy: A comparison of 'liberation' and 'gender' models for teaching and learning. *Journal of Education* 169, 91–100.

Weiler, Kathleen (1991) Freire and a feminist pedagogy of difference. *Harvard Educational Review* 61, 449–74.

*Women's Studies Quarterly* (1987) Nos 3–4 (Special issue on Feminist Pedagogy).

# Building Bridges Between Parents and the School

## Christian J. Faltis

### Overview

Up to this point, we have concentrated exclusively on providing for learning inside the joinfostering classroom, but for joinfostering to work optimally, the students' parents and communities also must have a significant role in education, both at home and in school. Your role is critical for building bridges between parents and the school by extending joinfostering principles into your students' homes and communities and enabling parents to reciprocate by becoming involved.

Involving parents, especially non-English speaking parents, and other family members in educational activities at home and in the school (the fourth joinfostering condition) is no simple matter. There are language barriers to consider as well as the various ways that parents in different cultures and communities view their roles and the school's role in educating their children. Within the Asian immigrant community for example, many parents feel that they are solely responsible for their children's learning, particularly the children's approach to learning, both at home and in school. The school's job is to provide a work place where children can be exposed to and practice basic skills (Cheng, 1987). In contrast, many recently arrived Mexican families see the school as the sole authority on what needs to be learned and how it should be done (Scarcella, 1990). At home, parents constantly teach their children to be respectful to elders, to care for family members, and to be accountable for their own actions, but they rarely work with their children on school-related activities (Delgado-Gaitán, 1987).

For many of these parents, school, not home, is the appropriate place for learning about content and basic skills. Within both cultural groups, parents are deeply concerned about the educa-tion of their children (Olsen, 1988; Yao, 1988). However, in both cases the ways that parents see their roles in schooling often differ considerably from the way that mainstream English-speaking communities view their relationship with schools (Leitch & Tangri, 1988).

Parents from mainstream communities, partly because they speak the language used in school and partly because most school personnel are members of their communities, tend to share with schools the view that parental involvement at home and in schools is positively related to school achievement (Epstein, 1991). Consequently, most mainstream parents agree that they are responsible for helping schools do their job and that they can do so by engaging in the following kinds of behaviors: ( 1 ) tutoring their children at home, (2) helping them with homework, (3) helping their children sell raffle tickets or candy to neighbors and friends, (4) attending class plays, (5) accompanying children on field trips, (6) attending parent–teacher conferences, and (7) helping out with the PTO (Parent Teacher Organization) activities. In addition to these more traditional parental involvement activities, many mainstream parents also function as *advocates for change* by attending school board meetings, as *co-learners* by attending workshops with teachers where participants learn more about children and schooling, and as *decision makers* by becoming members of advisory boards or school committees (Chavkin & Williams, 1989).

The fact that great numbers of mainstream parents perform these behaviors demonstrates the tremendous degree of familiarity that parents have with the way schools expect communities to support the education of their children. However, the fact that non-English speaking parents do not perform many of these behaviors does not mean that they are any less concerned about their children's education. In all likelihood, the reason that many of these parents are less involved in school-related activities than their English-speaking counterparts has as much to do with the school's unfamiliarity with non-English speaking communities as it does with these communities' unfamiliarity with the schools.

In this chapter, you will learn about ways to help your students' parents and other significant caregivers become increasingly familiar with how they can become more involved in schooling matters. At the same time, you will also learn how to become involved in your students' communities and to pay attention to the kinds of activities that parents and others feel comfortable doing in school and at home. A few words of caution are in order, however, before we continue.

It is important to understand that parental involvement in the joinfostering framework necessarily moves you outside of the classroom and into the communities you serve. This may come relatively easily in some cases, but it may cause you feelings of anxiety and insecurity in others. Moreover, building home–school relationships may also move you into school-level politics because some of the strategies we advocate may require support from your principal and other school-level authorities. Thus, you can expect many different kinds of resistance. For example, using a language other than English to invite parents to school functions or making sure that information about bus schedules is available in the parents' native language are political stances.

Garnering support for these kinds of actions may require you to get into some potentially bitter battles with colleagues and non-school people who do not share your perspective. Choose your battles wisely, and don't expect to fight or win every battle. Instead, look for ways to advocate for actions that you believe are clearly needed to improve education for all students and that you know your parents also support. Work with other teachers and with parents who share your views about joinfostering and the need for greater involvement of parents in the school and the school in the community. Lastly, rely on your personal stance to help your students and their communities join in the education process at home as well as in school.

With these caveats in mind, let us now proceed directly to Julia's classroom to learn how she is going to inform parents about the upcoming presentations her students have prepared on ways to preserve elephants in the wild. Following

this final episode in Julia's classroom, we will examine a structured two-way approach to parental involvement that divides the process of parental involvement and participation into four levels. At each level the involvement of parents in the school increases proportionately to the school's involvement in the communities it serves. For each level of involvement, we will discuss specific strategies and activities for teachers and parents alike.

## Episode Six: Almost all the Parents Showed Up!

Back to School Night is next Wednesday from 7:00 to 9:30 p.m. This gives Julia and her students less than one week to finish rehearsing their skits before presenting them to an audience of parents, family, and friends! The principal of the school selects Wednesday night after learning from a majority of both second-language and English-speaking parents across the grades that this is the best night for them to come to school. With the support of the principal's office, Julia and several other teachers make sure that the general invitations to Back to School Night are written in the language of the home and sent out at least one week before the event, and a short reminder goes home with students on Monday. Each invitation also asks the parents or other family members to bring one item of food or a beverage.

Julia's students also send out a personal invitation to their parents and other family members to come to the auditorium during Back to School Night to listen and watch as the students in her class present their skits and supporting materials to the entire school. Along with the invitation Julia sends a letter written by her students that explains the purpose of Back to School Night and the kinds of activities that they can expect. Since the letters are composed in English by the students, Julia hopes that the students will be able to read and translate them to their parents and other family members as needed. Julia knows that all of her second-language parents speak and understand very little English, but she is not sure about their English reading abilities.

With help from Jake, the bilingual resource teacher, and one of the teacher-aides, Julia also locates and talks with community workers who speak the four non-English languages in her class: Spanish, Korean, Chinese, and Vietnamese. She explains the presentations her students will be making and the other events that are planned for Back to School Night. Julia also inquires about the appropriateness of someone taking the teacher's place to contact parents by telephone and invite them to Back to School Night. All of the community workers feel certain that the parents will understand and will most likely welcome the invitation.

Julia asks the community workers to make one other request of the parents. On the general invitations, each household was asked to bring one item of food. One of the English-speaking mothers had already volunteered to help Julia call the English-speaking families and find out what they will be bringing. Julia wants the community workers to let parents know that she hopes they will bring a typical food from their respective countries. She also asks the community workers to share the telephone numbers of bilingual compatriot parents in other grades who are definitely bringing food with the hope that the parents will talk among themselves about the meaning and purpose of Back to School Night.

On Wednesday afternoon, Jake and three sixth-grade students go to the cafeteria to help Julia finish setting up the posters and the cardboard backgrounds for the skits. That evening, Julia's and her helpers' efforts pay off! Virtually all of the parents of Julia's students show up for the performance, and most stay afterward to visit her classroom to learn about their children's activities. Julia realizes that this is quite an accomplishment for many of the parents. For some of the second-language parents, this is the first time that they have attended a school function. Her next goal is to get her parents to feel comfortable contributing to classroom and school-level activities and, eventually, to school-wide decisions. To reach this goal, Julia knows that she has to continue her involvement with her students' families and communities and keep the families involved in school.

In the following sections, let's consider what you might do if you were in Julia's place, with her enthusiasm to build bridges between the home and school and with the ultimate goal of giving parents a voice in helping improve education for their children.

## A Two-way Parental–School Involvement Model

Refugee parents are frustrated. On the one hand they want to push their children academically, to become someone in society, to work hard and study well. On the other

hand, they cannot effectively intervene in the educational process. They cannot attend school functions, PTA meetings, even school conferences because of language and not understanding the process. *The relative solution would be two-sided. Parents have to be educated on how to access the system, how to be influential, what to go to. And on the other hand, the school itself needs to outreach to bring in the parents of the new students in the system, because unless the parents work cooperatively with the schools we will not get an education for the children that they need.* (Vu-Doc Vuong, Public Testimony, San Francisco, CA, in Olsen, 1988: 82–83 (emphasis added))

Most of the research on the relationship between parental involvement and academic achievement reports that parents who participate in their children's schooling experiences have a positive impact on attitudes toward schooling and, ultimately, school success (Bermúdez & Padrón, 1987; Epstein, 1991; Solomon, 1991). The relationship between parental involvement and school success is based on the assumption that children whose parents participate in school-related activities become more invested in school because their parents talk with them about the value of schooling for success in life.

The fact that parents are participating in school-related activities, however, presumes a familiarity with schools and a belief that schools provide access to a variety of professions and occupations in society (Ogbu, 1983). Accordingly, parental involvement is perceived as a one-way venture, from the parents to the school. That is, the school does not need to reach out to parents since parents implicitly understand the value of being involved in schooling matters. However, parents of second-language students — and particularly immigrant parents — may have little understanding about how US schools work (Olson, 1990), and the parents may not share the belief that schools prepare all children equally (Torres-Guzmán, 1991). The following statement by a Honduran mother captures the essence of these concerns:

My son needs an education here. That is the way for him to have a good life. I fear for him, though. Here the teachers don't keep an eye on the children. He misses school and the teacher doesn't discipline him. He says the teacher doesn't care if he does his work. I try to teach him respect for his teacher, but he says that is not how it is here. (Olsen, 1988: 82)

What can this parent do to allay her fear that her son is not getting a good education? And what could we do as representatives of the school to enable this parent to turn these concerns into action that would benefit not only her children but other children as well?

### A multi-level approach to home–school relationships

Building bridges between home and school inevitably rests upon the cooperative efforts of the school, teachers, and parents. However, teachers have the primary responsibility for initially getting parents involved in schooling matters. Reluctant parents won't get involved simply because the principal wants them to. Reluctant parents may get involved, however, if their child's teacher reaches out to them and gives them multiple opportunities to become involved at home and in school. The key to involving parents within the joinfostering framework, therefore, is to strike a balance between learning about the home environments of your students while the parents of your students learn about school-oriented activities and programs.

We can work toward this balance of involve-

ment by dividing the process of building bridges between the home and the school into four levels. This multi-level approach to parental and teacher involvement is based on the works of Pettit (1980) and Rasinski & Fredericks (1989). The approach is especially well suited for working in a culturally and linguistically diverse classroom because it begins with the teacher learning about the parents' community support systems and about stress factors related to living in a new environment; it ends with the parents actively contributing to curricular decisions. Figure 1 presents a visual representation of the four levels of teacher and parental involvement.

### Level I

Your objectives in Level I are (1) to learn about your parents' daily experiences and the community in which they live, (2) to initiate individual contact with the parents and other adult caregivers through informal chats, get-togethers, and home visits, and (3) based on the first two objectives, to begin to work with parents and other caregivers to show them ways to monitor their children's progress in school.

The most effective way of developing and establishing rapport with parents and learning about their particular community is through a home visit. A home visit enables you to gain first-hand knowledge of some of the constraints

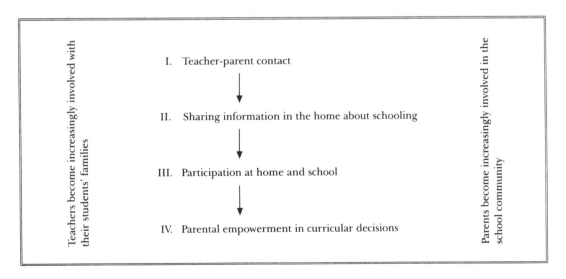

**Figure 1** A multi-level approach to teacher and parental involvement. (From 'Dimensions of parent involvement' by T. Rasinski & A. Fredericks (1989) *The Reading Teacher*, November, p. 181. Adapted by permission.)

that parents may face. For example, many second-language families live in crowded conditions with little room for study in isolation (Olsen, 1988). Children are often attended to by siblings and extended family members (Delgado-Gaitán, 1987), and parents may work long hours and sometimes have two or more jobs.

Begin scheduling your home visits early in the year and continue them on a regular basis, not just when a problem arises. Every visit you make should have a specific purpose, and the parents as well as the student should be aware of the purpose before the visit (Gestwicki, 1987). Also before you visit second-language parents, you should make inquiries about any special protocol or taboos of which you should be aware. Likewise, you will have a more successful encounter if you learn about greeting and leave-taking rituals and politeness formulae. (See Hoskins, 1971, for Vietnamese families; Kim, 1980, for Korean families; Yao, 1988, for Asian families; Delgado-Gaitán, 1987, for Mexican families; and Wong Fillmore, 1990, for Latino families.)

If there is not an adult in the household who can serve as an interpreter, bring a trusted translator from the school. But before you visit, talk with the translator about how you would like your interaction with the parents to be translated. Do you want paraphrased translations or word-for-word translations? It is important to have a translator who can translate literal information as well as cultural nuances. The translator may also be able to provide you with valuable information about the community and answer questions about appropriate cultural behavior.

In addition to making contact with your parents through home visits, you also should be learning about the community-based organizations that provide information and support services for different ethnic and language communities. Make an appointment to talk with a community worker or counselor at the local community-based organizations. In the meeting, try to learn about the services the organization provides and talk about the ways that you would like to involve parents over time. The community workers should be able to provide you with lots of information about the needs of the community. You should also ask about places in the community where families might shop for ethnic food and where they go for music and entertainment. Inquire about native-language religious services and places of worship. You may even attend a church service or visit a marketplace to get a better feel for the community.

Learning about the community enables you to tap into the 'funds of knowledge' that families rely upon for their daily experience. Greenberg (1989) refers to funds of knowledge as an 'operations manual of essential information and strategies households need to maintain their well being' (p. 2). These funds of knowledge may be useful to you in getting information out to the community and for developing thematic units around community-based topics. (See Moll & Greenberg, 1990, for an example of a community-oriented curriculum project.)

Your efforts to learn about the community and your parents at Level I should help you decide on the kinds of monitoring of schoolwork that you feel is most appropriate for parents. For example, suppose you learn that many of your second-language parents work at jobs that require long hours and that they have relatively little time to monitor their child's schoolwork at home; you also find out that a local neighborhood center offers after-school and weekend peer-tutoring services. You could inform parents about the services and help them set up a ride-share program if needed. Next, you could suggest a plan where you or students from a higher grade check the children's homework three days a week and the parents or other caregivers check it two days a week. You might also ask parents to spend at least three minutes every evening talking with their child about their schoolwork and any homework they have. You can even suggest the kinds of questions they might ask their child. Obviously, if you do not speak the language of the parents you will need to work with a bilingual liaison to assist you in your communication with parents.

In summary, your primary goals at this level are to establish contact with parents, begin learning about the community, and let parents know that you are there for them and that you will continue to support them throughout the school year. As you gain the trust of parents, you can begin suggesting ways to monitor schoolwork assignments completed in the home. You will increase the likelihood of getting parents involved in their child's schoolwork to the extent that your suggestions take into account the constraints under which the family operates.

*Level II*

The second level of involvement broadens the

kinds of communication that you have with parents. From your perspective, Level II involves informing parents through written sources, telephone calls, and informal conferences about their child's progress, classroom activities that may involve their community, upcoming events, and basic school policies. From the parent's perspective, the communication might range from providing you with feedback on how the child is responding to schoolwork at home to inquiring about holidays and bus routes.

At this level, involvement is tantamount to information sharing so that parents begin to feel comfortable relying on you for information about school policies and activities. At the same time, you increase your personal contact with them. Here is a list of some of the kinds of information that you might wish to share with parents:

(1) Important school dates (workshop days, half-days, holidays, registration days, report card days).
(2) Information about school events and meetings that parents should attend.
(3) Information about the school board and the issues that it is currently addressing.
(4) Summary of the minutes of school board meetings with a schedule of the next meeting.
(5) Information about changes in bus or school-day schedules.
(6) Information about and telephone numbers of bilingual liaisons who work for the school and the community.
(7) Information about community-based organizations.
(8) Information about upcoming television programs about the parents' community or country of origin.
(9) Information about local community events, such as music festivals, plays, carnivals, art displays, and speakers.
(10) Tips about the kinds of academic help that parents can provide at home.

To the extent possible, all of this information should be provided in the parents' native language, preferably by individuals who are native speakers and writers of the language. You will probably need help from bilingual liaisons working in the school or the district office. However, as the year progresses you may find a number of parents who would be interested in helping with this kind of information sharing.

Another way to inform parents about classroom and school activities is to send home a weekly newsletter primarily based on ideas generated by your students. The easiest way to produce a newsletter is to set aside a few minutes one day a week, and in a group meeting format, you and your students can generate news items, which you immediately write out on a ditto master or on a sheet of paper to be copied. News items can range from student discussions about what they are studying or what they liked about something they read or experienced in class, to the kinds of issues they would like to tackle in the coming weeks. The newsletter format should include a name (e.g. *Bruner Bobcat Weekly News*), a volume number, and a date at the top of the page. Most of the space on the paper should be reserved for student ideas. As the year progresses you occasionally may need to add a second page. You can also use 8-inch x 14-inch legal-size ditto masters or paper for an occasional longer edition.

The newsletter can also briefly announce upcoming field trips and special events, and other reminders to parents can be placed in a small rectangle at the bottom of the page, under the heading of 'Parent News.' In addition, the newsletter can devote a small space to a special phrase written in the native language of one of the groups represented in your class. For example, in a classroom such as Julia's where there are four languages in addition to English, each week Julia would write out a saying in one of the four languages and repeat the cycle at the end of every fourth edition. Gertrude Moskowitz's (1978) *Caring and Sharing in the Foreign Language Class: A Source Book for Humanistic Techniques* offers an extensive list of wonderful sayings in several different languages. In collaboration with your school librarian, you can also make suggestions about age-appropriate storybooks written in the native language highlighted that week.

Lastly, you can appoint two students a week to write a kind sentence about their family or their community. You can label this special section something like 'Our Community' and let the students write the sentences in their own handwriting on the ditto master. When the newsletter finally comes out it should look something like the one in Figure 2.

A weekly newsletter is a good way to get parents and other family members involved in schooling. Students enjoy reading about their classmates to just about anyone who will listen. Moreover, Hakuta (1990) has shown that bilingual children from the third grade on up are very

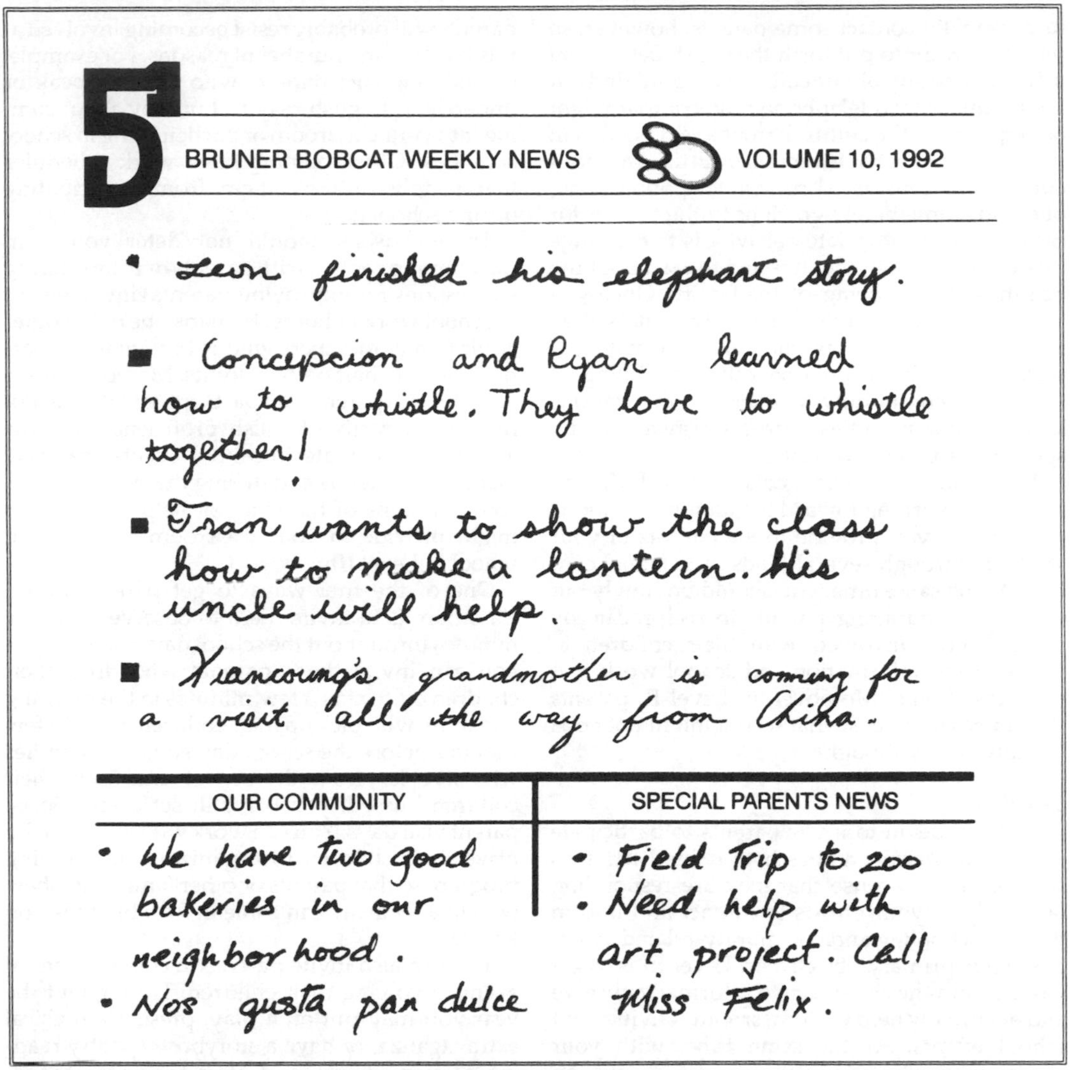

**BRUNER BOBCAT WEEKLY NEWS**     VOLUME 10, 1992

• *Leon finished his elephant story.*

■ *Concepcion and Ryan learned how to whistle. They love to whistle together!*

■ *Tran wants to show the class how to make a lantern. His uncle will help.*

■ *Xiancoung's grandmother is coming for a visit all the way from China.*

| OUR COMMUNITY | SPECIAL PARENTS NEWS |
|---|---|
| • *We have two good bakeries in our neighborhood.* <br> • *Nos gusta pan dulce* | • *Field Trip to zoo* <br> • *Need help with art project. Call Miss Felix.* |

**Figure 2** Newsletter example: *Bruner Bobcat Weekly News*

capable of translating from English to their native language and vice versa. Thus, your second-language students should be delighted to translate the newsletter for their parents and other family members!

You can also strengthen your relationship with parents by writing occasional personal notes and making telephone calls. In the personal notes addressed to the parents, you should share observations or anecdotes about how well their child is doing in class, especially in subjects that are of concern to parents. The notes should be brief and written in clear English or in the parents' native language. (You need to find out early on if there are adult family members who can read English. This will save you from having to rely so much on a translator.) Personal notes take less than five minutes to write. If you send out approximately ten notes a week, each student in your class will take at least one home every three weeks.

Telephone calls may be a bit more complicated if you need a translator because you will need a special telephone system for conference calls. Telephone contact may be the only way for you to personally contact some parents, however, so you may want to put forth the effort. Before you start making any phone calls, you should find out about any special telephone protocol that might be required in the cultural groups represented in your classroom. For example, in Latin American culture it is considered rude to telephone someone and immediately go right to the reason for calling. The appropriate behavior is to exchange relatively lengthy greetings and to ask about the health and well being of the family. Once you have completed this opening ritual, it is then acceptable for you as the caller to state the purpose of the telephone call. The bilingual liaison or community worker for the various language communities is probably aware of any special telephone protocol.

To summarize your goals in Level II, you should be working toward broadening the information that you provide to the parents of your students through several kinds of personal contact. At the same time, you should be slowly but steadily encouraging parents to reciprocate by getting more involved with their children in terms of the information and school work that you send home. Moreover, in Level II, parents should begin to sense that school might not be as foreign as they thought.

### Level III

You can begin to invite parents to participate in your classroom and in school-related activities as soon as you sense that they are responding favorably to your efforts to contact and inform them of schooling and community-related activities. Your primary objective in Level III is to get parents into the classroom to informally observe and eventually help with classroom activities and school events. At the same time, with your guidance, you also want parents to take on increasing responsibility for monitoring their child's study skills and work habits at home (Rasinski & Fredericks, 1989). In essence, you want the parents' experiences in school to serve as a model for the kinds of support and monitoring that they can provide for their children at home. That is, as a result of working in a joinfostering classroom environment, you want parents to try out strategies that they see occurring in the classroom when they assist their children with school tasks at home.

It is important to understand that although you may have contact with 100% of your parents as a result of your efforts in Levels I and II, some parents will probably resist becoming involved at this level for any number of reasons. For example, second-language parents who do not speak or understand English may feel uneasy about coming into your classroom or participating in school activities. Other parents have work schedules that simply prohibit them from participating during school hours.

These reasons should not deter you from maintaining contact with parents or from offering suggestions for improving parental involvement in school work at home. Perhaps one of the other adult family members who is bilingual can participate on behalf of the parents. Moreover, there are activities parents can participate in that do not require interactive English proficiency. Parents also can participate in school events that take place on weekends and during the evening. Let's consider some of the kinds of help that parents might provide in your classroom and for you school in Level III.

One of the first ways to get parents into a classroom is to invite them to observe for a few minutes throughout the school day. For example, you can invite those parents who drop their children off to stay a few minutes in the morning and those who pick up their children to visit a few minutes before the school day ends. For families who live far from the school and have their children bussed, you can still set aside special parent visit days. You can work with parents who drive their children to organize a ride-sharing program so that parents or other family members who live far away can come in for a brief visit on key days.

You can also invite parents to come to special events involving their children. Throughout the year you may put on a play, present a musical extravaganza, or have a storybook/poetry reading session. Before and after the presentation, students can show their parents around the room and talk about art, writing, science, and social studies projects that the class is currently undertaking. *This kind of informal involvement can be done in any language!* In fact, you should encourage parents to speak with their children in their native language in your classroom just as you should encourage them to do so in their homes.

In addition to the sheer enjoyment that parents receive from watching their children in your classroom, you can also help them become more aware of how learning takes place in your classroom by giving them a few tips on the kinds of actions and events to look for. For example, you can have parents pay attention to the different kinds of verbal and written interaction that the students use. Have parents watch you teach to the whole class or to a small group. Encourage them to notice the type of visual and nonverbal support that you provide as you teach. Both before and after parents observe your teaching, you might ask them to look for certain kinds of events and actions that you plan to emphasize in the lesson. Parents' observations of your teaching may give them ideas to improve interaction with their children at home. If you know ahead of time that second-language parents are coming to visit your classroom, try to have another bilingual parent or a bilingual liaison there to help you communicate with them.

As you learn more about your students' families, you are bound to uncover the wealth of experiences parents and other family members have. In fact, you may even wish to engage your students as budding anthropologists to learn about the 'funds of knowledge' that adults in their household rely on for any number of functions within their communities. Heath (1983) and Moll, Vélez-Ibañez, and Greenberg (1989) present ways for teaching students to use ethnographic techniques for studying community funds of knowledge. For example, Heath tells how students learned the best time to plant and harvest vegetables from local gardeners, and then they compared that with what the science books said. Moll and his colleagues had students discover what community members knew about banking and other important business concepts and then developed curriculum around the information.

One of the many benefits from gathering data and information from parents and other family members is that students learn about new sources of information in their own communities. Doing so elevates the status of community-based knowledge and makes it easier to invite family members into the classroom to share their personal knowledge about how things work and how things are done. For example, suppose your class were interested in finding out how people acquire sense about directionality (north, south, east, and west) and that you collected information from parents and family members. You could then invite several parents to share with the class how they tell about directions, and students could try out the various methods.

Parents who speak a language other than English can also be invited to share their knowledge of specific practices through a translator. The knowledge is important, as well as the fact that the parent is participating in the class. There is an additional benefit to having non-English speaking parents present a demonstration of a particular practice in their native language: students get to hear different languages, and they find out that teaching and learning can occur in any language!

There is one possible drawback to using ethnographic techniques to bring community knowledge and, ultimately, parents into the classroom. There are some kinds of community knowledge that adult members do not want children to bring into the school. To illustrate this point, Lipka (1989) tells a poignant story of a group of well-meaning educators and curriculum developers who were bent on developing a school curriculum that was responsive to the needs of the Yup'ik Eskimo community of Bayup in rural Alaska. One of the teachers involved in the project guided a group of students in producing a questionnaire to find out how the Community survived in the bitter winter months and how they gathered food. According to Lipka (1989), here's how the community responded:

> As soon as students began interviewing parents throughout the village, concerned community members got on the C.B. [radio] and warned everybody not to fill out the questionnaire. (p. 223)

The parents later explained that they felt threatened by attempts to take certain kinds of cultural knowledge outside the community and place them into the school. Their objection was essentially that 'if *kass'at* [white people] teach our culture to the students, then what is left for us? Our culture belongs to the community' (p. 223).

Subsequently, Lipka and his colleagues learned that the native community responded positively to efforts to construct curricula that dealt with contemporary issues of concern to the community. For example, community members were eager to work with the school on issues of land use and land management. Lipka learned from this experience that the information we gather from the community has to be relevant and purposeful to that community. In other words, rather than the community just being a resource for the school, the school has to become a resource for the community. For our purposes, this means that when we invite parents in to speak about their knowledge and practices we also need to consider ways that we can become resources for their needs as well.

Another way of involving parents in the classroom is to have certain parents help make bulletin boards and other kinds of decorations and building projects. For example, if you decorate your classroom around thematic units and festivities, parents can help you put up bulletin boards. You can set aside several locations in your classroom for non-English language bulletin boards. If you use the ceiling for decorations, as suggested in Chapter 3, you can ask a crew of parents help you put the students' work up and then add their own creations around a particular theme. Parents can also help prepare classroom materials. They can come into the classroom to work on assembling a stage for a classroom play, or they can sew and cut materials for a cooperative game. There are many ways that parents can help, regardless of their English-language proficiency.

Finally, at the school level, parents can observe and help with many of the same kinds of activities that they performed in your classroom. They can attend school functions, assemblies, and parties. They can be enlisted to help with food preparation and serving at these events. They can help set up and take down tables before and after the functions, assemblies, and parties. You need to be there, however, to support them and make them feel comfortable as they are learning to get involved in the school.

In summary, your goals in Level III are to get parents to participate in your classroom and in school, doing many different kinds of activities, while you increase your communication with them and show them how schools work. Parents will participate when they start to feel that the school is a comfortable place to be and that it is a potential resource for them.

### Level IV

In this fourth and highest level of parental and teacher involvement, the goal is to enable parents to play a more decisive role in school decisions and policies and at the same time to increase the level of confidence and trust that parents have in you as the teacher. This level is what Rasinski & Fredericks (1989) refer to as the 'empowerment' level. To achieve this highest level of involvement, you and the parents must have experienced each of the first three levels. Accordingly, Level IV is clearly not for every parent; in fact, few parents attain it. Reaching the level of empower-

ment depends in great part on the mutual trust and bond that forms between you and certain parents that want to invest extra time and effort in the schooling process (Rasinski & Fredericks, 1989). Those parents who do reach Level IV often become community spokespersons, to whom you and the school can look for both advice and support. In other words, due to their intense involvement in schools they become your colleagues in matters of curriculum and education in general. As such, you can ask for their opinions on classroom ideas and, as their participation progresses, for their advice on curricular decisions at the school level.

Your involvement with parents at this level is tailored primarily to providing suggestions to parents with the confidence that parents will implement the suggestions. For instance, if you suggest to Level IV parents that they organize a get-together to discuss community opinions about school plans to decrease the number of contact hours for physical education or to require all teachers to acquire an endorsement in teaching English as a second language within five years, you can be certain that they will do it. Moreover, because of your commitment to the various communities represented in your classroom, you may be asked to attend meetings and offer opinions at community-based organizations; you may even be asked to give rides to parents who lack transportation.

An excellent example of what empowered parents and teachers can accomplish is the Pájaro Valley Experience (Ada, 1988). The Pájaro Valley Experience is a family literacy program designed by the Spanish-speaking parents with the help of teachers in the Pájaro Valley School District near Watsonville, California. Each month, 60 to 80 Spanish-speaking parents come together to discuss children's literature in Spanish and to read the stories that their children have written in Spanish. Over time, the parents join in to write stories and poems along with their children. Parents also learn how to talk about books with their children and eagerly share the fruits of these discussions with fellow parents at the following monthly meeting. Ada points out that the program worked because a few parents worked to get others involved and because a few teachers helped with invitations, transportation, and book selections.

Establishing a family literacy program is one of many kinds of activities in which empowered parents can engage. Parents can also set up after-school tutoring programs. Padilla (1982) reports that parents in many communities throughout the Southwest have organized *escuelitas* (little schools) to help with schoolwork, promote Spanish language development, and reinforce Mexican culture. The *escuelitas* are run by parents and other students who volunteer to work with young children. Trueba, Moll & Diáz (1982) discuss a similar effort by Mexican immigrant parents in California, who organized 'Cafés de Amistad' (Friendship Coffees) for interested parents to come and share their concerns and knowledge about school.

Parents can also organize Parent Advisory Committees and work toward affecting change in school. Parent Advisory Committees represent the voice of the community on issues that concern their children. To be effective, parents who become involved in Parent Advisory Committees must 'be informed not only about the legal realities but also about the attitudes and activities of the local policy makers' (Curtis, 1988: 291). Moreover, the school district continually needs to be made aware of the parents' position on certain issues, just as the parents need to be apprised of their rights and of their power to impact school policy (Curtis, 1988: 291).

Again, due to the intense nature and relatively narrow focus of efforts, only a few parents participate in Level IV activities. The fact that some parents may eventually become involved in curricular and other school-wide decisions does not mean, however, that you lessen your communication and commitment to other parents. You still need to maintain contact with all of your parents and continue to encourage their involvement in school-related activities both at home and in your classroom.

In summary, your main goal at Level IV is to involve parents from the language groups represented in your class in advising, planning, and developing programs that you and they feel are needed for their children. Level IV parents have traversed the first three levels of involvement and are committed to working with you on improving education for their children. At this level you and the parents work with many people, from school board members and the school principal to fellow parents and local community leaders. Level IV involvement is intense and usually long-term, but the benefits are also rewarding and long lasting.

## Conclusion

This chapter began by emphasizing how difficult it may be to involve parents from diverse language and cultural backgrounds in school-related activities. In addition to language barriers, the ways that parents from different cultures view their role and the school's role in educating their children may be quite different from the expected pattern of school involvement. Despite language and cultural differences, however, there are ways to involve parents in schooling matters that minimize the barriers that language and cultural differences can create. The multi-level approach to home–school relationships is one such way to minimize barriers and instead build bridges between the home and the school. The success of this approach rests on you and parents working in tandem to learn about each other's worlds and, as a result, to get involved in helping the children make it in both.

As we witnessed in Julia's classroom, it takes lots of time and effort to bring about the social and pedagogical conditions that drive a joinfostering classroom. But joinfostering in the classroom is not complete unless parents are involved in schooling at the home and in the school. This is because joinfostering means that the teachers, students, and parents are inexorably connected in the process of education. From this perspective, no one should be left out of the education process due to a language or a cultural barrier. The multi-level approach to home–school relationships presented in this chapter gives you a means to complete the joinfostering mission of providing all parents variable access to and participation in schooling.

## Activities

(1) Contact a local elementary school and ask for a copy of the parent's handbook. Review the handbook, determine which sections might be difficult for second-language parents, and rewrite them using scaffolds, visuals, and other kinds of support. Work with an adult bilingual native speaker of one of the languages represented in the school and translate the section you rewrite.

(2) Using the parent's handbook as a guide, prepare a video in English and in the other major languages represented in the school to explain registration day and school policies concerning absences, the school lunch program, bus services, and discipline.

(3) Contact a local Parent Advisory Committee

and interview one of the members. Find out how the committee works and what some of the major issues have been in the last couple of years. Ask about committee membership of bilingual parents.

(4) Visit a community-based organisation serving a language minority community and interview one of the community workers. Find out about the history of the community and major community events and where the people in the community shop, worship, and go for entertainment. Based on what you learn about the community, attend an event or ceremony and notice (a) the roles that men and women play, (b) how and the extent to which children are involved, and (c) whether and under what conditions English is used for communication among members attending.

(5) Interview two parents from the same non-English speaking background to find out their perceptions of parental involvement. Try to find one parent who has minimal involvement in the school and one who is intensely involved in the school. Using the multiple-level approach to guide the interview, ask each parent to comment on how parents and the school can build better bridges at each level of involvement. Compare and contrast the responses given by each parent.

## References

Ada, F. A. (1988) The Pájaro Valley experience: Working with Spanish-speaking parents to develop children's reading and writing skills through the use of children's literature. In T. Skutnabb-Kangas and J. Cummins (eds) *Minority Education: From Shame to Struggle* (pp. 223–38). Clevedon: Multilingual Matters.

Bermúdez, A. and Padrón, Y. (1987) Integrating parental education into teacher training programs: A workable model for minority parents. *Journal of Educational Equity and Leadership* 7 (3), 235–44.

Chavkin, N. F. and Williams, D. L. Jr. (1989) Community size and parent involvement in education. *The Clearing House* 63 (4), 159–62.

Cheng, L. R. (1987) *Assessing Asian Language Performance*. Rockville, MD: Aspen.

Curtis, J. (1989) Parents, schools and racism: Bilingual education in a Northern California town. In T. Skutnabb-Kangas and J. Cummins (eds) *Minority Education: From Shame to Struggle* (pp. 278–98). Clevedon: Multilingual Matters.

Delgado-Gaitán, C. (1987) Parent perceptions of school: Supportive environments for children. In H. T. Trueba (ed.) *Success or Failure? Learning and Language Minority Student* (pp. 131–55). New York: Newbury House.

Epstein, J. (1991) Paths to partnerships: What we can learn from federal, state, district, and school initiatives. *Phi Delta Kappan* 72 (5), 344–9.

Gestwicki, C. (1987) *Home, School and Community Relations: A Guide to Working with Parents*. Albany, NY: Delmar.

Greenberg, J.B. (1989) Funds of knowledge: Historical constitution, social distribution and transmission. Paper presented at the annual meeting of the Society for Applied Anthropology, Santa Fe, NM.

Hakuta, K. (1990) Language and cognition in bilingual children. In A. M. Padilla, H. H. Fairchild and C. M. Valadez (eds) *Bilingual Education: Issues and Strategies* (pp. 47–59). Newbury Park, CA: Sage.

Heath, S. B. (1983) *Ways with Words: Language, Life and Work in Communities and Classrooms*. Cambridge: Cambridge University Press.

Hoskins, M. W. (1971) *Building Rapport with the Vietnamese*. Washington, DC: Government Printing Office.

Kim, B. L. (1980) *The Korean American Child at School and at Home*. Washington, DC: Government Printing Office.

Leitch, M. L. and Tangri, S. S. (1988) Barriers to home–school collaboration. *Educational Horizons*, Winter, 70–4.

Lipka, J. (1989) A cautionary tale of curriculum development in Yup'ik Eskimo communities. *Anthropology and Education Quarterly* 20, 216–31.

Moll, L., Vélez-Ibañez, C. and Greenberg, J. (1989) Community knowledge and classroom practice: Combining resources for literacy instruction. *Year and Progress Report*. Tucson: University of Arizona, College of Education.

Moll, L. and Greenberg, J. (1990) Creating zones of possibilities: Coming social contexts for instruction. In L. Moll (ed.) *Vygotsky and Education: Instructional Implications and Applications of Socio-Historical Psychology* (pp. 319–48). Cambridge: Cambridge University Press.

Moskowitz, G. (1978) *Caring and Sharing in the Foreign Language Class: A Source Book on Humanistic Techniques*. Rowley, MA: Newbury House.

Ogbu, J. (1983) Minority status and schooling in plural societies. *Comparative Education Review* 27 (2), 168–90.

Olsen, L. (1988) *Crossing the Schoolhouse Border: Immigrant Students and California Public Schools.* San Francisco: A California Tomorrow Report.

— (1990) Misreading said to hamper Hispanics' role in school. *Education Week* 9 (32), 4.

Padilla, A. (1982) Bilingual schools: Gateways to integration or roads to separation. In J.A. Fishman and G. D. Keller (eds) *Bilingual Education for Hispanic Students in the United States* (pp. 48–70). New York: Teachers College Press.

Pettit, D. (1989) *Opening up Schools: School and Community in Australia.* New York: Penguin.

Rasinski, T. and Fredericks, A. (1989) Dimensions of parent involvement. *The Reading Teacher,* November 180–2.

Scarcella, R. (1990) *Teaching Language Minority Students in the Multicultural Classroom.* Englewood Cliffs, NJ: Prentice Hall.

Solomon, Z. (1991) California's policy on parent involvement: State leadership for local initiatives. *Phi Delta Kappan* 72 (5), 359–62.

Torres-Guzmán, M. (1991) Recasing frames: Latino parent involvement. In M. McGroarty and C. Faltis (eds) *Languages in School and Society: Policy and Pedagogy* (pp. 529–52). Berlin: Mouton de Gruyter.

Trueba, H. T., Moll, L. and Diáz, E. (1982) *Improving the Functional Writing of Bilingual Secondary School Students.* (Contract No. 400-81-0023). Washington, DC: National Institute of Education.

Wong Fillmore, L. (1990, May) Latino families and schools. Remarks prepared for the Seminar on California's Changing Face of Race Relations: New Ethics in the 1990s. Sponsored by the Senate Office of Research. State Capitol, Sacramento, CA.

Yao, E. L. (1988) Working effectively with Asian immigrant parents. *Phi Delta Kappan,* 223–25.

## Questions

(1) What were the things that Julia did to prepare for Back to School Night that made it a success? How many of those things do you yourself do? Is there something else you do? What kind of success do you have with a Parents' Night? (If you are not teaching, reflect on your experience as a student.)

(2) Faltis outlines what he calls 'a structured two-way approach to parental involvement that divides the process of parental involvement and participation into four levels.' Explain first what Faltis means by a 'structured two-way approach to parental involvement.' Then list all the activities below. In a second column indicate which of the activities you practice, by putting a plus or negative sign next to the activity. In a third column, briefly explain your practice or give an explanation why you don't do it. (If you are not teaching, reflect on your experience as a student.)

A. Learning about parents and their communities
   (a) home visits;
   (b) visits to community-based organizations, shops, places of worship, places of entertainment.
B. Information sharing through:
   (a) weekly newsletter;
   (b) personal notes;
   (c) telephone calls.
C. Get parents to participate in classroom and in school by:
   (a) invitation to observe: time, days;
   (b) invitation to special events involving their children;
   (c) have parents help make bulletin boards and decorations;
   (d) invitation to school functions.
D. Parental empowerment in curricular decisions:
   Having parents advise, plan and develop programs that they feel are needed.

## Activities

(1) Find two parents, one working class and one professional, if possible in each of these four groups:
   (a) Asian;
   (b) Latino;
   (c) White Anglo;
   (d) African American or Black West Indian.
   Give them the list below and ask them to rate their participation as follows:
      'Frequently' = 3, 'Sometimes' = 2, 'Never' = 1
   Total the scores for each individual. Compare your findings across ethnolinguistic groups and also across social class.
   You may tabulate the responses from the entire class and make a poster with the findings.
   (a) Tutoring children at home.
   (b) Helping children with homework.
   (c) Helping children sell raffle tickets or candy.
   (d) Attending class activities.
   (e) Accompanying children on field trips.
   (f) Attending parent–teacher conferences/meetings.
   (g) Helping out with parent–teacher organizations.
   (h) Co-learners, attending workshops on children and schooling.
   (i) Decision makers, members of advisory boards or committees.
   (j) Advocates for change, attending school board meetings.
(2) Make a survey of the community-based organizations in your community that provide support services for the different ethnolinguistic communities. Try to identify especially if there are any services such as the ones described in the Pájaro Valley Experience, the *escuelitas*, or the Cafés de Amistad.
(3) Select an ethnolinguistic group represented in your classroom (or a classroom you choose). By observation and interview, make a list of the following:
   (a) the places where they shop (for food and clothing);
   (b) where they go for music and entertainment;
   (c) the places of worship and religious services they attend.
   For each of the places above, offer the following description:
   (a) How the minority language is used (either in oral interaction or signs and other written material).
   (b) Objects and other things (for sale, consumption, enjoyment or worship) that 'belong' to the minority culture and how they are used.
(4) For your classroom (or one of your choosing), design either a weekly newsletter to parents or a parents' handbook. Focus on language and cultural cooperation between home and school. Remember to decide on languages and their varieties, as well as content.

# Recasting Frames: Latino Parent Involvement

## Maria E. Torres-Guzmán

### Introduction

A number of inferences have been drawn about programs of parental participation in lower-working class and minority communities.[1] Much of what is written about parental participation is based on invidious comparison between white middle class and lower-working class and minority parental behavior. These comparisons are driven by preconceived notions of which participation behaviors are most important to students' school success. Consequently, empirical evidence confirms the general lay impression that parents in lower working class and minority communities have low participation rates and that this indicates they do not care about their children's education.

This paper presents a case study of parent involvement in an alternative high school located in one of the poorest Latino *barrios* in a large East Coast metropolis. The paper will focus on the 'invisibility' of certain important forms of parental involvement[2] which are made visible when naturally-formed parental networks are examined. I propose that these networks are meaningful modes of involvement within the context of the home–school relationships established by this school. Finally, the case will shed light on the limits of using a schema for parental participation derived from the behaviors of middle class parents. Specifically, I argue that the schema of middle class parent involvement fails to take into account the linguistic and cultural environment of the school as this frames for parents, students, and teachers, the home-school interaction that occurs.

### Prevailing Discourse Regarding Parent Involvement and Education

The literature is clear that parental involvement correlates positively with school achievement.[3] This literature presumes that parents who communicate the importance of schooling to their children will find their children more invested in educational activities and likely to experience successful academic achievement and school attainment levels. Parents demonstrate they care about the educational process by talking with their children about schooling and/or, more explicitly, by participating in school-related activities.[4]

The literature also supports a corollary proposition which is the inverse of the previous assertion. This proposition states that parents who do not talk to their children, who do not create conducive learning environments for their children, and/or who do not participate in school-related activities are implicitly communicating to the children that they do not care about their education.

Research studies have shown that middle class parents have positive attitudes toward involvement and generally participate in the education of their children at moderate levels (Stallworth, 1982; Melvin *et al.*, 1983). They also exert influence on schools and engage in extensive school/community networking (IRE, 1981). It is generally believed that minority and working class parents are not interested in school and that they rarely attend school-sponsored activities. This belief is partially substantiated by numerous accounts of school efforts that have not been very successful in attracting non-middle class parents. Factors identified as barriers to their involvement include language and cultural differences, lack of child care, lack of transportation, and lack of knowledge as to how to help their children. In comparison with working class and minority groups, the white middle class levels of parental involvement are higher, the networking is more extensive, and the influence on the school is more visible.

One would assume from the literature on parent involvement that participation rates of middle class parents would be high. This is true only in relative terms. When middle class parents are asked to describe their most frequently assumed roles in the education of their children, they mention tutoring their own children at home (helping out with homework) and school-wide or classroom activities that directly involve the children (helping the child sell raffle tickets or candy to the neighbors, attending class plays or accompanying children on field trips, attending parent–teacher conferences, etc.) or that indirectly provide school support (Melvin *et al.*, 1983). The participation rates among these parents in formal decision-making bodies is low (Stallworth, 1982). There has been an erosion in the confidence of the middle class in educational institutions over the years. Picchiotti (1969) has suggested that when parents are relatively happy with the programs, they feel no need to intervene formally in the day-to-day affairs of the school. This inference still resonates as a reasonable explanation for the low participation rates in governance activities.[5] It may be that only when parents lose that relative confidence in the teacher, a school program, or administrator, and want to express it, that the number of parents appearing at school board meetings, school council meetings, or the like, increases.

## Limitations of the Decontextualized Behavior Parent Involvement Schema

The schema of middle class parental involvement, as reported in the literature, focuses on specific desirable behaviors of parents and treats these behaviors analytically in a decontextualized way. Among the desirable behaviors cited are: attending school council meetings, attending parent teacher conferences, organizing school activities such as school tours, producing a PTA bulletin, etc. The rate of participation is a binary quantitative measure of the presence or absence of activity. The unit of analysis is the parent rather than the extended family, the parent–child dyad, or the home–school relationship.

Studies of parental involvement have ignored the interactive nature of parental involvement. They examine what parents do or don't do; they do not investigate how the parents respond to what is occurring in school or how the school defines its boundaries. The studies do not show how the parents' interpretation of what happens in schools is intertwined with how they behave toward schools. These studies rarely consider the school's contribution to the kinds and amounts of the parent–school interaction that may occur, i.e. how school personnel interpret what the parent/community can contribute and then define the home–school relationships and organize school initiated activities in accordance with that interpretation.

Thus, the studies of parent involvement show involvement behavior as decontextualized. The studies on parent involvement are not explicit about the social relationships that occur. Scholars appear to presume that the interpretive frame brought into the relationship is a positive one, i.e. that all parents and communities approach schools with the assumption that they are institutions organized to ensure that their students will become competent adults who are capable of surviving in and contributing to the mainstream society to which they belong. This posture ignores that schools can be seen as structured to achieve other systemic social goals (Bowles & Gintis, 1976) or even have competing or multiple social goals (Giroux, 1983). The extant model ignores the possibility of a frame of social conflict which can result in the alienation of parents from schools.

Parents may, in fact, understand schools as institutions organized to sustain social inequalities and discrimination (Ogbu, 1981). When this occurs, a logical role parents can play in the education of their children is to help them be successful at school failure, or stated in other words, parents can help their children develop alternative competencies of survival. This points to another limitation of the middle class schema; it is value laden. The schema is not inclusive of the view that parents can play a role in helping children make sense of the negative experiences they face in schools as positive. Parental participation aimed at academic and social success, as defined by the mainstream society we live in, is viewed as the only positive involvement, while parental involvement in helping children survive and be competent in alternative worlds is not.

### Recasting the frame

Most of the studies that have contextualized parent involvement have documented the social conflict between the dominant white middle class school system and working class and minority communities; the majority are accounts of alienation from schools. But this is not the total picture; there is diversity in home–school relationships among working class and minority populations.

In a study that examines differences between Latino caste-like minorities, i.e. Puerto Rican and Mexican Americans, and recent immigrants, Suarez-Orozco (1987) proposes that Latino caste-like minorities operate under, and reflect in their world view, aspects of the 'genre of depreciation':

> People know and are affected by the knowledge that they have been systematically depreciated for generations. Such 'remembrances of things past,' continued depreciation, and contemporaneous barriers to upward socio-economic mobility permeate how people view their 'place' in society and the role of schooling for their future. (Suarez-Orozco, 1987: 161)

The sense of powerlessness which results from the systematic oppression experienced by caste-like minority populations is manifested in the feelings of alienation from school. Suarez-Orozco contrasts Romo's (1984) findings of a study of Chicano families in Texas with those of the recent Central American Latino immigrants. Romo (1984) found that the Chicano families were the group most alienated from the school. In contrast, Suarez-Orozco finds that the new Central American Latino immigrants who fled from the tragic misery and destruction of war are embued with hope of better opportunities in the United States that were not as readily available in their homeland. They perceive success in school as a prerequisite or concomitant to helping the less fortunate at home. The perspective of the parents among these recent immigrants was that in the US their children would be educated, would learn English, and, ultimately, get a good job. 'They strongly believe that through study and hard work they *can* and *will* get ahead in this country' (Suarez-Orozco, 1987: 166).

Suarez-Orozco's distinction between caste-minority and recent immigrants is important in that it demonstrates that while both populations lived in similar conditions of poverty,[6] faith in the system's ability to 'equalize' the opportunities for the caste-minority was tinted by the community perceptions of historically embedded and extant societal power relationships. Extending the logic that what parents communicate, verbally and non-verbally, to the child is embedded in a broader belief system that is intrinsically connected with broader social and economic issues of power relationships suggests that home-school relationships are not solely determined by the socioeconomic status of the family or group.

Another way of proposing this is that home-school relationships exist within a frame of social conflict, i.e. that the parent perceives the school to be working against the best interest of the child and in favor of maintenance of the status quo.[7] When this is the case, involvement as defined by the school is not likely to occur. Instead, the kind of implicit participation of parents in the creation of school failure that Ogbu talks about is likely to occur. For schools to expect higher rates of participation or a change in the nature of participation with the establishment of a parent involvement program without recasting the frame is highly unreasonable.

While the social relationships established in the broader sociopolitical sphere may be framing the home-school relationships, at the local level and in the short run, experiences of home-school relationships where social conflict is not constitutive may provide information about ways in which this relationship can be transformed. Few studies have been reported and little is known about how the reframing of the home-school relationship may affect parental involvement. Using the experience of Esperanza High School, I will report on a case of reframing of home-school relationships and show that the school personnel were intuitively guided by their understandings of the child-parent, parent-school, and community-school dynamics within a cultural context. Building on their cultural knowledge and operating on the assumption that parents cared about their children's education, the school personnel recognized the potential areas of miscommunication between parents and their children regarding the role of schooling. Both their understanding of child development as well as cultural knowledge served to create a positive frame for the home-school relationship and an environment in which parents could be involved in a 'natural' way. The Esperanza High School was housed in a unique organizational cultural setting which made the reframing possible. I would further argue that parental involvement was not significantly different from what is found elsewhere among other groups. While Esperanza High School cannot claim to be a model of parent involvement, it was an example of a culturally congruent school community with naturally emerging home-school relationships.

## The Experience of Parent Involvement at Esperanza High

Esperanza High School is an alternative educational program housed in a community-based-organization (CBO) in a poverty stricken Puerto Rican/Latino *barrio* in New York City. The CBO is known in the neighborhood for providing comprehensive services in the areas of health and fitness, the arts, education, career development, social services, and community ecology to approximately 200 youth on a weekly basis. It is more importantly known for its advocacy work for youth and community empowerment.[8] The school began in February of 1987. It was studied during the second year which was the first full academic year in the life of the school.[9]

The school's goals have been to promote bilingualism, biculturalism, and create leadership for community development. Many of the students were limited English proficient, over-aged, and born in the United States. For the majority of these students. Esperanza High was perceived as the last hope in a long string of disappointing and alienating educational experiences.

### Esperanza High discourse on parent involvement

During the initial discussions about parent involvement, Esperanza High teachers expressed the urgent need to work with the parents so that messages to the students from the parents would not conflict with those of the school. The staff perceived the conflicting messages as centered on the value of a high school education. On the one hand, the staff felt that parents embraced Esperanza High as a place that represented hope for their children and viewed the teachers as second parents to which they entrusted their sons and daughters.

> Parents come here and they entrust their darlings to me. '*Aqui lo tienes. Mira ver si puedes ayudarme con el*'. (Here he is. See if you can help me with him.) Sometimes they tell their parents, '*Voy con la missi*'. (I'm going with the teacher.) And, the parents give them permission to go '*con el chispo ese*' (with that little bit). (Fieldnotes from meeting 9/10/87)

Some of those same parents, however, when confronted with issues of survival, discouraged their sons and daughters from attending school. The staff felt that some parents perceived the students to be wasting their time in school instead of participating in the workforce and helping the family financially.

The Esperanza High and the CBO staff understood that they needed to create alternatives for the students that would cushion the impact of the social and economic conditions the family faced, i.e. poverty, parents on drugs, parents attempting suicide, etc.

> A lot of them deal with a lot of social problems, they have to deal with poverty...they have to deal with loneliness, so on and so forth... A lot of their parents are dealing...with their own lives, they have to deal with their own shit... (Interview of CBO staff member, 2/18/88)

Thus, an operating assumption was that from time to time parents were incapable of creating supportive environments in the home and the parents became adversaries to the growth of the young person. Yet, a concurrent assumption was that parents did care about their children.

> Parents are willing...if they can help their young person, it may be a horrible dynamic going on, and they may not be able to communicate and they may not be even talking to each other, the student and/or the young person and the parent, but when you speak to that young [person], to that parent, they're receptive, and somehow whether they're alcoholics, whether they're child abusers, whether they're whatever, they're willing to hear and somehow they want to maintain that contact with that young person. And, they want to somehow overcome what difficulties and conflicts they're having at home They may not know how to do it. They may...be in this session for an hour and be receptive and do crying... They may not know how to do it. And they may leave this room and not talk to that young person, but their interest is still there. (Interview, 3/10/88)

The relationship of the youth to their families was relatively clear, in spite of the rhetoric about the importance of parents in the life of the young. After a few months of observation, the involvement of parents, as presented in the research literature, was still invisible. A parent–teacher conference had been organized where a handful of parents showed up; parents were invited to the

CBO public activities and holiday events (e.g. a Christmas party and the celebration of Dia de los Reyes (Epiphany)), but very few attended. Instead, there was evidence of school staff behaviors that kept the parents at a distance in order to protect the students. During a student strike in late fall (12/3/87), for example, the teachers made no effort to involve parents. On the contrary, one of the teachers indicated that calling parents could trigger in the parents the feeling that the students were wasting their time by going to school. This teacher felt, and other CBO staff concurred, that it was better to deal with the issues raised by the young people during the strike as part of the relationship between them and the students.

Confronted with this picture of parent involvement at Esperanza High and wanting to make sense of what was happening, we turned to the participants for an explanation. A series of interviews with the CBO staff, school personnel, and the students provided additional information as to how parent involvement was conceptualized. An implicit organizational framework of involving parents was discovered and can be summarized in the following way. The youth were the heart of the CBO activities; the activities were client-centered. The client was defined as the young person. What this meant was that prior to involving the home, a judgment was made about its appropriateness after consulting with the young person. This did not mean that the CBO staff abdicated its responsibility to the whims of the young people, but that the youth were included in the decision-making. While meeting the needs of the young person through agency services (i.e. health, education, and cultural activities), the CBO staff members strove to establish a relationship of respect and trust; respect for the young person and trust in the adults. A mutual relationship became central to creating bridges with the young person's parents. The following description captures the CBO's perspective:

> ...the parents are still very essential in the further growth and development of that young person...now we have parent involvement through the school, through the parents groups...and we...strongly advocate its component... *Always giving the priority and never losing the focus that the young person is the main reason why we want to involve the parent*. So that we have to have the consent of that young person. We have to

> [be] perceptive and sensitive enough that...if it's not good for the young person, ...then the parent cannot be part of that communication. So it's a very, very sensitive balance... (Interview with administrator, 3/10/88; my emphasis)

In other words, rather than elicit the parents' support for the child who is having problems in school, the CBO staff first considered the extent to which the home was a part of the problem and to what extent bringing in the parent would be a hindrance to the development of the young person. Since self-help is part of the CBO's philosophy, supporting the youth in resolving problems on their own was important. Yet, while understanding the centrality of the youth's perspective, the family was not negated. The family was viewed as an intrinsic aspect of the young person's life:

> ...it's hard work because you want to support that young person and at the same time you know that...the complete support of that young person is not looking at just the education... [it] is looking at the family unit and the family component that's ultimately going to support them throughout their life. So when you decided to separate services to the young person from those provided to the family, you're doing a disservice to that young person. (Interview with administrator, 3/10/88)

There was still another component. The CBO envisions bringing together the students, their parents, and the community-at-large on issues of community development. The CBO has modeled this involvement by participating in various community efforts which included struggles centered around education with the local school district, police brutality, and school board elections, etc. Thus, the CBO viewed parent involvement as encompassing more than a one-to-one parent–child relationship; it intricately interwove the process of growth and empowerment for youth with community development. The implicit framing of the social relationships established between parent and child as well as between parents and school was manifested as respect, trust, mutuality, and commitment.

In the school, three aspects of the participants' views were most informative: (a) the centrality of the parent–child relationship in promoting other forms of involvement; (b) the significance of the integration of the stage of development of the child and cultural traditions of parent–child relationship; and (c) the aim of community development. Much of what was defined as parent involvement was similar to that found in the literature. What the pattern of behaviors of parents meant to those involved, nonetheless, was different from what would have been anticipated. The following are descriptions of what the relationships looked like for the participants. For the purpose of this analysis, three categories of relationships were identified: participation of parents with their children, home–school communication patterns, and parental involvement in community development.

### Parent–child relationships

A relatively wide range of interactions were identified as a result of conversations with students. Most parents participated with their children by assuming the role of moral and emotional support, similar to what Delgado-Gaitán found in a study of Mexican-American parents (1986). Some Esperanza High students reported that parents were involved on a daily basis with their education. For example, one student's mother called in on a daily basis or followed the student to the school in order to ensure that he attended. Involvement consisted of the parent, usually the mother, asking the student about attendance or about homework.

How students characterized the on-going conversation with parents about schooling ranged from 'harassment' to *compañerismo* 'companionship'. Some talked about their parents 'getting on their back' because of school absences, homework, or tardiness. An area of tension and miscommunication between parents and students, for example, was homework. Whether homework was given or not, some parents expected the students to show evidence of their seriousness about school by bringing home and doing schoolwork. The students who faced this situation felt their parents did not know what to expect and that, as a result there was an intensification of conflicts between them.

At the parent–teacher conference held in the fall, questions about schooling from the parents turned into a discussion about homework The teacher chairing the meeting explained the school's philosophy. The homework questions during the parent/teacher conference and the students' accounts suggested a miscommunica-tion. While the parents perceived that seriousness entailed doing homework and that focusing on looking for evidence of school work in the home demonstrated that they cared about their children, the students felt the persistence to be a lack of understanding of what was expected of them by the school; therefore, these parental behaviors were uncalled for or 'harassment' rather than supportive. Some students reported that their parents did not ask them for homework, but instead waited for the end of semester grades. At the other extreme were students who described a close relationship with their mothers.

Interviewer: How do you relate to your parents?
Student:      Well to tell you the truth me and my mother, we're very close. We share a lot of things. An, if I have a problem, I'll tell her about it and when she has a problem she will tell me about it. We stick together a lot...
Interviewer: Does your mother ask you about your school or your homework?
Student:      Yes, she does... Most of the time I tell her what topic takes place...

Usually these were students who lived in single parent households and whose mother had returned to school. These students reported organized study periods which they shared with their mothers where they would both sit at the table to do their individual assignments.

The range of relationships from very close to almost non-existent, from 'too much' in a negative direction to an unusual amount of companionship. The types of relationships were made visible in the stories students told. A few students also described a very solitary existence, with little, if any, contact with parents or any adult outside the school environment. Either the student or the parents came home late and the opportunity to exchange more than a mere perfunctory hello on a daily basis did not exist.

### Home–school relationships

At Experanza High the staff were aware of the realities of students' home lives. One reason for this is that the staff organized their social lives in a way that brought them into contact with the students outside the classroom and with the parents in the community. One of the teachers had grown up and still lived in the neighborhood. Repeatedly, this teacher mentioned knowing what it meant to live in the neighborhood as an adolescent. The teacher knew some of the students' parents fairly well. Telephoning the parents, going over for supper, or accompanying the family to a service agency were reported by the teacher and confirmed in the student interviews. In fact, the closeness of this relationship between the teacher and parents was interpreted as 'too much' by some of the students. A few verbalized feelings of discomfort about some topics that became part of the conversation between the teacher and their parents because, as a result, their parents became privy to situations that students would have preferred to keep private.

> [Teacher's name] calls my house a lot. — she has this habit...she comes here to my house and talks to my mother and eats whatever and then — little by little says things in reference to what I do in school. Good and bad things... I hate it. — I understand she wants to do good for me but its not for her to judge what she thinks is right for me... (Student Interview 3/24/88)

In spite of these feelings, students seemed to respect the relationships of the adults around them and they managed to negotiate relationships that were generally comfortable for them. For example, one of the students reported having an unspoken agreement as to how far the teacher was allowed into her personal life and she felt the teacher respected this.

**Interviewer:** How about for you? Does the school reach out to your family?
**Student:** They wanted to but I always said not to relate to my father. I'm nineteen. I'm in this world by myself.
**Interviewer:** Independent?
**Student:** Yes... That's it. Nobody has to know my business and I am old enough to do what I got to do.

While each student's home situation was considered individually when decisions regarding home–school communication were made, for the most part the teachers acknowledged the need to maintain contact with parents as a way of eliciting emotional and moral support for the student.

There was more success in informal, interpersonal contact with the parents than in more formal, visible ways. For example, very few of the

parents showed up for the parent/teacher conference held during the first semester or to the Christmas party even though the teachers and the students encouraged the parents to attend. When researchers visited parents in their homes,[10] however, many expressed their gratitude for the work of Esperanza High and stated that they would be willing to attend or send a representative on their behalf to meetings which would help the school.[11] Of course, there were varying degrees of willingness.

**Interviewer:** *Estas dispuesta a ayudar?* (Are you willing to help?)
**Parent:** *Puedo tratar porque tengo niños chicos.* (I can try. I have small children.)

In this case the mother had small children which she felt were a future to fight for but also a hindrance to involvement. Other parents were working and thought it would be difficult to attend. Nonetheless, according to the interviewer's fieldnotes, the conditions of the *barrio* were a source of worry for the parents and they felt the school was a source of light for them and their children.

> *Estan muy agradecidos de haber encontrado [esta organización] para beneficio de su hijo. No tienen palabras para expresar su agradecimiento.* (The parents were pleased to have found an organization that would benefit their children. Words did not adequately express their gratitude) (Parent Interviewer fieldnotes, 7/88)

### Parent–broader community relationships

Parents of students at Esperanza High did not connect to the CBO community involvement activities in overt ways. Ecology became a focus of community involvement for both the school and the CBO. The Toxic Avengers were students who came together around environmental issues in the community as a result of the environmental science curriculum at Esperanza High. While their ultimate goal was to focus on a toxic waste disposal facility in the community, during their first year they began to practice understanding community organization, chemistry, politics, biology, etc., by targeting a chemical lot four blocks away from the school. They put pressure on the company that stored toxic waste in barrels on the lot to clean it up. In recounting the events in an interview with a newspaper reporter, one of the Esperanza High Toxic Avengers talked about her conversations with her mother regarding the community work. She said her mother was supportive and felt that the environmental science work in the community addressed issues of social justice. In various meetings and interviews, the teacher of the environmental science curriculum made explicit how parents would be important in the politics of community involvement around environmental issues. A toxic waste plant was located in the community; for the youth to advance the work begun in the environmental science class, the parents were important allies and the most important support base. While organizing parents had not occurred formally, the students were already eliciting support by conversing with their parents about the school work they were involved in.

An informal support network centered around the work of the Toxic Avengers was discovered accidentally. One day in March a young elementary school child was introduced to me as a CBO staff member's son. I began a conversation with the child on environmental health issues. He talked to me at length about the formation of an elementary school Toxic Avengers club[12] at his school. The Young Toxic Avengers were planning to take some samples of waste near their school playground. The boy's enthusiasm and clarity on the issues led to a conversation with the mother. It was in the mother's response that the parent networks created by younger children as a means for involving parents were made visible. The mother indicated that in an attempt to secure permission for the child's friend to stay after school to do Young Toxic Avenger work, the son had to explain the objectives of the group to his friend's mother. Because the friend's mother did not know English, the CBO staff member got on the phone and explained to the parent who the Toxic Avengers were and their objectives. This event revealed that many of the Esperanza staff are community members. Their histories in the community and networks of friends, families, and acquaintances kept information flowing from school to community to school to children.

## Rethinking Parental Involvement

The parental involvement found at Esperanza High, from the perspective of the schema presented in the literature, would appear to be in keeping with what has been found in the past in minority working class communities. The rate of participation is low at parent meetings and the Christmas events. Nonetheless, there is another way to explain the parents' behavior.

Much of the parental involvement that occurred was moral and emotional support rather than direct instruction, governance, or even financial support. Parental involvement of this type can easily go unnoticed. At Esperanza High the parents' role was to look after their children with respect to school attendance and homework; teachers and parents met at social occasions in the community, outside the school. Parents were generally informed of what was happening in the school and the community through their children, and they believed the school was organized to benefit their children. This type of 'invisible' behavior is no different than what is generally expected in the regular high schools.

In other words, when looking at how parents were involved in Esperanza High from a different set of assumptions, they appear to be active. For example, similar to the parental involvement reported in other high schools, while there was a range of involvement from nothing to 'too much' between parents and their children, the role parents can play was constrained by the stage of adolescent development. Thus, parental involvement was not as visible as during early childhood. Second, the 'invisible' involvement of parents in the education of their children (the moral, emotional, and financial support and the informal networking) sustained the formal parental involvement behaviors. In other words, it is from the network of parents and because of the relatively positive framing of the relationship between parents and schools that 'leaders' among parents naturally emerged, became representatives in more formal school activities, and established relatively non-adversarial relationships. Third, the linguistic and cultural congruency between home and school and the mission of the school were important in establishing the frame parents use to relate to the school. When these assumptions are taken into account, the level and nature as well as meaningfulness of parental involvement at Esperanza High are more evident.

### Parent involvement during adolescence

At Esperanza High the parental involvement was as invisible as one would expect at the high school level. A number of studies report that the higher the grade level of the children, the more likely there will be a decrease in the visible forms of parent involvement (McKinney, 1978; Epstein, 1986). By the time a student reaches high school, a shift in the process of decision-making about the student's education has occurred. It is during adolescence that children assert independence[13] from their parents in the most dramatic way; the youth generally prefer the lessening of parent involvement as was the case of the young girl who negotiated the teacher initiative with her father because she felt 'she was alone in this world'. The parent responds by deferring more to the child and, concurrently, the student exercises more control over his/her own as well as the parents' participation in the school environment. Parents become more peripheral and thus are more often engaged in supportive roles (providing guidance and emotional, financial and moral support) rather than the more visible roles assumed in primary grades (tutors, members of PTA and advisory councils, etc.). At the high school level it is very unlikely to find parents as involved in as many facets of school activity as at the elementary level. For elementary school children to ensure participation in activities, they must draw the significant adults in their lives into the organizing of activities. For example, the way in which the parents of the elementary school Young Toxic Avengers initiated school-related conversation would not have been as likely to occur among parents of the Esperanza High School students. At a high school level the young person will, for example, elicit moral support as was the case in the Toxic Avenger's account of the conversation with her parents about the toxic and hazardous waste in the community.

When the child was at the elementary level it was possible, if the parent knew English, to sit down and help with homework. At the high school level the instances of this type of interaction decrease. It is more likely that the parents and children would engage in conversation about homework, as was evident in Esperanza High, rather than being jointly involved in the actual doing.

## Parental networks

Informal parent networks serve to organize the students, parents, teachers and other staff in a set of activities which bond them together. These activities provide a sense of purpose and a support structure to connect the different actors to one another and to the school environment.

The middle class parent enjoys opportunities for creating informal, natural home–school networks given the congruency between this population's and the school's broad sense of mission, language, and culture. Their networks are usually embodied in the form of sustained informal interaction between the teacher and the parent. Whether it occurs during the arrival or leaving school periods at the elementary level, conversation about the school, the curriculum, and about factors at home which may affect the students are likely to occur periodically. Although both teachers and parents have unspoken agreements about when direct talk about both social as well as academic progress should occur (social behavior may be discussed more freely in informal conversation while academic talk is relegated to a parent/teacher conference or curriculum night except when there is an academic 'problem'), an expressed parental concern during informal talk is usually explored seriously. Most of the time problems are not posed as if in an adversarial relationship (Lightfoot, 1978). The discussions are undertaken and an assumption made is that parents are open to explore the causes of academic difficulties, including looking at what is happening at home. At the high school level the parent–teacher conversation continues but in an even more subtle fashion. The role of the parent is less of a mediator between the school and the child. At this point the child is more in the position to mediate for him/herself and the parent assumes the role of support for the child.

At Esperanza High the parents' main source of information about the school is the student. A secondary line of information comes through other parents. Parent–teacher conversation is the least frequent source of information for parents, and that occurs most often in informal events. This makes invisible much of the contact and information exchange between the school and the home.

In other words, on a day-to-day basis there appeared to be implicit understandings of what role each party had to play. The parents and teachers shared in the confidence that the institution was organized to act in the best interest of the child. In interviews parents seemed confident that the teachers had the best interests of the student at heart. There were also mechanisms for resolving problems when they emerged. In this sense, confidence in the institution did not differ from that found among mainstream parents with institutions organized to serve mainstream populations. Esperanza High was housed in a Latino community based organization perceived by the community to advocate for the community youth and for community development. The community was Latino and the teachers were, in majority, Latino. Not only was the staff ethnically identifiable as Latino, but the mission of the school was congruent with some of the community values and expectations, — especially those of *respeto* 'respect', *cariño* 'caring/loving', *familia* 'family',[14] and the dignity and celebration of the language, culture, and history of the community. Esperanza High was established with the specific goals of developing community leaders, of promoting bilingualism/biculturalism, and of creating educational alternatives for Hispanic children experiencing school failure.

The goals themselves embodied a posture between home and community that differed from most mainstream high schools. Thus, it was not only that the environment of the school was Latino; the school was also explicitly organized to serve the community by integrating its language and culture as ways of validating and promoting the development of the students, the parents, and the community. Many of the students and parents had experienced schools within their district as alienating environments in which school routines and conventional organization of instruction replicated in microcosm the conflicts and struggles found in the broader society. Because of this contrast between the experience of Esperanza High and previous schooling experiences, many parents implicitly felt confident enough to 'entrust their darlings' to the school even though the parents were unable to articulate the school's mission explicitly. Concretely, parents felt confident in raising issues with the teachers because of the access provided by a common language, Spanish, which was both a school medium of communication and a shared symbol of identity and co-membership.

## Summary

In conclusion, the decontextualized behavior schema of parent involvement is limited. It focuses on the frequency of participation in specified behaviors associated with academic achievement, but it ignores the meaningfulness of the behaviors of parents from the parents' point of view. The 'invisibility' of many specific interactions between the parents and children, as well as the school and community-at-large, are brought forth in the description. The goal was not to present an exemplary model of parent involvement, but a realistic picture of what occurs. The case demonstrated that while everyday ordinary, 'unnoticed' activity in this school was not much different from any other school, the framing of the home–school relationship gave it a meaning often ignored.

## Notes

1. Parent refers to the primary caretaker.
2. Involvement can mean any number of things: from giving the individual child emotional and moral support to participating in elections and in governance within the school. In between there are the parent activities involving direct instructional roles as well as those which are financially supportive of the school. A review of the literature on parent involvement and education includes discourse on who benefits from these activities. Benefit is not confined to the child through a direct relationship with a parent. The parents themselves benefit as their personal capacities are enhanced through the process of participation. The school, as an institution, also benefits, as it receives support from parents who assume ownership of the schooling process as a result of their closer working relationship, as does the community which benefits from the school's increased responsiveness to their needs when the parents, teachers, and administrators begin to talk the same language.
3. The evidence to support the proposed relationship is substantial. A review of the literature on parent involvement over the last two decades (SRI, 1973; Gordon *et al.*, 1979; Henderson, 1981; Tyler, 1981; Herman & Yeh, 1982; Moles, 1982; Robbins & Dingler, 1982; Smith & Nerenburg, 1982; Keesling, 1983; Epstein, 1986) provides evidence of a strong relationship between active involvement of parents and student academic performance. The relationship was found to hold when looking at specific areas such as preschool parent tutoring (Gilmer, 1969; McCarthy, 1968; Levenstein, 1969; and Karnes *et al.*, 1975), language achievement (Watson, 1972), student reading levels (Jackson, 1974; Spencer, 1978; Tyler, 1981), and math scores (Jackson, 1974). Various studies have found similar relationships between Latino parent involvement and educational achievement (Fernández, 1973; Cer-

vantes, Baca & Torres, 1979; Cadena-Muñoz *et al.*, 1982; García *et al.*, 1986).

4. While this assertion has widespread appeal among administrators, teachers, and the community-at-large, the evidence marshalled in its favor is not as convincing. At most, a 'blaming the victim' posture and the inverse logic of correlational studies which show that parent involvement is associated with school achievement are used to support this assertion. Two strands of research, nonetheless, have shown that parents play a role in the negative framing of schooling for their children. See the Office of Hispanic Education of the Michigan State Department of Education's (1984) study on Hispanic School Dropouts, and Ogbu (1974).

The 1984 Michigan study concluded that one of the most important contributing factors to the high Hispanic dropout rate was the lack of 'parental *interest* or involvement in a child's schooling'. While Ogbu (1974) also argued that the value of school is communicated by the parent, he does not make the assumption, as the Michigan study does that the lack of parent talk about school-related activities with their children is indicative of their lack of interest in the education of their children. Ogbu makes a more complex argument which proposes that parents participate in creating school failure by communicating to their children, implicitly, that schools fail many minority children and, thus, education does not work for them. Ogbu describes the communication of negative parental experiences with schools in daily talk (as in 'Well, when I was in school...') and proposes that recounting negative and failure experiences helps both the parent and child make sense of the difficulties children face in school. In this way the parent is supportive of the child (not necessarily blaming the child) while at the same time transmitting knowledge of the structure of society and their place within it (i.e. how systematic discrimination occurs across generations).

5. Wimpelberg (1982) found no connection between parental satisfaction and participation measures, but Herman & Yeh (1982) found that perceptions of influence were related to satisfaction.

6. In describing the salient characteristics of dropouts, both the income of the family and the educational background of the parents are significant factors. Barro (1984) found that twenty-two percent of students from low-income families as opposed to seven percent of those from high-income families drop-out of school. Additionally, students whose parents never completed high school were found about twice as likely as other students to drop out. Numerous other studies show a strong dynamic between parental involvement, poverty, and school failure (Rumberger, 1981; Steinberg *et al.*, 1984; Brown, Rosen, Hill & Olivas, 1986). Fernández & Shu (1988) found that poverty and dropping out functions a bit differently among Latinos. Among middle class Latinos, the leaving school behaviors are still more severe than the white middle class counterpart.

7. Erickson (1987) discusses institutional legitimacy and trust as important in framing face-to-face encounters between school staff and students and their parents.

8. The CBO has been involved in advocacy work around issues of education including a legal case of segregation of Latino children, school board elections, representation of Latinos on the city-wide school board, police brutality, educating the community on teen pregnancy, and AIDs education.

9. The data collected and analyzed herein came from a larger ethnographic study which documented the process of implementation of the alternative high school and was organized in the form of a research collaborative that included a university-based team and the CBO/Esperanza High staff. Parental involvement was, nonetheless, an important aspect of the study. Data from over 100 observations of classrooms, meetings, and community events as well as 75 formal and numerous informal interviews conducted throughout the year with the CBO staff, the Esperanza High School teachers, students, and parents served to bring together the different pieces of the story. It is not the intention of this paper to provide the entire story, but to present certain aspects that might illuminate some of the shortcomings of the national discussion on parent involvement in general and Latino parent involvement in particular.

10. Twenty-one out of 26 households were visited at least once.

11. It can be argued here that parents were responding in ways that they perceived were expected. Unfortunately, this was an area we

were unable to follow-up during the year and a half of fieldwork.

12. The Young Toxic Avengers were a group of elementary school children who organized themselves as an after-school group around the Esperanza High School Toxic Avenger's activities.

13. While one can argue that parental separation still continues and can be even more psychologically dramatic during later stages of adulthood, I refer here to the more concentrated and

overt attempts of adolescents to gain independence while also going from the stage of childhood to young adulthood.

14. Carrasco (1984) discusses *respeto* and *cariño* within the context of the classroom or *'el segundo hogar'* 'the second family'. The concept of *familia* emerged from discussions, observations, and interviews with the CBO and school staff in which the student and staff organizational participation patterns were viewed as paralleling that of family relationships.

## References

Barro, S.M. (1984) The incidence of dropping out: A descriptive analysis (Unpublished paper). Washington, DC: SMB Economic Research, Inc.

Bowles, S. and Gintis, H. (1976) *Schooling in Capitalist America*. New York: Basic Books.

Brown, G., Rosen, N., Hill, S. and Olivas, M. (1980) *The Condition of Education for Hispanic Americans*. Washington, DC: National Center for Education Statistics.

Cadena-Muñoz, R. and Keesling, J.W. (1982) *Parents and Federal Education Programs, Volume 4: Title VII*. Santa Monica, CA: Systems Development Corporation.

Carrasco, R.L. (1984) Collective engagement in the *'segundo hogar'*: A microethnography of engagement in a bilingual first grade classroom. Cambridge, MA: Unpublished Dissertation, Harvard University.

Cervantes, H.T., Baca, L.M. and Torres, D.S. (1979) Community involvement in bilingual education: The bilingual educator as parent trainer. *NABE Journal* 3 (1), 73–82.

Delgado-Gaitán, C. (1986) Parent perceptions of schools. In H.T. Trueba (ed.) *Success or Failure* (pp. 131–55). Cambridge, MA: Newbury House.

Epstein, J. (1986) Parent involvement. What research says to administrators. *Education in Urban Society* 19 (2), 119–36.

Erickson, F. (1987) Transformation and school success: The politics and culture of educational achievement. *Anthropology & Education Quarterly* 18 (4), 335–56.

Fernández, I. (1973) Parent involvement in bilingual education. Paper presented to the American Council on the Teaching of Foreign Languages Pre-convention Workshop, Boston, MA.

García, E.E., Baca, M. and Guerra-Willekens, M. (1986) Parents in bilingual classrooms. *NABE Journal* 11 (1), 47–60.

Gilmer, B.B. (1969) Intra-family diffusion of selected cognitive skills as a function of eudcational stimulation. *DARCEE Papers and Reports* 3 (1). Nashville: Peabody College.

Giroux, H. (1983) *Theory and Resistance in Education: A Pedogogy for the Opposition*. South Hadley, MA: Bergin & Garvey.

Gordon, I.J. *et al.* (1979) *Aspects of Parent Involvement in the Parent Education Follow Through Program*. Washington, DC: DHEW.

Henderson, A. (1981) *Parent Participation–Student Achievement: The Evidence Grows* (NCCE Occasional Papers). Columbia, MD: National Committee for Citizens in Education.

Herman J.L., and Yeh, J.P. (1982) *Some Effects of Parent Involvement in Schools*. Los Angeles, CA: California University, Center for the Study of Evaluation.

Hispanic Policy Development Corporation (1984) *Moving Up to Better Education and Better Jobs: Volume II*. Washington, DC.

Institute of Responsive Education (1981) *A Study of Citizen's Organizations. Citizen Participation in Educational Decision-making*. Boston, MA.

Jackson, A.H. *et al.* (1974) *Plan, Polish, Promote and Practice: A School Volunteer Program*. Florida Educational Research and Development Council.

Karnes, M.B. and Zehrback, R.R. (1975) Parental attitudes and education in the culture of poverty. *Journal of Research and Development in Education* 8 (2), 44–53.

Keesling, J.W. (1983) *Parents and Federal Education Programs: Preliminary Findings from the Study of Parental Involvement*. Santa Monica, CA: Systems Development Corporation.

Laosa, L. (1982) School, occupation, culture, and family: The impact of parental schooling on the parent–child relationship. *Journal of Educational Psychology* 74 (6), 791–827.

Levenstein, P. (1969) Cognitive growth in pre-schoolers through stimulation of verbal interaction with mother. Paper presented at 46th Annual Meeting of the American Orthopsychiatric Association, New York.

Lightfoot, S.L. (1978) *Worlds Apart: Relationships between Families and Schools*. New York: Basic Books, Inc.

McCarthey, J.L. (1968) Changing parent attitudes and improving language and intellectual abilities of culturally disadvantaged 4-year-old children through parent involvement. Unpublished dissertation, Indiana University at Bloomington.

McKinney, J. (1978) *Study of Parent Involvement in Early Childhood Programs*. Philadelphia School District, PA: Office of Research and Evaluation.

Melvin, J. *et al.* (1983) *Parent Involvement in Education Project (PIEP). Final Interim Report*. Austin, TX: SWEDL.

Moles, O. (1982) Synthesis of recent research on parent participation in children's education. *Educational Leadership* 40 (2), 44–7.

Office of Hispanic Education, Michigan Department of Education (1984) *Hispanic School Dropouts and Hispanic Student Performance in the MEAP Tests*.

Ogbu, J. (1974) *The Next Generation: An Ethnography of Education in an Urban Neighborhood*. New York: Academic Press.

— (1981) Origins of human competence: A cultural-ecological perspective. *Child Development* 52, 413–29.

— (1983) Minority status and schooling in a plural society. *Comparative Education Review* 27 (2), 168–90.

Picchiotti, N. (1969) Community involvement in the bilingual center. Paper presented at the Third Annual TESOL Convention, Chicago, IL.

Rumberger, W. (1983) Dropping out of high school: The influence of race, sex, and family background. *American Educational Research Journal* 20 (2), 199–220.

Smith, A.G. and Nerenburg, S. (1982) *Parent and Federal Education Programs. Volume 5: Follow Through. The Study of Parental Involvement*. Santa Monica, CA: Systems Development Corporation.

Stallworth, J.T. (1982) Identifying barriers to parent involvement in the schools. A survey of educators. Paper presented at the Annual Meeting of the American Education Research Association, New York.

Stanford Research Institute (1973) *Parent Involvement in Compensatory Education Programs*. Menlo Park, CA.

Steinberg, L., Blinde, P.L. and Chan, K.S. (1984) Dropping out among language minority youth. *Review of Educational Research* 54 (1), 113–32.

Suarez-Orozco, M.M. (1987) Towards a psychosocial understanding of Hispanic adaptation to American schooling. In H.T. Trueba (ed.) *Success or Failure*. Cambridge, MA: Newbury House Publishers.

Taylor, D. and Strickland, D.S. (in press) *Learning from Families: Implications for Educators and Policy*.

Tyler, R.W. (1981) Parent involvement in curriculum decision-making: Critique and comment. Paper presented at the Annual Meeting of the American Educational Research Association, Boston, MA.

Watson, K.I. (1972) *The 'Going Places' Classroom: A Community Involvement Program of Action Learning for Elementary Students* (Research Monograph No. 23). Gainesville, FL: Gainesville Florida University.

Wimpelberg, P.K. (1982) Redefining lay participation in education politics: Parental activity at the levels of school and classroom. Paper presented at Annual Meeting of the American Education Research Association, New York.

## Questions

(1) What is Torres-Guzmán's criticism of studies of parental involvement, especially with regards to working class parents? How does her position differ from the one by Faltis?

(2) Torres-Guzmán talks of Esperanza High as being 'an example of a culturally congruent school community with naturally emerging home–school relationships.' What does this mean? Describe the origin of Esperanza High School and its purpose. Also describe how parent involvement was conceptualized and how it was achieved.

## Activities

(1) Create a poster to display the practice of parental involvement in Esperanza High School. Make the poster a way of publicizing what Torres-Guzmán suggests is 'good practice.'

(2) What type of parental involvement in school exists in your community? Are there differing types of involvement (e.g. moral, emotional, social, financial, physical)? How interactive is such involvement? Does such involvement differ according to language group, social class, both, or neither? How does such involvement change with grade and age?

(3) Besides the Anglo conception of 'parental involvement,' there are other practices and philosophies prevalent in education in the United States today that do not always reflect the experience of language minorities. Read the following statements to at least five language minority professionals who have achieved well academically. Ask them to reflect on their experience growing up in a minority family, and to indicate whether the practice happened:

'Always' = 4, 'Frequently' = 3, 'Seldom' = 2, 'Never' = 1.

Then ask them to share with you other family influences that they think might have contributed to their academic success.

(1) My mother or father read to me before going to bed.
(2) There were children's books available to me.
(3) We went out to visit museums and other institutions.
(4) We went to the library to take out books.
(5) I had structured after-school activities and lessons.
(6) I belonged to 'clubs.'
(7) My mother or father helped me with my homework.
(8) My mother or father studied with me before a test.

(4) Use the list and scale above to interview five successful minority professionals, and five successful majority professionals. Are there differences in home literacy practices?

(5) Make a video of (a) a classroom with a mostly white language majority population and (b) a classroom with a mostly working-class non-white language minority population. Then select a student from each classroom. Visit the student at home, observe and record the following: language use at home, literacy practices, other child-rearing practices. If there are specific literacy events in the home, try to video-tape these. Contrast and compare both situations. Share the videos with the class.

## Further Reading

For an incisive treatment of how language use and literacy practices differ in the community, the home, and the classroom, see especially:

Heath, Shirley B. (1983) *Ways with Words: Language, Life and Work in Communities and Classrooms*. Cambridge: Cambridge University Press.

# Bilingual Classroom Studies and Community Analysis: Some Recent Trends

## Luis C. Moll

The questions and issues that underlie bilingual education are constrained by deficit views about the abilities and experiences of language-minority students. In general most research has emphasized how well students acquire English, assimilate into mainstream culture and perform on tests of basic skills. Employing a sociocultural perspective that acknowledges the many resources that are available to children outside of the school the author describes how research about children's communities can be used to enhance instruction. For this to work researchers and teachers must redefine their roles so that they enter into collaborative working relationships that focus on ways of bringing about educational change. (*Educational Researcher*, Vol. 21, No. 2, pp. 20–24)

Most children attending bilingual education classes in the United States are working-class students. Although rarely addressed in the literature, this fact has major implications for the goals and nature of instruction in these classrooms. In comparison with the schooling of peers from higher-income families, instruction for working-class students, be it in bilingual or monolingual classrooms, can be characterized as rote, drill and practice, and intellectually limited, with an emphasis on low-level literacy and computational skills (see, e.g. Anyon, 1980, 1981; Goldenberg, 1984, 1990; Oakes, 1986; also see Goodlad, 1984). This reduction of the curriculum is not only in terms of content, but in terms of limited and constrained uses of literacy and mathematics, the primary instructional means.

This working-class 'identity' of bilingual education is also reflected in the types of questions and issues that guide bilingual education research. In general, the dominant issues in bilingual education are related to English language learning and assimilation of students into the mainstream, with scant attention paid to academic development or broader social and instructional dynamics. Typical questions include how to determine language dominance; how long the first language should be used in instruction; when to mainstream or transfer students to English-only instruction; and, of course, what sorts of language tests to use to evaluate the effectiveness of one program versus another.

García & Otheguy (1985, 1987), in their revealing research on private bilingual schools located within Cuban working-class (and other) communities in Dade County, FL, have pointed out the myopia that seems to affect the field of bilingual education research. They report starting their study by trying to address some of the core bilingual education questions mentioned above (García & Otheguy, 1987: 85). They soon discovered that these questions were irrelevant or inapplicable to the schools they were studying. Indeed, their respondents could hardly make sense of their questions: 'These issues are not relevant at all to the people we interviewed. These community educators were only concerned about the best possible way of educating their own children. None of the [Cuban] schools focused solely on bilingualism or monolingualism as a goal. *In fact, there was remarkably little interest in language questions*' (p. 90, emphasis in original). Curricular issues common in bilingual education, such as remedial instruction, the categorization of children by language dominance, or the language of initial reading, were also dismissed by these educators as irrelevant if not nonsensical, and in some instances they had never even heard of them (pp. 90–92).

The primary concern in these schools, then, was not with the typical language issues associated with bilingual education, but with pedagogical issues and academic development, with providing a quality education for the children. Spanish and English fluency and literacy were simply expected and developed as unquestioned, valuable, obvious goals for Cuban children living and going to school in the United States. As the authors reported, in these schools, 'the use of both languages is considered the only natural — indeed the only conceivable — way of educating children' (1985: 13).

García & Otheguy (1987) concluded that their initial research questions failed because they had uncritically accepted the status quo in bilingual public schools and the limited vision of what is important or what counts as education for these children. They wrote: 'We too had framed our original questions within what one might call the majority context, that is, the intellectual and pedagogical context within which most US-born, white, English-speaking educators frame their thinking about the education of linguistic minorities' (p. 92). This is a context that focuses on 'disadvantages,' where explanations of these students' school performance usually assume they come from socially and intellectually limiting family environments, or that these students lack ability, or there is something wrong with their thinking or their values, especially in comparison with wealthier peers (Díaz, Moll & Mehan, 1986). This is also a context where the obsession with speaking English reigns supreme — as if the children were somehow incapable of learning that language well, or as if the parents and teachers were unaware of the importance of English in US society — and usually at the expense of other educational or academic matters. In short, to the extent that researchers and practitioners in bilingual education uncritically accept this limited vision of students, and the reductionist instruction that supports this vision, they help sustain beliefs and practices that severely constrain what bilingual teachers and students can accomplish .

## Some Recent Trends

In what follows, I present an example from a recent study in bilingual education that addresses broader social and academic issues than simply learning English, remedial instruction, or basic skills. This study takes what could be called a sociocultural approach to instruction (for additional examples, see Moll, 1990; Moll & Díaz, 1987; also see Cole, 1990; Newman, Griffin & Cole, 1989; Rosebery, Warren & Conant, 1990; Tharp & Gallimore, 1988). This approach, influenced in great part by Vygotsky's (1978) and Luria's (1981) formulation of how social practices and the use of cultural artifacts mediate thinking, highlights how classrooms (or households) are always socially and culturally organized settings, artificial creations, whose specific practices mediate the intellectual work children accomplish. When classrooms are viewed in this way, a key focus of study becomes how (and why) children come to use essential 'cultural tools,' such as reading, writing, mathematics, or certain modes of discourse, within the activities that constitute classroom life.

These studies, therefore, contribute to recent discussion in these pages and elsewhere on 'participatory' or 'apprenticeship' models of instruction that emphasize 'socializing' or 'enculturating' students into the important practices of, for example, a highly literate or scientific classroom community (see, e.g. Brown, Collins & Duguid, 1989; Palincsar, 1989; also see Farnham-Diggory, 1990; Goodman & Goodman, 1990; Heath & Mangiola, 1991; Hursch, 1989; Holt, 1990). As Resnick (1990) has recently explained in relation to literacy instruction:

> The shift in perspective from personal skill to cultural practice carries with it implications for a changed view of teaching and instruction If literacy is viewed as a bundle of skills, then education for literacy is most naturally seen as a matter of organizing effective lessons: that is, diagnosing skill strength and deficits, providing appropriate exercises in developmentally felicitous sequences, motivating students to engage in these exercises, giving clear explanation and direction. But if literacy is viewed as a set of cultural practices then education for literacy is more naturally seen as a process of socialization, of induction into a community of literacy practi*cers*. (p. 171, emphasis in original)

Creating the social and cultural conditions for this socialization into 'authentic' literacy practices, or into doing science and mathematics, is central to the studies cited above, and to the example presented below. Within this bilingual classroom, children are active learners using language and literacy, in either English or Spanish, as tools for inquiry, communication, and thinking. The role of the teacher, which is critical, is to enable and guide activities that involve students as thoughtful learners in socially and academically meaningful tasks. This emphasis on active research and learning leads to the realization that these children (and their families) contain ample resources, which we have termed *funds of knowledge*, that can form the bases for an education that far exceeds what working-class students usually receive.

Next I describe research that my colleagues and I are conducting in Latino (predominantly Mexican) households and bilingual classrooms in Tucson, AZ (Moll & Greenberg, 1990; Moll *et al.*, 1990). I first explain what we mean by funds of knowledge and then present an example of a teacher using this concept in the teaching of literacy to bilingual students. This study, I must emphasize, is only one of several that is helping facilitate a critical redefinition of bilingual education and its purposes (see, e.g. McCarty, 1989). Each in its own way attempts to create positive change in bilingual classrooms by taking full advantage of the sociocultural resources in the surrounding environment, including the children's developing bilingualism and knowledge, and in so doing, illustrates how easily we educators have come to accept notions of limitations and deficits in the education of these children.

## A Funds-of-Knowledge Perspective

The guiding principle in our work is that the students' community represents a resource of enormous importance for educational change and improvement. We have focused our analysis on the sociocultural dynamics of the children's households, especially on how these households function as part of a wider, changing economy, and how they obtain and distribute resources of all types through the creation of strategic social ties or networks (see, e.g. Vélez-Ibáñez, 1988; Vélez-Ibáñez & Greenberg, 1989). For present purposes, I will discuss only the breadth of the knowledge that these social networks can facilitate for a household.

In contrast to many classrooms, households never function alone or in isolation; they are always connected to other households and institutions through diverse social networks. For families with limited incomes, these networks can be a matter of survival because they facilitate different forms of economic assistance and labor

cooperation that help families avoid the expenses involved in using secondary institutions, such as plumbing companies or automobile repair shops. These networks can also serve other important functions, including finding jobs and providing assistance with child care, releasing mothers, if need be, to enter the labor market. In brief, these networks form social contexts for the acquisition of knowledge, skills, and information, as well as cultural values and norms. Given their importance to a household's well-being, family members invest considerable energy and resources in maintaining good social relations with others that make up the networks. These relations are maintained through participation in family rituals, such as baptisms, *quinceañeras* (adolescent girls' 'debutante' parties), and weddings, and through frequent, and sometimes strategic, visits (Vélez-Ibáñez, 1988; Vélez-Ibáñez & Greenberg, 1989).

From our perspective, the essential function of these social networks is that they share or exchange what we have termed *funds of knowledge*: the essential cultural practices and bodies of knowledge and information that households use to survive, to get ahead, or to thrive (see Greenberg, 1989). These funds of knowledge are acquired primarily, but not exclusively, through work and participation in diverse labor markets. With our sample, much of this knowledge is related to the households' rural origins and, of course, to current employment or occupations in what is often an unstable and highly segmented labor market (for examples, see Moll & Greenberg, 1990; Vélez-Ibáñez & Greenberg, 1989).

The knowledge and skills that such households (and their networks) possess are truly impressive. To make the point, consider the information presented in abbreviated form in Table 1. This information was culled from our field notes and interviews with a sample of 30 families. We have visited families that know about different soils, cultivation of plants, seeding, and water distribution and management. Others know animal husbandry, veterinary medicine, ranch economy, and mechanics. Many families know about carpentry, masonry, electrical wiring, fencing, and building codes. Some families employ folk remedies, herbal cures, midwifery, and intricate first aid procedures. And family members with more formal schooling have knowledge about (and have worked in) archaeology, biology, and mathematics.

We argue that these families and their funds of knowledge represent a *potential* major social and

**Table 1** A sample of household funds of knowledge

| Agriculture & Mining | Economics | Household Management | Material and Scientific Knowledge | Medicine | Religion |
|---|---|---|---|---|---|
| Ranging and Farming<br>Horseman-<br>ship (cowboys)<br>Animal hus-<br>bandry<br>Soil and irri-<br>gation systems<br>Crop planting<br>Hunting, Track-<br>ing, Dressing | Busines<br>Market values<br>Appraising<br>Renting and<br>selling<br>Loans<br>Labor laws<br>Building codes<br>Consumer<br>knowledge<br>Accounting<br>Sales | Budgets<br>Childcare<br>Appliance<br>repairs | Construction<br>Carpentry<br>Roofing<br>Masonry<br>Painting<br>Design and<br>architecture | Contemporary<br>medicine<br>Drugs<br>First aid<br>procedures<br>Anatomy<br>Midwifery | Catechism<br>Baptisms<br>Bible studies<br>Moral know-<br>ledge<br>and ethics |
| Mining<br>Timbering<br>Minerals<br>Blasting<br>Equipment<br>operation and<br>maintenance | | | Repair<br>Airplane<br>Automobile<br>Tractor<br>House mainten-<br>ace | Folk medicine<br>Herbal know-<br>ledge<br>Folk cures<br>Folk vetinary<br>cures | |

intellectual resource for the schools. Consider that every classroom has approximately 30 students in it; these students represent 30 households *and* their networks with their respective funds of knowledge. The key point is not only that there are ample funds of knowledge among these working-class households, but that this knowledge is socially distributed. When needed, such knowledge is available and accessible through the establishment of relationships that constitute social networks.

How can a teacher make use of these funds of knowledge within the usual classroom conditions? We have been experimenting with various arrangements, including having teachers conduct household visits to document funds of knowledge (see Moll, Amanti, Neff & Gonzalez, in press). Central to this work has been the development of after-school settings where we meet with teachers to analyze their classrooms, to discuss household observations, and to jointly develop innovations in the teaching of literacy, among other matters. These after-school settings represent social contexts for informing, assisting, and supporting the teachers' work: a setting, in our terms, for teachers and researchers to exchange funds of knowledge (for details, see Moll *et al.*, 1990).

Consider the work of a bilingual sixth grade teacher in our project, Ina A., and her development of what we have called the *construction module* (see Moll & Greenberg, 1990). She got the

idea for the module (or thematic unit) from the work of other teachers and researchers in the after-school setting, who were experimenting with an instructional activity centered around the topics of construction and building. Construction, it turns out, is a topic of considerable interest to the students and a prominent fund of knowledge among the households (see Table 1). Ina decided to implement this module in her classroom in an attempt to integrate home and school knowledge around an academic activity. Her efforts, summarized below, represent a good example of mobilizing funds of knowledge for instruction.

## Creating Strategic Social Networks for Teaching

After discussing with the students the idea of a module or theme study about construction, the teacher asked them to visit the library and start locating information, in either Spanish or English, on the topic. The students obtained materials, for example, on the history of dwellings and on different ways of building structures. Meanwhile, the teacher, through her own research in a community library and in the school district's media center, also located a series of books on construction and on different professions involved in construction, including books on architects and carpenters, and included them as part of the literate resources the class could use in developing the module. The students also built model houses or other structures as homework, using materials available in their homes, and wrote brief essays describing their research or explaining their construction (see Moll & Greenberg, 1990).

The teacher, however, did not stop there. She proposed to the class inviting parents or other community members who were experts on the topic to provide information that could expand the students' knowledge and work. The teacher reported that the children were surprised but intrigued by the idea of inviting their parents to the class as experts, especially given some of the parents' lack of formal schooling. The first two visitors were the father of one of the girls in the class, who worked for the school district, and a community member who worked in construction. The teacher was particularly interested in their describing their use of construction instruments and tools, and how they used mathematics in their work to estimate or measure the area or perimeter of a location, for example. The teacher described the visits as follows (from Moll & Greenberg, 1990):

> The first experience was a total success... We received two parents. The first one, Mr S., father of one of my students, works at [the school district] building portable classrooms. He built his own house, and he helped my student do her project. He explained to the students the basic details of construction. For example, he explained about the foundation of a house, the way they need to measure the columns, how to find the perimeter or area... After his visit, the children wrote what they learned about this topic. It was interesting to see how each one of them learned something different: e.g. the vocabulary of construction, names of tools, economic concerns, and the importance of knowing mathematics in construction. (p. 338)

Building on her initial success, the teacher invited others to make their expertise available to the class:

> The next parent was Mr T. He was not related to any of the students. He is part of the community and a construction worker. His visit was also very interesting. He was nervous and a little embarrassed, but after a while

he seemed more relaxed. The children asked him a great number of questions. They wanted to know how to make the mix to put together bricks... He explained the process and the children were able to see the need for understanding fractions in mathematics because he gave the quantities in fractions. They also wanted to know how to build arches. He explained building arches through a diagram on the board, and told the students that this was the work of engineers. (pp. 338–339)

What is important is that the teacher invited parents and others in the community to contribute *intellectually* to the development of lessons; in our terms, she started developing a social network to access funds of knowledge for academic purposes. In total, about 20 community people visited the classroom during the semester to contribute to lessons. The teacher used various sources of funds of knowledge, including the students' own knowledge and the results of their research, their parents and relatives, the parents of students in other classrooms, and the teacher's own social relationships, including other school staff, community members, and university personnel. These classroom visits were not trivial; parents and others came to share their knowledge, expertise, or experiences with the students and the teacher. This knowledge, in turn, became part of the students' work or a focus of study (Moll & Greenberg, 1990).

As the year progressed, these funds of knowledge became a regular feature of classroom instruction. The teacher also used homework assignments as a vehicle to tap the funds of knowledge of the students' homes and other locations, such as work sites. All of these activities, from the planning and interviewing to the preparation of a final product by the students, involved considerable reading and writing in both languages by the students. Literacy in English and Spanish occurred as a means of analysis and expression, not as isolated reading and writing exercises. To support the development of writing, and to enable individual assessments, the teacher organized peer-editing groups that focused on how to improve the writing to facilitate the clear expression of ideas, whether in English or Spanish. The teacher evaluated the students' progress by their ability to deal with new and more complex activities, and by their ability to read and produce more sophisticated writing to accomplish those activities.

Through the development of a social network for teaching, the teacher convinced herself that valuable knowledge existed beyond the classroom and that it could be mobilized for academic purposes. She also understood that teaching *through* the community, as represented by the people in the various social networks and their collective funds of knowledge, could become part of the classroom routine, that is, part of the 'core' curriculum. The teacher's role in these activities became that of a facilitator, mediating the students' interactions with text and with the social resources made available to develop their analysis, and monitoring their progress in reading and writing in two languages.

## Conclusion

A sociocultural approach to instruction presents new possibilities in bilingual education, where the emphasis is not solely on remediating students' English language limitations, but on utilizing available resources, including the children's or the parents' language and knowledge, in creating new, advanced instructional circumstances for the students' academic development. It is revealing, however, that our case study example, as well as other studies of this genre (e.g. Rosebery, Warren, Conant & Barnes, 1990), represent attempts at change that begin at the classroom level, with the teachers (and researchers) and the students actively shaping and giving intellectual direction to their work. These studies represent, therefore, positive examples, and perhaps a challenge to the instructional status quo, but certainly not systemic changes in bilingual education. It is, nonetheless, this focus on bringing broader research issues to bear on local circumstances that holds promise for change in bilingual education. As Goldenberg & Gallimore (1991) have remarked, 'The prospect of reforming schools depends on a better understanding of the interplay between research knowledge and local knowledge. The more we know about the dynamics of this interplay, the more likely it is that the research can have an effect on the nature and effectiveness of schools' (p. 2).

Our work, then, is an attempt at what could be called 'situated' change. We start with (or develop) the understanding that all classrooms are artificial creations, culturally mediated settings, in the Vygotskian sense, organized around beliefs and practices that control and regulate the intellectual life of the students. The role of the teachers within these systems is critical, as are their conceptions of what counts or is appropriate in the education of bilingual students, conceptions that are influenced by the larger school and societal context. We have found, as have others (e.g. Tharp & Gallimore, 1988), that although teachers may be quite willing to work for change, developing and implementing innovations is difficult and laborious work. Teachers, however, need not work alone; they can form study groups or other settings as special social and intellectual contexts to plan, support, and study change.

Within these settings teachers can collaborate with other colleagues, including researchers and parents, and receive assistance, as needed, in developing their thinking and their teaching. Creating and maintaining such supportive contexts with teachers seem to be indispensable aspects of obtaining positive change in education; that is, transformation in the conditions for teaching, and for thinking, is necessary if we are to obtain change in the students' classroom performance (see Richardson, 1990; Tharp & Gallimore, 1988, 1989).

The examples included herein illustrate that practical change can be socially arranged by using and developing the students', teachers', and communities' sociocultural resources, their funds of knowledge, in the service of that change. In doing so, researchers must redefine their roles, transform themselves from passive recorders or analysts of educational success or failure to collaborators in developing potential, exploring possibilities, and perhaps forging a vision of the children's future that will facilitate instead of constrain the education they experience in the present.

### Note

This study was funded by the Office of Bilingual Education and Minority Language Affairs (OBEMLA) of the US Department of Education, and formed part of the Innovative Approaches Research Project, directed by Charlene Rivera at Development Associates, Inc., in Washington, DC. The views expressed in this paper are those of the author and do not necessarily represent the views of OBEMLA.

## References

Anyon, J. (1980) Social class and the hidden curriculum of work. *Journal of Education* 162 (1), 67–92.

— (1981) Social class and school knowledge. *Curriculum Inquiry* 12 (1), 3–42.

Brown, J.S., Collins, A. and Duguid, P. (1989) Situated cognition and the culture of learning. *Educational Researcher* 18 (1), 32–42.

Cole, M. (1990) Cultural psychology: A once and future discipline? (CHIP Report No. 131). San Diego: University of California, Center for Human Information Processing.

Diaz, S., Moll, L.C. and Mehan, H. (1986) Sociocultural resources in instruction: A context-specifc approach. In California State Department of Education. *Beyond Language: Social and Cultural Factors in Schooling Language Minority Children* (pp. 187–230). Los Angeles: Evaluation, Dissemination and Assessment Center, California State University.

Farnham-Diggory, S. (1990) *Schooling*. Cambridge, MA: Harvard University Press.

García, O. and Otheguy, R. (1985) The masters of survival send their children to school: Bilingual education in the ethnic schools of Miami. *Bilingual Review/Revista Bilingue* 12 (1&2), 3–19.

— (1987) The bilingual educating of Cuban-American children in Dade County's ethnic schools. *Language and Education* 1 (2), 83–95.

Goldenberg, C. (1984) Roads to reading: Studies of Hispanic First Graders at risk for reading failure. Unpublished doctoral dissertation, University of California, Los Angles.

— (1990) Beginning literacy instruction for Spanish-speaking children. *Language Arts* 87 (2), 590–8.

Goldenberg, C. and Gallimore, R. (1991) Local knowledge, research knowledge and educational change: A case study of early Spanish reading improvement. *Educational Researcher* 20 (8), 2–14.

Goodlad, J. (1984) *A Place Called School*. New York: McGraw-Hill.

Goodman, Y. and Goodman, K. (1990) Vygotsky in a whole language perspective. In L.C. Moll (ed.) *Vygotsky and Education* (pp. 223–50). Cambridge: Cambridge University Press.

Greenberg, J.B. (1989) Funds of knowledge. Historical constitution, social distribution and transmission. Paper presented at the Annual Meeting of the Society for Applied Anthropology, Santa Fe.

Heath, S.B. and Mangiola, L. (1991) *Children of Promise: Literate Activity in Linguistically and Culturally Diverse Classrooms*. Washington, DC: National Education Association.

Hirsch, B. (1989) *Language of Thought*. New York: College Entrance Examination Board.

Holt, T. (1990) *Thinking Historically*. New York: College Entrance Examination Board.

Luria, A. (1981) *Language and Cognition*. New York: Wiley and Sons.

McCarty, T.L. (1989) School as community: The Rough Rock demonstration. *Harvard Educational Review* 59 (4), 484–503.

Moll, L.C. (ed.) (1990) *Vygotsky and Education*. Cambridge: Cambridge University Press.

Moll, L.C., Amanti, C. Neff, D. and Gonzalez, N. (in press) Funds of knowledge of teaching: A qualitative approach to connecting homes and classrooms. *Theory into Practice*.

Moll, L.C. and Díaz, S. (1987) Change as the goal of educational research. *Anthropology and Education Quarterly* 18, 300–11.

Moll, L.C. and Greenberg, J. (1990) Creating zones of possibilities: Combining social contexts for instruction. In L.C. Moll (ed.) *Vygotsky and Education* (pp. 319–48). Cambridge: Cambridge University Press.

Moll, L.C., Vélez-Ibáñez, C., Greenberg, J., Whitmore, K., Saavedra, E., Dworin, J. and Andrade, R. (1990) Community knowledge and classroom practice: Combining resources for literacy instruction (OBEMLA Contract No. 300-87-0131). Tucson, AZ: University of Arizona, College of Education and Bureau of Applied Research in Anthropology.

Newman, D., Griffin, P. and Cole, M. (1989) *The Construction Zone: Working for Cognitive Change in Schools*. Cambridge: Cambridge University Press.

Oakes, J. (1986) Tracking, inequality, and the rhetoric of school reform: Why schools don't change. *Journal of Education* 168, 61–80.

Palincsar, A.M. (1989) Less charted waters. *Educational Researcher* 18 (4), 5–7.

Resnick, L. (1990) Literacy in school and out. *Daedalus* 19 (2), 169–85.

Richardson, V. (1990) Significant and worthwhile change in teaching practice. *Educational Researcher* 19 (7), 10–18.

Rosebery, A.S., Warren, B. and Conant, F.R. (1990) Appropriating scientific discourse: Findings from language minority classrooms (Technical Report No 7353). Cambridge, MA: Bolt, Beranak and Newman.

Rosebery, A.S., Warren, B. Conant, F.R. and Barnes, J.H. (1990) Cheche Konnen: Collaborative scientific inquiry in language minority classrooms (OBEMLA Contract No. 300-87-0131). Cambridge, MA: Bolt, Beranak and Newman.

Tharp, R. and Gallimore, R. (1988) *Rousing Minds to Life: Teaching, Learning and Schooling in Social Context*. Cambridge: Cambridge University Press.

— (1989) Rousing schools to life. *American Educator* 13 (2), 20–25, 46–52.

Vélez-Ibáñez, C.G. and Greenberg, J. (1989) Formation and transformation of funds of knowledge among US Mexican households in the context of the borderlands. Paper presented at the Annual Meeting of the American Anthropological Association, Washington, DC.

Vygotsky, L.S. (1979) *Mind in Society*. Cambridge, MA: Harvard University Press.

## Questions

(1) How has instruction for working-class students usually been characterized? What does Moll mean by 'a sociocultural approach to instruction'? How does this relate to 'critical pedagogy'? (See Ada, this volume, and questions and activities following her paper.)

(2) What are 'funds of knowledge'? Make a list of the social networks that exist in your community and the funds of knowledge that they transmit. How are such 'funds of knowledge' shared among households?

(3) Contrast how households work with how classrooms work. Why are social networks extremely necessary in working-class families?

## Activities

(1) The guiding principle in Moll's work is 'that the students' community represents a resource of enormous importance for educational change and improvement.' Design a poster in which you list the resources in your community that are valuable to children and schools, and in particular to language minority students and schools interested in bilingualism.

(2) Visit two families from ethnolinguistic minorities and list their social networks and their funds of knowledge. Make a chart for the class.

(3) Imagine a school where parents and other community members contribute intellectually in the classroom. Compose a policy for the school that lists:
  (a) the aims and goals of this activity;
  (b) the frequency and process of the contribution;
  (c) the type of topics that would be included.

(4) Design a classroom unit based on the 'funds of knowledge' of your community. Involve community residents in the planning of the unit. Share it with the class.